111

subject. — I beg you will be so good as to let
Mrs. L. have a set of Chimney ornaments, which
you will chuse for her. She is so little fond of fine-
ry, that unless I undertake to provide her some
I will pass for a woman only higher dress. — I
have therefore resolved to spend 14 or 15 Dollars on
mantle pieces as she saves me twice as much
Year in beads, feathers & Gewgaws.

                    Yours affectionately

Please to call on Mr. Gilpin   B Henry Latrobe
                                    in market street above 8th when he comes to town

Samuel Mifflin Esq.   } Newcastle Nov. 7th 1803
      or son,   Philadelphia

            Smallman ought to have known better than to
have given you the trouble of enquiring after the
scale to the Drawings. They are full size excepting
the small drawing showing the whole stove the scale
to which is of no consequence, but I believe it is
either 1½ or 3 inches to the foot. Pray hurry them
after rec'd of this. In my letter of the 27th Oct. I gave
a particular description of the stove to which I
refer, and which was so written that it could be
torn off and given to Smallman. Perhaps a copy
would be best. — I am in great haste
                    Yours fct'ly   B H Latrobe
Adam Pasquard the bearer is afraid of finding the Green

The Papers of Benjamin Henry Latrobe

Edward C. Carter II, Editor in Chief

SERIES IV

Correspondence and Miscellaneous Papers

Benjamin Henry Latrobe, portrait by Charles Willson Peale, c. 1804.
Courtesy of the White House Collection.

The Correspondence and Miscellaneous Papers of Benjamin Henry Latrobe

VOLUME 1, 1784–1804

John C. Van Horne and Lee W. Formwalt, Editors

Darwin H. Stapleton, Associate Editor
Jeffrey A. Cohen and Tina H. Sheller, Assistant Editors

Published for The Maryland Historical Society
by
Yale University Press, New Haven and London
1984

The preparation of this volume was made possible (in part) by a grant from the Program for Editions of the National Endowment for the Humanities, an independent federal agency, and the National Historical Publications and Records Commission. This volume is published with the financial assistance of the National Historical Publications and Records Commission.

Designed by James J. Johnson and set in Baskerville Roman type by The Composing Room of Michigan, Inc.
Printed in the United States of America by Murray Printing Company, Westford, MA.

The paper in this book meets the guidelines for permanence and durability of the Committee on Production Guidelines for Book Longevity of the Council on Library Resources.

Library of Congress Cataloging in Publication Data

Latrobe, Benjamin Henry, 1764–1820.
   The correspondence and miscellaneous papers of Benjamin Henry Latrobe.

   (The papers of Benjamin Henry Latrobe. Series IV, Correspondence and miscellaneous papers of Benjamin Henry Latrobe; v. 1)
   Includes index.
   Contents: v. 1. 1784–1804.
   1. Latrobe, Benjamin Henry, 1764–1820. 2. Architects—United States—Correspondence. I. Van Horne, John C. II. Formwalt, Lee W. III. Maryland Historical Society. IV. Title. V. Series: Latrobe, Benjamin Henry, 1764–1820.

Papers of Benjamin Henry Latrobe. Series IV, Correspondence and miscellaneous papers of Benjamin Henry Latrobe; v. 1.
NA737.L34A3   1984   720'.92'4 [B]   83–27423
ISBN 0–300–02901–2 (v. 1)

Contents

Contents

Contents

Contents

Contents

Preface

This volume is the first of what will be three volumes of correspondence and miscellaneous papers, comprising Series IV of The Papers of Benjamin Henry Latrobe. This series represents the culmination of the work of this historical editing project on the life and works of Latrobe (1764–1820), America's first professional architect and engineer. In 1976 we published a comprehensive microfiche edition of all known Latrobe documents,[1] and it is from this extensive collection that the printed volumes in Series IV have sprung.

The journals that Latrobe kept intermittently from the time of his departure from England in November 1795 until his death in New Orleans in September 1820 have been published in their entirety.[2] Many of his engineering drawings, representing projects as diverse as the Philadelphia and New Orleans waterworks, the Susquehanna River improvement survey, the Chesapeake and Delaware Canal, and the development of steam power, have also been published.[3] Latrobe's architectural drawings, dealing with such important commissions as the Virginia State Penitentiary, the Bank of Pennsylvania, the United States Capitol, the Baltimore Roman Catholic Cathedral, St. John's Episcopal Church in Washington, D.C., and various private residences, are in the

1. Thomas E. Jeffrey, ed., *The Microfiche Edition of the Papers of Benjamin Henry Latrobe* (Clifton, N.J., 1976).

2. Edward C. Carter II et al., eds., *The Virginia Journals of Benjamin Henry Latrobe, 1795–1798*, 2 vols. (New Haven, Conn., 1977); Edward C. Carter II, John C. Van Horne, and Lee W. Formwalt, eds., *The Journals of Benjamin Henry Latrobe, 1799–1820: From Philadelphia to New Orleans* (New Haven, Conn., 1980).

3. Darwin H. Stapleton, ed., *The Engineering Drawings of Benjamin Henry Latrobe* (New Haven, Conn., 1980).

process of publication.[4] Also in press is a volume devoted to Latrobe's sketchbooks, his stunning visual description of the young republic that he traversed so widely and studied with such keen interest and insight.[5] Series IV, which will include selected letters to and from Latrobe and certain of Latrobe's published writings (such as pamphlets, newspaper articles and letters, and scientific papers), is intended to complement and supplement the other publications. In addition, at the conclusion of the project, the editors intend to publish an addendum to the *Microfiche Edition,* which will comprise about three hundred Latrobe documents accessioned after the first filming.

A word about the nature of the Latrobe Papers and the criteria we used in selecting documents for publication in this series is in order. Latrobe explicitly stated in May 1803, ". . . I do not keep Copies of my letters,"[6] and the contents of his surviving papers bears him out. In September 1803 Latrobe acquired from Charles Willson Peale a polygraph, a machine holding two pens that enabled a writer to make an exact copy as he wrote his letter. Latrobe was therefore able to retain polygraph copies of all his letters from then until December 1817, when his letterbooks abruptly end. It is presumed that his polygraph passed into the hands of his creditors during bankruptcy proceedings in December 1817 and January 1818. Latrobe's nineteen polygraph letterbooks, now in the collections of the Maryland Historical Society, contain approximately 5,700 letters. About 1,200 original Latrobe letters now reside among the papers of the recipients or in other manuscript collections. Although some of the latter are received copies of letters of which there are polygraph copies in the letterbooks, many (including those written before September 1803 and after 1817) are unique and serve to fill out the record of Latrobe's outgoing correspondence.

Letters to Latrobe are another matter, no collection having survived. In the summer of 1800, a chief clerk in Latrobe's Philadelphia office absconded with a large sum of money and "all [Latrobe's] books and papers of business"; Latrobe was left with "no copies of any letters previous to his flight."[7] Fifteen years later en route from Pittsburgh to Washington, Latrobe lost a wagon with "all my papers and correspon-

4. Charles E. Brownell et al., eds., *The Architectural Drawings of Benjamin Henry Latrobe* (New Haven, Conn., forthcoming).

5. Edward C. Carter II, John C. Van Horne, and Charles E. Brownell, eds., *Latrobe's View of America, 1795–1820* (New Haven, Conn., forthcoming).

6. BHL to Lenthall, 14 May 1803, below.

7. BHL to Joseph Norris, 25 Sept. 1809, LB (71/B2).

dence for 20 Years. . . ."[8] Although Latrobe sent a servant to search for
the wagon, it is not known whether the papers were ever recovered. In
addition, since virtually no letters to Latrobe from 1815 to 1820 are
known to have survived, it is presumed that letters from this period (and
perhaps from the earlier years) were lost after his death.

For letters to Latrobe, therefore, we have had to rely on the few
surviving original letters and, more usually, on copies of letters to him
retained by the writers. We have discovered somewhat less than three
hundred such documents. This imbalance in favor of letters written by
Latrobe is necessarily reflected in the contents of the volumes in this
series.

Series IV will print in full almost eleven hundred documents, or
approximately 15 percent of the collection. We have selected for inclu-
sion important documents that address such themes as Latrobe's intellectual, cultural, and scientific background and development; his
architectural theory and the attempt to establish architectural pro-
fessionalism; his creation of a tradition of monumental masonry architecture; his role in the transfer of European technology and its diffu-
sion in America and in the development of steam engineering; his role
in American economic development, particularly in the promotion of
internal improvements and a unified national transportation system; his
contributions in the realms of American science, art, and culture; his
relationships with Congress and the presidents, particularly Jefferson;
his observations on contemporary American life and politics; and of
course his personal affairs and family life. In selecting documents for
publication in this series, we have not eliminated from consideration any
particular categories of Latrobe's papers. Since Latrobe was not an elected official or a high officer of government, the collection contains virtually no routine papers such as letters from officeseekers and their
supporting testimonials, letters of appointment or commission, or other
official papers that he merely signed. The documents printed in this
series are thus representative of the collection as a whole and differ in
inherent importance, rather than in kind, from those that are not
printed.

Although few documents prior to September 1803 are extant, our
knowledge of his life prior to that time, while sketchy and impressionistic
in parts, is nonetheless fairly complete. The early part of this volume
traces quite clearly Latrobe's formative years before his immigration to

8. BHL to Henry Holdship, 18 July 1815, LB (126/C8).

America in 1795 at the age of thirty-one. At the outset, in an examination of his upbringing in Moravian schools and seminaries in England and Germany, we discover a restless and skeptical young man whose temperament changed but little over the course of his life. We discover, as well, the source of his abiding interest in natural history and drawing, in language and theology, in music and in engineering. In fact, Latrobe acquired his first training in civil engineering in Germany, and while traveling through England and Europe he observed public buildings, forts, canals, harbors, waterworks, and lighthouses, the knowledge of which stood him in good stead throughout his professional career.

Upon his return to England in 1783, having effectively rejected a career in the Moravian ministry, Latrobe entered into a world of privilege and opportunity. He and his family were numbered among the circles of such prominent figures as Samuel Johnson, Arthur Young, and Charles Middleton, later first lord of the Admiralty, and Latrobe was an intimate of the family of Dr. Charles Burney, the great musicologist. At first working in London in the government's Stamp Office (which administered the distribution of tax stamps), about 1786, Latrobe entered the office of John Smeaton, the foremost English engineer. Between that time and his departure for America, Latrobe was involved with projects to improve Rye Harbour, construct the Basingstoke Canal, and alter the route of the Chelmer and Blackwater Navigation. Likewise, he received excellent training from Samuel Pepys Cockerell, a prominent architect, in whose office Latrobe worked from about 1789. Under Cockerell Latrobe gained experience working on the house for the first lord of the Admiralty in Whitehall, London. Then in 1792 Latrobe began to receive his own public and private architectural commissions, designing Ashdown House and Hammerwood Lodge, both in Sussex, and serving as surveyor of the police offices in London.

In the meantime Latrobe had married, in 1790, Lydia Sellon, the daughter of an Anglican clergyman. After having two children, Lydia died in childbirth with their third child in November 1793. With his personal life shattered and his professional prospects set back by the war with France, Latrobe left his children in the charge of relatives and set sail for a new beginning in America.

The two and a half years that Latrobe spent exploring Virginia, well documented in his *Virginia Journals,* were disappointing professionally, his only major commission being the state penitentiary at Richmond. A
trip to Philadelphia in April 1798, ostensibly to study the innovative

Walnut Street Jail, afforded Latrobe the opportunity to view a thriving, cosmopolitan city in which his talents and training, unique in the United States, might be appreciated and utilized. And they were. By the end of the year Latrobe had been commissioned to design the Bank of Pennsylvania, which he considered his Neoclassical masterpiece; and early in 1799 the Philadelphia city councils adopted his ambitious plan to provide the city with water pumped from the Schuylkill River by steam engines. These two undertakings, each in their way a model for much American architecture and engineering to follow, were completed in 1801, and the pace of Latrobe's professional activity then slackened. (His personal life began to mend with his marriage in May 1800 to Mary Elizabeth Hazlehurst, a member of a prominent Philadelphia mercantile family, and with the arrival in America of his two children.)

Just how much his professional prospects had dimmed, and yet how much his talents were recognized by some, is reflected in a heartfelt letter of May 1801 from James Traquair, a Philadelphia stonemason who worked for Latrobe, to President Thomas Jefferson:

> Knowing how fond you are of every useful improvement, I have the pleasure to say the Water Works are about finished: the Engines answer exceedingly well, and now we have plenty of excellent water. It does great credit to Mr. Latrobe. As an Architect I think him the first I ever wrought under: he combineth taste with Strength and plainness with elegance and that, with the fewest expensive ornaments I ever saw. It is a pity that such Talents should be lost to the Country: not meeting with the encouragement his abilities had a right to expect. He proposes as soon as the Pennsylvania Bank is finished (which also doth him honor) to retire on a farm. If any thing is wanting either in public, or to private gentlemen, I think him a fit person as Architect or Engineer.[9]

By the fall of 1801 Latrobe undertook to assist his uncle Frederick Antes in the survey and improvement of a portion of the Susquehanna

9. Traquair to Jefferson, 30 May 1801, Massachusetts Historical Society, Boston.
    At about this time, prominent Philadelphian Thomas Cooper also wrote to Jefferson recommending BHL. He noted that BHL, "who certainly has taste and Science, and perseverance and integrity," had finished the waterworks and the bank, which "will do honour to the national taste by the unobtrusive, unoffending, and elegant chastity of the Stile in which they are finished." Cooper concluded by noting that BHL was "out of employ." Cooper to Jefferson, 17 May 1801, RG 59, National Archives.

River. Late in 1802 Thomas Jefferson did call Latrobe to Washington to design a naval dry dock and an extension of the Potomac Canal, and the following March he appointed Latrobe "Surveyor of the Public Buildings" in Washington. Because of the relative paucity of documentation for these early years, we are publishing a greater percentage of the extant papers than will be true of the later periods.

It was in 1803 that Latrobe began to take on more important commissions, and, with the beginning of his letterbooks, the documentation of both his personal and professional life begins to keep pace with his increased activity. Thus a great deal of the present volume is given over to Latrobe's work on the Capitol and the President's House during the early years of his tenure as surveyor of the public buildings (1803–12). There is much documentation as well on his work as surveyor and engineer of the Chesapeake and Delaware Canal Company (1803–06). In 1804 Latrobe also accepted an appointment as engineer to the Navy Department and began work on his monumental Baltimore Cathedral (1804–20). This volume thus comprehends both Latrobe's personal and professional beginnings and at least the genesis of the major works of his professional career.

Acknowledgments

In the course of preparing this volume for publication, the editors have incurred obligations to numerous individuals and institutions. We are especially grateful for continued financial support of our project to the National Endowment for the Humanities, the National Historical Publications and Records Commission, the National Science Foundation, and the Andrew W. Mellon Foundation. In addition, the American Academy in Rome appointed Edward C. Carter II, editor in chief of the Latrobe Papers, a visiting scholar in the fall of 1978, during which he was able to devote considerable time to work for the project. We must also express our particular appreciation to the American Philosophical Society, to which our project was transferred in September 1980 from the Maryland Historical Society, where it had been since its inception a decade ago. The transfer resulted from the appointment of Dr. Carter as Librarian of the American Philosophical Society. The Society has provided our project with excellent quarters, support services, and access to its outstanding collections.

Besides those editors whose names appear on the title page, many project staff members, past and present, have contributed enormously to this volume. They calendared and transcribed documents, proofread transcriptions, did initial research for annotation, typed notes, copy edited the manuscript, and read proof and indexed the volume. We thank William B. Forbush III, Geraldine S. Vickers, Thomas E. Jeffrey, Sally F. Griffith, Daniel J. Wilson, and Lisa Mae Robinson. Erik Kvalsvik did much of the photography for this volume. The editors reserve special thanks for Charles E. Brownell, formerly assistant editor for architectural history, from whose work on Latrobe's architectural drawings we drew liberally in composing editorial notes and annotation. Dr. Brownell also assisted in the selection of documents published in this volume and answered many queries that we put to him.

Mary Alice Galligan of Yale University Press did an admirable job of editing the manuscript and seeing it through publication.

For permission to publish transcriptions of documents in their collections we wish to thank the following repositories:

American Philosophical Society, Philadelphia, Pennsylvania
Archives of the Archdiocese of Baltimore, Baltimore, Maryland
British Library, London
Columbia University Library, New York City
Dickinson College Library, Carlisle, Pennsylvania
Essex Record Office, Chelmsford, England
Greater London Record Office, London
Historical Society of Delaware, Wilmington
Historical Society of Pennsylvania, Philadelphia
Library of Congress, Washington, D.C.
Maryland Historical Society, Baltimore
Morristown National Historical Park, Morristown, New Jersey
National Archives, Washington, D.C.
New York Public Library, New York City
Pennsylvania Historical and Museum Commission, Harrisburg
South Carolina Historical Society, Charleston
South Caroliniana Library, University of South Carolina, Columbia
Virginia Historical Society, Richmond
Virginia State Library, Richmond
Yale University Library, New Haven, Connecticut

Editorial Method

In producing transcriptions of Latrobe's manuscript correspondence and miscellaneous papers we have, in general, attempted to follow a "middle course" in presenting a printed text that stands between a type facsimile of the manuscript and a thoroughly modernized version. The objective is to produce a text that conveys the *meaning* of the original (even though it may not be in the precise form of the original), but which at the same time is free from the peculiarities of eighteenth-century orthography (and the editorial explanations that must accompany them). Happily, this is not a difficult task in our case, as Latrobe possessed a hand of admirable clarity and definition, wrote, spelled, and punctuated in a nearly modern manner, and did not employ unusual signs or abbreviations. Latrobe's letterbooks are generally free from unusual chronological or textual problems. Nearly everything he wrote, therefore, can be accommodated by modern typography, and his illustrative textual drawings can be reproduced readily.

While our general practice is to adhere as closely as possible to the original manuscript, textual alterations were sometimes necessary for the sake of clarity and comprehensibility. In some instances punctuation has been silently added or deleted. For example, commas have been added between components of a series where missing; periods have been supplied after abbreviations where missing; quotation marks have been added in dialogues and quoted material when an ambiguity or confusion arose without them; appropriate terminal punctuation has been added where missing; dashes used in place of commas, semicolons, colons, or periods have been replaced by the appropriate mark where necessary; and superfluous dashes have been eliminated, although dashes used to set off parenthetical expressions have been retained.

The original capitalization has been retained, except that all sentences begin with a capital letter. If it cannot be determined whether the author intended a capital or lowercase letter, modern usage is followed. The original spelling and syntax have been retained, except that obvious errors, such as the repetition of words and slips of the pen, have been silently corrected.

Ampersands have been changed to "and" except in the names of business firms and in the abbreviation "&c." Superscript letters have been lowered to the line of type, and the resulting abbreviation silently expanded if it is not easily recognizable (e.g., while "Pha." has been rendered "Philadelphia," "Phila." has been let stand). The thorn symbol (y) has been rendered as "th" and the tailed p ($\wp$) has been rendered as either "pre," "pro," or "per" depending on its usage. The tilde (~) has been silently omitted and the word expanded. All ships' names, book, periodical, and play titles, and foreign words have been italicized. Underlined italicized words are foreign words to which Latrobe gave emphasis or English words to which he gave special emphasis (usually by double underlining).

We have used square brackets to enclose, in italics, editorial insertions such as [*torn*] and [*illegible*], which, unless otherwise noted, indicate no more than two words in the text that are not conjecturable. Square brackets also enclose, in roman, editorial expansions, equivalents, conjectural readings, or words added to complete the sense of a sentence. Material added by the editors to correct an author's omission is bracketed without comment; material added by the editors to complete a sentence where the manuscript has been torn, blotted, and so forth is bracketed and the reason for the insertion is given in the bibliographic note following the document. A double ellipsis within brackets, [. .], indicates a blank space in the text. Angle brackets enclose, in italics, unless otherwise noted, material that was canceled in the manuscript and is legible and considered significant.

Printed sources have not been altered according to the editorial procedures above, except that obvious typographical errors have been silently corrected.

The editors have also effected certain procedures concerning the format of all documents, manuscript and printed. Latrobe frequently wrote the name (and sometimes the title and/or address) of the recipient xxii at the head or foot of a letter. These superscriptions and subscriptions have not been printed, and in instances when BHL addressed a letter by the title of the recipient, we have used the recipient's personal name in the heading of the document. For example, a letter addressed "To the Governor and Council of Virginia" is headed "To James Wood and the Council of Virginia." Any significant information about the document is presented in the bibliographic note or numbered footnotes. The dateline, in its original form, is printed at the head of each document at the right margin, regardless of its original location. The complimentary close is run together, regardless of its original form, but capitalization and internal and terminal punctuation are reproduced as in the manuscript.

Following each document is an unnumbered bibliographic note providing a description of the physical nature of the document, identifying its location, and providing the document number in Thomas E. Jeffrey, ed., *The Microfiche Edition of the Papers of Benjamin Henry Latrobe* (Clifton, N.J., 1976). The abbreviations and descriptions we used are:

ALS	Autograph letter signed. Both the text and the signature are in the hand of the author.
LS	Letter signed. Only the signature is in the hand of the author, with the text of the letter in the hand of a clerk or secretary.
Polygraph Copy	Copy made with the use of a polygraph.
Letterbook Copy	Copy entered into a letterbook, either by the author or a clerk or secretary.
Letterpress Copy	Copy made with the use of a letterpress.
Copy	Contemporary manuscript copy other than a polygraph, letterbook, or letterpress copy.
Draft	Draft of a document of which the final version is not extant.
ADS	Autograph document signed. A manuscript other than a letter entirely in the hand of, and signed by, the author.
AD	Autograph document. An unsigned manuscript in the hand of the author.
DS	Document signed. Only the signature is in the hand of the author, with the text of the document in the hand of a clerk or secretary.
Printed Copy	Document transcribed from a printed source, such as a newspaper, report, pamphlet, or article.

xxiii

Typed Copy	Document transcribed from a typescript when neither the original manuscript nor a contemporary manuscript or printed copy exists.

The bibliographic note provides, as well, any pertinent information concerning addresses, endorsements, enclosures, and damages to the manuscript. (Although no address folios exist for Latrobe's polygraph or letterbook copies, the address of the recipient usually given at the head of the document is included in the bibliographic note preceded by "addressed.") The bibliographic note also includes references to other extant contemporary manuscript and printed versions, except that polygraph (letterbook) copies of letters printed from a received copy are usually not noted. In all cases, significant differences between versions are noted.

In the annotation of this volume, the editors have attempted to explain fully what was necessary to clarify the immediate text or to place larger passages or events in historical perspective. *Editorial Notes* generally precede documents that require substantial commentary or explanation. They vary in length, depending on the matter under discussion. *Footnotes*, numbered consecutively within each document, have been employed by the editors to explain their textual changes, identify persons and places whenever possible, give scientific citations, translate foreign phrases, gloss obsolete terms, provide the sources of literary references whenever possible, and clarify events that have not been touched upon in editorial notes. On occasion, Latrobe himself annotated his text by means of traditional footnotes or marginal commentary keyed to the manuscript by "NB," an asterisk, or some other sign. Whether these have been set in the text or transposed into footnotes carrying numbers or symbols, Latrobe's authorship is noted in all cases. It should be pointed out that it is not our policy to append footnotes reading "Not identified" or "Letter not found" each time an obscure or elusive person or document is mentioned in the text. We have identified all persons mentioned insofar as it was possible, generally at the first mention. The lack of an identifying footnote indicates that our research turned up nothing significant to add to the text. Likewise, if a letter or other document is referred to that is extant, a note will refer the reader to it. The lack of such a note indicates that it could not be traced.

References to documents, whether letter, drawing, journal, or
other, that have been or will be published in any of the nine volumes of

The Papers of Benjamin Henry Latrobe are to the published version rather than the manuscript. References to other Latrobe documents include the repository and microfiche number. Those documents that have been accessioned since the compiling of the *Microfiche Edition* will be included in an addendum. References to such documents include the repository and the phrase "microfiche add.," in lieu of a number.

All quotations from the Bible are taken from the King James Version. In most instances, full bibliographical citations have been provided in the annotation for sources. However, the editors have not cited such basic reference works as the *Dictionary of American Biography,* the *Dictionary of National Biography,* the *Dictionary of Scientific Biography,* the *Biographical Directory of the American Congress,* the *Encyclopedia Britannica, Appleton's Cyclopedia of American Biography, Drake's Dictionary of American Biography,* the *Oxford Classical Dictionary,* the *Oxford English Dictionary,* and general works such as The Cambridge Modern History, nor have we indicated the source of information gleaned from city directories; lists of patents; *University of Pennsylvania: Biographical Catalogue of the Matriculates of the College . . . 1749–1893* (Philadelphia, 1894); "Former Members of the Society," in *The American Philosophical Society Held at Philadelphia for Promoting Useful Knowledge: Year Book 1975 . . .* (Philadelphia, 1976), pp. 69–110; Nikolaus Pevsner, John Fleming, and Hugh Honour, *A Dictionary of Architecture,* rev. and enlarged ed. (Woodstock, N.Y., 1976); and Francis B. Heitman, *Historical Register of Officers of the Continental Army during the War of the Revolution, April, 1775, to December, 1783,* new, rev., and enlarged ed. (Washington, D.C., 1914) and *Historical Register and Dictionary of the United States Army, from Its Organization, September 29, 1789, to March 2, 1903,* 2 vols. (Washington, D.C., 1903).

In the notes the reader will encounter many citations to published works such as pamphlets, books, and government documents. It should be pointed out that such works printed in America before 1820 are reproduced in microcard form in the *Early American Imprints* series published by the American Antiquarian Society.

Short Titles and Abbreviations

Annals of Congress
  The Debates and Proceedings in the Congress of the United States [1789–1824], 42 vols. (Washington, D.C., 1834–56).
APS
  American Philosophical Society, Philadelphia.
ASP
  American State Papers. Documents, Legislative and Executive, 38 vols. (Washington, D.C., 1832–61).
Aurora
  Aurora. General Advertiser (Philadelphia).
BHL
  Benjamin Henry Latrobe.
BHL, *Architectural Drawings*
  Charles E. Brownell et al., eds., *The Architectural Drawings of Benjamin Henry Latrobe* (New Haven, Conn., forthcoming).
BHL, *Correspondence,* 2
  John C. Van Horne et al., eds., *The Correspondence and Miscellaneous Papers of Benjamin Henry Latrobe, 1805–1810* (New Haven, Conn., forthcoming).
BHL, *Correspondence,* 3
  John C. Van Horne et al., eds., *The Correspondence and Miscellaneous Papers of Benjamin Henry Latrobe, 1811–1820* (New Haven, Conn., forthcoming).
BHL, *Engineering Drawings*
  Darwin H. Stapleton, ed., *The Engineering Drawings of Benjamin Henry Latrobe* (New Haven, Conn., 1980).
BHL, *Journals*
  Edward C. Carter II et al., eds., *The Virginia Journals of Benjamin Henry Latrobe, 1795–1798,* 2 vols. (New Haven, Conn., 1977). (Referred to as *Journals,* 1 and 2.)

Edward C. Carter II, John C. Van Horne, and Lee W. Formwalt, eds., *The Journals of Benjamin Henry Latrobe, 1799–1820: From Philadelphia to New Orleans* (New Haven, Conn., 1980). (Referred to as *Journals,* 3.)

BHL, *Latrobe's View of America*
 Edward C. Carter II, John C. Van Horne, and Charles E. Brownell, eds., *Latrobe's View of America, 1795–1820* (New Haven, Conn., forthcoming).

C & D Canal Company Papers
 Chesapeake and Delaware Canal Company Papers, Historical Society of Delaware, Wilmington.

C & D Committee of Works Journal
 "Ches. & Del. Canal Co. Commit. of Works Journal," Salem County Historical Society, Salem, N.J.

C & D Report
 "Copy of Reports of the Engineer," Chesapeake and Delaware Canal Company Papers, Historical Society of Delaware, Wilmington.

C & D Survey Committee Minutes
 "Chesapeake & Delaware Canal Co. Com. of Survey: Minutes," Chesapeake and Delaware Canal Company Papers, Historical Society of Delaware, Wilmington.

CHS, *Records*
 Records of the Columbia Historical Society.

CVSP
 Calendar of Virginia State Papers and Other Manuscripts, 1652–1869, Preserved in the Capitol at Richmond, 11 vols. (Richmond, Va., 1875–93).

Ellis and Evans, *History of Lancaster County*
 Franklin Ellis and Samuel Evans, *History of Lancaster County, Pennsylvania, with Biographical Sketches of Many of Its Pioneers and Prominent Men* (Philadelphia, 1883).

Gray, "Early History of C & D"
 Ralph D. Gray, "The Early History of the Chesapeake and Delaware Canal—Part I: Early Plans and Frustration," *Delaware History* 8 (1959): 207–64.

Hamlin, *Latrobe*
 Talbot Hamlin, *Benjamin Henry Latrobe* (New York, 1955).

Jefferson Papers
 Thomas Jefferson Papers, Library of Congress, Washington, D.C.

JLCHS
 Journal of the Lancaster County Historical Society.

Johnston, *History of Cecil County*
 George Johnston, *History of Cecil County, Maryland, and the Early Settlements Around the Head of Chesapeake Bay and on the Delaware River, with* xxvii

Sketches of Some of the Old Families of Cecil County (Baltimore, 1972 [orig. publ. 1881]).

LB
Letterbooks of Benjamin Henry Latrobe, Papers of Benjamin Henry Latrobe, Maryland Historical Society, Baltimore.

Lowry, ed., *Architecture of Washington*
Bates Lowry, ed., *The Architecture of Washington, D.C.* (microfiche edition), 2 vols. (Washington, D.C., 1976).

MdHS
Maryland Historical Society, Baltimore.

MEL
Mary Elizabeth Latrobe.

Microfiche add.
See p. xxv, above, for explanation.

National Intelligencer
National Intelligencer and Washington Advertiser (Washington, D.C.).

Nelson, "Herrnhut"
David Nelson, "Herrnhut: Friedrich Schleiermacher's Spiritual Homeland" (Ph.D. diss., University of Chicago, 1963).

Pa. Statutes, 1682–1801
James T. Mitchell and Henry Flanders, comps., *The Statutes at Large of Pennsylvania from 1682 to 1801,* 16 vols. (Harrisburg, Pa., 1911).

Pa. Statutes, 1802–1805
James T. Mitchell et al., comps., *The Statutes at Large of Pennsylvania from 1802 to 1805* (Harrisburg, Pa., 1915).

PBHL
Papers of Benjamin Henry Latrobe, Maryland Historical Society, Baltimore.

Peale Letterbooks
Peale Letterbooks, Peale-Sellers Papers, American Philosophical Society, Philadelphia.

PHMC
Pennsylvania Historical and Museum Commission, Harrisburg.

PLCHS
Papers of the Lancaster County Historical Society.

PMHB
Pennsylvania Magazine of History and Biography.

Pursell, *Steam Engines in America*
Carroll W. Pursell, Jr., *Early Stationary Steam Engines in America: A Study in the Migration of a Technology* (Washington, D.C., 1969).

RG 26
Records of the U.S. Coast Guard.

RG 42
Records of the Office of Public Buildings and Public Parks of the National Capital.

RG 45
Naval Records Collection of the Office of Naval Records and Library.

RG 46
Records of the U.S. Senate.

RG 49
Records of the Bureau of Land Management.

RG 59
General Records of the Department of State.

RG 77
Records of the Office of the Chief of Engineers.

RG 107
Records of the Office of the Secretary of War.

RG 128
Records of the Joint Committees of Congress.

RG 217
Records of the U.S. General Accounting Office.

RG 233
Records of the U.S. House of Representatives.

RG 351
Records of the District of Columbia.

Illustrations

Benjamin Henry Latrobe, portrait by Charles
Willson Peale, c. 1804. *frontispiece*

MAPS   *page*

Chronology

1793 *November*	Lydia Latrobe dies in childbirth
1793	Designs and builds Ashdown House in Sussex
1795 *November 25*	Sails for America on the *Eliza*
1796 *mid-March*	Arrives in Norfolk, Virginia
1796 *March*	Designs the William Pennock House, Norfolk, his first American house design
1796 *June 7–17*	Makes informal survey of the Appomattox River for the Upper Appomattox Navigation Company
1797 *June 6–27*	Visits property of the Dismal Swamp Land Company as an engineering consultant
1797 *June 22*	Appointed by Gov. James Wood to build the Virginia State Penitentiary, Richmond
1798 *January 6*	Completes design for the Richmond theater, assembly rooms, and hotel complex
1798 *March–April*	Visits Philadelphia to examine Walnut Street Jail
1798 *July*	Draws plans for fortifications at Norfolk, Virginia
1798 *December 1*	Leaves Richmond to establish residence in Philadelphia, having been selected as architect of the Bank of Pennsylvania
1798 *December 19*	Submits paper on Cape Henry sand hills to American Philosophical Society
1799 *March*	Plans for Philadelphia Waterworks adopted by the City Councils and ground broken
1799 *July 19*	Elected to the American Philosophical Society, Philadelphia
1799 *December 18*	Submits paper on bay alewife and fish louse to American Philosophical Society
c. 1799	Designs the Gothic villa, Sedgeley, in Philadelphia
1800 *January 26*	Finishes design for a national military academy
1800 *May 1*	Marries Mary Elizabeth Hazlehurst (1771–1841)
1800	Designs mausoleum/national monument to honor George Washington
1801 *January 27*	Centre Square engine house pumps first water at the Philadelphia Waterworks

1801 *June 29*	Birth of Juliana Latrobe (died 11 August)
1801 *August–September*	Appointed engineer and contractor of the Susquehanna River Survey
1801	Designs alterations for Chestnut Street Theater, Philadelphia
1802 *October 4*	Loses competition for design of New York City Hall
1802 *November*	Accepts President Jefferson's invitation to design a covered naval dry dock at Washington
1802	Plans restoration of Nassau Hall at Princeton
1803 *January 21*	Submits paper on two species of wasp to American Philosophical Society
1803 *March 6*	Appointed "Surveyor of the Public Buildings of the United States at Washington" by President Jefferson
1803 *May 4*	Birth of John Hazlehurst Boneval Latrobe
1803 *May 18*	Completes set of drawings for Dickinson College, Carlisle, Pennsylvania
1803 *May 20*	Submits paper on steam engines in America to American Philosophical Society
1803 *July 5*	Begins survey for the Chesapeake and Delaware Canal Company
1803 *September*	Acquires polygraph machine from Charles Willson Peale
1804 *c. January*	Appointed engineer to the Navy Department
1804 *January 25*	Appointed engineer of the Chesapeake and Delaware Canal Company
1804 *February 5*	Draws plans for the first Washington Canal Company
1804 *April 10*	Offers to donate his services in designing the Roman Catholic cathedral at Baltimore
1804 *May 2*	Ground broken for the Chesapeake and Delaware Canal feeder
1804 *July 7*	Birth of Juliana Elizabeth Boneval Latrobe
1804 *December 17*	Designs furnishings and rearrangements of Senate Chamber for the Chase impeachment trial

Genealogy

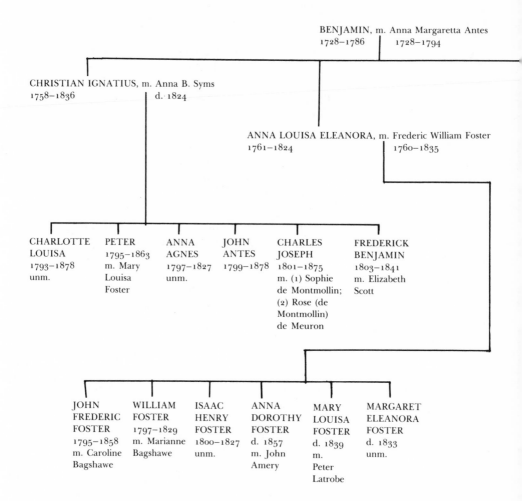

BENJAMIN, m. Anna Margaretta Antes
1728–1786   1728–1794

CHRISTIAN IGNATIUS, m. Anna B. Syms
1758–1836   d. 1824

ANNA LOUISA ELEANORA, m. Frederic William Foster
1761–1824   1760–1835

CHARLOTTE
LOUISA
1793–1878
unm.

PETER
1795–1863
m. Mary
Louisa
Foster

ANNA
AGNES
1797–1827
unm.

JOHN
ANTES
1799–1878

CHARLES
JOSEPH
1801–1875
m. (1) Sophie
de Montmollin;
(2) Rose (de
Montmollin)
de Meuron

FREDERICK
BENJAMIN
1803–1841
m. Elizabeth
Scott

JOHN
FREDERIC
FOSTER
1795–1858
m. Caroline
Bagshawe

WILLIAM
FOSTER
1797–1829
m. Marianne
Bagshawe

ISAAC
HENRY
FOSTER
1800–1827
unm.

ANNA
DOROTHY
FOSTER
d. 1857
m. John
Amery

MARY
LOUISA
FOSTER
d. 1839
m.
Peter
Latrobe

MARGARET
ELEANORA
FOSTER
d. 1833
unm.

*All persons on this chart are Latrobes unless otherwise stated.
A more detailed genealogy of Latrobe's ancestors and descendants is found in BHL, *Journals,* 1: lxv–lxvii.

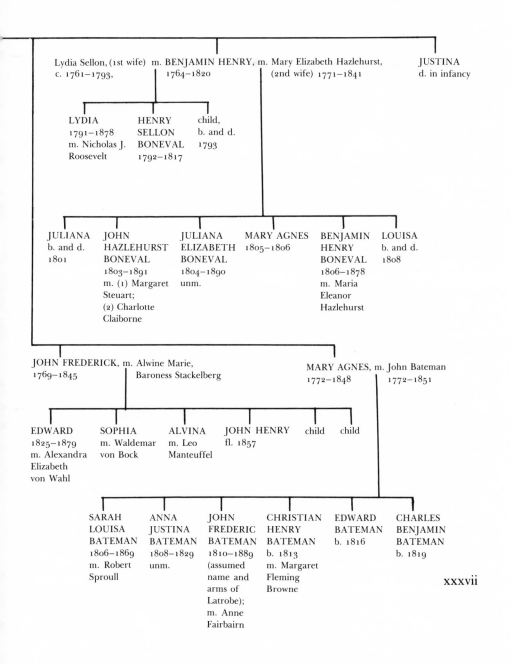

Lydia Sellon, (1st wife) m. BENJAMIN HENRY, m. Mary Elizabeth Hazlehurst, JUSTINA
c. 1761–1793,   1764–1820   (2nd wife) 1771–1841   d. in infancy

LYDIA   HENRY   child,
1791–1878   SELLON   b. and d.
m. Nicholas J.   BONEVAL   1793
Roosevelt   1792–1817

JULIANA   JOHN   JULIANA   MARY AGNES   BENJAMIN   LOUISA
b. and d.   HAZLEHURST   ELIZABETH   1805–1806   HENRY   b. and d.
1801   BONEVAL   BONEVAL   BONEVAL   1808
                   1803–1891   1804–1890   1806–1878
                   m. (1) Margaret unm.   m. Maria
                   Steuart;   Eleanor
                   (2) Charlotte   Hazlehurst
                   Claiborne

JOHN FREDERICK, m. Alwine Marie,   MARY AGNES, m. John Bateman
1769–1845   Baroness Stackelberg   1772–1848   1772–1851

EDWARD   SOPHIA   ALVINA   JOHN HENRY   child   child
1825–1879   m. Waldemar m. Leo   fl. 1857
m. Alexandra von Bock   Manteuffel
Elizabeth
von Wahl

               SARAH   ANNA   JOHN   CHRISTIAN   EDWARD   CHARLES
               LOUISA   JUSTINA   FREDERIC   HENRY   BATEMAN   BENJAMIN
               BATEMAN   BATEMAN   BATEMAN   BATEMAN   b. 1816   BATEMAN
               1806–1869   1808–1829   1810–1889   b. 1813   b. 1819
               m. Robert   unm.   (assumed   m. Margaret
               Sproull   name and   Fleming
                                               arms of   Browne
                                               Latrobe);
                                               m. Anne   xxxvii
                                               Fairbairn

Correspondence and Miscellaneous Papers
1784–1804

Moravian Education

EDITORIAL NOTE

Latrobe's upbringing within the *Unitas Fratrum* (United Brethren, or Moravian church) laid the foundation for his abiding interests in natural history, engineering, languages, theology, music, and drawing. He was born on 1 May 1764 at the Moravian community of Fulneck near Leeds in England[1] and was the son of the Rev. Benjamin Latrobe (1728–86), a leading Moravian minister. There is scant documentation of Latrobe's years at Moravian schools and seminaries in England and Germany. It is evident, however, that his Moravian background played a crucial role in shaping his intellectual interests and moral character, though he would eventually reject membership in the Moravian church.

The Moravian faith had its origins in the Hussite rebellions of the fifteenth century in central Europe, but it did not flourish until the 1720s, when Count Zinzendorf took a group of its adherents under his protection in Saxony. Thereafter the Moravians developed a strong evangelical movement which spread their faith to the rest of Europe, the Americas, and Africa. In addition to embracing traditions of simple living and devotion to Christ similar to those of Pietist movements in German Protestantism, the Moravians believed that formal education was a bulwark of faith and normally established schools in their settlements, such as Fulneck. All Moravian children were expected to enroll in school at an early age and to follow their education as far as their personal talents could take them. The church provided support for those children whose families could not afford to keep them in school. By the latter part of the eighteenth century, the Moravians had developed a rigorous and vital educational system which was among the best in the Western world.[2]

Moravian communities of Latrobe's era were arranged by age and sex into

1. Journal of baptisms at the chapel of the United Brethren, at Fulneck, Fulneck Congregational Archives, Fulneck, England.

2. Edward Langton, *History of the Moravian Church* (London, 1956), pp. 15–75, 143, 147–62; Gillian Lindt Gollin, *Moravians in Two Worlds: A Study of Changing Communities* (New York and London, 1967), pp. 4–6, 102–03; Nelson, "Herrnhut," p. 104.

groups called choirs, which generally had common eating and living quarters. Boys and girls passed through their respective little, middle, and great choirs, and at about age twenty they moved into the single sisters' or single brothers' choirs. Married members, widows, and widowers each formed a separate choir.[3] These choirs were often closely knit, and moving from one choir to another was an occasion of solemn and often tearful community observance.[4] Though the family was an important social unit in the Moravian church, choirs played a significant role in the spiritual and personal development of the individual.

In 1767, at the age of three years and one month, Latrobe became a member of the little boys' choir at Fulneck. There were about fifty-five children in the Fulneck children's choirs, a number that remained approximately the same during Latrobe's years there. The curriculum for children of his age included spelling and reading for an hour every morning and afternoon during the week, as well as religious devotions daily.[5] On his fourth birthday Latrobe ceremonially received "brethren clothing" as a visible sign that he had joined the Moravian fellowship. Three months later Latrobe's parents left Fulneck to take leadership roles in the governing bodies of the Moravian church in London, although they returned to Fulneck for weeks at a time during the next several years. Latrobe's older brother, Christian Ignatius, and his older sister, Anna Louisa Eleanora, remained with him at Fulneck. Later his younger sister Justina, younger brother John Frederick, and uncle James La Trobe joined them.[6]

As he became older Latrobe had a fuller academic schedule. Arithmetic, writing, grammar, geography, Bible history, music, and "the rudiments of the Latin tongue" were standard elements of his instruction.[7] His teachers included a succession of men who were the managers of the school, as well as other adult members of the community. Overseeing the course of education was a conference of church elders, which included Latrobe's father.[8]

3. The memorabilia at the end of 1788 in the Fetter Lane congregational diary (Archives, Moravian Church House, London) lists this structure, except for the middle boys' and girls' choirs, which are mentioned in the Fulneck congregational diary at various places (Fulneck Congregational Archives). Gollin, *Moravians in Two Worlds*, pp. 67–70; Nelson, "Herrnhut," pp. 79, 113.

4. Nelson, "Herrnhut," p. 109. E.g., Fulneck congregational diary, 21 Oct. 1771, Fulneck Congregational Archives.

5. "List of Teachers and Boys in the Oeconomy, with Timetable of School, 1761," in "Children's Economy at Fulneck, 1755–76," Fulneck Congregational Archives; Joseph Jackson to Brother Okerhousen, 9 Aug. 1767, and "Account of the Expences of the Children's Oeconomy in Fulneck from Midsummer to Michaelmas 1776," in box labeled "Sundry Papers and Accounts," Moravian Church House.

6. Justina died while BHL was at Fulneck. Fulneck congregational diary, 1 May, 4 Aug., 5 Aug. 1768, 22 Apr. 1769, 18 Apr. 1772, 27 Aug. 1774, 13 Feb. 1776.

7. "List of Teachers and Boys in the Oeconomy, 1761"; "Congregational Accounts 1777. Week the 52d. Reports of the Oeconomies of the unity for the year 76 and 77," in "U. E. C. Letters and School Statements," Fulneck Congregational Archives.

8. Minutes of the Children's Economy Conference for Fulneck, 1761–1774, Fulneck Congregational Archives.

The religious experience at Fulneck centered on daily worship and, beginning in 1771, weekly instruction in the principles of Christianity. "Love feasts," which ritually confirmed each person's commitment and affection for the other, were held at regular intervals. A succession of special occasions, such as the little boys' festival, and the celebration of each person's birthday, as well as the observance of Christmas and other holidays, also enlivened the community worship.[9] Music was always a part of worship and new hymns and instrumental pieces were composed and played by members of the Fulneck community.

Yet the school at Fulneck had difficulties. It was often in severe financial distress, in part because of the Moravian church's attempt to give every member's child an education. There were frequent appeals to English congregations for contributions to support indigent students, as well as requests for parents to remit tuition on time.[10] The Moravian hierarchy exhibited concern with the educational system and early in Latrobe's years at Fulneck criticized the school for allowing "the Children . . . too much time to spend without any employment, which is a great damage to them."[11] In addition, the church's evangelical activity provided a constant stream of new members, some of whom in time became dissatisfied with the discipline of the community and the rigor of the school's curriculum. Latrobe's father was instrumental in dismissing many of the discontented in the early 1770s, and many others left of their own accord.[12]

In 1776 Latrobe was a central figure in two ceremonies at Fulneck. On 7 January he was admitted to the great boys' choir, and on 16 September he and three other boys were honored by a love feast in celebration of their imminent departure from England. On 17 September Latrobe left for the Moravian school at Niesky in Saxony (in what is now southeastern East Germany), following the path of his brother Christian Ignatius by five years.[13] By a synodical decree of 1769 the Niesky Paedagogium had been designated the school for children of missionaries and church officials who, since they traveled a great deal or were in remote locations, wanted to insure that their children received an adequate

9. Fulneck congregational diary, 31 May 1771; Adelaide L. Fries, *Customs and Practices of the Moravian Church* (Bethlehem, Pa., 1949), pp. 33–47, 54–62; Nelson, "Herrnhut," p. 104.

10. Benjamin La Trobe, Account of visit to Fulneck, Aug. 1774–Jan. 1775, parcel C, box A1, Moravian Church House.

11. Fulneck congregational diary, 29 Apr. 1768; "Minutes of the General Synod at Marienborn, July 1–September 17, 1769," and "The Conclusions of the Synod of the Unity of the Brethren held at Barby in the Year 1775," both in the Moravian Church House.

12. Benjamin La Trobe, Account of visit to Fulneck.

13. Fulneck congregational diary, 7 Jan., 17 Sept. 1776. In 1741 the 16th of September was set aside as a memorial day for ministers in the Moravian church. Presumably BHL and his classmates, who were headed for Niesky, were honored on that day because it was believed that they would become ministers in the church. The 17th of September seems also to have been the traditional matriculation day for Barby students. Fries, *Customs and Practices of the Moravian Church*, pp. 57–58.

education.[14] Even so, tuition had to be paid, and Latrobe was admitted despite the fact that the English Moravian School Diaconate would pay only half tuition for his first two years because of its poor financial condition.[15]

When Latrobe arrived in Niesky in the fall of 1776, the school was in the capable hands of Christian Theodor Zembsch (1728–1806). Zembsch had studied theology at Jena and taught at the Moravian school at Grosshennersdorf from 1750 to 1760. Inspired by the classical curriculum instituted there, he moved to Niesky in 1760 and in 1769 or 1770 became its superintendent. Zembsch had by this time published a work on Greek logic, and he ardently advocated the study of Latin, Greek, and Hebrew. Under him the Niesky curriculum also included geometry, trigonometry, arithmetic, music, French, history, and drawing.[16] Latrobe's class schedule for 1779 has survived (see fig. 1). The students had weekly religious instruction under the local Moravian minister at Niesky and were expected to use their free time wisely. The school had an excellent library, the nearby von Schachmann family home had an art collection which was open to the students, musical concerts were held twice weekly, and natural history was a popular avocation for both students and faculty.[17]

The intellectual environment of the Niesky Paedagogium was indeed stimulating, and it may have provided the best education in Europe for boys between twelve and eighteen years old. Latrobe's classmates included Karl Gustav von Brinkmann (1764–1847), who became a Swedish diplomat and man of letters, and immediately following Latrobe at Niesky was Friedrich Schleiermacher (1768–1834), who became one of the leading European theologians of the nineteenth century.[18] Other contemporaries of Latrobe became major figures in the Moravian church.

Late in 1781 or early in 1782 Latrobe left Niesky and went (or was sent) to the Moravian settlement at Gnadenfrey in Silesia (now Pilawa Górna, Poland). This may have been an attempt to accommodate Latrobe's growing feeling that his future profession would not be in the ministry. He found at Gnadenfrey a wide variety óf craftsmen, and he probably carefully examined their shops as his

14. *Geschichte des Pädagogiums der evangelischen Brüder-Unität* (Niesky, 1859), p. 6.

15. Minutes of the Unity Elders' Conference, 26 Apr., 8 July 1776, Archiv der Brüder-Unität, Herrnhut, East Germany.

16. BHL's drawing teacher for 1778, Charles Gotthold Reichel, concurrently assisted in the construction of a major new building at Niesky. "Lebenslauf des 18ten April 1825 in Niesky selig entschlafenen verwitweten Bruders Carl Gotthold Reichel, Bischofs der Brüderkirke," *Nachrichten aus der Brüder-Gemeine* 4(1826) : 763–64.

17. Heinrich Casmir Gottlieb Graf zu Lynar, *Nachricht von dem Ursprung und Fortgange, und hauptsächlich von der gegenwärtigen Befassung der Brüder-Unität* (Halle, 1781), pp. 145–47; *Geschichte des Pädagogiums*, pp. 7–9; E. R. Meyer, *Schleiermachers und C. G. von Brinkmanns gang durch die Brüdergemeine* (Leipzig, 1905), pp. 94–99.

18. *Allgemeine Deutsche Biographie* (Berlin, 1971), s.v. "Brinkmann, Karl Gustav"; Meyer, *Schleiermachers und C. G. von Brinkmanns gang durch die Brüdergemeine;* Martin Redeker, *Schleiermacher: Life and Thought,* trans. John Wallhauser (Philadelphia, 1973); Nelson, "Herrnhut."

Fig. 1. BHL's course of study at the Moravian Paedagogium at Niesky, 1779.

Subject	Sessions per week (one hour each)	Texts	Instructors
Latin	9	class 1: Cicero, *Orations* class 2: Cicero, *Letters* [Hieronymus] Freyer, *Fascikel*	class 1: J. Christian Beatus Neumann class 2: Johann Gottfried Cunow
Greek	6	[Johann Matthias] Gesner, *Chrestomathie* New Testament	Johann Gottfried Cunow
Geometry and Trigonometry	4	unknown	Christian Theodor Zembsch
History	2	unknown	J. Christian Beatus Neumann
Hebrew	2	Genesis	Johann Gottfried Cunow
French	2	Abrégé*	Johann Gottfried Cunow
Piano	2		Christian Ignatius Latrobe
Violin	2		Freydt
Drawing	1		[Charles G.?] Reichel

*Probably Fenelon's *Abrégé des vies des anciens philosophes.*

Sources: Graf von Lynar, *Nachricht von dem Ursprung und Fortgange*, pp. 145–46; manuscript catalogue of Niesky paedagogium, 1779, R.4.B. IV. a. 7, Archiv der Brüder-Unität, Herrnhut, East Germany.

brother Christian Ignatius did on a visit to the settlement several years later.[19] While there, Latrobe made the acquaintance of Heinrich August Riedel (1749–1810), a Prussian government engineer, spent weeks or months observing his activities and learning about engineering, and also talked with other Prussian military engineers.[20]

In August 1782 Latrobe's educational standing was brought to the attention of the Unity Elders' Conference, the highest governing body of the Moravian church, which was charged with training, calling, and ordaining ministers. Latrobe's father asked that his son be permitted to enter the seminary at Barby, in what is now western East Germany, where his eldest son Christian Ignatius had been enrolled in 1776. The conference agreed that Latrobe could scarcely continue his formal education at Gnadenfrey, but found it difficult to decide whether Latrobe was spiritually ready to enter Barby. The conference minutes record that "he is confused and confesses his sins, but he still has no comfort and has not taken hold of the Savior."[21] Latrobe himself later recalled that by this age he was an "indifferentist," that is, he could not find any reason to affirm one particular set of Christian beliefs above another. During his stay in Silesia, he heard a powerful sermon in a Lutheran church which emphasized that it was far better to constantly search for a valid doctrine and even to hold vehemently to a false one than to believe that any would do. Latrobe recalled that he was "so staggered by this Sermon, that untill his [the preacher's] arguments yielded to time and amusements, I really was quite unhappy."[22] In spite of such spiritual beliefs, or perhaps because "one was inclined to be charitable to young Benjamin Latrobe in accordance with his father's wishes," Latrobe was admitted to Barby in the fall of 1782.[23]

The Moravian church regarded Barby as the pinnacle of its educational system. The seminary's primary purpose was to train future ministers, missionaries, and teachers, although it made some provision for students who intended to become lawyers or physicians. Teachers strictly regulated the daily life of students in the belief that all activity during the years of seminary training should center on intellectual growth and the development of personal piety. Little intercourse with the outside world was permitted.

19. Christian Ignatius Latrobe journals, 29 Nov., 10 Dec. 1788, John Rylands University Library, Manchester, England.

20. BHL to the Mayor and Corporation of the City of New Orleans, 10 June 1816, and enclosure, "On the means of preventing, meeting, and repairing the calamities occasioned by innundations," New Orleans City Archives, Louisiana Division, New Orleans Public Library (225/c1); BHL, ed., *Characteristic Anecdotes and Miscellaneous Authentic Papers, Tending to Illustrate the Character of Frederick II, Late King of Prussia* (London, 1788), p. 11n(140/B1); Johann Christoph Adelung, *Fortsetzung und Ergänzungen zu Christian Gottlieb Jöchers Allgemeinem Gelehrten-Lexico*, 6 vols. (Hildesheim, West Germany, 1960–61), 6 : 2112.

21. Minutes of the Unity Elders' Conference, 6 Aug., 11 Aug. 1782.

22. BHL, *Journals*, 3 : 225–26.

23. Minutes of the Unity Elders' Conference, 11 Aug. 1782; D. Paul Kölbing, ed., *Die Feier des 150 jährigen Bestehens des theologischen Seminariums der Brüdergemeine in Gnadenfeld am 24. Mai 1904* (Leipzig, 1904), p. 75.

Instruction in the sciences was regarded as complementary to the seminary's purpose. There was instruction in physics and botany, and the seminary was equipped with a cabinet of natural history, an astronomical observatory, and pneumatic apparatus for experiments.[24] The major intellectual force behind the scientific activity was Friedrich Adam Scholler, who was director of the seminary from 1772 to 1782. Scholler's primary interest was botany and in 1775 he published a *Flora Barbiensis*. Scholler was succeeded as director by Johann Gottfried Cunow (formerly at Niesky), who taught mathematics and physics. The primary focus of studies, however, at least in a student's first year, was ancient languages, followed by philosophy, history, Bible history, and theology.[25]

Latrobe apparently did well as a student at Barby, but his spiritual state remained a matter of concern to church officials. The issue was brought to a head in March 1783 during an investigation of the seminary conducted by August Gottlieb Spangenberg, the most eminent Moravian of the time. Among many observations he reported:

> Doubt and disbelief concerning the truth of evangelical teaching is expressed by a number of students, most of whom however are at a loss as to how to deal with this and let themselves be freed from their doubts through the Savior's grace. Only one, or at most two, find pleasure in persevering in this state. This is particularly the case with Benjamin Latrobe, whose continued stay here at the seminary seems very questionable and would cause a great deal of damage.[26]

Latrobe's unwillingness to at least outwardly conform to Moravian doctrine persisted in spite of a strong letter from his father, and in late June 1783 the members of the Elders' Conference decided that they had no other course but to require Latrobe's departure from Barby. He left the next month and arrived in London on 28 August 1783.[27]

The primary cause of Latrobe's departure was his religious unorthodoxy, but his preliminary choice of vocation (apparent in his activities at Gnadenfrey) presented further difficulties. In June 1783 when the members of the Elders' Conference finally decided to dismiss him, they recorded in their minutes that Latrobe wanted to go to Vienna in order "to perfect his inclination toward fortification [i.e., military engineering]."[28] That his initial interest in engineering

---

24. Graf zu Lynar, *Nachricht von dem Ursprung und Fortgange,* p. 151; Redeker, *Schleiermacher: Life and Thought,* pp. 12–14; Minutes of the General Synod at Marienborn, 1 July–17 Sept. 1769, Moravian Church House.

25. Graf zu Lynar, *Nachricht von dem Ursprung und Fortgange,* p. 151; Hermann Plitt, *Das Theologische Seminarium de Evengelischen Brüder-Unität in seinem Anfang und Fortgang* (Leipzig, 1854), pp. 54, 56; Kölbing, ed., *Die Feier des 150 jährigen Bestehens,* pp. 65, 75; Meyer, *Schleiermachers und C. G. von Brinkmanns gang durch die Brüdergemeine,* pp. 94–95; BHL to John Law and Walter Jones, 11 Dec. 1810, LB (80/D7).

26. Minutes of the Unity Elders' Conference, 27 Mar. 1783.

27. Ibid., 9 Apr., 26 June 1783; Fetter Lane congregational diary, 28 Aug. 1783, Moravian Church House.

28. Minutes of the Unity Elders' Conference, 26 June 1783.

was directed toward military concerns is understandable because Continental engineers frequently had military training and held military rank even in civilian positions. But Latrobe's choice of vocation must have shocked his Moravian elders, to whom pacifism was a cherished tenet of faith, and it made his departure from Barby the more necessary.

Thus, at the age of nineteen Latrobe was in London, and by the following year he had obtained employment in the government Stamp Office. The following document is his earliest extant writing.

TO JOHANN FRIEDRICH FRÜAUF

London, August 5, 1784.

My dearest friend:[1]

I have been so busy ever since Br. Loretz[2] has been here, that I could not find time, to write to you before the very last moment. I rec'd your very kind letter duly, and thank you for it; you put me indeed quite to shame by your kindness in writing to me, and tho I certainly should always have esteemed it as such, yet as your's was the only letter I have received from my Barby friends, it was doubly agreeable to me. Tho I may have outwardly appeared otherwise to you, yet I can from my heart assure you, that the regard I conceived for you the first time I saw you, and which you will perhaps recollect, has never ceased. If I look over the whole list of friends, and half friends (which last I should not mention) in Germany, the sincerity with which you always have treated me, would be abused if I did not find you foremost among them. Accept in return all I can give, my most hearty love and friendship, and a regard I feel to very few. As we expect Br. Deichen from Jamaica every day, and I shall have an opportunity of writing to you by him, I shall defer most of what I have to say to you, till then, especially as my time is at present so short. I am here agreeably situated, beyond expectation of which I shall give you a substantial account in my next. I hope that by some opportunity or other I shall be able to shew you my regard in more than mere words, as I can have many trifles here at almost no expence, which are difficult to purchase abroad, I therefore expect you will not spare me, if you should think of anything you particularly want. As I have no time to write to anybody but you, I must trouble you with a commission or two. Tell Mr. Sheube, that nothing but a good opportunity is wanting for me to send his orders over. If I send them alone, they will cost double, before they reach him, and Br. Loretz cannot take in, the least trifle more, as he is

10

already overladen. I have left in Barby a bed, a pillow, [. .] a bolster. I do not know what they are worth, but I suppose they are not worth sending. Pray take care that they are some how or other disposed of, and apply the money to the payment of any small debts I may perhaps have left, tho I know of none. If there are none, pay Br. Quandt[3] the money who will remit it to me, but first let me know how much it amounts to. Br. Loretz will at any time forward a mail letter to me, if [someone] should honor me with a line or two. I shall answer yours punctually. My direction is [. .] to Mr. Benjamin *Henry* La Trobe, Stamp office, London,[4] which will distinguish me from my father, in whose house I lived. Scold Sprecher for not writing to me.[5]

Typed Copy: PBHL (microfiche add.). Addressed to Früauf at Barby Seminary. Endorsed as received 27 August. Bracketed ellipses indicate words or phrases omitted in the type-script; a notation on the typescript indicates they were in German.

1. Johann Friedrich Früauf (1762–1839) studied at Niesky and Barby with BHL. In 1788 he settled in Pennsylvania, where he was a teacher and minister at several Moravian settlements and congregations. There is no record that BHL met with Früauf in America, but he did write to Früauf in 1813 regarding the possibility of enrolling an acquaintance's child in a Moravian school. "Report of Unity Schools, 1776–1777," *Gemein-Nachrichten,* 1777, 52d week, 1st part, Moravian Archives, Bethlehem, Pa.; Ministers' book, Moravian Archives; Früauf to G. H. Loskiel, 30 Dec. 1803, Letters from Philadelphia, Moravian Archives; BHL to Früauf, 7 Jan. 1813, LB(106/B14); Kölbing, ed., *Die Feier des 150 jährigen Bestehens,* p. 75.

2. Johann Jacob Loretz (1737–1818), an official of the Moravian church in Germany and a friend of BHL's father. "Der am 31sten Mai 1818 in Sarepta selig entschlasene verwitwete Brüder Johann Jacob Loretz hat von seinem Lebenslauf folgende Nachricht hinterlassen," *Gemein-Nachrichten* 1 (1820) : 133–56; Daniel Benham, ed., *Memoirs of James Hutton; Comprising the Annals of His Life, and Connection with the United Brethren* (London, 1856), pp. 508–09.

3. Johann Christian Quandt (1733–1822), a teacher and minister at Barby. "Lebens-lauf des Bruders Johann Christian Quandt, *Senior civilis* der Brüder-Unität, heimgegangen den 24 März 1822 in Herrnhut," *Gemein-Nachrichten* 33 (1851) : 432–68.

4. BHL apparently began his employment in the Stamp Office after the beginning of 1784. He was employed there at £60 a year as a comptroller's clerk until 1794. *The Court and City Register; Or Gentlemen's Complete Annual Calendar . . .* (London, [1790–93]); *The Royal Kalendar; Or Complete and Correct Annual Register for England, Scotland, Ireland, and America . . .* (London, [1789], [1794]).

5. Johann Andrew von Sprecher (b. 1764) studied with BHL at Niesky and probably arrived at Barby before BHL returned to England. "Report of Unity Schools, 1776–1777"; Kölbing, ed., *Die Feier des 150 jährigen Bestehens,* p. 76.

TO ARTHUR YOUNG

Stamp office, Somerset place May 22d. 1788

Dear Sir,[1]

We have been waiting for your arrival in town *impatiently* for the week past, and, I am afraid, we must now make up our minds to wait *patiently* a great deal longer, as the passing of the Wool bill has not been able to bring you to town.[2] By the Word, *We,* I mean my brother,[3] our friend the *Lord of slaves,*[4] myself, and I dare say it includes 50 other people whom I have not the honour of knowing. *We,* have been these days past laying our heads together, to find out some method of *doing you honour in effigy* in order to make up to you in some measure the disgrace you have undergone, (as is credibly reported about town) of being burnt in effigy by the wool Manufacturers at Bury.[5] My brother is for procuring your effigy, and after having crowned it with a wreath composed of turnip-roots, cabbage-leaves, potatoe-apples, Wheat ears, oats, straw &c. and tied with a band of Wool, thinks it ought to be placed upon its pedestal (being the Volume of Virgils *Georgics*)[6] to be worship'd by the real patriots; Mr. Heithausen thinks a plain ribbon a sufficient honour for a man whose ideas can admit of the belief of the existence of Slavery in Silesia: and as for myself, I am of opinion that a man whose life has been devoted without fee or reward to the service of the public has so great a reward arising from the consciousness of having done good, and so just a Claim to honour, that shall not trouble my head about methods *to encrease it.*

But I must beg your pardon for this ladylike chat, though your having been burnt in effigy, is enough to make any pen run wild, and only beg the favour of you to consult the next page for the performance of a promise, I ought to have fulfilld sooner. The table will explain itself and will I hope be satisfactory. I could wish that a favour I have to beg of you were not inconvenient to you. In my book relating to the king of Prussia I have occasion (in order [to] save myself the trouble of writing out a new account) to refer to the state of Servitude of Silesian peasantry as stated in Baron Heithausens answers to your Queries. If you could insert these answers in your next number viz for June, I could allude to them in this manner: Vide the *Annals of Agriculture* No. 54 for June 1788 by Arthur Young Esqr.[7] As the sheet will soon go to press you would infinitely oblige me by desiring any body ⟨*Miss Young*⟩ to write upon a scrap of paper the word Yes, or No, sealing it up and sending it to town, *quam celerrime.*[8]

The Burneys, Francises[9] &c. &c. &c. &c. are all well. London begins to *swarm* (that is like a Bee hive, perhaps this is the wrong expression in Suffolk, in Yorkshire it is right) every body is getting into the Country. If I go on I shall leave no room for my table, and can therefore only assure of the sincerity with which I am Your most humble and obedt. Servant,

B. H. Latrobe

ALS: Additional Manuscripts 35126, folios 420–21, British Library (140/A1).

1. Arthur Young (1741–1820), agriculturist, founder and editor of *Annals of Agriculture* (1784–1809), and author of numerous treatises on agriculture.

2. Young had been deputed by the wool growers of Suffolk to support a petition against the wool bill, which prohibited the exportation of wool. He wrote a number of articles in his *Annals of Agriculture* opposing the bill, and in the spring of 1788 he published two pamphlets on the subject. Young was in London in April 1788 attending Parliamentary sessions and reporting on the bill's progress in the *Annals*. On 22 and 23 April he testified against the bill in the House of Commons, but the House passed the bill on 19 May 1788 and sent it to the House of Lords. On 7 June, Young testified before that body, but the Lords also ignored his views and the wool bill became law. *Journals of the House of Commons* (1788), vol. 43, p. 483; John G. Gazley, *The Life of Arthur Young, 1741–1820* (Philadelphia, 1973), pp. 215–17.

3. Christian Ignatius Latrobe (1758–1836), BHL's eldest brother, was at this time an ordained minister of the *Unitas Fratrum* and secretary of the Moravian Society for the Furtherance of the Gospel. The brothers lived together at No. 6, Rolls Building. Christian Ignatius was to become a prominent figure in the Moravian church, a musical composer, and the compiler of *Selection of Sacred Music from the Works of the Most Eminent Composers of Germany and Italy*, 6 vols. (1806–25). Christian Ignatius Latrobe journals, 23 Feb. 1789, John Rylands University Library, Manchester, England.

4. This refers to Ch. [Christian?] Heithausen, mentioned again later in this letter. He was a German Moravian, apparently, and he resided with BHL and Christian Ignatius at least from April 1788 to February 1789. Christian Ignatius Latrobe journals, 4 Apr. 1788, 23 Feb. 1789.

5. Although BHL says the incident took place in Bury St. Edmunds, Suffolk County, Young himself says it occurred in neighboring Norfolk County in Norwich. M. Betham-Edwards, ed., *The Autobiography of Arthur Young with Selections from his Correspondence* (London, 1898), pp. 172–74.

6. Virgil's *Georgics* (completed 30 B.C.) is a didactic poem on farming that praises Italy and the farmer's way of life.

7. In 1788 BHL published *Characteristic Anecdotes, and Miscellaneous Authentic Papers, Tending to Illustrate the Character of Frederic II, Late King of Prussia, with Explanatory Notes and Observations, by B. H. Latrobe* (London, 1788) (140/B1). BHL described this volume in the preface as "chiefly translated and compiled from a German work, now publishing in numbers in Berlin, under the authority of the present king" (p. iii).

"Queries Concerning Silesia: Answered by Baron Von Heithausen, Lord of Krausche,   13 near Buntzlau," is in Young's *Annals of Agriculture* 10, no. 54 (1788) : 132–38. In query 2, Young asks whether slaves or free peasants are involved in the weaving of linen. BHL cited Heithausen's response to this question in *Characteristic Anecdotes,* p. 193.

    8. Trans.: As swiftly as possible.

    9. Arthur Young's wife, Martha Allen, was the sister of Elizabeth (Allen) Burney, second wife of Dr. Charles Burney, for whom and for the Francises, see the following letter, n. 1.

TO CHARLOTTE ANN (BURNEY) FRANCIS

Norwich Aug. 4th. 1788.

Dear Madam[1]
Here I am,
Eleven miles from Aylsham[2]
With a melancholy story to tell
But what that can be you must guess
For as to my health, I am perfectly well.
And so is my host and my hostess.
But health, you know, without content
Philosophers have said,
May in sad misery be spent.

But this is not the thing
For Browne[3] begins to sing
And now that horrid creature
Has sent me off my metre
And I'll be hang'd if in my head
I find one word to rhyme to "said."
And So in prose I will proceed
As rhymes are scarce, and I must speed
And therefore surely t'will be better
Steads of bad verse, to write a letter.

Now you must know, Madam, that Mr. Francis is to be out this
    morning,
14 As Mrs. Browne with her usual omniscience is me informing:

Therefore I take the liberty upon this present occasion to write his
    wife
And it is of some importance that this letter is read directly, upon my
    life.
For, I must tell you this, William the coachman has taken back every
    drawing;
And if I had him here I'd give him a clapperclawing.
They were in the same Chaisse pocket from which he took my buckles
And I appeal to you whether or no he does not deserve a rap o' the
    knuckles.

But I have now to request, that you'll do your best
To send in quest, of somebody or other to do your behest
And bring the roll of drawings and musick and the rest
By Tomorrow morning to me here at Norwich, where at present I eat
    my porridge.

Now tho' I am in a most violent hurry
I must not forget a message from Dr. Murray
Which is that when Mr. Francis sends any thing to the Eastindies
He'd be so good as to let the Doctor know, as he wishes to put a
    parcel int'his.

Now I *must* likewise tell you that we are *just* now going in the broiling
    heat of the Sun
To Mr. Garlands house at Framlingham, and when we get there I
    believe we shall be pretty well done.

Tol de rol dol, fal de ral tit
Lack a day, what a foine string of wit.

If you can't send the drawings by to morrow morning's light,
By no means send them up to London quite,
But as there's musick with them belonging to Mr. Browne,
Send them to him at Norwich town
And he will send them me,
As soon as *may be.*
And Now to conclude, with eyes full of tears
                                       15

Conjur'd up by affection, by laughing, by fears
That it will be a long time before I again
Shall see your sweet faces; I lay down my pen.

B.L.T.

ALS: Henry W. and Albert A. Berg Collection of English and American Literature, New York Public Library (microfiche add.). Addressed to Mrs. Francis at Aylsham. Endorsed as answered 14 August (letter not found). Although BHL did not employ standard verse form throughout, the editors have transcribed the entire manuscript in this manner.

1. Charlotte Ann (Burney) Francis (1761–1838) was the daughter of the musicologist and Latrobe family friend, Dr. Charles Burney, and the sister of the novelist Fanny Burney. In 1786, she married Clement Francis (d. 1792), a surgeon who had served in India as secretary to Warren Hastings (see BHL to Charlotte Francis, 10 Mar. 1789, n. 3, below). Six years after Francis's death, she married Ralph Broome (1742–1805), who had also served under Hastings in India and who chronicled the governor general's impeachment trial in *Letters of Simpkin the Second, Poetic Recorder, of All the Proceedings upon the Trial of Warren Hastings* (1789). BHL later described Charlotte as " a Lady, for whom, to use the coldest possible expression, I felt so much sincere friendship, and such unfeigned admiration. . . ." BHL to Charlotte (Burney) Broome, 20 Nov. 1815, in BHL, *Correspondence*, 3; Joyce Hemlow, *The History of Fanny Burney* (London, 1958), pp. 193, 228, 280.

2. A small town in Norfolk County, England, home of the Clement Francises. BHL was on his way to London after having spent about a month in Aylsham.

3. Richard Brown (d. 1843) matriculated at Magdalen College, Oxford, in 1778, and he later served as lay clerk at Norwich Cathedral. Charlotte Francis described him as "one of my prime favourites, a very superior man indeed, an excellent companion, and a fine singer." Charlotte (Burney) Francis to Fanny Burney, 14 July [1788], in Annie Raine Ellis, ed., *The Early Diary of Frances Burney, 1768–1778*, 2 vols. (London, 1889), 2 : 319–20; Joseph Foster, *Alumni Oxonienses: The Members of the University of Oxford, 1715–1886*, 4 vols. (Oxford, 1887–88).

TO CHARLOTTE ANN (BURNEY) FRANCIS

London, March 10th. 1789.

Dear Madam

Very well I thank you! and how does yourself and Signor Placido? Hah? I am glad to hear that your little sweeten, neaten, discreeten, compleaten talks and walks, but she "*like any thing*" is an ambiguous appendage;[1] you do not mean to insinuate that she walks like a duck, and talks like a magpye? Or that she walks like a Ghost and talks like a Madman? I should suppose her, (to make her as amiable as I can) that

16

she talks and walks like her Mammy. Hope no offence! I did really not mean to call you a *thing*, Tho' I should be sorry to say that you are *nothing*. So much for that.

Did You or did you not receive a long queer letter in answer to your last dated January the 2d. wherein I gave you some account of Old batchelor-ship. Since then I have had the misfortune to have been turned out of doors with my family consisting of an old Mother of 76, a wife and 3 Children. I lodged in No. 6 Rollsbuildings at the house of one Bowen, an attorney. The villainy of this fellow may be brought in a small degree within your comprehension by this one plain fact. When Mrs. Bowen, who is a Lady of a superior family and education was brought to bed of her last Child, she was left by him for about a week without any thing to *support* herself, her family and nurse, but one shilling; so that most of her Clothes went to *support* her in that situation, as he had *robbed* her of her private fortune and grossly affronted all her friends who might have *supported* her. Upon his return home, she expostulated with him upon the cruelty of his conduct, which so enraged him that he drew an old rusty hanger which hung in the room, and had the instrument not been very blunt, he would have wounded her mortally across the breast. He however merely raised the skin, but threw her into a situation which occasioned the death of her Child, and put her own life into very imminent danger. This fellow having neglected for a Year and a half to pay either the rent or the taxes due upon his house, two Warrants of distress were taken out against the furniture, by which Your humble servant was a loser to a considerable amount, and had besides with the kind assistance of some friends, the above mentioned family to support for near 3 Months during the severe weather of last Winter, in order to keep them from positive *starvation,* as Bowen himself could nowhere be found, but had absconded with a woman he had lived with, for about a twelvemonth before. I am now housed at No. 4 Staples inn buildings, and cannot help being angry with Swift for having painted the *Yahoos* in colors much more favorable than they deserve.[2]

I have this morning enquired after the abode of Mr. Hastings and find that he lives at No. 12 Wimpole street, Mary bone. The disappointment Mr. Burke has lately met with, will I hope inspire him with a new stock of abuse and blackguardism, with which I heartily wish he may splash Mr. Hastings as copiously as ever, nothing being, in my opinion, a more effectual way of *serving* that much injured Man.[3]

By the bye I am 3 Guineas in your debt, which I have half neglected   17 and half forgotten to pay to young Mr. Francis, but which I ought long ago to have refunded. Indeed I have lost the direction of Mr. Francis, and if you please I will postpone the discharge of this enormous debt till your arrival which I am glad to hear will be in April.

Mr. Hutton has been extremely ill of a violent noise in his head. He is at present better but not quite well. I saw him a few days ago; his spirits are superior to his strength I think.[4]

I most heartily join you in rejoicing with exceeding joy upon the joyful Subject of the Kings recovery. Tonight the whole town will be illuminated, and I mean to be one of the *Mob,* and to have some *fun.* The Bells of every Church in the town are now thwacking their tongues against their jaws, Guns are firing from every quarter, all is din and uproar. There's poetical prose for you!!![5]

My views from Aylsham are, allas! not yet all finished. Some of them are however in great forwardness, and that of your house &c. &c., shall be ready for you when you arrive.

I thank you for your account of the weal and woe of our dear Aylshammers. Poor John Bell is I hope better off than he has been for this Year or two past. I am glad to see you in so much better humor [*torn*] this world than I am, (and I do not think myself [*torn*] of the least happy) it shows that you are happy in it. But to be so in London is impossible. Who could be either in love with his shape or his existence when he daily sees so many villains, fools, tormenting wives, Lords, pickpockets, beggarly rich men, false friends, and conceited fools, who bear evident marks of having an affinity to ones self. Nero would have done more justice, than injustice had he conjured all mankinds necks into one, and cut it off at one blow; so much greater a number of bad Yahoos, than of tolerable Men compose the human race.

My compliments to Mr. Sewell and family, if I can recommend him any scholar I shall be happy. My best respects, eke, to the Adeys, love to Miss Hardingham, compliments to the Hollys, a hearty shake o' the hand for my good honest friend Jack Repton,[6] a formal bow to the Murrells, love and respects to Bulivers, and Elvins families, do. to Mr. R. Francis and family, especially the little charming creature Nancy, item the folks at What ye call ums, down there at the bottom, where the Mill is, God-bless my soul for a stupid blockhead who can't remember names! But I mean the Parmeters! And when you have done all this, contrive some method, the most effectual you can think of, to assure Mr. Clement that I respect, esteem, regard, revere, venerate, and reverence him, with all

18

the warmth I am capable of. A kiss to Charlotte, and a low bow, and what else you allow me from Your sincere friend and nonsense talker

B. Latrobe
for yourself

P.S. Remember I won a kiss from you in St. Martins street 4 Years ago for which I only got a Shake by the hand.[7]

ALS: Henry W. and Albert A. Berg Collection of English and American Literature, New York Public Library (microfiche add.). Addressed to Mrs. Francis at Aylsham, Norfolk.

1. Charlotte Francis (1786–1870), later known as Charlotte Francis Barrett. She edited the personal papers of her aunt, Fanny Burney, in *Diary and Letters of Madame D'Arblay*, 7 vols. (London, 1842).

2. In Jonathan Swift's *Gulliver's Travels*, the land of the Houhynhnms was inhabited by horses who behaved with reason and men, called Yahoos, who behaved like beasts.

3. Warren Hastings (1732–1818), first governor general of British India (1774–84), was impeached by the House of Commons in 1787. Among his chief prosecutors was Edmund Burke (1729–97), who gave vent both to his frustrations with the defeat of the India Bill of 1783, and to his contempt for the corruptions of the British government in India, in a vigorous and lengthy attack on Hastings. The proceedings against Hastings extended over seven years, by the end of which time "Burke's reputation, rather than [Hastings's], was in need of repair." J. Steven Watson, *The Reign of George III, 1760–1815* (Oxford, 1960), p. 322.

BHL may have known Hastings through his architectural apprenticeship with S. P. Cockerell at precisely the time when Hastings's country house, Daylesford House in Gloucestershire, was being designed in Cockerell's office. Hastings's diary gives a date in July 1788 for early contacts between architect and client. Paul F. Norton, "Daylesford: S. P. Cockerell's Residence for Warren Hastings," *Journal of the Society of Architectural Historians* 22 (1963) : 127–33.

4. James Hutton (1715–95), founder and leader of the Moravian church in England and a close friend of the Burneys.

5. On the night of 10 March 1789, Englishmen celebrated the recovery of George III from a prolonged period of physical illness and mental derangement. Ida Macalpine and Richard Hunter, *George III and the Mad-Business* (London, 1969), pp. 90–91.

6. John Adey Repton (1775–1860), architect, son of landscape-gardener Humphry Repton.

7. St. Martin's Street, Leicester Square, was the home of the Charles Burney family from 1774 to 1787. There the Burneys lived in the house previously occupied by Sir Isaac Newton. Joyce Hemlow, *The History of Fanny Burney* (London, 1958), pp. 51–52, 198.

The Chelmer and Blackwater Navigation

EDITORIAL NOTE

Latrobe's survey for the improvement of the navigation of the Chelmer and Blackwater rivers was his first independent engineering commission. The River Chelmer, which joins the River Blackwater at the small port of Maldon, connects Chelmsford, the inland county seat of Essex, with the coast. By the early 1790s the navigation through Maldon had become too shallow for large vessels, and a number of Essex residents petitioned Parliament for an act incorporating a company to improve the river navigation by constructing a canal that would bypass Maldon and terminate below the town at Collier's Reach. Maldon residents opposed the proposed legislation, and the port's mercantile community hired Latrobe as an expert witness to testify against the bill when it was examined by a committee of the House of Lords in the spring of 1793. The bill passed, however, and the undaunted Maldon merchants, led by John Strutt, prepared to present, at the next session of Parliament, an alternative plan which would have retained the navigation through their port.[1] They turned to Latrobe in October 1793 to make the necessary surveys and plans for the new navigation proposal. After about two weeks of surveying, Latrobe drew up the plan and report, printed below, in which he advocated straightening and deepening the channel in the River Blackwater from Collier's Reach to Maldon. He suggested that the cost of improvement could be reduced by selling the ballast which was removed in deepening the river. Latrobe proposed the construction of a canal from Maldon to Beeleigh Mill, where the navigation would enter the River Chelmer and proceed on to Chelmsford.[2] Shortly before the Latrobe scheme was introduced in the House of Commons in March 1794, the engineer changed his mind regarding the location of the canal from Maldon to Beeleigh Mill. Latrobe described the change and the reasons for it in his letter of 24 February 1794 to John Strutt, also printed below.

Perhaps because the last minute changes violated the standing rules of the Commons regarding the length of time that navigation schemes had to be advertised, the Commons committee killed the plan.[3] The Maldonites decided to make another effort to change the original Chelmer and Blackwater Navigation Act in the spring 1795 session of Parliament. Latrobe was again hired to make a

---

1. BHL to Strutt, 24 Feb. 1794, below; A. F. J. Brown, *Essex at Work, 1700–1815* (Chelmsford, England, 1969), p. 90; John Booker, *Essex and the Industrial Revolution* (Chelmsford, England, 1974), pp. 138, 142; *Journals of the House of Commons* 48 (1793): 224, 923, 938–39.

2. BHL, "A Survey of the Course of the River Blackwater . . . ," watercolor map, 11 Nov. 1793, Q/RUm 1, and BHL, "Report upon the Practicability and advantage of making the River Blackwater navigable . . . ," 30 Dec. 1793, D/DQs 135, both in the Essex Record Office, Chelmsford, England (260/B1, 154/A11).

3. William Birch, bill "In Matter of an Applicatn. for obtaing. an Act of Parliament for improvg. the Maldon Navigation &c.," 14 May 1795, D/DRa o13, Essex Record Office.

new survey and plan which incorporated his changes of early 1794.[4] He appeared before a Commons committee, chaired by John Strutt's son, Joseph
Holden Strutt, and Thomas Berney Bramston. Satisfied with his testimony that
the plan was "very practicable" and that the standing orders of the Commons
had been complied with, the committee reported to the Commons that a bill
should be prepared for altering the 1793 Chelmer and Blackwater Navigation
Act according to Latrobe's plan. But before the bill could be approved it was
amended to death by supporters of the Chelmer and Blackwater Navigation
Company, and subsequently the navigation was completed in 1797 according to
the original plan.[5]

   In the meantime, Latrobe had difficulty collecting his fees from the Maldon
group. He wrote John Strutt on several occasions in 1795 asking him to take care
of the matter, but it is not known whether the engineer was ever paid before
leaving for America in November of that year.[6]

   4. Ibid.; BHL, "A Map or Plan of the intended Improvement of the Navigation of the
Rivers Blackwater and Chelmer . . . ," watercolor map, [30 Sept. 1794], Q/RUm 1, Essex
Record Office (260/B5); BHL, "Report upon the plan of the intended Improvement of the
rivers Blackwater and Chelmer . . . ," 28 Oct. 1794, D/DRa 016, Essex Record Office
(154/E5), enclosed in BHL to Strutt, 28 Oct. 1794, below.
   5. *Journals of the House of Commons* 50 (1795) : 184; Birch, bill "In Matter of an Applicatn. for obtaing. an Act of Parliament for improvg. the Maldon Navigation &c.," 14
May 1795; Thomas Wright, *The History and Topography of the County of Essex*, 2 vols. (London, 1836), 1 : 95.
   6. BHL to John Strutt, 17 July, 29 Aug. 1795, both in D/DRa 022, Essex Record
Office (microfiche add.); BHL to Strutt, 8 Sept. 1795, below.

REPORT ON THE CHELMER AND BLACKWATER NAVIGATION

London, Decr. 30th. 1793.[1]
No. 6 Grafton street Fitzroy square

Report upon the Practicability and advantage of making the
River Blackwater navigable for Vessels not drawing more than
12 feet of Water, from Colliers-reach to the Hithe, and from
thence to Fullbridge at the upper end of the town of Maldon in
Essex.

In consequence of an Act of Parliament having passed in the last
Session, authorizing a certain Company of Proprietors therein named
under certain regulations and restrictions,[2] and according to a plan
delivered in, to carry into effect a Scheme for making the river Chelmer   21

navigable from Chelmsford to Beely Mills, and to construct a Culvert and navigable Canal over Langford Oldstream from thence into the River Blackwater which being rendered navigable as far as Heybridge is to be continued by means of a forced Canal across the Marshes to Colliers reach; the Work has been begun in several places above Beely-Mills, and is in some degree of forwardness. Contrary however to the usual practice in constructing navigable Canals, to begin at the lower end, in order to gain a Navigation as soon as possible, there is no appearance of an intention to carry that part of the Scheme into execution which lies below Beely Mill. It seems moreover to be the intention of the Company, wholly to abandon that part of the Navigation, and apply for an act to construct a Bason in Pottman marsh connected with the navigable river at Beely Mill by a barge-Canal, and with Colliers Reach by a Ship-Canal, running nearly parellel to the old Channel of the River. The Injury the present Owners of Property on the old Stream at Maldon will suffer by this Scheme if carried into execution need not be pointed out. It is self evident. But independent of the Injury it would occasion to the town and port of Maldon, its expence must be enormous even if its practicability were well ascertained. Upon the sort of Estimate that it is possible to make of a scheme with the detail of which I am not acquainted, I will venture to affirm that it will cost at least £25.000, to carry it in execution in such a manner as appears to me to be necessary to make it answer the purposes naturally to be expected from so great an undertaking; and to give it that degree of Strength and durability which is requisite to avoid future expence.

It must be evident upon examining into the means of connecting the old with the new navigation, that the easiest method would be to render the old Channel navigable to such a distance from the Sea, that the Effect of the Swell shall not prevent the Canal-Barges from taking in their loading from the Ships, or endanger them while lying in the River or going up or coming down the Stream.

Could it be made clear that this can be done and at a small comparative expence the advantages obtained thereby in diminishing the expence of the Navigation, in the preservation of the advantages long enjoyed by the town and port of Maldon, and in the security obtained by the Owners of Land, Wharfs, and Warehouses upon the River of an undiminished Value in their property, would, it is presumed render all further argument against the Pottman Marsh-Scheme unnecessary.

22   With this view I have taken a very minute Survey of the Channel of

the River Blackwater, and am of opinion, that few Navigations may be improved more easily and at a smaller expence. This must in some measure appear from this circumstance that though no method whatever has been pursued within the memory of the oldest Navigators of the River in order to obtain more water upon the Shoals above Colliers reach, excepting by heaving Ballast for the use of the Colliers, yet wherever a shoal has been lowered by this means, the water has remained of the same depth for a considerable time without being again filled either by drift sand, or the loamy Sediment of the river.

The situation of all the Shoals in the River Blackwater, from Hilly pool point to Fullbridge, points out the natural means of preventing their reaccumulation when once removed. Wherever there is an angle or bend in the Channel, there is deep Water at the point, and a Shoal on each side of it. By cutting off these angles therefore the cause will be removed: and though it would be difficult and very expensive to render the Channel perfectly straight, the bends may be made so easy that the accumulation of Shoals can be well prevented.

The line which I would propose to be followed in making the new Channel is marked upon the map in blue. The old Channel is marked by dotted lines in Orange.[3]

I must here observe that the soil through which the River Blackwater runs consists of a very smooth loamy earth which resists the effects of the stream and the tide. Below this stratum is another of hard coarse gravel. On the South side the stratum of loam is very thick. But on the North Side the Gravel lies so near the surface and is so easily removed by the action of the Stream, or of the Tide that the Channel has for some Years past and is still gaining upon the North and leaving the South shore. Within the memory of many of the Bargemen now navigating the River the Channel directed its course across the Sand hill near to Parsonsness and was then deeper and freer from Shoals than it has been since it quitted that direction, for one more curved.

The expence of removing many of the Shoals will in a great measure be repaid by the Sale of the Ballast of which they consist. I have therefore set down half of this expence as the utmost sum likely to be required.

Estimate of the expence of rendering the River Blackwater navigable for Vessels of Burthen to the Hithe at Maldon, and from thence to Fullbridge.

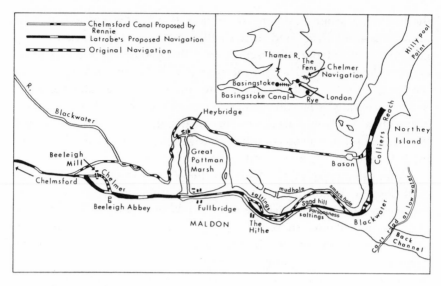

Map 1. The Chelmer and Blackwater Navigation. By Mike Chu.

1. To lowering the Shoal at Colliers point, one feet six inches, so as to procure 13 feet of Water at spring tides. This shoal consists of good clean Ballast; half the expence_____ 44. 0.0 £ s d

2. To cutting a new Channel across the Sand hill by Parsonsness into the old Channel to the West of the Mudhole, removing the Soil into Smack hole and mudhole_____ 880. 0.0

3. To deepening the Channel and making a new Cut across the point to the Hithe_____ 618.13.4

4. To deepening the River from the Hithe to the Bridge so as to render it freely navigable at all tides for large Sloops and Barges, by procuring 11 feet 6 inches Water all the Way. The whole of this is Clean Ballast, one half paying its own expence_____ 141.13.4

5. To further deep'ning the Channel so as to procure 12 ft. 6 i. of Water from the Hithe to the Bridge, that large Vessels may warp up._____ 177. 1.8

6. In order to connect the Navigation of the Blackwater with the navigation of the Chelmer above Beely Mill, it will be necessary to remove the present Bridge and to erect a new one, through which Barges may more

conveniently pass and repass, the expence of which,
if built in timber will be————————————————— 865. 0.0

7. A lock must be constructed above the Bridge in the
situation pointed out in the Map, which if 70 feet
long in the Clear, built in Brick, and facing and
pairing bricks bedded and jointed in tarras,[4] and
coped with Granite will cost————————————— 830. 0.0

8. The expence of a navigable Cut from the lock at the
bridge to the lock below the Culvert at Beely Mill,
will be————————————————————— 748. 0.0

9. Expence of utensils, barges, superintendance, &c. &c.   520. 0.0

10. Purchase of Land from Beely Mill to Fullbridge being
5 Acres 2 Roods, worth at an average of 20 s. per
Acre at 30 Years purchase——————————— 165. 0.0

11. Purchase of the small Quantity of Land in the
saltings at Parsonsness and the Hithe point————— 50. 0.0

Total 5.049.8.4[5]

I will only add that it would be of very little, if of any use to render
the River navigable for large Vessels up to the Bridge from the Hithe.
The river is from thence to the Bridge much narrower and should at any
time a ship of burthen warp up, she would considerably impede the
navigation, and prevent the smaller Craft from coming in, or going out.
Besides it is impossible for the Canal-barges to lie or load more safely,
than they may at the Hithe, or indeed any where between the Hithe and
Colliers reach point.

P.S. It is my opinion, although it does not enter into the present
scheme that the Navigation of the River Blackwater would be rendered
much more safe and certain, were the Gut between Northey Island and
the South Shore of the River entirely stopt up, by raising the present
Cart road to the Highth of the Seawalls. The Cross tide which sets in
from the Back of the Island occasions more inconvenience than any
other circumstance attending the navigation. This might be done at an
expence of about 2.500 pounds. But should even nothing be done in this
respect, the Back channel is daily filling up by the sediment of the Water,
and there is a certain, though a distant prospect, that time will at last
effect it.

B. H. Latrobe   25

ADS: D/DQs 135, Essex Record Office (154/A11).

1. A reason for BHL's month-and-a-half delay in writing this report (he made the survey from 25 October to 11 November 1793) may have been the tragic death of his wife, Lydia, in childbirth on 25 November. According to BHL's brother, "the loss of his first wife . . . quite deranged his affairs and almost his mind." Christian Ignatius Latrobe to John Frederick Latrobe, 10 Apr. 1794, 18 Sept. 1821, both in John Henry de La Trobe Collection, Hamburg, copies in PBHL.
2. Chelmer and Blackwater Navigation Act, 33 Geo. III, cap. 93.
3. "A Survey of the Course of the River Blackwater . . . ," watercolor map, 11 Nov. 1793. See Map 1, based on a similar map that BHL drew a year later: "A Map or Plan of the intended Improvement of the Navigation of the Rivers Blackwater and Chelmer . . . ," [30 Sept. 1794]. The original maps are reproduced in BHL, *Engineering Drawings*, pp. 114–15.
4. Tarras is one of the names for hydraulic or waterproof cement, which in BHL's time was widely used for canal structures.
5. This total is in error. The correct figure should be £5039.8.4.

TO JOHN STRUTT

Grafton street, London Feby. 24th. 1794.

Sir,[1]

As I found some difficulty in procuring admission to the Office of the Clerk of the Peace at Chelmsford yesterday, (being Sunday), I have been under the necessity of delaying my plan a day longer than I hoped to have done. It will however be completed early tomorrow morning.[2]

Upon very mature consideration of every circumstance relating to the communication of the Maldon navigation, with the Chelmer canal at Beely mill, I cannot help being decidedly of opinion, that both the expence of obtaining an act of Parliament to carry it in the line proposed, North of the Chelmer, and the money expended in attempting it, should an act be obtained, will be thrown away. The best level, and the best Ground is certainly on the South side of the river. In my examination before the committee of the house of lords in the last Session, I gave it as my opinion, an opinion then founded upon reasons, which further consideration has more strongly confirmed, and of the substantiality of which I am thoroughly convinced, that the scheme of going by means of a Culvert across Langford old Stream was impracticable. I mean, that though it might in a fortunate season free from floods, be effected, the first high tide, in opposition to a full fresh flood, would immediately

26

blow it up, though built in the most durable manner. The reasons I gave for this opinion, were not even attempted to be refuted, and were hardly animadverted upon by Mr. Rennie's people.[3] I cannot therefore with any hope of making good my evidence, insist upon that part of *our own scheme,* should the opposite party, who have taken notes of my former evidence, rest upon it.

When I was last at Maldon, the Gentlemen whom I had the honor of consulting with, impressed my mind with very different ideas, from the new light in which the matter is taken up. Their utmost wish seemed to be this, to prevent, by the introduction of a plausible scheme of improving the old Channel at a small expence, the passing a bill for making a bason in Pottman-marsh, and a canal for ships leading from Colliers reach into it. Whether the new plan ever took effect or not, whether even it were feasible or not, seemed to them not of so much importance, provided that object were attained. I received directions to go down to Maldon on the 20th. of October. I could not arrange my affairs to go down till the 25th. What use I made of the very short time between that day and the 11th. of Novr. my survey will best prove. Indeed my exertions were as great as in very short days, and excessively bad weather they could be.

Had I supposed that a scheme intended to take full effect, and to dispose of the money of my employers were in view, I should at once have declared, that a fortnight was too short a time, finally to determine upon so important an object, or even to take the necessary plans and levels; and I should at once have given the whole weight of my advice against the idea of carrying the canal of Communication on the north side of the river.

As far however as my plan goes, namely from Hilly pool point to above Fullbridge, I cannot possibly make it more correct than it is, nor do I conceive that any estimate can be more exact, than that I have formed upon my survey. I can also vouch for the greatest possible accuracy in that part of my estimate which relates to the lock above Fullbridge, and to a Canal of the length, depth, and width of the Canal of Communication from that lock to the Lock below the Culvert.

In regard to the plan proposed by my reference[4] it was agreed upon between myself and the Gentlemen of Maldon, to have it open as much as could be done—either to go immediately into the Blackwater river above the Fullbridge lock at the point shown in my plan, or to pass through the grounds described upon the plan in the Reference, which 27 appeared completely sufficient for the purposes they had in view. Now the fact is, that if the canal of Communication be carried on the North side of the river, there is no reason why it should not join the Navigation of the Blackwater in the point nearest to the lock, excepting, that by going into Mr. [Robert] Barnard's Mill-head, it might injure his mill. The same injury however would be done to Mr. Crosier's mill by the scheme, introduced into my estimate, though in a less degree, as there is already a lock proposed in that situation.

Upon reading a Copy of the petition, I find that if it be opposed, an objection may be made that the plan does not support it, to its whole extent. For though all the lands, with the names of the owners and tenants are described upon the plan, they are not actually laid down, nor was it possible in the time, independent of the views of the Gentlemen of Maldon, to push my surveys to that extent.[5]

Considering the state and merits of the objects aimed at by both parties, I cannot help remarking, that the proprietors under the last act, as if not sufficiently embarrassed by this present burthensome undertaking, seem likely to obtain nothing even by a successful application to Parliament for the Pottman marsh scheme, but a new incumbrance; and if the Maldon trade be preserved till it be carried into execution, it will be long enough before it is lost.

On the contrary, nothing appears to me more practicable at a small comparative expence, than to make the present Channel of the river Chelmer navigable for barges at all tides from Fullbridge to almost opposite to Beely abbey, there to construct a lock, and to go from thence into Beely Mill head on the South side. This is certainly the only scheme to which I would advise subscriptions, a scheme likely to be productive of all the advantages pointed o[ut] by Mr. Birch, and which alone, I should of my [own ac]cord recommend, and with a full expectation of seeing its success.[6]

I have the honor to be Sir Your most obedient humble Servt.

B. H. Latrobe

P.S. The time is so short, that I am under the necessity of requesting that you will have the goodness to accept my apology for sending this rough copy to you.

ALS: D/DRa 018, Essex Record Office (microfiche add.).

1. John Strutt (1727–1816), M.P. for Maldon from 1774 to 1790, was a wealthy country squire and progressive farmer. He began building his manor, Terling Place, in

1772, and by 1781 his estates included over 5,000 acres which earned nearly £3,500 a year. A staunch Tory, Strutt was active in local affairs in the borough of Maldon and in the county. In 1790, his son, Col. Joseph Holden Strutt (1758–1845), succeeded him in the House of Commons. Sir Lewis Namier and John Brooke, *The History of Parliament: The House of Commons, 1754–1790*, 3 vols. (New York, 1964), 3 : 493–95; Charles R. Strutt, *The Strutt Family of Terling, 1650–1873* (n.p., 1939).

2. According to the standing orders of the House of Commons, certain requirements had to be fulfilled before a canal or river improvement bill could be introduced. These orders required that a map of the project and a book of reference be deposited with the clerk of the peace of the appropriate county and that notices of the planned improvements be inserted in the county newspapers. Apparently BHL wished to examine the map and book of reference he had deposited with W. Bullock, the Essex County clerk of the peace, the previous November. O. Cyprian Williams, *The Historical Development of Private Bill Procedure and Standing Orders in the House of Commons*, 2 vols. (London, 1948–49), 1 : 43–44; BHL, "A Survey of the Course of the River Blackwater . . . ," watercolor map, 11 Nov. 1793, Q/RUm 1, Essex Record Office, Chelmsford, England (260/B1).

3. John Rennie (1761–1821), the leading civil engineer in England in the early 1790s, was in charge of constructing three major canals (Kennet and Avon, Lancaster, and Rochdale) at the time he undertook the Chelmer and Blackwater commission in 1792. Therefore, he assigned his assistant, Charles Wedge, to make the actual survey for the canal and river improvement. BHL's testimony in the House of Lords had been against the Rennie/Wedge plan which bypassed Maldon. C. T. G. Boucher, *John Rennie, 1761–1821: The Life and Work of a Great Engineer* (Manchester, England, 1964), pp. 15–16; John Booker, *Essex and the Industrial Revolution* (Chelmsford, England, 1974), p. 142.

4. This was the book of reference that BHL submitted with his plan to the Essex clerk of the peace in November 1793.

5. This failure to include the details of all the land through which the entire navigation was to pass may have been the impediment which resulted in the defeat of BHL's scheme in the spring 1794 session of Parliament. According to William Birch, the Maldon group's attorney-lobbyist, objections were made to the BHL plan "on the Ground of informality as to the advertisemt. plan and Book of reference." Birch, bill "In Matter of an Applicatn. for obtaing. an Act of Parliament for improvg. the Maldon Navigation &c.," 14 May 1795, D/DRa 013, Essex Record Office.

6. No copy of BHL's new plan of February 1794 has been found; however, his changes were incorporated in the plan he submitted the following November. "Report upon the plan of the intended Improvement of the rivers Blackwater and Chelmer . . . ," 28 Oct. 1794, D/DRa 016, Essex Record Office (154/E5), enclosed in BHL to John Strutt, 28 Oct. 1794, below.

TO JOHN STRUTT

Grafton street Octr. 28th. 1794.

Sir,

I herewith transmit to you my report and estimate of the proposed improvements in the Navigation of the Rivers Chelmer and Blackwater, and of the New Canal of communication proposed to be Cut at Beleigh   29

Mill.[1] I have very carefully examined my old estimate of the improvements of the lower Channel and find nothing to alter or amend. That part therefore stands as formerly. You will find that I have separated the expence of cleaning out the Channel above the Hithe for Sloops and Sailing Barges, and the expence of rendering the same navigable for Ships of Burthen. This is, I believe what you wished for in your favor of last Week.[2]

I shall set off tomorrow evening upon a journey of business into Yorkshire. I propose staying some time with Sir Christopher Sykes at *Sledmere near Malton, York;*[3] where any letter you may do me the honor to write will find me.

I beg still to observe that I have valued the Land cut through by the Canal, or occupied by the Bridge or towing path, at the rate paid by the Proprietors of the Chelmsford Navigation, £90 an acre. The whole, excepting about 1 Rood and 3 Pole belonging to Mr. Shuttleworth, is Mr. Crosiers, and I have measured into the Quantity that part of his Meadow on the South side that will be liable to be much under water and therefore deteriorated in Quality.

I have the honor to be Sir Your most obedt. hble. Servt.

B. H. Latrobe

ALS: D/DRa o16, Essex Record Office (154/E2).

1. BHL, "Report upon the plan of the intended Improvement of the rivers Blackwater and Chelmer . . . ," 28 Oct. 1794, D/DRa o16, Essex Record Office, Chelmsford, England (154/E5).
2. BHL estimated the cost of deepening the channel from the Hithe to Fullbridge "so as to render it freely navigable at all tides for large Sloops and Barges by procuring 11 f. 6 i. of water all the Way" at £141.13.4. To deepen the channel further "so as to procure 12 feet 6 inches of water . . . that large vessels may warp up" would cost £177.1.8.
3. Sir Christopher Sykes (1749–1801), second baronet, of Sledmere, Yorkshire, was a graduate of Oxford and represented Beverly in the House of Commons (1784–90). He was a prominent figure in the agricultural development of the Yorkshire Wolds. The nature of BHL's business is not known. Peter Townsend, ed., *Burke's Genealogical and Heraldic History of the Peerage, Baronetage and Knightage,* 105th ed. (London, 1970), p. 2603.

The London Police Offices

EDITORIAL NOTE

In 1792, Parliament passed the Middlesex Justices Act providing for the establishment of seven police (or public) offices in London at Queens Square, Hatton

Garden, Worship Street, Whitechapel, Shadwell, Southwark, and Great Marlborough Street. Latrobe was appointed architect for this commission, probably through the influence of his friend Sir Charles Middleton, whose relative, Henry Dundas, was home secretary. According to Latrobe, Dundas attempted to get him to approve of some graft in the acquisition of supplies for the project. Latrobe later recalled, "I hesitated and refused. From that moment I found obstacles to all I attempted, and could not get a shilling out of the treasury."[1]

Latrobe's work on the police offices was limited to repairs and alterations since the offices were housed in already existing buildings. Part of his work included the examination of accounts of tradesmen, merchants, and housekeepers who worked on, or provided supplies for, the police offices. A number of these accounts. which Latrobe approved as late as November 1795 (the month of his departure for America), are in the Middlesex Records, The Greater London Record Office.[2]

1. BHL to Christian Ignatius Latrobe, 5 Jan. 1807, in BHL, *Correspondence*, 2.
2. Hamlin, *Latrobe*, pp. 46–47.

LONDON POLICE OFFICES ACCOUNT

[February 1795]

John Reeves Esqr. Receiver of the Public Offices,[1]
established by an act of the 32d. Year of Geo: III, Dr. to
Benjn. Henry Latrobe, Architect.

1792.	£	s	d

1792 July 29th. to Decr. 31st.	To various attendances at each of the seven houses afterwards converted into Public Offices and upon the Receiver to adjust the plan of a Report to the Privy Council, making an Estimate for that purpose, surveying sundry houses proposed but not taken, sundry attendances at the Secretary of State's Office, and at Wimbledon upon Mr. Dundas,[2] and upon the Landlords of the several offices, attendances upon Messrs. Spurrier and Phipps, and the agent of Mr. Hamilton	31

Rowan to remove difficulties respecting the possession of the house in Great Marl- borough street, and to making sundry arangements unconnected with the repair, alteration, or erection of any of the build- ings and a voluminous correspondence with Magistrates Clerks &c. 75 — —

To actual expences in postage, porter- age, Cartage of rubbish, expenditures of Clerks, stationary, and sundry ready monies paid } 16 10 —

1793.

March 12th. To a joint Survey of the house and premises in Great Marlborough street taken with Mr. Saml. Robinson, surveyor by order of the Secretary of State, to a report upon the same, and attendances upon the Receiver and at the Secretary of States Office } 10 10 —

To Cash paid Mr. Saml. Robinson, as above 10 10 —

To designs, particulars, and an estimate of a new Public office proposed to be built in Whitechapel, which design was laid aside after the Contract was made, at 630 at 2-1/2 per Ct. } 15 15 —

To a new design, particulars, estimate and Contract, for the same, which was after- wards executed } 7 10 —

April 8th. To taking an inventory of the furniture &c. of Great Marlborough street, and transfer of the same from Mrs. Isabella Wilson to Mrs. Sexton, her Successor 2 2

To Do. at Whitechapel from Mrs. Nolan to NN 2 2

To actual expences in postage, porterage, removing furniture, expenditure of Clerks, stationary and sundry ready monies paid from January 1st. to Decr. 31st. 1793 } 23 8 9

1794.

		£	s	d
from Jany. 1st to Decr. 31. 1794	To actual expences in postage, porterage, carting rubbish, expenditure of Clerks, stationary, and sundry ready monies advanced }	13	8	7
	To attendances at each of the public Offices by order of the Treasury upon the survey directed to be made by Mr. Groves, at the Works executed under my direction.[3] 12 days at £3.3s. per day }	37	16	—
	To commission upon £5,414.2.2 being the sum expended under my direction at 5 per Ct. }	270	14	—

Total Mr. Latrobe's Bill	485	6	4

To Cash paid

Housekeepers and Messengers.

	£	s	d
Mrs. Morrison Housekeeper Queensquare West, for Wages and Necessaries	12	15	6
Mr. Hatch, Messenger do.	1	1	—
Mrs. Isabella Wilson, Housekeeper, Gt. Marlboroughstreet, Wages, Necessaries &c. from Aug. 25th. 1792 to June 1793 }	39	9	6
Mr. Ogden, Messenger, dismissed	8	15	—
Mr. Davies do.		10	6
Mrs. Sexton Housekeeper do.	12	12	—
Mrs. Nolan, do. at Whitechapel from Augt. 21st. 1792 to Feby. 16th. 1793, 26 Wks. @ 10/6	13	13	—
do. allowance for Necessaries @ 2/6 per Wk.	3	10	—
do. Mops, Brooms, pails, Matts &c. &c.	4	14	—
Mr. Nolan Messenger from Aug. 21st. 1792 to Augt. 25th. 1793 }	27	6	—

	609	12	10

33

Dr.   609 12 10

Current Expences

Paid Mr. Nelson for Coals to Queensquare	10	5	—
Do. Do. Great Marlboroughstreet	10	7	6
Paid Mr. Walker for Oil do.[4]	6	13	—
Paid Mr. Dickinson for do. Hatton Garden	2	10	6

£29.16.0

Incidental Expences for

scouring, cleaning the houses in Queen-
square, Great Marlboroughstreet, Hatton-
street, Union hall, and matts, brooms &c.   7 8 5
Paid Ashby linnendraper for towels for the
Magistrates   8 10 9

£15.19.2

£655 8 —

2d. Cash advanced certain tradesmen as per
General acct.   2538 18 10

£3194 6 10

1st. Discount and stamps	10	9	6
Expences of an action Rogers v. Latrobe	5	3	7
Do. Younger[5] v. do.	3	2	3
Do. Smith v. Burton[6] & Do.	9	7	6

£28.2.10

£3222 9 8
2453 1 —

£769 8 8

Cr.
1792
Septr. 1st.   By a draft on Hammersley & Co.   150 — —
      20   By a do.   50 — —
               By a do.   100 — —
               By a do.   50 — —
34   By a do.   30 — —

1793				
Novr. 5th.	By a Bill at 3 Mo. due Feby. 8th. 1794	300	—	—
		680	—	—
1794	By a draft on Hamersley & Co.	35	—	—
Jany. 3d.	By a do. do.	40	—	—
Feby. 19	By a draft do.	170	—	—
March 15	By a Bill at 2 Mo.	100	—	—
18th.	By a Bill at 2 Mo.	90	—	—
Aprl. 8th.	By a draft on Hammersley & Co.	40	—	—
22d.	By a Bill at 2 Mo.	150	—	—
May 3d	By a draft on Hammersley & Co.	20	—	—
9th.	By sundry acceptances	265	—	—
June 3d	By do.	500	16	—
Octr. 31st	By a Bill	5	5	—
Novr. 13	By do.	84	—	—
Decr. 5th.	By do.	100	—	—
23	By do.	48	—	—
		2328	1	—
1795				
Jany. 2	By a draft on Hammersley & Co.	35	—	—
24	By a do.	50	—	—
"	By a Bill at 6 Wks.	40	—	—
		2453	1	—
	Balance due to Mr. Latrobe	769	8	8
		3222	9	8

AD: Middlesex Records, Greater London Record Office (155/A12). Endorsed: "Mr. Latrobe in Account with John Reeves Esqr. Receiver of the police, Febry. 1795."

1. John Reeves (1752?–1829), in addition to serving as receiver of the public offices, was at various times chief justice of Newfoundland, superintendent of aliens, and king's printer. He published widely on legal and religious subjects. BHL to William Lovering, 20 June 1811, LB (85/G1).

2. Henry Dundas (1742–1811), one of the most powerful Scottish politicians in his day, was the secretary of state for home affairs from 1791 to 1794. A member of the House of Commons (1774–1802) and the House of Lords (1802–11), Dundas held such important posts as treasurer of the navy (1782–1800), privy councillor (1784–1805), secretary of war (1794–1801), and first lord of the Admiralty (1804–05). In 1802 he was created

Viscount Melville of Melville in the county of Edinburgh. He was impeached and nearly convicted in 1806 for misuse of navy funds.

3. Groves "ascertained and passed" a number of the bills of tradesmen who worked on the police offices. BHL, "General Acct. of Monies due and paid to the Police Trades-men, Febry. 1795," Middlesex Records, Greater London Record Office (155/B9).

4. John Walker supplied "fine Spermaceti Oil," "Glass Cillinders," lamp shades, and candles for the Great Marlborough Street police office. Police Office Accounts of Mr. Walker, Oilman, 20 Dec. 1794–11 Apr. 1795, Middlesex Records.

5. BHL had paid bricklayer Thomas Younger £32.18.9 for his police office work. BHL, "General Acct.," February 1795.

6. In 1795, R. Burton performed over £46 worth of carpentry and joiner's work at the Great Marlborough Street police office. Carpenter's Bill, Great Marlborough Street Police Office, Jan.–Nov. 1795, Middlesex Records.

TO JOHN STRUTT

Grafton street Fitzroy Square
Septr. 8th. 1795.

Sir,

Previous to my intended Journey to Ireland,[1] I took the liberty to send you the enclosed Bill,[2] for which Mr. Birch had very frequently asked me. I confess, that I should have been much less reluctant to have troubled you with my account had your endeavors in favor of the port of Maldon been successfull, and even now I am almost ashamed of the amount of my bill. I hope you will have the goodness to make your remarks to me with the utmost freedom upon it, and I assure you that nothing would be more distressing to me, than that you should think I had overrated the services I have endeavored to be of to you.

My actual expences, of which I have kept a very particular account, amount to very near £30.0.0, with the balance of my former account.[3]

I have now most particularly to entreat you, that you will have the goodness to favor me with a remittance as soon as convenient at least of some part of my account, and should I have the misfortune to appear to you to have overcharged you, I assure you that I consider myself as open to correction upon any particular article. Some particular *family* occurrences press at this moment most heavily upon me,[4] I have been cruelly disappointed in my expectations from Ireland, and in short, any part of my account remitted to me at an early period would most essen-
36 tially serve me, and prevent very great inconvenience to me. At all

events, I hope you will forgive the urgent manner in which I have addressed you, and be assured that I am with the greatest respect and gratitude Your faithful obedt. servant

B. H. Latrobe

ALS: D/DRa 022, Essex Record Office (microfiche add.). Addressed to Strutt at Terling Place, Witham, Essex. Also in BHL's hand: "To be forwarded as soon as possible."

1. BHL may have intended to go to Ireland on business relating to some land there ("a little piece of a Dunghill") that had belonged to his mother. Christian Ignatius Latrobe to John Frederick Latrobe, 25 Sept. 1792, 6 Apr. 1795, both in John Henry de La Trobe Collection, Hamburg, copies in PBHL.

2. The bill (D/DRa 022, Essex Record Office; microfiche add.), which covered expenses BHL incurred between 1793 and 12 May 1795 for traveling, attending Commons, making a survey, making maps, etc., came to £83.7.6. He had received £5.5.0 from a Mr. Bernard, leaving a balance due of £78.2.6.

3. BHL's enclosed bill included an entry for £30.0.0 for "making a compleat survey of the Ground and levels of the proposed Navigation from Fullbridge, and of the proposed new Cut to the South of Beleigh Mill, with an Estimate of making the same and a report and Correspondence thereupon."

4. BHL may be referring to his difficulties in collecting that part of William Sellon's (his father-in-law) estate which had been left to BHL's children upon the death of their mother. BHL's brothers-in-law, John and William Sellon, were in charge of the estate and they never paid BHL the money before he left England. In fact, years later in America, he was able to obtain only a small fraction of the amount due before William Sellon went bankrupt, ending all hopes of remuneration. BHL, *Journals*, 1 : 203; BHL to Christian Ignatius Latrobe, 7 May, 4 Nov. 1804, both below, and 7 Mar. 1808, LB (64/A3); BHL to John Baker Sellon, 4 Feb. 1806, in BHL, *Correspondence*, 2; Hamlin, *Latrobe*, p. 30.

POEM: "GEORGE KING TO KING GEORGE"

[ante 1796]

The petition of a capital Convict to the late King, by which he gained his pardon.

Poor George King to King George presents his petition,
And prays King George will consider poor George King's condition,
And if King George will to George King grant a long day,
George King for King George forever will pray.

as in Duty bound &c. &c. &c.

AD: British Library (155/D8).

POEM: "FOOTE & QUIN"

[ante 1796]

As Quin and Foote one day went out,
To view the country round,
In merry mood they chatting stood,
Hard by the village pound.
Foote from his poke, A shilling took,
And said I lay a penny,
In this same place, Before your face
I'll make this piece a guinea.
Upon the ground, Within the pound,
The shilling soon was thrown,
You see says Foote, The thing's made out,
For here is One pound, one.
I wonder not, Says Quin that thought,
Should in your brain be found,
For that's the way, Your debts you pay,
One shilling in the pound.

[To] the censor of wit,
[With] Mr. B. H. La Trobe's Complts.

AD: British Library (155/D11). The bracketed words in the final couplet are conjectural readings, the manuscript being torn.

TO GEORGE WASHINGTON

Richmond Augt. 22d. 1796.

Sir,

The plough which you did me the favor to say you would try, is now ready, and I shall send it, directed to the care of Mr. Porter, merchant, Alexandria, by the first vessel that is bound from hence to that port.[1] Its merits in working you will easily ascertain upon trial, and should you be satisfied on that head, you will, I believe, find, that with very little care and precission your own people may repair or copy it. I am sorry I could not procure for you in time a cast iron Mould-board. I shall be able to send you one soon. The *turn* of the board appears to me to be the most perfect possible, and applicable to any plough whatever.

Mr. Gilbert Richardson under whose direction this plough has been made, has been in the habit of using the heavy Rotheram plough in England, and perfectly understands its construction. I should conceive myself particularly favored by your sending me the stock of your plough, which the loss of your iron work has rendered useless to you; as I think I can get it perfectly reinstated here. Should your engagements permit your attention to these lesser objects, I should be extremely flattered by your suffering me to show my sense of the very polite reception with which you honored me at Mt. Vernon in endeavoring to be of the slightest assistance to your agricultural views.

We have had such constant rains *here,* and lower down upon James river, that almost all the lowland corn is much injured, and a great quantity totally destroyed. The highland crop looks and promises well should the weather become more favorable. There has been no fresh, nor even a considerable rise in James river notwithstanding the daily rains of the two months past.

I have the honor to be Sir Your most obedient hble. Servt.

Benjn. Henry Latrobe.

ALS: George Washington Papers, Library of Congress (microfiche add.). Endorsed as received 17 September.

1. BHL visited Mt. Vernon in July 1796 and described his conversation with Washington on "the different merits of a variety of ploughs" which the president had tried. Washington preferred "the heavy Rotheram plough from a full experience of its merits. The Berkshire iron plough he held next in estimation. He had found it impossible to get the iron work of his Rotheram plough replaced in a proper manner otherwise he should never have discontinued its use." Latrobe promised to send the president "one of Mr. Richardson's ploughs of Tuckahoe, which he accepted with pleasure." BHL, *Journals,* 1 : 170.

Porter was probably Thomas Porter (d. 1800), an Alexandria merchant who was elected secretary to the first board of directors of the Bank of Alexandria in 1792. CHS, *Records* 8 (1905):5; *Tyler's Quarterly Historical and Genealogical Magazine* 9 (1927–28):159.

The Virginia State Penitentiary

Editorial Note

In the late eighteenth century an international group of thinkers and reformers, some of them motivated by Enlightenment rationalism and some by Christian 39 piety, attacked the traditional penal standards of the Western world. They argued for the reduction of capital punishment to a minimal number of crimes, the substitution of imprisonment for the death penalty, and the transformation of jails, workhouses, and prisons from sordid places of confinement to healthy, secure institutions of moral reform. Their exertions were especially fruitful in Great Britain and Pennsylvania. In Britain the writings of John Howard and Jeremy Bentham, and the prisons built by the obscure but distinguished prison architect William Blackburn, laid a basis for the future development of a penal system. In Philadelphia, Quaker humanitarianism, stimulated by Howard's writings, brought about a new cell house built from 1790–91 in the yard of the Walnut Street Prison. Here was instituted a reformative program of solitary confinement and labor, and the restriction of the death penalty to first degree murder in 1794.[1] In 1796, twenty years after Jefferson had first attempted to revise the "sanguinary code" of Virginia, the state legislature revised the penal code in imitation of Pennsylvania's, and provided for a "penitentiary house" at Richmond. The new spirit of a rationalized and humanitarian penology had at last penetrated Virginia, and now posed a relatively novel architectural problem.

By early 1797 Latrobe had begun a design for the Virginia State Penitentiary which his friend Meriwether Jones, a member of the Virginia Council of State, showed to Governor James Wood. On 25 June 1797 Latrobe learned that he had won the competition for the design of the penitentiary. He supervised construction until his removal to Philadelphia in December 1798, after which Major John Clarke completed the building during 1799–1806 with extensive modifications of Latrobe's design. The prison was constructed throughout of vaulted masonry as a fire preventive; permitted a 180-degree view of the semicircular range of cells from a central building; provided both individual cells and workrooms for communal labor; showed attention to ventilation; and displayed an advanced neoclassical style. As such the design reflected new, international penological and architectural thinking. Nonetheless the penitentiary proved to be an unsuccessful experiment in penology, due primarily to the manner in which it was administered. After numerous alterations, the last traces of Latrobe's work disappeared in 1928. For a more detailed discussion of Latrobe's work on the penitentiary, see BHL, *Architectural Drawings*.

1. For the Walnut Street Prison, see Thorsten Sellin, "Prisons of the Eighteenth Century," in *Historic Philadelphia: From the Founding until the Early Nineteenth Century* (Philadelphia, 1953), pp. 326–30; Orlando F. Lewis, *The Development of American Prisons and Prison Customs, 1776–1845* (Albany, N.Y., 1922), chap. 3; Rex A. Skidmore, "Penological Pioneering in the Walnut Street Jail, 1789–99," *Journal of Criminal Law and Criminology* 39 (1948–49):167–80.

TO JAMES WOOD

Richmond January 25th. 1797.

Sir,[1]

I have the honor to return herewith the Map with the Loan of which I have been favored, and to express my thanks for your liberality in permitting to me the use of it. I will take the liberty of waiting upon you, on my return to town to request the favor of seeing the sketches you were so good as to mention in your letter to me.

There is another subject, on which it was my intention to have intruded myself upon the notice of the Executive whenever it should have appeared to me that I could have done so with propriety, namely, to offer my services in the design of the Penitentiary house voted by the last Legislative Assembly.[2] For this purpose I waited till I could obtain information of the Ground resolved upon by the Governor and Council of State, in order that I might have had the means of presenting a design wanting little or no explanation, and adapted to every circumstance attending the building: but as Mr. Jones[3] has anticipated much of what I should have submitted to your Excellency and the Council of State, by laying before You a very rough drawing, intended only to elucidate my private conversations with him, I have now only to express my extreme gratification in the indulgence shewn by the Executive to that plan; and to beg permission that whenever the steps taken by Government shall have sufficiently ripened the business, I may be allowed to lay before them for consideration whatever former experience, or the particular demands of the plans proposed for this State, may suggest.

I have the honor to be with the greatest respect Your Excellency's most obliged humble Servant

B. H. Latrobe.

ALS: State Penitentiary Papers, Virginia State Library (155/E1).

1. James Wood (1750–1813) represented Frederick County in the House of Burgesses (1775), in the 1776 Convention, and in the House of Delegates (1776, 1784). He began his military career during the Revolution as a colonel in the Eighth Virginia Regiment, and by the time the war was over he had risen to the rank of brigadier general of the state troops. In 1784 he was elected to the Council of State and by seniority became lieutenant governor. He was governor from 1796 until his resignation in December 1799. Under his direction the Richmond armory and Richmond penitentiary (designed by BHL) were constructed. He was again elected to the Council of State after his resignation and served until 1813. He was president of the Virginia abolitionist society (1801) and of the 41

Society of the Cincinnati (1802–13). Earl G. Swem and John W. Williams, *A Register of the General Assembly of Virginia, 1776–1918 and of the Constitutional Conventions* (Richmond, Va., 1918), p. 448; Lyon Gardiner Tyler, ed., *Encyclopedia of Virginia Biography,* 5 vols. (New York, 1915), 2 : 46; Robert A. Rutland, ed., *The Papers of George Mason, 1725–1792,* 3 vols. (Chapel Hill, N.C., 1970), 1 : cix.

2. In December 1796 the Virginia General Assembly passed "An Act to amend the penal laws of this Commonwealth," the seventeenth article of which authorized the governor to purchase land in or near the city of Richmond for the construction of a penitentiary capable of accommodating at least 200 prisoners. Samuel Shepherd, *The Statutes at Large of Virginia, from October Session 1792, to December Session 1806, Inclusive, in Three Volumes (New Series), Being a Continuation of Hening,* 3 vols. (New York, 1970 [orig. publ. 1835]), 2 : 5–14.

3. Probably Meriwether Jones (1766–1806), ardent Republican editor of the Richmond *Examiner* (established 1798). In 1796 he was elected to the Council of State, from which he resigned two years later, after he had been elected public printer. He was reelected annually to this patronage position until 1804. In 1799, when political passions ran high in Richmond, Jones "frequently superintended his press with his pistols within his reach." The editor had a keen interest in education and humanitarian causes and was appointed an inspector of the penitentiary in 1801 and a trustee of the Richmond Academy in 1803. BHL, *Journals,* 2 : 544.

TO HENRY BANKS

Richmond, Aprl. 19th. Wednesday [1797].

Dear Sir,[1]

Major Claiborne[2] delivered to me your note and commission the morning after you left town, and I have since then bestowed all the time that the very unfavorable weather would permit, to the compliance with your wish. It has rained part of every day during my survey, and yesterday and today have been so *stormy* and cold as to render it impossible to proceed: I should otherwise have dispatched the drawing by the post of tomorrow. I may however promise that the post which leaves this place on Saturday shall convey to you *a compleat map of your Canal estate,* with *a section* of the whole ground shewing the difference of level between the Canal and the river from one end to the other, by which the power and eligibility of every millseat can be ascertained exactly.[3] If the weather permit you shall also have a continuation of the survey to Richmond showing the connection of your canal estate with the town. I intended to have proceeded to the Locks but must, I fear, give that up for the present. That you may be able to speak with certainty upon the subject, I will just mention that *the line of Millseat,* extending from the Culvert, at

Washington's boundary, to the great Overfall at the extent of your land, and the beginning of Watkins' is 108 Ch. 86 Links, or One Mile, 2 Furlongs, 8 Chains, 86 Links. From this must be deducted that part which belongs to Mauls Mill of which I have not at present information.

To the above drawings I will add my Ideas of the Value of the Estate and of what constitutes that Value, and it has occurred to me that if I could procure the signatures of some of the most respectable Men here, such as Bushrod Washington, Carrington, Marshall, Pollard, Pickett,[4] &c. &c., or of one or two only of them to my statement it might be usefull to you. Claiborne can assist me in getting them.

The weather will scarce permit my sending on a view of your garden. But I will write something about it. I understand that you have a survey of the ground by Paine.[5]

Arthur wrote to Dubois for a Telescopic level which has I believe been made for me in Philadelphia. I sent drawings and dimensions for it. If it is made accordingly it is a valuable instrument, and if you happen to see Dubois and can get it it will be valuable to you whatever you do with your Canal Estate excepting selling it outright, and besides I have a design upon it myself. I just tell you this that you may do as you please or as you can. I have scrawled this at full gallop as you may see. I saw Mrs. Banks[6] an hour ago. She looks and is well, but wants you back again. Believe me very truly Yrs.

B. H. Latrobe.

ALS: Henry Banks Papers, Virginia Historical Society (155/E5). Addressed to Banks at the City Tavern, Philadelphia.

1. Henry Banks (1761–1836), Richmond merchant and lawyer, was the author of numerous articles on political and historical topics. Following the Revolution, Banks acquired large tracts of land in Kentucky and Virginia, much of which he owned jointly with Richard Claiborne. At the time of BHL's association with Banks, however, the latter's fortunes were in a state of decline. Nevertheless, Banks gave BHL much-needed support during his first years in America, in exchange for which BHL made several surveys of Banks's lands. Contract of sale of lands between Richard Claiborne, Henry Banks and James Trenchard, 1794, Henry Banks Papers, Virginia Historical Society, Richmond; Joseph I. Shulim, "Henry Banks: A Contemporary Napoleonic Apologist in the Old Dominion," *Virginia Magazine of History and Biography* 58 (1950):335–45.

2. Richard Claiborne (c. 1756–post 1818) was an officer in the Continental army and an assistant deputy quartermaster for Virginia during the Revolution. In 1805 BHL described Claiborne, a land speculator, as "a ruined Man, now wandering some where in Louisiana, and I would not trust him with 10 Dollars, so exceedingly indiscreet is he." Claiborne later became judge of Rapides Parish in the Orleans Territory (1808–13). By 1814 BHL's opinion of Claiborne had tempered to the point where he wrote, "You are the

same good hearted, wild animal I always knew, and I shall always esteem you for your sincerity, and even for your passionate candor." Like BHL, he pursued an active interest in science and technological improvements. He claimed the invention of a device for propelling boats, the "Duck's-Foot Paddle," the patent rights of which he seems to have at some time offered BHL, but which BHL never officially received. While in New Orleans, Claiborne published an essay on steam navigation, and in 1818 the Louisiana legislature granted him exclusive rights to navigate and propel boats by the "'hinge or duck-foot paddle' method within the boundaries of the state for a period of fourteen years." BHL to Nicholas J. Roosevelt, 18 Dec. 1805, BHL to Claiborne, 8 Jan. 1814, both in LB (46/E2, 114/B14); Curtis Carroll Davis, "A National Property: Richard Claiborne's Tobacco Treatise for Poland," *William and Mary Quarterly*, 3rd ser., 21 (1964):92–117.

3. Banks apparently owned land on the north bank of the James River between the James River Canal and the shore of the river, as well as some adjacent rocks and islands in the river. The land between this segment of the canal and the river was a valuable mill seat because the water in the canal was considerably higher than the river level and thus had waterpower potential. Mauls' Mill, one owned by Banks, and several other mills were already utilizing this power source (see the map in Henry Banks Papers contemporary with this letter). For this privilege the millowners paid a "water rent" to the James River Company, a source of income for the company which became very significant in the next two decades.

Banks wanted BHL to survey his property so that the "fall" (in this case the difference between the canal level and the planned tailrace) could be determined for any particular site in the millseat. Typical falls developed for waterpower in this period were five to twenty-five feet. Wayland Fuller Dunaway, *History of the James River and Kanawha Company* (New York, 1922), pp. 29, 34, 39n; Louis C. Hunter, *Waterpower in the Century of the Steam Engine* (Charlottesville, Va., 1979), pp. 62–63.

4. Bushrod Washington (1762–1829), Richmond lawyer, U.S. Supreme Court justice (1798–1829), and nephew of George Washington; Edward Carrington (1749–1810), officer in the Continental army during the Revolution, delegate to the Confederation Congress (1785–86), and marshal of Virginia appointed in 1789 by President Washington; John Marshall (1755–1835), lawyer, chief justice of the U.S. Supreme Court (1801–35); Robert Pollard (c. 1755–1842), treasurer and secretary of the James River Company (1793–1823); and probably George Pickett (c. 1752–1821), a Richmond merchant in partnership with Pollard. *William and Mary Quarterly*, 1st ser., 10 (1902):202; Samuel Mordecai, *Richmond in By-Gone Days* (Richmond, Va., 1856), pp. 72–73, 234; *Richmond Portraits in an Exhibition of Makers of Richmond, 1737–1860* (Richmond, Va., 1949), pp. 152–53.

For BHL's characterizations of Bushrod Washington and John Marshall, see BHL, *Journals*, 1 : 133.

5. Banks owned nearly five acres of land along a hillside in Richmond adjoining Shockoe Creek to the west, known as "Falling Gardens." William G. Payne surveyed the land for Banks in February 1797. Henry Banks Papers.

6. Martha Koyall (Read) Banks (1775–1804). BHL, *Journals*, 2 : 534–35.

TO JAMES WOOD AND THE COUNCIL OF
STATE OF VIRGINIA

Richmond, May 12th. 1797.

Honorable Sirs,

I beg leave to acknowledge with sincere gratitude the receipt of One hundred Dollars, on account of the plan of a Penitentiary House which you have done me the favor to take under your consideration. I receive it as a gratuity; for I had no claim whatever upon your liberality unless you had thought the plan worthy of being executed; having in common with others purchased *the possibility of preference* by the pains I have taken to merit it. Had you therefore found any other design more eligible and returned mine, I could not have complained that I had employed my time unprofitably.[1]

As a proof of the sense I have of your generosity, I beg to be permitted to add to the drawings contained in the book, the detail of the square part of the building, and such other designs as I omitted on account of their not being perfectly necessary to the explanation of my ideas.[2] I have the honor to be with great respect Your most obedient humble Servt.

B. Henry Latrobe.

ALS: State Penitentiary Papers, Virginia State Library (155/F1).

1. In July BHL received an additional $150 as compensation for his penitentiary drawings and design. BHL to Wood, 20 July 1797, State Penitentiary Papers, Virginia State Library (156/B7).

2. On 1 June, BHL sent to Wood and the council two more sheets of drawings of the square part of the prison (State Penitentiary Papers; 155/F12).

TO HENRY BANKS

Richmond May 29th. 1797.

Dear Sir,

I did not receive your letter d. May 1st. till Saturday. By what accident this can have happened is impossible for me to guess, as I have been daily at the Post Office from whence I have taken many letters, and have been exceedingly impatient to hear from you and of the opinion you have of my Map. I cannot express to you how much I am vexed at not having executed you two Commissions.[1] I am now engaged in them both but doubt the possibility of sending them to you before Thursday or perhaps Saturday. I do not remember the day on which my Map was sent, but it was on a Saturday. On the Monday following I saw Mrs. Banks, who was doubtful whether you would receive it in time. I therefore determined to wait till the next Post. Mr. Macraw[2] arrived by the following stage, and told me you had not received the Map when he left you, but that you would come home by the stage succeeding that which brought him forward. Still I did not hear from you. Major Claiborne told me in answer to my anxious enquiries about the Map, that you had written, that it came in time and that it was *a Cup.* I could make little of the phrase but took it of course as a Compliment. I enquired constantly about you, but neither Mrs. Banks nor Major Claiborne told me any thing respecting what you wished to be done. I would not write to you as my letters could not be worth postage. Thus you see how innocently I have disappointed you.

Mr. Mayo is now building a Mill in the very falls of which you speak, in an eligible Spot. I have been there two or three times with him.[3]

In the mean time I have been hard at work for Major Claiborne with whom I mean to go to Morgantown. I have connected almost all his Surveys, and have drawn several Maps from Surveys in the Land office. But the connecting them is a dry and laborious business indeed. I am exerting myself to procure agencys in which I have partly succeeded. Major Claiborne is to let me have 2,000 Acres of his Cheat or Kenhawa Land for which I am to pay as far as it will go in professional Assistance.[4] The Executive Council have not yet adopted or rejected my plan,[5] but have however very generously given me 100 Dollars for the trouble I have already had and have promised more if my plan be approved: so that you are now my only [Credi]tor and I am quite easy.

Mrs. Banks has been at Hanover the [*illegible*] Weeks. She was well though lowspirited when she left town. Major Claiborne and myself mean to pursue your hint of an Agency office in Morgantown upon which I must write to you another time. I have done much towards my map already. I hope soon to see you here in the mean time believe me truly Yrs.

B. H. Latrobe.

In great haste 9 o'clock.

The Mr. Latrobe you mention must have been my father. He belonged to the Society of Moravians when he died in 1787.[6] His astonishing talents and conspicuous virtues, and the very extensive *fashionable* connexions he had, added some celebrity to that very quiet silent set of Christians, but he was not at their head. However he was the most learned and accomplished Gentleman of their Society, and was distinguished from them, and their rather morose address of the others, by his elegant and winning manners. His Children did not follow his example excepting one of my brothers.

ALS: Henry Banks Papers, Virginia Historical Society (155/F7). Addressed to Banks in Philadelphia.

1. Banks had apparently commissioned BHL to do two drawings: one of Banks's property in the falls of the James River, and one of "Falling Gardens," which Banks wished to promote and sell. See BHL to Banks, 5 June 1797, with enclosure, "Description of Property in the Falls of James River, belonging to Henry Banks Esqr.," Henry Banks Papers, Virginia Historical Society, Richmond (155/G6).

2. Probably Samuel McCraw (1762–1823), a Richmond lawyer who served as state senator from 1795 to 1798. Earl G. Swem and John W. Williams, *A Register of the General Assembly of Virginia, 1776–1918, and of the Constitutional Conventions* (Richmond, Va., 1918), pp. 45, 47, 49.

3. John Mayo (1760–1818), wealthy planter and member of the Virginia House of Delegates (1785–86, 1791–96). BHL, *Journals,* 2 : 547.

4. In 1788, while in England, Richard Claiborne attempted to sell part of his extensive acreage on the Cheat River in western Virginia. Writing to Thomas Jefferson, he explained: "I mean to return to Virginia in the Spring, and settle in Monongalia County, and cultivate plantations on 55,000 Acres which I have on Cheat River, through which the Main Road runs that forms the Line of Communication from Potomac River to Cheat or Monogalia. My views are, to have Farms productive by the time the navigation of the Potomac is completed; and to avail myself of the Trade down that River on one side of the property, and the Western waters on the other." According to Claiborne's prospective buyer, part of his lands were "contiguous to Morgan's Town on the Monongalia." Claiborne to Jefferson, 30 Dec. 1788, and Edward Luttrell to Jefferson, 11 Jan. 1789, both in Julian Boyd, ed., *The Papers of Thomas Jefferson* (Princeton, N.J., 1950–), 14 : 402–03, 434–35.

5. For the penitentiary in Richmond.

6. The Rev. Benjamin Latrobe actually died on 29 November 1786. For a brief discussion of his life and accomplishments, see BHL, *Journals,* 1 : xvii–xviii.

TO HENRY BANKS

Richmond June 2d 1797

Dear Sir,

I wrote to you in great haste by the post of last Tuesday[1] but had not time to thank you for half the obliging things your letter of May 1st contains. Let me therefore do it at once, and assure you that I feel myself so much in your debt for your kind conduct and sentiments towards me that no exertion I can myself make will easily satisfy my opinion of what I owe you.

I told you, I believe, in my last what I have lately been about. Since then I have been engaged by the old Dismal Swamp Company to survey their whole patented Land in the Swamp to take all the Levels of their drains and to give them a compleat report upon their concerns there. I ought to have gone thither this day with Mr. Macaulay who came hither for me, but as *I wish* to send you *what you wish*, before I go I have obtained a furlough till Tuesday next.[2]

I have not yet been able to stir one step towards getting a survey of your Rocks. Mr. Mayo has been since I received your letter at the Races at Petersburg, till this morning. I got him, immediately upon his arrival, to go with me to the river and to point out the line of your location. He did so, but as there is not an Island in the whole bundle of Rocks which is accessible, I am not much the wiser. From Mr. Mayo I learned that you bought the *Rocks and Water* of one Martin Hoskins.[3] In your own name I could not find any thing in the Land office relating to this purchase. I shall now search in that of Mr. H. But after all I shall be reduced to the necessity of laying down this scene of Cataracts from my eye, and making the best looking thing I can of it. I will accompany it with an acct. of the advantages which belong to it, though to tell you the truth I do not conceive them to be great.[4] In the case of Marshall and Picketts location of Rocks the Chancellor decided against their right.[5] The advantage they promised themselves was to enjoy the exclusive fishery. I conceive the same decission would be given against you, although I believe, that were you to erect works upon these Rocks you could not be ousted, and might then exact toll from those who would bring their fish ashore upon the rocks thus *colonized*. However I will do the best, and all I say of the *capability* of the Mill seats will be true.[6]

Major Claiborne has written to you fully, as I understand, about our 48 Morgantown intention. When *we are there*, your good offices with your brother Landholders will no doubt be useful to us, and we will then solicit them.

Mrs. Banks came to town a few days ago. I have seen her daily since. She looks well, and is by her own account in excellent health. *Do send for her!* Believe me most sincerely your affectionate friend

B. H. Latrobe.

ALS: Henry Banks Papers, Virginia Historical Society (155/G1). Addressed to Banks in Philadelphia.

1. See the preceding letter.
2. The Dismal Swamp Land Company was organized in 1763 by a small group of Virginia planters led by George Washington in order to exploit forty thousand acres of rich timber and farmland in the Dismal Swamp. Eventually, harvesting of the swamp's lumber, much of it exported in the form of shingles, replaced farming as the company's major source of income. Since the company's land had never been surveyed, by the 1790s poachers were making incursions on the company's valuable timber preserves. In addition, the company needed a new canal to replace or supplement the increasingly inadequate Washington's Ditch, a drainage canal that carried the lumber out of the swamp. To solve these problems, Alexander Macaulay (1754–98), a Yorktown merchant and acting director of the Dismal Swamp Land Company, turned to BHL. On Tuesday, 6 June 1797, Macaulay and BHL began their trip from Richmond to examine the swamp. After touring the company's facilities, they laid plans for BHL's survey. But before he could begin, BHL was called to Richmond to undertake the more important commission of constructing the state penitentiary there. For BHL's account of the Dismal Swamp expedition, see BHL, *Journals,* 1 : 229–39. Dismal Swamp Land Company Papers, Duke University, Durham, N.C.; BHL, *Journals,* 2 : 546; Robert H. Reid, "History of the Dismal Swamp Land Company of Virginia" (M.A. thesis, Duke University, 1948), pp. 7–32; *Virginia Cavalcade* 4 (Winter 1954):26.
3. Banks bought the property from Martin Hawkins. See "Certificate of Martin Hawkins respecting 116 Acres in the falls of James River," 30 Apr. 1795, Henry Banks Papers, Virginia Historical Society, Richmond.
4. BHL's account of the advantages of Banks's property in the James River is found in "Description of Property in the Falls of James River . . . ," cited in BHL to Banks, 29 May 1797, n. 1, above.
5. The Chancellor, or judge of the High Court of Chancery, was George Wythe (1726–1806). This case has not been traced.
6. For BHL's discussion of James River fish tolls, see BHL, *Journals,* 1 : 94–95.

FROM JAMES WOOD

Richmond 22d. June 1797.

Sir,

I have the pleasure to inform you that the Board after examining the different Plans before them, have unanimously agreed to adopt yours.[1] We have two hundred thousand Bricks already burned and wish to begin digging the foundation without loss of time. I hope it will be convenient to you to repair to this place immediately, as it is our Wish that you should make a Survey of the ground &c. I have the honor to be with great respect &c.

James Wood.

Letterbook Copy: Executive Papers of Governor James Wood, Virginia State Library (microfiche add.). BHL received this letter on 25 June. BHL, *Journals*, 1 : 239.

1. Others who submitted plans for the penitentiary included Vice-President Thomas Jefferson, George Hadfield, and Samuel Dobie. Jefferson, who had sent a design from Paris as early as 1786, sent another copy to Governor Wood in March 1797. Hadfield (1763–1826), architect and brother of Jefferson's friend Maria Cosway, studied at the Royal Academy. In 1795 he was appointed superintendent of the U.S. Capitol, but was dismissed three years later after quarreling with the city commissioners and William Thornton over the design and construction of the building. BHL, who had met Hadfield in England, later employed him as an assistant at the Capitol for several months. Dobie (b. 1730), surveyor of the public buildings in Richmond in 1790, had acted as supervisor and contractor of the Virginia State Capitol in Richmond. He revised portions of Jefferson's design, and many aspects of the building's interior have been attributed to him. Dobie also submitted plans for the U.S. Capitol in the 1792 competition. In August 1797 Dobie demanded compensation from Governor Wood for his rejected penitentiary plans. Julian P. Boyd, ed., *The Papers of Thomas Jefferson* (Princeton, N.J., 1950–), 9 : 222, 237; BHL to Jefferson, 28 Feb. 1804, below; BHL to Hadfield, 12 July 1812, LB (100/G14); BHL, *Journals*, 3 : 72; *CVSP*, 8 : 445; George S. Hunsberger, "The Architectural Career of George Hadfield," CHS, *Records* 51–52 (1951–52):46–65; Jeanne F. Butler, "Competition 1792: Designing a Nation's Capitol," *Capitol Studies* 4 (1976):24–29; Saul K. Padover, ed., *Thomas Jefferson and the National Capital, 1783–1818* (Washington, D.C., 1946), p. 511; Howard Colvin, *A Biographical Dictionary of British Architects, 1600–1840* (London, 1978), p. 375.

The drawings BHL submitted appear to have allowed for (or included alternate plans for) more than one proposal regarding the form of the penitentiary house. The "lines of the Building . . . perfectly ascertained" for foundation digging two weeks later are those of the front, rectangular part of the complex, that to be constructed first. As late as September 1797, however, it was still undecided as to whether the rear portion would be round or polygonal ("Half of a dodecagon"). For reasons of planning convenience and economy, BHL recommended the round shape, despite the client's initial preference for the other. BHL to James Wood and Council of State of Virginia, 6 July 1797 (below), and 29 Sept. 1797 (Virginia State Library, Richmond; 157/B1).

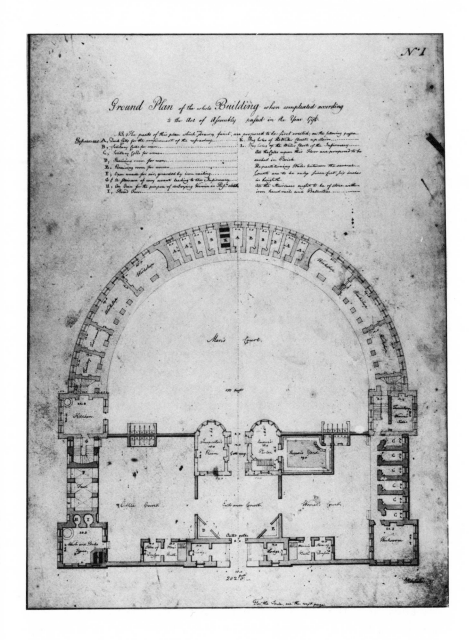

Fig. 2. BHL, Ground plan of the Virginia State Penitentiary, 1797. Courtesy of the Plans and Drawings Collection, Archives Branch, Virginia State Library, Richmond, Virginia.

TO JAMES WOOD AND THE COUNCIL OF STATE OF VIRGINIA

Richmond, July 6th. 1797

The Report of B. Henry Latrobe, architect,
respecting the Penitentiary House, now to be erected
at Richmond, Sheweth,

That, having laid out the foundations of the Building according to the plan, approved by the Executive, the following circumstances appear to him to require as early an attention, as you may please to bestow upon them.

In considering of the best means of supplying the building with a sufficient quantity of Water, two Wells were examined which have been dug upon the Ground for the use of the Brickmakers. They afford in the present dry Season, scarcely a sufficiency of Water for the purpose for which they were dug; and not nearly a supply adequate to what will be the common demand of the prison.[1] He therefore turned his attention to the rivulet which runs in the Eastern Valley. It is now much lower than usual, and yet there is a very sufficient stream for any possible occasion. A spot therefore being fixed upon at the stream, in the Grounds of Mr. Rutherford, a level was struck to the nearest part of the Hill to the Building, and the depth of it was ascertained to be 39 feet 10½ in. below the Summit.[2]

It does not occur that there is any cheaper, or more eligible mode of bringing the water from thence within the reach of an Hydraulic engine, than to drive a Tunnel or Drift into the Body of the Hill to meet a Shaft sunk in the Men's court. The length of this Tunnel would be about 60 Yards. It is unable to ascertain its expence, as this kind of Work is new here, but considering the necessity of the Object it is to accomplish, it must be comparatively small, perhaps only £200.0.0.

It will however at all events be necessary that the Shaft or Well be sunk within a few days, in order to supply Water to the Bricklayers.

The lines of the Building being now perfectly ascertained, the foundations should be immediately dug out. Indeed every day in which this is delayed, is lost to the Work.

Your reporter also begs leave humbly to represent, That, there are many articles which ought to be purchased for the public use, and some labor to be employed in order to carry up with truth and certainty, the

52

walls of the building: such as a few Axes, saws, and other tools, planks and nails to be converted into, squares, levels, plumbs, gages, and trammels; and he begs further to submit to your consideration whether it be not necessary to erect a slight wooden building in which these things, and the current account books should be kept, and for the shelter of the Gentlemen employed in the Superintendance and direction in foul Weather.

B. Henry Latrobe.

ALS: State Penitentiary Papers, Virginia State Library (156/A1).

1. For BHL's sections of the wells dug at the penitentiary site, see BHL, *Journals,* 2 : 402, 403, 405.

2. Thomas Rutherfoord (1766–1852), Scottish immigrant, became a wealthy Richmond merchant, entrepreneur, and real estate developer with lands in Virginia, Kentucky, and Ohio. In May 1797 Governor Wood and the Council of State agreed to pay Rutherfoord $1,208.75 for the land on which the penitentiary was to be built. Journal of the Council of State, 5 May 1797, Virginia State Library, Richmond; *Richmond Portraits in an Exhibition of Makers of Richmond, 1737–1860* (Richmond, Va., 1949), pp. 182–83.

TO HENRY BANKS

Richmond Aug. 15th. 1797.

My dear Sir,

Your very friendly Letter of the 4th. of June did not reach me till this morning, having travelled after me to Norfolk where it remained some time before I saw in a Norfolk paper that there were some letters for me in the Office and sent for them.[1] I thank you a thousand times for all the kind things you say to me in your letter, and the *many* you have *done* for me, teach me how to appreciate their sincerity. I should have written to you before this, but as you requested that your friends would apply to Mr. Hargrove upon *business,* I was unwilling to encrease your postage by matters and expressions of friendship.[2]

I am now in much business here. The Penitentiary house is going on entirely under my direction, I am in full and encreasing confidence with the Executive, the James River Company have consulted me upon some difficulties that have occurred, and I have every prospect of being permanently employed by them.[3] I have hitherto received but little hard

53

Cash. I have done what I possibly could in the reduction of your account against me. It has been but little but it shall always be in *my memory*, that you *did not "wish it to be upon your mind."*

I am most happy that Mrs. Banks is with you and Pray assure her of my sincerest esteem.

I have received a letter from Mr. Hunt of New York. He has been non-suited for want of certain papers which you have had to manage for him through the Land Office. Pray let me know how this matter stands? I will take any trouble for you or for him.[4]

We have no news here. **ALL** the fish in James river are dead and the shores are covered with them, and they swim in shoals upon the Water. This is the most curious event I have to relate.[5]

I am Dear Sir In great truth Yrs.

B. Henry Latrobe

Claiborne has written to me from Winchester where his wife lies in. A letter in his own stile.

ALS: Henry Banks Papers, Virginia Historical Society (156/C1). Addressed to Banks in Philadelphia.

1. BHL arrived in Norfolk from the Dismal Swamp on 13 June to order supplies and equipment for his survey expedition. Due to a shortage of funds, he had to stay there until the Dismal Swamp Land Company could pay his expenses. He returned to Richmond after receiving Governor Wood's letter of 22 June informing him of the acceptance of his design for the state penitentiary. BHL, *Journals*, 1 : 239; BHL to Thomas Swepson, 21 June 1797, Dismal Swamp Land Company Papers, Duke University, Durham, N.C. (microfiche add.).

2. John Hargrave, Banks's agent in Richmond, wrote to Banks several times in the summer of 1797 reporting his unsuccessful efforts to collect BHL's debt to Banks. Hargrave to Banks, 28 June, 12 July, 21 July 1797, all in Henry Banks Papers, Virginia Historical Society, Richmond.

3. The James River Company was chartered in 1785 to make the river navigable from the "highest place practicable" to the beginning of the great falls above Richmond at Westham. From there the company was to bypass the falls with canals and carry the navigation to tidewater below the city. The canal bypassing the upper falls was completed in 1789, and the second canal passing the lower falls and carrying the navigation into Richmond was "nearly completed" when BHL first saw it in April 1796. At that time the company directors were planning to construct the part of the navigation from the basin in Richmond to tidewater at Rocketts Landing below the city. The English engineer William Weston was consulted, and he advised the company to construct a tier of locks to complete the navigation. BHL disagreed with Weston's plan and offered an alternative, but the company directors chose Weston's scheme. BHL later outlined his own scheme in a report to Albert Gallatin in 1808. The locks were finally built in 1810, when the company hired Ariel Cooley, of Springfield, Massachusetts, to construct a chain of thirteen locks linking Richmond and the tidewater. BHL, *Journals*, 1 : 92–94, 2 : 363–64; BHL, Report to Albert

Gallatin on Internal Improvements, 16 Mar. 1808, in BHL, *Correspondence,* 2; Wayland Fuller Dunaway, *History of the James River and Kanawha Company* (New York, 1922), pp. 28–29; Joseph Hobson Harrison, Jr., "The Internal Improvement Issue in the Politics of the Union, 1783–1825," (Ph.D. diss., University of Virginia, 1954), p. 96; James Poyntz Nelson, *The Chesapeake and Ohio Railway* (Richmond, Va., 1927), p. 187.

4. Jesse Hunt, former sheriff (1781–85) and town supervisor (1785–86) of Rye, Westchester County, N.Y., wrote to Banks about this time "respecting the registers rect. for issueing patents for sundry tracts of Land," which he had left with Banks. John Hargrave to Banks, 20 Sept. 1797, Henry Banks Papers; J. Thomas Scharf, *History of Westchester County, New York, Including Morrisania, Kings Bridge, and West Farms,* 2 vols. (Philadelphia, 1886), 1 : 483, 655–56.

5. BHL made more extensive comments on this fish kill in *Journals,* 1 : 272.

REPORT ON THE PENITENTIARY

Augt. 17th. 1797

Report upon the State of the Works at the Penitentiary House at Richmond, in Virginia.

1.) State of the Walls.

The Walls of the Gateway and Front enclosure are so far advanced, that on Saturday evening (the Watertable) *the Basement course* will be laid. In the progress of the Work it has been necessary to make [three?] reversed Centers. These have been executed by Mr. John Shortis, who has performed all those small Jobs which occur in every building and cannot always be foreseen, with such skill and fidelity that I conceive the interest of the public to require that I should recommend him to the Honble. Board particularly.[1]

2.) Centers of Groins and Arches.

I have taken the liberty with the consent of the Superintendant[2] to order Mr. Shortis to make the large Centers of the Gateway, and they are now ready.

About a month ago I pressed the necessity of beginning to make the Centers of the lower arches and the groins of the Cellar story. The Honble. Board were then informed that they were not required till the house should be covered in. Upon hearing my sentiments upon this subject, the board seemed to be convinced, and I have since then daily urged the absolute necessity of beginning them. Hitherto no steps whatever have been taken, and the plank which has been delivered by Mr.

Paine[3] for the purpose of making them, has been employed to other uses; such as laying platforms for the mortar, and building a Lime house, and another house for safely keeping tools, materials, and books. Notwithstanding that these latter works were indispensable, I cannot deny that the progress of the work must now be injuriously delayed by the neglect of the Centers, as scarce any exertion can get them ready in time.

In order to convince the Honorable Board how impossible it is to proceed more than 5 feet 10 inches above the foundation without the Centers I have annexed a drawing in which that part of the work which does not depend upon the Center is colored red, and that which does, yellow. The Honble. Board will see that without the yellow part of the Work all above it is suspended in air. A very slight inspection of the drawings in the large book of designs would have been sufficient to prove the fact.

By adding sufficiently to the thickness of the Walls, the Arches might undoubtedly have been postponed till the completion of all the other Works. It would however have been at the expence of 850.000 Bricks, additionally and unnecessarily expended, and at the risk of cracking every wall by the addition of a new and heavy weight acting in a direction different from that under which the work had settled. These things however are familiar to every one who has thought upon the subject.

3.) Plank required to be procured.

When I had last the honor of speaking to the Board upon the subject of Plank, I was not very well informed respecting the difference of Virginian and Northern pine. Since then I have particularly examined the two sorts, and seen them worked upon, and find that they differ exactly as *yellow* and *white* deal do in Europe. The former is more durable, resists the effects of Wet, and retains a better color than the latter. It is fuller of turpentine. On this account it is more usefull for all external Works, for floors, and for every thing that is not to be painted. The clean and best sort works well under the plane, and for general uses it is as good as the best plank in the World. But it has qualities which peculiarly and wholly unfit it for the purpose of centers. It cannot be nailed without boring, and when nailed it holds the nail so fast and splits so easily, that the nail, or the plank, or both, is lost, in taking the Center asunder. Now every Center made of Northern plank may be used, and altered
over and over again and not a nail or plank be lost. This is an object of

infinite importance as to expence. The expence of the first Centers will perhaps surprize, especially as to the article of Nails, but when once incurred the labor only of the succeeding ones is to be paid for, for the planks and nails which supported the groins of the Cellars, will carry the arches of the uppermost Cells, and after that retain a Value.

Besides these considerations, which, I think, are decisive the Northern plank has straight edges, which is *necessary,* it is in general broad, which saves very much in cutting it out, it works with uncommon ease, *and costs only 13 Dollars per thousand.* The Virginian plank is difficult to work, seldom exceeds 14 or 15 inches in breadth, and has a crooked edge. I now speak of the cheapest sort which is proposed to be delivered at 16 1/2 Dollars per thousand. In working up a thousand feet of Virginian plank into Centers there will be a difference of time, that is, of labor and expence, of 2 1/2 Dollars a thousand, making in all in favor of Northern plank a difference of 6 Dollars per thousand. I need not say anything further. I have said thus much, because it appears not to be intended to receive either the balance of the order given to Mr. Paine nor to extend this order to replace the quantity expended to other uses.
4.) Timber and Scantling.

About 3 Weeks ago I furnished the Superintendant with a bill of Scantling of all the Timber necessary for the Works to be executed this Year excepting the Floors, Sashes, and Doors of the lodges. It is now high time the Timber were upon the spot and the Carpenters at work upon it. I beg leave to urge that measures to this end, be no longer delayed.
5.) Stone Basement course.

I have taken the liberty to order of Mr. Whitelow the Stone absolutely required in the present instance for the Gateway.[4] There is only 40 feet running of it, and I beg the Honble. Board will forgive and confirm this order, as it could not be delayed till a meeting of the Council.
6.) Arch bricks.

The bricks which have been burned in the only kiln which is now ready for delivery are so very rough and tender, that the Gateway arch cannot possibly by turned in them. It is intended to burn some thousand better and cleaner moulded bricks, for this purpose, in the second kiln, which will not be ready for delivery till next month. These bricks, I am informed, will cost 50/ per thousand. I have small hopes of their proving very good. The earth has never been well tempered and is not of the best 57 sort. The Brick maker is not much in fault. But besides, they cannot be delivered *in time,* by more than a fortnight. The number wanted will be about 4.000. I have therefore made enquiry elsewhere, and have found from 3 to 5.000 most excellent bricks, (of which I send in *one*) which will be delivered at the Pond head at 51 s. per thousand. I beg leave to recommend *strongly* to the board to purchase these bricks, having the refusal of them for only a few days longer. They came as ballast in a Vessel, and are at the disposal of Mr. Orris Paine.[5]

7.) Delivery of Materials.

It is a very disagreeable part of my duty to make the most serious complaint of the manner in which the Bricks and Lime are delivered at the Building. The Contractor for laying the Bricks[6] suffers materially by it, but the public suffers still more. Many days, I have seen all the Brick-layers and laborers idle for one third of their time for want of bricks, and this morning the bricklayer has been obliged to employ his Laborers to bring bricks from the Kiln to the Wall upon their Heads. I should not have troubled the Board with this Complaint, had not very frequent and pressing representations been useless.

If I have exceeded the boundary line of my duty in these represen-tations, I humbly hope the Honble. Board will forgive my zeal to justify the confidence with which they have honored me.

B. Henry Latrobe
Architect.

ADS: State Penitentiary Papers, Virginia State Library (156/C6).

1. Shortis was nearly killed in a fracas among penitentiary workers the following year. For BHL's description of the fight, see BHL to Wood, 26 Oct. 1798, in BHL, *Journals,* 2 : 440–41.

2. Maj. Thomas Callis was appointed superintendent over the construction of the Richmond penitentiary on 23 March 1797. BHL experienced numerous difficulties in working with him. For sarcastic remarks on Callis and his superstitious beliefs, see BHL, *Journals,* 2 : 359–62. Journal of the Council of State, 23 Mar. 1797, Virginia State Library, Richmond.

3. Probably Jesse Payne, a contractor who furnished lumber for the manufactory of arms in Richmond in 1800. *CVSP,* 9 : 175, 355.

4. Thomas Whitelaw, "a stone mason celebrated for faithful execution of his work," delayed in filling the order and Superintendent Thomas Callis turned to another mason for the needed stone. See BHL to Wood and Council, 31 Aug. 1797, below. *CVSP,* 9 : 258.

5. Paine was a Richmond merchant and owner of coal pits west of the city. *ASP. Miscellaneous,* 1 : 808.

6. Martin Mims (c. 1753–1819), Revolutionary War veteran, continued to supervise the brickwork at the penitentiary through 1803. From 1800 to 1807 he served as keeper of

the penitentiary. He was murdered in 1819. *CVSP*, 9 : 100, 357, 502; *Virginia Magazine of History and Biography* 35 (1927):448.

TO THOMAS CALLIS

Swan Tavern[1] [Richmond], Augt. 26th. 1797.

Sir,

As you have thought proper to tell the Governor, that the bill of Mr. Shortis up to the present date—to which I have affixed my name—is *double* in its amount to what it ought to be, I hereby give you notice, that at the next Board, which will probably meet on Tuesday, I shall lay the matter before the Executive, when you may prepare yourself either to prove your assertion, or to acknowledge its falsehood.[2] As you have also taken upon yourself to deny my authority to direct what work shall be done at the penitentiary house, and to assert to *four* Gentlemen, whom I mean to bring forward as witnesses, that I am appointed *only to assist you* in setting out the building, I also apprize you, that it is my intention at the time to endeavor to prove to the board your total incapacity to fill the place to which *you* are appointed. I think it fair to give you this notice, because you are not always prepared to decide by previous examination, upon the subjects you are called upon to discuss.

I am Sir Yours &c.

B. Henry Latrobe.

ALS: State Penitentiary Papers, Virginia State Library (156/E1). Enclosed in Callis to James Wood, 28 Aug. 1797, ibid. (156/D9).

1. On Broad Street between Eighth and Ninth streets. Virginius Dabney, *Richmond: The Story of a City* (New York, 1976), p. 36.
2. Shortis's carpentry bill for £74.2.0 was approved by BHL on 24 August 1797. John Shortis account, 23 Aug. 1797, State Penitentiary Papers, Virginia State Library, Richmond.

FROM THOMAS CALLIS

Richmond Augt. 28. 1797.

Sir,

Yesterday evening, at dark, I received your letter of the 26th. instant[1] and if your apparent candor were real it would deserve and receive my thanks.

It has however not had a tendency to convince me, that I have erred in my opinion, that Mr. Shortis's bill, up to the present day, is double the amount it ought, in justice to the Commonwealth, to be; or that your object in thus obtruding yourself upon the public Notice, perhaps contrary to the wish of the Executive, has been to drive me, by *finesse* and *intrigue,* from the office to which I have had the honor to be appointed.

Having met that appointment, I am unacquainted with any authority which you have to direct any work whatever to be done at or about the penitentiary house after having in conformity with the request of the Governor (and being very liberally paid for it) laid off the ground upon which it is to stand.

I trust Sir, that the Conduct which has provoked your resentment, will meet the approbation of the Executive, who will thereby perceive, that I am not unduly to be influenced to Sacrifice the public interest to accommodate you or your friends.

As self interest (and not the public good) is the motive which induces your present conduct, I have no doubt but it will meet the *attention* which it merits.

It is unnecessary for me further to notice your letter, than by assuring you, that the insinuation which closes it, receives that which it is only entitled to, my most hearty contempt.

I am, Sir

Thomas Callis

Copy: State Penitentiary Papers, Virginia State Library (156/E4). Addressed to BHL at the Swan tavern. Enclosed in Callis to James Wood, 28 Aug. 1797, ibid. (156/D9).

1. See preceding letter.

TO JAMES WOOD AND THE COUNCIL OF STATE OF VIRGINIA

Richmond. Augt. 31st. 1797.

Honorable Sirs,

I beg leave to solicit Your attention to two occurences in which the public interest, not less than my personal character is engaged. On the 21st. inst. the Superintendant being indisposed retired from the Penitentiary ground, and continued absent till the 24th. On that day early Mr. Shortis requested that I would apply to the Honble. the Board of Council for the discharge of his Bill for building certain temporary houses, and making centers. I directed him to bring his books to my apartment, and having examined them, I drew out the bill herewith sent in, according to the form which I had constantly observed in my office, and which is the rule of all the Architects in Europe. I put my name to the corner of the Bill, leaving room for that of the Superintendant, and Shortis delivered the Bill to him. He refused to sign it, and waiting upon his Excellency the Governor he informed him, *"that it was double in its amount to what it ought to be."*

If I am either so ignorant as to be imposed upon in the Value of work performed under my professional eye, or so dishonest as to assist another in imposing upon the commonwealth, I am very unfit to enjoy the confidence of the Executive, and the sooner I retire the less will that confidence be abused. I hope however to prove satisfactorily to the Honble. Board that in no instance do I deserve the imputation of total ignorance, still less of dishonesty, and I beg that I may be indulged in defending my conduct upon Mr. Shortis's bill *vivâ voce.* I enclose two Statements. The first is an exact extract from Mr. Shortis's books which I believe to be honest and correct, having seen all the Men therein mentioned employed upon the Work during the time stated: the other is a collateral examination of the reasonableness of the bill, by comparison with the Value of the same Work in England.[1] To both the papers I would beg leave to speak, and to produce both Mr. Shortis's book, and the *printed* book of London prices, as vouchers.[2] If necessary the Men employed by Mr. Shortis are ready to make Oath to their accounts.

Another more serious injury arises to the public from the declaration of the Superintendant to the Brickmaker, and the Mechanics employed at the Penitentiary house, *that I have no authority to direct in any instance,* and that I have only been appointed to *assist* him in setting out   61 the Site of the Building. On Thursday the 24th. inst. I expostulated against the Bricks delivered. They were almost wholly unfit for use; and as it had no effect, I ordered a Load to be carried back to the Kiln. Mr. [William] Rawleigh informed me that though he was willing to take back any bad bricks on being rejected by the Superintendant, *I* had no authority either to receive or reject, and that the Superintendant had informed him so.[3] Having ordered the Stone of Mr. Whitloe which has been wanting this fortnight past, (and the Want of which has obliged me to employ the tender bricks of the first kiln in the Women's Wing instead of the Gateway, a most injurious circumstance) the superintendant superceded my order and gave it to Mr. Robinson the plaisterer who gave it to Mr. Beard the mason. As it was wholly neglected, I applied several times to Beard to dispatch it, but was treated with so much coldness, and received such evasive answers, that I enquired into the cause, and found that he had also been taught to consider me as wholly without authority in what I did. I could quote several other instances in which similar delay has taken place from the same cause.

On the 26th instant I wrote to the Superintendant informing him that I meant to lay before the executive both the above complaints. I thought it fair to do so, as he was ill, and the proof of his first charge required examination, being positively certain that he had not measured nor examined Mr. Shortis's work.

I received an answer, not written, but only signed by the Superintendant, in which he asserts: *"that Mr. Shortis's bill is double the amount it ought to be in justice to the commonwealth; that my object is to obtrude myself upon the public notice contrary to the wish of the executive; that having laid off the Ground on which the Penitentiary house is to stand and having been most liberally paid for it I have now no authority what ever to direct any thing to be done at or about the Ground, and that Self interest is the motive of my conduct."*

I now appeal to the Board, and to the individual feelings of every member of it, whether I ought any longer to appear upon a ground, on which I daily receive opposition and insult, on which I daily see the public interest sacrificed or neglected, on which instead of 120 busy hands laboring under my eye, there are only 4 solitary Bricklayers in a corner, and on which I can neither glean reputation, nor the public, advantage. Since the first setting out of the Ground I have been absent only 4 days, I have declined every other engagement, I have, and I assert it boldly, directed every thing from the first shovellfull of earth, to the position of the last brick, and I now find my exertions branded with the name of dishonesty, and my assiduity stigmatised as *"unauthorized obtru-sion upon public notice."*

Still however I commit myself to the scrutiny and disposal of the Honorable board.

I have the honor to be Your most obedt. faithfull Servt.

B. Henry Latrobe

PS. I beg leave to press once more upon the board the consideration of my report of the 17th. of Augt. There are many other things requiring immediate direction which I am ready to state.[4]

ALS: State Penitentiary Papers, Virginia State Library (156/E7).

1. The statements are now in the Virginia State Penitentiary Papers with this covering letter. The first statement listed Shortis's ten journeymen carpenters and the number of days each spent working on the temporary houses and on the centers. The men worked a total of 77 days on the houses and 131 3/4 days on the centers at six shillings each per day. Shortis himself spent 10 days on the houses and 16 days on the centers at 7s.6d. per day. The second statement itemized the dimensions and costs of the three classes of centering executed by Shortis and his men.

2. In the second enclosure, BHL stated that he calculated the worth of Shortis's work according to "the price book of the Board of Works in London," which listed prices "lower than any other prices allowed in England by the Measurers." This book may have been the "printed book" he enclosed; if so, it has not been identified. Alternatively, if the enclosed printed price book were other than some such officially sanctioned list of prices for governmental purposes only, it would probably have been of one of the two kinds of builders' price books common at the time: books intended as an internal standard of valuation by a group of associated craftsmen; or those published for a larger audience as a general guide for estimates and calculation. Books of the first of these two groups were numerous in early America, as Dr. Louise Hall has shown, and BHL was frustrated early in his American career in obtaining access to them, as Jefferson would be later. Jefferson, however, apparently had success in obtaining a book of the second type. By 1805 he owned a copy of *The Builder's Price Book: Containing a Correct List of the Prices Allowed by the Most Eminent Surveyors in London, to the Several Artificers Concerned in Building* (London, 1788), a book issued in more than a dozen editions between 1775 and 1806. It is possible that BHL too owned a book of this type and referred to it here. Louise Hall, "Artificer to Architect in America" (Ph.D. diss., Harvard University, 1954); E. Millicent Sowerby, ed., *Catalogue of the Library of Thomas Jefferson*, 5 vols. (Washington, D.C., 1952), 1 : 533–34; Roger W. Moss, Jr., "The Origins of the Carpenters' Company of Philadelphia," in Charles E. Peterson, ed., *Building Early America* (Radnor, Pa., 1976), pp. 35–53; Peterson, ed., *The Rules of Work of the Carpenters' Company of the City and County of Philadelphia, 1786* (Princeton, N.J., 1971). See also BHL to William Waln, 22 Jan. 1807, n. 3, in BHL, *Correspondence*, 2.

3. According to Callis, Martin Mims, who was the contractor for laying the bricks and who served as acting superintendent during Callis's illness, had "no motive for admitting any to be laid but such as are of the quality stipulated by the Contract to be furnished." Callis to Wood, 28 Aug. 1797, State Penitentiary Papers, Virginia State Library, Richmond (156/D9).

4. The dispute over Shortis's bill continued for a fortnight. Referees, appointed to valuate the carpenter's work, disagreed with BHL on the value to be assigned to certain types of more difficult work. BHL finally reduced his valuation about £11 to £63.2.5. BHL to Wood, 7 Sept. 1797, BHL to John Courtenay, 9 Sept. 1797, BHL to Wood and the Council of Virginia, 14 Sept. 1797, all in State Penitentiary Papers (156/F9, 156/G1, 157/A1); Council Minutes, 31 Aug. 1797, Anderson Barret to Wood and the Council of Virginia, 4 Sept. 1797, Shortis to Wood and Council of Virginia, n.d., all ibid.

TO HENRY BANKS

Richmond Novr. 28th. 1797.

Dear Sir,

I should have written to you long before now, were I not convinced that nothing I could write would be worth the postage or the expenditure of your time. Nor should I now have troubled you, were I not anxious to redeem my character from the imputation of ingratitude which, in your opinion expressed to Mr. Hargrove in the letter he read to me rests upon it. In order to do this, I must first request of you that you will believe me that I have a very due sense of your kindness to me in relieving me from the most unpleasant situation I was in respecting Radford.[1] As far as *sentiment* goes I have nothing but *assertion* to offer, and you must decide, upon what you have seen of me, whether or no it is possible for me to entertain *grateful sentiment* in the highest degree, without possessing pecuniary abilities to prove them.

But in respect to *conduct,* I can more substantially reply. Since March the 25th. to this day I have received 400 Dollars and no more for my *Penitentiary house* services. Of these I expended 75 in going down to the Dismal swamp and commencing a survey for the Company. I had but just begun my operations when I was recalled by the Governor to attend the progress of the Penitentiary Works by which I lost all I had expended in the Dismal Swamp and my engagement into the bargain. But I had a choice of difficulties, and I fear I chose wrongly. Since then (June 22d) I have not stirred from hence. I have paid to your acct. 70 Dollars, and for Clothes and Victuals, (and God knows I have incurred no other expence) for these last *8* Months, the remainder having been obliged to pay my board and lodging at the swan up to Novr. 30th. at which time I agreed to quit to make room for Legislators.[2] I have now a Doghole of my own at a high rent. So much for inability.

In respect of my charges against you, it is false that I ever charged you £20 for what I have done for you. I charged *nothing* against you nor ever intended it till Mr. Hargrove, though he knew my situation, and saw my exertions to lessen my debt to you, threatened to arrest me for £40, the stated balance of my account. I then told him that I in that case would certainly make a set off of my services. I charged 50 Dollars for the two Maps I sent you a charge as reasonable as your compensation of 20 Dollars is ridiculous and have had occasion to employ the County surveyor Williamson in a dispute with Rutherford on the public account about boundaries, and he charges 5 Dollars for every attendance.[3] My labor is, (without any vanity) worth more than his (per Day even), and at the rate of 5 Dollars per Day I should have charged you 80 Dollars at least for the surveys, the Levelling your Mill seats in 6 places, and the Maps of the Canal and the Fall Estate. Major Claiborne estimated them at still more and he *saw* what I did. As to Airy plains, I never dreamt of charging you any thing for what I did there.[4] Had I however, instead of exerting myself to supply Mr. Hargrove and Sydnor,[5] very much to my distress, cancelled my whole debt by purchasing *your* bond at 5/ in the Pound, when it was offered to me, with 6 Months credit, I should indeed have behaved very much like a rascal—but certainly with much prudence—and have escaped the hint that I ought to pay 5 per Cent per Month for what I owe you.

As to Mr. Hargrove it appears to me that the excessive difficulties he is under, have betrayed him to make a wrong statement to you merely thro' haste and inadvertence. He appears to be the most industrious and faithful agent I had almost said *Slave* to your affairs that you could have found in all America. I honor his attachment, nor am I angry with him for his threat or his mistatement, but I wish to set your opinion to rights.

I will now make my own declaration. I think myself more obliged to you than to any man in Virginia unless it be to Mr. [Meriwether?] Jones who has supported my public interests most generously. I mean to pay you every farthing of the balance against me as soon as I can with interest, But before I will be arrested for £40, I will make the offset of 50 Dollars, as above, and purchase your bond for the remainder. Pay you, I will notwithstanding, and with my first monies, but I will neither go to jail nor will I ask any man to be my security, *while I live,* for a debt. I will borrow money, but never accept bail. I have lost too much by being bail for *honest* men, ever to lead others into the same risk though conscious of my own honesty. You see I have written in the style you use, *open* and *decided.* And now lets shake hands and be friends, for I feel not only gratitude, but sincere affection for you.

How does Mrs. Banks? Pray remember me to her. So Mr. Norwood is married. To a philosopher I hope. As for myself, I shall do well *in time;* But my affairs are like the Countryman's road which had a good bottom, but it has a d——d long way to it. Believe me very truly Yrs.

B. Henry Latrobe

ALS: Henry Banks Papers, Virginia Historical Society (157/E1). Addressed to Banks in Philadelphia.

1. William Radford (1759–1803) was proprietor of the Eagle Tavern in Richmond. BHL had earlier lodged at the Eagle, and the "most unpleasant situation" may have been BHL's inability to pay the rent. BHL, *Journals,* 1 : 186. *Richmond Portraits in an Exhibition of Makers of Richmond, 1737–1860* (Richmond, Va., 1949), p. 167.

2. On 1 December, BHL took up quarters at Maj. Alexander Quarrier's Court, on the canal at the foot of Seventh Street. BHL, *Journals,* 2 : 332. Martin S. Shockley, *The Richmond Stage, 1784–1812* (Charlottesville, Va., 1977), p. 386.

3. The dispute concerned access to a stream which was largely on the property of Thomas Rutherfoord. The stream was needed as a source of water for the Richmond penitentiary. BHL to Wood and Council, 6 July 1797, above, and 19 Oct. 1797, State Penitentiary Papers, Virginia State Library, Richmond (157/C5).

4. BHL made a ground plan of Airy Plain, Banks's estate on the York River in New Kent County, opposite West Point, Virginia, probably in March 1797. See BHL, "Sketch of the Estate of Henry Banks Esqr. on York River," Historical Society of Pennsylvania, Philadelphia (313/A4); and another version, "Sketch of Airy Plain Estate," Sketchbook II, PBHL (248/C3), both reproduced in BHL, *Latrobe's View of America.*

5. Robert Sydnor (d. 1804) supervised the construction of Banks's forge and mill on the James River Canal. John Hargrave to Henry Banks, 26 June 1797, Henry Banks Papers, Virginia Historical Society, Richmond.

RICHMOND THEATER PROPOSAL

Richmond, January 22, 1798.

It is Proposed to Erect in the City of Richmond, a
Building to Contain an Hotel, Assembly-Rooms, &c.
a Commodious Theatre[1]

To comprize the particulars of the scheme in an advertisement, would be impossible, but the following are its principle features.

A subscription shall be opened, consisting of 270 SHARES of 100 Dollars each, payable by instalments of 10 Dollars per month, during the course of the present year.

A specific contract for the completion of the building in conformity to the design, and in a given time will be entered into with the most ample security for its performance, whereby the usual disappointments in Building by subscription will be avoided.

The whole proceeds, or rents of the Building shall be divided half yearly, among the subscribers. At the rate of rent now established in Richmond, the shares are calculated to produce 9 1/4 per cent.

The site of the Building, is the ground upon which the Theatre now stands. Conditional agreements highly advantageous to the subscribers, have been entered into with Mr. West,[2] who has undertaken to build the interior parts of the Theatre at his own expence, and according to the design. All the Building except the internal part of the Theatre will be vested in the Subscribers, or their representatives in perpetuity.

All the Designs are finished, and Mr. Latrobe, the Architect, will attend every morning from 10 to 12 at Major Quarrier's[3] to exhibit, and explain them.

Alexander Quarrier.

B. Henry Latrobe, B.[4]

Printed Copy: *The Observatory; Or, a View of the Times* (Richmond), 14 June 1798 (158/A1).

1. BHL spent December 1797 and early January 1798 preparing his "Designs of a Building proposed to be erected at Richmond in Virginia, to contain a Theatre, Assembly-Rooms, and an Hotel" (Prints and Photographs Division, Library of Congress; 310/A3 ff.), reproduced in BHL, *Architectural Drawings*. The new theater was to replace the oversized wooden structure built in 1785 and later bought by Thomas Wade West, the energetic theatrical impressario. Apparently West requested BHL's design for the new theater. The "Designs," BHL's incomplete set of presentation drawings, demonstrate the architect's interest in introducing up-to-date ideas, show his earliest known work of such civic scale and spatial complexity, and include drawings of exceptional richness and vivacity.

Upon completion of his theater plans, BHL wrote a play which was performed on 20 January (see BHL to Scandella, 24 Jan. 1798, below). Several days later the old Richmond Theater burned down, but even this did not bring about the needed financial support to get BHL's proposed theater project off the ground. For the next decade Richmond theater-going audiences attended plays in a temporary theater, Market Hall, until that building was destroyed in the tragic fire of 1811. In the 1960s a group of Richmond citizens once more tried to develop support for the BHL theater project, but this effort also failed. Abe Wollock, "Benjamin Henry Latrobe's Activities in the American Theatre (1797–1808)" (Ph.D. diss., University of Illinois, 1962); Martin S. Shockley, *The Richmond Stage, 1784–1812* (Charlottesville, Va., 1977), pp. 134–40, 385–90.

2. Thomas Wade West (c. 1745–1799), actor and theatrical producer, arrived in Philadelphia from England in 1790 and formed a company of actors to tour Southern towns. West built five theaters in America (Norfolk, Va., 1792; Charleston, S.C., 1793; Petersburg, Va., 1796; Fredericksburg, Va., 1797; Alexandria, Va., 1797). His company performed BHL's play, *The Apology*, on 20 January 1798. BHL, *Journals*, 2 : 334; Susanne

K. Sherman, "Thomas Wade West, Theatrical Impressario, 1790–1799," *William and Mary Quarterly,* 3d ser., 9 (1952):10–28.

3. Alexander Quarrier (c. 1746–1827), Revolutionary War veteran and Philadelphia coachmaker, moved to Richmond in 1786. In 1798 he applied for and was granted the post of commandant of the Armory Guard. He obtained a state contract for supplying gun carriages and was also a land speculator. BHL, *Journals,* 2 : 550.

4. The "B." stands for Boneval. For BHL's mistaken notion that the Latrobes descended from the French noble family of Bonnevals, which BHL spelled with one *n,* see BHL to Du Bourg, 25 Mar. 1804, n. 3, below.

TO GIAMBATTISTA SCANDELLA

Richmond, Virginia, Jany. 24th, 1798.

My dearest Sir,[1]

Since your departure, the multiplicity of my business has not prevented my daily regret at not hearing from you. My pleasure was therefore great indeed when on the back of a letter which I found lying upon my table on my return home this evening, I recognized your handwriting. Having read your very kind letter through, I immediately hastened to the Postoffice in search of your first letter, and found that by the mistake of the Clerk it had been put into the pigeon hole marked B (Boneval) when my letters usually find lodgings under protection of the Letter L. Permit me *most* sincerely to thank you for both of them. I should not have waited for a letter from you had I known how to have directed to you. I hope I shall not again lose the trace of you, but be able to follow you *with letters,* wherever it may be the will of "your blind fortune" to carry you, as you so *coldly* express yourself. Happy is it for you that she is blind! With *your* heart and *your* understanding you will be able to lead your conductress into paths of happiness she perhaps never intended to travel. But, to tell truth, I am too much concerned for you to be able to indulge in any thing but very serious reflections on your feelings, and those of your friends, who are so dear to you. [*At this point about twenty lines, or 400 words, have been cut out of the manuscript.*]

My dear friend, I am a very unfit man to write to you. You labour under the same disease with myself. A morbid sensibility. I threw down my pen to collect my mind from wandering among the Alps, among the mountains the plains and the Cities of your native country—a country I so much love—in order to *think* myself into a more pleasant state of

68

mind, and to give my letter a brighter tint. But I rambled into a house I never saw, into a family of whom I know only one individual, and yet I found myself perfectly at home. I saw beauty, sincerity, and kindness in the eyes of the women, the power and the desire to bestow happiness in their looks, in the men, manly grace, polished virtue, independence of soul, and affections untethered by selfish and mean considerations. There was a silent thoughtfulness that seemed to communicate more of sentiment, to ripen and concentrate well digested resolutions better than the most eager debate could have done. I thought I saw the picture of the same heroism the same courageous prudence in every face, "*in vario sembiante, l'istessa virtú.*"[2] Nothing was spoken, but every thing was said. "This is not the time, but Venice is our country, and Venice *shall* be free" was the translation I gave to the "act of Assembly," if I may so call the common sentiment.[3] The many imperfect hints, but hints so intelligible and so impressive which you have at various times given me, had introduced me into the midst of your family. I cannot persuade myself that the illusion is much unlike the truth.

Your first letter is dated the 8th of Decr. 1797: Your last the 9th of Jany. I am heartily vexed that they have both been so long in finding me out. The *manner* of the first is so affectionate, that not an atom of its worth to me has evaporated in the mechanical lodging it has occupied for 6 Weeks. I wish I knew Dr. Thornton.[4] I hope I shall know him. If he is the man I fancy him—and I assure you my opinion of him is highly favorable—I will positively use no introduction to him, but to tell him what is so flattering to me, that you are my friend. As to the foederal City, I have never seen it, but I am sure your judgement of it is correct. Do you remember a passage in Citizen Fauchet's intercepted dispatch, published in our friend Edmund Randolph's vindication, wherein he asks, speaking of the vices and corruption of our young government, "*if this be the decrepitude of its youth, what will its old age be?*"[5] I was reminded of the passage by your very comic comparison of the city to a Giant with pigmy limbs. My dear friend; considering you are a physician, you ought to have known better. The limbs are in a natural state, but the Child is *strumous*, afflicted with scrophula and ricketts, laboring under an Hydrocephalus, badly treated at [worst?] and I fear somewhat tainted with the King's evil. Were I inclined to pun, I might say, that a blister of Spanish flies [*torn*][6] (which is likely enough to be thus applied) would discover the nature of its disease. It must [*At this point about twenty lines, or 400 words, have been cut out of the manuscript.*] it into her head to avoid the possibility 69 of my speaking to her, or even sitting near her, and *I*, like a fool, to desire more than anything in the world, to be in her company. We have now played at bo-peep for 6 weeks, and might have entertained our friends still longer, had not her vanity come to the assistance of my philosophy, by instigating her publicly to mortify me at the Theatre. This roused the remains of french blood in my veins, and like the French, whose despair, if it can but evaporate in a *petit chanson*, never was known to kill them, I gave the following extempore answer to a friend who asked me the question, "how am I to translate that look of yours, *Latrobe?*"

> Ingulph me, Earth! crush me, ye Skies,
> My quiv'ring soul is on the Rack,
> On John she's turn'd her beauteous eyes,
> On me _____ her back![7]

And now I am heart-whole again, and you may laugh as loud as you please. Having thus furnished you with a *Thema*, upon which your wit may compose Variations ad infinitum, I was just going to indulge in a few *quirks* and *cranks* myself, when I fell into a profound reverie upon the Analogy of *Sexual desire* to *Chemical affinity*, from which I am awaked as grave and serious as a judge, perfectly convinced that nothing but your assistance will ever render so important an enquiry successful.

I have a thousand things more to say to you, and have not room for half of them. Our state assembly broke up this day. This *annual Mob*, as Colonel Innes[8] called them, has done no great mischief and some good. They have voted 25,000 Dollars towards the completion of the Penitentiary house. There was a petition to repeal the Law, and leave was asked to bring in a bill for that purpose. Forty Members out of 200 were found to vote in favor of the Bill, but it was not permitted to show its face. Shakespeare put into the mouth of J. Caesar these words. *"Caesar ne'er did wrong, but with just cause."*[9] Our assembly adopted this confused idea, and voted a censure, and had almost voted an impeachment of a Foederal Grand Jury for having *"presented as a real evil"* some printed letters of a Mr. Cabell to his constituents in which he accused the Foederal Government of gross misconduct and corruption, and, more than insinuated, that it is in the pay of Britain. The letters were ill written, and made up in wormwood what they wanted in salt. The conduct of the Grand jury was certainly justifiable by the powers and duties belonging to them. They are to *present* for prosecution all evils and nuisances, and whatever may be liable to occasion a breach of the peace. Their own judgements must certainly direct them to these objects. If they thought my walking stick in my hands a dangerous weapon, they certainly might present it, at the risk of being laughed at, and of the presentment being neglected, as that of *Cabell,* was. Error is no fault in their proceedings: they are not final, and there is no obligation in the court to notice them. All they had therefore done was innocent, excepting as far as *an opinion* delivered by a Grand Jury in the form of a *Presentment* might *influence* the liberty of the press, for it could not controul it. Our grave Assembly however spent 4 days in debate upon this point; impeachments, remonstrances to congress, and twenty other angry resolutions were discussed. At last the *brutum fulmen*[10] of a string of resolutions condemning the conduct of the Grand jury and pointing out its bad tendency was passed. It was an odd anomalous production, full of good sense and crabbed cramped language. As much as I think the Grand jury to blame, as having betrayed a fretful boyish jealousy for the power of the foederal government, and having chosen a very silly manner, and a very silly subject to exhibit it, I cannot help thinking that the Legislature has done worse. Juries are our guardians against the despotism of our own Legislatures. They are *ourselves.* The Legislature ought not to interfere with their proceedings. I mention this circumstance at large, because it has made much noise among us.[11]

My time has been almost entirely occupied in designing a building to contain a Theatre, an Hotel, and Assembly rooms. It is proposed to build it by subscription, and it may perhaps be erected this Year. The subscription however is not yet full. I have bestowed my best talents and experience upon it and am satisfied to have made the drawings by way of keeping my hand in, should nothing else result from it. I have also written a Comedy which has been acted with a mixture of violent Applause and as violent opposition. The Author was not known till the next morning. The subject was Hamilton's *Apology,* and the most *comic* character, Peter Porcupine, under the name of *Skunk,* who does all the dirty work of the piece.[12] It was written in two days, the idea being started among a few friends and immediately pursued. The fact is, that it *ought* to have been *damned.* Not on account of any very great demerit in the [play?] but because not one of the performers knew half his part, excepting Green, who acted Skunk most admirably. I believe the loude[st], [*illegible*] laughter during the representation was occasioned by 5 performers being on the stage at once, not one of whom knew what to say, 71 and as the Company is not worth a prompter, they walked off and left the scene unfinished. You may guess at my feelings. The house was more crouded than it had ever been before. It was full of Ladies, or we should have had a tournament between the friends of Hamilton and those of liberty and morality. I intended to publish it, and it was advertised, but I believe I shall keep it, *ut nonum [novum?] prematur in annum.*[13] I will however, if I can find time, send you a copy in manuscript.

Our very good friends at Belvidere have been most seriously sick for a Month past: Mr. [Bushrod] Washington of a pleurisy, and his wife of a violent sore throat. His life was once despaired of. They are now both recovering. You are often very affectionately enquired after, and the regret you express at your very short acquaintance with them, is equally felt on their side. I have purchased of Mr. Washington an island in the midst of the Falls of James river. It is a beautiful, fertile and romantic spot. It contains about 80 acres of good land, and its scenery would not disgrace the magic rivers of Italy. I mean to live there. I am oppressed by the meanness of our Executive. I am called an extortioner because I have asked 1000 Dollars for my services at the Penitentiary house. To attend to that work I gave up my more profitable engagement with the Dismal Swamp [Land] company and refunded 200 Dollars I had received. I travelled from Norfolk and paid my expences there amounting to 100 Dollars more. They have seized my drawings and will not suffer them to be in my possession even to direct the work. I am yet unpaid. I have half ruined myself by living in this expensive city upon my own moderate capital. I mean therefore to be independent, and shutting myself up in my island to devote my hours to litterature, agriculture, friendship, and the education of my children, whom I hope to see here this Spring. And yet if I thought that in any part of America my talents, my acquired knowledge, and my honest intentions (of all which I have learnt to think myself possessed, from seeing the want of these qualifications in those who are here confided in) would meet with moderate respect, I believe I should be happier in the *active* pursuit of professional reputation. Indeed I am here truly unhappy. My only friend is Washington. He can feel with me, and I believe loves me. But yet he is only a Lawyer, and I have the itch of Botany of Chemistry, of Mathematics, of general Literature strong upon me yet, and yawn at perpetual political or legal discussion especially conducted in the cramp, local manner in which it is treated in Virginia. I never missed any friends in my life as much as I did you and Mr. McClure after you were gone.[14] I rambled about silently for a week afterwards and a hundred times walked into your empty room to see if it were possible you could be there. The disappointment threw me into low spirited reveries. What is such a shattered, weak brain as mine good for? My destiny is not blind. She has a keen active eye to discover thorny paths for me to walk in.

You are infinitely kind to have thought of my india ink, and the *Zoonomia*.[15] The best way to send them is by any vessel coming hither, directed to the care, either of Mr. McClure's house; or of Mr. James Brown who is usually so kind as to take care of my little affairs of this kind. May I again take the liberty of using your friendship to purchase me a pair of spectacles, silver frames, oval eyes, with concave (shortsighted) glasses ground to fit them, namely 2 pair of Glasses No. 6, 2 pair No. 7, and 2 pair No. 8. No. 7 suited my eye in England, but it may have altered its convexity by the change of Climate. If Mr. McClure will draw upon me for the amount I will pay it with many thanks. It depends much upon the *common sense* of our Executive whether I shall reach Philadelphia this spring. They seem to consider me as a disease that they would get rid of if they knew how. They see that they cannot do without me, and therefore do every thing but quarrell with me, but they heartily repent ever having employed me. I am an animal they do not understand. They cannot haggle with me about Dollars. I will not suffer my services to be underrated by way of beating down their reward. To this they are not accustomed. I have refused any arbitration upon them, because I deny the capacity of any man here to judge of them. You see therefore that it is ten to one that I shall be no longer employed. The last assembly ordered an Arsenal to be built. Passing by *me*, an Officer in the corps of Artillerists and Engineers in the Militia of this State, and the only *Engineer* in the Corps, they have already consulted a *Millwright*, who never saw a military work in his life.[16] Should I be laid on the shelf as useless, I shall not have any call to Philadelphia nor will the Expence of the Visit be convenient to me. I hope however that I may be able to settle matters more to my satisfaction when our new Members of Council take their seats. They are *my friends*, but such friends are not very zealous, and I have an *active* enemy at the board, whose hatred does me great honor.

I am convinced that I owe to your partiality the favorable opinion formed of my talents by Mr. Lownes.[17] I beg you to assure him that I will lose no time in making very exact drawings and descriptions of our Penitentiary house for him. All I beg in return is, that he will favor me with an exact account of the details of the Philadelphia institution *should*

73

I write for it—for if I either come to Philadelphia myself, or am laid upon the Shelf, it will be unnecessary to give him that trouble. I had the happiness to inherit from my father the friendship of the great Mr. Howard whom I knew during the last years of his stay in England, and from whose conversation all the little knowledge I may possess of what is a good, secure, and humane mode of confinement, is derived.[18] I had some experience in England of the practice also, as Architect to the Police of London and Middlesex. If I have occasion, but not otherwise I will take the liberty of troubling Mr. Lownes, through you with a series of questions, the answers to which will convey to me all the information I want. The drawings shall be in Philadelphia in three Weeks.

I heartily wish I could make the remaining slip of paper convey to you how much I esteem and love you. Insulated as I am here, separated from my *friends* by their want of similar taste and knowledge, and from those who possess both, by want of friendship, I was charmed beyond description by my most fortunate acquisition of your acquaintance. The remembrance of your talents, your gentleness and manners, and your sensibility will always be dear to me. I hope I shall always deserve to retain your good opinion and your affection.

Believe me most affectionately Yours

B. Henry Latrobe B.

ALS: The first page of this letter is in Jefferson Papers (158/A3); the second page is in Accessions, No. 24313, Virginia State Library (158/B1). About six inches of the first page appear to have been deliberately cut out and the page has been taped back together. This has created gaps in the text where noted. Addressed to Scandella in Philadelphia.

1. Dr. Giambattista Scandella (c. 1765–1798), Venetian physician, graduated from the University of Padua medical school in 1786 and was admitted to the practice of medicine that year. In 1790 he published a treatise on fertilizers in the Venetian *Nuovo giornale d'Italia*. He then moved to London, where he served as secretary of the Venetian legation. Within a year after BHL's arrival in America in 1796, Scandella landed in Quebec and visited many parts of North America. He met BHL while traveling through Virginia and stayed for a time in Philadelphia, where his friend Count Constantin Volney was residing. In April 1798 he was elected to the American Philosophical Society. After the passage of the Alien and Sedition acts, Scandella went to New York in September 1798 to embark for Europe, but he contracted yellow fever and died. Antonio Pace, "Giambattista Scandella and His American Friends," *Italica* 42 (1965):269–84; Hamlin, *Latrobe,* pp. 80, 127, 133; Harry R. Warfel, *Charles Brockden Brown: American Gothic Novelist* (Gainesville, Fla., 1949), pp. 118–20.

2. Trans.: In a different outward appearance, the same virtue.

3. BHL refers here to recent political events in Venice. The Republic of Venice, in existence since the late Middle Ages, collapsed during the French Revolution. The government offered no resistance to Napoleon, and Ludovico Manin, the last doge, was deposed

in May 1797. A provisional democratic municipality was set up in place of the republican government, but in the same year Venice came under Austrian control.

4. Dr. William Thornton (1759–1828), amateur architect, inventor, and public official, received his M.D. degree from Aberdeen University (1784). He came to the U.S. in 1787 but did not practice medicine. In 1793 he won the competition for the design of the U.S. Capitol and from 1794 to 1802 he was a commissioner for the city of Washington. The dispute between Thornton and BHL over BHL's alterations to the design of the Capitol became the subject of newspaper and pamphlet exchanges between 1804 and 1808. The dispute culminated in BHL's libel suit against Thornton, initiated in 1808 and decided, in BHL's favor, in 1813.

5. The dispatch from the French minister to the United States, Joseph Fauchet, to his government, dated 31 October 1794, was intercepted by the British. Its disclosure led to allegations that Secretary of State Edmund Randolph had made indiscreet intimations to Fauchet. Randolph resigned when confronted with the allegations but later published *A Vindication of Mr. Randolph's Resignation* (Philadelphia, 1795), which included a transcript of Fauchet's dispatch. BHL quoted the sentence: "What will be the old age of this government, if it is thus early decrepid!" (*Vindication,* p. 46).

6. Four or five words are missing.

7. Mrs. Green (née Willems), an actress who emigrated from England in 1794, asked BHL the question. BHL wrote "the name of the young Lady whose cruelty could be the cause of the above expressive look" in Hebrew script in his journal, the transliteration of which is Black Louise (or Lucy) Nelson. The woman has not been identified. BHL, *Journals,* 2 : 333, 335n.

8. Col. James Innes (1754–98), Revolutionary War veteran well-known for his remarkable oratorical skills and "colossal stature," served in the Virginia House of Delegates as a representative of James City County (1780–81) and Williamsburg (1781–82, 1785–87). He succeeded Edmund Randolph as attorney general of Virginia in 1786. Innes died in Philadelphia while serving as commissioner to negotiate damages awarded to citizens under Article VI of the Jay Treaty, a position to which he had been appointed in 1796. BHL, *Journals,* 1 : 130, 132, 2 : 543–44.

9. From *Julius Caesar,* act 3, sc. 1, lines 47–48: "Know, Caesar doth not wrong, nor without cause will he be satisfied."

10. Trans.: brute thunderbolt.

11. These events took place between May and December 1797. A federal grand jury meeting in Richmond, presided over by Federalist Supreme Court Justice James Iredell (1751–99), presented "as a real evil the circular letters of several members of the late Congress, and particularly letters with the signature of Samuel J. Cabell, endeavouring at a time of real public danger to disseminate unfounded calumnies against the happy government of the United States." Cabell (1756–1818), a Republican congressman, was defended by the Virginia House of Delegates, which adopted a resolution condemning the grand jury presentments as a violation of free speech and as an unlawful interference by the judiciary in congressional affairs. Noble E. Cunningham, Jr., ed., *Circular Letters of Congressmen to Their Constituents, 1789–1829,* 3 vols. (Chapel Hill, N.C., 1978), 1:xxxvii–xxxix, 39–43, 67–72, 115–20.

12. The original manuscript of *The Apology* has not been discovered, and no known copy of the play exists today. The play was a satire on Alexander Hamilton's affair with Mrs. Maria Reynolds and the public apology issued by Hamilton following the episode. Hamilton had privately revealed his illicit relationship with Mrs. Reynolds and the resulting blackmail by her husband, James, in December 1792. The episode did not become public until the publication of *The History of the United States for the Year 1796* (Philadelphia,

1797) by James T. Callender. Hamilton responded with *Observations on Certain Documents contained in Nos. V. and VI. of "The History of the United States for the Year 1796," in which the Charge of Speculation against Alexander Hamilton, late Secretary of the Treasury, is fully refuted* (Philadelphia, 1797), in which he acknowledged his liaison with Mrs. Reynolds but denied any malfeasance in office while serving as secretary of the Treasury. BHL's play was performed in Richmond on Saturday, 20 January 1798. Abe Wollock, "Benjamin Henry Latrobe's Activities in the American Theatre (1797–1808)" (Ph.D. diss., University of Illinois, 1962), chap. 2.

William Cobbett (1763–1835), one of the founders of American party journalism, emigrated from England in 1790 and soon moved to Philadelphia. In 1797 he began publishing *Porcupine's Gazette and Daily Advertiser,* a high Federalist paper which advocated alliance with England and war against France.

For the published exchange of letters over the merits of *The Apology* in the *Virginia Gazette & General Advertiser* (Richmond), see BHL, *Journals,* 2 : 343–46, 350–52, 353–56.

13. Trans.: So that it may be printed in the ninth [new?] year. The second Latin word is unclear, and could have either meaning.

14. William Maclure (1763–1840) was born in Scotland and emigrated to America in 1796 after making his fortune as a merchant. While in Europe as a commissioner to settle spoliation claims between the United States and France, he studied geology and natural history. Upon his return to America Maclure made a geological map of the United States, the first map of its scope in the history of geology (1809). In 1812 he became one of the first members of the Academy of Natural Sciences of Philadelphia, and served as its president from 1817 to 1840. He was also president of the American Geological Society.

15. Erasmus Darwin, *Zoonomia; Or the Laws of Organic Life,* 2 vols. (London, 1794–96).

16. On 23 January 1798 the Virginia General Assembly passed "An Act to establish arsenals and a manufactory of arms." The "millwright" consulted was Maj. John Clarke (1766–1844), whom Governor Wood described as a man "who is known to be extremely well skilled in the erection of Works of every denomination and whose respectability as a citizen has been long established." Later in 1798 Clarke succeeded BHL as director of the construction of the Richmond penitentiary, and in 1802 Gov. James Monroe appointed him the first superintendent of the armory. Giles Cromwell, *The Virginia Manufactory of Arms* (Charlottesville, Va., 1975), pp. 4, 11–12; *Virginia Magazine of History and Biography* 48 (1940):60.

BHL had "been appointed, without solicitation Engineer to the 4th regiment of Artillery attached to the first division of the Virginia Militia." BHL, *Journals,* 2 : 356.

17. Caleb Lownes, a Philadelphia Quaker, was an active member of the Pennsylvania Prison Society and served as a member of the Board of Inspectors of the Pennsylvania state penitentiary from 1790 to 1799. He was the author of *An Account of the alteration and present state of the penal laws of Pennsylvania, containing also An Account of the goal and penitentiary house of Philadelphia and the interior management thereof* (Philadelphia, 1793). Lownes was an iron merchant, and supplied Thomas Jefferson with much of the iron for his nailery. He also served as secretary of the Philadelphia Committee, which organized the city's resistance to the yellow fever plague of 1793. LeRoy B. DePuy, "The Walnut Street Prison: Pennsylvania's First Penitentiary," *Pennsylvania History* 38 (1951):130–44; Edwin M. Betts, ed., *Thomas Jefferson's Farm Book* (Princeton, N.J., 1953), pp. 426–29; John H. Powell, *Bring Out Your Dead: The Great Plague of Yellow Fever in Philadelphia in 1793* (Philadelphia, 1949).

18. John Howard (1726?–90), English philanthropist and prison reformer, erected model cottages on his Cardington estate, provided elementary education for the village children, and encouraged the individual industry of the villagers. For BHL's description of Howard's Cardington establishment, see BHL, *Journals,* 1 : 269–70.

TO JAMES WOOD

Richmond Feby. 14th. 1798.

Sir,

In complying with the desire of the Executive expressed to me by you in September 1797, by herewith submitting my charge for professional Services at the Penitentiary house, I have been unwilling to accompany it with any observations, lest I should appear to doubt either the liberality of the Executive, or the fairness of my bill. As however both the employment of an architect and its concomitant expence appears to be new to the public Works of this State, and some question may arise relative to it, I take the liberty to trouble you with the following explanatory remarks, leaving it to your discretion whether or no they ought to be respectfully submitted by me to the Executive.

It is in France, Germany, and England the established custom of Architects, (in England confirmed by many decisions of the Courts) to charge for their works, 1.) a commission of 5 per Cent on the whole amount of the expence incurred in executing their design; 2.) a certain sum for fair drawings, if furnished, according to their difficulty, number, or beauty; 3.) if the work be at a distance from the usual residence of the Architect, all travelling expences, and a certain sum per day for loss of time. All the English architects of eminence charged in 1795, five Guineas per day, and no surveyor or measurer less than one Guinea. If surveys, reports, or agreements are drawn, these are separately charged. If drawings and descriptions alone are made, without further direction of the work, either personally or by letter, 2½ per Cent *upon the Estimate* is charged, whether the work be executed or not. This latter charge is established by several decisions of the Courts.

I never was of opinion that the charge of a regular sum per Cent upon all buildings was a fair mode of recompence. Upon very small works of taste it is much too little, upon very extensive ones, it is often too much. It is however difficult to contrive any other more eligible method, and compared with the charge of merchants for their negotiations, it is in all instances very reasonable. In an hour a merchant can by means of a Clerk execute a commission which requires no ability acquired at a great expence, and his charge of at least 2½, often of 5 per Cent is admitted without dispute. To execute a commission to no larger an amount, an architect or engineer must perhaps attend in all weathers for many months, and his charge is no greater. The talents necessary to 77 his profession are care, and a more expensive education is requisite to none. His services however if honestly applied, are of the utmost importance to his employers, and independent of the utility and convenience of his works, it is in his power to save much more than any reasonable recompence can amount to.

It may be said, that the customs of the old countries ought not to govern the practices of this State. Admitting the justness of the observation, I beg leave to compare my charge to one actually paid to a professional man employed in this city. Mr. Western came from Philadelphia to Richmond, being sent for by the James river company to give designs for the completion of their Navigation.[1] He staid not more than eight days, and left drawings, plans and profils, of eight locks, with the necessary descriptions and estimates. His bill at the tavern, and his travelling charges were paid, besides his account for professional services. In all they amount to 1.200 Dollars.[2] From Richmond he went to Petersburg, expecting to meet the Appomattox Superintendants. He was disappointed and returned the same day. I was present when his bill of 50. Dollars, and 13 or 15 Dollars for expences was ordered to be paid, at the meeting of the Company at Chinquopin Church.[3]

It would be hypocrisy in me to say that either my experience, or my opportunities of acquiring professional knowledge were less than his, and his testimony in my favor renders comparison unnecessary.

I will now mention only one more circumstance which affects me personally. When my plan was so honorably to me both in the manner and in the gratuity accompanying it adopted by the Executive, I was engaged by the old Dismal Swamp Company to make a survey of all their Land in the Swamp, to cut a compleat Lane round it, and to lay off canals for the supply of Jericho and Smiths Mills. I had been residing a fortnight at Suffolk, from whence I visited and ascertained the situation of the West side of the Swamp and the Lake, and had staid another fortnight at Norfolk, where at the expence of the Company I was furnished with the necessary conveniences for exploring the whole Swamp, in which it was calculated I should encamp about 3 weeks, without being able to command any assistance or food, but what I carried with me. All the expence attending these preparations was incurred, when I received Your letter informing me that my attendance at Richmond would be required to survey the situation and set out the building of the Penitentiary house. Mr. McCaulay the President of the Company delivered me the letter, and consented to the postponement of the intended expedition. I was under the necessity of staying a few days longer at Norfolk,

78

and of returning to Richmond *at my own expence*. It was however impossible for me after wards to resume my operations, and the Company took my bond for 120 Dollars (which was about the amount of their expences) payable on the 1st. of May 1798 in case I should not proceed in this business. This bond will, I presume, at all events be forfeited.

The sum expended under my direction is about 15.000 Dollars. On this I have charged 5 per Cent including all my expences, and every other possible charge, and I have no doubt but that it will appear to the board that is has been my intention to charge as moderately as possible, and my books will prove that I have charged less than I ever did before. Should the Executive still employ me, it is my earnest wish to have a fixed Salary, the amount of which, were I permitted to name it, would be not more than at the rate of 2½ per Cent on the money likely to be expended at the Penitentiary house in the course of the present Year, and I would then consider myself as bound to give my professional assistance to the Executive in *every public* Work at *Richmond*.

I am with great esteem and sincerity Yrs.

B. Henry Latrobe B.

ALS: Executive Papers of Governor James Wood, Virginia State Library (158/B10).

1. William Weston (c. 1752–1833), English civil engineer, was employed in the United States (1793–1800) on numerous projects, including the Schuylkill and Susquehanna Navigation Company (Pa.), the Middlesex Canal (Mass.), the Potomac Company, the Western Inland Lock Navigation Company (predecessor of the Erie Canal), and the Schuylkill River Permanent Bridge. He went to Richmond in 1796 to advise the James River Company. Before BHL's arrival in America, Weston and Christian Senf were the only professional canal engineers in the country. Joseph Hobson Harrison, Jr., "The Internal Improvement Issue in the Politics of the Union, 1783–1825" (Ph.D. diss., University of Virginia, 1954), pp. 96, 112; Richard Shelton Kirby, "William Weston and His Contribution to Early American Engineering," Newcomen Society for the Study of the History of Engineering and Technology, *Transactions* 16 (1935–36):111–25.

2. See BHL to Banks, 15 Aug. 1797, n. 3, above.

3. Weston met with superintendents appointed by the trustees of the Upper Appomattox Company which had been incorporated in 1795 to improve the navigation of the Appomattox River. BHL met with the trustees on 5 May 1796 at Chinquopin Church in Amelia County; it was probably at this meeting that Weston's expenses were approved. At the meeting BHL made preliminary arrangements for a survey expedition on the river, which he made in June 1796. In 1799, BHL noted that "the observations made upon this trip decided the present attempt to render the river navigable, which, if successfully conducted, will open a source of prosperity to all the counties bordering upon the river from the tide of James river [into which the Appomattox flows] to the Blueridge." Samuel Shepherd, *The Statutes at Large of Virginia, from October Session 1792, to December Session 1806, Inclusive, in Three Volumes (New Series), Being a Continuation of Hening*, 3 vols. (New York, 1970 [orig. publ. 1835]), 1 : 390–94; BHL, *Journals*, 1 : 98, 137–55, 2 : 530.

TO JAMES WOOD

Richmond, March 5th. 1798

Sir,

In answer to the proposal with which you favored me on Friday last, I beg leave to say, that I accept of a Salary of £200.0 per Annum as a compensation for my direction of the Work at the Penitentiary house.[1]

At the same time I beg leave to state that though I am perfectly well acquainted with every thing that has been done in Europe to render prisons safe, convenient and wholesome, I am unwilling to remain without the advantage of having seen what has been done at Philadelphia, and it seems to me to be of importance to the public that I should know it.[2] I have also many private reasons for the journey, among which the first is, that since my arrival in America, I have not seen my very near and numerous relations in Pensylvania, the Antes family. Previous to my departure I will leave in writing the most ample directions should the work commence before the middle of April, before which time I shall return, but as the contracts for work and Materials cannot be made before the middle of the present month, and the season is still very early, I hope no possible delay can arise from my absence: and when the Executive takes into consideration that since the beginning of the Work I have never quitted the spot, I hope I shall be permitted to take this journey without forfeiting my salary or engagement. In the mean time I have begun to draw the necessary directions, and should my absence not be inconsistent with the wishes of the Executive, I will deliver them to Your Excellency before my departure on Thursday morning.[3] I am with great respect Yours &c.

B. Henry Latrobe B.

ALS: Dreer Collection, Historical Society of Pennsylvania (158/C6).

1. BHL later recalled that he had received $1,000 for his work before accepting this annual salary of £200 (about $670). The $1,000 he received may represent 5 percent of the $15,000 up to then expended ($750), plus the $250 he had earlier received for his drawings. The £200 salary would correspond to 2 1/2 percent of an estimated outlay of about $27,000. BHL to Wood and Council, 12 May 1797, above; BHL to Robert Mills, 12 July 1806, in BHL, *Correspondence*, 2.

2. On 26 March 1798 BHL arrived in Philadelphia for a two-week visit during which he studied the Walnut Street Jail.

3. BHL, "Directions to the Superintendant of the Penitentiary house to be followed in case the Work should proceed during the absence of Mr. Latrobe, the Architect," 8 March 1798, and BHL to Wood, 10 Mar. 1798, both in the Executive Papers of Governor James Wood, Virginia State Library, Richmond (158/C10, 158/D5).

TO THOMAS JEFFERSON

Francis's Hotel [Philadelphia] March 28th. 1798

Sir,[1]

I should have taken the liberty to deliver to you the enclosed letter from Mr. Randolph immediately on my arrival two days ago, had he not told me, that he has therein done me the favor to recommend me to you, with a view to interest your kind offices for me in an application I had intended to make to the Executive of the United States, during my stay at Philadelphia. I had understood that it was the intention of the Government to erect an Arsenal and a Manufactory of arms at Harpers ferry,[2] and as I am now engaged in Virginia, in the Penitentiary house, and am consulted by several of the Canal companies, to have designed and directed a Work of such magnitude as, I suppose, this Arsenal will be, would have at once decided me to sell my Pensylvanien property and consider myself as a Virginian for the rest of my life. But upon some previous enquiry, I am told, that although I have very strong recommendations to several Gentlemen highly in the confidence of the President, I am not likely to succeed, should I apply; and that it will not avail me to have had an education entirely directed to the object of becoming useful as an Engineer and Architect, and to have given proofs of some degree of skill, for I am guilty of the crime of enjoying the friendship of many of the most independent and virtuous men in Virginia, and even was seen at the dinner given to Mr. Monroe.[3] I have therefore resolved not to run the risk of a· refusal, and should esteem it a mark of favor in you to permit the enclosed letter to pass for a *general* recommendation. Since my arrival in America, it is been my very anxious wish to become known to you, and to improve an old acquaintance with, and admiration of your works, into a personal knowledge of you.

If you will permit me, I will do myself the honor to wait upon you in your apartment tomorrow morning, being engaged for this evening to meet Mr. Caleb Lownes.[4]

I am, with the sincerest respect Yours

B. Henry Latrobe B.

ALS: Jefferson Papers (158/D9).

1. At this time Jefferson (1743–1826) was vice-president of the United States.

2. The federal government purchased land at Harpers Ferry for an arsenal and armory in 1796. An act of 4 May 1798 provided $100,000 for the development of federal 81

armories and foundries, and by September of that year Joseph Perkin, a Philadelphia gunmaker, was engaged as superintendent of construction of the Harpers Ferry facilities. Merritt Roe Smith, *Harpers Ferry Armory and the New Technology: The Challenge of Change* (Ithaca, N.Y., 1977), chap. 1; Stuart E. Brown, Jr., *The Guns of Harpers Ferry* (Berryville, Va., 1968), pp. 9–10.

3. On 26 January 1798 in Richmond, BHL "dined with a large party of Gentlemen at the Eagle who assembled to do honor to Mr. James Monroe, our late ambassador *near* the french republic" (BHL, *Journals*, 2 : 336). Monroe was appointed U.S. minister to France in June 1794, about the time John Jay arrived in England to negotiate an Anglo-American commercial treaty. Monroe was decidedly pro-French, and he found the task of reconciling France to the Jay Treaty impossible. Unable to satisfy either the French government or the Federalist administration at home, Monroe was recalled in 1796. On his return Monroe published *A View of the Conduct of the Executive, in the Foreign Affairs of the United States* (Philadelphia, 1797), a vindication of his mission.

4. Two days earlier, on 26 March, Julian Ursyn Niemcewicz "spent the evening at the house of Mr. Launs, . . . Director of the [Walnut Street] Prison. Latrobe, architect from Virginia, was there. They discussed only the prison." Niemcewicz, *Under Their Vine and Fig Tree: Travels Through America in 1797–1799, 1805, with Some Further Account of Life in New Jersey*, trans. and ed. Metchie J. E. Budka (Elizabeth, N.J., 1965), p. 53.

TO HENRY ANTES

Philadelphia, April 8, 1798.

My Dear Uncle:[1]

Since my arrival in America, two years ago, it has been my particular wish to see you. Expecting to arrive in winter, I took my passage in a ship bound for Virginia, and intended to travel through the more southerly States previous to my settling in Pennsylvania. A great variety of public business, which was offered me, rendered it impossible to accomplish my desire of settling near you. I came to Philadelphia about a fortnight ago, partly upon business entrusted to me by the Executive of Virginia, partly with the intention of spending a week with you. I have, however, found it out of my power to take a journey to so great a distance without staying so long away from my engagements in Virginia as to run the risk of their suffering injury in the meantime. I must, therefore, postpone the pleasure of seeing you till another opportunity, which I shall endeavor to procure as early as possible. I have been extremely fortunate in meeting my cousin, Mr. Snyder, here; he will tell you how much I am interested in becoming acquainted with a branch of my family, the only one now remaining.[2] My father, when he died in 1787, had not a single relation on his side but his children. I have two brothers, one elder and one

82

younger than myself. The elder is married, and has two or three children in England; the younger is a physician in Russia. I have also two sisters, the elder of whom is married to a Mr. Foster, and has four children; whether the younger is married I cannot tell; it was expected she would be when I last heard from her. I myself was married seven years ago, but had the misfortune to lose my wife before we had lived three years together. Her loss so afflicted my mother that she survived her not quite a month. I have two children, a boy and a girl. The latter is the eldest and is now six years old. They are in England with my sister.[3] I have written to you at least three letters, but I fear you never received them. I entrusted them to private hands, not knowing how to direct to you by post, and suppose my friends either neglected or found themselves unable to gain intelligence of your abode. I hope to correspond in future with you, whenever it may be convenient to you. I shall be happy to receive a line from you, but shall think it my duty to write to you as frequently as possible.

Having received a literary education, I turned my thoughts early to the study of architecture and to receive instruction necessary to an engineer, and having improved myself by having traveled through a great part of Europe, I commenced business in England a little before my marriage, and was engaged in many public and private works, having been architect to the Police of Middlesex and Westminster, and engineer to three or four canals and harbors.[4] The loss of my wife made business irksome to me, and I therefore resolved to leave a country where everything reminded me how happy I had been and how miserable I was. On my arrival in Virginia, however, I so far recovered my spirits and health as to have resolved to recommence my professional pursuits. I am at present engaged for twelve months by the State of Virginia, but though I have purchased land in that State, I have bought a lot in the city of Richmond,[5] I have seriously thought of settling in Pennsylvania. I will take the liberty of consulting you upon the subject whenever it becomes a more immediate object to me. In the meantime I hope you will believe that the affection which my mother taught me to bear to you by her frequent and affectionate mention of you remains undiminished and can only be increased by a personal acquaintance of your character. I beg you to give my best love to my aunt and my cousins and all my relations when you see them, and to believe me, very truly,

Your affectionate nephew, Benjamin Henry Latrobe. 83

Printed Copy: Edwin MacMinn, *On the Frontier with Colonel Antes* (Camden, N.J., 1900), pp. 491–93 (158/D13).

1. Col. Henry Antes (1736–1820), a native Pennsylvanian and a Revolutionary War hero, was a brother of BHL's mother. He served as sheriff of Northumberland County. Edwin MacMinn, *On the Frontier with Colonel Antes* (Camden, N.J., 1900), p. 487.
2. Simon Snyder (1759–1819), later governor of Pennsylvania, was at this time a member of the state House of Representatives. He was married to BHL's cousin Catherine Antes (d. 1810).
3. BHL's father actually died in 1786. BHL's older brother, Christian Ignatius Latrobe, a Moravian clergyman, had married Anna B. Syms (d. 1824) and eventually had six children. BHL's younger brother, John Frederick Latrobe (1769–1845), married Alwine Marie, Baroness Stackelberg and had six children. BHL's older sister, Anna Louisa Eleanora Latrobe (1761–1824), married Frederic William Foster (1760–1835), a Moravian clergyman, and had six children. BHL's younger sister, Mary Agnes Latrobe (1772–1848), married John Bateman (1772–1851) and had six children. See Genealogy, above.
   BHL married Lydia Sellon (c. 1761–1793) on 27 February 1790 and had two children, Lydia (1791–1878) and Henry Sellon Boneval (1792–1817). BHL's wife and her third child died in childbirth in November 1793. BHL's mother, Anna Margaretta (Antes) Latrobe (1728–94), actually died four months later on 17 March 1794. Later BHL noted that his daughter went to live with Frederic William and Anna Louisa Eleanora (Latrobe) Foster, while his son stayed with Elizabeth (Sellon) White, BHL's sister-in-law. After BHL remarried in 1800 the children came to live with their father in America. BHL to Erick Bollmann, 30 Aug. 1805, in BHL, *Correspondence, 2.*
4. BHL worked on the following engineering works in England: the Rye Harbour improvement project (c. 1786–87), the Basingstoke Canal (c. 1788–89), and the Chelmer and Blackwater Navigation (1793–95). For the latter, see BHL, Report on the Chelmer and Blackwater Navigation, 30 Dec. 1793, above. BHL, *Engineering Drawings*, pp. 5–7, 113–15.
5. On 30 April BHL wrote that he had rented the land south of Col. John Harvie's property on Byrd Street between Third and Fourth. "The lots to the East I had before purchased." BHL to Giambattista Scandella, 30 Apr. [1798], in BHL, *Journals*, 2 : 383.

TO GIAMBATTISTA SCANDELLA

Richmond Aprl. 17th, 1798.

My dear friend

I arrived here last night, oppressed by the fatigue of the most disagreeable journey and by the most violent cold, I ever experienced. I found every place as I passed along and every individual agitated by the political impulses that are at present operating. As the air grew warmer and the trees greener by the influence of the Sun, in my progress to the Southward, the opinions of those with whom I conversed grew gradually more unfettered by presidential veneration. On arriving in Virginia all our Passengers, except one Philadelphian, were exchanged for Democrats. Till then, Mr. Clopton[1] (of Congress) and myself were in the minority. As I got nearer Richmond I heard of nothing but instructions against War to representatives, Petitions to Congress, remonstrances to the Executive. I called in the course of the evening upon most of my friends, and found them all over heads and ears in political discussions. Even the peaceful fireside of Mr. [Bushrod] Washington is disturbed by political fanaticism. What news? what news? what news? assailed one on every side. XYZ and the Lady &c., was my answer. Shocking indeed! Who should have thought it of the virtuous French? exclaimed one party. Nothing else could be expected from the bloodsucking rascals, cried the other. War, war, war—or national disgrace, and slavery, on one side. Peace, peace, at all events and all hazards on the other. Pray, my very good friends, how will you make war? and you others, how can you preserve peace?[2] Let alone your discussions, and read Gulliver. The book is both entertaining and instructive, and has a very pretty story in it about the Land of Brobdingnag.

In order to give you a more clear idea of *doings* here, I send you a paper full of descriptions of *storms* in a teapot *de chambre*. Among the dashing waves you will see floating a paper, being a petition to be forwarded to Congress. I need not comment upon it. It is, I think, a proof, that we have men of sense, of firmness, of clear conception, of love of truth, and of powerful *pens* in Virginia, and that the writer Colonel John Taylor is one of them.[3] I am heartily sorry however to see the effect of this *dose* of XYZ &c., upon a great number of *honest* men, who know not the tricks of the world, and cannot comprehend that nothing has been administered to them but the faeces that settle to the bottom of every diplomatic brewage.

You see, my dear friend, how the politicomania has seized me even, for had not my barber come to shave me, and thus broken the thread of my political discussion, I should perhaps have filled this whole sheet with an extension of it. But indeed, at the present moment the great convulsions of empires and nations, are so violent, that they lay hold of, and move individuals with an effect unknown in the former wars of kings. The surface—the great men of every nation—were once the only part of the mass really interested. The present storm is so violent, that the ocean is moved to the very depth, and you and I who inhabit it, feel the commotion.

Mr. Palmer who is so good as to take charge of this letter is now   85 waiting for it. Forgive its want of length and of matter. I need not tell you how often I think of you, and your invaluable friends—invaluable for superior understanding highly cultivated, but still more so for minds devoted to truth and to benevolence. I shall be the happier and the better throughout my life for having spent a fortnight among you. I would say so much to Mr. Maclure, to Mr. Volney, to Mr. Lownes, and to Mr. Jefferson, and Mr. Maclure Junr. that I cannot say in any reasonable compass that I must beg you to be my interpreter. You cannot mistake my sentiments, unless you err in expressing too little of grateful friendship for them all. An early post shall carry letters to each. In the mean time believe me Yours most affectionately

B. H. Latrobe B.

Mr. Palmer is an excellent man and deserves to be loved by every body. I owe him much. I believe Mr. Maclure knows him.

ALS: Wetmore Family Papers, Yale University Library (158/E1). Addressed to Scandella at "Mr. Maclures So. 11th. street, Philadelphia."

1. John Clopton (1756–1816), a graduate of the College of Philadelphia (now the University of Pennsylvania) in 1776, served as a lieutenant and captain in the Virginia militia during the Revolution. He represented New Kent County in the Virginia House of Delegates (1789–91) and served in the U.S. Congress as a Republican (1795–99, 1801–16), having lost the closely contested 1799 election to John Marshall by 108 votes. Between congressional terms, he served on the Virginia Council of State. BHL, *Journals,* 2 : 538.

2. John Marshall, Charles Cotesworth Pinckney, and Elbridge Gerry had been appointed envoys extraordinary and ministers plenipotentiary to France by President John Adams in May and June 1797. Upon their arrival in Paris, they were approached by agents of Charles Maurice de Talleyrand-Périgord, the French minister of foreign affairs. The agents (Nicholas Hubbard, English partner in an Amsterdam banking firm; Jean Conrad Hottinguer, a Swiss financier; Pierre Bellamy, a Hamburg banker of Swiss origin; and Lucien Hauteval) attempted to obtain a bribe of $250,000 for Talleyrand and the Directors as well as a loan to the French government of $12 million as a prerequisite for the negotiations. The Americans refused to comply, and their dispatches, detailing the solicited bribes and the failure of the mission, arrived in Philadelphia in March 1798. Adams submitted the dispatches to Congress in April, substituting the letters W, X, Y, and Z for the names of the French agents. The lady, another Talleyrand agent, was never identified. The publication of the XYZ dispatches sparked a popular outcry for war with France, and contributed to the resurgence of the Federalist party. William Stinchcombe, *The XYZ Affair* (Westport, Conn., 1980).

3. This petition of the citizens of Caroline County to Congress, printed in the *Virginia Gazette, and General Advertiser* (Richmond) on 10 April 1798, denounced Federalist foreign policy and claimed that "war makes individuals richer, by making the people poorer." The petition blamed the war scare on those who wanted to protect British commerce, and it advocated the maintenance of friendly relations with France. Richard R. Beeman, *The Old Dominion and the New Nation, 1788–1801* (Lexington, Ky., 1972), p. 177.

John Taylor of Caroline (c. 1753–1824), political writer and politician, was an Anti-federalist in 1788 and later a Jeffersonian Republican. He served in the U.S. Senate (1792–94, 1803, 1822–24). Taylor used his literary talents to oppose federalism and any strong centralizing tendencies in the national government. He introduced resolutions into the Virginia legislature in 1798 opposing the Alien and Sedition acts. BHL, *Journals*, 2 : 555–56.

TO JAMES WOOD

[Richmond] July 9th. 1798.

Dear Sir,

I have this day most attentively examined that part of the Arch of the Cellar under the Kitchen of the Penitentiary house which has been supposed to have settled, and find that the place, where the bricks have been driven down, is not at all under the pillar above. Upon enquiry, Mr. Duke[1] could inform me, that Beard the Stonemason occasioned this apparent failure by hammering the Base stone there. In no other instance is there the smallest failure. I have marked out upon the arch the exact spot over which the pillar stands, and should be extremely obliged to you to examine it. You will be convinced that the pressure of that Stone has done no mischief. In the SE Cellar the whole weight of the Octagon groin-Butments is upon the Crown of the lower Arch, and no sign of settlement is to be seen. *There,* there is not even a Capstone to relieve it. But although I am myself satisfied of the security of the Work, I should be very much to blame, were I to hold out obstinately against your opinion, and I have requested Mr. Callis junior[2] to point out to you the mode by which every possible danger may be avoided. I beg leave to express to you my very sincere gratitude for your kind anxiety for the success of my works and I shall always remember, that if I ever arrive at any professional eminence in Virginia, I owe it to your early patronage.

I have this day ordered part of the Centering of the Octagon groin to be struck for your inspection. Every thing is going on in the very best manner, and I have left directions in writing and drawings for 6 Weeks to come.[3]

Inclosed is the proposed Advertisement for Carpenters' Work and the account of State.

I beg most seriously to represent to you the necessity of thinking soon of supplying the house with Water. The well is now empty and Mr.   87

Mims receives only 2 Hogsheads per day of bad Water from it. Even the Brickmakers have given up their Wells. There can be no doubt but that in November we may receive Prisoners.[4] In Philadelphia there is a natural stream which clears their Sewers, and yet they keep constantly 2 pumps going for the house and the Works. To supply Water in any Way will require two Months preparation, and we cannot well begin the work till August.

I have drawings of all the Philadelphia Machines for making nails. We ought to think of making some. I am willing to take any trouble and give any assistance.[5]

Believe me with sincere respect, Yrs.

B. Henry Latrobe.

ALS: Executive Papers of Governor James Wood, Virginia State Library (158/F1). Enclosed BHL, Proposed Advertisement for Carpenters' Work, below.

1. James Duke, a carpenter employed at the penitentiary. *CVSP*, 8 : 486, 9 : 175.
2. This is probably William Callis, Jr., grandson of Superintendent Thomas Callis. William Callis, Jr., and his father, William Callis, Sr. (son-in-law of Thomas Callis), were both employed as carpenters on the penitentiary in 1798. William Callis, Sr., to Wood, 26 Oct. 1797, State Penitentiary Papers, Virginia State Library, Richmond; *CVSP*, 8 : 486.
3. Shortly after writing this letter, BHL left for Norfolk to undertake his first federal commission, "to survey and report upon the fortifications at that place." See BHL to Jefferson, 22 Sept. 1798, below.
4. The first six convicts to be incarcerated at the penitentiary did not arrive until spring 1800. *CVSP*, 9 : 334.
5. BHL also made drawings of the Philadelphia nail cutting machine for Thomas Jefferson. See BHL to Jefferson, 22 Sept. 1798, below. A shop for the manufacture of cut nails was set up at the penitentiary and George Anderson Stile was hired in 1800 "to instruct and work with the prisoners in nail-making." An unintended use of the nails and nailer's tools occurred in 1803 when two prisoners used them to help in their escape. *CVSP*, 9 : 120, 352, 479.

ENCLOSURE: PROPOSED ADVERTISEMENT FOR CARPENTERS' WORK

Proposals will be received &c. for executing the following Carpenters and Joiners Work.

1.) Laying single joists upon Arches.
2.) Framing principal roofs according to directions and drawings to be given by the Architect. A specimen of the mode of framing may be seen over the Gateway.
3.) Planking the Walls of the Cells with 1½ inch Oak plank driven full of clinched nails, and ploughed and tongued.

4.) Laying straight joint pine plank floors, askewnailed.

5.) Boarding for Slate with inch plank close joint.

6.) Planing and fixing the principal joists of the Galleries in Locust

7.) Framing the (pine) Floors of the same and boarding them

8.) Making rebated Window frames to all the external openings, with cambered heads and sunk Cills, in Locust

9.) Making rebated Locust door frames, double heads, rebated,

10.) Six pannelled 2 inch bead and flush doors

11.) Six pannelled 1½ inch do.

12.) Making six pannelled 1 inch double doors bead and flush with a plate of iron between them, and bolted with 8 bolts to the foot.

13.) 1½ rebated and beaded linings

14.) Superficial Moulded work (per foot)

15.) 1½ sashes, dowelled and franked.

NB. All this carpenters Work must be delivered in its place: the doors must all be hung, and the sashes fixed.

Slating

200 Square.

The slates must hold 18 inches in length and show 5.[1] All the eves must be doubled. They are to be laid dry, and pointed in the inside. NB. As the building itself cannot be burned, might shingles do for the prison and slates *only* for the Gate and Keepers house.

AD: Executive Papers of Governor James Wood, Virginia State Library (158/F5). Enclosed in BHL to Wood, 9 July 1798, above.

1. While on the stage after departing Richmond, BHL realized that he had erred in this statement. On arriving in Petersburg he wrote Wood to correct the mistake: "The Slates should be, either 14 inches long to show 5 inches or 18 inches long to show 7½ inches." BHL to Wood, 10 July 1798, Executive Papers of Governor James Wood, Virginia State Library (158/F9).

TO JAMES WOOD

Richmond Septr. 8th.1798

Sir,

Having now nearly compleated the Road to the Penitentiary house the Contractor's Workmen are ready to proceed with the Sewers. Great progress has been made in the proposed Chains for securing the West

Wing, which still remains exactly in the State in which it appeared on striking the Centers;[1] but for want of another good Smith and striker, the Iron Work goes on heavily. Mr. Paul is a very good Nailor.[2]

The superintendant's illness, has prevented the report upon the Stonework being in readiness to be submitted to the Executive this day. It will be laid before you in the next Week.

I beg leave once more to remind the Executive of the very great urgency of considering the means of Supplying the Penitentiary house with Water, and to refer to my reports of the last Season, upon this Subject. I had hoped, that the building would have been ready to receive convicts in December. My exertions however have been ineffectual. But as the Woodwork may be done during the Winter, it cannot be doubted that the square part of the Prison, will be compleated early in Spring. Without a very copious supply of Water, it will then be unfit to be inhabited.

I received about 14 days ago, the intimation of the Executive that a proposition had been made at the Council, to remove me from my Office as Architect to the penitentiary house. It was my intention to have immediately applied for a decision upon a subject of so much importance to my present and future interests: but as I am convinced that such intimation was given to me from motives of attention and delicacy, I have been unwilling to trust myself with an early expression of my feelings on the subject, lest they might betray me into any thing that might not appear consistent with my respect for the honorable Board. In the mean time, I hope, I shall be pardoned in saying, that conscious as I am, that I have very far exceeded the limits of my precise duty in my exertions to be useful to the public, that I have sacrificed, and am at this moment sacrificing situations infinitely more eligible in point of emolument, to my determination not to forsake the employment in which I first embarked; knowing that I have now educated a set of workmen, capable of finishing the Work, who when I first met them, were unable to execute any thing beyond the commonest arch, that I have done the duties of *two* situations ever since I was appointed, that it is impossible with justice to charge me with the slightest infidelity or neglect, and that, in fact, no such charge has ever been made. I hope, I shall be pardoned in saying, that such a record of disgrace, as now appears against me upon the books of the Honorable the Council of State, entered without my having the most distant conception of the accusation against me, or knowing against what charge and against whom, I have to defend
90 [myself, is] to me a punishment, which could only be due to some

flagrant and proved misconduct. I am unwilling to anticipate the determination of the Executive respecting the day fixed, nor has the anxious and lengthened suspence in which I am held diminished my zeal to fulfill my duty; but if the Honble. Board would indulge me with a hearing on Tuesday next, I should feel myself infinitely obliged to your Excellency to express such my request, and I should feel myself sincerely obliged.[3]

I am Sir with true respect Yours &c.

B. H. Latrobe B.

ALS: Executive Papers of Governor James Wood, Virginia State Library (160/B1). Bracketed words are obscured by the seal of the letter. Enclosed BHL, Account, below.

1. Seven individuals, including BHL and Thomas Callis, sent the governor a signed statement informing him that there was no need to take down the arches in the west wing of the penitentiary because of the appearance of cracks. They agreed "that the expedient proposed by the Architect in chaining together the opposite walls will secure it from a further injury and enable it to bear the encreased weight of another story of Brickwork." Nathaniel Quarles et al. to Wood, n.d., State Penitentiary Papers, Virginia State Library, Richmond (157/G13).

2. In 1797 Robert Paul wrote the governor offering to make nails of the best quality for the use of the state at 1s. per pound at his Richmond factory. *CVSP*, 8 : 450.

3. On 29 September the governor affirmed the need for the continued services of BHL and Thomas Callis. Journal of the Council of State, Virginia State Library.

ENCLOSURE: ACCOUNT

Mr. Paul's account of 8 days work.

$$\left.\begin{array}{l}\text{Paul } 8.6 \\ \text{Son } 6.0\end{array}\right\} \text{per day}$$

Making a Tew iron and jobs, one day 14.6		
Brick borer. . . . . .4-½ days	3. 3.3
Two plain chains and jobs . . . . 2-½ 1.16.3	
	5.14

The brickborer is worth at most 1/6 per pound.
It is badly executed, and has been new bitted by Featherstone.[1]
Its weight 12 lb.

Value . . . . 18.

Cost the public

Iron, independent of Waste, at 4d ½. 4.6

Steel 1.3

Labor 3. 3.3

£3. 9.0   91

AD: Executive Papers of Governor James Wood, Virginia State Library (160/B5). Enclosed in BHL to Wood, 8 Sept. 1798, above.

1. The following month BHL had to dismiss Featherstone, a smith, when he flew into a rage and started a fight in which Paul, William Callis, and other workers were injured. BHL to Wood, 26 Oct. 1798, in BHL, *Journals*, 2 : 440–41.

LATROBE AND THOMAS CALLIS TO JAMES WOOD

Penitentiary House, Septr. 22d. 1798.

Sir,

We have attentively examined and measured the Stonework executed by Messrs. Baird and Robertson at the Penitentiary House, from the 25th. of July to the present date, and find the same to amount to

1.802 ft. 1. superfl. work at 2s.9	£247.16s.6d.
69 " 7 Cube Ashler at 3s.0	10. 8 .9
148 " 10 supfl. scapelling to do. at 1s.6d.	11. 2 .7-½
	269. 7 .10-½

These dimensions include every part of the Work which is charged in the bill delivered to the Executive on the 1st. of Septr. amounting to £199.19.9½, and also all that has been wrought and set from the 27th. of August up to the 20th. of September.

Of this amount only £167.6s.4d. is accounted for in the Estimate laid before the Legislative Assembly in the last Session. The remaining Sum of £102.1.6½ is a charge for Work which was not contemplated at the time of making the Estimate. This extra Work consists of Stone Pillars to support the Groins of 6 rooms, stone imposts to all the external Arches, stone Corbels in the Spandrils of the Arches, and Keystones to the large Groins. The tenderness of the Bricks, and the rapidity with which the Work has been carried on, has rendered it highly necessary to employ stone in all these situations. The Expence of Brickwork saved by the use of this Extra stone, in pillars, and in the diminished Size of Arches and Spandrills, amounts to:

18.750 Bricks and laying at £3 per m.	£56.5.0
336 feet of cut splays at 9d.	12.2.0
	£68.7s.0d.

So that the extraordinary expence of Stonework in the whole Estimate up to this day is £33.14.6½: and the building has thereby gained a solidity in its weakest parts, that will forever secure it from danger. Much room has also been acquired, by substituting small stone pillars for massy Brick piers.

The Work *already* executed, and specified in the Estimate falls rather below the estimated amount, and there still remains somewhat more than 300 pounds worth of Work still to be executed.

All the stone which will be required this season is now on the Ground and we are informed that the greatest part of the remainder is ready in the Quarry.[1] In about a fortnight the Gate will be compleated, and the front Wall coped.

The particular dimensions of every stone are recorded in the measuring book of the Work.

We are with the greatest respects Your most obedt. hble. Servants.

B. H. Latrobe B. Architect
Thos. Callis Superintendant.

ALS:Executive Papers of Governor James Wood, Virginia State Library (160/B7). The letter is in BHL's hand; both signatures are in autograph. Enclosed BHL, Estimate of the Expense of Altering the Penitentiary Roof Design, 22 Sept. 1798, below.

1. "All the stone, which is employed in the building [of the penitentiary] comes from a Quarry upon the land of Graham and Heron, near their Coalpits, about 3 Miles above Tuckahoe and 20 Miles by Water from Richmond." BHL, *Journals*, 2 : 390.

ENCLOSURE: ESTIMATE OF THE EXPENSE OF ALTERING THE PENITENTIARY ROOF DESIGN

Penitentiary house, Saturday Septr. 22d. 1798

Estimate of the Expence of altering the Design of the Roof of the Penitentiary house, from a Hip-roof to a Gabell roof.

NB. If the roof be covered with Slate, the Hips of the Hip-roof must be leaded, and also the Vallies.

If the roof be a Gabel roof, the Ridge of the Gabell must be leaded, and the fillets of the lower roof where it meets the Gabel Wall.

The fillets are equal to the Valleys. The Ridge of the Gabell roof is 29 feet long, the top of the straight cornice is 28 feet long making in each roof 57 feet. The hip rafters are 20 feet long, making in each hip roof 80 feet. So that there will be in each hip roof 23 feet more of lead than in the Gabel roof. This lead must be 1 ft. 6 i. wide, and weigh 6 pound to the square foot. This will make the hip roof more expensive in lead, as follows:

$$33 \text{ f. } 6 \text{ i. supfl. at } 6 \text{ lb. to the foot} \qquad 201 \text{ lb.}$$
$$\text{say 2 Cwt.}$$
Two Cwt. of lead at 8 Dollars the Cwt. is 16 Doll.
$$\text{For four roofs} \quad \underline{4}$$
Total additional expence in lead 64 Doll.

There will be some more expence in cutting the Shingles to the Hip which at the highest calculation may be estimated at 36 Dollars, making the Hip roofs more expensive than the Gabel roof........ 100 Dollars
    In every other respect the Hip roof and the Gabell roof are equal. The same number of Shingles will cover each, and although the Hip roof is stronger and takes less timber, as it requires no Wind braces no Gabel plates, I shall not calculate up this circumstance in favor of the Hip roof:
    The Gabel roof will cost beyond the Hip roof the following:

8 Gabells will take 36.500 Bricks which at 10 Dollars for
   laying and Materials is............................. $365.00
Each Gabell or Pediment has 36 feet of raking Cornice
   which in timber, Joiners Work, nails, and painting cannot
   possible be estimated at less than ⅞ per foot, as it projects
   1ft. 6i., and cannot now be altered, the roof being framed
   to that additional span: nor would the very high Walls be
   properly protected by a less projection.
8 Pediments make 288 feet of Raking cornice at $1.25   360.00
Waste of timber framed to a Hip roof, new timber for the
   Gabell roof, and new framing; cannot be less than   100.00
                               Dollars 825.00
Deduct saving of lead &c.   100

                                          725.00

    Thus it appears, that in order [to] change the original design of the roof from a Hip roof to a Gabel roof, it will cost the public 725 Dollars, a sum which would execute ¾ths. of the work necessary to supply the House with Water.

As to the sacrifice of Taste and professional feelings it is not my province to speak. The drawings herewith added, will do it, for me.[1]

B. H. Latrobe, Architect

ADS:Executive Papers of Governor James Wood, Virginia State Library (160/B11). Enclosed in BHL and Callis to Wood, 22 Sept. 1798, above.

1. When executed, the penitentiary was built with gables.

TO THOMAS JEFFERSON

Richmond Septr. 22d 1798

Dear Sir,

A round-about application has just now been made to me respecting a navigation in your neighbourhood, between Milton and Charlottesville, for which, I am told, a very considerable subscription is already raised. It comes from a very honest work man here, who presses me to go up, and see it. But as the thing seems to stand not quite upon so good a footing as the negotiations of Messrs. W X Y and Z and the Lady &c., I take the liberty to mention it to you, and if my talents as an Engineer can be of the smallest service to you—for I take it for granted that you are at the head of any work of public utility within your sphere of agency—I beg you will draw upon them to any amount. I consider our improvements in navigation in their infancy, to require a little *nursing* by the hand of public spirit, and to speak plainly, when I offer my assistance to you, it is infinitely more with a view to be useful than to exhaust your funds by my emoluments. Little can be done this Year, if any thing be intended, but I shall be happy to wait upon you to advise or to plan for the next season, if you think proper.[1]

Since I had the pleasure to see you at Fredericsburg, I have been upon a strange errand at Norfolk—to survey and report upon the fortifications at that place. I spent about three Weeks in performing this service, and having planned a new Fort for Point Nelson, and alterations for Fort Norfolk, and besides, designed Barracks for both places, an officer carried my papers to the Secretary at War. All that I had proposed was ordered to be carried into immediate execution, and strange to tell, the business was taken out of the hands of the Military Commander of the Garrison, and put into those of the Collector of the port. All this was consistent with the operations of a Government for the sake of a Revenue. Of myself not the slightest notice has been taken, *because a man of my politics is not to be trusted in so important a case as the defence of the Country against the French.* My *politics* I presume have been found out since my appointment to survey and report, for surely there was as much danger in permitting me to design, as to construct a Work.[2]

The late accounts of the Paris negociation have made some impression here. Marshall stands for Henrico district, but his election is doubtful. Bushrod Washington, who offers for Westmoreland district stands little chance. His zeal against *the subverters of all Government,* has decided the wavering John Heath against him, than whom no one in the District has more influence, so that we shall most likely see Dr. Jones again in Congress. Upon the whole, I think the aspect of things in this part of the country favors the republican side. But you have no doubt better intelligence from your more informed correspondents than I can give you. John Mayo, had distributed 500 Copies of the *Cannibals progress* in Henrico district to pave the way for himself. Captn. Billy Austin has sent a packet of Addison's pedantry to Bedford; Carrington scatters X W Y Z over the state, and another packet consisting of the speeches of Goodloe Harper and [Fisher] Ames is dispersed by a subscription of citizen subjects. But little I believe is effected by all this expence.[3]

I have taken the liberty to have several of your mould boards made for my friends.[4] I do not apologize to you for so doing, as I know that your object is to be extensively useful. I have been astonished at their performance.

As I am somewhat uncertain whether or no you will ever receive these lines I forbear enclosing in them the drawings of the Philadelphia Nail cutting Machine which I have long made for you, but which I have never had an opportunity to send.[5]

I have now only to beg that you will excuse the liberty I have taken to write to you upon the subject of your Navigation upon the very informal application to me, and to assure you of the truth of the sentiments of esteem and respect with which I am Your faithful Servant

B. Henry Latrobe B.

ALS: Jefferson Papers (160/C1). Endorsed as received 1 October.

1. Milton, six miles southeast of Charlottesville, was the furthest navigable point on the Rivanna River. Jefferson favored improving the river between those points because his

lands lay upriver from Milton and his produce had to be carried there and then transferred to larger boats for shipment to Richmond. Between 1776 and 1803 Jefferson built a canal at his Shadwell estate on this stretch of the Rivanna to power mills. In his reply of 18 October 1798 (Jefferson Papers; 160/C6), while his canal was still under construction, Jefferson wrote Latrobe that as the longer canal "would pass through my lands, except a few hundred yards, it connects itself in different ways with some petty interests of mine, not enough to be felt by myself, yet quite enough to enable those, so disposed, to ascribe any thing I should do to interested views, and perhaps to injure the undertaking were I to meddle. I sincerely wish it done on the broad principle of general good which must also effect particular good. But I have avoided taking any active part in it, wishing that others should do it whose situations clear them of particular imputations. I have made your letter the occasion of stirring them up but I am very doubtful whether it will be with effect. If any thing should be done and I know the benefit they would derive from your aid, I shall not fail to acquaint them with your kind offers." The project materialized in 1806 with the incorporation of the Rivanna Navigation Company, but Jefferson encountered difficulties. Since Jefferson had built a dam at the site of his mills, "some way had to be provided for boats to pass either through or around the dam." A long controversy ensued between Jefferson and the company over riparian rights, the location of locks, and other subjects. Edwin M. Betts, ed., *Thomas Jefferson's Farm Book* (Princeton, 1953), pp. 343–44; Malone, *Sage of Monticello*, pp. 38–39.

   2. Forts Nelson and Norfolk had been largely destroyed in the British bombardment of the city during the Revolution. They began to be rebuilt in 1794, the initial work being done by the military engineer John Jacob Ulrich Rivardi. As the fortification of America's eastern seaboard took on added significance during the Quasi-War with France, BHL's republican sympathies apparently led to his losing the commission to carry out his planned renovation. Jefferson replied to BHL's letter on 18 October 1798: "I am glad the works at Norfolk were put into so good hands for projection. That the execution should have been given to others may be consistent with the new code of morality the principles of which are daily developed to and in the practices of the exclusive friends of order and religion" (Jefferson Papers; 160/C6). BHL's "Plan of Fort Nelson, in Virginia, shewing the exact state of the Works in July, 1798" and his "Design for compleating Fort Nelson Virginia" are in RG 77, National Archives (309/B1, 309/B3).

   The secretary of war was James McHenry (1753–1816); the collector of the port was Col. Francis Otway Byrd (1756–1800). BHL, *Journals*, 2 : 536.

   3. In the congressional elections held in April 1799, John Marshall defeated the incumbent Republican, John Clopton, in a very close contest. Bushrod Washington was challenging another incumbent Republican, Dr. Walter Jones (1745–1816), for the Northern Neck seat when President Adams nominated Washington to the U.S. Supreme Court. Following Senate confirmation of the nomination, Washington withdrew his candidacy and was replaced by Federalist Gen. Henry "Light-Horse Harry" Lee, who defeated Jones. John Heath (1758–1810), Republican congressman (1793–97), had resumed his private law practice in 1797 in Heathsville, the Northumberland County seat named after him. Mayo was distributing copies of *The Cannibal's Progress, Or, The Dreadful Horrors of French Invasion! As Displayed by the Republican Officers and Soldiers, in the Perfidy, Rapacity, Ferociousness, and Brutality, Exercised Towards the Innocent Inhabitants of Germany. Translated from the German, By Anthony Aufrer, Esq.* (1798, editions published in Albany, N.Y.; Amherst, N.H.; Boston; London; New Haven ,Conn.; Newburyport, R.I.; Portsmouth, N.H.; Savannah, Ga.; Vergennes, Vt.; Walpole, Mass.; and Philadelphia). Capt. William Austin (d. 1807) of the Richmond Troop of Horse in 1798, was distributing works by Alexander Addison (1759–1807), Scottish immigrant, Pennsylvania lawyer and jurist, and Federalist political pamphleteer. BHL, *Journals*, 2 : 542, 544; CVSP, 9 : 22; Richard R. Beeman, *The*   97

Old Dominion and the New Nation, 1788–1801 (Lexington, Ky., 1972), pp. 204–08; David Hackett Fischer, *The Revolution of American Conservatism: The Federalist Party in the Era of Jeffersonian Democracy* (New York, 1965), pp. 332–33, 380–82.

4. Jefferson's "mould-board of least resistance," an important improvement in the wooden plough, was developed in the early 1790s. Jefferson presented a description of it to the American Philosophical Society in 1798; the Society published the description in its *Transactions* 4 (1799) : 313–22.

5. Jefferson had erected a nailery at Monticello in 1794 and had acquired a nail-cutting machine in 1796. Always interested in technical improvements for his machinery, Jefferson may have solicited BHL to draw up the plans of the Philadelphia machine. Caleb Lownes and other Philadelphia merchants supplied Jefferson with most of his nail-rod and iron. BHL's drawings have not been found. Betts, ed., *Thomas Jefferson's Farm Book*, pp. 426–28.

TO JOSEPH PERKIN

[Richmond, 7 November 1798]

Dear Sir:[1]

On my return from Norfolk yesterday, I found two letters from Harper's ferry, which deserve my sincerest thanks. Be assured that your friendly information affects me with the truest esteem for you, and that this new proof of your good disposition towards me will not be forgotten.

You have perhaps heard that I have already been employed by the United States Government to survey and report upon the fortifications at Norfolk, and to design such additional works as might be necessary. This business I finished in August last, and it seems much to the satisfaction of the Government, for everything I had suggested is ordered to be carried into execution. You know however that I am a bad hand at making bargains. In this instance I stipulated nothing beforehand, because the extent of the business could not be ascertained. I have not therefore as yet heard what I am to get by all this business, and only know that I am to be paid something, for, in a very flattering letter, enquiry has been made, what I demand.[2] By this means, you will observe I am already known to the Secretary at War, and I believe under very favorable impressions. It is my intention to be in Philadelphia in about a fortnight or three weeks. It will be impossible for me to arrive sooner, with convenience. In the mean time I hope the usual slowness of Government affairs will prevent any other appointment. I shall bring with

98

me strong letters of recommendation, and "stick a black cockade into my hat," which will vouch for my ability for anything.[3]

But to be serious, you would exceedingly oblige me by mentioning me in the way you think of me to the Sec. at War; and if you think the plan you were so good as to accept of, could be of any service, I am sure you will use it to the best advantage by showing it.[4]

Our arsenal here, has at last been designed by the millwright Clarke. It will be a very inelegant building, much too large in size and too weak in construction. But the machinery will no doubt be very excellent, for he is, independent of his worth as a man and a citizen, a very good machinist. That he is no architect nor engineer he cannot help, and the fault is with those who have employed him. The ground plan is taken from the Penitentiary house, but the elevations are very different, and from some circumstances, I believe he had seen your plan, while the Governor had it.

I reckon upon your son as a pupil. When I come to Philadelphia, I shall kidnap him.

Pray remember me to Mrs. Perkins and Your Children.[5]

Typed Copy: PBHL (microfiche add.). Addressed to Perkin "near the Moravian Chapel, Philadelphia." Postmarked Richmond, 8 November 1798. Endorsed, perhaps by BHL, "Not found" and "Put into my hand by the postmaster general—a dead letter."

1. Joseph Perkin (d. 1806) was an English Moravian and gunmaker who emigrated to America about 1774. At the beginning of the Revolutionary War he worked for John Strode, a well-known businessman and manager of the Rappahannock Forge near Falmouth, Va. At the end of the war he moved to Philadelphia and set up a small gun shop with Samuel Couty where he made arms for both public and private patrons. In 1792 he became superintendent of the federal arsenal at New London, Campbell County, Va. When the installation was abandoned in 1798, Perkin was appointed superintendent of the arsenal at Harpers Ferry, then under construction by the War Department, where he died of malaria in 1806. Merritt Roe Smith, *Harpers Ferry Armory and the New Technology: The Challenge of Change* (Ithaca, N.Y., 1977), pp. 38, 54.

2. BHL eventually received $500 "for a weeks survey of forts at Norfolk and all my expences." BHL to Eakin, 13 Mar. 1803, below.

3. The Federalists adopted the black cockade as their party badge during the XYZ affair with France in 1798. It was intended to be a reminder of the American Revolution, when the black cockade was worn as a symbol of patriotism. The Republicans had earlier adopted the French tricolor cockade as an outward sign of their sympathy with republican France. Andrew C. McLaughlin and Albert Bushnell Hart, eds., *Cyclopedia of American Government*, 3 vols. (New York, 1930), 1 : 133; Hans Sperber and Travis Trittschuh, *American Political Terms: An Historical Dictionary* (Detroit, 1962), p. 40.

4. This may have been "the plan of an Armory designed by Mr. Latrobe" (not found) that Perkin showed to Secretary of War Henry Dearborn in 1802. Dearborn to Perkin, 27 Sept. 1802, RG 107, National Archives.

5. Perkin and his wife, the former Willhelmina Henman, had four children: John (b.

1781), Maria Henman (b. 1783), Henry Henman (1786–c. 1801), and Juliana (b. 1791). Records of the First Moravian Church, Philadelphia, in *Collections of the Genealogical Society of Pennsylvania*, vol. 47 (Philadelphia, 1900): 34, 78; John W. Jordan, comp., "The Inscriptions on the Grave-Stones & Tablets in the Moravian Burying Ground (N. W. Corner Franklin & Vine Streets) Philadelphia," in *Collections of the Genealogical Society of Pennsylvania*, vol. 262 (Philadelphia, 1911): 109.

LATROBE AND THOMAS CALLIS TO JAMES WOOD

Richmond, Novr. 28th. 1798

Sir,

In compliance with your directions "that the Architect and Superintendant of the Penitentiary, report upon the State of the building as to its progress, and furnish an estimate of such materials as may be requisite for the completion of the same" we beg leave to lay before you the following Statement.

1797. At the Close of the last Season (1797) The Basement story of the East Wing containing six solitary Cells, a Washhouse and a store cellar had been carried up as high as the Ground line (Watertable) all the Arches were turned, and the Centers struck.

The Walls of the West Wing were raised to the springing of the Arches, and all the Centers were made and put into their situations.

The front Walls were built as high as the Ground line, and considerable progress had been made in erecting the Gate and the Offices attached to it.

1798. The late and unfavorable Spring prevented the Workmen from resuming their operations untill the first Week in May, and the very early and severe Frost has obliged them to desist a month sooner than last Year. But notwithstanding these disadvantages, and the delay and inconvenience occasioned by the uncommonly heavy rains of the Months of June and August the Work has proceeded with considerable rapidity, and is at present in a state of forwardness not much short of our expectations.

East Wing. The East Wing, which is intended for the confinement of female Convicts, has been carried up from the Ground line to the Eaves of the roof. The Arches of the Ground story and second floor have been turned, and the Centers of the third story are made, and in their places.

100

The Ground story contains six solitary Cells, the Guard room of the Women's Ward, and one Workroom.

The second story contains 4 Workrooms, and the upper story 4 Dormitories. A staircase is in the North East Angle.

The roof of this Wing is finished ready to be raised, as soon as the upper Arches shall be turned.

West Wing. The arches of the Basement story have been turned, and the story compleated.

The Ground story has been compleatly carried up and arched.

Of the second story every part is erected excepting the North end.

The West Wing contains in the Basement story, the common dining room for the Men, to which the access is from their Court. The whole Wing may be appropriated to this use, when their numbers may render it necessary.

The Ground floor contains the Kitchen and Bakehouse and an open Arcade, the use of which is to admit air into the Area of the building from the Westward, the Quarter from which the Summer winds most usually blow.

Upon the second story is the infirmary for the Men.

These apartments are arched over, and the Wing would have been compleated this Season, had the weather continued mild as long as is usually the case.

The Gate. The Gateway is carried up to its utmost highth, and will be perfectly finished during the winter. It contains two lodges for a porter and Guards, and on each Wing, a bath and storeroom, on the East for the Women, on the West, for the Men.

The South Walls are also carried up, and will, in the course of the Winter, receive their Coping and Iron railing.

Men's Court. Of the semicircular Building, which is to contain the Workshops, the Dormitories and the Cells of the Men; the foundations are laid, and the external Wall is raised to the highth of five feet.

The Sewers are dug out, and a road has been made from the City line to the Gateway.

The Smiths are at present employed in making the Iron Grates to the external Windows, and during the Winter will compleat all the Work necessary to render the East Wing, and South front secure.

The Carpenters have already finished a considerable number of Window frames, and may during the Winter compleat all the Work necessary in the East and West Wings.

It is intended that all the external Walls shall be lined with strong Oak plank, thickly nailed. Much of the plank is delivered and this necessary Work will also be performed during the Winter.

Most of the Stone is already quarried, and much of it is delivered upon the Spot. The experience of the present Season, and the nature of the Brick has pointed out the necessity of a greater quantity of Stonework than was at first intended, to the amount of 850 dollars.

There are ready for the work of the next Spring about 750.000 Bricks upon the Ground.

The expence of completing the Work according to the design will be as follows. We must however beg leave to suggest the fluctuating state of the prices of Materials and Labor, which has been already so much experienced as liable to occasion uncertainty in our Estimate. We have endeavored to be as accurate as possible, calculating from what has been done, upon the expence of what still remains to be performed.

Brick Work,	5.324.12.6
Deduct 250.000 Bricks, already paid for at 38/	475. 0.0
	4.849.12.6 — 4.849.12.6
Stone Work	554. 0.6
Carpenters Work	2.997. 0.3
Joiners Work	1.204.13.1
Painters' Work	307. 7.4
Plaisterers' Work	126. 4.0
Ironwork	1.460.19.2
Finishing the Keeper's house, independent of Brick, stone, and iron work	450. 0.0

£ 11.949.16.10
Dollars 39.832.80 Cts.

We have the honour to be Your Excellency's faithful and obedient Servants

B. Henry Latrobe B. Archt.

Thos. Callis supt.

ALS: Executive Papers of Governor James Wood, Virginia State Library (160/D7). The letter is in BHL's hand; both signatures are in autograph.

Paper on the Cape Henry Sand Hills

EDITORIAL NOTE

Latrobe's American Philosophical Society paper on the sand hills at Cape Henry was the first public result of his newly aroused interest in geology. Although he was exposed to mineralogy and geology as part of his natural history studies at Niesky and Barby, and thereafter made occasional geological observations, Latrobe did not focus his scientific curiosity on that field until his Virginia years. Late in 1797 and early in 1798 he became acquainted with three scientifically inclined Europeans: Giambattista Scandella, Constantin-François de Chasseboeuf, comte de Volney, and William Maclure. All three savants were later elected to the American Philosophical Society, and Volney and Maclure made fundamental contributions to the study of American geology.[1]

Latrobe's journal entries and his letters soon reflected his discussions with them and his geological expeditions in their company. Just prior to submitting this paper, Latrobe had traveled with Maclure from Richmond to Philadelphia (1–2 December 1798), taking the opportunity "to investigate the nature of the soil and stratification of the Stone at Fredericsburg on the Rappahannoc, and from George town to the little falls, on the Potowmac."[2] Latrobe then took up residence with Maclure's family and was quickly initiated into Philadelphia scientific circles.

The sand hills paper is the first of Latrobe's three widely separated but coherent publications on the relation of the ancient oceans to the piedmont and coastal geology of the Middle Atlantic region. In this paper he discusses the current theory that water deposition was responsible for Virginia's coastal geology and suggested that a currently observable process of sand deposition by wind at Cape Henry could produce similar results in the future. Several years later he related his examination of the freestone being quarried in northern Virginia and attributed its origin to wind deposition on an ancient seacoast, in a manner such as he had seen at Cape Henry.[3] Finally in 1817 Latrobe proposed his theory of the formation of the Columbia marble of Virginia, Maryland, and Pennsylvania, suggesting that in that instance the wave action of an ancient ocean was responsible.[4]

---

1. For an analysis of BHL's knowledge of geology, see BHL, *Journals*, 2 : 384–90. For his earlier comments on geology, see ibid., pp. 346–50, 379–81, 390–414, 453–54. See also ibid., pp. 329, 357–59, 381–84. For Maclure, see BHL to Scandella, 24 Jan. 1798, n. 14, above.

2. BHL, *Journals*, 3 : 7.

3. BHL, "An account of the Freestone quarries on the Potomac and Rappahannoc rivers," [19 Feb. 1807], APS, *Transactions* 6 (1809) : 283–93, in BHL, *Correspondence*, 2.

4. BHL to Joseph Gales and William Seaton, 18 Jan. 1817, in BHL, *Correspondence*, 3.   103

PAPER ON THE CAPE HENRY SAND HILLS

Memoir on the Sand-hills of Cape Henry in Virginia.
By B. Henry Latrobe, Engineer.

[Philadelphia] December 19th, 1798.

From the falls of the great rivers of Virginia over the out-runnings of the granite strata, the general level of the land gradually approaches the level of the ocean. At the falls it is elevated from 150 to 200 feet above the tide: on the sea shore at Cape Henry, the original coast rises not more than 15 feet above high water mark.

That the whole of this extensive country, from the falls to the coast, is factitious, and of Neptunian origin, appears far from being hypothetical;[1] and the fossil teeth and bones, which accompany this memoir,[2] and which with many hundred more, were dug out of a well at Richmond, from the depth of 71 feet,[3] prove that the deposition of the superstrata is not of a date sufficiently removed to have destroyed the soft and almost cartilaginous part of the joints, or to have injured the enamel of the teeth. The Neptunian theory of geogeny, has now very generally taken place the old volcanic system, and, as far as conjecture and hypothesis can forward science, it is certainly more generally applicable.[4] But along the coast of Virginia,[5] a process is going forward, the result of which will be exactly similar, and in which water has' no immediate share.

The shore, and the bed of the Atlantic near the shore, consist of a fine sand. The daily action of the flood tide carries a certain quantity of this sand above high water mark, which being dried by the sun and air, is carried further in land by the winds. The most violent winds on this coast, blow from the points between the N. West and the East; and besides, a gentle easterly breeze prevails the whole summer, during some part of almost every day. This easterly wind, which is in fact a trade wind, is felt as high as Williamsburg. It is said to be felt, at this day, higher in land than formerly, and to be annually extending its influence; and it will no doubt, when the woods shall be more cleared away, blow health and coolness over a portion of lower Virginia, which is now considered as extremely unhealthy.[6]

These easterly winds blowing during the driest and hottest season of the year, carry forward the greatest quantity of sand, and have amassed hills, which now extend about a mile from the beach. The natural level of the land, elevated little more than 10 feet above high water mark, has

104

a very gentle declivity to the east. It is now a swamp[7] of about five miles square (25 square miles.) The soil below the surface, is a white loamy sand, and if the water falling upon, or rising in it, had a free discharge to the ocean, it would probably be perfectly dry: this, however, the sand hills prevent, and the water is discharged into the sea to the southward, and into the mouth of the Chesapeak to the northward, by small creeks, which find vent from the westerly extremities of the swamp. Lynhaven creek is the most considerable of these drains. The swamp, or as the neighbouring inhabitants call it, the Desart, is overgrown with aquatic trees and shrubs; the gum (*L. styraciflua*), the cypress (*cup. disticha*), the maple (*acer rubrum*), the tree improperly called the sycamore (*platanus occidentalis*), the magnolia glauca, the wax myrtle (*myrica cerifera*), and the reed (*ar. tecta*) are the principal.[8] Of these many thousands are already buried in the sand, which over-tops their summits, and threatens the whole forest with ruin. Their destruction is slow, but inevitable. Upon the extreme edge of the sand hills towards the swamp, the wind opposed by the tops of the trees, forms an eddy: the sand carried along with it is precipitated, and runs down the bank into the swamp. Its slope is very accurately in an angle of 45°. By gradual accumulation, the hill climbs up their trunks, they wither slowly, and before they are entirely buried, they die. Most of them lose all their branches, and nothing but the trunk remains to be covered with sand, but some of the cypress retain life to the last.[9]

The Desart abounds in deer, bears, racoons, and opossums. Its skirts are more thickly peopled than the sterility of the soil would give reason to suppose; but the inexhaustible abundance of fish and oysters in the creeks, and the game, render it easy to support a family.

The light house,[10] which was built about sixteen years ago, is an octangular truncated pyramid of eight sides, rising 90 feet to the light, and sunk 18 feet below the basement course.[11] Within a few yards of the light house, is the keeper's dwelling, a wooden building of two stories. Both are surrounded by a platform of plank, and, without any such design in the architect, this platform has preserved both these buildings from being buried in the sand.

When the light house was built, it was placed upon the highest sand hill at the Cape. Its distance from the beach may be 6 or 7 hundred yards, and the elevation of its base above high water, not less than 90 feet. At that time there was from the foot of the building, the most expanded view of the ocean, the Desart, the Chesapeak and its eastern 105 shore. At present, a mount of sand surrounds them, which overtops the keeper's dwelling, and has buried his kitchen to the eaves. The platform, which was laid upon the former level of the sand, is an accurate standard from whence to ascertain its accumulation. The winds meeting in their course the elevated tower of the light, form a perpetual whirl around it, which licks up the sand from the smooth surface of the timber, and heaps it around in the form of a bason. Where the platform ceases, the sand accumulates. The sandy rim, while it protects the keeper from the storms, renders his habitation one of the dreariest abodes imaginable. This rim is sometimes higher, at others lower, according to the direction and strength of the wind. Since the establishment of the light, the hills have risen about 20 feet in height (measuring from the platform) and have proceeded into the Desart about 350 yards, from a spot pointed out to me by the keeper. I stepped the distance as well as I could, while at every step I sunk up to my ancles in the sand. The height of the hill at the swamp, is between 70 and 80 feet perpendicularly. It is higher nearer the sea, the inner edge being rounded off, and I think at its highest point, it cannot be less than 100 feet above high water mark. If the hills advance at an equal ratio for 20 or 30 years more, they will swallow up the whole swamp, and render the coast a desert indeed, for not a blade of grass finds nutriment upon the sand.

Should this event take place, and some future philosopher attend the digging of a well *in the high sandy country, on the coast of Virginia,* his curiosity would be excited by fossile wood, 100 feet below the surface. He would there discover a bed of vegetable and animal exuviæ, and going home, he might erect upon very plausible ground, a very good-looking hypothesis of a deluge, sweeping the whole upper country of its sand, and depositing it along the line of its conflict with the waves of the ocean.

B. Henry Latrobe.

To Samuel Harrison Smith, Esq.
one of the Secretaries of the American Philosophical Society.[12]

P. S. The annexed drawing is a section of the Cape, in a direction N.E. and S.W. The scale is of course unequal, but the effect is true.

Printed Copy: American Philosophical Society, *Transactions* 4 (1799): 439–43 (160/E5). Read by the Society on 21 December 1798 and referred to Samuel Harrison Smith, who recommended publication on 27 December, to which the Society agreed. BHL's drawing

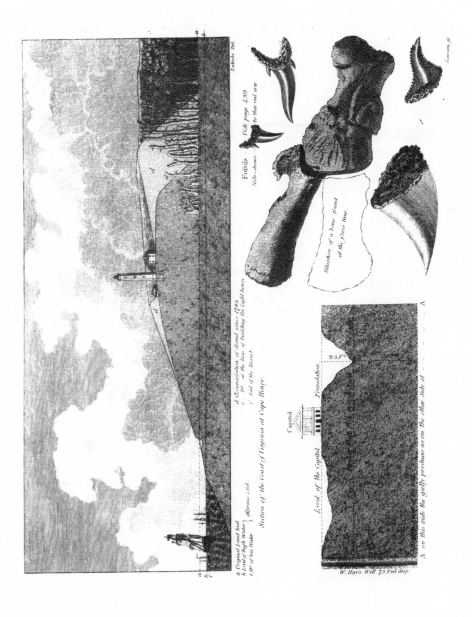

Latrobe Del.

a Original Land level
b Level of High Water
c Dº of low Water
d Accumulation of Sand since 1783
e Dº at the time of building the Light house
f Soil of the Desert

Section of the Coast of Virginia at Cape Henry

Fossils   Vide page 439
Note—those refer to that red one

Situation of a bone found at the same time

Capitol

Level of the Capitol

Foundation

25 F.

W. Hays Well 75 Feet deep

A on this side the gully produces as on the other Side of ⸺ A was engraved by Alexander Lawson. In writing this article BHL relied heavily on notes in his journals of 1796–98, some of which have been lost or destroyed. See BHL, *Journals,* 2 : 393–414.

1. The Neptunian thesis suggested that most observable rock formations resulted from mineral precipitation and sedimentation in an earlier ocean which covered the earth. The primary exponent of the thesis in BHL's time was Abraham Gottlob Werner (1749–1817), professor of the Bergakademie at Freiberg, whose early publications BHL could have read while studying at Niesky and Barby. The first systematic exposition of his views appeared in 1789.

2. BHL's footnote here reads: "The teeth appear to be those of a shark. They are highly enamelled and extremely sharp: their roots are perfectly sound and entire, and the minute and almost transparent jags of many of them are as perfect as the rest. They are found in every well, dug in or near Richmond, to a sufficient depth; and, *as I am informed,* in every deep well for many miles below the city. The stratum in which they lie consists of highly sulphurated blue clay, abounding in pyrites, and which has the appearance of having been mud. They were first discovered in the beds of rivulets, which had worn their channels to the depth of this stratum; and obtained the name of *Indian Dart-points,* in the same manner, as the immense oysterbeds, which have been quitted by the ocean, are vulgarly called *Indian* oyster-banks.

"The bones were dug from the same stratum. Among them are two out of six bones, which formed a *paw* of some animal unknown to me. Many very sound vertebræ of fish, and a remarkably perfect thigh bone of a large bird have been in my possession."

3. This refers to the well at the Virginia State Penitentiary. In his journal BHL carefully recorded the strata encountered in its excavation, although through an error in addition he calculated the depth at 71 feet instead of 81 feet, an error he repeated here. BHL, *Journals,* 2 : 402–03, 409–11.

4. Since volcanic deposition is one of the few observable means of rock formation, it has appealed to many geological theorists as a major means of rock formation.

5. BHL's footnote here reads: "I speak only of the coast of Virginia at Cape Henry: for although I have the best reason to believe that the same natural process has produced all the sand banks, islands, and sand hills from the Delaware to Florida: I have only *examined* that part of the coast, which is the subject of the present memoir."

6. For half a century European and American philosophers had disputed the character of the American environment, its effect on the health of the colonists, and the climatic result of clearing the land. BHL here takes the position advanced by James Madison and Thomas Jefferson that clearing the woods of Virginia had permitted the deeper inland penetration of salubrious sea breezes. Gilbert Chinard, "Eighteenth Century Theories on America as a Human Habitat," APS, *Proceedings* 91 (Feb. 1947):31–33, 36, 41–44; Jefferson, *Notes on the State of Virginia,* ed. William Peden (Chapel Hill, N.C., 1955 [orig. publ. 1787], p. 77.

7. BHL's footnote here reads: "By a swamp I exclusively mean a piece of ground, the surface of which is wet and soft, but which has a sound bottom. In this it differs from the Dismal swamp, much of which is a *bog* or *morass.* Into the latter, a pole of any manageable length may be forced with great ease."

8. Respectively, the sweetgum, *Liquidambar styraciflua;* bald cypress, *Taxodium distichum;* red maple, *Acer rubrum;* American plane tree, *Plantanus occidentalis;* sweetbay, *Magnolia virginiana;* myrtle or southern bayberry, *Myrica cerifera;* switch or small cane, *Arundinaria gigantea tecta.*

9. BHL's footnote here reads: "That the swamp with its trees extended to the sea coast, perhaps *within* a century, is very evident from this circumstance: between the summit

of the sand hills (see the drawing) and the sea shore, and more especially on the Chesapeak side, the undecayed, though mostly *dead* bodies of trees still appear in great numbers. Being on the windward side of the sand hills, they have not been more than half buried. At the light house there are none of the trees, (see the section) but to the westward and southward are many."

10. BHL's footnote here reads: "It is a good solid building of Rappahannoc freestone, but has the unpardonable fault of a wooden stair case, which being necessarily soaked with oil, exposes the light to the perpetual risk of destruction by fire. Such an accident might be attended with an incalculable loss of lives and property, the mouth of the Chesapeak being perhaps the inlet to more ships than any other in the United States."

11. Although in the early 1780s the state of Virginia planned for a lighthouse at Cape Henry and gathered materials to construct it, the site was ceded to the federal government in 1789, and the lighthouse was completed only in 1792. It is often cited as the nation's first public works project under the Constitution. The tower remains standing but is no longer in use as a lighthouse. U.S. Coast Guard, Public Information Division, *Historically Famous Lighthouses* (Washington, D.C., 1972), pp. 85–87; Ellis L. Armstrong, ed., *History of Public Works in the United States, 1776–1976* (Chicago, 1976), p. 24.

12. For Samuel Harrison Smith, member (elected 1797) and secretary (1798–1800) of the APS, see BHL to Smith, 24 Dec. 1803, n. 1 below.

The Philadelphia Waterworks

Editorial Note

The Philadelphia Waterworks was Latrobe's greatest and most successful engineering work.[1] It was the first urban utility in the United States (in the modern sense), and it was the first convincing display of steam power in the Western Hemisphere. With the completion of the waterworks, Latrobe's engineering career in America was begun and thereafter he was almost constantly engaged in that branch of his profession.

Waterworks for urban water supply have been known since antiquity. The Greeks designed elaborate networks of tunnels and canals to bring water to their cities, and Roman engineers made them a characteristic amenity of their cities. Whereas the Romans often brought water by gravity flow from miles away, since the Middle Ages engineers have used pumps to raise water directly from the rivers on which major cities were located. Latrobe was familiar with the eighteenth-century London waterworks which raised water from the Thames or other sources by waterwheels and steam pumps.

The primary reason for urban waterworks in the eighteenth century was to provide copious supplies of drinking water, since naturally occurring water was often too distant or unfit for consumption, while wells ran dry or turned foul, particularly in summer months. Other urban water demands included fire-fight-

---

1. For a detailed examination of the design and construction of the Philadelphia Waterworks, see BHL, *Engineering Drawings*, pp. 28–36, 144–98. A more general view is provided by Nelson M. Blake, *Water for the Cities* (Syracuse, N.Y., 1956), chap. 2.

ing, street flushing, public fountains, and, increasingly, industrial and food preparation requirements. Finally, many observers thought fresh water desirable because they saw a connection between dirty, smelly water and the epidemic and endemic diseases of the cities. In 1793 Philadelphia experienced what still ranks as one of the worst epidemics of yellow fever in American history. During that summer perhaps one-tenth of the city's residents died of yellow fever, even though many people (particularly the wealthy) left the city until the epidemic had passed.[2] There were lesser incidents of the fever in 1797 and 1798, and occasionally thereafter until 1820.

Contemporary explanations of the etiology of yellow fever varied widely. Latrobe, after his first visit to Philadelphia in the spring of 1798, considered three frequently cited causes: lack of ventilation, excessive accumulation of filth and debris, and contamination of wells by sewage. Each of these was a symptom of urban concentration and was to some degree a source of illness or disease, but none was a primary cause of epidemic yellow fever, which we now know was caused by a virus transmitted by certain mosquitoes. Latrobe, however, considered contaminated wells to be the most likely contributing factor, and he showed how the effluvia from backyard privies was easily communicated by groundwater seepage to the front yard wells common to Philadelphia.[3]

Many citizens shared Latrobe's analysis of the cause of yellow fever, and in November 1797 the city councils appointed a joint committee to investigate the possibility of bringing pure water into the city. The committee's attention first turned to the unfinished Delaware and Schuylkill Canal north of the city, but it was soon obvious that the canal company was incapable of completing its work rapidly. The committee then considered a plan submitted by a Connecticut artisan, but it was unsatisfactory. When Latrobe arrived in Philadelphia in December 1798 to direct the construction of the Bank of Pennsylvania the committee was no closer to providing the city with ample pure water than it had been when appointed a year earlier.

The president of the Bank of Pennsylvania, Samuel M. Fox, was a member of the committee, and he undoubtedly discussed the water supply problem with Latrobe. On 27 December 1798, John Miller, Jr., the chairman of the committee, formally requested a report from Latrobe on how supplies of water might be obtained from Spring Mills north of the city and from the Schuylkill River on its western edge. Latrobe's report, printed below, is dated two days later. Its effect was convincing and immediate. Preliminary commitments to execute the work were made within a month, and three months later the city councils formally approved Latrobe's revised plan for the waterworks.

2. Mathew Carey, *A Short account of the Malignant Fever, lately prevalent in Philadelphia . . .* , 4th ed., improved (Philadelphia, 1794); John Harvey Powell, *Bring out Your Dead: The Great Plague of Yellow Fever in Philadelphia in 1793* (Philadelphia, 1949).

3. BHL, *Journals*, 2 : 379–81. Cf. Thomas Condie and Richard Folwell, *History of the Pestilence, Commonly Called Yellow Fever, Which Almost Desolated Philadelphia, in the Months of August, September & October, 1798* (Philadelphia, [1799]), pp. 6–9, 27.

VIEW OF THE PRACTICABILITY AND MEANS OF SUPPLYING THE CITY OF PHILADELPHIA WITH WHOLESOME WATER

Philadelphia, December 29th, 1798.

Sir,

Agreeably to your request,[1] I now submit to you my ideas upon the subjects which you have communicated to me for consideration, *viz.*

I. To supply the city of Philadelphia with a sufficiency of wholesome water for culinary purposes:

II. To introduce an additional supply of water for the purpose of washing the streets, and, if possible, of cooling the air of the city.

The season and the weather are at present both unfavorable to an investigation of all the circumstances, which may affect a measure of so much importance; and indeed the time allotted to me has been so short, that it cannot be expected that my opinion should extend far into the minutiæ of estimate and execution: I have, however, endeavored to establish general principles, which cannot be affected by any variations of detail, and to which every attempt to accomplish your object must be made to bend.

The indispensible requisites, of every work which may be executed, appear to me to be the following. Indeed so indispensible do I consider them, that every proposal in which they do not meet, ought, I think, to be at once rejected. Their importance is in the order in which I have arranged them.

I. The works must be in full operation before the end of July, 1799.[2]

II. They must be *certain* in their effects, and *permanent* in their construction.

III. They must not be liable to interruption from ice or freshes, but be equally useful in the severest winter, and in the wettest summer.

Having maturely considered all the schemes, which I have seen published, or have heard mentioned in conversation, I shall proceed to state to you, what appear to me to be the *only* means of concentring all these requisites in *one* work; and, having laid before you what I propose to accomplish, with the means, and the probable expence of effecting it, I will then give you my reasons for rejecting every other proposal.

The nearest waters to the center of the city of Philadelphia are those of the Delaware and Schuylkill. I conceive them both to be wholesome, 111 for reasons which I will mention in a postscript, in order that I may not interrupt this consideration of the principal object.

It is evident that the exertions of only seven months, cannot in this country bring water from a greater distance.

In choosing between the waters of the Delaware and Schuylkill, the following considerations occur:

 I. In favor of the Delaware: It is true that works erected upon the margin of the river would supply water to the city immediately, from the river upwards, and save all the expence, which must, in the other case, be incurred between the Schuylkill and the center square.[3]

 II. Against the Delaware will operate, the impurity of its water, which is subject to a strong running flood tide, and which must be supposed to be contaminated by the decayed vegetables of the marshes over which it passes; independently of the filth, thrown from the numerous vessels lying along the wharves, or running into it from the public sewers.[4]

 III. In favor of the Schuylkill: The principal circumstance is the uncommon purity of its water; its bed is every where narrow and rocky, its sources lie entirely in the lime-stone country, and the tide opposite to the center of the town does little more than raise the water by accumulation.[5]

 IV. On the other side; the extraordinary expence of works from the banks of Schuylkill to center square may be alleged.

I believe however that you will agree with me in thinking, that, as the difference of expence on the largest estimate cannot exceed thirty thousand dollars, there ought not to be a moment's hesitation in preferring the Schuylkill. I shall therefore confine my remarks to that river.

Neither the waters of the Delaware, nor of the Schuylkill can become useful, unless they be raised to an elevated level, commanding every part of the city. To do this, in sufficient quantity, very powerful machinery will be required; and, I am very certain, that human ingenuity has not hitherto invented any thing capable of producing the proposed effect with constancy, certainty and adequate force, excepting the *Steam-engine*.

Taking therefore all the preceding principles for granted, I submit to you the two following proposals, which are in effect the same; and the choice between which must depend upon the practicability of the *first*.

 N.B. The distribution of the water over the city being the same under every scheme that may be adopted, I shall postpone its consideration to the last.

The objects which I propose to accomplish are:

I. To raise a reservoir in center square. It is not sufficient that this reservoir should be elevated so high, that it will discharge its water into the distributing pipes: I think it should be forty feet above the level of the pavement, in order that the pressure of the water, in so elevated a head, may not only propel it to every part of the city, but throw it up in fountains in every street, wherever it may be required.

II. To bring to the reservoir the waters of the Schuylkill.

III. To raise them into the reservoir.

A culvert, or tunnel, six feet in diameter, carried under ground, the bottom of which should be level with the bed of the Schuylkill, would bring the water into a reservoir in center square, at the depth of about forty feet. I am not perfectly informed of the levels, but ten feet more or less, would affect the expence very inconsiderably. Over or near this reservoir, which ought to be a cylindrical well of at least twenty-five feet diameter, the Engine-house should be erected. It may, at the same expence that would render it useful, be made an ornamental building.[6] Upon the top of the Engine-house should be the reservoir. With the reservoir all the distributing pipes are to be connected. The engine will keep it perpetually full, being of a power sufficient to supply every possible demand of the city.

There is however a circumstance, which may render the scheme impracticable, or at all events unadviseable. It is this. The gravel stratum, to which all the wells of this city are sunk, seems to be nearly on a level with the waters of the adjoining rivers, and to be supplied by them with that inexhaustible quantity of water, for which it is remarkable.[7] Should it so happen, as I believe it will, that the tunnel lay near, or in, this stratum, it might be difficult, if not impossible to keep the work sufficiently dry; and I doubt, whether, at any rate workmen could be induced to labor in this subterraneous situation, which will always be wet, and the safety of which may depend upon the certainty of working the pumps above. I shall therefore make another proposal, which is liable to no inconvenience in the execution, but which, though not more expensive at first, will, as it requires two engines, be liable to more *annual* expence.

II. A reservoir being made on the banks of the Schuylkill, an engine will throw up a sufficient quantity of water into a tunnel, carried from thence to a reservoir in center square. This tunnel should be sunk so low, that three feet of earth may cover it, in its whole length. The reservoir in center square, might be sufficiently elevated to supply all the streets from Water-street to Fourth or Fifth-street with water for culinary uses. To supply the rest, and to raise fountains for the purpose of washing the streets, a smaller engine and an elevated reservoir would still be necessary.[8]

It is very evident, that in either of these proposals, the three requisites meet: the supply of water would be inexhaustible; the work might be accomplished in a few months; the ice would never obstruct the operations of the works, as the tunnel would be inaccessible to frost; and the power employed is that, of which the amount, and the effect depends not on the variable seasons, nor on the natural advantages of situation, but solely on the *option* of man. In every species of machinery in which mechanical powers alone operate, the bulk, the friction, and the unwieldiness of the works, encrease nearly in proportion to the effect required; in the chemical operation of a Steam-engine, power is encreased in a ratio far outstripping the bulk and the price of the engine, and when the first expence is incurred, the *two* men that are necessary to attend the smallest, can manage the most gigantic mechanism. The expence would be 75,000 dollars.

Having accomplished thus much of the proposed object—enough to substitute pure, for putrifying water, and effectually to provide for the cleansing and cooling the streets—a very important part of it, still remains unfinished, but which may be a work of more leisure. This is to bring to Philadelphia the spring, which turns the mill, called Spring-mill, for the sole purpose of supplying the city with water for culinary use.

It has been generally supposed, and perhaps with great truth, that limestone water has a medicinal effect in bilious cases. The mill-springs form a rivulet gushing from a limestone bason, and, as nearly as I could ascertain it, under all the disadvantages of the season, and the want of instruments, it would run through, and fill a trunk of from four to five feet in section, not calculating upon any head.

This quantity would give a perpetual supply to 2,880 pipes, the bore of which should be equal to ¼ of an inch square, and supposing the water were permitted to run only twelve hours each day, it would supply 5,760 houses with a quantity more than ten times their possible consumption. As the aqueduct, before it reached Philadelphia would gain a very considerable head, the same supply would be received, but in less time. A more detailed calculation is at present unnecessary: this is enough to show that the spring produces water in sufficient quantity.

The spring has never been known to increase in wet or to diminish in dry seasons. Its temperature is, as I am well informed, lower than that of most other springs, being only forty-two or forty-three degrees of Farenheit, and the water issues in such quantities that it maintains a warmth above the freezing point, in a course of three miles down the Schuylkill, keeping the river open for canoes in the severest winters. Even the winter of 1796 did not affect it. To the information which I received of this fact, from several most respectable men in the neighbourhood, I can add that it was open as far as I could see it, on the twenty-seventh of this month, when every other part of the river was frozen over.

The practicability of bringing this spring to the city is ascertained by the practicability of the canal, near the proposed bank of which it rises.[9] Its level is four feet higher than that of the canal, it would go over better ground, the distance would be shorter, and it is to the south and eastward of all the rocky knolls. I have good reason to think that the distance would not exceed twelve miles.

In executing this work, only two objects of indispensible consideration occur.

I. To prevent the quantity of water from being diminished by evaporation or absorption.

II. To preserve its temperature, both in summer and winter.

Both these ends would be attained, by conducting the water in a close tunnel (say an eliptical culvert of three feet by six feet)—three feet at least under the surface of all the natural ground, provided with the necessary air-holes, and air-traps—and carrying it in light aqueducts of segment arches across all the vallies, avoiding every attempt at a forced canal of earth.

The expence of bringing the water as far as the city would not exceed 275,000 dollars.

It is evident, that in this work the water would never freeze, nor yet acquire any perceptible degree of heat. Only while passing along the aqueducts, it would lose, in winter, and gain heat, in summer.

But supposing even that the aqueducts amount to a mile in length, and that the course of the water be only two miles an hour, it would never be exposed to an atmosphere hotter or colder than itself, for more than thirty minutes. We have seen that it will retain a temperature above the freezing point for near three miles, though it has passed a mill, and is mixed with the colder water of the Schuylkill. As the aqueduct would be in short lengths, the water would re-acquire in the tunnels, the temperature it might lose in the open air

Should the mill spring at any time be found insufficient, the aqueduct, once constructed, might receive, in its course, supplies from all the neighbouring springs, which rise in levels sufficiently elevated; and perhaps convey water to the city, sufficient in quantity to render the Steam-engine on the Schuylkill unnecessary.

Even when the first supply arrives, the engines may be dormant, from the month of November to the beginning of August.

I have now to consider the works necessary in the city itself.

In the *first instance,* they will consist of wooden pipes of four inches bore, leading from center square in the following arrangement:[10]

I. Four pipes down Market-street, supplying at their extremities, ranges of cross pipes of three inches bore, running north and south, in Water-street, Front-street, Second and Third-streets. These pipes will lie under or near the gutters. From them will branch laterally the leaden pipes which supply each house. The detail of cocks, public spouts, fountain and fire plugs, would be particularly attended to. These four mains will be served from the bason in center-square, and they must be so connected, as at option to be served also from the reservoir upon the Engine-house.

II. Four pipes down Chesnut, and four down Arch-street, to supply the cross streets upon the same principle, as high as Eleventh-street. If no more could be accomplished in the first year, it would be sufficient, as the pumps above Eleventh-street furnish as yet very good water.

If time permit, *before,* and certainly *after,* these pipes are in operation, the east and west pipes must be doubled so as to serve separately, one the north, the other the south streets. In the course of time, they ought to be replaced by cast iron pipes of nine inches bore.

This may be done gradually, beginning with the longest.

In all the pipes, plugs or cocks will be fixed which, when drawn, will throw up fountains playing to a hight proportionate to the elevation of the reservoir, the lower cock being previously closed. A main of four inches bore, for instance, will, when closed at the lower extremity, throw up, in different parts of the same street, twelve fountains of an inch diameter each, and thus the whole city may be alternately cleansed and cooled.

116

In case of fire, these fountains will fill the engines without manual labor, by the proper application of a hose. This is of itself an object worthy of the whole expence of distribution.[11]

The pipes ought to lie at least two feet below the pavement. Wooden pipes require much attention and repair.[12] I cannot in the short time allowed me, furnish any probable calculation of the annual expence of these repairs. The experience of the London new river company shows, that notwithstanding their frequency, the water can be supplied, and all the works kept up at a small annual water-rent, reserving a very large income to the company.

Neither can the original expence of laying down the pipes be very exactly calculated, without better information than I have been able to procure. My enquiries however lead me to believe, that the pavement may be opened, the pipe manufactured and laid down, and covered again, for half a dollar a foot, allowing for plugs, cocks and hoops.

On this supposition, and allowing 10,000 feet of pipe (or nearly two miles) to Front-street, 8,000 feet to the three next, 5,000 each as high as Eleventh-street, and 35,000 in the east and west mains, the whole amount will be 104,000 feet, making 52,000 dollars.[13]

This expence would distribute water through all the crouded parts of the city, and render the pumps wholly unnecessary. The expence, of laying the water by small leaden pipes from the main to the private houses, should be borne by the individuals. It would amount to fifty cents per foot, and in no case exceed twenty-five or thirty dollars, an expence which I think every family would cheerfully incur to avoid the inconveniences arising from the necessity, as at present, of sending their servants to the pumps. For these pipes, a rent would be paid. The poorer inhabitants would supply themselves from the public plugs, without any charge. I think half the expence of laying down the main pipes, *i.e.* twenty-five cents per foot, if assessed upon the city, would not be objected to. The rich would pay in proportion to their fronts, the poor would be slightly affected; the expence in fact would fall upon the landlord. Corner houses should pay only for one front. This assessment would pay the whole expence, one half being levied on each side of the street. If a tax is to be levied on the city for the work, a lighter and a juster could not perhaps be devised. It would in fact be the *purchase money* of health and convenience, and occur only once. Every new house, would pay its share, as it was built, and thereby contribute to the future repairs.

But I ought to apologize for these suggestions. I have made them only to show, that the effort, which it is proposed to make, is much within the powers of this wealthy city.

Recapitulation of expence:

Erecting the Engines and bringing water from Schuylkill to
    Center-square, ... 75,000
Bringing the Mill-spring to the city, ... 275,000
Distributing the water throughout the city—first expense, ... 52,000

Dollars 402,000

A further expence will be necessary to extend the distribution to every distant part of the town. This may be executed in Anno 1800. The expence cannot easily be ascertained.

I will furnish you, at any time you please, with the detail of my estimates, which I believe will not be found short of the reality.

In order to ascertain the probable proceeds of the works, I will suppose, that of six thousand houses, four thousand families will supply themselves with water from the main. The water-rent which I paid while residing in London, in a house of twenty-four feet front, was thirty-six shillings, sterling, or eight dollars.[14] Fixing ten dollars as the first average rent—which, as the funds become prosperous, may be annually lowered—this alone would produce an annual rent of 40,000 dollars, independently of extra supplies to brewers, distillers, or very large families.

	Dollars.	Cts.
40,000 dollars rent, at 6 per cent. per annum, is equivalent to a capital of.........	666,666	66

I will now add a few remarks upon the following proposals, which have been supposed to be worthy of consideration, and which indeed are the only schemes that have come to my knowledge, that deserve attention.

I. To complete the canal immediately.

II. To conduct Wissahikon-creek to the city.

III. To erect water-works to be driven by one of the two rivers.

IV. To collect water from any practicable source, and bring it over hill and dale in wooden, or perhaps, in iron pipes, to Philadelphia.

If, and I presume it will not easily be disputed, the three requisites of (*1st.*) *immediate* utility, (*2d.*) permanence, and (*3d.*) security against *frost*, be indispensible, I may dismiss these proposals in a few words.

I. The first is deficient in the first, and, I fear, in the last.

II. The second, (if at any time the water were sufficient) in the first and last.

III. The third in the second and third.

IV. The fourth in permanence, and, I think, in efficiency.

I. As to the canal, I am convinced that the very eminent and acknowledged abilities of the Engineer Mr. Weston, could overcome any obstacles which art dare combat; and that a work, in which he has already done himself so much honor, would not want completion if it depended upon his genius or his industry. If, therefore, the work could be accomplished in time, it certainly would render great part of the expence, which I have proposed, unnecessary. But, from what I have heard, doubt may be entertained of the possibility of the necessary expedition. But I confess myself very imperfectly informed. I fear the ice would embarrass the winter-supply for culinary use, but to every other purpose its waters would be amply adequate.[15]

II. Wissahikon-creek has, I believe, not a sufficient quantity of water. Besides, to get the water upon a proper elevation, it would be necessary to purchase two mills, and then to bring the water to town over very unfavorable ground. The creek has been, even this winter, almost frozen to the bottom, and yielded little water.[16]

III. The examples of London, (London bridge works,) Versailles, (Marly,) and Bremen, would forever deter me from attempting works to be driven by a river subject to ice and freshes.[17] The expence of keeping up the timber-work is enormous, and equal to re-building once in seven years. To give such works *power*, they must be unwieldy. *Cranks*, which are their necessary appendage, are the very worst things in mechanism. In the Delaware or Schuylkill, the works might stand still six hours in twenty-four—perhaps during the raging of a fire. I once saw several houses in London burn down, while the works were waiting for the tide. This happens not unfrequently. In winter they would be wholly useless.

IV. To bring water, in pipes of any description, a yard further than necessity requires, is very bad œconomy. All water has more or less sediment, and pipes cannot be cleansed without taking them up. It is difficult often to find where the fault lies. Metal pipes are very liable to injury from the frost, and in a long extent every part could not be equally secured.[18] Wooden pipes, like every thing else that is wooden, are a perpetual source of expence, repair, and interruption. The inconvenience attending them in distributing the water must be borne, because it cannot be avoided, but where it can be avoided, it ought not to [be] borne.

By the length of this letter, you will see that I have endeavored to comply fully with your request—by the want of detail, you will observe that I have been straightened in time.

I am, Sir, With great esteem, Your's faithfully,

B. Henry Latrobe.

To John Miller, Esquire, *Chairman of the Committee of the Select Council of the city of Philadelphia.*

POSTSCRIPT.

I am induced to add still the following remarks, as connected with the subject of my letter.

I. *Prejudice against River-water.*

Although most men prefer spring, to river water, it may be doubted, whether the latter be not the most wholesome. It is certainly supposed by Physicians to be more generally free from noxious ingredients. The Indians, I am informed, from motives of health now grown into habit, never drink water from a spring, when they can procure it from a stream. London is entirely supplied with river water. It is taken from the Thames in different places, from the New River, and from the river Lee; and has nothing to boast of the cleanliness of its aqueducts. The water is received in each house in wooden, or leaden cisterns, where it deposits a black impalpable mud. When boiled the New River water crusts the vessels with a calcareous precipitate, so as in time to choak the spouts of the tea kettles. I believe that the country, in which the river rises, has a basis of chalk. The water must, therefore, be similar to that of the Schuylkill in quality, though very inferior in purity. The houses in London are supplied only once in two days. The water then runs about three hours. Yet during some years residence in London I thought it very pleasant, and I am certain it is very wholesome. It is preferred to the water of any spring in the two cities and suburbs, and those that have any fame, (such as St. Paul's, or Aldgate,) owe it to their coldness, not their superior salubrity. I must remark, that I never knew a deficiency of water in my family, notwithstanding the distant intervals between the supplies. The cisterns always ran over during the last hour of the water's coming in. This shows how sufficient our own resources are.

In this hot climate, however, cool water is more valuable than in London, and, perhaps, absolutely necessary. The Mill-spring seems to possess every desireable quality, in a degree which our most sanguine wishes could scarce have expected.

II. *Fountains.*

The Engine proposed for Center-square, may be considered as a necessary and unavoidable expence, by whatever means the water be brought to town. It may be rendered an ornament to the city. Its use is to supply water to the higher levels of the town, and fountains to all the streets. They are the only means of cooling the air. The air produced by the agitation of water is of the purest kind, and the sudden evaporation of water, scattered through the air, absorbs astonishing quantities of heat, or to use the common phrase, creates a great degree of cold. Coal mines, which are troubled with foul air, are supplied with pure air by the simple means of pouring a small stream of water through a trunk, down the shaft into a cask. The air extricated in the trunk and cask, is conveyed by means of pipes to distant parts of the works. When the shaft is deep it will blow out so strongly, that a man cannot stand against it. The water blast, used in Switzerland in the furnaces, which is produced by the same simple means, is the strongest that can be devised, and on account of the purity of its air, partakes of the superiority of the chemical oxygen furnace.[19]

As to the mechanism of the fountains, it consists merely of a short wooden pipe, set perpendicularly into the main, and stopped by a cock, which is turned, when the fountain is not in use. The *name* produces an idea of great expence, but they may be realised at a very small one.

III. *Public Baths.*

I have often wondered, that while in many despotic countries, all ranks of men have been provided with the convenience, and the wholesome pleasantness of public baths, fountains, and porticoes, the American people do not indulge themselves, in the smallest gratification, as salubrious, as it is innocent, of this kind. Our abstinence is commendable, as it arises from industry, and our attention to more serious pursuits, but highly blameable as it injures our health. We retain indeed both in our buildings, our diet, and our modes of life, the habits of our Northern ancestors, and have not yet learned how to live healthily in a hot climate. In the city of Philadelphia, I think baths almost an absolutely necessary means of health. When the engine in center square is at work it will with great ease supply a requisite number of baths. I mention this only as a hint. It might be worth while to look forward to some such thing in the arrangement that may be thought of, provided the preparation may be made without expence. I think it may. Such baths would be a source of a large revenue and perhaps it might not be bad policy in the citizens of this primary metropolis of North America, to counterbalance the fashionable inducements which point to the Potowmac, by conveniences, and advantages which cannot for many years be thought of in a city, which is at present almost destitute of dwellings.

IV. *Steam Engines.*

For want of the necessary information of what can be executed in this city—which I have not had time to procure—some uncertainty in the estimates, in which the Steam Engines are concerned, must be expected. I have said nothing of their power, because it is perfectly at your option from the supply of five hundred to any higher number of gallons per minute. I have no doubt but that this city can produce Smiths capable of constructing very efficient Engines, under proper direction.

The annual expence of each Engine, and repairs, will not exceed three thousand dollars.[20]

Printed Copy: *View of the Practicability and Means of Supplying the City of Philadelphia with Wholesome Water. In a Letter to John Miller, Esquire, from B. Henry Latrobe, Engineer. December 29th. 1798.* (Philadelphia, 1799) (160/F1). Printed by order of the Corporation of Philadelphia.

1. On 27 December 1798, two days prior to this letter, BHL visited Spring Mills, the site of an abundant natural spring in Montgomery County on the north bank of the Schuylkill River about ten miles from Philadelphia. BHL was accompanied by John Miller, Jr., and other Philadelphia gentlemen who were interested in BHL's opinion of the spring as a source of drinking water for the city. Miller, as chairman of the Philadelphia city councils' joint committee on watering the city, then asked BHL to write this extended

comment on Philadelphia's water supply. *Report to the Select and Common Councils, on the Progress and State of the Water Works, on the 24th of November, 1799* (Philadelphia, 1799), p. 6.

2. The yellow fever season normally extended from July to October.

3. Centre Square, where Broad and High (Market) streets met, is the site of the present-day City Hall.

4. A contemporary account gave the following description of the Delaware River adjacent to Philadelphia: " . . . there are also many vacancies on the bank of the river, which are covered with a thick bed of miery filth; the wharves, likewise, at times, become filled up with impure substances from the adjoining streets; and, during the summer, emit, at low water, a very offensive smell." Condie and Folwell, *History of the Pestilence, Commonly Called Yellow Fever,* p. 7.

5. Many of the Schuylkill's tributaries rise in the Great Valley of southeastern Pennsylvania, which has many limestone outcrops. However, the sources of the Schuylkill River itself are beyond the Blue Mountains where limestone formations are less abundant. Benjamin Leroy Miller, *Limestones of Pennsylvania* (Harrisburg, Pa., 1934), p. 208.

6. When the city councils adopted BHL's waterworks plan they accepted his idea that the Centre Square Engine House should be ornamental, and he designed a neo-classical structure which was a city landmark while it stood. See BHL, *Architectural Drawings.*

7. BHL's footnote here reads: "The perfect permeability of this stratum is evident from the connection of the wells with each other, and with the sinks and privies, from whence arises the extreme unpleasantness of the water in the crouded parts of the city. It is worth considering, whether the pumps do not act as chimnies to bring up volumes of noxious Gas from the putrifying water, which may predispose the inhabitants to receive the Yellow-fever." See BHL, *Journals,* 2 : 379–81; BHL, "Designs of Buildings . . . in Philadelphia," [1799], p. 1, Historical Society of Pennsylvania, Philadelphia (294/A1).

8. It was this second plan which was eventually adopted by the city.

9. The Delaware and Schuylkill Canal was begun in 1792 but only partially completed before funds ran out in 1795–96. It began at Norristown, followed the north bank of the Schuylkill River to near Philadelphia, then turned east to the Delaware River.

10. Bored-out logs had considerable use as pipes from the late Middle Ages. BHL was familiar with their use by the London waterworks. In the *Federal Gazette* (Baltimore) of 11 February 1799, BHL advertised for 104,000 feet of white oak logs for use at the Philadelphia Waterworks. H. W. Dickinson, *Water Supply of Greater London* (London, 1954), pp. 31–33.

11. It was a common feeling that Philadelphia needed water for cooling the air, cleaning the streets, and fire-fighting, as well as drinking. Just after BHL's waterworks plan was adopted, one citizen commented: "It would be endless to expatiate on the benefits of this establishment. Abridgment of labour, by the spontaneous flow of that which has hitherto been raised with difficulty from wells, and transported from a toilsome distance; the promotion of health by the substitution of wholesome and pure water, for what is polluted, and poisonous, and nauseous, are the immediate, certain, and best effects of this scheme.

"It is no less conducive to the cleanliness of the streets, through which purifying torrents may, at any time, be made to roll; and to the salubrity of the atmosphere, which may be incessantly filled with dewy exhalations. Conflagration, the great pest of American cities, if it cannot be wholly prevented, may be extinguished in its birth." B., "Philadelphia Water-Works. June, 1799," *The Monthly Magazine, and American Review* 1 (June 1799):181.

12. In 1801 James Todd and John Davis reported to the Watering Committee on the problems and advantages of using wooden pipe. Todd and Davis to the Watering Commit-

tee, 16 Nov. 1801, in *Report of the Committee Appointed by the Common Council to Enquire into the State of the Water Works* (Philadelphia, 1802), pp. 76–81.

13. In December 1801, near the end of the Waterworks' first year of operation, only 29,963 feet of pipe had been laid. Ibid., p. 48.

14. BHL's house on Grafton Street in London was provided water by the New River Company. Charles S. Singer et al., eds., *A History of Technology*, 7 vols. (New York and London, 1954–78), 4 : 496.

15. BHL's dismissal of the Delaware and Schuylkill Canal was not taken lightly, and it initiated a brief pamphlet war during January 1799 between BHL and the canal company. *Address of the Committee of the Delaware and Schuylkill Canal Company to the Committees of the Senate and House of Representatives on the Memorial of Said Company* (Philadelphia, 1799); BHL, *Remarks on the Address of the Committee . . .* (Philadelphia, 1799) (161/D1); *Remarks on a second Publication of B. Henry Latrobe . . .* (Philadelphia, 1799).

In spite of this antagonism, BHL was later employed as a consultant to the company. Delaware and Schuylkill Canal Co. minutes, 16 Nov. 1799, Union Canal Co. Papers, RG 174, box 1, Pennsylvania Historical and Museum Commission, Harrisburg (microfiche add.).

16. Bringing water to the city from Wissahickon Creek had been a favorite project of Philadelphians for many years. Benjamin Franklin's will included a bequest to aid it. Codicil, 23 June 1789, in *Gazette of the United States* (New York), 29 May 1790.

17. The London Bridge Waterworks, with waterwheels in the Thames between the bridge's piers, was established in 1581. The famous Marly machine with fourteen waterwheels pumped water from the Seine into the gardens of Versailles. Bremen was partially supplied with water by a waterwheel pump in the Wesser River. Abraham Rees, ed., *The Cyclopedia; or Universal Dictionary of Arts, Sciences, and Literature*, 1st American ed., 40 vols. (Philadelphia, 1805–24), s.v. "Bremen" and "Water, motion of;" Dickinson, *Water Supply of Greater London*, pp. 491–92; Eugene S. Ferguson, "The Steam Engine Before 1830," in Melvin Kranzberg and Carroll W. Pursell, Jr., eds., *Technology in Western Civilization*, 2 vols. (New York, 1967) 1 : 262–63.

18. Experiments were made with iron pipe at the Philadelphia Waterworks as early as 1801, but such pipes were not readily available in America. In 1818 the Watering Committee obtained models of iron pipes and stopcocks from England in order to set standards for American producers. Significant quantities of iron pipe were laid in the 1820s. *Report of the Watering Committee to the Select and Common Councils. November 1, 1804.* (Philadelphia, 1804), p. 4; *Report of the Watering Committee to the Select and Common Councils. Read January 22, 1818* (Philadelphia, 1818), p. 3; *Report of the Watering Committee to the Select and Common Councils, 14 January 1819* (Philadelphia, 1819), p. 3; Nelson M. Blake, *Water for the Cities* (Syracuse, N.Y., 1956), p. 83.

19. By his comments regarding the water blast and the chemical furnace, it is very likely that BHL had read William Lewis's *Commercium Philosophico-Technicum; or, the Philosophical Commerce of Arts: Designed as an Attempt to Improve Arts, Trades, and Manufactures* (London, 1763). Lewis begins the work with a lengthy description of a "Portable Furnace for making experiments," and later on gives considerable attention to the water blast, which he describes as "a stream of water, falling through a pipe . . . [carrying] air down with it; and this air, . . . may be so collected, as to have no other vent than a pipe which shall carry it to the furnace" (p. 269). In an appendix Lewis states that he has "received an account, from a worthy correspondent in Swisserland, of a [water blast] machine which he has constructed for a smelting furnace" (p. 631). Lewis, however, does not discuss the use of the water blast for ventilating mines, nor does he discuss the use of oxygen in the chemical furnace, since it had not yet been isolated as a separate gas. Possibly in the hurry

of writing this letter BHL's own imagination supplied these aspects of his remarks.

20. After the first twenty-two months of operation the expense of both engines had been $17,946.14, or about $4,900 per engine per annum. *Report of the Joint Committee Appointed by the Select and Common Councils for the purpose of Superintending and Directing the Water Works* (Philadelphia, 1802), p. 16.

TO JAMES WOOD

Philadelphia, Feby. 23d, 1799.

Sir,

I acknowledge with many thanks the receipt of your favor of the 16th current which has just now come to hand.[1] Ever since the latter end of December 1798 I have endeavored so to arrange my affairs, as to be able to return to Virginia, and have more than once fixed the day of my departure. Notwithstanding the highly advantageous circumstances which have detained me, I beg you to believe, that I feel extreme chagrin at not having been able to accomplish my wish. On my arrival here the Directors of the Pensylvania Bank to whom I had given a design 12 Months ago, by a very liberal compensation, rendered it a duty in me to arrange and make all their contracts, and to put their work into progress. In my engagement with them, I made an express stipulation that I should be permitted to give every necessary attendance to the Penitentiary house of Virginia, and I should have been with you nearly two months ago, had I not been very unexpectedly called upon to give my advice in a much greater and more immediately important Work—the supply of this City with Water from the Schuylkill. My proposal was adopted in its fullest Extent. You have no doubt seen it in some of the Philadelphia papers. The opposition however of the Delaware & Schuylkill Canal company occasioned delay both in the measures taken by the State Legislature, and by the Corporation, and thus the month of February, which I had intended, and could have otherwise devoted to my duty in Virginia has slipt by without my being able to stir from hence. On these accounts it is impossible for me, without most materially injuring the public interests in this place, to obey my desire to proceed immediately to Richmond. The strong personal interest I feel in the first great Work which your confidence, and that of the council of state gave me an opportunity of planning in America, as well as the object of the building itself, weigh strongly with me, against every other interest which I have; and although it is at present 125 out of my power *immediately* to attend your directions, I promise to make every exertion to be with you in as short a time as is practicable.

In the mean time I hope you will permit me to give in writing all the direction which I could personally offer. I am well aware of the difference of the effect of written and oral instructions, as it is impossible that the same zeal which I feel in the cause of the building should actuate any other person. I hope however that what I shall transmit to you may not be entirely useless. The necessary immediate instructions to the Bricklayer I enclose, the rest will follow by the next and the succeeding posts.

The necessity of employing an active and intelligent Clerk of the Works, or Superintendant, I took the liberty of pointing out very early in the correspondence which I had the honor of addressing to you in the Summer of 1797. The age and infirmities of Mr. Thos. Callis, rendered his integrity of less avail, and embarrassed a little the progress of the building; and perhaps the worst consequence resulting from it was, the total neglect of every species of regular account. I much fear that the loss of materials *delivered and paid for,* which was very considerable before I left Richmond, may have still encreased during the Winter. Perhaps the first measure of importance should be, to make a very exact inventory of all that remains. By the next post I will take the liberty of transmitting to you a page of all the books which form the system of accounts which are kept at the Pensylvania Bank building, and without which I believe it impossible—for I have always found it so—to conduct a public work with oeconomy and regularity. An abstract of this system is I believe to be found in some of my first letters.

I hope you will not ascribe it to a presumptuous desire to intrude the services of any individual upon you, if I venture to mention Mr. William Callis to you, as a person highly qualified to be useful to the public, though not exactly in the last mentioned capacity, which requires at least the assistance of a good Accountant. He understands my whole system of construction, both in respect of Arches and all Brickwork, as also of every species of Woodwork; and in making Centers, I know he has not a superior in Virginia. Since my arrival here I have not heard of, or from him, although I have enquired by letter, more than once. It was my intention to have made him Clerk of the Works to the Pensylvania Bank, to which situation a Salary of $1.000 per Annum is annexed; but as he has a family, and there is a risk of the return of the yellow fever, and I also hope to serve him in a more independent Way, I have appointed another. In the mean time I earnestly wish, that you may find it to the public interest to continue him in the public employ, for the assigned reasons; which, I solicit, you will accept as an apology for my giving this unasked recommendation. He will compleatly understand all my directions, and not only know how to follow them himself, but also to instruct others. Every part of the Work, as it now stands has been set out by his assistance, he is intimately acquainted with its most intricate detail, and, which is a very material point, every Workman at the building had the fullest confidence in his skill and integrity, when I left Richmond.

I beg once more to assure that it is with real regret that I cannot immediately comply with your wish for my return. I beg you to receive my thanks for the very polite and obliging manner in which you have communicated it to me, and to accept of the assurance of my most perfect esteem.

I am, Sir, with great respect Yours faithfully

B. Henry Latrobe B.

ALS: Executive Papers of Governor James Wood, Virginia State Library (161/F1). Enclosed BHL, Directions to the Bricklayer, 23 Feb. 1799, below.

1. Wood wrote BHL: "We have determined, to begin laying bricks at the Penitentiary House on the first of the next month, and deem your presence at that time essentially necessary as it is our wish to continue you in your appointment for the ensuing year." Wood to BHL, 16 Feb. 1799, Governor's Letterbook, 1794–1800, Virginia State Library, Richmond (microfiche add.).

ENCLOSURE: DIRECTIONS TO THE BRICKLAYER

Directions to the Bricklayer of the Penitentiary house, Richmond in Virginia

Philadelphia Feby. 23d. 1799

1., It is more than probable that the Lime which was burned last season has been much injured during the Winter. On this, and on every other account, I most earnestly recommend, that before any part of the Work be begun, at least 100 bushels of Lime be wrought up into mortar, and the same Quantity be always kept beforehand. I tried in vain to procure the Lime to be water slacked last Season, and the difficulty of procuring an abundant Supply of Water will perhaps continue to render it impracticable. This renders it doubly necessary that a large heap of Mortar should be made up, before a brick is laid. The interests of the Bricklayer, as well as of the public demand it. He paid for more time lost by the Bricklayers at the Wall, because they had to wait for Mortar, then can be easily calculated.

2., East Wing. The Centers of the Octagon being fixed, and the iron 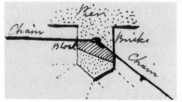 chain in its place already, it is necessary that an Oak block should be cut to fit each angle nine inches high, and reaching across each pier, for the arch to but against. This block should be two inches thick at its thinnest ends. This being done, turn the groin.

3., The Range of Cell Arches from East to West have the Centers and Chains fixed already. Turn them in nine inches, and level the Spandrils with the top of the Arch.

4., The Centers used below for the flat arches must be fixed again for this last story. Turn the arches in 9 inches.

5., The Groin of the N. E. Angle ought not to be turned untill the Circular building is carried up to its Springing. At present there are two Chains remaining to be put up at each end, in a direction from East to West, which lay hold of the bond timber in the Walls. Future directions for this arch will be given.

6., The Centers of the two Groins in the Circular court, East end, should be immediately struck, and fixed at the West side, and the Groins turned.

B. Henry Latrobe B. Archt.

ADS: Executive Papers of Governor James Wood, Virginia State Library (161/F5). Enclosed in BHL to Wood, 23 Feb. 1799, above.

The Bank of Pennsylvania

EDITORIAL NOTE

Latrobe made his first design for the Bank of Pennsylvania during his visit to Philadelphia in spring 1798, and it was the acceptance of this design that resulted in his move from Richmond to Philadelphia in December 1798. At the instance of Samuel M. Fox, the bank president, Latrobe adopted the Jeffersonian goal of giving to a modern public building the general form of an antique temple. Between 1799 and 1801, he supervised construction of the bank, a fireproof structure of permanent masonry vaulting that culminated in a domed 128 circular banking hall. The building had a marble exterior with two Greek Ionic porticoes and was surrounded with an enclosed garden. Finely executed because of a liberal budget (including Latrobe's $4,000 fee), the bank set a standard for civic buildings and became one of the most influential prototypes for early nineteenth-century American architecture. Latrobe, who took it as a point of reference for numerous later designs, regarded it as his masterpiece. The federal government demolished the building in 1867 but fragments still survive. For a detailed analysis of Latrobe's design, see BHL, *Architectural Drawings*.

AGREEMENT FOR EXECUTING THE MARBLE WORK OF THE BANK OF PENNSYLVANIA

[26 February 1799]

Agreement made this twenty Sixth day of February 1799 between the President, Directors and Company of the Bank of Pennsylvania on the one part,[1] and James Traquair, John Miller, and John Bennett Marble Masons and Contractors for executing the Marble work of the Said Bank,[2] and John Ross and Robert Patterson Sureties for the Said Contractors,[3] Jointly and Severally, on the other part.[4]

Whereas the President, Directors and Company of the Bank of Pennsylvania have resolved and undertaken to erect a Building for their use and convenience as a Banking Company, upon a certain lot of ground, bounded on the east by Second Street, on the west by Dock Street, and go forth Alley, on the North by Lodgealley, on the South by the City Tavern Alley, agreeably to the designs and descriptions made by Benjamin Henry Latrobe Architect. And whereas a considerable part of the work of the Said building is intended to be executed in Marble, it is therefor agreed between the Said parties to these presents.

First, On the part of the Said President, Directors and Company of the Bank of Pennsylvania, that convenient Sheds or Shops shall be erected at the expence of the said President, Directors and Company of the Bank of Pennsylvania upon the lot abovementioned for the use of the Said Contractors in which they shall be at full liberty to bring, deposit, and work the Marble to be used in the erection of the Bank.

2d. That should the Sheds and Shops so erected be insufficient to deposit and work the Marble to be employed in the said Building, the Contractors shall be at liberty to work the Marble which shall be ordered for the Building in their own yard or yards, and after it is wrought it shall be removed to the Building at the expence of the said President, Directors, and Company.

129

3d. That every Species of Tackle, Machinery, Rope, Plank, and Scaffolding for Setting the Marble when wrought shall be provided at the expence of the Said President, Directors, and Company excepting as excepted in Article 3d of the 2d part, but no tool, implement or Banker used in working the Same.

4th. That the work which may be finished shall be measured, whenever the Contractors shall require it and the account or balance of account that is Justly due Shall be paid on certificate by the Architect, or in his absence from the City, by any other agent of the said President, Directors and Company duly authorized.

5th. That the Contractors shall at all times be furnished on demand with every Drawing, Direction, or Mould which shall be necessary to the execution of their contract, and the Architect shall be personally accountable to the contractors for the wages of all workmen who shall be prevented from proceeding in the execution of the Contract to their full amount for the time for which they Shall be idle for want of Such Drawing, Direction or mould.

6th. That the Said President, Directors, and Company Shall pay, or cause to be paid to the contractors the wages of all such Masons, Labourers and other workmen who shall be employed in Setting the work after it is finished at the following rates per day of ten working hours.

For every Masson	Twelve Shillings and sixpence
For every Labourer used to masons work and entered by the Architect as such	Seven Shillings and Sixpence

And for the purpose of avoiding all doubt respecting the time employed in Setting the work, that every Mason or Labourer who Shall be thus employed shall be entered with the clerk of the works previously to his being thus employed, together with the time for which he is to be rated to the said President, Directors and Company, and the Clerk of the works shall also keep an exact account of every time at which such Setting work shall be completed.

Second, on the part of James Traquair, John Miller, and John Bennett Contractors, and John Ross and Robert Patterson their Sureties,

1st. That all Marble used in the building of the Bank of Pennsylvania, shall be quarried, brought to the yard of the Building, unloaded,

130

banked and wrought ready to be Set in its place at the Sole and proper charge and expence of the Contractors, Save only Such marble work as shall be finished ready to be Set at the yard or yards of the Contractors in the City of Philadelphia for want of room in the yard of the Bank, which Marble, and none other shall be hauled from the yard or yards of the contractors to the yard of the Bank at the expence of the said President, Directors and Company as expressed in Article 2d on the part of the Said President, Directors and Company.

2d. That the Contractors shall in every respect, both in working and setting the marble, Strictly conform to the Designs, Directions, Drawings and moulds which shall be delivered to them by the Architect, nor shall they be responsible for any mistake, error, or failure of any work for which they can produce a voucher of having been directed in its execution by the Architect. On the other hand they shall if required alter, take down, remove and correct any work which they may have done contrary to, or different from the Direction, Design, Drawing or mould given to them by the Architect, at their own proper cost and expence. And it is clearly understood, that as no responsibility whatsoever lies upon the Contractors for the Success or failure of any part of the work if executed according to direction, so also they alone are to answer to the damage or failure occasioned by any deviation from such direction, and in order to prevent the possibility of Doubt or dispute upon this Subject, no direction will be admitted as authentic unless it be in writing or drawings Signed by the Architect.

3d. That the Contractors shall whenever required thereto by the Architect, or Clerk of the works, and receiving one days notice, employ their masons and Labourers in Setting such work as Shall be finished, and Shall enter such men as are to be thus employed, with the Clerk of the works, being jointly responsible for their industry and attention during Such Setting and as expressed in the Sixth article on the part of the Said President, Directors and Company. The Contractors shall at their own proper charge furnish the following tools and implements for the purpose of Setting the work, Crowbars, Betles,[5] Mallets, Trowels, Setting tools, Louises[6] and Rollers, and none other.

4th. The Contractors shall discharge from their work at the yard of the Bank, any workman whether Mason or Labourer, to whom the Architect shall object in writing, giving him notice to the end of the week for which he may be engaged.

5th. The work shall be measured and paid for when required by the   131

Contractors as expressed in article 4th on the part of the Said President, Directors and Company. The Architect Shall measure on the part of the Said President, Directors and Company, and the Contractors or any one they may appoint on their own part. Should any dispute arise the matter Shall be refered to two persons appointed, the one by President, Directors and Company of the Bank, and the other by the Contractors, whose decision if unanimous, if not, that of an Umpire chosen by the Referees shall be final, and bind both the Said President, Directors and Company, and the Contractors, and the work shall be measured according to the following rules, and paid for according to the affixed prices.

1st. All Cubic Blocks of Marble in the bases and shafts of the Collumns, the bases, Shafts and Capitals of the Pilasters, Architraves, and cornices of the Porticoes, Cieling of the Porticoes, Front steps, Upper courses of cheek blocks, the Angle blocks of the recessed Flank Cornice, the Impost mouldings of the Flank Windows, the Piers and Imposts of the lower Windows of the west front, the Architraves of the three great Doors, and all other blocks which Shall exceed ten feet in length, one foot, Six Inches in width, and one foot in thickness, shall form one class of Marble and be paid for in its rough State at the rate of one Dollar and twenty five Cents per Cubic foot.

And in order to ascertain its rough dimensions the following rule Shall be observed.

	ft.	in.	
for every ten feet in length and so in proportion	1	6	Shall be allowed for waste and
one foot in heighth Do.		3	added to the
one foot in width Do.		4	neat extreme dimensions

Excepting only in the Shafts of the Collumns, which shall be rated to contain thirty feet in heighth, four in width and four in thickness of rough marble amounting in each to four hundred and eighty cubic feet.

Each of the Capitals of the Collumns shall [be] finished in the best Stile of Sculpture which can be produced, agreeably to the Drawings and descriptions contained in a Book hereby referred to, and which Drawings and Descriptions are Signed by the Contractors and Architect and

Fig. 3. BHL, North flank of the Bank of Pennsylvania, 1800. Courtesy of the Historical Society of Pennsylvania.

form part of this agreement, and shall be Set in its place for the Sum of two hundred Dollars, including all charges of materials, workmanship and Setting.[7]

All plain, Sunk, tooled, or Sanded works, the faces and soffits of Architraves and circular plain work wrought on the above mentioned blocks shall be measured neat at the price of one Dollar twenty five cents per foot Superficial.

All Sunk moulded work shall be girt from the external edge of the upper moulding to the lower edge of the lowest moulding and charged at two Dollars and twenty five cents per foot Superficial.

All plain straight work, all joints, beds, and weatherings measured neat at the price of Seventy five Cents per foot Superficial.

The circular sunk mouldings of the bases of the columns, shall in *this* instance, on account of the particular manner in which they are to be wrought, be charged at four Dollars and fifty cents per foot Superficial, but this price is not to furnish any precedent for future charges.

2d. Class. The like unwrought marble in all other moulded work not enumerated above shall form a Second Class. One Dollar per cubic foot shall be charged for it, and it shall be measured according to the following rule.

Fig. 4. The Bank of Pennsylvania, engraving by William Birch, 1804, hand colored. Courtesy of the American Philosophical Society.

For every ten feet in length and so in proportion	1 foot	⎞ Shall be allowed
Heighth be what it may	3 Inches	in addition to its extreme neat dimensions

and one foot shall be allowed for the bed in all cases. All moulded work on the above marble shall be charged at two Dollars, twenty five cents per foot Superficial, according to its Girt.

All Beds and Joints shall be rated nine inches deep, and one bed and one Joint allowed to each stone, seventy five cents per foot superficial.

3d. All other marble measured cube shall form a third class and be charged at one Dollar per Cubic foot. The Marble of the Frize all round the building shall be measured thus.

For every ten feet in length	one foot	⎞ Shall be allowed
The height	3 Inches	in addition to its extreme neat dimensions

134   and nine inches in all cases for the bed.

The plain face, measuring in addition *one* 9 Inch Joint and *one* 9 Inch bed to each stone shall be charged at Seventy five cents per foot Superficial.

For all the Ashler in the flanks and front of the building and round the Dome, and also for all the paving, no cubic dimensions shall be charged but One Six Inch bed and one Six Inch Joint shall be allowed to each stone, and it shall be charged according to its Neat Superficial dimension at the rate of 66⅔ Cents per foot.

For every Single Joggle shall be charged	10 Cents
For every running Joggle and Grove per foot running	10 Cents
For every double dovetail Joggled and fitting	$1.60

And it is hereby agreed by and between both parties to this agreement that So much of the description of the Building of the Bank as relates to the marble work, and to the quality of the marble, and Such drawings as describe or represent any part of the marble work and are contained in a certain Book entitled "Designs for the Bank of Pennsylvania at Philadelphia by Benjamin Henry Latrobe Boneval—Richmond 1798," and to which the Contractors and the Said Benjamin Henry Latrobe Boneval have Set their hands, are to all intents and purposes part of this agreement, and of equal force and validity.

And for the true and faithful performance of all and Singular the convenants herein before particularly recited the Subscribers hereunto bind themselves jointly and Severally their and each of their Heirs, Executors and Administrators in the penal Sum of Twenty Thousand Dollars.

Signed by

> (James Traquair)
> (John Miller)
> (John Bennett)
> (John Ross)
> (Robert Patterson)

Sealed and delivered in the presence of
(Thomas Annesley)[8]
(Joseph A. Bedford)[9]
> attest (Jonathan Smith Cashier)[10]

Copy: Miscellaneous Bank Papers, Historical Society of Pennsylvania (microfiche add.). 135

1. The Bank of Pennsylvania, incorporated in 1793, had twenty-five directors including the president; three directors were appointed annually by the state senate, three by the state house of representatives, and the remainder by the stockholders. James Mease, *The Picture of Philadelphia, Giving An Account of Its Origin, Increase and Improvements in Arts, Sciences, Manufactures, Commerce and Revenue* (Philadelphia, 1811), pp. 105–06.

2. James Traquair (1756–1811), "a Capitel stonecutter" and sculptor, emigrated to Philadelphia from Scotland in 1784 and set up a stonecutting yard with John Miller in 1788. Traquair did the marblework on BHL's Centre Square Engine House of the Philadelphia Waterworks. He and his son, Adam, made marble mantels, many of which BHL obtained later for the U.S. Capitol and the President's House. In 1799 Traquair's cutting yard was at Tenth and Market streets, as was the establishment of Miller & Bennet. John Bennet also provided BHL with marblework for the Capitol. BHL to Bennet, 19 July 1807, LB (58/A3); BHL, *Engineering Drawings*, p. 30; Saul K. Padover, ed., *Thomas Jefferson and the National Capital, 1783–1818* (Washington, D.C., 1946), pp. 163–64; Hamlin, *Latrobe*, pp. 134–35; *PMHB* 54 (1930):184, 58 (1934):18.

3. John Ross (1729–1800), Scottish merchant, immigrated to America before the Revolution and was a strong financial supporter of the American cause. He carried on an extensive overseas trade and was well respected in Philadelphia mercantile circles. *PMHB* 23 (1899):77–85.

Dr. Robert Patterson (1743–1824), mathematics professor at the University of Pennsylvania (1779–1814), was a member of the Select Council of Philadelphia and became its president in 1799. In 1805 President Jefferson appointed him director of the mint. Patterson was a member of the American Philosophical Society and was elected its president in 1819.

4. BHL negotiated the contract on behalf of the bank. Some years later he wrote that after an earlier contract had fallen through, he "had to begin anew with Mr. Traquair, Miller and Bennet, with whom I at last made a contract for the *prices* of the work in Marble, all the rest of the Work being done by the day." BHL to the President and Directors of the Bank of Pennsylvania, 4 Sept. 1809, in BHL, *Correspondence*, 2.

5. Obsolete form of beetle.

6. Louis: variant form of lewis.

7. This document, "Designs for the Bank of Pennsylvania at Philadelphia by Benjamin Henry Latrobe Boneval—Richmond 1798," is now lost.

8. Philadelphia merchant.

9. In 1801 Bedford was a porter to the Bank of Pennsylvania.

10. Jonathan Smith remained cashier at the Bank of Pennsylvania until 1816 when he left to become cashier at the Bank of the United States.

TO HENRY BANKS

[Philadelphia, February 1799]

My dear Sir,

I am very sorry that your letter arrived when I have several people with me on Bank business. I had already determined although I did not

136 know how to till yours, to draw some money from the Bank in order to

absolve part of the obligations I owe to you, and I mean this very evening to have called upon Mrs. Banks in order to make her my Messenger, and spare me what I ought to say. You will excuse my saying more at present. I have sent you within a dollar all I have by me. You shall have more as fast as I can manage it. Your much obliged srvt.

B. H. Latrobe

ALS: Henry Banks Papers, Virginia Historical Society (161/E9). Addressed to Banks in Philadelphia. Dated from endorsement, presumably in Banks's hand.

STATEMENT CONCERNING PHILADELPHIA WATERWORKS AND AN ACCOUNT OF STEAM ENGINES

An Answer to the Joint Committee of the Select and Common Councils of Philadelphia, on the Subject of a Plan for Supplying the City with Water, &c.

Philadelphia, March 2d, 1799.

Gentlemen,

In compliance with your desire—"that I should state in as concise and clear a manner as possible, the detail of the plan proposed to be executed for supplying the city of Philadelphia with pure and whole-some water," which has been adopted by the councils, "and also, the progress which has been made towards carrying the same into effect"—I now submit to you the following statement:

It is proposed that a short canal shall be cut from the Schuylkill, near the middle ferry, to terminate at the foot of the bank at the end of Chesnut-street, upon which stands an old redoubt. This canal is to be deeper than the lowest water-mark, and may be so furnished with gates, as to receive only the water of the ebb. When the canal arrives at the foot of the hill, it will be continued through a short tunnel into a well, sunk in the old fort, of about eight feet diameter. Over this well will stand the first engine-house. From the engine-house along Chesnut-street and Broad-street, a brick tunnel of considerable dimension, and lying at least

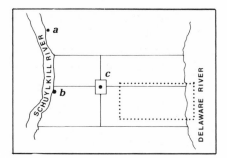

a. Sedgeley
b. Schuylkill Engine House and basin for waterworks
c. Centre Square Engine House for waterworks
d. Alterations to University of Pennsylvania (President's House)
e. Medical Hall, University of Pennsylvania
f. Markoe house and proposed "neighbors"
g. Burd house (attributed)
h. Goodwin house
i. Base projected for statue of William Penn, Pennsylvania Hospital
j. Masonic Temple project; initial Waln house project

k. Sansom's row
l. Meany house
m. Waln house
n. Harrison stable
o. Chestnut Street Theatre
p. Second Bank of the United States project
q. Bank of Philadelphia
r. Washington Hall project
s. Alterations to Bingham mansion
t. Bank of Pennsylvania
u. Philadelphia Exchange project
v. Insurance Company of the State of Pennsylvania

Map 2. BHL's buildings and unexecuted projects in Philadelphia, 1798–1818.

three feet below the surface, will convey the water pumped into it by the engine, into Centre-square. The steam engine will be of sufficient power to supply in twenty-four hours, whenever required, three million of gallons. Supposing that 10,000 houses are to be supplied,[1] the daily demand, in the winter months, cannot often exceed 300,000 gallons. In rainy weather, when the river may be turbid, the demand will also be confined to domestic consumption, and cannot easily exceed the same quantity. The tunnel will contain about 8,000,000 gallons, being a supply for a much greater length of time than any rain can, in common seasons, be expected to continue. In the tunnel the water will not only become cool, but should it have been pumped up in a turbid state, which will scarcely ever be necessary, it will deposit its sediment.

An engine of a power twice as great as that proposed, might not only have pumped up the water from the Schuylkill, but have forced it into the reservoir in Centre-square, and thus have rendered a second engine unnecessary. No immediate saving would have been effected by this means; such an engine could not have been constructed in America, but might have been imported. Expense might have been saved during the time of the greatest supplies, as the power of an engine increases in a greater ratio than its consumption of fuel. But the advantage of the tunnel, considered in the point of view stated above, and the avoiding of those risks to which pipes are liable, far outweigh any trifling saving which could thus have been made.

In Centre-square another engine is to be erected, which, raising the water to an elevated reservoir, will, from thence, distribute it in wooden pipes over the whole city and suburbs. Every citizen will have the choice of supplying his family, either at the public plugs, or by leading the water through private pipes to any part of his house, at an easy water rent. There are few houses in Philadelphia, to the highest apartments of which it could not be conducted, and during the day it may run a constant stream. The subscribers to the proposed loan, will, on the terms offered by the corporation, have the advantage of receiving it for three years free of rent.[2]

At every square, opposite to the public alleys, a fire plug will be placed. By this an inexhaustible quantity of water will be supplied to the fire engines, in cases of fire; and as the method used in London may be adopted, the engines will be filled by means of leathern hose or pipes, and the citizens, being relieved from the fatiguing duty of handing the buckets, will be at liberty to give the most active assistance to the preservation of the lives and property of the sufferers.

Considerable progress has been already made towards the completion of this plan. The steam engines are already ordered, and some progress is made in their construction: and although a great variety of obstacles have occurred, and some delay has thereby been occasioned, there is still remaining a very reasonable hope that they will be completed by the time originally contemplated.[3] The expense, at which these engines are contracted for, does not exceed the estimate which has been stated to the committee. One of the principal persons engaged in constructing them, was the agent of Messrs. Bolton & Watt in Holland, where he put up a very large engine for the purpose of draining a lake, the success of which was complete.[4] Under his management, and that of several other very skillful workmen, an excellent engine has already been constructed in this country; and any gentleman, to whom it may be convenient to call at Mr. Rooseveldt's works, on Second River, near Newark, in the Jerseys, may convince himself how well founded are the expectations that I have entertained on this subject. Very accurate information respecting the maintenance of the engines is before you, and it is evident from thence that their annual expense will not, at an average of their greatest and smallest supply, very materially exceed the annual expense of the pumps, with which I have been furnished.

Several other conditional contracts have been entered into, all of which are for less sums than the estimate submitted to you, and especially in the very important article of distribution, conditional agreements have been made for logs, and boring, which authorize me to believe that the estimate of half a dollar per foot will cover every expense contemplated under it. Thus far the business has proceeded, and I think a reasonable hope may now be entertained, that no common obstacles can prevent an early completion of the work under your direction.

The many attempts which have been made in this country to adapt steam engines to the navigation of boats against the stream, and which have miscarried,[5] have occasioned a prejudice against them, which does not exist in Europe, where also every attempt to apply them to the same purpose has failed, but where, in every other respect, they have completely succeeded.

Another prejudice, respecting the repairs of steam engines, prevails, which I am anxious to remove. It is necessary that the joints of the machine should be frequently oiled; and the piston of an engine in constant work, requires *packing*, or refurnishing with tow, perhaps once a week—this is the work of an hour, and is done by the man who attends the fire. Other repairs are trifling, and arise in general from the bad original construction of some detailed part of the work. But *once* in ten years it is necessary to furnish the engine with new valves. The valves are the only part of an engine *liable*, from their necessary construction, to injury. The contractor for the city engines estimates, in this contract, the renewal of this part of the engine at 500 dollars, which appears to me to be a reasonable charge. As to the annual repairs, they form the least considerable item in the contract for maintenance.

Unwilling to recommend to you any scheme which has not been ascertained, and the success of which might be therefore precarious, I subjoin the following account of engines which are applied to the use of supplying large cities in Europe with water. As many of our fellow-citizens have been in Europe, its authenticity may be easily verified; and, though I state it from memory, I believe there is no reason to doubt its perfect correctness.

I am, with great respect, Yours, faithfully,

B. Henry Latrobe, Engineer.

Account of Steam Engines, &c.

Philadelphia, March 2d, 1799.

The cities of London and Westminster are in part supplied with water by the following engines.

I. Chelsea water-works: Two engines. The water is received from the Thames at high-water, into several basons and canals, through flood-gates which shut when the tide falls, and prevent its return. The water supplies the lower parts of Westminster, and is in part forced up into Hydepark by the engines. A smaller engine forces it still higher than the park reservoir. This reservoir and the smaller engine supply the extreme north-western part of the town.[6]

II. Hungerford water-works. A large, but badly constructed, atmospheric engine, near the Adelphi, raises the water to the top of a high tower, from whence it supplies a considerable part of the town about the Strand.

III. The new River-head, is sufficiently elevated to supply a very extensive portion of the cities, but not sufficiently for some parts about

Islington and Mary-le-bone. A large quantity is therefore raised by an engine near Sadler's wells, into an elevated reservoir, from whence it is then distributed. In the year 1794, a cast iron main had been nearly completed, by which the New River water was to be conveyed across a very deep valley, falling, and again rising, with the ground. A steam-engine was to be erected at the end of Tottenhamcourt road to raise the supply to an elevated reservoir. By this measure near a million feet of wooden pipe will be saved.

IV. Stratford le Bow. A very large engine forces the water of the river Lee into an elevated reservoir, from whence many eastern parts of the town are supplied.

V. Wapping near Shadwell: This is the largest engine in London, and receives its waters from the Thames.

VI. Lambeth Marsh on the south side of the Thames, takes also its water from the river.

In Southwark there are more engines than one. My memory does not retain their exact situations. Mr. Whitebread's brewery, Mr. Thrale's, Mr. Dickinson's, and Mr. Sellon's, and many others, have all engines of considerable power, which pump the liquor, and do all the other work.[7]

For the purposes of manufactories, &c. their number is also very great.

The city of Worcester is entirely supplied with water by a very excellent engine. There are many other cities in England of which I know that they are in the whole, or in part, supplied with water by steam engines; but as I cannot detail the extent of their power or effect, I omit to mention them.

Every one who has been at Paris, knows that water was carried about in the streets by innumerable water-porters, whose cry had something remarkable in it, to the ear of a foreigner. This was very inconvenient, and (I believe in the year 1784 or 1785) a very extraordinary steam engine was erected in Paris, for the purpose of raising and conveying the water by means of pipes, to different parts of the city. It was constructed in England, by Mr. Wilkinson, and was (if I am not mistaken) the largest double engine which, till then, had been made. Its cylinder is, I believe, 4 feet, 2 inches in diameter. It was in operation in the year 1788, and I have good authority for asserting, that lately the shares in this concern were sold at an advance of 600 per cent. upon their original cost.[8] Soon after the invention, steam engines were justly considered as dangerous, man had not yet learned to controul the immense power of steam, and now and then they did a little mischief. A steam engine is, at present, as tame and innocent as a clock.

B. H. Latrobe, Engineer

Printed Copy (161/F8).

1. BHL probably refers to the number of houses that would ultimately be served. About 1800 there were probably only about 6,600 dwelling houses in the city proper, and perhaps another 4,600 in the surrounding parts of Philadelphia County. James Mease, *The Picture of Philadelphia* (Philadelphia, 1811), pp. 31–34; John K. Alexander, "The Philadelphia Numbers Game: An Analysis of Philadelphia's Eighteenth-Century Population," *PMHB* 98 (1974):323.

2. On 7 February 1799 the Philadelphia city councils authorized the raising of a 6 percent loan of $150,000 in shares of $100 each. More than six hundred shares were subscribed by the end of the month, but few more were forthcoming and installment payments were tardy. The resulting financial crisis in the summer of 1799 was relieved by the imposition of a special tax. *Report to the Select and Common Councils, on the Progress and State of the Water Works, on the 24th of November, 1799* (Philadelphia, 1799), pp. 8–9, 16–18.

3. In January 1799, the joint committee sent BHL to Nicholas Roosevelt's Soho Works near Newark, N.J., to assess Roosevelt's capability of manufacturing two steam engines for the waterworks. BHL made a conditional contract with Roosevelt which the councils approved. The engines were expected to be ready in the summer of 1799, but difficulties continually intervened, and the engines were not in place and operable until the winter of 1800–01. Ibid., pp. 10, 24–25; Minutes of the Select Council, 23 Jan., 2 Feb. 1799, Archives of the City and County of Philadelphia; BHL, *Journals*, 3 : 8.

Nicholas J. Roosevelt (1767–1854), inventor and entrepreneur, manufactured steam engines for various enterprises at his Soho Works. In 1811 Roosevelt, in partnership with Robert Fulton, built the *New Orleans*—the first steamboat to descend the Ohio and Mississippi rivers from Pittsburgh to New Orleans. Roosevelt had married BHL's daughter Lydia in November 1808, and she accompanied him on the maiden voyage of the *New Orleans*. BHL was involved in a number of financial schemes with Roosevelt, including a rolling and slitting mill at the Philadelphia Waterworks and the promotion of Roosevelt's New Jersey copper mine. See Morris to BHL, 24 Dec. 1800, below. John H. B. Latrobe, *The First Steamboat Voyage on the Western Waters* (Baltimore, 1871); Hamlin, *Latrobe*, pp. 170–71.

4. James Smallman (died c. 1822) was in the early 1790s a highly regarded employee in the steam engine company of Matthew Boulton (1728–1809) and James Watt (1736–1819) in England. In the fall of 1793 the partners sent him to Mijdrecht, Holland, to erect one of their engines, remarking to the purchaser that he was a "quiet, inoffensive, industrious man who we hope will give you satisfaction, as he has done wherever we have sent him." After successfully completing the installation of that engine in the summer of 1794 Smallman decided to immigrate to the United States. He eventually came into the employ of Nicholas Roosevelt, who in 1793 had formed a company to work an old copper mine in northern New Jersey. The acquisition of Smallman may have been the primary reason why Roosevelt's company turned to steam engine manufacture, first working on an engine for Chancellor Livingston's steamboat (1798), and then two engines for the Philadelphia Waterworks (1799–1800). Smallman was the chief engineer of both projects. Smallman supervised the erection of the waterworks engines in 1800 and subsequently remained in Philadelphia. Until 1805 he was Roosevelt's agent and chief engineer at both the waterworks and the Schuylkill rolling mill. Thereafter he went into business for himself as an engine 143

constructor and consultant. His most successful commission was a steam engine for the Washington Navy Yard, erected in 1810. BHL considered Smallman "the best Engine maker in America." BHL to Andrew Hazlehurst, 19 Oct. 1810, in BHL, *Correspondence*, 2; Boulton and Watt to J. D. Van Liender, 7 Oct. 1793, James Watt, Jr., to Smallman, 16 Aug. 1794, both in Letterbooks, Boulton and Watt Collection, Birmingham Reference Library, Birmingham, England; Jennifer Tann, "Marketing Methods in the International Steam Engine Market: The Case of Boulton and Watt," *Journal of Economic History* 38 (June 1978): 375–76; Pursell, *Steam Engines in America*, pp. 28–31, 42–44; BHL, *Engineering Drawings*, pp. 34–35, 51, 52–54, 214–33.

    5. BHL was referring primarily to the steamboats of John Fitch (1743–98) and James Rumsey (1743–92). Pursell, *Steam Engines in America*, pp. 18–24.

    6. BHL apparently drew heavily on his knowledge of the Chelsea Waterworks, located on the site of what is now Victoria Station, in designing the Philadelphia Waterworks. Similar elements included the use of a tidal river for a water supply, a settling basin with floodgates, and raising the water with two steam engines in series. Hugh Phillips, *The Thames About 1750* (London, 1951), pp. 148–50; H. W. Dickinson, *Water Supply of Greater London* (London, 1954), pp. 56, 68.

    7. These brewers were Samuel Whitebread (1720–96); Henry Thrale (c. 1728–1781), whose wife Hester befriended Dr. Samuel Johnson; Rivers Dickinson, the father-in-law of BHL's brother-in-law John Baker Sellon; and BHL's brother-in-law William Marmaduke Sellon. BHL, *Journals*, 1 : 206–07, 269.

    8. In 1778 Jacques-Constantin Périer founded La Compagnie des Eaux to supply water to Paris, and in 1779 he reached an agreement with Boulton and Watt to build one of their newly patented steam engines for pumping water. John Wilkinson made the cylinder of about 60 inches (1.52 meters) diameter, Boulton and Watt made some other parts, and the remainder of the engine was manufactured at Périer's new foundry at Chaillot along the Seine in Paris. The engine was erected at Chaillot in 1781. Jacques Payen, *Capital et machine à vapeur au XVIIIe siècle: les frères Périer et l'introduction en France de la machine à vapeur de Watt* (Paris, 1969), pp. 32, 107, 112, 122, 123.

TO JOHN MILLER AND HENRY DRINKER

June 5, 1799.

Gentlemen,[1]

I have received your letter of the 5th of June, recommending to me the immediate consideration of the Instrument put into my hands about a week ago, and reproaching me with the delay which has taken place.[2]

In order to prevent further delay, I will in a few words put it in your power, to terminate the business.

In my letters which *you have fairly quoted*,[3] I have made proposals which I will abide by. In these proposals I in no manner whatsoever contract to execute the work for a certain Sum, but demand 5 per Cent on whatever it may cost. In the Contract submitted to me, my Recompence is fixed at a sum certain which may be more or less than 5 per Cent. Most probably less, and I am made the contractor for the work without any chance of making the profit which a contractor ought to have to cover his work, which profits (if any) are shared among many other contractors; and under the penalties of the loss of every compensation, and perhaps of my whole fortune.

The only chance for me would be in a Court of Equity to which it might be submitted to decide, to *whose* fault an excess of estimate ought to be attributed.

The negociations with Roosevelt have taught me to avoid negociation.[4]

I therefore, leave to you the choice between the following proposals.

1st. I will sign a contract, containing terms exactly the same with those contained in my letters, excepting only that I do not insist upon a compensation exceeding the sum of 6,350 dollars,[5] stipulated in the contract offered me, or

2d. I will sign the contract offered me, rather than dispute about it, because I do not think that you would have offered me an instrument for signature, upon which you did not think it your duty to insist, as organs of a body deserving and having my highest respect; and because I cannot believe that the terms contained in that instrument would have been proposed to any person (considered in his official capacity) to whom the fear of pain and penalties were not supposed to be necessary to tie him to his duty, and although this will be the first contract of any kind signed by a man of my profession, and the first instance in which the profession itself has been degraded below that of a Merchant, a Lawyer, or a Physician; to whom property and life are intrusted without any restraint by deeds or other legal fetters, yet, rather than be an actor in scenes like those exhibited in the case of Roosevelt, and rather than devote that time to dispute, which is scarce sufficient to the performance of my duty, I will sign my contract, and should the worst happen, I will trust to the liberality of a Jury,[6] or

3d. I will release you from every engagement with me, and having carried the work to a stage in which it requires only honest management and perseverance in my plans, to insure its success, I will sit down contented with the reputation I have already acquired, and of which no one can rob me; if the arrangements already made are only carried to their end under the Managers and workmen whom I have employed and instructed.

Your expressions of politeness to me are the more flattering, because they are, I am sure, sincere. I am gratefully sensible of the confidence placed in me hitherto; and am more anxious to justify you in having given it to me, than to gain pecuniary emolument in the work under my care. The plain sentiments I have expressed above, are perfectly consistent with the respect I feel for you. I know the responsibility of your situations, and have given a proof of my wish to act, with a view to your duty to the Corporation, as well as my duties to you, in agreeing to enter into a written contract with you, and in modifying my terms of recompence to your wish. The former of these points I have refused to the Directors of the Pennsylvania Bank, and am under no contract but what my letters create. I hope, therefore, that you will still continue to believe me.

Your sincere Friend, and Faithful servant,

B. H. Latrobe.

Printed Copy: *Poulson's American Daily Advertiser* (Philadelphia), 26 Oct. 1801 (163/G13). Enclosed in Henry Drinker to Zachariah Poulson, 24 Oct. 1801, ibid.

1. John Miller was the select council and Drinker the common council representative of the Joint Committee on Supplying the City with Water (the Watering Committee).

Henry Drinker (1757–1822), son of John Drinker (1733–1800) and Susanna Allen, was for many years cashier of the Bank of North America. He should not be confused with Henry Drinker (1734–1809), a prominent Philadelphia merchant. Eliza Cope Harrison, ed., *Philadelphia Merchant: The Diary of Thomas P. Cope, 1800–1851* (South Bend, Ind., 1978), pp. 416, 610.

2. Miller and Drinker to BHL, 5 June 1799, in *Poulson's American Daily Advertiser* (Philadelphia), 26 Oct. 1801 (163/G12).

3. At this point, *Poulson's* editor added the following footnote: "Letter from B. H. L. dated 18th, April, 1799. 'My compensation shall, let the expence be what it will, not exceed 5 per cent. on the estimate of 127,000 dollars, if less be expended, it shall be reduced to 5 per cent. on the actual expences.'"

4. BHL concluded a preliminary contract with Nicholas Roosevelt for the waterworks' engines in January 1799, but Roosevelt and the city of Philadelphia did not sign a final contract for them until 23 May 1799. Minutes of the Select Council, 23 Jan., 2 Feb., 1 Aug. 1799, Archives of the City and County of Philadelphia; *Report of the Committee Appointed by the Common Council to Enquire into the State of the Water Works* (Philadelphia, 1802), pp. 21–36; BHL to Samuel Mifflin, 18 Oct. 1805, LB (45/B5).

5. Five percent of the $127,000 estimate.

6. The contract finally signed by BHL on 20 August 1799 allowed him the fee of $6,350 but stipulated that "for the ultimate success [of the waterworks], he will, and hereby doth hold himself, unless prevented as aforesaid, completely responsible, and bound under the penalty, in case of failure, of forfeiting all emoluments or compensation to which otherwise he would be entitled by these presents, and of refunding unto the said Mayor, Alderman and Citizens, the sums or sum which may have been advanced to him in part payment, of such compensation." The city in turn agreed to release him from the contract if it could not adequately fund the construction of the waterworks.

146   BHL's conflict with the Watering Committee over the terms of his employment re-

flects a fundamental disagreement and perhaps a misunderstanding over the role of a professional engineer. BHL thought of himself as a skilled consultant who provided his mental labor, plans, and competent oversight for a project, and whose integrity was measured by the full exercise of those skills rather than by the technical success of a project, which might be due to other factors. The merchants and businessmen who sat on the Watering Committee, however, were used to establishing personal integrity by the fulfillment of legal obligations, and they could not understand BHL's objection to signing a contract which bound him to erect a waterworks "of a permanent stability, and good and perfect in kind." *Report of the Committee* (1802), pp. 36–44; Miller and Drinker to BHL, 5 June, 8 June 1799, both in *Poulson's American Daily Advertiser*, 26 Oct. 1801 (163/G12, 163/G13); BHL to Constantin Volney, 28 July 1811, in BHL, *Correspondence*, 3.

DESIGN OF THE PENNOCK HOUSE, NORFOLK

Design of the House of Captain William Pennock
in the Main street, Norfolk

[8 September 1799]

This design was made in consequence of a trifling Wager laid against me by Captn. Pennock that I could not design a house which should be approved by Mr. Luke Wheeler; which should have only 41 feet front; which should contain on the Ground floor, 3 Rooms, a principal Staircase, and backstairs; and, which was the essential requisite, the front door of which should be in the Center.[1] I won the Wager, and on leaving Norfolk in March 1795,[2] I gave him the drawing, drawn to a very small scale. He had then no idea of executing the plan. About two months afterwards, I dined at the Eagle tavern in Richmond, where accidentally, Colonel Kelley of Norfolk was also present.[3] In the course of general conversation he related, that some time ago, a frenchman was at Norfolk, who had given Captn. Pennock the most preposterous design, which he had ever seen; that Captn. Pennock had been mad enough to attempt to execute it, and that having carried up part of the Walls he was now perfectly at a stand, as none of the Workmen knew how to proceed. From his description, interlarded with many oaths and imprecations against the Frenchman, I learnt that my own design was meant. I wrote immediately to Norfolk, but before my letter could arrive, I received one from thence, soliciting my advice how to proceed with the work. Soon afterwards I went down to view it, and found that it was in the Hands of Mr. Hill, a ship joiner,[4] and Mr. Gracie an ingenious Scotch joiner, but obstinately wedded to the heavy wooden taste of the last century. It was with much difficulty that I could repair the mischief already done. No part of the plan had been accurately set out. The front was totally altered: all the sash frames, instead of being in reveals, were solid, and placed on the outside, and no two sides of the bow window were equal, or set out from the same center. The Chimnies occupied double the space requisite for them; and in general it was necessary to accommodate the original plan to the blunders committed by the workmen, to combat their prejudices and obstinacy, and to inform their ignorance as well as I could.

These are the reasons, why the house, as it has been executed, is by no means so perfect even as the design, and in respect to its situation, my intentions have been entirely overthrown, by the prejudice in favor of placing the house upon the street, "in order that one may see what is going forward." To accomplish this end, the dust, the noise, and the smells of a sea port have been encountered, and the prospect of the river, and of an open airy expanse of Water sacrificed. It was my intention to have built the house upon a small rise in the Garden, and to have occupied the street by two small, and ornamental stores, which would have yielded a very good rent. On this account, I have arranged all the communications along the entrance front; whereas, had I known how much interest would be taken in what is going forward in the street, I should have given the ladies a good room in front, at least upstairs. Below is the design, as I intended it. The dimensions of the garden are not very correct, but the relative situations are right.

The Walls are built of very bad bricks. The front is faced with red Philadelphia bricks, which being thinner than the others are badly

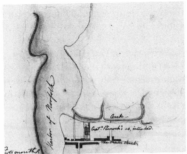

bonded, and the wall has given way, and is bulged about four inches. The woodwork in general is indifferently performed, excepting that executed by Gracie, which includes the staircase. The cornices which I designed, were deemed too plain, and Mr. Ferguson was employed to furnish such as were *tastier,* and *finer.*[5]

After the Design was finished, the front was extended from 41 to 43 feet.

Elevation on the Main Street.

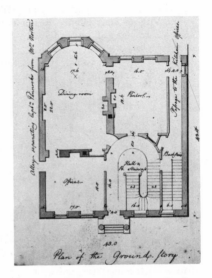

Plan of the Grounds Story

Fig. 5. BHL, Designs for the Pennock house, Norfolk, [March 1796], from "Designs of Buildings Erected or Proposed to be Built in Virginia." Courtesy of the Library of Congress.

AD: Prints and Photographs Division, Library of Congress (307/A3). Date supplied from title page of album cited in n. 1, below.

1. William Pennock (c. 1752–1816), a native of Maryland, became a merchant in Richmond at the end of the Revolution. About 1789 he moved to Norfolk, where he was a merchant and also became a shipowner. BHL, *Journals,* 2 : 550. In addition to the two illustrations shown in figure 5, BHL drew plans of the chamber story and second floor, and a perspective of the stair hall. All these drawings, in an album BHL titled "Designs of

149

Buildings Erected or Proposed to be Built in Virginia, By B. Henry Latrobe Boneval. From 1795 [1796] to 1799" (Prints and Photographs Division, Library of Congress; 307/A1 ff.), are reproduced in BHL, *Architectural Drawings.*

Luke Wheeler (d. 1827), alderman and justice of the peace in Petersburg, Va. (1793), moved to Norfolk, where he served as alderman (1805) and mayor (1806). He was one of the directors and later president of the Dismal Swamp Canal Company. His daughter, Susan, married Stephen Decatur in 1806. BHL designed a house for the Decaturs in Washington, D.C., in 1817. BHL, *Journals,* 2 : 557; *Annual Report of the President and Directors of the Board of Public Works, to the General Assembly of Virginia* (Richmond, Va., 1818), pp. 24–27.

2. I.e., 1796.

3. George Kelly (d. 25 October 1796) served as mayor (1783–84, 1788–89) and common councilman (1780–82, 1791–96) of Norfolk. A land- and slaveowner, Kelly held stock in the Dismal Swamp Canal Company. *Norfolk Herald,* 27 Oct. 1796; Norfolk Borough Hustings and Corporation Court Will Book, No. 1, 1784–1800, folios 138–40, microfilm, Virginia State Library, Richmond; Brent Tarter, ed., *The Order Book and Related Papers of the Borough of Norfolk, Virginia, 1736–1798* (Richmond, Va., 1979), pp. 203, 213–20, 264–77, 296, 381.

4. Probably Thomas Hill, Norfolk carpenter.

5. Finley Ferguson, Norfolk plasterer.

TO ROBERT STEWART

Philadelphia, October 29th, 1799.

Sir,[1]

As far as it is possible to comply with your wish, that I should give you some idea of the probable expence of supplying the city of Baltimore with water from Jones's falls, taking it from some part of the tail race of the last mill above the city—I will with pleasure attempt it. From my general knowledge of the situation of Baltimore from several visits to that city, I believe *that* part of Jones's falls which runs behind the courthouse, would be the most convenient spot from whence to raise the water. It would be well to throw it up to the height of about 80 or 90 feet, so as to command with a strong head, not only all that part of the city which is already built, but such situations as may be built upon in future, and which lie higher up the sloping ground, ascending, if I recollect right, in every direction from the water. A powerful head is also necessary to ensure a quick passage of the water to the most distant parts of the city, as Fell's Point, &c. And indeed the difference of expence, either at first or annually, in the machinery which may be employed to elevate the water to a height of 50 or of 80 feet, though considerable, will bear no proportion to the advantages to be obtained by being able to command the supply in the most effectual and redundant manner. My objections to water-wheels, or any machinery depending only upon the combination of mechanical powers, are detailed in the pamphlets published by the corporation of Philadelphia, upon the subject of watering this city. The effect of frost in winter, and the perpetual destruction of wet wood work by the rot, are of themselves decidedly against water wheels: but their total deficiency in power to throw up a sufficiency of water in proportion to their bulk and unwieldiness, for all the purposes of such a city, is insuperable.

I must therefore recommend, as I have done here, the erection of a steam engine; a machine, powerful to an almost incredible degree—the increased power of which is in an immense proportion to its increase of bulk, which is not liable to be affected by weather, by freshes, or frost, of which the repairs are very inconsiderable, and the maintenance can be accurately calculated; and which by being put into a strong and fireproof building, may be secured against every accident arising from the usual course of nature. Such an engine can be constructed in this country, as well as in England, and with considerable improvements. A specimen may be seen at Soho, near Newark, and I hope in a few months to exhibit its effects in this city, upon a very large scale.[2]

For the distribution of the water, the best pipes are those of white oak. To pine pipes, two objections may be made, which I think more than counterbalance their cheapness, straightness and durability—they affect for many months, and in so large a distribution, perhaps for years, the taste of the water; and they are, from the straightness of their grain, liable to split and burst easily. Pipes of potter's ware or iron, are inadmissible, because they do not admit of small side pipes for the supply of private houses. Those of lead are poisonous when of such extent, as to detain the water long in them.

Taking for granted, then, that a steam engine be built on Jones's falls, to throw up the water to the height of, say 80 feet, and to supply to the city from three to four millions gallons of water a day, a quantity equal to any possible wants for culinary uses, washing the streets, extinguishing fires or supplying ships, the estimate would stand nearly thus:

151

	Dollars.
Purchase of ground, &c. say	10,000
Steam engine, put up complete,	25,000
Engine house, reservoir, forcing main, &c.	25,000
100,000 feet of white oak pipe of distribution, (which I think will be sufficient for Baltimore and Fell's Point for some years to come) at 50 cents per foot, including stop cocks, mud cocks, hydrants or street cocks, for public distribution, supply of fire engine, &c.	50,000
Incidental expences,	20,000
	130,000
The interest of which sum, at 6 per cent, amounts to an annual expence of	7,800
Annual maintenance of steam engine in fuel and attendance,	6,000
Street expences and salaries of turn cocks,	1,500
	15,300

Against this must be set, not a *speculative income*, but an annual revenue, which will be as certain as the efficiency of the works, and which I will set down as low as possible.

Annual water rent from 3000 dwelling houses, at eight dollars per annum. N.B. This rent arises from such houses, who by small leaden pipes, taken from the great main, lead the water into the kitchens or any other part of their buildings. The bore of all such pipes is determined by a brass ferule furnished by the corporation, measuring not more than three fourths of an inch. All supplies above this measure must be paid extra.	24,000
Extra supplies to brewers, distillers, stables, and a great variety of manufacturers, equal to at least 1000 pipes, at 8 dollars	8,000
Supply of shipping, at least	5,000
	37,000

It will be evident to you, that this annual income cannot, as stated, be exaggerated. Both the estimate of expence and of revenue, are laid
152 down under every disadvantage of want of accurate information and of

time. The former, however, may be tolerably depended on, excepting as to the first and last article, and unless there are difficulties in the way, such as I cannot imagine to myself. Such as they are, I hope you will receive them as proofs of my respect, and of my wish to give you every possible assistance in your public spirited endeavors.

I am, With true respect, Your's faithfully,

B. H. Latrobe,
Engineer to the city of Philadelphia.

P.S. On reconsidering what I have written, I think I may safely vouch for the first cost and annual expence of the engine. As to the engine house, it may be made an ornament to the city, and its expence may be thereby increased—but 25,000 dollars will build a *sufficient one.*

B. H. L.[3]

Printed Copy: *Federal Gazette* (Baltimore), 21 Feb. 1801 (162/C4).

1. This is the first evidence of BHL's role in the establishment of the Baltimore Waterworks. Essentially he provided here free consultation, based upon his Philadelphia experience, presumably in the hope that he would become the project engineer. Baltimore began seriously considering a waterworks late in 1798 (about the same time as Philadelphia) and made an attempt to pipe local spring water into the city during the succeeding months. The attempt proved abortive, however, for lack of funds and proper legal authority. Thus, concerned Baltimore citizens were looking to the accomplishments in Philadelphia.

Robert Stewart (c. 1746–1826), a native of Scotland, was a Baltimore stonecutter who became prominent in the city's affairs. He was on the First Branch of the City Council (1798–1801 and 1804) and he represented the city in the Maryland House of Delegates from 1806 to 1808. He owned an acre of land on an island in Aquia Creek from which BHL later procured stone for the U.S. Capitol. BHL to Thomas Jefferson, 15 Jan. 1804, Jefferson Papers (171/B1); Dielman-Hayward File, MdHS; J. Thomas Scharf, *History of Baltimore City and County* (Baltimore, 1881), pp. 187, 194.

2. At this point the editor noted: "Should the information be desirable, Mr. Latrobe can now answer every question as to its superiority and effect in Philadelphia, the water works of that city being now in operation."

3. After several years of discussion and debate, the City Council in February 1803 appointed a committee (including Stewart) to look into the water problem. Subsequently BHL received an inquiry from Robert Goodloe Harper, a promoter of the waterworks, and Edward J. Coale wrote to Thomas Pym Cope for copies of the newspapers that carried the extensive Cope-Latrobe debate over the Philadelphia Waterworks in 1801. The committee reported in February 1804 in favor of the formation of a private water company. On 20 April 1804 a Baltimore newspaper published a "Sketch of a Plan for supplying the city of Baltimore, in every part of it, with an abundance of Good Water" which relied heavily on the example of the Philadelphia Waterworks. A citizens meeting called the same

day appointed a committee (including Harper) to look into the feasibility of a waterworks company, and in the next month the Baltimore Water Company was formed. Although the company chose to employ water power rather than the steam engine which BHL proposed, it did use Jones Falls as the source of water, and the water was pumped up to a central reservoir as he suggested. John Davis, who was BHL's clerk of the works in Philadelphia, designed the Baltimore Waterworks in the fall of 1804 and became president of the company the next year. In 1816 Davis was succeeded by Robert Mills, one of BHL's pupils. BHL to Harper, 28 Mar., 15 May 1803, below; Coale to Cope, 12 May 1803, Cope Collection, Haverford College, Haverford, Pa.; *Federal Gazette* (Baltimore), 20 Apr., 27 Apr., 24 May 1804; Nelson M. Blake, *Water for the Cities* (Syracuse, N.Y., 1956), pp. 69–75; "Autobiography of John Davis, 1770–1864," *Maryland Historical Magazine* 30 (1935): 15–17, 23–24; H. M. Pierce Gallagher, *Robert Mills: Architect of the Washington Monument* (New York, 1935), p. 159.

A DRAWING AND DESCRIPTION OF THE BAY ALEWIFE AND THE FISH LOUSE

Philadelphia, December 18th, 1799.

To Thomas P. Smith, one of the Secretaries
of the American Philosophical Society.[1]

Sir,

I beg leave, through your means, to communicate to the American Philosophical Society, an account of an insect, whose mode of habitation, at least during some part of his life, has appeared to me one of the most singular, not to say whimsical, that can be conceived.

In the month of March 1797, illness confined me for several days, at the house of a friend on York river in Virginia, during his absence.[2] My inability to move further than to the shore of the river, gave me leisure to examine carefully, and in more than an hundred instances, the fact I am going to mention.

Among the fish that at this early season of the year resort to the waters of York river, the alewife or oldwife, called the *bay-alewife* (*clupea nondescripta*) arrives in very considerable shoals, and in some seasons their number is almost incredible. They are fully of the size of a large herring, and are principally distinguished from the herring, by a *bay* or red spot above the gill-fin.[3] (see the drawing) They are, when caught from March to May, full-roed and fat, and are at least as good a fish for the table as the herring.

In this season, each of these alewives carries in her mouth an insect, 154 about two inches long, hanging with its back downwards, and firmly

Plate 1.

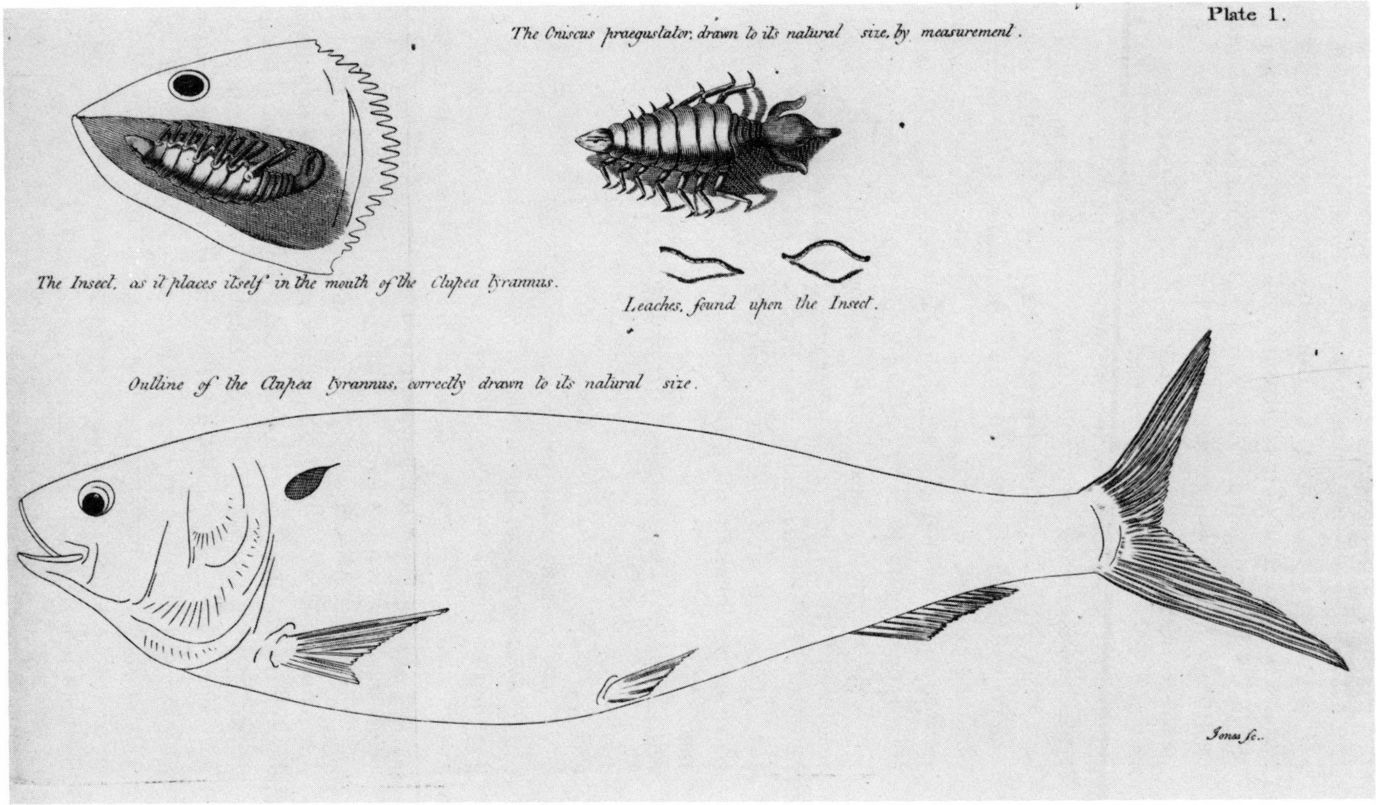

The Oniscus persequutator, drawn to its natural size, by measurement.

The Insect, as it places itself in the mouth of the Clupea tyrannus.

Leeches, found upon the Insect.

Outline of the Clupea tyrannus, correctly drawn to its natural size.

Jones Sc.

holding itself by its 14 legs to the palate. The fishermen call this insect *the louse*. It is with difficulty that it can be separated, and perhaps never without injury to the jaws of the fish. The fishermen therefore consider the insect as essential to the life of the fish; for when it is taken out, and the fish is thrown again into the water, he is incapable of swimming, and soon dies. I endeavoured in numerous instances to preserve both the insect and the fish from injury, but was always obliged either to destroy the one, or to injure the other. I have sometimes succeeded in taking out the insect in a brisk and lively state. As soon as he was set free from my grasp, he immediately scrambled nimbly back into the mouth of the fish, and resumed his position. In every instance he was disgustingly corpulent, and unpleasant to handle; and it seemed, that whether he have obtained his post, by force, or by favor, whether he be a mere traveller, or a constant resident, or what else may be his business where he is found; he certainly has a *fat* place of it, and fares sumptuously every day.

The drawings annexed to this account were made from the live insect, and from the fish out of whose mouth he was taken. I had no books to refer to, then; but examining the *Systema Naturæ* of Linnæus, I was surprized to find so exact a description of the insect as follows (see Salvii *editio*, Holmiæ 1763. p. 1060. also Trattner's Vienna edition, same page).[4]

"*Insect. apt.* ONISCUS, PEDES XIV.
Antennæ setaceæ
Corpus ovale.
O. Physodes, abdomine subtus nudo, caudâ ovatâ.
Habitat in pelago; corpus præter caput, et caudam ultimam, ex septem segmentis trunci, et quinque caudæ. Antennæ utrinque duo, breves. Caudæ folium terminale omnino ovatum; ad latera utrinque subtus auctum duobus petiolis diphyllis, foliolis lanceolatis, obtusis, caudâ brevioribus. Caudæ articuli subtus obtecti numerosis vesiculis longitudine caudæ."[5]

From the particularity with which the *oniscus physodes* is described by Linnæus, it is evident that he had the insect before him, or a description by an attentive observer. It appears also from the "*Habitat in pelago,*" that the *O. physodes,* if this be the insect, is found detached from his conductor. There are a few points in which the *O. physodes* differs from my insect. I did not observe the antennæ, perhaps for want of sufficient attention, or of a microscope. The petioli of the tail were not, to appearance, *two-leaved,* and I am certain that the segments of the tail, and the tail itself, were without the *vesiculi longitudine caudæ.*

156   There are many circumstances, to ascertain which is essential to the

natural history of this insect. The fish whose mouth he inhabits comes, about the same time with the chad,[6] into the rivers of Virginia from the ocean, and continues to travel upwards from the beginning of March, to the middle of May; as long as they are caught upon their passage up the river, they are found fat and full of roe. Every fish which I saw had the *oniscus* in his mouth; and I was assured, not only by the more ignorant fishermen, but by a very intelligent man who came down now and then to divert himself with fishing, that, in 40 years observation, he had never seen a bay alewife without the louse. The chad begin to return from the fresh water lean and *shotten,* about the end of May and beginning of June, and continue descending during the remaining summer months. No one attempts then to catch them, for they are unfit for the table. Whether the bay alewife returns with the chad, I could not learn, but it is certain that after June it is not thought worth the trouble to catch them. No one could tell me *positively* whether the *oniscus* still continues with them, but it was the opinion of my informant, that, like every other parasite, he deserts his protector in his reduced state, for he could not *recollect* that he had ever seen him in the mouth of those accidentally caught in the seine in July or August.

I consider, therefore, the natural history of the *oniscus,* which I now communicate, as very imperfect; and it were to be wished that some lover of natural science would follow up the enquiry, by endeavoring to ascertain whether he continue with, or quit the fish before his return to the ocean, and also whether he be the *oniscus physodes* of Linnæus, *qui habitat in pelago.*

Should he be an insect hitherto undescribed, I think he might be very aptly named *oniscus prægustator.*[7]

The bay alewife is not accurately described in any ichthyological work which I have seen; nor can I from my drawings, which were made with a very weak hand, venture a description. From his having a regular *prægustator,* I would suggest that he ought to be named *clupea tyrannus.*[8]

The *oniscus* resembles the minion of a tyrant in other respects, for he is not without those who *suck* him. Many of those which I caught had two or three leaches on their bodies, adhering so closely, that their removal cost them their heads. Most of the marine *onisci* appear to be troublesome to some one or other fish. The *oniscus ceti* is well known as the plague of whales, and many of the rest are mentioned in Linnæus and Gmelin,[9] as *pestes piscium.*

Benjn. Henry Latrobe, F.A.P.S.   157

P.S. A gentleman well skilled in entomology informs me that he believes, that in Block's *History of Fishes,* a work not to be had in Philadelphia, this *oniscus* is mentioned.[10] But, from a late examination of Gmelin and Fabricius,[11] I am convinced that the *oniscus prægustator* is a species not hitherto accurately described—Gmelin had probably seen the Linnæan insect, having changed the *antennæ utrinque duo,* to *antennis quaternis,* and left out most of the long description given by Linnæus. Neither he, Linnæus nor Fabricius mention the circumstance of habitation in the mouth of the fish, and the industrious and copious Fabricius, who having changed the names of the genera, calls him *cymothoa physodes,* copies the description of Gmelin, excepting the mention of the 4 antennæ, which in his arrangement form a character of the genus.

Printed Copy: "A Drawing and Description of the *Clupea Tyrannus* and *Oniscus Praegustator,*" American Philosophical Society, *Transactions* 5 (1802):77–81 (162/D2). Read before the society on 7 February 1800. Referred to Benjamin Smith Barton, who recommended publication on 17 February 1800. The society approved on 21 February 1800.

1. Thomas Peters Smith (c. 1776–1802), chemist and mineralogist, was a student of Robert Patterson and Benjamin Smith Barton. He was elected to the American Philosophical Society on 19 July 1799, the same day as BHL. The two men made chemical analyses of Maryland marble before Smith left for a European tour in 1800; he died on the return voyage. For BHL's comments on Smith and his humor, see BHL, *Journals,* 3 : 14–16. Wyndham Miles, "Thomas Peters Smith: A Typical Early American Chemist," *Journal of Chemical Education* 30 (1953):184–88.
    2. BHL stayed at Henry Banks's estate, Airy Plain, in New Kent County on the York River opposite West Point.
    3. The adult alewife may reach 15 inches. In fresh specimens, overlaying silver pigment often masks the spot.
    4. The Salvius, or twelfth edition, was published in Stockholm in 3 volumes (1766–68). The Vienna edition, edited by Johann Thomas von Trattner, was published in two volumes in 1767–70.
    5. Trans.: Wingless insects. Oniscus, fourteen feet.
Antennae bristling
Body ovate.
Oniscus physodes, with abdomen bare below, tail ovate.
    Inhabits the sea; the body apart from the head and apex [has] seven trunk [segments] and five tail segments. On each side [of the head] are two short antennae. The apex of the tail [is] completely ovate; with two minute bifoliate feet [protruding from] underneath [the terminal plate] on each side, [and armed] with lanceolate laminae, obtuse, and shorter than the tail. For their [entire] length, the tail segments [are] covered underneath with numerous vesicles.
    6. For BHL's earlier remarks on the shad migration, see BHL, *Journals,* 1 : 94–95.
    7. *Praegustator* means "the taster." This parasitic isopod, a crustacean, not an insect, is now known as *Olencira praegustator* (Latrobe). The complete life cycle of the alewife is not known, but the isopod is thought to stay in the mouth until it dies.
    8. BHL's specific name, *tyrannus,* is now used for a related species, the menhaden,

Alosa tyrannus. The alewife is now *Alosa pseudoharengus,* although efforts are currently underway to restore BHL's name to the alewife.

9. Johann Friedrich Gmelin (1748–1804) edited the thirteenth (posthumous) edition of Linnaeus's *Systema Naturæ,* published in Leipzig in 3 volumes (1788–93).

10. Marcus Eliéser Bloch, *Ichtyologie, Ou Histoire Naturelle, Générale et Particulière des Poissons* (Berlin, 1785–97).

11. Johann Christian Fabricius (1745–1808), a student of Linnaeus, was one of the greatest early entomologists.

The Washington Monument

EDITORIAL NOTE

Within two weeks of the death of George Washington on 14 December 1799, Congress resolved to place a marble monument in the U.S. Capitol to commemorate the military and political events of the president's life and, if possible, to bury him beneath this monument. A committee was appointed, chaired by Congressman John Marshall and including Henry Lee, to consider the measures for commemorating Washington. William Thornton and Latrobe both made recommendations for a Washington monument. Latrobe designed a pyramidal monument, which he justified in his letters to Lee and Congressman Robert Goodloe Harper, printed below.[1] Marshall's committee favored Latrobe's design for a time, but, on 8 May, Henry Lee, who had succeeded Marshall as chairman, recommended resolutions to construct a marble monument in the Capitol and to erect an equestrian statue in front of the Capitol. Meanwhile, Latrobe sought the assistance of Harper (see letter of post 24 April 1800, printed below), who introduced the pyramidal design into the discussion on 8 May. The House of Representatives approved it on 10 May, but the bill died in the Senate two days later.[2]

The Washington Monument proposal was renewed in December 1800 in the following session of Congress. A new design by the British architect George Dance, the younger, however, won the approval of the House. The bill died in the Senate in March 1801, though, and nearly half a century passed before a national monument to Washington was begun in the nation's capital.[3]

1. Five drawings of BHL's proposed monument survive in the Prints and Photographs Division, Library of Congress (312/A1, 312/B5) and in PBHL (312/A7, 312/B1, 312/B3), reproduced in BHL, *Architectural Drawings.*

2. *Annals of Congress,* 6th Cong., 1st sess., pp. 178–79, 181, 203–06, 207–09, 708, 711–12.

3. Ibid., 6th Cong., 2d sess., 732, 733, 735, 736, 737, 738, 758, 792, 796, 799–804, 817–20, 837–38, 855–65, 874–75, 1003, 1071–72. See also BHL, *Architectural Drawings.*

For BHL's revived and revised pyramid design as a mausoleum for the victims of the Richmond Theater fire of 1811, also unexecuted, see BHL to John Wickham, 21 Jan. 1812, in BHL, *Correspondence,* 3; and BHL, *Architectural Drawings.*

TO ROBERT GOODLOE HARPER

[post 24 April 1800]

Dear Sir[1]

As the Committee have reversed the report in favor of the Mausoleum, during the absence of General Marshall, I take the liberty of referring you to my letter to General Lee,[2] accompanying the Plan of which I enclose a Copy, for general arguments in its favor and if you could get hold of Trumbull's letter it would be very serviceable perhaps.[3]

A very striking proof of the folly of expecting that any statue will be always respected exists in Williamsburg, where Lord Botetourts statue which had remained untouched during the whole war, was mutilated, and decapitated by the young collegians, in the first frenzy of French revolutionary maxims, *because it was the statue of a* **Lord.**[4] The statue now graces Mrs. Hunt's Garden in a very mutilated state. The pedestal has these inscriptions which remained the libel of the country and age, beneath the decapitated statue in 1797.

America behold your friend, who leaving his native country declined the additional honors which were there in store for him, that he might heal your wounds and restore tranquillity and happiness to this extensive continent. With what zeal [and] anxiety he pursued these glorious objects, Virginia **thus** bears her grateful testimony.

On another side

Deeply impressed with the warmest gratitude for his Excellency's the Rt. Honble. Lord Botetourt's prudent and wise administration, that the remembrance of those many public and social virtues which so eminently adorn[ed] his illustrious character **might be transmitted to the latest posterity,** the General Assembly of Virginia, on the 20th of July 1771 resolve[d] with one united Voice to erect this statue to his Lordships memory.

I could furnish you with many other proofs of the perishability of statues, and the immortality of pyramids, from Rome, Westminister Abbey, the cidevant place Louis XV, the cidevant Church St. Genevieve, Egypt, Greece and Italy, and (if Mr. Reed will permit) from South Carolina.[5]

General Washington's statue at Richmond has already lost a spur.[6] We know that even his virtues are hated, by fools and rogues, and unfortunately that sort of animals crawl much about in public buildings. Yours in haste

B. H. Latrobe

ALS: Records of Joint Committees of Congress, RG 128, National Archives (162/E10). Addressed to Harper at the House of Representatives. The bracketed portions of the third and fourth paragraphs are taken from BHL's sketchbook (see BHL, *Journals*, 1 : 88).

1. Robert Goodloe Harper (1765–1825), of South Carolina, served in the American Revolution, graduated from the College of New Jersey (Princeton) in 1785, and served in the South Carolina House of Representatives from 1790 to 1795. Elected as a Republican congressman in 1795, he quickly became a Federalist and served until 1801. After he had lost his reelection bid in 1800, Harper moved to Baltimore, where he married Catherine Carroll, daughter of Charles Carroll of Carrollton. In Baltimore, Harper engaged in a successful law practice and became prominent in civic affairs. He helped organize and was a member of the first board of directors of the Baltimore Exchange Company in 1815. It was through his efforts that BHL secured the commissions for designing the Baltimore Exchange and the Baltimore Library Company, the latter not executed. The Latrobes and Harpers were close friends, and after BHL's death in New Orleans Harper became the family advisor. At his suggestion, MEL returned to Baltimore, where he gave the family assistance and trained BHL's son, John H. B. Latrobe, in the law. Hamlin, *Latrobe*, p. 458.

2. See below. Gen. Henry ("Light-Horse Harry") Lee (1756–1818), father of Robert E. Lee, gained fame during the Revolution for his cavalry attacks on the British. An active Federalist in post-Revolutionary Virginia, Lee served as governor of the commonwealth (1791–94) and congressman (1799–1801). At the Philadelphia memorial service for Washington, Lee eulogized him as "first in war, first in peace and first in the hearts of his countrymen."

3. The letter from painter John Trumbull (1756–1843), then in England, has not been found.

4. Norborne Berkeley (1718–70), Baron de Botetourt, was governor of Virginia from 1768 to 1770. Authorized by the Virginia Assembly in 1771, the Botetourt statue was carved by British sculptor Richard Hayward (1728–1800) and arrived in Virginia in 1773. In 1801 the College of William and Mary moved the statue to its grounds and repaired it. The restored statue, one of the oldest public statues extant in North America, now stands in the college library. For BHL's sketches and further comments on the statue, see BHL, *Journals*, 1 : 87–89. Wayne Craven, *Sculpture in America from the Colonial Period to the Present* (New York, 1968), pp. 49–50.

5. Sen. Jacob Read (1752–1816), of South Carolina, was a Revolutionary War veteran who served in the state legislature (1781–84, 1789–94) and the Continental Congress (1783–85) before his election as a Federalist to the U.S. Senate (1795–1801). He was one of Adams's midnight judges and served on the U.S. district court for South Carolina from 1801 until his death.

6. Jean-Antoine Houdon (1741–1828), French neoclassical sculptor, was commissioned in 1785 to carve a statue of George Washington, authorized by the Virginia legislature the previous year. That year Houdon visited America briefly to make a study for the statue. He completed the work in France by 1791, and the statue was shipped to Virginia in 1796 and installed in the state capitol. Gilbert Chinard, ed., *Houdon in America: A Collection of Documents in the Jefferson Papers in the Library of Congress* (Baltimore, 1930), pp. xiv–xv,

161

xviii–xix, xxi; H. H. Arnason, *The Sculptures of Houdon* (New York, 1975), pp. 72–77, fig. 153, plates 98–101; Craven, *Sculpture in America,* pp. 51–52.

ENCLOSURE: TO HENRY LEE

[24 April 1800]

I do myself the honour to submit to you a design for the monument to the memory of Genl. Washington, A sketch of which you have already seen to request you will lay the same before the Committee of the Legislature appointed upon this subject and that you will permit me to make a few observations upon the ideas which have governed me in the choice of the plan. It appears desireable that a Monument erected to the Memory of the Founder of American Liberty should be as durable as the Nation that erected it. Single statues either in Marble, Basaltis or Bronze, and indeed any species of sculpture is liable to injury and destruction, I believe that not a single statue has come down to us from antiquity uninjured in many of its most material parts, small projections very soon are broken off, by the wantoness of the spectators. The statue of Washington in the state house at Richmond has already lost several of its smaller parts. Bronze is not so easily broken but it has nothing but durability to recommend it, the utmost skill cannot render its appearance agreeable, and the value of the material has in all revolutions devoted the bronze of Ancient statues either to the purposes of money or to the manufacture of Military implements. More Roman Marble buildings have been destroyed for the sake of the bronze Cramps, than have been spared, and very few statues indeed remain. It appeared therefore to me more proper that I should offer to the Committee the design of a building, the construction of which should secure it against the slow effects of time and weather as well as against violence, and which by the simplicity of its form and the plainess of its decoration should defy the criticism of fashion, to which all complicated works must submit, as well as concord with the character and the progress in art which at present exists in America.

The building is a Pyramid, upon a base of 13 steps, of 100 feet side and height. It contains one chamber, 30 feet square, in the Center of which is a plain Sarcophagus or tomb, and opposite the door a niche for a statue of the General. This Chamber is lighted by 4 Windows, arched, one in each side. The pannels may be filled by representations, either in

162

bas relief, or fresco painting, of the principal events of the life of Washington. A Platform encircles the upper part of the Pyramid.

The material I should propose to be of Granite, which abounds in the Potomac, the Walls of the Chamber, and the Columns of white marble, either from Pennsa. or from the County of Loudon in Virginia.

The site which struck me as the best, is an elevated spot on the bank of Potomak, in the federal City, where a fort is planned in the Map of the City. As the spot is commanded from all sides, I presume no fort will ever be erected there.[1]

With these remarks, I beg leave to submit my design to the Committee, and am with true respect Your faithfull Servant

(Signed) B. H. Latrobe,
Archt. and Engr. to the City of Philadelphia

Sketch of an Estimate for the monument

100 feet side

Plain stone work	55.000
Marble	12.500
	67.500

The statue of Lord Rodney, erected by the Legislature of Jamaica was executed by Bacon for 1.000 Guineas, with its pedestal contained 4 Basso relivo's. Bacon, Flaxman and Banks are the best English Sculptors, Hedourin [Houdon], I believe the best parisian, and Canova, not only the best Italian but I believe the first European Artist.[2]

(Signed) B. Henry Latrobe

Copy: Records of Joint Committees of Congress, RG 128, National Archives (162/E14). Enclosed in BHL to Harper, [post 24 Apr. 1800], above. Date supplied from endorsement.

1. This eminence south of E Street, N.W., and west of 23d Street, N.W., was later the site of the first Naval Observatory, built in 1843. The building is now used as the Potomac Annex of the U.S. Navy Bureau of Medicine and Surgery. Nancy B. Schwartz, comp., *Historic American Buildings Survey: District of Columbia Catalog* (Charlottesville, Va., 1974), pp. 104–05.

2. Admiral Lord George Brydges Rodney (1719–92), naval hero in the Caribbean action against the French and Spanish during the American Revolution, was rewarded by

Parliament for his wartime services with a barony and an annual pension. The statue (1786) commissioned by the Jamaica legislature to honor him was carved by British sculptor John Bacon (1740–99) and now stands in the main square of Spanish Town, Jamaica.

John Flaxman (1755–1826), eminent British Neoclassical sculptor and draftsman, exercised an international influence. BHL, who felt great admiration for him, carried this influence to America. See BHL, *Architectural Drawings* and *Latrobe's View of America.*

Another important British Neoclassical sculptor, Thomas Banks (1735–1805), did work for a number of major buildings, including Samuel Pepys Cockerell's Daylesford House in Gloucestershire (1788–93). BHL, who worked for Cockerell, may have met Banks in connection with this commission.

The Italian sculptor Antonio Canova (1757–1822) was one of the greatest masters in the Neoclassical movement. In 1805, BHL corresponded with Philip Mazzei concerning the idea of commissioning from Canova a statue of liberty for the Hall of Representatives at the U.S. Capitol, but Canova was too busy with other projects he had already promised and was unable to undertake the work. BHL to Mazzei, 6 Mar. 1805, and Mazzei to BHL, 12 Sept. 1805, both in BHL, *Correspondence*, 2; Rupert Gunnis, *Dictionary of British Sculptors, 1660–1851* (London, 1968), pp. 24–28, 37–40.

TO ROBERT LISTON

Second Street [Philadelphia] June 18th. 1800

To his Excellency; Robert Liston Esqr. His Brittanic Majesty's Minister Plenipotentiary to the United States of North America,[1] I should neither have the presumption, nor, as an artist jealous of his professional merits, the imprudence to commit the rude sketches contained in the six volumes herewith sent. But to Mr. and Mrs. Liston to whom I owe so much on the score of friendly and polite treatment, I commit them with pleasure, and with the certainty of indulgent inspection.

B. Henry Latrobe

There is an index to most of the Books. The last Volume is miserably mildewed.[2]

ALS: Sir Robert Liston Papers, Library of Congress (162/F9).

1. Sir Robert Liston (1742–1836), at his death called "the father of the diplomatic body throughout Europe," served as chief British diplomat in Spain (1783–88), Sweden (1788–93), the Ottoman Empire (1793–96, 1811–21), the United States (1796–1802), and the Batavian Republic (1802–04). In 1796, Liston married Henrietta Marchant, daughter of Nathaniel Marchant of Jamaica.

In July and September 1800 BHL drew several "Sketches for a round House for Mr.

Liston" (Sketchbook 6, PBHL; 252/B6 ff.), reproduced in BHL, *Architectural Drawings*. It appears that the drawings were done for intellectual exercise or playful fancy and that neither Liston nor BHL viewed the matter in dead earnest.

2. There are five extant sketchbooks that BHL employed between 1795 and 18 June 1800, the first two of which have indexes by the artist.

FROM GOUVERNEUR MORRIS[1]

Washington 14 Decr. 1800

Sir,

I have had the Honor to receive your Letter of the fourth and am the more bound to thank you for the Compliments it contains as I know them to be far beyond what I can justly pretend to. As yet nothing has come from the other House respecting the Mausoleum and there is some Reason to beleive that the *Evidence* of our national gratitude will be greatly reduced from the Size first intended.[2] Perhaps the *Sentiment* itself was not so great as the wise might wish and the virtuous alone can feel.

Letterbook Copy: Gouverneur Morris Letterbooks, Library of Congress (162/G6). Addressed to BHL in Philadelphia.

1. Gouverneur Morris (1752–1816), Federalist politician and diplomat, played a prominent role in New York politics during the Revolution. He served in the Continental Congress (1777–80), as assistant minister of finance (1781–85), and in the Federal Constitutional Convention of 1787. After a tour of duty as minister plenipotentiary to revolutionary France (1792–94), he returned in 1798 to his mansion at Morrisania (now the Bronx, N.Y.). He was elected to fill a vacancy in the U.S. Senate in 1800 and served until 1803.

BHL visited Morrisania on his wedding trip of May–June 1800. In 1808 Morris married Anne (Nancy) Cary Randolph, whom BHL knew from his Virginia years. Morris later played a leading role on the New York Canal Commission and in 1810 sought BHL's technical advice on the western navigation linking Albany with the Great Lakes. BHL, *Journals*, 1 : 144n, 3 : 18n; BHL to Morris, 10 Apr. 1810, and Morris to BHL, 25 Apr. 1810, both in BHL, *Correspondence*, 2.

2. On 1 January 1801 the House of Representatives passed a mausoleum bill appropriating $200,000, the estimate for Dance's 150–foot pyramid, by a vote of forty-five to thirty-seven. The bill, however, died in the Senate in March. BHL, *Architectural Drawings*.

FROM GOUVERNEUR MORRIS

Washington 24 Dec. 1800

Sir,

I had the Honor to receive your Letter by Mr. Roosevelt. It does not appear as yet that we shall have any Thing to say about the Copper Company in our House, and if it should be brought before us I beleive it will be my Duty to oppose the Incorporation for Reasons which I explain'd to Mr. Roosevelt.[1] They turn on two Points. 1st, a serious doubt whether the Implication by which a Power of making Corporations is vested in Congress can in fair Construction extend to a Case like the present and 2ly, a full Conviction that the Exercise of such Power on such Occasions might be inexpedient and perhaps unjust. In Effect, if the Intention and probable Operation be analized we shall find that the Intention is to obtain for the Stock Holders a Chance of great Profit with a Security against great Loss; and that the Operation involves the following Dilemma: If the Company obtain from the Public no Credit beyond their Capital the Act of Incorporation is of no Use; if they do obtain such Credit it is not the Company but the Public who run the Risque of Loss while it is not the Public but the Company who have the Chance of gain.

Letterbook Copy: Gouverneur Morris Letterbooks, Library of Congress (162/G8). Addressed to BHL in Philadelphia.

1. BHL had been appointed an agent by Nicholas J. Roosevelt and his associates to lobby for a congressional act of incorporation of a "Mine and Metal Company" in New Jersey. In 1793 the New Jersey Copper Mining Association was formed, which leased the Schuyler Copper Mine between the Passaic and Hackensack rivers. The mine, discovered in 1719, had yielded "superior quality" copper ore in the colonial period. But events of the Revolutionary War era disrupted operations until the new company took control in 1793. By the late 1790s, Roosevelt had purchased the whole interest of the company. But in order to attract the necessary capital for exploiting the mine Roosevelt needed a charter of incorporation from Congress. BHL's friendship with Roosevelt and his residence in the capital city made him the logical choice for lobbyist. An even more important reason for BHL's support of the plan was that Roosevelt's lease of the Schuyler Copper Mine served as his bond should he fail to fulfill his contract with the city of Philadelphia to provide the two waterworks steam engines. Roosevelt's petition for incorporation was presented to the House of Representatives on 23 December 1799 and a bill incorporating the Passaick Copper Company passed the House on 29 April 1800. The Senate, however, killed the bill on 10 May 1800. That year BHL published a pamphlet detailing the copper mine's history and advocating the incorporation of Roosevelt's company, but the bill was not reconsidered in the next congressional session. In 1801, however, the New Jersey legislature incorporated the Soho Company, comprising Roosevelt, Arent J. Schuyler, John Stevens, Robert R. Livingston, Samuel Corp, and James Casey. BHL, *American Copper-Mines* (n.p., [1800]) (163/B8); *Annals of Congress*, 6th Cong., 1st sess., pp. 168, 180, 207, 684, 691; Harry B. and Grace M. Weiss, *The Old Copper Mines of New Jersey* (Trenton, N.J. 1963), chap. 2.

TO GOUVERNEUR MORRIS

Philadelphia Decr. 29th, 1800

Dear Sir

I ought to have acknowledged the receipt of your favor of the 14th Decr. before now.[1] The extreme pressure of the business which has occupied me, the first introduction of the Water of the Schuylkill into the city about the time I had the honor to receive it, will I hope plead my apology. Your candid opinion, has decided me to remain here, rather than suffer my ambition, to lead me into a field of controversy in which all my reasonings might be plausibly ascribed to personal motives. It must certainly appear to you, however, as it does to me, singular, that the opposers of a plain Pyramid, should advocate a Bronze equestrian Statue, with 4 historic pannels in Basso relievo on the pedestal—a work, which if executed as it ought to be by Banks, Flaxman, or Bacon, would be much more expensive.

Please to accept my sincerest thanks for your friendly Candor, and believe me with the truest respect Your obedt. humble serv.

B. Henry Latrobe

ALS: Gouverneur Morris Papers, Columbia University Library (162/G11). Enclosed in BHL to Morris, 30 Dec. 1800, below.

1. See Morris to BHL, 14 Dec. 1800, above.

TO GOUVERNEUR MORRIS

Philadelphia Decr. 30th, 1800

Dear Sir,

Since writing the enclosed (yesterday) I have been honored by your letter of the 24th Decr.[1] The principle upon which all incorporations are desired, is certainly that of diminishing the *natural risk* of expensive projects; nor is the Schuyler-Mine Company, as petitioned for, an exception to the rule. But if the question be answered in the affirmative—"Is it not desireable in every political point of view that we should not be dependent upon foreigners for the means of protecting our coasts by a Navy?"—and it be also admitted, that the actual *prejudices* of monied men are such, that an adequate capital *cannot* be raised but by the contribu-

167

tions of *many,* and under the protection of an act of incorporation—then perhaps the general principle might be safely and indeed beneficially sunk in the question of National policy. On this ground alone, does such an act appear to be defensible, and when we consider that Great Britain has rendered the importation of Sheet copper a matter of extreme difficulty and expence, that German Sheet copper is of a very bad quality, and that we possess the means of supplying ourselves, by a little stretch of power and principle perhaps, but still without any obvious detriment to the public, are not the reasons for and against an Act of Incorporation nearly balanced?

I feel while I am writing that I have no claim to the right of endeavoring to combat your arguments, or to influence your opinion: but that I have abundant reason to express to you my acknowledgements for the reception with which you honored my friend Mr. Roosevelt. I have since seen him, and although the opinion you expressed to him on the subject of his application to congress has almost entirely discouraged him, his respect for your personal character will never be obliterated.

I am with the truest respect, Your very obliged humb. Servt.

B. Henry Latrobe

ALS: Gouverneur Morris Papers, Columbia University Library (163/B4).

1. For both letters, see above.

FROM GOUVERNEUR MORRIS

Washington 5 Jany. 1801

Sir,

I have duly received yours of the 29th and 30th of last Month.[1] Your Reasons on the Ground of *Expedience* deserve Consideration. Can they outweigh those which are founded on *Right*—Can they supply the Defect of Power, must also be considered.

Letterbook Copy: Gouverneur Morris Letterbooks, Library of Congress (163/C3). Addressed to BHL in Philadelphia.

1. For both letters, see above.

THE WATERWORKS

[14 March 1801]

From the time at which the mode of supplying the city of Philadelphia with water, became a subject of controversy between the Delaware and Schuylkill canal company and the corporation, before the state
legislature to the present, we have cautiously refrained from any remarks either in praise or in censure of an undertaking which in its
progressive state, we were not competent to decide upon. Where we
could neither praise nor censure with judgment, we deemed it right to
be silent.

The work having lately proved the practicability of supplying our
city abundantly with water, by its complete success as far as the pipes are
yet laid, we have thought it our duty not to pass it over with silence; and
as it is undoubtedly the greatest as yet executed in the United States, to
give (with the assistance of Mr. Latrobe) a concise and intelligible account of it: we do this more especially as the body to whose execution it
has been entrusted have permitted the public opinion to take its own
course, and have never thought proper to explain their conduct to their
constituents, excepting only by means of a few pamphlets of limited
circulation which were printed for the use of the councils.

The first idea of the present work was started in December 1798,
when Mr. Latrobe's first scheme was published. The corporation having
adopted his proposals, applied to the legislature for aid: but the Delaware and Schuylkill canal company conceiving the right of supplying the
city with water to be vested in them by their incorporating act, opposed
the application, and prayed that the funds for which the city solicited,
might be appropriated to the completion of the canal so as to render it
capable of bringing water into the city. By the collision of these parties,
neither obtained their object, and the corporation, after fruitless negociation with the company, opened a subscription for a loan of 150,000
dollars, toward the execution of the work. The contending interests of
the parties, and especially the eight per cent, loan of the U. States which
was opened at the same time, among its many other pernicious effects,
prevented the subscription of more than about 70,000 dollars.

The work was, however, begun in May 1799; and notwithstanding
the yellow fever of that year, and the scanty state of the city finances its
progress gratified the expectations of its patrons. During this year the
canal and the subterraneous tunnel on the Schuylkill were cut through 169

Fig. 6. The Centre-Square Engine House, engraving by William Birch, hand colored. Courtesy of the Athenaeum of Philadelphia.

the solid rock: the lower engine house was built, the brick tunnel extending from thence to the centre square, was finished, and the engine house in the square was raised to a considerable height. Nearly three miles of pipes were also laid in the streets. The exertions of the year 1800 have brought the work to its present state. The bason has been sunk into the bed of the river, and the bason wall has been built where was formerly 11 feet of water. Its foundations were laid upon the rock at the south end 12 feet below the bed of the Schuylkill. The pipes in the streets now extend nearly 6 miles: the engines have been set to work.

The leading features of this work, which at first view appears so complicated, are extremely simple. A bason or enclosure made in the river itself, receives the water. In this bason where the river is muddy its sediment is deposited, and from it, if the water be received in a clear state at the commencement of rains, the muddy fresh can be excluded. From this bason the water has free access through the canal, and the

170

subterraneous tunnel into a well, sunk above 50 feet deep from the top of the high bank on which the city stands. The cleansing, as well of the bason, as of the canal, and, the tunnel is provided for by successive sluices. Over the well the engine-house is built, in which a double steam engine of 39 inch cylinder is erected. The pump worked by the engine has a barrel of 18 inches in diameter. The stroke of the engine is 6 feet. The water is discharged by the pump into the long cylindrical tunnel which is carried to the Centre-square. This tunnel passes over an aqueduct of three arches near Second-street, Schuylkill, and is in its whole length (which wants little of a mile) covered with at least 3 feet of earth. It is of hard bricks laid in cement, its diameter is six feet, and its depth below the surface near Broad-street, is 18 feet. It has a fall towards Schuylkill of 10 inches, for the purpose of scouring it, and is terminated at each end by a chamber of solid marble in very large blocks. In the lower chamber is a sluice, in the upper is placed the upper pump. The tunnel passes from the Schuylkill engine house into Chesnut-street, is continued in a straight line to Broad-street and from thence twins[1] into Centre-square, where its bottom is about 12 feet below the natural level of the ground. The engine-house in Centre-square is finished only so far as to contain the engine. The present reservoir of wood is temporary. It contains 7,500 gallons. The permanent marble reservoir will hold 25,000 gallons, and will be elevated about 45 feet above the street. The pump worked by the engine in Centre-square is of the same size with that at the Schuylkill. The water is raised by the two engines, to the height of about 115 feet above the level of the river. From the reservoir the water descends into a chest of cast iron. This chest is furnished with brass cocks of six inches bore. Each of these cocks supplies a principal branch of the distribution. Those of Market, Arch, and Chesnut streets are complete.

The pipes are of white oak. The principal pipes are six inches bore, and these diminish in proportion to the supplies required of them 4½, 3½ and 3 inches. From these pipes the water is furnished gratis to the public, by means of Hydrants. The Hydrants are upright pipes rising 3 feet above the pavement, in each of them are 2 cocks, one of ¾ of an inch bore, for common use, the other of 2½ bore to be used only to water the streets, and in cases of fire. The Hydrant near Fifth-street, in Market-street discharges through the small cock 4 gallons in 11 seconds, or an hogshead of 63 gallons in less than three minutes.

The funds that have carried on the work have been: 171

1. A Loan by Subscription, about   70,000[2]
2. Cash received by the sale of the scite of the
   permanent Bridge,   20,000[3]
3. A Water Tax,   50,000[4]
4. Saving from various appropriations of City
   revenue, fines, amercements, &c.,   15,000
5. Appropriations of revenue raised for paying the
   interest on the Loan and the maintenance of the
   Engines in 1799 and 1800, and which were not
   called for, on account of the deficiencies of the
   subscription, and the delay in setting the Engines
   to work until 1801, about   175,000

This sum of 175,000 dollars is nearly the amount of the monies already expended, and we find that it is supposed that a further sum of about 25,000 dollars will be required to finish the work in its various parts to extend the distribution, and to pay off the arrears which may be due on the settlement of the last years accounts.

The first expence of this undertaking considerable as it is, having been borne, and cheerfully borne by the majority of our citizens, works being yet incomplete, we have endeavoured to gain accurate information as to the burthen likely to be entailed upon our fellow-citizens, by the maintainance of the engines, in order to ascertain in how far her advantages likely to result to the city by the supply of water might authorise the annual expence, by which it is obtained. If the Corporation had been empowered by their charter to supply the citizens with water upon the principle of the Manhattan Company,[5] the new river company, and other water companies in England, the expence of two steam engines perhaps would have borne but a small portion to the emoluments of the monopoly. But as the water is supplied gratis to those who chuse to send to the Hydrants in the streets, the revenues arising from supplies to private houses will be limited, and perhaps for some years, inadequate to the annual expence of maintenance and repair of pipes.

On this subject Mr. Latrobe has on our application, furnished the following information.

"By the original contract for the steam engines, the contractor was bound to furnish to the City, two engines capable of supplying three million gallons in twenty-four hours. This, it was supposed would be the

172 greatest consumption of water in the hottest summer months for many

years to come. It was not expected that more than 200,000 gallons per day could be consumed during the winter months. Two hundred and fifty thousand gallons per day is the utmost supply to the city of New-York, contemplated by the Manhattan Company (*See Dr. Brown's Pamphlet.*)[6] It is therefore evident, that the engines must waste, during the supply of quantity of water below, 3 million gallons, a large portion of their power which might be otherwise advantageously employed. The right of employing this extra power, as it has been called, has been made the foundation of the contract, at present subsisting for the maintainance of the engines. By the lowest calculation that could be made of the prime cost of maintaining the engines with fuel, attendance, repairs, and a great variety of materials constantly required in working them—it appeared that their usual expence would not be less than 4000 dollars per annum each engine, in the hands of persons skilled in their management, and interested in their expence.

"It could not be believed, that under the management of the Corporation, by persons wholly uninterested in their expence, they would cost rarely so small a sum: nor could it be expected that persons sufficiently skillful and honest, could be procured for every duty attached to them, while those who had the appointment, however zealous in the public service, could not possibly be judges of all the qualifications required. The following terms were therefore agreed upon with the contractor, for the maintainance of the engines.[7]

1. That he shall be at liberty to encrease the stipulated power of the engine on the river Schuylkill, at his own expence.

2. That he shall have a lease of the extra power of that engine, and of sufficient ground for the erection of works contiguous to the engine house, for 42 years.

3. That he shall maintain both engines in every expence of fuel, attendance, repairs, &c. during the term of his lease, supplying to the city daily, all the water which the pipes can possibly consume, to any amount not exceeding 3 million gallons.

4. That he shall pay to the corporation a rent for the ground occupied by him, encreasing during the term of his lease from 500 to 1800 dollars per ann.

5. The corporation shall pay to the contractor for the maintenance of each engine the annual sum of 3000 dollars, so long as he shall supply daily, not more than one million gallons. That for every day on which the supply exceeds one million gallons, he shall receive a further sum, 173

diminishing in such ratio that for two million gallons he shall be paid only as much per day, as for the first one million. The rate of the additional payment is settled by the contract.

"The effect of this agreement is this: During eight months of the year, even when the distribution of water throughout the city shall be compleat, it is almost impossible that more than one million gallons can be consumed by supplies from the hydrants and to private houses. The average consumption of the four other months may be estimated at 2,000,000 gallons per day at the utmost: as though for 60 days 3,000,000 may perhaps be consumed, yet the intervention of rains and of cool weather, and the absence of many citizens in the country will, probably, keep down the remaining supply for the remainder to 1,000,000.

"The annual payment to the contractor on these principles would be as follows:

Regular payment for 1,000,000 gallons	6000
Payment for four months at average supply of 2,000,000 gallons	2000
	8000
Deduct average rent of the extra power for 42 years, from 500 to 1800 dollars per annum	1150
Annual expence of the engines Dols.	6850

"By the terms of the water loan, every subscriber is entitled to supply a house for three years with water, free from rent. The number of shares is about 700. If every subscriber avail himself of this privilege at first, it is not probable that the water revenue will be considerable for three years. It will also require a few years to make evident the solid advantages of having a constant supply of soft water in the house for domestic purposes. But after the public opinion on this subject shall have been settled—there can be no doubt but that few houses will be without a rented pipe—and of 6000 dwelling houses which are supposed to be in the city, 4000 will be then supplied. If the rent be the same which is paid to the New River Company, in London, about 8 dollars a year—the water-rents, independently of supplies to manufactories, would amount to 32,000 dollars per annum, and thus be not only fully adequate to the annual expence of that system, but considerably contribute to the relief of the city from taxes.

174   "As much doubt has existed on the subject of the maintenance of

the engines—I have with pleasure complied with your desire for information on the subject. The arrangement made by the watering committee is so advantageous to the city, that the thanks of their fellow-citizens, will not fail to be bestowed, when their conduct is perfectly understood. At the same time the contractor may certainly employ a very large capital to his own advantage, and that of the city in the establishments to be connected with the extra power, which at a very enormous expence he has created upon the Schuylkill.

"As a professional, and an interested man my testimony to the patriotism of the water committee, cannot perhaps be thought of much value, otherwise I should not let slip the opportunity you have given me of doing them now that justice which they will undoubtedly meet from their fellow-citizens, in the course of a few years. The laborious attention which they had given during two years to a work, to which neglect, but for a short time, would have been fatal, the attacks of ignorance, of illiberality, and of interested enmity which they have patiently borne, sacrifices of time, and private business which they have made—the large sums which in periods of embarrassment they have individually advanced—the personal responsibility to which they have subjected themselves in the loans made of the U.S. bank; while the smallest advantage, or emolument has not accrued to a single individual of the committee— deserve a degree of public gratitude which few public agents have ever had the virtue to merit."[8]

"B. HENRY LATROBE."

Printed Copy: *Aurora. General Advertiser* (Philadelphia), 14 Mar. 1801 (163/C10). Titled "The Water-Works."

1. Probably a misreading of "turns."

2. See BHL, Statement Concerning Philadelphia Waterworks and an Account of Steam Engines, 2 Mar. 1799, n. 2, above.

3. On 12 December 1799 the Philadelphia city councils sold to the Schuylkill Permanent Bridge Company a plot of land where Market Street meets the Schuylkill River. Minutes of the Common Council, 13 Mar. 1800, Archives of the City and County of Philadelphia.

4. On 5 August 1799 the Philadelphia city councils passed an ordinance levying a special tax (the "water tax") to raise $50,000 for the waterworks. *Report to the Select and Common Councils, on the Progress and State of the Water Works, on the 24th of November, 1799* (Philadelphia, 1799), pp. 18–23.

5. In 1799 the Manhattan Company began supplying water to portions of the city of New York. Depending upon their size, private residences were charged from $5 to $20 annually for water. Nelson M. Blake, *Water for the Cities* (Syracuse, N.Y., 1956), p. 59.

6. *Proceedings of the Corporation of New-York, on Supplying the City with Pure and Whole-*

some Water; with a Memoir of Joseph Browne, M.D., on the same subject ([New York], 1799).

7. Roosevelt's contract for the extra power was signed on 24 December 1799. *Report of the Committee Appointed by the Common Council to Enquire into the State of the Water Works* (Philadelphia, 1802), pp. 30–36.

8. Thomas Pym Cope, a Philadelphia merchant and member of the Watering Committee, made the following comment upon reading this article: "It is, as might be expected, a shrewd artful composition, calculated to ensnare and mislead. Some things are asserted which perhaps no person but a member of the Committee or some one in their service could contradict. I suppose they must pass; it is but a gull for the gapers, and a pill for the croakers. The concluding paragraph contains a high compliment to the *patriotism, disinterestedness* and *virtue* of the Committee. It will have its effect. He wants a birth as surveyor and engineer under the distribution ordinance. I know him well and therefore shall not be taken in by this trash, but some of my brethren love tickling, and having their elbows rubbed, will scratch his back." Thomas Pym Cope diaries, 15 Mar. 1801, Haverford College Library, Haverford Pa.

TO JAMES EAKIN

Philadelphia, April 10th, 1801

My dear Cousin[1]

A blot at the outset is ominous. But this is my last sheet of letter paper, and I had saved it on purpose to show you my respect, and to offer you my thanks for the very obliging manner in which you have undertaken my little application.[2] Mr. Newman, who will deliver you this, has laid me under great obligations by his very polite advice and exertion on the subject of my claim.[3] I have given him a letter to Colonel McHenry, and I hope you will meet with no difficulties. All I could do in return was to show him my works, and I dare to say that my vanity was on that occasion as much liable to be expected, as my civility might be admired; and perhaps I am, when making my exhibitions, often compared to those indiscreet mothers who, in order to be very civil, cram their slobbering brats down your throat. But indeed I am highly obliged to Mr. Newman, and hope he will remember that my door and my hand are always open to receive him.

As to marriages, deaths, and bankruptcies, I can say but little in the way of news. Mr. Cooper's affair with Miss Abby Willing is off.[4] Mrs. Bingham, as the last recourse for life goes this day on board a Vessel intended to carry her to Lisbon. Her husband and daughter, and Abby Willing accompany her and as she is scarcely expected to live a week her leaden Coffin is part of the Cargo. What a melancholy Set![5]

God bless you. I have only time to assure you of mine and Mrs. Latrobe's undiminished affection.[6]

Believe me very truly Yrs.

B. Henry Latrobe

ALS: Society Collection, Historical Society of Pennsylvania (163/D10). Addressed to Eakin in Washington.

1. James Eakin, a cousin of BHL's wife (for whom see n.6, below), was the son of a Presbyterian clergyman from Delaware and a sister of Joanna (Purviance) Hazlehurst, BHL's mother-in-law. He worked as a clerk for the accountant of the U.S. War Department in Washington until the early 1830s. In 1830 he was listed as chief clerk in the Second Auditor's Office. BHL to Eakin, 28 May 1801, below; BHL to Joshua Gilpin, 1 Nov. 1803, and BHL to Henry Clay, 2 Nov. 1813, both in LB (27/A5, 113/A2); Noble E. Cunningham, Jr., *The Process of Government under Jefferson* (Princeton, N.J., 1978), p. 330; James McLachlan, *Princetonians, 1748–1768: A Biographical Dictionary* (Princeton, N.J., 1976), pp. 113, 426–27.

2. For BHL's claim against the War Department, see the following document.

3. John Newman, chief clerk of the War Department. CHS, *Records* 9 (1905):230.

4. Abigail Willing (1777–1841) was the daughter of Philadelphia banker Thomas Willing. After her engagement with a Mr. Cooper, she was courted by Louis Philippe, duke of Orleans. On 1 March 1804 she married Richard Peters, a nephew of Judge Richard Peters (1744–1828). Robert C. Alberts, *The Golden Voyage: The Life and Times of William Bingham, 1752–1804* (Boston, 1969), pp. 307–08, 412, 526.

5. Anne (Willing) Bingham (1764–1801), an older sister of Abby Willing, married William Bingham II (1752–1804) in 1780. Bingham was a Philadelphia merchant, land speculator, banker, and U.S. senator (1795–1801). The Binghams had two daughters and one son. Their youngest daughter, Maria Matilda (1783–post 1826), accompanied the Binghams on the voyage to Bermuda, which Mrs. Bingham's doctors had prescribed as a treatment for her "galloping consumption," a rapid form of tuberculosis. She died at St. George Island on 11 May 1801. Ibid., pp. 94, 96, 113, 129, 394, 411–13, 438.

6. BHL and his second wife, Mary Elizabeth Latrobe (1771–1841), were married in Christ Church, Philadelphia, on 1 May 1800. MEL was the eldest child and only daughter of Philadelphia merchant Isaac Hazlehurst (for whom see BHL to MEL, 10 Nov. 1801, n. 4, below). Frank Willing Leach, "Old Philadelphia Families: Hazlehurst" (no. 59), *The North American* (Philadelphia), 19 July 1908.

TO JAMES EAKIN

Philadelphia May 28th, 1801

My dear friend,

I formerly wrote to you upon the subject of a demand which I have against the War office, for designs, an estimate, and a report, relative to the establishment of military Schools, which were made by desire of the 177 late Secretary at War, Colonel McHenry.[1] But it appears that the packet miscarried. I now trouble you once more to receive the amount of my account which is 200 Dollars, should the Secretary pay it without hesitation.[2] If however, in consequence of the change of Administration, and the probable destruction of the papers by the fire, any difficulty in passing my account should occur, I will beg the favor of you to manage matters for me as well as you can, and to inform me of what may be required to substantiate my claim.[3] On this account I send you the letter I have written to the Secretary, *open,* begging you to seal and deliver it, and to put into a proper cover. The drawings cost me much time and trouble, and as a work of supererogation, I am willing to furnish a copy. I am sorry to put you to so much trouble and heartily wish I had the means of requiting your kindness.

By letters from Richard Hazlehurst received yesterday, it appears that he will sail for England from Charleston on the 6th of April. A better fellow never crossed the Atlantic. We all wish him safe back again, after having had a sufficient regale of English Roast beef and Colchester Oysters.[4] When shall we see you here again? Our little circle of boys is reduced amazingly by your, Richard, and Andrews[5] absence. God know whether we shall ever get together again. You, no doubt mean to pay us a visit in the course of 1801. Your good mother is daily expected here on her way home; though it is not impossible but that she and your fair Sisters may stay the Summer in Delaware state. But Isaac[6] supplies you no doubt with all the family news hot and hot. We married folks are out of the merry ring in which Novelty is bandied about, and at the first glance you will no doubt observe the difference between the communications of a married and a single cousin.

Having written to you on business, I have no doubt, but that you will not give me all the credit I deserve in writing to you also on the pose of sincere regard. But I beg you notwithstanding to be assured, that with the most affectionate family sentiment I am, Your faithful friend and Cousin

B. Henry Latrobe

Mary desires me to tell you that she has a pair of bouncing twins to introduce you to who can already walk alone, and ask more questions in 10 Minutes than she can answer in an hour. She begs her love to you.

178 ALS: Jefferson Papers (163/E3). Addressed to Eakin at the War Office, Washington, D.C.

1. BHL's six "sketches for a Design of a Military Academy to accomodate seven Professors, and fifty Students," dated 26 January 1800 (Prints and Photographs Division, Library of Congress; 277/B1 ff.), are reproduced in BHL, *Architectural Drawings*. BHL's estimate for executing his scheme was $40,000. Secretary of War McHenry submitted both BHL's and Jean Foncin's plans to Congress on 31 January but the bill for establishing the academy died later in the session. In 1802 Congress authorized the establishment of the military academy at West Point but BHL's plans were not employed. In 1807 when the Jefferson administration considered moving the academy to Washington, BHL reminded West Point superintendent Jonathan Williams of his 1800 design, which survived in the War Department. But Congress left the academy at West Point and BHL's plans on paper. BHL to Williams, 28 Dec. 1807, in BHL, *Correspondence*, 2.

2. In 1801 the secretary of war was Henry Dearborn (1751–1829), a Massachusetts physician, soldier, and congressman. He served in Thomas Jefferson's cabinet from 5 March 1801 until 16 February 1809.

3. When the seat of government moved to Washington in 1800, the War Department occupied a building on the south side of Pennsylvania Avenue between 21st and 22nd streets. On 8 November 1800 the building was destroyed by a fire caused by a defective chimney in an adjoining house. Only a few of the public records were saved. Some of the Republican newspapers charged that the fire in the war office, along with the fire that broke out in the Treasury office on 20 January 1801, was part of a Federalist scheme to destroy the public records and eliminate evidence of misgovernment and misappropriation of funds. A committee of the House of Representatives investigated the causes of both fires and concluded that they were accidental. Joseph Hodgson, the owner of the house leased to the war office, brought suit for damages but lost his case in the federal courts. Wilhelmus Bogart Bryan, *A History of the National Capital from Its Foundation through the Period of the Adoption of the Organic Act*, 2 vols. (New York, 1914–16), 1 : 384–85; L[urton] D. Ingersoll, *A History of the War Department of the United States with Biographical Sketches of the Secretaries* (Washington, D.C., 1879), p. 109.

4. Richard Hunter Hazlehurst (1778–1831), MEL's brother, graduated from the University of Pennsylvania in 1794 and joined his father's mercantile firm (for which see BHL to MEL, 10 Nov. 1801, n. 4, below). He visited BHL's sister, Mary Agnes Latrobe, in Fairfield, England, in February 1802, while promoting the family business in England. Mary Agnes remarked to her brother John Frederick that Richard was "above six foot high, and so like one of our Family—that you wou'd think him our own Br." Hazlehurst told Mary Agnes that "his whole Family loves Benjamin very much—they speak of his abilities in the highest terms." Hazlehurst traveled on the Continent, led a "very extravagant" life, and "was considered the principal cause" of the failure of the mercantile firm in 1809. Mary Agnes Latrobe to John Frederick Latrobe, 26 Feb.. 2 Mar. 1802, John Henry de La Trobe Collection, Hamburg, copies in PBHL; Frank Willing Leach, "Old Philadelphia Families: Hazlehurst" (no. 59), *The North American* (Philadelphia), 19 July 1908.

5. Andrew Purviance Hazlehurst (1781–1819), MEL's youngest brother, graduated from the University of Pennsylvania in 1795 and established a mercantile house in Baltimore with his brother Isaac, Jr. (see below), in partnership with their father's Philadelphia firm. He married Frances Purviance, of Baltimore, a relative of his mother, Juliana (for whom see BHL to MEL, 10 Nov. 1801, n. 4, below). He lived with Frances in Baltimore until his death. Leach, "Old Philadelphia Families: Hazlehurst."

6. Probably Isaac Hazlehurst, Jr. (1779–1855), BHL's brother-in-law. Isaac, Jr., was a graduate of the University of Pennsylvania (1794) and a Baltimore merchant. He later moved to St. Croix, West Indies, where he managed the plantation of his sister-in-law Elizabeth Baynton (Markoe) Hazlehurst (for whom see BHL to McKean, 20 Oct. 1801, n. 4, below). He eventually became owner of the estate and died in the West Indies. Ibid. 179

The Susquehanna River Improvement

EDITORIAL NOTE

In August 1801, Pennsylvania Governor Thomas McKean appointed Latrobe surveyor and assistant to Frederick Antes, his maternal uncle, to improve the navigation of the Susquehanna River from Wright's Ferry (Columbia), Pennsylvania, to tidewater. The appointment was authorized by a 1799 Pennsylvania statute incorporating the Chesapeake and Delaware Canal Company and providing for the improvement of the lower Susquehanna River.[1] The improvement project was a joint venture of the Pennsylvania government, whose agents were Antes and Latrobe, and the Susquehanna Canal Company (a Maryland corporation building a canal along the Susquehanna from the Pennsylvania boundary to tidewater), whose agents were Sebastian Shade and his engineering assistant, Christian P. Hauducoeur. Shortly after his arrival at the Susquehanna to begin his duties, Latrobe learned of his uncle's serious illness.[2] Upon his uncle's death on 20 September 1801 Latrobe assumed control of the Pennsylvania half of the project and worked with his Maryland counterparts in accomplishing two tasks: a complete survey of the river from Wright's Ferry south; and the clearing of the natural obstacles for safe downstream navigation in spring freshets. Both objects were quickly achieved. In November 1801 Latrobe presented a report to the governor on the improvements he made (below), and in the report's appendix he provided a guide for navigators descending the river.[3] During the winter of 1801–02 he completed a seventeen-foot-long watercolor map of the river.[4] By mid-March 1802, Latrobe brought his map to the governor in Lancaster and began a lobbying effort in the Pennsylvania legislature to secure $2,000 to complete the river improvements he had nearly finished the previous fall. Latrobe's letter to his wife of 18 March 1802 (below) presents some of his impressions of the legislators he was trying to influence. Latrobe's efforts were successful, the appropriation was passed, and the improvements were completed in 1802.[5]

---

1. *Pa. Statutes, 1682–1801*, 16 : 338–40.

2. For BHL's detailed description of his uncle's fatal illness, see BHL, *Journals*, 3 : 22–27.

3. BHL, "Appendix. Description of the works performed towards effecting a safe Navigation of the river Susquehannah, from Columbia to Tidewater, and instructions for performing the same," 28 November 1801, Susquehanna River Improvement File, PHMC (164/E1); also printed in the *Aurora*, 30 Mar. 1802.

4. "The Susquehanna from Columbia to the Pennsylvania line and thence to Havre de Grace" (PBHL) is reproduced in BHL, *Engineering Drawings*, pp. 91–109.

5. *Pa. Statutes, 1802–1805*, p. 226. For a detailed analysis of the Susquehanna map, see BHL, *Engineering Drawings*, pp. 73–109.

TO THOMAS McKEAN

Philadelphia Octr. 17th, 1801

Sir[1]

Agreeably to your verbal instructions, and the sanction you gave to the directions I had given since the death of Coll. Antes,[2] I have let to different contractors all the Work in clearing the Susquehannah which can be accomplished by the appropriation of 10.000 Dollars. On the opposite side is an Abstract of the account of the expenditure of 3.000 Dollars issued by you to that object, and I have now to request that you will please to issue the further sum of $2.000, to satisfy the pressing demands of such contractors as have finished their Work. In the course of 3 Weeks from the present date, I have no doubt but that every part of the Work will be compleated which has been contracted for this Season. I am with true respect Your faithful hble. Servt.

B. Henry Latrobe

ALS: Susquehanna River Improvement File, PHMC (163/F14). Enclosed BHL, Account, below. Enclosed in BHL to McKean, 20 Oct. 1801, below.

1. Thomas McKean (1734–1817), Delaware and Pennsylvania politician and statesman, was a member (1762–79) and speaker (1772–73) of the Delaware Assembly. He represented Delaware in the Continental Congress during the Revolution. Although he was chief justice of Pennsylvania from 1777 to 1799, McKean continued to hold political office in Delaware. A Federalist in 1787, he urged adoption of the Constitution, but by 1794 he had become closely associated with the Jeffersonians. In 1799 he won a bitterly contested gubernatorial election and served as governor of Pennsylvania until his retirement in 1808. G. S. Rowe, *Thomas McKean: The Shaping of an American Republicanism* (Boulder, Colo., 1978).

2. Frederick Antes (1730–1801), younger brother of Anna Margaretta (Antes) Latrobe, was an iron founder who cast some of the cannons used by the American Revolutionary forces. During the war he moved to Northumberland County, and he was elected to the Pennsylvania House of Representatives in 1784. In 1790 Gov. Thomas Mifflin appointed him one of the commissioners to survey the headwaters of the Delaware, Lehigh, Schuylkill, and East Branch of the Susquehanna rivers. The Susquehanna Canal Company of Maryland employed him in 1798 to make improvements on the lower Susquehanna near Columbia. His work was interrupted in 1799, however, when the Pennsylvania Assembly declared such improvements by private individuals or corporations illegal. On 7 July 1801, Gov. Thomas McKean appointed Antes to undertake the improvement of the lower Susquehanna River on behalf of the state of Pennsylvania. BHL, "The Susquehanna from Columbia to the Pennsylvania line and thence to Havre de Grace," watercolor map, c. 1802, PBHL (306/A1); *PMHB* 3 (1879):98; *Colonial Records of Pennsylvania*, 16 vols. (Harrisburg, Pa., 1838–53), 14 : 167, 169, 16 : 319; Gertrude MacKinney, ed., *Pennsylvania Archives*, 9 ser., 10 vols. ([Harrisburg, Pa.], 1931–35), 3 : 1755–56; *Pa. Statutes, 1682–1801*, 16 : 338–40; Edwin MacMinn, *On the Frontier with Colonel Antes* (Camden, N.J., 1900), pp. 333, 446.

ENCLOSURE: ACCOUNT

The Works on Susquehannah,

Dr.

To so much issued by the Treasury $3.000.

Cr.

By monies actually expended by Coll. Antes in Wages, tools, powder, and payments on contracts	1.555.16½
By balances since expended left in the hands of Geo. Stoner, superintendant, Burkhalter's ferry[1]	135.08½
Chrn. Wisler, do. Turkey hill,[2]	48.75
By, his salary 81 days at 4$.oo per day	324.00

By, Cash paid by B. H. Latrobe

To Jo. Gundacker for powder,[3]	130.00 ⎫	
To Works at Turkey hill	200.00 ⎬	680.00
To Do. at Burkhalters ferry	350.00 ⎭	

By balance in hands of the Superintendant's expended but not settled in acct.	257.00
	3.000.00

E.E.

          B. Henry Latrobe Engr.

NB. All the monies stated above as balances have been paid over to Contractors, whose accounts are still to be settled.

ADS: Susquehanna River Improvement File, PHMC (163/G2). Enclosed in BHL to McKean, 17 Oct. 1801, above.

 1. Earlier George Stoner had received $1,040 for work he had supervised at Burkhalter's Ferry. Stoner (b. ante 1754), probably the son of Lancaster County clockmaker Rudy Stoner, was a Conestoga Township farmer who served as town supervisor in 1810. BHL, Field Books and Accounts, Aug.–Sept. 1801, PBHL (13/A1); Ellis and Evans, *History of Lancaster County,* p. 739; Stacy B. C. Wood, Jr., "Rudy Stoner, 1728–69, Early Lancaster, Pennsylvania Clockmaker," *JLCHS* 80 (1976):119. For BHL's description of Stoner, see BHL to McKean, 17 Jan. 1802, below.

 2. Christian Wisler had earlier received $250 for work he supervised at Turkey Hill. BHL stayed at Wisler's house at Turkey Hill during part of his surveying expedition of 29 October–14 November 1801. BHL, Field Books and Accounts, Aug.–Sept., Oct.–Nov. 1801, both in PBHL (13/A1, 14/A1).

3. John Gundacker, Lancaster merchant, was a stockholder of the Philadelphia and Lancaster Turnpike (1792) and manager of the Lancaster and Middletown Turnpike Company, incorporated in 1804. A charter member of the Active Fire Company (1792) in Lancaster, Gundacker was also director of the Farmers' Bank of Lancaster (1810). He sold black powder ($9 a cask) and brimstone and steel for use on the Susquehanna project. BHL, Field Book and Accounts, Aug.–Sept. 1801; *PLCHS* 13 (1909):92, 22 (1918):94, 40 (1936):27; Ellis and Evans, *History of Lancaster County,* p. 313.

TO THOMAS McKEAN

Philadelphia, Octr. 20th, 1801.

Sir,

Agreeably to your appointment, I waited upon you yesterday, (Monday) but found that you had just set off for Lancaster. I had written the enclosed letter, which will give you an account of the manner in which 3.000 Dollars have been expended issued to Coll. Antes.[1] Although I may state his accts. to the proper Officers on my own responsibility, I find I cannot *pass* them without a power of attorney from his Administrator for which I have written, and which I hope soon to receive.

I have this day received the most pressing letters from Mr. Shade[2] and from the Contractors at Burkhalters ferry, for a settlement of account, and I take the liberty to solicit that while you are at Lancaster you will please to issue a Warrant for 2.000 Dollars, to be left for me with your Secretary[3] for the payment of such Contracts as I shall find compleated on my arrival at Lancaster on Monday next. Previous to that day it will be impossible for me to be there, both on acct. of my business here, and from a circumstance in the family, the marriage of Mrs. Latrobe Brother to Miss Markoe, from which I cannot well absent myself.[4] I flatter myself that I shall have the honor of meeting you either at Lancaster or on the road. I have made every arrangement to comply with your wishes in being fully prepared with my report and survey on the 20th of November.

I am with the truest respect Your very faithful humble Servt.

B. Henry Latrobe

ALS: Susquehanna River Improvement File, PHMC (163/F10).

1. BHL to McKean, 17 Oct. 1801, above.
2. Sebastian Shade had "upwards of eighteen years" experience as a "navigator on the river." *Oracle of Dauphin, and Harrisburgh Advertiser,* 15 Mar. 1802. For BHL's favorable assessment of Shade, see BHL, Report on the Susquehanna River Improvements, 28 Nov. 1801, below.
3. Either James Trimble (1755–1837), deputy secretary of Pennsylvania from 1777 to 1837, or Thomas McKean Thompson, McKean's nephew and secretary of Pennsylvania from 1801 to 1808. *PMHB* 5 (1881):83, 102 (1978):236n.
4. Philadelphia merchant Samuel Hazlehurst (1772–1849) married Elizabeth Baynton Markoe (1778–1842) on 22 October 1801. A graduate of the University of the State of Pennsylvania (1789), Samuel Hazlehurst became a partner in the firm of Isaac Hazlehurst & Son and was a member of the First Troop City Cavalry of Philadelphia from 1796 to 1810. Frank Willing Leach, "Old Philadelphia Families: Hazlehurst" (no. 59), *The North American* (Philadelphia), 19 July 1908. For BHL's comments on the Markoe family, see BHL, *Journals,* 3 : 80–82.

TO MARY ELIZABETH LATROBE

Martick Forge[1] Novr. 10th, 1801. Tuesday morng.

My beloved Wife

We are this moment going to leave Mr. Brien for Mr. Reed's 3 Miles below Burkhalter's.[2] Mr. Brien will take this letter to Lancaster. I wrote to you on Saturday from Lancaster a letter which you must receive about this time. Yesterday we made a great exertion to forward our work, and returned at night so entirely fatigued, that none of us could write or you would have had a more circumstantial letter now. But we must depart immediately, or do no business today. I expect to meet Mr. Hauducoeur[3] a few miles below Mr. Reed's. As soon as we meet, my labours are at an end.

Your letters have not yet reached me. Mr. Shade on hearing at Columbia from somebody who saw me there that I was at Lancaster, sent them back again, and I am now hunting after them by means of every person whom I can entrust with the enquiry.

I know not how it is, but whenever I sit down to write to you I feel as gloomy and agitated, as if I had neither reflection to reconcile me to our separation, nor confidence in your exertions to bear it. If I could bring myself to write to any one but you, I could furnish a letter entertaining enough. The little incidents of our journey have been often extremely laughable, and almost always curious. The very reception we have met with has been so various, that I could fill a letter with descriptions of

184

character, and mannars that would often make you laugh. And as to the natural scenery in which we have been engaged, it is so savage in many instances, and so beautiful in others, that I could not fail to find in that alone matter enough for twenty letters. But after writing the first words of my letter, after calling you, my dearest Mary, my dearest wife, my beloved wife, the whole world vanishes from my imagination, and I see none but you: I seem to stretch my arms from the rocky Walls of the Susquehannah in vain towards you, all my spirits, and strength exhaust themselves in the exertion, and I scarcely am capable of guiding my pen, just to give a bare dry narrative of our daily labors. But why should I point to you the weakness of my mind; when you perhaps, and God grant it be so, have long become satisfied that it is little less than impious to cast away the happiness that is within our reach, because the necessary circumstances of our lives, refuse to permit to us the enjoyment of *all* that we can paint to our selves as *possible*. When I think of you, my dearest love, my heart melts at first into tenderness, such as I never before knew; but it soon rests itself firmly upon that superiority of mind, that soundness of reasoning, and that command of your feelings which I know you possess, and then I take my level on my shoulder, and march forth as strong as a lion to push forward to the end of my labor, when your arms and your kisses, if I dared to think of them, shall reward all my fatigues. Oh my love! what virtue can deserve such a woman as you are! Were I but half worthy of you, how superior to all should I be, and how just would be my pride!

Our health has been uninterruptedly good, and though weather browned and lip chapped, we eat and sleep as well as farmers. The weather also has favored us exceedingly, for we have lost only 1½ days. Today again we were apprehensive of rain, but the Sun has climbed over the mountain, and looks cheerfully on my paper. I pray God you may have been well. Love to the Children and to our father and mother, and to the *boys*.[4] Your most tenderly affectionate husband

B. Henry Latrobe.

ALS: Mrs. Gamble Latrobe Collection, MdHS (164/B2). Addressed in care of Isaac Hazlehurst, 117 N. Second St., Philadelphia.

1. Martic forge was on Pequea Creek, a tributary of the Susquehanna River, in Martic Township, Lancaster County, Pennsylvania. Thomas F. Gordon, *A Gazetteer of the State of Pennsylvania* (Philadelphia, 1832), p. 273; Burl Neff Osburn, "Mysteries of Martic," *JLCHS* 63 (1959):161–82.

2. Edward Brien (1769–1816), ironmaster at Martic Forge, was born in County Tyrone, Ireland. In 1799 his uncle and Robert Coleman, part-owner of the forge, hired Brien as manager of the forge. Under his care, a slitting mill (1801) and rolling mill (1803) were added. In 1804 Brien became a partner with Coleman in the forge. Slaves provided much of the labor at Martic Forge before and during Brien's management. Brien was one of the original stockholders of the Columbia Bridge Co. in 1811. In 1802 he married Dorothy Hand (1777–1862), daughter of Gen. Edward Hand (1744–1802). Brien sold nearly $40 worth of iron to Sebastian Shade for use on the Susquehanna River Improvement.

John Reed had a $500 contract to improve a portion of the river navigation. He lived in Lancaster County, on the Susquehanna River opposite Reed's Island. BHL, Field Books and Accounts, Aug.–Sept., Oct.–Nov. 1801, both in PBHL (13/A1, 14/A1); Osburn, "Mysteries of Martic," pp. 167, 177; Ellis and Evans, *History of Lancaster County,* pp. 45, 977; Robert H. Goodell, "The First Columbia Bridge," *PLCHS* 46 (1942):97.

3. Christian P. Hauducoeur, a Maryland engineer who had published a map of the Maryland portion of the Susquehanna River in 1799, was employed by the Susquehanna Canal Company "to make a map of the Maryland part of the River." In addition, he surveyed the lowest section of the Pennsylvania portion of the river (from McCall's Ferry to the Maryland line) and supplied this information to BHL for the latter's report and survey map. Hauducoeur spent six days in Philadelphia "drawing out" his map which BHL apparently used in compiling his own map of the Susquehanna. BHL, "The Susquehanna from Columbia to the Pennsylvania line and thence to Havre de Grace," watercolor map, c. 1802, PBHL (306/A1); BHL, Field Book and Accounts, Oct.–Nov. 1801; Hauducoeur, *A Map of the Head of Chesapeake Bay and Susquehanna River . . .* (Philadelphia, 1799); BHL, *Engineering Drawings,* pp. 77, 82.

4. "The Children" refers to Henry Sellon Boneval Latrobe (1792–1817) and Lydia Sellon Latrobe (1791–1878), BHL's children by his first wife, recently arrived from England. "The *boys*" probably refers to MEL's brothers: Samuel, Richard, Isaac, Jr., and Andrew. MEL's brother Robert (1774–1804), a graduate of the University of Pennsylvania (1792) and Philadelphia lawyer, was assisting BHL on the survey expedition. (Another brother, John, born in 1775, had died of yellow fever in South Carolina in 1796.) "Our mother and father" refers to Isaac Hazlehurst (1742–1834) and Juliana (or Joanna) (Purviance) Hazlehurst (1741–1804). Isaac Hazlehurst was born in Manchester, England, worked in a London business firm, spent some time in Paris, and immigrated to America around 1768 with his brother Robert (1755–1825), who eventually established a branch of Isaac's Philadelphia mercantile firm in Charleston, S.C. In 1769 Isaac married Juliana Purviance, daughter of Philadelphia merchant Samuel Purviance. During the American Revolution he played an important role as a signer of colonial notes. Although he suffered financially as a result of the war, he reestablished a prosperous mercantile house in Philadelphia, which he maintained until it failed in 1809. BHL to Samuel Hazlehurst, 3 Sept. 1809, LB (70/D9); BHL, Field Book and Accounts, Oct.–Nov. 1801, PBHL; Frank Willing Leach, "Old Philadelphia Families: Hazlehurst" (no. 59), *The North American* (Philadelphia), 19 July 1908.

TO WILLIAM BARTON

Peachbottom [Pa.] Novr. 14th, 1801

My dear friend,[1]

I herewith return you your Son, improved I hope in knowledge, and I believe in health.[2] I cannot say too much in favor of his talents, his disposition and his conduct. You have reason to be proud of him, and may look forward with more confidence to comfort and pleasure from him, than most parents have reason to do. There is an innate decency and chasteness of mind in him which I have rarely met with, and which it will not be in the power of any company, which he may and probably will fall into before he is twenty, entirely to warp. Society may expect from him a most valuable and prominent citizen, and your and his mothers[3] sound judgement will be able to set him so agoing that the comunity may not lose the benefit of his talents. He certainly is more inclined to pursue science and *art,* than to enter into any profession of *conjecture* or of words. Whether medecine may be called in a great measure a profession of *conjecture* your brother[4] may decide. You can answer for the Lawyer. Should my profession flourish, and your Son wish to acquire such a knowledge of it, as would enable him to live by it, my office is open to him. Two Years of previous education at a College would be necessary to put him in the first rank of the profession. I intend this merely as a *hint,* among your future views for this most amiable youth, whom I shall always love most sincerely, and who has secured to himself an interest in the affection of Mr. Hazlehurst, that will be lasting.[5]

I will send you from Philadelphia a draft for 15 Dollars. I know not here how my account with Kirkpatrick stands.[6]

My best respects attend all your family. My hands are so cold I can scarcely write more than that I am with much affection Yours

B. Henry Latrobe

ALS: Vertical File, MdHS (164/B7). Addressed to Barton in Lancaster.

1. William Barton (c. 1754–1817), one of the six children of the Rev. Thomas Barton (1730–80) of Lancaster, was a local jurist and staunch Republican supporter of Gov. Thomas McKean.
2. William Paul Crillon Barton (1786–1856) assisted BHL on his Susquehanna River survey. He would later collaborate with BHL on the proposed establishment of a naval hospital in Washington. See BHL to Barton, 10 Nov. 1811, in BHL, *Correspondence,* 3.
3. Elizabeth (Rhea) Barton (b. 1759) was the daughter of John and Mary (Smith) Rhea

of Portsmouth, N.H. Edward Carpenter and Louis Henry Carpenter, comps., *Samuel Carpenter and his Descendants* (Philadelphia, 1912), p. 92.

4. Benjamin Smith Barton (1766–1815), Philadelphia physician and naturalist, was William Barton's younger brother. A professor at the University of Pennsylvania from 1791, he was a member of the American Philosophical Society and its vice-president from 1802. His *Elements of Botany* (1803) was the first botany textbook written in America. Jeannette E. Graustein, "The Eminent Benjamin Smith Barton," *PMHB* 85 (1961): 423–38.

5. William P. C. Barton went on to the College of New Jersey (now Princeton), where he received a classical education and graduated with distinction in 1805. After studying medicine at the University of Pennsylvania under his uncle, Dr. Benjamin Smith Barton, he was appointed surgeon in the U.S. Navy. Throughout his long career he maintained his affiliation with the navy and in 1842 became the first chief of the navy's Bureau of Medicine and Surgery. Barton also was an accomplished botanist. Appointed professor of botany at the University of Pennsylvania, he published a number of botanical works including *Vegetable Materia Medica of the United States* (1817–19) and *Flora of North America* (1821–23).

6. William Kirkpatrick (d. 1838), Lancaster merchant and philanthropist, played an important role in the town's affairs in the late eighteenth and early nineteenth centuries. He was a Lancaster borough (later town) official and was a strong promoter of internal improvements in the Lancaster area. He held stock in the Philadelphia and Lancaster Turnpike Company and the Columbia Bridge Company and served as president of the latter in 1823. Kirkpatrick belonged to a number of voluntary organizations, often serving in leadership positions. An elder of the Presbyterian Church, Kirkpatrick also assisted Lancaster blacks in securing the establishment of an African Methodist Episcopal Church. *PLCHS* 5 (1901):114, 22 (1918):94, 33 (1929):114–16, 34 (1930):137, 235, 35 (1931):130, 133, 140, 36 (1932):89, 46 (1942):97, 126; Ellis and Evans, *History of Lancaster County*, pp. 373, 374, 387, 478, 490.

REPORT ON THE SUSQUEHANNA RIVER IMPROVEMENTS

To His Excellency Thos. McKean, Governor of Pennsylvania. Report on the improvements in the Navigation of the river Susquehannah, from Columbia to the Pennsylvania line, and from thence to tide water, in consequence of the appropriation of 10.000 dollars to that purpose by the State of Pennsylvania, and of 8.500 Dollars expended by the Susquehannah canal Company during the year 1801.

Philadelphia Novr. 28th. 1801.

Sir,

In order to improve the navigation of the river Susquehannah, within the state of Pennsa. by such gradual means as the appropriation of the Legislature would permit, and by a concert with the Susquehannah company of Maryland to render this improvement effectual to tide water, I received your Excellency's instructions to repair to the river to make a compleat survey of the same below Columbia; and in concert with the late Colonel Antes, so to direct the work within Pennsylvania, that the most material obstructions might be removed, should the limitation of expenditure prevent the completion of a *perfect* navigation this Season.

The death of Colonel Antes, soon after my arrival at Columbia, deprived the State and myself of the benefit of his very extraordinary talents and integrity. He had however viewed the river from the Tide to Columbia, jointly with Sebastian Shade, Esqr. and lived long enough to communicate his general ideas upon the State of its Bed and its future improvement.

The judgement and experience of Mr. Shade in the navigation of the Susquehannah, are well known. He was engaged jointly with Col. Antes, to superintend the works below the Maryland line, and his knowledge has been most essentially serviceable to both States. After my uncles death he was so obliging as to view once more with me those parts of the river of which the navigation was the most difficult, and a common principle of improvement was agreed upon. He also undertook to see those works performed, which were necessary immediately above the Pennsylvania line, contiguous to those in Maryland.

Since the month of August, in which I received your instructions, I have executed a compleat and I believe very accurate survey and map of the river, and every exertion has been made to forward the works.[1] The Season has been so favorable that I have now the satisfaction to report to your Excellency the completion of all that could be effected by the appropriation of the Legislature: and although much remains to be done before a clear inshore channel, entirely free from danger and affording a back navigation can be made; yet the work of this Season has removed all the obstructions which were formerly so formidable, as to render the attempt to descend the river hazardous to the lives of those who undertook it.

The principles that have guided the direction of the improvement, have had a view to the prosecution of the work to perfection at a future period. No money has been laid out to get over a difficulty, by means, which in future would be laid aside. As far as it has been carried, the work is part of a straight, clear inshore channel on the East side of the river; between the Western Boundary of which and the Shore, as 189 marked by trees or high rocks, no danger shall exist, so that the simple direction, *to keep the shore close,* shall be a perfect chart of the navigation to the head of the Susquehannah Canal, and thence to the Bald friar.[2] At the Bald friar, natural obstructions, not to be overcome by any reasonable expenditure will always oblige the vessels to cross to the Western Shore. The obstructions to crossing are removed, and a good channel is made thence to the tide.

The detail of the works, which have been actually executed, are contained fully in the directions for navigating the new channel, which are hereunto annexed and I beg leave here only to report generally on the subject.[3]

The most formidable obstruction in Pennsylvania below Columbia was perhaps Turkey hill fall. The river after spreading to the width of nearly two miles, suddenly contracts itself on breaking through the mountains to the width of 60 Chains, or ¾ of a mile. The whole bed is obstructed by high ridges of Rocks extending in regular lines directly across from shore to Shore, while at the same time it is choaked by rocky islands; this state of the river continues about a mile, still contracting its width. A natural channel on the Eastern Shore, generally from 50 to 100 feet deep, and from 60 to 100 feet wide then commences; through which, in the autumn, the whole river is discharged with astonishing rapidity. In this channel there is no danger. The difficulty has been to enter it round the point of Turkey hill.[4] In the year 1798 the Maryland Company[5] expended a considerable sum, under the direction of Col. Antes, in endeavors to clear a channel on the Eastern shore, by blowing away the rocks. This work was interrupted by a law of Pennsylvania,[6] and though some improvement had been made, still the place remained highly dangerous. During the present season the channel has been further opened and straitened, and it is the opinion of persons who are well acquainted with the river that *enough* has been done. Others and I believe a majority of experienced pilots, whom I have consulted, agree with me in judgment, that some money still remains to be expended on this spot before it can be called a safe channel, and I should recommend, that of any future appropriation a portion should be applied to open Turkey-hill falls entirely, so as to leave nothing in passing them to extraordinary skill and management.

Below Turkey hill the next most dangerous rapid is called Eschelmann's Sluice. It is situated ½ a mile below the mouth of Conestogo.

There was no possibility of avoiding this sluice without making an entire new channel to the Point falls. This has been done, and the channel has been continued, below the Point falls so as to render that very dangerous part of the river safe to the Indian steps should the force of the current carry Vessels out of the most common direction. The Appendix hereunto annexed more fully explains what has been done.

No obstructions occur below the Indian steps which may not be easily avoided, till you arrive at the foot of the bear Islands. For though Culley's falls are among the roughest parts of the river, I cannot learn that any wrecks have happened there, as the course is tolerably straight, and the direction easy. Below these falls a clear channel continues to the end of the Bear Islands where the river again spreads to the width of two miles across, and becomes a more quiet stream, shallow, and sprinkled over with rocks from side to side. Along the Eastern shore a channel has been made by the removal of all obstructions to the Maryland line.

A law of the state of Maryland was passed in 1800 loaning to the Susquehannah Company the sum of 30.000 Dollars, on condition that 5.000 Dollars of this sum should be expended in rendering the bed of the river navigable for Arks and rafts in the spring season.[7] This sum was evidently very inadequate to the object, and after a compleat view of the river by Mr. Shade and myself, in which the expence of several proposals was minutely considered, a plan was finally arranged; to carry which into execution, the sum of 3.500 Dollars[8] appeared requisite. It also appeared that it would be necessary to expend within the State of Pennsylvania the sum of 1.500 Doll. beyond the appropriation of 10.000 Dollars; in order to unite the works of the states in a proper manner. As several Gentlemen of the State of Maryland interested in the navigation of the Susquehannah, had on a former occasion offered to raise a large Subscription, to be expended in its improvement, a meeting with them and the Governor and Directors of the Company[9] was obtained at Baltimore in October, to which I submitted the plan and estimate. It was adopted, but as the resources of the private Individuals who met could not be immediately called into action, the Susquehannah Company directed their own funds to be applied to its execution, and the Work is in such progress that I cannot doubt its completion this season. By this plan all obstructions to crossing the river at the Bald friar will be removed, and the most dangerous part of the navigation in Maryland, Amos's falls, will be cleared.

It will appear by what I have herein reported to your Excellency, and by the Appendix hereunto annexed, that a navigation perfectly safe, 191 in comparison to what it has hitherto been, is already effected from Columbia to tidewater. But much remains still to be done, before this *unfriendly river* can be made fit for the common purposes of a convenient intercourse between the country, so immense in extent and population, which it waters, and the commercial cities. For a few months in the Year indeed, the produce of the most distant parts of Pennsylvania, and even of some parts of the State of New York, can be hurried to the tide. But by the shortness of the period to which the supply of the commercial market, with this produce is limited, the market becomes overstocked, and the Back-country Pennsylvanian deals to disadvantage among so numerous competitors. The Arks always, and often the boats, must be sold for a mere trifle, although they contain much value in labour and materials. Then, the returns of manufactured and imported goods is circuitous and slow; for it is impossible to carry any bulk of goods up the river; and land carriage, for at least part of the way, must be resorted to.

It will be for your Excellency to consider in what manner you may please to recommend to the Legislature to provide the means to over-come these difficulties. That they *may* be overcome, at a less expence of labour and money, than on a first view their magnitude would suggest, cannot be doubted; and I comply with your desire in suggesting what ought to be done to that end.

1.) To compleat an inshore channel on the Eastern side from the line to Columbia, and thence to the Chickisalunga Rocks;[10] and to render the present perfectly safe.

2.) To make a towing path for horses, above the reach of ice and freshes, along the river, in the following progression: 1. from the mouth of Conestogo to Turkey hill; 2. From the foot of the bear Islands to Fultons ferry; 3. From Columbia to Chickisalunga Rocks. From the Maryland line to the foot of the bear Islands, from Fultons ferry, to the mouth of Conestogo, and from Turkey hill to the falls above Columbia the river is shallow enough at all seasons to admit of poling.

3.) To render the inshore channel navigable in at least 2 feet of water at all seasons, either by deepening the bed of the river, or (which is the cheapest and easiest method) by erecting low wing dams at proper places to throw in the stream.

4.) To continue the towing paths where omitted.

The improvements in the navigation of the river above Chick-
192 isalunga Rocks are not within the scope of my instructions, or of my

knowledge. The map hereunto annexed has been made with scrupulous care, and is I hope exact.

I do not venture to lay before your Excellency any estimate of works so various and extensive. An Annual appropriation of 20.000 Dollars would however in my opinion accomplish them *all* in five years.

I beg leave to add that upon every subject contained in my report and the appendix, I have made use of the information of Mr. Shade, and of every experienced pilot whom I could meet with, so that even where opinions should differ from those I have expressed, I may venture to assure you, that my own judgment is not unsupported by the experience of many respectable men who have made the navigation of the river a principal business of their lives.

I am with true respect Yours faithfully

B. Henry Latrobe
Engineer

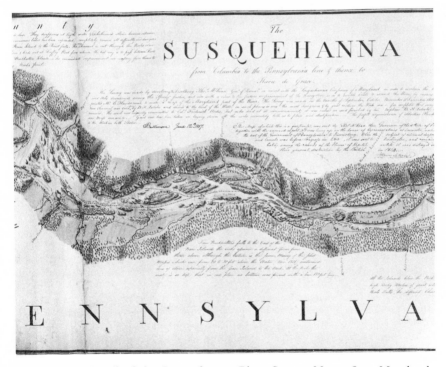

Fig. 7. BHL, Detail of the Susquehanna River Survey Map, 1802, Maryland Historical Society.

DS: Susquehanna River Improvement File, PHMC (164/C11). Printed in *Aurora*, 29–30 Mar. 1802 (microfiche add.) and *Report of the Governor and Directors, to the Proprietors of the Susquehanna Canal, at Their Semi-Annual Meeting Held in the City of Baltimore, October 25th, 1802* (Baltimore, 1802), pp. 13–20 (dated 24 Nov. 1801) (164/F1).

1. BHL actually completed the map in early 1802. BHL to McKean, 15 Jan. 1802, Susquehanna River Improvement File, PHMC (165/A10).

2. The ferry at Bald Friar was "said to have been kept at one time by a bald-headed man, called Fry, at which time it was called Bald Fry's Ferry." Johnston, *History of Cecil County*, p. 345n.

3. See The Susquehanna River Improvement: Editorial Note, n. 3, above.

4. "Turkey Hill [is] so-called from having formerly been famous for wild turkey shooting, tho' now, thanks to the boundless liberty of killing game at all seasons and the total lack of protection from game laws, these excellent birds are scarcely ever to be met with in this part of the country. Turkey Hill is situated six miles to the left [southeast] of Columbia and twelve [southwest] from Lancaster." Richard Beale Davis, ed., *Jeffersonian America: Notes on the United States of America Collected in the Years 1805–6–7 and 11–12 by Sir Augustus John Foster, Bart.* (San Marino, Calif., 1954), pp. 222–23.

5. I.e., the Susquehanna Canal Company.

6. See BHL to McKean, 17 Oct. 1801, n. 2, above.

7. The act was passed 3 January 1800. William Kilty, ed., *Laws of Maryland . . .* , 2 vols. (Annapolis, Md., [1800]), vol. 2, 1799–1800 session, chap. 17. Joshua Gilpin, a Philadelphia merchant and friend of BHL's, described the Susquehanna arks as "vessells of the rudest and strongest construction, a flat frame of timber is laid for the bottom very strong on which strong parts are placed upright and boards fastened on the outside, which are roughly tho securely caulked—they are in fact nothing more, than a vast, rough, and unwieldy box of this shape, being flat bottomed and perpendicular at the sides, about 60 to 90 feet long, from 15 to 20 wide and about 5 feet deep—they are so rough as to be put together only with wooden pins or dowells. They carry an immense quantity, and draw about 2 feet water . . . they have neither oars or sails but depend solely on the velocity of the current and are guided by a long oar at each end—thus strong they bounce and tumble over the falls and rapids, it being only necessary to keep them from running aground." Joseph E. Walker, ed., *Pleasure and Business in Western Pennsylvania: The Journal of Joshua Gilpin, 1809* (Harrisburg, Pa., 1975), pp. 11–13.

8. In his errata to the *Aurora* version of this document (30 Mar. 1802; microfiche add.), BHL noted that the figure should be $8,500.

9. The governor or president of the Susquehanna Canal Company, incorporated in 1783, was Robert Gilmor; the directors included William Smith, William Cooke, and Mark Pringle. Gilmor (1748–1822), a Scottish immigrant and Federalist, became one of the wealthiest Baltimore merchants and acquired a reputation in international mercantile circles. *Report of the Governor and Directors of the Susquehanna Canal Company* (Baltimore, 1802), p. 12; Robert Gilmor, *Memoir, or Sketch of the History of Robert Gilmor of Baltimore* (n.p., 1840), pp. 3, 27, 32.

10. The Chiquesalunga Rocks, also called Chickies Rock or Chickies Ridge, are at the mouth of Chiquesalunga Creek north of Columbia in Lancaster County. The name derives from the Indian word Chickiswalungo, or "place of the crawfish." Ellis and Evans, *History of Lancaster County*, p. 875; George P. Donehoo, *A History of Indian Villages and Place Names in Pennsylvania* (Harrisburg, Pa., 1928), p. 29.

TO THOMAS McKEAN

Philadelphia Jany. 17th, 1802.

Sir,

Since I had last the honor to request of Your Excellency to grant a Warrant for 1.080.73 to Sebastian Shade Esqr. in order to the full discharge of the expenses of the Work in clearing the Susquehannah from the Maryland line to Niel's point (a distance of seven Miles) I have received the very flattering information, that Messrs. Haldiman and Strickland took advantage of the fresh which about 3 Weeks ago raised the river four feet, to navigate the new Channel from Columbia to the tide, and that they have found it perfectly safe, and easily kept.[1]

The work at Burkhalter's ferry is now the only part which has not been compleatly paid for. The Contractors have become impatient for their balances, which amount to about 2.000 Dollars. Of this Sum whatever is deficient in the Pensylvania appropriation will be made up by the Susquehannah Company, and I have already drawn upon them for 600 Dollars. I am unwilling further to press them, untill it shall be known whether the Legislature are disposed to grant the further appropriation of 2.000 Dollars recommended in your Excellency's communication to be granted for the repayment of their advance.[2]

One of the principal Contractors being now in town, I have taken the liberty once more to use the expedient for his relief, which I have already used in favor of Mr. Shade; namely to send to you a blank Endorsement for a Warrant, to be filled up at your Excellency's pleasure, for 800 Dollars, which sum will perfectly satisfy all pressing demands; and should untill I arrive. The balance of the appropriation of 10.000, in our Treasury, will then be 120. Dollars.

At Turkey hill there remains due only the sum of 49$.74cts., all accounts for that part of the Work being settled, and the Vouchers in my possession.

I have endorsed the blank Warrant to Geo. Stoner, a very respectable farmer living at Burkhalters ferry, to whom the late Coll. Antes entrusted the resident superintendance of that part of the Work, whenever he was absent at other parts of river, who will see the money faithfully distributed agreeably to the directions I have sent to him.

I beg to assure you of the sincere respect with which I am Your Excellency's obliged hble. Servt.

B. Henry Latrobe

195

ALS: Susquehanna River Improvement File, PHMC (165/B1). Sent by George Stoner.

1. John Haldeman (1753–1832) and Jacob Strickler (1763–1812) bought a grist mill near Columbia in August 1801. Haldeman, a wealthy merchant and partner of Robert Ralston of Philadelphia in the China trade, served in the Pennsylvania General Assembly. In 1790 he built a grist mill at the mouth of Conoy Creek and sent flour and produce down the Susquehanna River in keel boats to Wright's Ferry (Columbia), from which point it was shipped overland to Philadelphia. Strickler was engaged in the lime-burning business in Hempfield, Lancaster County. He served in the state militia as major (1797) and lieutenant colonel (1799) and was also a member of the state legislature (1797–1800). Strickler was one of the three commissioners appointed to superintend the removal of the state's effects from Philadelphia to Lancaster when the state's capital changed in 1799. Haldeman's and Strickler's interest in opening the river to navigation below Wright's Ferry probably prompted their voyage through the channel newly opened under BHL's direction. Thomas Lynch Montgomery, ed., *Pennsylvania Archives*, 6 ser., 15 vols. (Harrisburg, Pa., 1906–07), 4 : 582, 746; *PLCHS* 48 (1944):104, 55 (1951):8; Alexander Harris, *A Biographical History of Lancaster County: Being a History of Early Settlers and Eminent Men of the County* (Lancaster, Pa., 1872), pp. 257, 598; William Henry Egle, *History of the Counties of Dauphin and Lebanon in the Commonwealth of Pennsylvania: Biographical and Genealogical* (Philadelphia, 1883), p. 498; Ellis and Evans, *History of Lancaster County*, pp. 549, 750, 878.

2. On 5 December 1801 McKean had requested the Pennsylvania legislature to appropriate the $2,000 needed to complete the river improvement project. *Journal of the House of Representatives of the Commonwealth of Pennsylvania* (1801–02), p. 24.

TO THOMAS McKEAN

Philadelphia January 27th, 1802

Sir,

By the bearer, Mr. Stoner, I again take the liberty to trouble you with a blank Warrant for 125 Dollars, indorsed to him. I must at the same time mention to your Excellency, that Mr. Stoner was placed in the situation in which he has continued since my appointment, by the late Colonel Antes, and was, upon his death bed, strongly recommended to me, by him as a man of strict probity, and attention to business. He has amply deserved that Character since I have known him, and the works at Burkhalter's speak sufficiently for him. By their means the most dangerous part of the river, next to Turkey hill falls, comprising Eschelman's Sluice, Burkhalters falls, and the point falls, is now among the safest parts of the Navigation. Without Mr. Stoner's exertions in superintending them daily they would scarcely have been completed this season. If any thing has been whispered against him, it is by those to whom nothing appears a greater crime than republicanism. I take the liberty particularly to state thus much of Mr. Stoner, because Francis Murray, after breaking my orders in order to obtain the last warrant for 800 Dollars, has I understand endeavored to obtain for himself a degree of character, which, if he had deserved, wóuld have induced me to have paid his demand without submitting it to Mr. Stoner's discretion.[1] I am truly sorry that my absence has occasioned trouble to your Excellency which I would, if possible have spared you. But though I can walk about my business without pain, I still can[not] get my wound to heal entirely, and am detained. Hoped every day to set off [to] Lancaster, and finding myself disappointed.[2]

The balance still due will be paid on my draft by the Susquehannah company, but I have delayed drawing untill I shall see whether or no the Legislature will do anything for the Susquehannah navigation.

I am with the truest respect and gratitude for the obligations I am under to your Excellency Yr. faithfull hble. Servt.

B. Henry Latrobe

ALS: Susquehanna River Improvement File, PHMC (165/B11).

1. Francis Murray of Chanceford, York County, had a joint contract with Barney Rogers and Ferdinand O'Donnell to clear part of the Susquehanna River channel below Pequea under the general supervision of George Stoner. By late October 1801 only $20 of the $1,000 contract had been paid. Murray was apparently still attempting to obtain his money in January 1802 by deception (in BHL's view), if necessary. BHL, Field Books and Accounts, Aug.–Sept., Oct.–Nov. 1801, both in PBHL (13/A1, 14/A1); John "D" Stemmons, ed., *Pennsylvania in 1800* (Salt Lake City, 1972), p. 446.

2. Besides the wound mentioned, BHL had also suffered from a "very severe attack of sickness" with which the rest of his family was soon stricken. A second attack hit the Latrobe household in February. BHL to McKean, 15 Jan. 1802, Susquehanna River Improvement File, PHMC (165/A10); BHL to Miller, 25 Feb. 1802, below.

TO WILLIAM MILLER

Philadelphia Feby. 25th. 1802.

Sir,[1]

A second very severe attack of sickness, and the delay in receiving such information from Virginia as I have now procured, has prevented till this day my decision as to the contract for the Lighthouses at New and   197

Old point comfort, and at Smith's point.[2] Having now before me all the data upon which to form an opinion, I am sorry that I cannot prudently engage in the undertaking under the limitation of the sum appropriated. I have planned three lighthouse adapted to the situations, and of the highths mentioned, and calculated upon as small a scale as my determination, not to offer to the public any thing but what should be *incombustible* and *permanent* in its construction, would admit. These three plans, if no accident should happen to increase the expense, but every thing succeed to my expectation, might be executed for $17.500 dollars, leaving as a profit or compensation, only $1.500. For this sum, it is evident, that I cannot prudently leave my family and business for so long a time as would be required only to set the work a going.

As much therefore as I feel myself obliged and flattered by your very polite communication, I am under the necessity for declining the contract. But I am ready to furnish to you any ideas on the subject which might be thought useful, in the form of a report, and also the plans I had made. I considered stone staircases as of the first importance, and I believe that a construction of the light upon the principles of Argand's lamp would be highly important and easily practicable.[3] The construction of the light destined for a light[house] designed by me in England, also [will b]e furnished.[4]

I beg you to accept of my sincerest thanks for your politeness on this occasion, and that you will believe me with great esteem Yours faithfully

B. Henry Latrobe.

ALS: Records of the U.S. Coast Guard, RG 26, National Archives (165/C1). Addressed to Miller at the Treasury Department, Washington. Bracketed portions of the text are conjectural readings, the manuscript being torn.

1. William Miller, Jr., was commissioner of the revenue, U.S. Treasury Department. In repealing all internal taxes after June 1802, Congress abolished Miller's post. Noble E. Cunningham, Jr., *The Process of Government under Jefferson* (Princeton, N.J., 1978), pp. 98–99.

2. Miller had written to BHL, Henry Dearborn, and John McComb, Jr., the previous November requesting them to submit plans and estimates for the erection of three lighthouses on Chesapeake Bay at Smith's Point, Old Point Comfort, and New Point Comfort. The appropriation for Smith's Point was $9,000, for Old Point Comfort $5,000, and for New Point Comfort $5,000. Stone was the preferred construction material and the plans were to include "an Oil Vault and a moderate sized Frame Dwelling for the Keeper and his family." Miller to BHL, Dearborn, and McComb, 17 Nov. 1801, RG 26, National Archives (164/C1).

The three men each had previous experiences with American lighthouses. In early November 1798, BHL and Miles King had offered a joint bid of $3,000 for the Old Point

Comfort lighthouse authorized by Congress in April 1798. However, due to his change in plans and departure for Philadelphia the next month, BHL did no further significant work on the lighthouse plan until Miller approached him in 1801. Dearborn entered into a contract in 1798 to construct a lighthouse on Cape Hatteras, North Carolina. In 1806 the Treasury Department consulted BHL on the value of Dearborn's light. McComb (1763–1853), builder and mason, built three lighthouses in the 1790s, at Cape Henry, Virginia, and at Montauk Point and Eton's Neck, both on Long Island. BHL, *Journals*, 2 : 448–49; Richard Harrison to BHL, 22 Nov. 1806, RG 217, National Archives (186/B14); Agnes Addison Gilchrist, "John McComb, Sr. and Jr., in New York, 1784–1799," *Journal of the Society of Architectural Historians* 31 (1972): 10, 15–16.

3. About 1782 Aimé Argand invented a lamp with a tubular wick that allowed a current of air to pass along both the inside and outside of the flame, thus achieving more perfect combustion and a brighter light.

4. This is the only hint in BHL's extant writings that he designed a lighthouse before leaving England in 1795. No further evidence of this has been found.

TO MARY ELIZABETH LATROBE

Lancaster, March 18th. 1802.

My dearest Wife

I have written to you twice since my arrival, by Dunwoody's stage,[1] and I hope you have not failed to receive my letters. I intend this to go by post, but I shall also write a few lines by the stage. I expect today to receive a letter from you, and promise myself the happiness of hearing that you are well and cheerfull, contented and happy in the degree of enjoyment of which the unavoidable course of human affairs, renders us capable, and in the certainty that whether absent from you, or the happiest of men by *your side,* your husband's heart is full of the truest and tenderest affection for you.

Having dined and spent a late evening at Mr. Thompson's I arranged my papers for this day, and have got my demands put upon the appropriation list.[2] I have attended the house this morning, and regretted that I durst not use my pencil as freely as I wished. Depend upon it, it is the true original ugly Club.[3] Some of the figures there exhibited, are *morceaux* fit only for the pencil of Hogarth. I counted only 12 combed heads, and 2 woolen nightcaps. The rest dressed in the fashion of James W-lc-ks.[4] There is neither form nor comeliness in them that we should desire them.[5] Some of the countenances unite coarseness and brutality with stupidity in a superior degree. And yet I was most disappointed in 199 hearing sound sense proceed from many of the least promising in appearance, though dressed in very uncouth language.

All these are strong likenesses, and not caricatured.[6]

After the house broke up, I had occasion to go to the Governor. He had just received a petition from Meadeville on lake Erie praying for the removal of a Mr. Kennedy, a prothonotary whom he had appointed, and who is said to be a very worthy man.[7] He was stated to be an aristocrat, a tyrant and a tory. The petition was signed by more than 500 names, written on papers of various sizes pasted together so as to form a roll of about 7 feet long. On looking over the roll is appeared, that the signatures consisted of old Muster rolls, of the signatures to other petitions the heads of which were cut off, and so clumsily pieced, that the words *"as in duty bound shall ever pray,"* were not even destroyed and on separating two pieces, the head showed the names to be a list of taxable inhabitants of Erie county. So abominable a forgery, excited a little of His Excellencys choler, and the fellows who brought it sneaked away in the utmost confusion.

I am now going to dine at Mr. Hopkins', who called here this morning to invite me.[8] All the Barton's, the Governor's family and half the town are to be there. I shall finish this letter on my return.

I intended to have sent this letter by post. But Mr. Francis who is arrived has prevented me, by keeping me beyond the hour, and I have no letter from you!!!!

Mrs. Hopkins tells me that *by some untoward accident* she was prevented from calling upon you during your stay here, which she much regretted, and so did I, you may be assured. However she was pointedly apologizing and polite, and Mr. Hopkins did every thing a Gentleman could and ought [to heal] the smart of the neglect which they seem [conscious] to have occasioned. There were exactly 20 at table. The Barton's 4; McKeans 4; Miss Jones from Newcastle, had seen aunt Greeman;[9] Miss Ross; Mr. Ross;[10] three or four young Gentlemen; Miss

Coakley; and a splendid dinner; but what care I for them or for dinners, when I have scarcely paper left, to say how all things and people pass before me like the figures of a magic lanthorn, while my heart and soul is entirely engrossed by thinking how much more I should enjoy every thing were you but with me. Heav'n bless thee my own dear Mary. Your most affectionate husband

B. H. Latrobe

ALS: Mrs. Gamble Latrobe Collection, MdHS (165/C6). Addressed to Mrs. Latrobe, 186 Arch Street, Philadelphia.

1. John Dunwoody (d. 16 December 1802), Revolutionary War veteran, owned the Sign of the Spread Eagle Tavern as early as 1792 and moved it to the corner of Ninth and Market streets around 1800. Dunwoody's inn was the eastern terminus of the Philadelphia-Lancaster stage, which, in 1802, left Philadelphia each weekday morning for Lancaster and returned in the evening. *Journal* (Lancaster), 4 July 1802, quoted in John "D" Stemmons, ed., *Pennsylvania in 1800* (Salt Lake City, 1972), p. xvi; *PMHB* 46 (1922):360.

2. For Thomas McKean Thompson, see BHL to McKean, 20 Oct. 1801, n. 3, above. The demands were for $2,000 that BHL had calculated as necessary for completion of the Susquehanna improvement project. The Pennsylvania House of Representatives granted $2,126 for the river project on 29 March 1802. Governor McKean signed it into law on 6 April 1802. *Journal of the House of Representatives of the Commonwealth of Pennsylvania* (1801–02), pp. 451, 502; *Pa. Statutes, 1802–1805*, p. 226.

3. The story of the ugly club, or the "Club of Ugly-Faces," was one popularized by Edward Ward (1667–1731) in his *Satyrical Reflections on Clubs . . .* (London, 1710). This collection presented some thirty-two clubs, many of which were caricatures in varying degrees of actual and rumored gatherings among London's tavern and coffee house habitués. Ward's book went through seven editions by 1756, when it appeared as *A Compleat and Humorous Account of All the Remarkable Clubs and Societies in the Cities of London and Westminster. . . .* The Club of Ugly-Faces, however, seems to have been written of before Ned Ward's account, appearing in *The Wandering Spy, or the Way of the World Inquired into*, no. 12 (August 1705), pp. 18–25.

The ugly club was not unknown in America; in 1808, for example, the putative George Town Ugly Club made an appeal for new members who might possess "a *huge nose, goggle eyes, hump back, wide mouth*, or some other distinguished and prominent mark of merit." *Washington Federalist* (Georgetown, D.C.), 27 July 1808; Howard William Troyer, *Ned Ward of Grub Street* (Cambridge, Mass., 1946), pp. 151–68.

4. James S. Wilcocks was a brother of MEL's girlhood friend, Mary Wilcocks. Hamlin, *Latrobe*, pp. 197–99.

5. "For he shall grow up before him as a tender plant, and as a root out of a dry ground: he hath no form nor comeliness; and when we shall see him, *there is* no beauty that we should desire him." Isa. 53 : 2.

6. George Jacob Follmer (Folmer, Fullmer) (c. 1738–1804) married Anna Catherine Walters (1742–1808) in 1760. A member of the Pennsylvania state senate, he died in Northumberland County. *Baltimore American*, 6 Sept. 1804; William Curry Harllee, *Kinfolks: A Genealogical and Biographical Record of Thomas and Elizabeth (Stuart) Harllee*, 3 vols. (New Orleans, 1934), 2 : 984.

7. Dr. Thomas Ruston Kennedy (d. 1813) was appointed prothonotary of Crawford

County by McKean on 13 March 1800. Kennedy, a son of Revolutionary War surgeon Samuel Kennedy, owned a large amount of land in western Pennsylvania. He was surgeon on Andrew Ellicott's expedition to lay out the town of Presqu'Isle (now Erie, Pennsylvania), in 1795. In July 1802 Kennedy married Ellicott's daughter, Jane Judith. Gertrude MacKinney, ed., *Pennsylvania Archives*, 9 ser., 10 vols. ([Harrisburg, Pa.,], 1931–35), 3 : 1611; Charles W. Evans, *Biographical and Historical Accounts of the Fox, Ellicott, and Evans Families* (Buffalo, N.Y., 1882), p. 193; Catherine Van Cortlandt Mathews, *Andrew Ellicott: His Life and Letters* (New York, 1908), p. 124.

8. James Hopkins (d. 1834), admitted to the Lancaster bar in 1787, became an eminent lawyer and developed "the largest and most lucrative" practice in nineteenth-century Lancaster County. He trained many young lawyers including future president James Buchanan. Hopkins served as a churchwarden of St. James Episcopal Church (1827–34) and was a director of the Lancaster branch of the Bank of Pennsylvania (1803). He also was a promoter of internal improvements, serving as a manager of the Falmouth and Elizabethtown Turnpike Company (1810) and securing a state charter for the Conestoga Slack-Water Navigation Company (1820). Ellis and Evans, *History of Lancaster County*, pp. 228, 313, 317, 466, 511; Alexander Harris, *A Biographical History of Lancaster County: Being a History of Early Settlers and Eminent Men of the County* (Lancaster, Pa., 1872), p. 319.

9. Aunt Greeman was a sister of MEL's mother, Juliana (Purviance) Hazlehurst. She was first widowed by a Mr. Eakin, a Presbyterian clergyman from Delaware, and then by a Dr. Greeman (or Greenman). BHL to Henry Clay, 2 Nov. 1813, LB (113/A2).

10. Probably George Ross, Jr., son of the signer of the Declaration of Independence. In 1791, Gov. Thomas Mifflin appointed the younger Ross as register and recorder of wills for Lancaster County, a position which he held for eighteen years. MacKinney, ed., *Pennsylvania Archives*, 9 ser., 1 : 176; Harris, *Biographical History of Lancaster County*, pp. 501–02.

TO [JOHN EWING COLHOUN]

Philadelphia Aprl. 17th, 1802.

Sir,[1]

I am highly flattered by your polite letter of the 14th currt. and if anything could induce me to enter into such a competition as is proposed by the Advertisement of the trustees of the S. Carolina College, it would be the letter you have written to me.[2] But there are reasons, which your politeness renders it proper for me to state to you, which have long prevented men who have a reputation to lose, and who do not absolutely depend upon a *chance* of business for support, from encountering the sort of rivalry which a public notice calls forth. The merit of the design of a *professional* man of experience and integrity is, that nothing is proposed but what is *practicable; permanent; oeconomical*, with a view to ultimate expenditure; and in point of taste, capable of encountering the severest criticism. But these are merits of which it is not easy for *unprofessional* men to judge *in a plan* (drawing); and on that account the decission is not always according to the merits. I have now before me a most seductive design in point of drawing and coloring, and which has also some excellent points of arrangement, which has been submitted to me, to decide, whether it shall be executed or not. It is drawn by a most ingenious Amateur. But the chimnies cannot be carried up: the staircase has not head way enough by two feet, and lands so that the doors are inaccessible, and some of the upper walls have no support. These errors appear only on scrupulous examination, and no one was more surprised on discovery of them, than the designer. *Elegant,* but *impracticable* designs, which in their execution bring discredit on the art, are however not the only unpleasant rivals of those of professional men. Workmen, who are supposed to know more of expense and construction, than mere tasteful amateurs, are always deficient in arrangement. In private building their own *wants* and *habits* govern their plans of dwellings for gentlemen of quite different *wants* and *habits;* and in public buildings they generally have recourse to books. Excepting when books describe and delineate works of merit, actually executed, they generally have been published by men, whose want of business, and of course, of experience, has given them leisure to speculate, and to build *castles in the Air.* Of this kind are almost *all* the books of Architecture with which I am acquainted, as Thomas's, Paine, Swan's, &c. &c. &c. out of all which a judge of architectural merit, can gather valuable materials; but in which those, who usually have recourse to them, are incapable of distinguishing beauties from defects.[3]

Having determined never to submit a plan to any public body which should not be so digested in its minutest arrangements as to satisfy my own mind of its practicability, and eligibility; and which, in case of my death or absence, should not be sufficient to guide my successor to its perfect completion, I find it extremely inconvenient and humiliating to devote a month's time to making a complete set of drawings and calculations, and to collecting such information respecting the materials to be had, the contracts to be procured, and the expense attending them as would authorise a risk of reputation, and this only for the *chance* of being preferred to the Amateur, and workman who may enter the lists against me. It is the misfortune of our country, that in most instances men of natural Genius, who have had little instruction, and less opportunity of improvement are preferred to men, who have expended the best part of their lives in endeavoring to acquire that knowledge which a good Architect and Engineer ought to possess. I have in all those instances, in which I have taken my chance with others, been thrown out by some such Genius, and I have an habitual dread of them. They have, either as possessing the confidence of building committees, or holding a seat in the committee often made me repent that I have cultivated my profession in preference to my farm. And it is because I have no means of preventing the inroads of these Gentlemen upon the steadiness, the consistency, and energy of my system of operations, unless I were on the spot, that I feel particularly reluctant to offer a plan for a work to be erected at so great a distance.

But should even my plan be adopted, the sum of 350 Dollars (which is the reward offered by the S. Carolina Trustees) is a very inadequate reward only for the labor it would cost me, deducting the actual expense of my office. For before the fair and decissive drawings can leave the office a voluminous mass of drawings of the whole detail must be made, first in the rough, and then in two fair copies, one for myself, the other for my employer.

In one late instance, however, similar to the present the flattering request of a Gentleman high in the public, as well as in my private respect has induced me to give a design for the City hall in New York. I have done so under the express stipulation, that I shall not be considered as a Candidate, if even my design shall be preferred, unless I have the sole direction of the work, appointing my own superintendant, and at the same time rendering myself fully responsible for the success of my plans, and for the conduct of the Superintendant.[4] On these terms I have executed the two great works which have been committed to my care here.[5] They have secured to the public a consistency, an uniformity and a promptness of operation, which cannot be expected from the measures of any Committee; and to myself, the satisfaction of perfect success.

After taking up so much of your time, for which I hope you will pardon me, I beg leave to say, that I will send to *you* a design for the S. Carolina College; not laboriously elaborated, but fairly sketched, and leave it you to do with it as you please, provided, if it should be thought worthy of preference, I shall be permitted to send a person to superintend the work. I will then send also the detailed drawings and instructions, and if possible visit the spot myself once, which will be sufficient. As to compensation, there will be no difficulty in arranging it with me. I shall be very *easy* on the subject, if the terms of contract over the erection are liberal, and I can assure myself, that my character will not, (as it does most disgracefully at Richmond in Virginia) depend upon the *improvements* and embellishments of another. I must however solicit, that you will please to inform me what number of Professors and Students it is intended to accomodate in the house, and whether Stone or Brick is to be employed. Great accuracy is not required; your ideas, if you have not perfect information, will be sufficient.

I hardly know how to apologize for having taken up so much of your time and patience in answering your polite letter. I beg you will however consider my readiness to transmit to you a design, as it sincerely is intended, as a proof of my wish to prove to you how respectfully I am, Your obliged faithful hble. Servt.,

B. Henry Latrobe.

The many marks of haste in the above arise from my wish to answer by return of post, and I must beg you to excuse them.

ALS: Colhoun Papers, South Caroliniana Library, University of South Carolina (165/E6). Although the name of the addressee does not appear on the document, the letter is among Colhoun's manuscripts.

1. John Ewing Colhoun (1750–1802) was a U.S. senator from South Carolina from December 1800 until his death on 26 October 1802, although he had received a leave of absence to return to South Carolina on 8 April 1802.

2. In 1801 the South Carolina legislature passed "An Act to Establish a College at Columbia." In February 1802 the board of trustees of the new South Carolina College (now the University of South Carolina), presided over by Gov. John Drayton (1767–1822), advertised the competition for the college's design, which attracted over half a dozen entries. It seems doubtful that BHL's offer to provide a "fairly sketched" design was accepted; no later record of it is known. On 26 May 1802 the board decided to adopt none of the proposed plans, but rather to draft its own plan based on the principles in the designs submitted by Richard Clark (d. 1808) and Robert Mills (1781–1855), soon to be BHL's pupil. When the college opened in 1805, the first building, Rutledge College, was ready to receive nine students, the president, and one faculty member. John Morrill Bryan, *An Architectural History of the South Carolina College, 1801–1855* (Columbia, S.C., 1976), pp. 3, 4, 12, 14, 30, 59.

3. BHL veiled his disapproval of the authors whom he mentioned. Not only had none of them been an architect with a substantial practice, but two of them had been artisans who wrote for other artisans, and all of them had worked in styles that to BHL seemed not simply old-fashioned but in fact invalid. Abraham Swan (fl. 1745–68) and William Pain (fl. 1758–93), British carpenters, each produced a succession of builders' guides, a number of which had gone into American editions in the late eighteenth century. William Thomas (d. 1800), a minor British architect, published his *Original Designs in Architecture* in 1783. Howard Colvin *A Biographical Dictionary of British Architects, 1600–1840* (London, 1978),   205

pp. 606–07, 799, 822–23; Henry-Russell Hitchcock, *American Architectural Books* (New York, 1976), pp. 74–75, 103.

4. Vice-President Aaron Burr of New York persuaded BHL to enter the competition for the design of a courthouse and city hall building for New York City, announced by the common council of the city on 20 February 1802. During March BHL prepared his city hall plans and perspective, in which he drew heavily on his Bank of Pennsylvania design. His presentation drawings (Prints and Photographs Division, Library of Congress; 291/A1 ff.) are reproduced in BHL, *Architectural Drawings*. The competition, which elicited twenty-six entries, was finally judged on 4 October 1802. Despite Burr's promised influence, BHL's plan lost to one submitted by Joseph François Mangin in collaboration with John McComb, Jr. For BHL's opinion of the Mangin-McComb scheme, which has continued to serve the city, see BHL to Christian Ignatius Latrobe, 4 Nov. 1804, below. See also Damie Stillman, "New York City Hall: Competition and Execution," *Journal of the Society of Architectural Historians*, 23 (1964):129–42.

5. The Philadelphia Waterworks and Bank of Pennsylvania.

The Chesapeake and Delaware Canal

EDITORIAL NOTE (PART 1)

Soon after the seventeenth-century Swedish and Dutch settlement of the narrow-necked Delmarva Peninsula between the Delaware and Chesapeake bays, visionary residents began to see it would be possible to build a canal across it. Such a canal would allow water travel on protected inland waters from the falls of the Delaware River (the site of Trenton, New Jersey) to the capes of the Chesapeake, possibly to great economic benefit. It was not until the late eighteenth century that Philadelphia merchants realized that the growing trade of the interior of Pennsylvania had found its natural route down the Susquehanna River to the Chesapeake and the infant port of Baltimore rather than to their city. In 1769 a surveying party sponsored by the American Philosophical Society and financed by Philadelphia merchants examined several possible routes across the peninsula and estimated the cost of digging a canal along each.

After the Revolutionary War, interest in the canal continued, but political geography hindered action: the project concerned Philadelphians principally, yet all the routes lay in Delaware and Maryland. Moreover, the legislatures of the three states were reluctant to make complementary laws without mutual concessions. Finally, in 1799 the Chesapeake and Delaware Canal Company was incorporated in Maryland, and over a year later in both Pennsylvania and Delaware. Part of the impetus for passage by Maryland was Pennsylvania's stipulation that the improvement of its part of the lower Susquehanna depended on Maryland's incorporation of the canal company.[1] The company was organized in 1802 and began selling shares to residents of the three states. As Latrobe reported to

1. Gray, "Early History of C & D," pp. 223–39; Ralph D. Gray, "Philadelphia and the Chesapeake and Delaware Canal," *PMHB* 84 (1960):402–07.

Jefferson later that year (see below), public response was unenthusiastic and prospects for undertaking the canal appeared bleak without federal assistance.

Latrobe had been interested in such a canal for some time prior to the canal company's incorporation. As early as August 1799, he had examined part of Maryland's Eastern Shore for a potential route. Latrobe's concern for the canal was not surprising considering his interest in internal improvements and his residence in Philadelphia, headquarters of the canal movement. In Philadelphia he met merchant and canal enthusiast Joshua Gilpin, a future director of the canal company, who from the start was a "uniform friend" of the engineer.[2] Although the canal would benefit primarily Philadelphia, Latrobe saw the project as one of vital national interest, thus his attempt to secure Jefferson's agreement to federal support of the scheme.

Places mentioned in this and later correspondence related to the Chesapeake and Delaware canal may be found on map 4.

2. BHL, *Journals,* 3 : 8; BHL to Samuel M. Fox, 11 May 1805, LB (39/G4).

TO THOMAS JEFFERSON

Philadelphia October 24th. 1802.

Sir,

I beg leave to transmit to you by my particular friend, and near relation, Mr. Eakin of the War-office the enclosed letter, in which I have taken the liberty to give to you all the information which I possess on the proposed plan of a canal communication between the Delaware and Chesapeake bays. I have done this with a view to suggest the propriety of this subject being taken up by Congress as an important national object; which is now in the way of being either irretrievably lost, or advantageously accomplished, and which, I am convinced, that your recommendation would call into the notice it deserves. Mr. Eakin possesses lands in the probable neighborhood of the canal, and with a clear and impartial judgement possesses much information on this subject. On this account, and as a young man of no common merit, I beg leave to recommend him to your polite notice.

I am with true respect Your faithful hble. Servt.

B. Henry Latrobe.

ALS: Jefferson Papers (165/F9). Enclosed BHL to Jefferson, 27 Mar./1 June/24 Oct. 1802, below. Endorsed as received 20 November "by Eakin."

ENCLOSURE: TO THOMAS JEFFERSON

Philadelphia March 27th 1802

Sir,

For taking up a portion of your valuable time by this Letter I find sufficient apology to myself in the many personal civilities I have received from you, and in my warm personal attachment to you and I hope the public nature of the object, to which I wish to lead your special consideration, will with *yourself,* plead my excuse. Without any further preface I will therefore take the liberty to detail to you the Ideas which have occured to me on a subject that at present agitates the public mind in Baltimore, Philadelphia and the state of Delaware, though in a much less degree than it ought. I mean the Cross cut, as it is called, which is intended to connect the Waters of the Chesapeake and Delaware bays.

Having viewed the ground in all those parts, which lie between the granite ridge, and sassafras-creek, from bay to bay, I am well assured of the easy practicability of the project; and shall not take up your time with proving it. The Professional consideration of the scheme is that which is the least important. The practi[ca]bility being granted, the principal difficulty will be to procure to the public, to the *union* in peace and war, the best communication, and to prevent the jealousies of the two rival cities, Baltimore and Philadelphia, from executing an imperfect or useless work, occupying perhaps the best situation, and thereby excluding improvements by Law and Charter. I will endeavor to bring the whole subject into view as concisely as I can.

I.) Baltimore: has no water communication with the back country, which naturally and therefore *necessarily* brings its produce to that market. It must fear that on one side the Conegocheage will in a few years carry a great part of the produce of the Western Counties of Pennsylvania to the foederal City, and on the other, the Susquehanna, daily becoming an object of greater attention in Pennsylvania, will drain off by its South and Western streams, (many of which may be easily canalled and rendered navigable) most of the Maryland and Pennsylvania produce which now goes to Baltimore by land carriage. The Susquehannah produce will have three vents. 1.) By the upper canal to the Schuylkill and thus to Philadelphia. For notwithstanding its failure for the present, that Canal must naturally be compleated in a few Years.[1] 2.) By the turnpike road now nearly extended as far as Wrights ferry, to Philadelphia.[2] 3.) By the natural bed of the River to Havre de grace.

208

I believe the thinking men of Baltimore forsee this natural course of things. They depend perhaps too much upon the reluctance of Capital to leave an established channel of activity, and upon the exertions of their monied men to procrastinate it; and in the general encrease of our prosperity and productive powers, Baltimore may perhaps by these means retain as much trade as she now has; but can hardly be expected to encrease in proportion to those Citys, which will enjoy encreasing advantages. The interests of Baltimore as they respect the Cross cut, and as they are, I think, correctly viewd by their influential men, are these: 1. to prevent its becoming an easy means of Water Communication between Philadelphia and the coasts and waters of the Chesapeake, as far as Richmond and Fredericksburg; 2. to prevent its becoming a means of conveying easily the Susquehanna produce to Philadelphia; 3. to prevent its assisting the growth of Havre de grace by being an easy communication with New York and the Eastern States from thence. 4. If possible to delay, or prevent its execution altogether. There is one simple means of accomplishing these objects: It is, To procure the Canal to be cut as far down the Chesapeake as possible, And to make it a mere barge navigation of about 4 feet water. If this be done the bay craft cannot enter it; nor can the canal boats navigate the bays. A ruinous shifting of cargoes at each end of the Canal must therefore take place: And the vicinity of the Delaware and to the Ocean would render it useless in time of War, without a protecting fleet.

II. The interests of Philadelphia are in all these respects opposite to those of Baltimore; but I do not conceive that the cross cut will conduce so largely to the trade of our City, as many of its Mercantile Men persuade themselves. The principal convenience to the Philadelphia trade will be this: that when the Market price of produce is higher in Philadelphia than at Baltimore, adding to the Baltimore price the Canal toll, *then* the Susquehanna produce will go to Philadelphia. Some convenience will also be obtaind in carrying on the Chesapeake trade, and the communication with Norfolk. The voyage will be shorter and safer and the tolls may not counterbalance these advantages. It is very evident however, that these conveniences and advantages can only be procured by making the Canal so deep that the bay craft and coasting vessels can pass thro' it. That is, to give it 8 feet of Water at least: and it is also important to bring it as high up the two bays as possible; to Reedy Island, at least, in Delaware; and not lower than Sassafras in the Chesapeake.

III. Havre de Grace. The Baltimore gentlemen are apt to profess very little fear of this infant City. Depending on their capital, on their 209 having the *start*, on the supposed unhealthiness of the place, on its want of convenient Wharves and stores and on the difficult navigation of the Susquehanna, they do not dread its becoming their rival.

But it appears to me impossible to prevent the Natural advantages of Havre de Grace from overcoming in time all these impediments. It is in the first place the natural entrepot of all the produce that passes Wrights Ferry. Already have Baltimore merchants sent their ships round to Havre, to take in the produce which must otherwise have been brought round in Shallops. Already Factors for Baltimore merchants purchase and store at Havre the Cargoes of the Arks and Keel boats which cannot get further. For though a parade has been made of the arrival of two arks at Baltimore it should be known that they were towed thither by Sloops at a very great risque: and the nature of the river Susquehanna forbids its being ever navigated by Vessels so constructed as to live in the swell of the Bay. Havre de Grace has been hitherto kept down by the impracticability of the river Susquehanna. The produce stopped at Wrights ferry and crossed the peninsula to Philadelphia by land, a distance of 74 miles, along the turnpike road. But this obstacle is in a very great degree removed during the last summer: 25.000 Dollars having been applied below Wrights Ferry in the clearing of the river; and as the expenditure passed through my hands, I may venture to say that it has effected *much*. An ark may in a moderate swell of the river, that is, from March to June pass in 7 hours from Columbia to Havre, a distance of about 47 miles. 50.000 Dollars more would render this navigation practicable in all seasons. A full report on the subject has been laid before the Legislature of Pennsylvania and is publishd in the Aurora of ? March.[3] It will no doubt be a work of time to render the river which for the last 40 miles of its course is a continued cataract, navigable upwards, so as to return in imported commodities the value of the produce brought down. But this would not perhaps be of so much importance as the bulk of the latter exceeds that of the former so exceedingly, as to render it capable of bearing carriage upwards by land; at least as far as Columbia, from whence it can be boated. If good roads were made, to that distance this expence could be easily borne: and at all events it is evident, that Havre de Grace necessarily has all the advantage of the improved navigation of the Susquehanna, *in the first instance,* and without the expence of freight and time at which Baltimore obtains it. This is already so fully perceived that one Million of Bricks were laid during the year 1801 in building stores and houses in Havre de Grace and double that number is expected to be laid this year. I have omitted to mention, what is of the first importance namely, that Havre has on the east side as deep a harbor as Baltimore. On the advantage which the Canal will produce to Havre de Grace there is no occasion to dwell. In the first period it will render Havre de Grace a store house to Philadelphia, as well as to Baltimore. By degrees like every other entrepot, of which the history is recorded, it will enrich itself by the Trade of the Cities to which it is subservient, and set up for itself. Palmyra is the most magnificent instance of this kind. When Havre is thus advanced the Canal will then shorten her eastern and northern Coasting trade, about 600 miles, and open to her the whole of the Trade of south Jersey, an important Timber and Iron Country, to which it will be as contiguous as is Philadelphia. The interests therefore of Havre de Grace, as they respect the Canal, coincide with those of Philadelphia. They require a deep Canal, in a situation not below Sassafras.

IV. To the state of Delaware this Canal is of immense importance, although the blind policy of the Legislature of that State have retarded its execution, clogged it with a charge on its profits, and made its existence depend upon the liberty *to copy deeds in the Pennsylvania Land Office without paying Fees.*[4] In the latter part of this Letter I will take the liberty to lay before you my Ideas of the best mode of executing the Canal from which these advantages will more particularly appear.

V. The importance of the Canal to the union is very evident, and I am sure, Sir, I need say very little on the subject to you. It is a link in a chain of inland Navigation which may be stretched from Georgia to New York; which will unite our most distant states and in War, give that safety to internal communications, to which, if carried on by our Coasting trade, a powerful fleet, might not be always adequate. But the advantages it would afford would be very imperfect, unless the Vessels which navigate the Chesapeake and Delaware Bays could pass from one to the other, without shifting the Cargo.

June 1st. 1802.

When I began this Letter, it was my intention to have sent it to you sufficiently in time to have the subject submitted to Congress, should you have thought proper to have made it immediately a subject for national consideration. But circumstances have occurred to prevent my compleating it, and as I am sure you will forgive my occupying part of   211 your time with it during the recess, I will proceed without further apology. There are three principal lines at which the Cross cut is proposed to be effected and three or four seperate local interests which are waiting the opportunity of making exertions for themselves without regard for the public. The highest of these is from the head of Elk to Christiana Bridge and thence down the creek to Wilmington. The second from Bohemia to Drawyers Creek or Apoquinimink. The third from Sassafras to Apoquinimink. Lately a very indifferent map of the Delaware state, has been published by a very amiable and entertaining French Gentleman, Major Varley, but who is certainly not as well acquainted with the mathematical science and practical engineering, as with Music. A new route for the Canal is laid down in this map, which strikes the Delaware at *Hamburg*.[5] Not being acquainted with this ground, I cannot form an opinion, as to its practicability. But all the Gentlemen of that part of the Country whom I have seen, ridicule the scheme, which having the great disadvantage of wanting a good harbour on the Delaware bay, is said to possess no merit but that of enhancing the value of the lands of the Major's Patron. It has sometimes been proposed to cut the Canal still lower down by going into Chester River, and thence to Blackbird or Duck Creek. This latter scheme would exactly suit the interests of Baltimore; but in every other point of view, is inadmissible, on account of the danger in Delaware bay, both from the Enemy, and from the weather. Also, because the communication with the Susquehanna is too circuitous. I will shortly point out what strikes me as being the advantage and disadvantage of each of these lines.

1. Elk River to Christiana Bridge.

The advantages are, a certain and copious supply of Water to the upper levels, and an entrance in the Delaware above Reedy Island. This latter circumstance is stated to be of much importance in time of War, because Reedy Island affords a harbour, and at least a good shelter to a fleet which might protect the shores above, while those below might easily be molested by an enemy keeping the Ocean and the Bays and even by the Desultory attacks of Privateers.

The disadvantages are, Water daily growing shallower and filling up at Frenchtown,[6] and thence up to Elkton, by the wash of the Country, which comes down with the many rapid streams that tumble from the Granite Ridge; a rough and rocky Country, which the Canal has to pass from the tide of Chesapeake, to the tide of Delaware at Christiana Bridge; and a very circuitous navigation down Christiana creek to the

Delaware, which is also much interrupted by the ropes of Ferrys, which are a most serious nuisance to Navigation however convenient they may be in crossing. And from the best judgement I can form without an actual survey and level, it appears impossible to cross on this line without at least *two* locks at each end which certainly should be avoided if it be possible to execute the Work elsewhere, with only *one*.

2nd. From Bohemia to Drawyers Creek or Apoquinimink. Drawyers creek is a branch of Apoquinimink and it is of little consequence excepting perhaps as to expence which route is taken. The advantages of this route are: Good Water at Bohemia River, which is not so liable to be filled as Elk because no considerable or rapid streams fall into it; better and lower ground for the Canal; a short cut to the Delaware which may be made quite strait through the marshes saving a distance of more than ten miles.

The disadvantages are, a dubious supply of water to the upper level, and an entrance into Delaware bay below Reedy Island.

3.) From Sassafras to Apoquinimink.

This line is in most respects circumstanced as the last, but has the disadvantage of an entrance lower down the Chesapeake, and is also at a greater distance from a supply of water for the upper level by this stream and the higher country.

If it be thought of great importance to the utility of this Canal in time of War, that its entrance in the Delaware should be in a situation in which it be easily defended by a Fleet, or military works, it will then certainly be best to carry it from Frenchtown to Wilmington; for Wilmington is capable of being made an excellent military position as Reedy Island is the lowest safe road in the Delaware for a fleet. But on no other account ought this line to have the preference, according to my Idea of the ground, and the distance to be encountered.

Bohemia and Sassafras on every other account will afford the cheapest and easiest cutting and which ever line be adopted I will take the liberty to give you my opinion of the principles which should govern the work.

The Canal should carry 8 feet at least of Water, and each end should be a lock of not more than eight feet lift at high water, and if the entrance of the Canal be made practicable at half tide (which be still better) the lift on the Delaware at high Water should be only 5 feet. I have heard so many contradictory assertions as to the difference of the levels of high Water in Delaware Bay, and in Chesapeake, that I do not

213

venture to rely on any of them. The tide in Chesapeake at Turkey Point rises from two to three feet, in Delaware and Reedy Island from 7 to 8. The more northern situation of the mouth of Delaware Bay, and the vicinity of the Ocean must be the cause of this difference in the rise of tide. But I should suppose, that the low water of both bays cannot materially differ, and that if there be a difference, that of the Chesapeake will be the highest.

The gentlemen who surveyed and levell'd across the middle ground, and whose operations are described in the *Transactions* of the American Philosophical Society,[7] have found that its highest elevation above the tide is 66 feet: if my memory does not fail me. Mr. Levi Hollingsworth, one of the few of them who survive, assures me that their work was correct, and stood the test of several trials.[8] This Elevation cannot however extend for the whole neck is full of Ravines, coming up from each Bay, and ground may no doubt be chosen low enough to save much digging. Indeed the mere digging will not be the most expensive part of the Work. The solid work in stone which will be required at each end will demand the most skill and money. But whatever digging may prove necessary it ought to be encountered rather than multiply locks at each end. The expence in maintaining and delay in passing which, would be a permanent and irremediable evil.

It is my opinion that although the streams which at present run into Bohemia, Sassafras, and Drawyers or Apoquinimink Creeks, seem to be sufficient for the supply of a number of Mills, yet when the Earth shall be cut down to a depth probably below the strata in which they lie, and the land shall be cleared of its Woods which will be a necessary consequence of cutting the Canal, and when the Water which they supply will be exposed to evaporation in a surface of 60 or 80 feet wide and perhaps 10 miles in length, they will be found very insufficient to keep up the water in the upper level to the necessary height. Such an event would ruin the work. It may be avoided by a measure easy of execution, and which would render the Canal much more useful to the Country immediately adjoining it. I would propose to cut a Canal of only 3 feet of Water from the high land about the source of Christiana Creek along the middle ground to serve both as a feeder to the summit level of the Grand Canal, and as a means of conveying to it the produce of all the Country on each side; from whence it might choose its market at Philadelphia, Havre de Grace, or Baltimore. This Canal would necessarily have many descending locks towards the grand canal and would terminate in a large Reservoir near it. The head waters of Christiana creek including white clay Creek, and of Elk river rise in the granite ridge. They are not liable to fail from the same cause which would effect the streams of the lower country and may be relied upon for a certain supply and it is my opinion however low down the Peninsula the cut be made the upper Country must be resorted to for a supply of the summit level. For the whole of the soil below the Granite ridge is factitious, Sand, clay, Gravel and then generally unfathomable sand. The water lies on the first Clay.

October 24th. 1802

Sickness, and a variety of very pressing business has prevented my concluding this letter which at two former periods I began to write to you, till the present moment. I beg you will permit the subject itself and my sincere respect for your opinion to apologise for the intrusion upon your time of which I am guilty. I have now to lay before you the State in which the business of the Crosscut is suspended.

Under the different acts of the Legislature incorporating the Canal Company,[9] the books were opened for Subscriptions on a fixed day, in places within the different states. By this simultaneous mode of opening the Subscription, it was intended, that the individuals of each of the three states, Pensylvania, Maryland and Delaware, should have an equal chance of influencing the measures of the Company, and of choosing such Directors, or Managers as would exert themselves for their local interests in the plan of the Work.

The whole capital of the company is fixed at 500.000 Dollars in shares of 200 Dollars each: and by the law of Delaware one half or 250.000 must be subscribed before the Company can be formed, and the work commence. Of this Sum of 250.000 or 1.250 Shares, no subscription has been obtained in Baltimore, as far as is known to me, or the Committee here. In Delaware about 210 Shares have been taken. It was supposed that when the books should be opened in Philadelphia the subscription would at once be filled. But no such thing took place. The book was shifted from compting house to compting house, and the Merchants and monied Men were *pressed* to come in. At last, *heavily* and slowly 216 Shares have been put down. The friends of a sloop Canal feared that the moment the Baltimorians should know the event of the Subscription in Philadelphia they would fill up the Shares; thus obtain- 215 ing a Majority of Votes, and with it, the means of totally defeating the Work, or of executing it in a manner to subserve only to the interests of Baltimore. But even this has not yet happened: and after much enquiry, though without any immediate information from Baltimore, I find the subscriptions to stand nearly thus:

		Shares		amount
Philadelphia,		216,		43.200$
Delaware,	about	210,		42.000
Maryland scattering and a few known in Pensylvania, but not in the subscription book,	say	74		14.800
				100.000
			Deficiency	150.000
				250.000

It seems now to depend upon the opinion which the national Legislature may form of the importance of this communication, to obtain the full controul over its execution, for the Government of the United States. If the Government were authorized by an act to subscribe a commanding number of the deficient Shares a Canal might then be executed, planned with a view to the general good of the Union, and in which local interests, and private speculation might be deprived of that influence over the Work, which has ruined almost all attempts at great public Works in America.

The Legislature of Delaware, besides clogging the Work with a tax on its Profits, and with other trifling and unworthy obstructions, have also limited the existence of its incorporating act to some time in May 1803, unless half the Shares shall by that time be subscribed. I do not doubt, nor do the Gentlemen who compose the Canal Committee in Philadelphia[10] in the smallest degree doubt, but that the Subscription will fill rapidly, if either the National Legislature, or any of the State Legislatures especially that of Pensylvania should subscribe largely to the Work. But from the Legislature of Pennsylvania nothing is to be expected, not even an assent to borrow of one of the banks in our city, which is ready to lend the whole capital at 6 per Cent, redeemable only by the excess of the produce of the tolls beyond the Interest. We have been very unfortunate in the choice of our Representatives for some

Years past, and men of Sense seem to be ineligible in the unanimous opinion of the Majority.

The facts and remarks in this long letter I submit to your consideration, and to your intimate knowledge and care of the internal interests of your country,[11] and am, with the most respectful attachment, Your very hble. Servt.

B. Henry Latrobe

ALS: Jefferson Papers (165/C12). The portions written on 27 March and 1 June are in MEL's hand. Enclosed in BHL to Jefferson, 24 Oct. 1802, above. Endorsed as received 28 November.

1. The incorporation of the Schuylkill and Susquehanna Canal Company in 1791 was followed the next year by the incorporation of the companion Delaware and Schuylkill Canal Company. The two projected canals were the crucial links in an all-water route from the Susquehanna River to Philadelphia. Work began on the project in 1792 and the companies drew on the expertise of the English engineer William Weston. But the companies soon ran out of funds and in 1795 the work was discontinued. In 1811 the two companies were merged into the Union Canal Company, but the project did not again get off the ground until 1821. A 77-mile canal connecting the Susquehanna with Philadelphia's "back door" on the Schuylkill was finally completed six years later. James Weston Livingood, *The Philadelphia-Baltimore Trade Rivalry, 1780–1860* (Harrisburg, Pa., 1947), pp. 102–08.

2. The Philadelphia and Lancaster Turnpike Company, incorporated in 1792, completed its turnpike four years later. The road extended westward to Columbia (Wright's Ferry) on the Susquehanna between 1801 and 1803. This Lancaster and Susquehanna turnpike completed the 74-mile improved overland route between Philadelphia and the Susquehanna River. Livingood, *Philadelphia-Baltimore Trade Rivalry*, pp. 41–45.

3. See BHL, Report on the Susquehanna River Improvements, 28 Nov. 1801, above. At the request of the Roads and Inland Navigation Committee of the Pennsylvania legislature, BHL had his report, with the appendix, published in the Philadelphia *Aurora* (29 Mar., 30 Mar. 1802; microfiche add.), a strong Republican sheet with a nationwide circulation.

4. The Delaware law of incorporation required the C & D Canal Company to pay the state one-tenth of all its profits "whenever and so long as the net profits arising from the said tolls shall amount to ten per centum per annum or more." In addition, Delaware required Pennsylvania to pass two laws before the company could be incorporated: (1) a law allowing agents of Delaware "to have free access to the papers in their [Pennsylvania's] land office and to transcribe and copy . . . all such warrants surveys resurveys patents grants and other original papers" which related to lands in Delaware; and (2) a law repealing "certain provisions and regulations contained in the quarantine laws" of Pennsylvania which adversely affected the Delaware ports of Wilmington and New Castle. *A Collection of the Laws Relative to the Chesapeake and Delaware Canal; Passed by the Legislatures of the States of Maryland, Delaware, and Pennsylvania, Subsequent to the Year 1798* (Philadelphia, 1823), pp. 32–34.

As a result of the Delaware law, 1,656 land records were transferred to Delaware by 1808. In 1946, sixty-eight newly uncovered Delaware land documents were given to the state according to the 1801 law. Gray, "Early History of C & D," pp. 237–38n.

5. [P. Charles Varlé], "A Map of the State of Delaware and Eastern Shore of Maryland With the Soundings of the Bay of Delaware From actual survey & soundings made in 1799, 1800, & 1801 by the Author," (Philadelphia, [1801]). The map shows five proposed canal routes; the route from Frenchtown to Hamburg is labelled "the best course according to the Author." A copy of the map is in the Hall of Records, Dover, Del.

Peter Charles Varlé, a native of France, "learned the theory of canals, turnepike roads and bridges" in the province of Languedoc. He immigrated to Santo Domingo (now part of Haiti) at the beginning of the French Revolution, where he worked as a civil engineer. The Haitian revolt of 1793 forced Varlé to flee to America, and by 1794 he had settled in Philadelphia. After a short stint as an engineer in the War Department and employment in Maine and Massachusetts (where he worked on the Middlesex Canal connecting the Merrimack River with Boston Harbor), Varlé by 1798 moved to Maryland, where he served as superintendent of the Susquehanna Canal Company. Varlé published two maps of counties in Maryland and Virginia as well as maps of Santo Domingo, Philadelphia, the United States east of the Mississippi, and the map of Delaware and Maryland cited above. He also published a pocket guide to Baltimore that included a map of the city. Varlé presented several papers to the American Philosophical Society, one of which BHL critiqued in 1807. Richard W. Stephenson, "Charles Varlé: Nineteenth Century Cartographer," *Proceedings of the American Congress on Surveying and Mapping, 32d Annual Meeting* (Washington, D.C., 1972), pp. 189–98. See also BHL to Peale, 4 Mar. 1807, in BHL, *Correspondence*, 2.

6. Frenchtown was on the Elk River two miles south of Elkton. The name derived from a settlement of French Acadians expelled from Nova Scotia by the English in the mid-eighteenth century. According to BHL, "the packets which sail from hence for Baltimore render frenchtown a place of some trifling importance. The houses are only the tavern, a store and Mr. Frisby Henderson's dwelling. He is the proprietor of the whole estate." BHL, *Journals*, 3 : plate 6; BHL, *Latrobe's View of America*.

7. "An Abstract of sundry Papers and Proposals for improving the Inland Navigation of Pennsylvania and Maryland, by opening a Communication between the Tide-Waters of Delaware and Susquehannah, or Chesopeak-Bay; with a Scheme for an easy and short Land-Communication between the waters of Susquehannah and Christiana-Creek, a Branch of Delaware; to which are annexed some Estimates of Expence, &c.," APS, *Transactions* 1 (1771):293–300.

8. Levi Hollingsworth (1739–1824), Philadelphia merchant, was elected to the American Philosophical Society in 1768. On the 1769 APS expedition, he along with three other men surveyed and leveled the ground between the navigable part of the Christina (formerly Christiana) River and Elkton. When the C & D project was revived in 1803, Hollingsworth was one of the more active supporters and BHL consulted with him on a number of occasions. BHL to Hollingsworth, 10 Mar., 10 June, 6 Aug. 1804, all in LB (30/A10, 32/G7, 34/C13); "An Abstract of sundry Papers and Proposals," p. 295; Henry Simpson, *The Lives of Eminent Philadelphians Now Deceased* (Philadelphia, 1859), pp. 539–42.

9. *Laws of Maryland* . . . (Annapolis, Md., [1800]), chap. XVI, passed 7 Dec. 1799; *Laws of the State of Delaware* . . . , III (Wilmington, Del., 1816), pp. 170–88, passed 29 Jan. 1801; *Pa. Statutes 1682–1801*, 16 : 549–53, passed 19 Feb. 1801. All three statutes of incorporation are reprinted in *A Collection of the Laws Relative to the Chesapeake and Delaware Canal*, pp. 3–15, 19–34, 42–46.

10. Apparently an unofficial group of C & D Canal supporters which probably included such Philadelphia canal enthusiasts as Joshua Gilpin, James C. Fisher, George Fox, George Roberts, and William Tilghman, all of whom eventually sat on the C & D board of directors. Gray, "Early History of C & D," p. 242.

11. Jefferson was interested in the Chesapeake and Delaware Canal but he did not, at

this time, find it in the power of the national government to assist it. Writing to Secretary of the Treasury Albert Gallatin the following spring, the president warned that "while we pursue, then, the construction of the Legislature, that the repairing and erecting light-houses, beacons, buoys, and piers, is authorized as belonging to the regulation of commerce, we must take care not to go ahead of them, and strain the meaning of the terms still further to the clearing out the channels of all the rivers, &c. of the United States." By 1805, however, Jefferson had come to approve of federal support of internal improvements, if a constitutional amendment authorizing them were passed. Jefferson to Gallatin, 21 Apr. 1803, in H. A. Washington, ed., *The Writings of Thomas Jefferson: Being His Autobiography, Correspondence, Reports, Messages, Addresses, and Other Writings, Official and Private,* 9 vols. (Washington, D.C., 1854), 4 : 478; Jefferson, Inaugural Address, 4 Mar. 1805, ibid., 8 : 41.

Naval Dry Dock and Potomac Canal Extension

EDITORIAL NOTE

In late 1802 President Thomas Jefferson called Latrobe to Washington to design a dry dock for United States Navy frigates. Under an act of March 1801 that gave the president discretion to reduce the navy from the size it had attained during the quasi war with France to thirteen frigates (six of which had to be in active service), and in accord with his party's principles of economy and peace, Jefferson was overseeing a radical reduction in the fleet. For the inactive vessels that were subject to weathering and decay, Jefferson developed a plan for building a huge covered dry dock at the Washington Navy Yard in which ships could be stored and economically readied for service when necessary.[1] Jefferson prepared some sketches of his design, and by the fall of 1802, Thomas Tingey, commandant of the Washington Navy Yard, had examined several possible sources of the water required to float ships in and out of the dry dock—Tiber Creek, Stoddert's Spring, and the Potomac [River] Company's Little Falls canal.[2]

On 2 November 1802 Jefferson asked Latrobe (below) to come to Washington, and within three weeks Latrobe was there working on the dry dock design. Although limited in his approaches to the task by the broad outlines of Jefferson's conception, it is likely that Latrobe drew liberally on his knowledge of European canals, docks, and harbor improvements. His report of 4 December 1802 (below) favored an eight-mile canal traversing the city of Washington to supply the proposed dry dock with water. The feeder canal was to originate at the Potomac Company's Little Falls canal (completed in 1795), which lay to the northwest of Washington along the Potomac River. It would then follow the river to Rock Creek, crossing it by an aqueduct, and enter a tunnel through the

---

1. Dumas Malone, *Jefferson the President: First Term, 1801–1805* (Boston, 1970), pp. 102–03, 247–49, 263.

2. Tingey to Robert Smith, 22 Oct. 1802, in *Message from the President of the United States, Transmitting Plans and Estimates of a Dry Dock, for the Preservation of Our Ships of War* (Washington, D.C., 1802), pp. 21–24.

hill on the opposite side.[3] No drawings of Latrobe's plans for the rest of the route are extant, but comments he made in letters to Jefferson ([c. 22 Nov. 1802], [28 Nov. 1802], both below) suggest that he hoped to construct the canal on or near Pennsylvania Avenue from the tunnel to the Capitol, then tunnel through Capitol Hill, and turn south to the Washington Navy Yard on the Eastern Branch (or Anacostia River). Latrobe reasoned that a canal connected to the Potomac Company's works would be of great economic importance to the navy yard by carrying stores from the interior directly to the yard. He believed that such a canal could be built by a private company, possibly the Potomac Company, which had built the canals and locks around Great Falls and Little Falls on the Potomac River, or the Washington Canal Company, for which a charter had recently been granted. In his report Latrobe also estimated the cost of the Tiber Creek and Stoddert's Spring feeder canals.

After locating the site of the dry dock itself on what promised to be firm ground at the navy yard, Latrobe designed two large masonry locks to raise vessels from tidewater to the level of the dry dock. Each was to be about 110 feet long and 50 feet wide, about large enough to accommodate one frigate. After ascending both locks the vessel would enter a short canal communicating with the dry dock. Latrobe designed the canal long enough so that it could form the axis of a turning basin to be excavated in the future. With the turning basin, vessels leaving the dry dock could be rotated so that they could enter the Eastern Branch bow first.[4]

Latrobe designed the dry dock generally in accordance with Jefferson's dimensions and architectural suggestions. The president called for an "upper bason" measuring 800 feet by 175 feet (more than three acres), to be covered by a roof "in the manner of that of the Halle au blé at Paris, which [needs] no underworks to support it."[5] Latrobe proposed a vast, open, arcaded hall of masonry faced with Aquia sandstone, measuring approximately 780 feet by 165 feet internally and roofed with sheet iron. Latrobe estimated that the dry dock could be built in a year at a cost of about $225,000. The locks, he thought, would cost another $170,000.

The House of Representatives received Jefferson's message on the dry dock and Latrobe's plans, sent them to committee, debated them briefly on the floor in January 1803, and tabled them.[6] Jefferson did not easily give up the scheme

3. Four sheets of BHL's project for this part of the canal (dated Dec. 1802), containing detailed watercolor sections and plans, are in Geography and Map Division, Library of Congress (267/A1 ff.). Details of these sheets are reproduced and discussed in BHL, *Engineering Drawings*, pp. 116–24.

4. BHL's section and plan of the locks and his plan, section, and elevation of the dry dock, both dated 4 Dec. 1802, are in Prints and Photographs Division, Library of Congress (278/A1, 278/A2), and reproduced in BHL, *Engineering Drawings*, pp. 119–20.

5. Jefferson to BHL, 2 Nov. 1802, below.

6. *Annals of Congress*, 7th Cong., 2d sess., pp. 343, 401–11, 443; *Report of the Committee Appointed on the 17th Ultimo, to Whom Was Referred So Much of the Message of the President of the United States as Relates to Our Navy Yards and the Building of Docks* ([Washington, D.C.], 1803), pp. 3–4; Eugene S. Ferguson, "Mr. Jefferson's Dry Docks," *American Neptune* 11 (1951):112–14.

and told Latrobe in March that he thought the long-term savings from preserving the fleet would soon persuade Congress to accept the dry dock plan.[7] During Jefferson's administration the dry dock idea was not, in fact, revived. It was, however, the first project of Latrobe's long association with public works in Washington, and, from a technical standpoint, the design of the Potomac Canal extension foreshadowed his plans for the Chesapeake and Delaware Canal feeder.[8]

7. Jefferson to BHL, 6 Mar. 1803 (Private), below.
8. For further discussion of BHL's dry dock plans, see BHL, *Engineering Drawings*, pp. 9–11, 116–18; and BHL, *Architectural Drawings*.

FROM THOMAS JEFFERSON

Washington Nov. 2. 1802

Dear Sir

The placing of a navy in a state of perfect preservation, so that at the beginning of a subsequent war it shall be as sound as at the end of the preceding one when laid up, and the lessening the expense of repairs, perpetually necessary while they lie in the water, are objects of the first importance to a nation which to a certain degree must be maritime. The dry docks of Europe, being below the level of tide water, are very expensive in their construction and in the manner of keeping them clear of water, and are only practicable at all where they have high tides: inasmuch that no nation has ever proposed to lay up their whole navy in dry docks. But if the dry dock were above the level of the tide water, and there be any means of raising the vessels up into them, and of covering the dock with a roof, thus withdrawn from the rot and sun, they would last as long as the interior timbers, doors and floors of a house. The vast command of running water, at this place, at different heights from 30. to 200 feet above the tide water, enables us to effect this desireable object by forming a lower bason, into which the tide water shall float the vessel and then have it's gates closed, and adjoining to this, but 24 feet higher, an upper bason 175 feet wide and 800 f. long (sufficient to contain 12. frigates)[1] into which running water can be introduced from above, so that filling both basons (as in a lock) the vessel shall be raised up and floated into the upper one, and the water then being discharged leave her dry. Over a bason, not wider than 175. feet, a roof can be thrown, in the manner of that of the Halle au blé at Paris, which needing no underworks to support it, will permit the bason to be entirely open and free for the movement of the vessels.[2] I mean to propose the construction of one of these to the National legislature, convinced it will be a work of no great cost, that it will save us great annual expence, and be an encouragement to prepare in peace the vessels we shall need in war, when we find they can be kept in a state of perfect preservation and without expence.

The first thing to be done is to chuse from which of the streams we will derive our water for the lock. These are the Eastern branch, Tyber, Rock creek, and the Potomak itself. Then to trace the canal, draw plans of that and of the two basons, and calculate the expence of the whole, that we may lead the legislature to no expence in the execution of which they shall not be apprised in the beginning. For this I ask your aid, which will require your coming here. Some surveys and levellings have been already made by mr. N. King, a very accurate man in that line, and who will assist in every thing you desire, and execute on the ground any tracings you may direct, unless you prefer doing them yourself.[3] It is very material too that this should be done immediately, as we have little more than 4 weeks to the meeting of the legislature, and there will then be but 3 weeks for them to consider and decide before the day arrives (Jan. 1.) at which alone any number of labourers can be hired here. Should that pass either the work must be over for a year, or be executed by day labourers at double expence. I propose that such a force shall be provided as to compleat the work in one year. If this succeeds, as it will receive all our present ships, the next work will be a second one, to build and lay up additional ships. On the subject of your superintending the execution of the work it would be premature to say any thing till the legislature shall have declared their will. Be so good as to let me hear from you immediately, if you cannot come so soon as you can write. Accept my best wishes and respects.

Th: Jefferson

Letterpress Copy: Jefferson Papers (165/F13).

1. In January 1801 the Adams administration had proposed that a peacetime navy have only thirteen frigates in service. Jefferson effectively accepted that standard since it was consonant with his attempt to reduce federal expenditures. *Naval Documents Related to the Quasi-War Between the United States and France. Naval Operations.* 7 vols. (Washington, D.C., 1935–37) 7 : 80.

2. Jefferson was very much taken with the dome added in 1782–83 to the Paris grain market, or Halle au Blé, by J.-G. Legrand and Jacques Molinos. They adapted a construc-

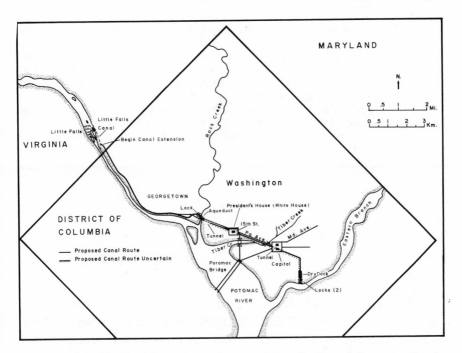

Map 3. BHL's 1802 proposals for the Naval Dry Dock and Potomac Canal Extension. By Stephen F. Lintner.

tion technique developed by the Renaissance architect Philibert Delorme that used composite arched ribs made up of small wooden segments to support a roof, leaving the space underneath free of columns. The Halle au Blé roof also had skylights between the ribs that allowed the interior to be flooded with sunlight. Although Jefferson here refers specifically to the Halle au Blé, he in fact did not take that round building as his immediate prototype. His copy of Delorme's *Nouvelles inventions pour bien bastir et à petits fraiz* (1561) provided the model: Delorme's design for a *"grande salle comme une basilique, ou lieu Royal,"* a rectangular banqueting hall of 150 by 240 feet roofed with the same kind of composite ribs later used at the grain market.

3. Nicholas King (1771–1812), English immigrant, came from a family of surveyors that included his father, Robert King, Sr. (d. 1817), and his younger brother, Robert King, Jr. Upon his arrival in America in 1794, Nicholas King's reaction to American mapmaking was similar to BHL's reaction to American architecture. He found cartography in the hands of amateurs and he spent much of his life attempting to professionalize it. In 1796 King went to Washington to do survey work for the Robert Morris syndicate, which had bought large amounts of land in the city for speculative purposes. Once in Washington, he took a position in the surveyor's office at the request of the city commissioners. He relinquished this position to his father when the latter immigrated in 1797. Accompanying his father were Nicholas's sister Jane (1780–1852), who later married John Lenthall, BHL's clerk of the works at the U.S. Capitol; and his brother Robert, who later became surveyor of the city from 1812 to 1813 and from 1815 to 1817 (the latter stint, a joint appointment

223

with BHL). Between 1797 and 1803 Nicholas King carried out surveying and related tasks for private parties. Upon his father's resignation from the surveyor's office and his return to England in 1802, Jefferson appointed King surveyor of the city, a post he held from 1803 until his death. In 1803 he completed a major survey map of Washington. King was also active in political and civic affairs in Washington. A Republican, he was elected to the City Council for six one-year terms between 1802 and 1812 and was serving as president of the Council's Second Chamber at the time of his death. Ralph E. Ehrenberg, "Nicholas King: First Surveyor of the City of Washington, 1803–1812," CHS, *Records* 69–70 (1969–70):31–65; Maud Burr Morris, "The Lenthall Houses and Their Owners," CHS, *Records* 31–32 (1930):1–35.

TO THOMAS JEFFERSON

Philadelphia Novr. 9th. 1802

Dear Sir,

In the haste in which I was under the necessity of answering your letter of the 2d inst.[1] I fear I could not do justice to my sense of the obligation I owe to your kindness.[2] If any thing I have written should have borne the slightest appearance of false pride, or of a mercenary disposition, I have done the greatest injustice to my sentiments of respectful attachment to you, as a public, and as a private character. I cannot better convince you of my sincerity than by candidly stating to you the exact situation in which I am now placed.

During the 3 first Years of my residence in Philadelphia, I have expended in erecting the Bank of Pensylvania and in supplying the city with Water, near 500.000 Dollars. Both works are completed, and their adequacy to the purposes for which they were designed, and the oeconomy and integrity with which they have been conducted, is not disputed even by those who have used the public prints as the vehicle of their calumnies against me. And yet my emoluments have been disputed with me inch by inch, and I have the prospect before me, of a lawsuit with the city, for a considerable part of my compensation, which has been awarded to me by two references, by a joint Committee of both councils, by the Select council, but which the common council has neglected or refused to vote to me.[3]

I will not take up your time by stating many other instances in which I have devoted time, talents, and have incurred expence without any return. The labor of the mind, is not *here* supposed to be a *merchantable article.*

224

The result of all this has been that my private fortune, and the slow and hardly earned proceeds of my professional employ have barely supported me and my family in the enjoyment of those indulgences, and of that society in which I have been educated, and in which all my habits have been formed; and having for the last twelve month been wholly without professional employment, I have turned my attention to business of more permanent and independent emolument.

The Gentleman who erected the Steam engines of the Waterworks contracted for the use of all the power which they should possess, beyond that used in the daily supply of the city with water, and in order to increase this power, the size of the Engine on Schuylkill was doubled. As the funds of this Gentleman failed, some of my friends were induced, by their confidence in my statements, to join with him in attaching rolling and slitting works to the Engine; and I also placed the whole of my own capital in those works. Their expence has been very great, and they have as yet produced nothing. My honor with my friends, my reputation with the public, and my own fortunes are at risk in their Success. Within these few weeks we have begun to manufacture Iron, and our most sangine wishes begin to be accomplished. But the daily support of my family depends upon an allowance, in advance of future profits, paid to me in the manner of a Salary by my partners, who themselves have received nothing. This allowance is at the rate of 2.500 Dollars per Annum, and is absolutely my only resource. It depends on my personal attendance, and is suspended during occasional absence.[4]

Since I last had the honor to see you, I have married the daughter of Mr. Isaac Hazlehurst of this city, who is I believe known to you. I have also two Children. Were I single I should have waited upon you before this letter could arrive, and should not have incurred the possibility of a doubt of my confidence in You. The noble plan suggested by your letter is sufficient to excite the ambition of a man much less an enthusiast in his profession than I am. But independently of ambition, and the fair prospect of future emolument, I should have required no motive but to have been called upon by You.

I have now only to beg that you will think as favorably of my disposition, as you have done me the honor to conceive of my talents. In the mean time, I am preparing to leave Philadelphia in a few days. I hope to hear again from You, and am with the highest respect Your obliged Hble. Servant

B. H. Latrobe.

ALS: Jefferson Papers (165/G5). Endorsed as received on 12 November.

1. See preceding document.
2. BHL to Jefferson, 8 Nov. 1802, not found. Jefferson referred this letter to Secretary of the Navy Robert Smith, who wrote BHL on 12 Nov. 1802 (Mrs. Gamble Latrobe Collection, MdHS; 165/G10). See following document.
3. While BHL's original waterworks contract stated that he could claim no further compensation for his service as engineer than that stipulated, on 28 January 1802 he memorialized the Philadelphia city councils to pay him for services rendered beyond those required by his contract. His memorial was referred to a joint committee, which reported it favorably to the councils. The Select Council accepted the recommendation on 6 May 1802, but not until early 1805 did the Common Council also assent to the additional payment. Minutes of the Select Councils, 28 Jan., 25 Feb., 1 Apr., and 6 May 1802, Archives of the City and County of Philadelphia; BHL to William Cramond, 26 Jan. 1805, LB(37/E3); Eliza Cope Harrison, ed., *Philadelphia Merchant: The Diary of Thomas P. Cope, 1800–1851* (South Bend, Ind., 1978), pp. 179–80.
4. As part of his contract with the city of Philadelphia to construct engines for the waterworks, Nicholas Roosevelt gained the right to use the surplus power of the Schuylkill engine for industrial purposes. At first he intended to erect a mill to roll copper for naval vessels, but eventually the mill was set up to make sheet and rod iron. BHL designed some elements of the mill and commission merchants Erick and Lewis Bollmann became investors. Production commenced by the fall of 1802 but operations were never profitable, and the mill ceased manufacturing within three years. Despite BHL's statement here that he was salaried, he later claimed that he had received no compensation for his professional services. BHL, *Engineering Drawings*, pp. 48–52; BHL to Richard Peters, 14 Feb. 1807, LB(55/A12).

FROM THOMAS JEFFERSON

Washington Nov. 13. 1802.

Dear Sir

Your favor of the 9th.[1] is recieved as that of the 8th. had been the day before. On recieving that of the 8th. I was immediately sensible I had omitted in mine[2] to say any thing on the subject of a just compensation for the preliminary business of a survey, estimate etc. I therefore referred your letter to the Secretary of the Navy (who was now returned, having been absent at the date of my letter) and he yesterday wrote to you to assure you of a proper compensation,[3] and at the same time to mr. George Harrison[4] to make you an advance of (I believe) one hundred dollars. The work I propose is to contain the vessels we now possess, but that finished, and answering, as cannot be doubted, another will be proposed for building vessels under, and laying them up as built, so that the two will take some time for construction. The first however we should push as much as possible, to get our present vessels put out of the way of decay. I shall hope to see you here as soon as possible, because our estimate must be ready before the meeting of Congress.[5] Accept assurances of my esteem and respect.

Th: Jefferson

Letterpress Copy: Jefferson Papers (165/G13).

1. See preceding document.
2. Jefferson to BHL, 2 Nov. 1802, above.
3. Secretary of the Navy Robert Smith assured BHL that the government would "not fail to provide an adequate compensation" for his services. Smith to BHL, 12 Nov. 1802, Mrs. Gamble Latrobe Collection, MdHS (165/G10).

Smith (1757–1842), brother of Gen. Samuel Smith (1752–1839), practiced law in Baltimore before serving as Jefferson's secretary of the Navy (1801–09) and Madison's secretary of state (1809–11). Smith has been viewed by many historians as a weak appointee, but a recent study argues that the navy secretary was a competent administrator who "took steps to improve the efficiency of the department." Noble E. Cunningham, Jr., *The Process of Government under Jefferson* (Princeton, N.J., 1978), pp. 15, 133.

4. George Harrison (1762–1845) was navy agent at Philadelphia from 1799 to 1833. In 1807 BHL would design a brick stable and coach house for Harrison. John Hill Martin, *Martin's Bench and Bar of Philadelphia* (Philadelphia, 1883), p. 134; Edward L. Clark, *A Record of the Inscriptions on the Tablets and Grave-Stones in the Burial-Ground of Christ Church, Philadelphia* (Philadelphia, 1864), p. 552.

5. Congress was to meet on 6 December 1802.

TO JOHN VAUGHAN

Archstreet, Novr. 14th. 1802

Dear Sir,[1]

I have not a Copy of the last information I gave to you on the Steam engine, and therefore cannot explain anything contained in it. But I can give you *such* additional information as is required by your communication from Mr. Pinckney's letter.

I have no accurate experiment as to the difference of *effect* in raising Steam, which is produced by different species of Wood fuel, or of Coal. All that has been done in England with *Coal*, in experiments upon Iron-boilers of different construction may been seen in the *Encyclopedia,* and the *Repertory of Arts.*[2] *Here,* I have had only an opportunity of ascertaining the relative effect of Pine, oak, and coal on *wooden* boilers, and as the experiment was made by my Clerk in my absence, and much interrupted by the officiousness of some of the Members of the Water committee, I can only give the general result, which is this, that *the expence* of maintaining our Upper Engine with Coal at 30 Cents per Bushel is less than if maintained with Pine at 3$ per Cord or with Oak at 4$.50, but that the difference is trifling.[3]

The Papers on this Subject were mislaid or lost in the frequent Removals of the Water office during the finishing of the Center Engine house. A correct opinion of the comparative expence may thus be formed, the price of Coal and wood in any given place being known. For instance: we burn 20 Bushels per day when the boiler flue is neither very free, nor much clogged with soot: These 20 Bushel cost us, 6$.oo, of course we should burn in the same time about 2 cords of pine wood, and 1½ of Oak, which is nearly the fact. But Coal is more convenient as lying in a smaller compass; and being easily loaded into a bucket, we haul it up by the power of the Engine, to the door of the boiler. On this account we always use Coal though the price is sometimes 42 Cents.[4]

I would advise by all means that the Cylinder should not be less than 18 inches, though 14 inches might suffice. The difference of expence is trifling, 2 or 300 Dollars; that of power, very great. The Stroke 4 feet 6 i. or perhaps 4 feet only; such an Engine would make from 25 to 30 strokes per Minute. The Flywheel, if on the Sun and Planet-plan of Bolton and Watt (which I think has many disadvantages and requires a Beam), would make double that number of revolutions. If on a different plan without a Beam the flywheel would also make from 25 to 30 Revolutions per Minute.[5] When Rice is not to be shelled or h[u]lled, such an Engine would carry 2 Saws of 10 feet stroke each and cut from 3.500 to 5000 feet of boards in 24 Hours, or turn two pair of Millstones of 4 feet diam: The Slabs would half maintain her.[6] The late Robt. McKean's patent, is by the bye, no obstacle to sawing timber by steam, provided the *three* Methods specified are not used, and indeed they are the only three Methods which a good Mechanic would not use.[7]

Of course all expences are included in the annual sum of 1.500 Dollars for maintenance and fuel, *and repairs:* But only *one* Man is *allowed* to attend the Engine, and one man is enough for 15 Hours per day. No expence of attendance on the mill, or indeed any expence beyond the Flywheel, from whence all motion is derived, is included. As to repairs, both our large engines have not cost us 50 Dollars in repairs since they were erected 2 Years ago.

In respect to very *minute* calculations, my time has never permitted me to make them as you well know. We have labored under a thousand disadvantages, in getting Engines erected at all. In future I shall have leisure, and the means of knowing exactly what our improvements on the Airpump and boiler will do for the saving of fuel. I am with much truth Yrs. affecty.

B. H. Latrobe.

ALS: St. Julien R. Childs Collection, South Carolina Historical Society (microfiche add.).

1. John Vaughan (1756–1841), a Philadelphia merchant who had been born in England, was a Unitarian and a generous friend of the poor. He devoted much of his life to the American Philosophical Society, to which he was elected in 1784, serving as its secretary (1789–90), treasurer (1791–1841), and librarian (1803–41). Vaughan was also a member and promoter of virtually every other learned and benevolent society in the city. *Recollections of Joshua Francis Fisher, Written in 1864* (n.p., 1929), pp. 256–58; Biographical File, APS.

2. BHL here refers to the London technological journal *Repertory of Arts and Manufactures . . .* , begun in 1794, and perhaps to the article "Coal" in *Encyclopaedia; Or, a Dictionary of Arts, Sciences, and Miscellaneous Literature . . .* , 18 vols. (Philadelphia, 1798).

3. The Centre Square or upper engine of the Philadelphia Waterworks had a wooden boiler. BHL, Report on Steam Engines, 20 May 1803, below; BHL, *Engineering Drawings*, pp. 181, 184, 185.

4. Six months later BHL reported that the Centre Square engine burned "25 to 33 bushels of Virginia coal of the best sort" during 16 working hours every day. The coal storage was in the basement story below the engine. BHL, Report on Steam Engines, 20 May 1803; BHL, *Engineering Drawings*, pp. 174, 178.

5. Steam engines without working beams to connect the steam cylinder and the drive shaft were still in an early stage of development in England. In 1807 Henry Maudslay, an English mechanical engineer, patented a steam engine without a beam. R. J. Law, *The Steam Engine* (London, 1965), pp. 15, 17; H. W. Dickinson, *A Short History of the Steam Engine* (Cambridge, England, 1938), p. 109.

6. Apparently Pinckney had inquired about an engine for a rice-hulling mill. BHL had learned of such mills from his recent experience of preparing an engraving of a water-powered rice mill for John Drayton's *A View of South-Carolina, as Respects Her Natural and Civil Concerns* (Charleston, 1802), but it was more than twenty years before significant numbers of rice mills were steam powered. BHL, *Engineering Drawings*, p. 247; Pursell, *Steam Engines in America*, p. 75.

7. Robert McKean (1766–1802), son of Gov. Thomas McKean, was a merchant and auctioneer for the city of Philadelphia (1800–01). He received his patent for a steam sawmill in 1798. G. S. Rowe, *Thomas McKean: The Shaping of an American Republicanism* (Boulder, Colo., 1978), pp. 321–22; Thomas Green Fessenden, *The Register of Arts* (Philadelphia, 1808), p. 388.

TO THOMAS JEFFERSON

[Washington, 22 November 1802]

Mr. Latrobe presents his respectful Compliments to the President of the U. States:[1]

In preparing for his survey of the line of Potowmac Canal, Mr. L. has obtained access to the records of the Commissioners, which happen to be perfect as to the levels of the Streets, N. West of the Presidents house, and South of the large Street **K** and also as to those of some streets about the Capitol. The page marked by this letter (32) exhibits the level above high water of that part of the Pennsylvania Avenue which is immediately in front of the six buildings.[2] It appears that the level on the highest point marked ✳ is 76 feet 10 i. 9/10 above highwater. Should the Canal be carried along this line there will of course be a difference between the level of the street and of the Water of 44 feet (the fall at the locks being only 32 f. 6 i. or thereabouts). This difference will Mr. L. fears, be fatal to the idea of carrying the Canal along the line of the Pennsylvania Avenue, for a navigable tunnel from Rock Creek to the descent of the hill East of the President's house would be cheaper than such an open Canal.

As there is lower Ground both to the right and left of the Pennsylvania Avenue Mr. L. examined the book as to a variety of Streets running across or along the lowest situations, and finds that there is not any track between the Pennsylvania Avenue and the high Ground intended for the University,[3] which is lower than from 50 to 54 feet above high Water, giving a difference between the level of the Street, and of the Water in the Canal of at least 20 feet. From the bank of the Rocky Creek, North of the Pensylvania Avenue towards the Tiber, *the hollow,* (which appears to run along the Wide street marked **K,** and then to follow the Massachusets Avenue to the Tiber) does not seem lower for a very considerable part of its extent than that between the Pennsylvania Avenue and the University hill, so that no advantage would be gained by leading the Canal into that *"uninteresting"* part of the City, as the natural level of the Ground must be about 50 feet above high Water. Of the levels of the streets in this direction Mr. L could not find any record in the office of the City surveyor.

It appears from these facts that if the Canal be made not very different in its level from that of the street, the streets near the river must be resorted to. The line indeed of the Cut will be circuitous, and

230

the Ground often disadvantageous, but the thing is practicable; and its execution might perhaps be attended with the advantage of unloading the Country produce near to the Stores from which it must be exported, and which will naturally arrange themselves near the Potowmac. As the weather forbids operations in the open Air, Mr. Latrobe will employ himself in making the drawings of the dock and Locks, untill he receives further instructions from the President, upon whom he will wait at the first convenient moment.

Washington Secretary's Office P. U. S.
Monday morning

Mr. N. King is in possession of an accurate detailed plan, and sections of Georgetown, from Fayette street to Rocky Green, which will render Mr. Ls. operation through that City unnecessary.[4] Indeed there does not appear to be more than one weeks surveying necessary to obtain all the requisite data for a very detailed estimate.

AD: Jefferson Papers (166/A4). Jefferson endorsed the document 22 November 1802, which was a Monday.

1. BHL received Jefferson's letter (13 Nov. 1802, above) on the sixteenth and promised the president to "come on by the Mail" which was to leave Philadelphia on the eighteenth. Within four days, BHL had arrived in Washington, begun his surveys, and made this first report to the president. BHL to Jefferson, 16 Nov. 1802, Jefferson Papers (166/A1).

2. The Six Buildings, rowhouses erected in the 1790s, were part of James Greenleaf's speculative venture in Washington. They were on the northwest corner of Pennsylvania Avenue and 21st Street, N.W. Constance McLaughlin Green, *Washington: Village and Capital, 1800–1878* (Princeton, N.J., 1962), p. 4; James M. Goode, *Capital Losses: A Cultural History of Washington's Destroyed Buildings* (Washington, D.C., 1979), p. 140.

3. The high ground was south of Tiber Creek along the south side of the Mall. President Washington set aside nineteen acres in the city for a national university and he provided for its support in his will. Congress, however, delayed in acting on the measure. In 1816 BHL, as surveyor of the city, drew a plan for the university for a congressional committee considering the matter. The institution in BHL's plan was to be located at the western end of the Mall on the Capitol axis, southeast of the President's House. But a national university, supported by Congress, never got off paper. BHL, "Plan of the West end of the public Appropriation in the city of Washington, called the Mall, as proposed to be arranged for the Site of the University," Jan. 1816, Geography and Map Division, Library of Congress (266/A3), reproduced in BHL, *Architectural Drawings;* Green, *Washington,* p. 42.

4. BHL used a large scale map on which were "laid down the Natural Levels as well as the proposed Graduation of the Streets of George Town, which were accurately ascertained by Mr. Nicholas King in the Year 1800" including "the buildings then Standing."

BHL, "No. III, of Plans, and Sections, of the Proposed continuation of the Canal at the Little Falls of the Potomak to the Navy Yard in the City of Washington," Dec. 1802, Geography and Map Division, Library of Congress (267/B1).

TO MARY ELIZABETH LATROBE

Washington, November 24, 1802.

Having employed my morning in my business I went to dine with the President. His two daughters,[1] Mr. and Mrs. Madison,[2] Mr. Lincoln (Attorney General),[3] Dr. Thornton, a Mr. Carter from Virginia, and Captain Lewis (the President's Secretary)[4] were the party. The dinner was excellent, cooked rather in the French style (larded venison), the dessert was profuse and extremely elegant, and the knicknacs, after withdrawing the cloths, profuse and numberless. Wine in great variety, from sherry to champagne, and a few decanters of rare Spanish wine, presents from Chevalier D'Yrujo.[5] The conversation, of which Mr. Madison was the principal leader, was incomparably pleasant, and though Mr. Jefferson said little at dinner besides attending to the filling of plates, which he did with great ease and grace for a philosopher, he became very talkative as soon as the cloth was removed. The ladies stayed till five, and half an hour afterwards the gentlemen followed them to the tea table, where a most agreeable and spirited conversation was kept until seven, when everybody withdrew. It is a long time since I have been present at so elegant a mental treat. Literature, wit, and a little business, with a great deal of miscellaneous remarks on agriculture and building, filled every minute. There is a degree of ease in Mr. Jefferson's company that every one seems to feel and to enjoy. At dinner Mrs. Randolph was asked by Mr. Carter to drink a glass of wine with him, and did so. Mr. Jefferson told her she was acting against the health law. She said she was not acquainted with it, that it must have passed during her absence. He replied that three laws governed his table—no healths, no politics, no restraint. I enjoyed the benefit of the law, and drank for the first time at such a party only one glass of wine, and, though I sat by the President, he did not invite me to drink another.

Printed Copy: John E. Semmes, *John H. B. Latrobe and His Times, 1803–1891* (Baltimore, 1917), pp. 12–13 (166/A9). Semmes published only an extract of the original, addressed to MEL in Philadelphia.

1. Jefferson's daughters were Martha (1772–1836), who married Thomas Mann Randolph (1768–1828) in 1790, and Mary, or Maria (1778–1804), who married John Wayles Eppes (1772–1823) in 1797. Dumas Malone, *Jefferson the Virginian* (Boston, 1948), pp. 428, 432, 434.

2. James Madison (1751–1836) and his wife Dolley (Payne) Madison (1768–1849). At this time Madison was secretary of state.

3. Levi Lincoln (1749–1820), a native of Massachusetts and a graduate of Harvard (1772), served as attorney general from 1801 until his resignation at the end of December 1804.

4. Meriwether Lewis (1774–1809), like Jefferson a native of Albemarle County, Va., served in the militia during the Whiskey Rebellion and then entered the regular army in May 1795. He became the president's private secretary shortly after the inauguration in 1801 and held that position until 1803, when he and Capt. William Clark of Louisville began their famous expedition. After their return to Washington in 1806, Lewis resigned from the army and Jefferson appointed him governor of the Louisiana Territory, the position he occupied at his death.

5. Don Carlos Maria Martinez d'Yrujo (1763–1824) came to the U.S. in 1796 as envoy extraordinary and minister plenipotentiary of Spain. In 1798 he married Sally McKean (1777–1841), daughter of Pennsylvania Governor Thomas McKean. *Gilbert Stuart: Portraitist of the Young Republic, 1755–1828* (Providence, R.I., 1967), p. 81.

TO THOMAS JEFFERSON

6 buildings, Washington Sunday morning.
[28 November 1802]

Dear Sir,

An unfortunate scratch across the end of my Nose which I received among the briars in the Neighborhood of the Navy Yard, has given me so disgraceful an appearance for the last four days, that I have confined my Labors to the Survey of the Canal, and to my Chamber. I have now nearly finished the Ground work of my Estimate and have every reason to believe, that the Canal from the Locks to the Navy Yard, perforating both the Capitol hill, and that extending from Rocky Creek to Eastward of the Presidents house, cannot be executed for a less Sum than 250.000 Dollars, of which the perforations will consume 116.320 or thereabout (if the plan of the City be at all correct). If the hill be followed it is possible that 50.000 Dollars of the whole expence may be saved. In two or three days (about Wednesday) I will exhibit to you a compleat section of the Canal, and the Plans of the Docks and locks, all which are in a

233

greater or less degree of forwardness or ready.[1] I am with the truest respect Your faithful hble. Servt.

B. Henry Latrobe.

ALS: Jefferson Papers (166/A11). Endorsed as received 28 November.

1. These plans, dated 4 Dec. 1802, are in the Prints and Photographs Division, Library of Congress (278/A1, 278/A3), and are reproduced in BHL, *Engineering Drawings*, pp. 119–20.

TO MARY ELIZABETH LATROBE

Washington City Novr. 30th. 1802

My dearest Mary,

Yesterday I wrote to you a long letter for which you will have to pay treble postage, but if you value my letters, as I do yours you will not complain. I had dined with the president: his invitation was to meet a small party of friends, and accordingly I found only 3 besides myself. I was introduced to them all, but their names were pronounced in so slovenly a way by Capt. Lewis, the President's secretary, that I only half understood them and had in ten minutes forgotten them entirely, for my head was full of a previous conversation on the Drydocks. Their names are however of no consequence: they were all men of science, one of them had a broad Scotch accent and seemed lately arrived. The conversation turned on the best construction of arches, on the properties of different species of Limestone, on cements generally, on the difference between the French and English habits of living as far as they affect the arrangement of their houses, on several new experiments upon the properties of light, on Dr. Priestley,[1] on the subject of emigration, on the culture of the time,[2] on the dishonesty of Peter Legoux and his impudence,[3] on the domestic manners of Paris, and the orthography of the English and French Languages, by this time the President became very entertaining and told among others the following anecdote of a Friend, Dorcas.[4]

A number of English, and some french Ladies with their husbands were assembled at Dr. Franklin's, who spoke wretched French. Dorcas whose proficiency was not much greater, undertook on several points to set him to rights, and had become very ridiculous by some of her corrections. At that moment Temple Franklin[5] entered, and in one of his freaks of assurance kissed the Lady who stood nearest to the door, and then went round the room saluting each of them; and last of all he kissed Mrs. Jay.[6] Mrs. Jay unused to such gallantry blushed so deeply that Dr. Franklin observing it, asked why she blushed. Mrs. M[ontgomery] immediately answered, *"Parc'qu'il a **lui** baissé **la derriere,**"* instead of ***la derniere.*** Poor Dorcas might as well have used the broad English phrase of Moll Turner, as to the feelings of Mrs. Jay, or the entertainment of the French Men.[7]

Yesterday night I wrote thus far, I was then absolutely driven by the cold into bed, for as it was the first day of the Races, every body had gone out, and there was no Wood split. This is one of my grievances, for the wood comes home in long logs and must be cut up by the Servants. The races have brought hundreds to this city, and among the rest Judge and Mrs. Washington[8] who called upon me for ten minutes, and appeared, and I am sure were so unfeignedly glad to see me, that I have not felt so much pleasure since I left home. You are absolutely bespoke for Mount Vernon, and no denial is to be taken.[9] Several other of my Virginia acquaintance are here and have called, but I have not [been] out of my room, not even to spend the evening with Judge Washington as I was invited to do, or with Chevalier d'Yrujo as I also ought to have done, for it rained violently all the evening and night, and I was glad of the excuse, for I cannot afford the time, and as to amusement I find none in any party. I did not receive a letter from you yesterday, for no mail arrived but today expect a few lines with certainty. You ought to have received a letter from me daily, for I have not once missed, nor do I intend it. Would to God I could return to you on the day you mention, Monday, but you forget that that is the *day* on which at *soonest* I can leave this Place, for it is the day on which Congress opens, and of course I must stay till then. Then there are *three days of travelling* to be got over before I can again embrace you. I shall not be able to say with certainty what day I can return till *Saturday* next. God keep you my best beloved wife. Take care of yourself and of your dear infant,[10] and believe me unalterably Yours,

B. Henry Latrobe

Printed Copy: Hamlin, *Latrobe,* pp. 576–77 (166/B1).

1. For BHL's earlier comments on Dr. Jospeh Priestley (1733–1804), scientist, educator, Nonconformist minister, and Jeffersonian Republican, see BHL to Giambattista Scandella, 30 Apr. 1798, in BHL, *Journals*, 2 : 381–83.

2. Probably a misreading of "vine." See next note.

3. Peter Legaux (1748–1827), a native of France, served as *conseiller* of the Parlement of Metz and *avocat* at the supreme court of Lorraine before leaving France late in 1781. He spent four years in Guadeloupe, where he served in civil capacities, before emigrating to Philadelphia in 1785. Legaux established himself at Spring Mill, his estate on the Schuylkill several miles northwest of Philadelphia, where he took meteorological readings and engaged in the culture of grapes for winemaking. From 150 imported plants in 1787, his vineyard had expanded to 18,000 plants by 1793, when the newly-created Company for the Promotion of the Cultivation of the Vine adopted it. BHL subscribed three shares of the Company at $20 per share in 1800. Legaux to Thomas Jefferson, 25 Mar. 1801, enclosure, Jefferson Papers; Biographical File, APS.

4. Mrs. Dorcas Armitage Montgomery, a wealthy Philadelphia widow who went to Europe in 1781 to supervise the education of her son Robert. Communication from The Papers of Benjamin Franklin to the editors, 6 Jan. 1981, PBHL.

5. William Temple Franklin (1762–1823), son of Benjamin Franklin's son William (c. 1731–1813). Leonard W. Labaree et al., eds., *The Papers of Benjamin Franklin* (New Haven, Conn., 1959–), 1 : lxii.

6. John Jay (1745–1829) married Sarah Van Brugh Livingston, daughter of William Livingston (1723–90) of New Jersey, in 1774.

7. This incident, which undoubtedly took place at Franklin's lodgings at Passy, outside Paris, must have occurred between June 1782 and May 1784, when the Jays were for the most part in France. Since Jefferson did not arrive in Paris until August 1784, after the Jays had returned to America, he could not have witnessed the incident.

8. Bushrod Washington married Julia Anne Blackburn, daughter of Col. Thomas Blackburn, in 1785. BHL, *Journals*, 2 : 535, 557.

9. Bushrod Washington inherited Mount Vernon from his uncle and lived there from 1802. The Latrobes were frequent visitors to Mount Vernon during their Washington years.

10. At this time MEL was pregnant with John H. B. Latrobe, who was born on 4 May 1803.

TO THOMAS JEFFERSON

Saturday morning Decr. 4th. 1802

Dear Sir,

I should be happy to wait upon you with the result of my calculations at 2 o'clock, if you could then make it convenient to devote half an hour to me. I propose that hour because it is the very earliest that I can mention, and I believe you to be desirous of obtaining the information which I can give as soon as possible; but a later hour will be equally convenient to me. I am anxious that you should believe that if during my

residence here I have been wanting in the respect of personal attendance upon you, it has been, because my whole time has been engrossed
by unremitted attention to the subject you have committed to me; and
that if I could use expressions to which no meaning of adulation could
be possible attached, I should not be at loss, as I am, to express to you my
sense of your personal kindness to me, and to tell you how much my
attachment to your public character, which my parents instilled into me
before I saw you, and which has never varied, has spread itself over that,
which belongs to you as an individual. I hope you will pardon this invol-
untary effusion of my feelings, they are sincere, and disinterested, and I
should have much less sensibility than I do, and much less gratitude than
I ought to, possess, were I to feel otherwise. I have perhaps taken an
improper opportunity to express them, but my tongue cannot to do, but
my conduct may.

I am with great truth Your faithfull hble. Servt.

B. Henry Latrobe

ALS: Jefferson Papers (166/B5). Endorsed as received 4 December.

REPORT ON PROPOSED NAVAL DRY DOCK

To Robert Smith Esq.
Secretary of the Navy

Washington Decr. 4th. 1802

Sir

In conformity to your instructions, I repaired to the city of Washington and have since my arrival devoted my best attention to the several
objects committed by you to my consideration. I now beg leave to submit
to you the result.

I. Site of a dry dock or naval arsenal.

The principle of a dry dock or naval arsenal in which twelve frigates
of 44 guns could be laid up, had been already so far matured by the
President of the United States before my arrival, that I have only to lay   237

before you a description of the situation in which it can most advantageously be erected, and designs and estimates of the works which are necessary to carry it into effect.

The Harbour of the Eastern Branch of the Potowmak has, in almost every part, a bottom of mud, into which the wharves which have been erected, sink to a great depth and which affords in very few places a prospect of a good building foundation at a moderate depth and expence. But at the end of the street marked 9 east of the Capitol which bounds the navy yard to the East a Spit of hard gravel runs out near to the channel which promises to furnish a solid foundation for the erection of the first Lock necessary to raise the ships into the Dock. Another circumstance points out this spot as advantageous. A Valley runs up in the direction of the street, the greatest part of the distance to which the works must be extended. This will save more than half of the digging, which would otherwise be necessary. To render the situation as advantageous as possible it will be requisite that the streets should be vacated so far as the square in which the Virginia and Georgia avenues intersect each other, and to purchase the squares east of the street No. 9 as far as No. 10. But should any objection occur to the vacating of the streets to such an extent, or to the terms on which the lots could be purchased the plan herewith submitted may be executed at nearly the same estimated expence, by vacating the streets only to the extent of the navy yard, according to its present limits, and by placing the arsenal at right angles with the Locks, extending the same from East to West. A circle is marked on the plan representing a turning dock which would also be useful as a repairing and graving Dock for three frigates, if necessary to execute the same. Its expence is included in the Estimate herewith submitted.[1] Should this mode of executing the plan be adopted it will render the purchase of only 100 feet by 250 feet necessary, to the eastward of the street no. 9, at the distance of about 400 feet from the present shore. As however this plan has many disadvantages, it will [have] to be considered in how far the present purchase of the Eastern Squares could be effected by the sum which the erection of the turning Dock will require; for if the arsenal be in a line with the Locks, the erection of the turning Dock may be well postponed until the extension of the arsenal, or the construction of repairing or graving Docks be found necessary. And should great part of the navy yard be occupied by the arsenal the space which ought to be open for the erection of Store Houses, will not only be much curtailed, but their situation deteriorated. If the Eastern Squares be

238

obtained, a range of Store Houses, East of the Locks will not only enclose and protect the works but be in the most advantageous situation for the delivery of the Stores to the ships, as they arrive from the arsenal at the Pier Heads. For the perfect comprehension of the situation, I beg to refer to the maps of the city.[2]

II. Works necessary to be erected.

The first works to be erected are two Locks of 12 feet lift each. The lowest of these Locks being sunk 23 feet below high water receives the ship from the channel of the harbour. The lower Gates being shut the lock is filled by water from the upper Lock until it rises to the heighth of 12 feet above high water at which level the Vessel will find 23 feet of water in the upper Lock into which she then enters. The water in the upper Lock being then raised 12 feet higher, the vessels will be admitted to the Dry Dock or arsenal into 23 feet of water. Her keel being then (if she draw 23 feet) one foot above high water mark, whenever the number of Vessels intended to be docked or laid up have been raised into the dry dock by this process (which is more fully explained by the model which I shall in a few days submit to you) all the water is permitted to discharge itself into the harbor, and the vessels being properly shored as the water leaves them, settle upon the blocks which are prepared upon the slips marked in the drawing No. 2, fig. 1.[3] It is very evident to use the words of the Presidents letter to me "that a Vessel thus secured from the weather from above, and placed with her keel one foot above high water mark, may be perfectly drained and rendered as safe against decay as the internal timbers of a house." In order to get rid of the foul air which is the most rapid cause of rot, and also perfectly to drain the Vessels, it may be necessary, on laying them up to take off one streak on each side, on each floor below the gun deck from stem to stern. In this dock a Vessel may be built or repaired at leisure. A single vessel may be docked for repair between the dry dock and the Locks without filling the Dry Dock.

The naval arsenal as appears by the drawing hereto annexed, is to be so constructed as to admit the free passage of the air from every Quarter. It was essential that it should be permanent in its mode of Construction and secure from fire. The walls are, therefore, of solid masonry. For so extensive a span without a pillar no better roof could be adopted than that recommended by the President and of which he has   239 furnished me with the model, namely that of the Hal au bled or corn market at Paris, and of incombustible roofs that covered with painted or varnished Sheet Iron, is certainly the cheapest and I think the best. The drawings and estimates are therefore calculated for such a Building and roof. As to the ornamental parts of the design they are not included in the estimate nor are they within the compass of the arts in America at present.

III. The means of supplying the Dock with Water.

In the letter of the President to me two modes of supplying the Dock with water were submitted to examination: 1. from the Potowmak Canal, 2d. from the Tiber.[4]

1. There cannot be one moment's hesitation as to the abstract merits of each of these methods of supply. The Potowmak Canal may be brought by continuation from the Locks at the little falls through George Town to Rocky Creek and through the City to the navy yard. This Canal would not only fill all the works in twelve hours, but convey to the Navy Yard all the timber, stores and provisions which the whole range of the upper navigation of the Potowmak could supply, comprehending not only a great part of Virginia and Maryland, but also a very considerable portion of the most fertile Western Counties of Pennsylvania. To this part of the subject I have paid particular attention and have fully digested a plan which appears to me the best, and perhaps under all the circumstances of the property and the levels of the ground in the city, the only feasible means of accomplishing such a navigation. Being however instructed by the President to separate the consideration of this project from my present report, on account of its large expence, I will only mention here, that the plan of a company either by way of extension of the old Potowmak Canal Company,[5] or of a new company for this separate object has been suggested, which, if formed under the sanction of the Legislature would give to the nation all its advantages both as to the Docks and the supply of stores, on no worse terms than those on which private citizens would obtain its commercial facilities.

2d. The Tiber

Captain Tingey[6] and Mr. King by your orders[7] have measured and levelled the ground between the Hill on the Tiber which belonged to the late Mr. Notley Young,[8] and also between the Spring known by the name of Stodderts Spring,[9] and the navy yard. I have proceeded in my calculations of the expence of bringing the water of the Tiber to the navy yard, upon their Survey. The correctness and fidelity of Mr. King as a Surveyor are well known and may always be depended upon. I have also carefully gone over the ground, with a view to its quality and to the best line of conducting the water. Nothing can be more easily effected than the canals, the whole of the ground being remarkably easy to be dug. At the navy yard, however, no more than a head of twenty four feet above high water is wanted while the head of water of Youngs mill[10] is forty six feet seven inches, and the level of Stodderts Spring is thirty two feet three inches above high water. This difference of elevation while it offers the advantage of large reservoirs to contain a Sufficient Quantity of water to fill the Docks rapidly renders it necessary to construct works of some expence to hold up and discharge the water in such a manner that it shall not destroy the Banks of the Canal by its rapidity and fill the docks with the earth and sand brought down by the Stream. For this reason a dam weir and Sluice at Youngs mill must be built—the sluice to discharge the water from the reservoir in order to cleanse it, the weir to prevent injury to the works in time of heavy rains, and the dam to hold up a considerable body of water at all times. The works at Youngs mill must be so constructed as to lower the water at once to the level of Stodderts spring, by means of a Sluice which shall be capable of being so regulated as to keep a constant slow stream in the canal to prevent stagnation; or to discharge into it the whole of the water necessary to keep the canal full, when the Sluice which fills the Dock shall be drawn. The Reservoir on the Piney Branch[11] must be nearly on a level with Stodderts Spring below which, on the most convenient place, another weir and sluice must be erected to lower the water to the Canal which supplies the Dock. The last Sluice must be at the Dock itself, where no Weir is required, as it will be constantly under inspection. The whole quantity of water required to fill the works at the Dock is 3.515.200 Cubic feet. If the Quantity of water yielded by the Tiber and Stoddert's Spring at the time of Captain Tingeys survey (see his Report)[12] were not made to accumulate in Reservoirs, it would require a month (29 days) to fill the Dock and locks allowing nothing for evaporation and Soakage; for the joint streams yield only 125,088 Cubic feet in twenty four hours. But by collecting the water at Youngs mill, and in the Reservoir on the Piney branch of Tiber, and by making the Canal of large dimensions as 241 proposed, namely, sixteen feet on the surface, six at the bottom, and three feet deep, the works may be completely filled in three days.

The expence of these works is annexed in Estimate no. 2.[13]

IV. The time of completing the works

Should the works be undertaken immediately while the very numerous skilful and experienced workmen who have been collected and in part educated in the execution of large and difficult works at the Pensylvania Bank and the works for supplying the city of Philadelphia with water are within reach, I have not the smallest doubt that with the assistance of those collected in the city of Washington, and in a tolerably favorable season a frigate may ascend the locks and be placed above high water mark before the end of the year 1803 and that the naval arsenal may be completed before the end of the year 1804. The supply by means of the Tiber may probably be effected in the year 1803; but if not, the *Locks* only may be filled in Decr. 1803 by means of the pumps employed in their erection in three days. The Potowmak canal could not be completed before the end of the year 1805; but would by that time, with tolerable seasons, discharge itself into the Dock.

I need not mention to you Sir that the operations of the ensuing year depend in a great measure upon very active preparations before the first of March. By that time every good Workman has usually planned and engaged in the employment of the season.

In respect to the estimates I must beg leave to remark that as to the rate of charge for materials and Workmanship, they are founded upon the experience of expence in works in Philadelphia the nature of which is similar and, as far as they are designated and described in the drawings, I trust that no material difference will arise. There are however two points of expence upon which I must make an observation. The first is, the price to be paid for Land, on which it is impossible to be, at present, informed; and in which it is easy to commit a mistake. The other is, the uncertainty of the foundations below the bed of the harbor, for though there is no indication of a failure of solid foundation at the place at which the lower lock chamber is proposed to be founded, yet as the rest of the bed of the River is muddy, it is possible that mud may be found below the gravel, in which case, piling to the extent of perhaps 10,000 dollars may be necessary.

With these observations I submit to you the result of my attention to your instructions and hold myself in readiness to offer such additional information and Explanations as you may please to command.

I am with true respect your faithful Hble. Servant

(Signed) B. Henry Latrobe

Copy: Records of the U.S. House of Representatives, RG 233, National Archives (166/B9). Another copy is in Records of the U.S. Senate, RG 46, National Archives (166/D1). Also printed in *Message from the President of the United States, Transmitting Plans and Estimates of a Dry Dock, for the Preservation of Our Ships of War* (Washington, D.C., 1802), pp. 7–19 (166/E6). Enclosed BHL, Estimate of the Locks and Naval Arsenal, 4 Dec. 1802, and BHL, Estimate of Supplying the Canal with Water, 4 Dec. 1802, both below. Smith forwarded BHL's report to Jefferson on 8 December. Jefferson transmitted the report to Congress in his message of 27 December. The report and the first enclosure also appeared in *National Intelligencer*, 7 Jan., 12 Jan., and 19 Jan. 1803.

1. See below.

2. The published map of the city was executed by surveyor Andrew Ellicott, *Plan of the City of Washington in the Territory of Columbia . . .* (Philadelphia, 1792). Also available was James Reed Dermott's unpublished map of 1795, which had been approved by President Washington in 1797 and President Adams in 1798 as the official map of the city. Ralph E. Ehrenberg, "Nicholas King: First Surveyor of the City of Washington, 1803–1812," CHS, *Records* 69–70 (1969–70):46.

3. Reproduced in BHL, *Engineering Drawings*, p. 120.

4. Jefferson actually suggested four sources for the water: the Eastern Branch (Anacostia River), Tiber Creek, Rock Creek, and the Potomac River. Jefferson to BHL, 2 Nov. 1802, above.

5. The Potomac Company was chartered by the states of Maryland and Virginia in 1784–85 to make the Potomac River navigable for boats carrying the equivalent of 50 barrels of flour. By 1802 obstructions had been removed from portions of the river, and canals had been built around five falls, including the Great Falls and Little Falls near Washington. Walter S. Sanderlin, *The Great National Project: A History of the Chesapeake and Ohio Canal* (Baltimore, 1946), pp. 29–36.

6. Thomas Tingey (1750–1829), naval officer, was born in England and served in the Royal Navy and merchant marine. After the Revolutionary War he settled in Philadelphia and commanded American merchantmen. In 1798 he was appointed a captain in the United States Navy, and in January 1800 he was appointed superintendent of the new Washington Navy Yard on account of "being a man of understanding and having seen the navy-yards of England." Tingey, a fixture in Washington society for the next twenty-nine years, became a close friend of BHL's. The two men were involved in several projects in the capital, including work on the Washington Navy Yard and the Washington Canal. Henry B. Hibben, "History of the Washington Navy Yard," U.S. Congress, Senate, Executive Document 22, 51st Cong., 1st sess. (1889–90), p. 25; Constance McLaughlin Green, *Washington: Village and Capital, 1800–1878* (Princeton, N.J., 1962), pp. 20, 51.

7. Robert Smith to Tingey, 13 July 1802, RG 45, National Archives, referred to in Tingey to Smith, 22 Oct. 1802, printed in *Message from the President of the United States, Transmitting Plans and Estimates of a Dry Dock, for the Preservation of Our Ships of War* (Washington, D.C., 1802), pp. 21–24.

8. Notley Young (c. 1736–1802) owned large tracts of land in Prince George's County, Md., a portion of which was incorporated into the newly created District of

Columbia in 1791. Young's hill was in the extreme northeastern part of Washington City. His other holdings included land in the southwestern part of the city where his home, Mansion House (G Street between Ninth and Tenth streets, S.W.), was located, and in Washington County, D.C., north of the Washington City limits. A portion of Young's vast wealth was tied up in about 250 slaves. A Roman Catholic whose relations included the Brents, Carrolls, and Casanaves, Young was a leader of the Catholic community in the Washington area. His daughter and son-in-law, Washington Mayor Robert Brent, lived with him at Mansion House until his death. CHS, *Records* 2 (1899):236, 3 (1900):215, 16 (1913):5–6, 35–36 (1935):76.

9. Stoddert's Spring, or Cool Spring, belonged to Benjamin Stoddert (1751–1813), Georgetown merchant, Washington speculator, and the first secretary of the Navy. The spring had its origins in Washington County, D.C., just north of the easternmost section of Washington City, near the corner of present-day Sixteenth and Rosedale streets, N.E. CHS, *Records* 12 (1909):70.

10. Notley Young's mill on a branch of Tiber Creek was near the south side of N Street, N.E. between First and Second streets, N.E. Young's Mill became known as Casanave Mill when his daughter, Ann (Young) Casanave, inherited it after his death. CHS, *Records* 31–32 (1930):83.

11. Of Tiber Creek, not to be confused with Piney Branch of Rock Creek in the western part of the city.

12. Tingey to Smith, 22 Oct. 1802, cited in n. 7, above.

13. See below.

ENCLOSURE A: ESTIMATE OF THE LOCKS AND NAVAL ARSENAL

Washington 4th. Decr. 1802.

Estimate of the Locks.

20,160 yards.	Earth to be removed to make the flanks of the Coffre Dam, digging and carting @ 30 Cents......................	6,048
	Coffre Dam, framed piled and puddled, if rated agreeably to the actual cost of a similar dam erected at Phila. which measures 292,800 cubic feet, and cost in labor, Machinery and all materials 30,000 dollars nearly, it would stand in 10 cents per foot.	
54,000.	Cube of Dam @ 10 Cents............	5,400
244 29,756 yards	Digging below high water mark Lower lock pit @ 25 cents	7,439

14,878 do.	Upper lock pit @ do. do..............	3,719.50
14,875 do.	above high water @ 15 cents..........	2,231.70
	This will account for all the digging of the Lock and turning dock; for the amount accounted to the flank dams will come out of these places.	

Walling.

384 Perch	In wings @ 3$......................	1.152
4,992 do.	In piers and round the gate recesses @ 4$................................	19,968
	Faced with Acquia stone[1] above high water and the whole bedded and jointed in Taves.	
2,932 perch	Lock Chamber in common stone @ 3.50$.............................	10,262
1,579 do.	Above in Ashler @ 5$...............	7,895
2,240 perch	Gate and sluice Walls to upper locks @ 4$................................	8,960
1,579 do.	Lock Chamber below high water @ 3.50$.............................	5,226[2]
2,932 do.	Do. above in Ashler @5$............	14,660
2,956 do.	In the turning dock @5$............	14,780
4,836 do.	Gates to the dry docks and arsenal @ 5$................................	24,180
1,896 do.	Paving in lock chambers and gates @ 3$................................	5,688
2,660 feet	Cube @ 25 cents, labor and workmanship in each of 6 pair of Gates 665	
2,000 lb.	Iron work @ 20 Cts. 400	
	1,065	6.390
12 Sluices	@ 150$...........................	1,800
	Pumping, being the expence incurred in a similar work in Phila.............	3,000
	Scaffolding and Utensils.............	10,000
		152,699[3]

To this sum must be added 10 per Ct.
for incidental expences of direction,

Superintendance, Office Expences and
other small charges, impossible to be
foreseen or enumerated   15,269
Total . . . .   167,968.

Naval Arsenal

13,703 Perch.	in the Dock @ 3.50$.	47,960
21,210 do.	in the Dock @ 5$	106,050
	8 Capitals @ 200$.	1,600

There is nothing about the building but
plain masonry, faced with Acquia stone,
excepting only the cornices of the piers
and the Capitals of the columns. 5$ per
perch is a good allowance for the whole
of the work including arches; the small
quantity of moulded work which is in
the Piers, and for the stairs which have
been measured as solid.

1,374 squares of compound ribs, labor, nails and all
materials including sheeting @ 10$.   13,740

1,374 Square of sheet iron roof, laid down and
painted @ 20$.   27,480

Scaffolding and Utensils beyond what
has served for the locks, say,   5,000
201,830

Add 10 per Cent for incidental charges
as on the other side   20,183
Dolls.   222,013

signed

B. Henry Latrobe
Engineer

Copy: Records of the U.S. House of Representatives, RG 233, National Archives (166/ C10). Enclosed in BHL, Report on Proposed Naval Dry Dock, 4 Dec. 1802, above.

1. Aquia freestone or sandstone had been used in the construction of the north wing of the Capitol in the 1790s. BHL later used the stone, which came from the area around Aquia, Va., in his construction of the south wing of the Capitol.

2. This figure should be $5,526.50.
3. This figure should be $159,099.70, making the total $175,009.67.

ENCLOSURE B: ESTIMATE OF SUPPLYING THE CANAL
WITH WATER

Washington 4th. Decr. 1802

Estimate of the Expence of supplying the Canal
by means of the Tiber and Stodderts Spring

Yards	Perch	Items	$	cts.	Dolls.
	720	Masonry and sluices and weirs at Young's Mill @	5		3600
	360	at the second reservoir on Piney Branch	5		1800
7200		dam at Young's Mill		25	1800
9680		Canal		15	1452
17500		Dam at Piney Branch 2d. Reservoir		20	3500
31,680		(3 miles) Canal to the Navy Yard		15	4752
	192	Sluice to discharge into the Dock	5		960
	3	Sluices	150		450
		Purchase of Land at Notleys Mill			4000
		Purchase of ditto along the line of the Canal 30 feet wide, about 5 acres, at an average of	300		1500
		Purchase of Lands for Reservoirs in Piney Branch.			1000
					24814.
		Add 10 per Ct. for direction, Superintendance and incidental Exps.			2481
				Dolls.	27.295

E.E.

B. Henry Latrobe
Engineer   247

[Jefferson appended the following:]
Recapitulation

The two lower docks	167,968
The Dry dock or Arsenal	222,013
Water of the Tyber	27,295
	417,276

Copy: Records of the U.S. House of Representatives, RG 233, National Archives (166/C13). Enclosed in BHL, Report on Proposed Naval Dry Dock, 4 Dec. 1802, above.

TO THOMAS JEFFERSON

Philadelphia Decr. 15th. 1802.

Dear Sir

Captain Dale, of the Un. State's Navy, called upon me this morning, and in conversation upon the Naval Arsenal or Dry Docks proposed by You to be erected at the Federal City, which he most warmly approved, he informed me that the Swedish Government had lately conceived the idea of adopting the same means of preserving their Navy in times of peace.[1] The Swedish Admiral Söderstrom described to him the situation of the Dock which was then in the progress of construction.[2] It was intended to contain 8 Ships of 74 Guns, and another was projected to contain 12, in all making provision for 20 Ships of the line. The situation was remarkably favorable. Deep water close to a perpendicular rock which can be easily wrought, gives the opportunity of excavating the dock, the rock forms the Wall; and the roof is laid over, at such a higth that the ships go in with their lower Masts standing. Captain Dale did not exactly know how the ships were worked into the dock, but from his description of the situation I presume they are tide docks. Admiral Söderstrom said, that the Vessels were to be washed with fresh Water, perfectly drained, and opened to a circulation of Air, and that he had no doubt of their remaining in perfect repair in the dock for a Century, and gave many reasons for his opinion which were convincing.

This *example* of Sweden, added to that of *Venice*,[3] may perhaps outweigh, the argument with which our Philadelphian federalists hope to answer every thing that can be said in their favor, *"the British have never erected them,"* of course they cannot be worth erecting. I hope you will excuse this intrusion on your time, as perhaps you are already acquainted with the facts, I have related. Should they however be new, they may be useful in the hands of those who have to combat objections, such as are made by party men, who consider not[hing] an improvement worth adopting, that has [not] the sanction of Europaean practice.

I am with the sincerest respect, Your much obliged hble. Svrt.

B. Henry Latrobe.

ALS: Jefferson Papers (167/B1). Addressed to Jefferson in Washington. Endorsed as received 22 December. The manuscript is torn, obscuring two words in the last paragraph.

1. Commodore Richard Dale (1756–1826), born near Norfolk, Va., became an officer in the American navy during the Revolutionary War and was promoted to captain in 1794. He resigned from the service in December 1802 and settled in Philadelphia. Although a Federalist, Dale disagreed with the sentiments of his political compatriots in Philadelphia regarding the need for the dry docks. *PMHB* 4 (1880):499.

2. Research by Svante Lindqvist of the Royal Institute of Technology Library in Stockholm failed to turn up a Swedish admiral named Söderstrom. The man was probably Richard Söderström, who was the Swedish consul general at Philadelphia from 1794 to 1813.

3. In the latter medieval period the Venetians built ship construction facilities and supply stores generally known as the "arsenal." BHL and Jefferson would have known of the facility through the classic works of Dante (*Inferno* 21. 7–15) and Galileo Galilei (*Two New Sciences: Including Centers of Gravity and Forces of Percussion,* trans. Stillman Drake [Madison, Wis., 1974], p. 11). By BHL's time, the Venetian dry docks were, apparently, of little significance.

PAPER ON TWO SPECIES OF WASP

On two species of Sphex, inhabiting Virginia and Pennsylvania,
and probably extending through the United States.
By B. Henry Latrobe.

Philadelphia January, 21st, 1803.[1]

The two species of Sphex to which this memoir is confined, are well known under the names, blue wasp, mason, and dirt-dauber. Among all the remarkable insects belonging to the order of hymenoptera of Linnaeus, they appear to be most distinguished by their singular and cruel mode of providing for their young.

The two species are distinguished from each other in their manner of building, and in the form of their bodies; but agree exactly in their 249 mode of life, in the materials of which they build their cells, and the food provided by them for their offspring.

The first, No. I. Plate I. is probably the Sphex coerulea of Linnaeus, of which the following is the description:

Coerulea, alis fuscis: habitat in America septentrionali.[2]

This sphex, is by far the most common of the two species: the antennae are pointed and stand up when he is at work. His nose is furnished with a strong beak, with which he works sideways, leaving ridges on his cells which make them appear to be plaited; his thorax is thick, the abdomen petiolated. From the scutum attached to the petiole, is extended a strong hook, which is very serviceable to him in securing his prey.[3] His sting is not very painful, and soon ceases to be troublesome.[4] The wings which Linnaeus describes as brown, play between a beautiful green, brown, and blue. The joints of the feet are yellow, the whole of the head, body, and legs are blue. I have however seen some individuals which had yellow spots on the thorax, in front of the wings.

The other sphex, No. II. Plate I. (probably the Pennsylvanica of Linnaeus) differs from the former in many particulars of form and colour. Linnaeus's description runs thus:

Nigra, abdomine petiolato atro, alis subviolaceis. Habitat in Pennsylvania.[5]

The specific differences are as follows:

The head is broad, the nose blunt and emarginate, his thorax is longer in proportion, the petiole of the abdomen very long, the hook is wanting, the abdomen conical and elegantly formed. The general colour is a dark blue approaching to black, but on the thorax are many yellow spots, and the legs, thighs, and feet are also spotted with yellow. His antennae are longer than in No. I. and he carries them less upright, and often curls them. No. II. Fig. 2. is an enlarged view of his head.

The figures both of the coerulea and Pennsylvanica are exactly the size of the live insects, and an attempt is made to imitate accurately their manner when alighting on their cells.

The cells both of the S. coerulea and Pennsylvanica are built of clay collected in moist places; but their appearance, and mode of construction is very different.

The S. coerulea chuses, in the open air, the south side of a rock, or of the trunk of a tree for his structure. He then seeks by the side of a stream for his materials. He scrapes the clay together with his feet, and

SPHEX.

N.º I. Caerula.

1.

2.

3.

4.

c.

b.

a.

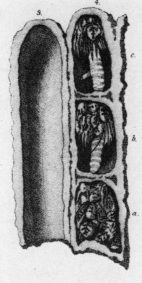

6.

5.

N.º II. Pennsylvanica.

2.

1.

N.º III.

1.

2.

3.

4.

3.

4.

working it into as large a round ball as he can well carry off, he begins by plaistering the stone or wood with a thin coat. He spreads the clay with his head, uttering a shrill sound during his work. He then flies off for another lump, and by degrees forms the upper ridge of his cell. He afterwards adapts a second ridge to the first, working alternately on each side, frequently going into the tube thus formed, and making it perfectly smooth in the inside. In this manner he compleats a tube of 3 or 4 inches long, before any attempt is made to carry in provisions for the young brood.

In the inside of houses, nothing furnishes both these species of sphex with a more convenient situation for their cells than the backs of picture frames; for they are fond of building in places which have a very moderate degree of light, and the back of a picture frame hanging against the wall has also the advantage of furnishing two sides of the cell. A hollow moulding of a pannel has also its strong temptations, or the internal angle of the frame of a table. In the wooden houses of Virginia they occupy all these situations in great numbers. I have seen the hollow space in the front of the books in a library occupied by a whole tribe of the sphex coerulea, which thereby saved themselves much trouble, as they had only to close the space between the edges of the binding.

The sphex Pennsylvanica differs exceedingly from the coerulea in the construction of his cells. Instead of a series of long tubes divided into separate cells, the former builds separate horizontal apartments close to each other. They are perfectly smooth internally, but roughly finished on the outside. See No. II. Fig. 3 and 4: of both these species of cells the figures give an exact representation, both as to size and form.

The food provided by both species for their offspring is however exactly the same, namely *spiders* of every genus and species, chiefly however of those who do not fortify themselves by extensive webs. There is a common yellow spider which they collect in the greatest numbers. I have however observed both the Pennsylvanica and coerulea attack large spiders, in the midst of their webs and of the dead bodies of other insects which had fallen victims to them; especially in a remarkable instance: the sphex flew nimbly at the spider and stung him. He then retired to clean himself from the cobwebs. This he did in the manner of a fly, using his hind legs to wipe his wings, and his fore legs to [wipe] his head. After several attacks the spider at last attempted to escape by letting himself down to the floor, by a thread. He then ran away, but his enemy fol-
252 lowed him, and frequently stinging him attempted to carry him off: but

the spider was too large and heavy; and though the sphex endeavoured to lighten his load by biting off the spider's legs, he could not succeed while I observed him, which was for at least half an hour.

The spiders thus collected are not killed; life enough seems to be still left to preserve them from putrefaction or drying. In all the cells which I have opened, they were in a languid state capable of motion, but not of crawling along. Nothing more cruel than their condition can well be conceived. They are closely and indiscriminately packed together, waiting to be devoured piecemeal by the young worm, for whose support they are destined.[6] See No. I 4, and No. II. 4.

Each of the cells of the sphex, Pennsylvanica being separately contrived to enclose a sufficient number of spiders, they are separately made. But the sphex coerulea, having formed a long tube, crams into it as many spiders as he judges sufficient, and encloses them, together with an egg, by a cross partition of clay. He then puts a new head to the next cell and having filled it, encloses it as the first. Thus he proceeds to the amount sometimes of 4 or 5 cells in one tube.

The egg appears to be soon hatched after deposition, though I found it impossible to ascertain the time between the closing of the cell and the escape of the young sphex.

No. I. Fig. 3 and 4, exhibit the exact state in which I found two ranges of cells at Ripponlodge in Virginia.[7] The cells were made at the back of a picture frame, from which I cut them carefully with a table knife. The figure shows the side next to the frame. Fig. 3, is an empty tube, ready to be divided into cells. Fig. 4a, is the last filled cell of the other range. It is full of spiders, the worm having been just hatched, and eaten nothing. b. contains a worm more advanced which has consumed half his store. c. contains another in a still greater progress to maturity, which has but little provision left. Fig. 5, exhibits the worm, which after consuming all the stock of spiders, is prepared to spin its involucrum. Fig. 6, represents the chrysalis, broken. The dots exhibit its full size.

In the first range of the cells, No. I. Fig. 2; and in No. II. Fig. 3, are seen the holes by which the young sphex escapes. No. II Fig. 4, shews the inside of two cells, carefully separated from the board on which they were built.

As I had always found the number of spiders in each cell unequal, but apparently regulated by their size, I opened a range of cells of the sphex Pennsylvanica, and having weighing the contents I found the result as follows. See No. III.

253

The lowest contained 19 spiders and a small worm, which   grains.
    seemed lately hatched, and had eaten nothing. See Fig.
    I. The spiders weighed 7 1/2
The next contained 17 spiders and one empty skin, the
    worm, Fig. 2, weighed 1/4 of a grain, the spiders 6 1/4
The third contained 19 very small spiders and a few empty
    skins, weighing 5 3/4
The worm, Fig. 3, weighed 1/2
The fourth contained only the empty skins of the spiders.
    The worm, Fig. 4, seemed lean and weak, he was just
    beginning to spin. I think he must have had a short
    allowance provided for him, or have been sick: he
    weighed 3 1/4
The fifth contained an involucrum in which was a large grub
    not yet changed to a chrysalis. The involucrum and
    worm being heavier than the last, weighed 3 1/2
    The 6th and 7th cells were open at the point, the young sphex
having escaped.

This examination proves that the sphex exercises a nice degree of
judgment in the quantity of provision he lays up. For the cell No. 3. must
have contained 22 or 23 spiders, and I have often counted only 6 or 7 in
one, but they were of a large size. It also appears that the full-grown
worm weighs about half as much as the food that reared him.

If it be further necessary to break the line which has formerly been
drawn between reason and instinct, the economy of the whole class of
hymenoptera, and especially of the sphex, will contribute towards it.[8] I
will relate a singular instance of conduct in which instinct appears to be
out of the question.

In order to examine one of these insects (the Pennsylvanica) at
work, I raised a picture frame a little from the wall. In doing this, I
injured several of his cells, for the dirt sticking to the wall was torn off,
and left holes in them, through which the spiders and young worms
were visible. I kept the frame about an inch from the wall so as to see
plainly behind it. In a few moments the sphex returned, bringing with
him a round lump of clay. He had just begun a new cell, but seeing his
former work disturbed, he ran rapidly over the cells, in apparent doubt
what to do. At last he put down the clay on the margin of one of the
holes, and began to spread it with his nose, pushing it out before him

with the action of a hog which is rooting. While he did this he made a shrill buzzing noise. Having plaistered up the hole very perfectly and neatly, he flew away. In 4 minutes he returned with another lump of clay. He put it down at once by the next hole, and stopped it in the same manner. He repeated this four times, and having finished his repairs, and satisfied himself by ranging over the cells several times, he flew for another lump, with which he proceeded to compleat his new cell.

If reason be exhibited in the modification of conduct to unexpected circumstances, this surely was an instance of reasoning. The sphex saw the unexpected dilapidation of his work: it had happened in his absence: the clay he brought was for the new cell: seeing however, the injury done to his work, he thoroughly repaired the old cells, instead of building new ones.

Printed Copy: American Philosophical Society, *Transactions* 6 (1809):73–78 (167/B6). Read by the Society on 21 January 1803 and referred to Benjamin Smith Barton, who recommended publication on 15 July 1803. A slightly edited version of this paper, without the plate, was published in the London, Edinburgh, and Dublin *Philosophical Magazine* 25 (Aug. 1806):236–41.

1. In writing this article BHL drew on observations he had made in Virginia. John Bartram (1699–1777), the pre-eminent American naturalist of his era, earlier described the same species of wasps in letters to his London correspondent Peter Collinson. Collinson published Bartram's remarks (accompanied by sketches of the wasps and their nests), which are briefer and less descriptive than BHL's. Bartram did, however, report his observations of the wasps building nests and storing food for their young in much the same manner as BHL. BHL, *Journals*, 1 : 157–60, 239–42, 2 : 502–03; John Bartram, "An Account of some very curious Wasps Nests made in Clay in Pennsylvania," Royal Society of London, *Philosophical Transactions* 43 (1744–45):363–66, figures; John Bartram, "Observations made by Mr. John Bartram, at Pensilvania, on the Yellowish Wasp of that Country," Royal Society of London, *Philosophical Transactions* 53 (1763):37–38.

2. Trans.: Blue, wings dark: it inhabits North America. The blue mud-dauber wasp, *Sphex caerulea* (Linneaus), is now *Chalybion californicum*.

3. Bartram's earlier description and sketches had omitted these anatomical details.

4. Only the female of the species has a true stinger.

5. Trans.: Black, with petiolated black abdomen; wings violet. It inhabits Pennsylvania. The yellow mud-dauber, *Sphex pennsylvanica* (Linnaeus) was reclassified in 1801 as *Sceliphron cementarium*, but BHL was apparently unaware of the change.

6. BHL's "worm" is the wasp in its larval state.

7. Rippon Lodge, in Prince William County, Va., was the estate of Col. Thomas Blackburn (1740–1807). BHL visited it in July 1796 and made a watercolor of some wasps and their cells which he observed there. BHL, *Journals*, 1 : 159–60, plate 16; 2 : 535.

8. Here BHL challenged the prevailing notion that only man possessed reason while other animals were lower in the chain of nature and acted from instinct. Arthur O. Lovejoy, *The Great Chain of Being: A Study of the History of an Idea* (New York, 1936), pp. 231–36.

TO JOHN LENTHALL

Philadelphia March 5th. 1803

My dear Sir,[1]

I am ashamed not to have written to you sooner. Old Men may be the wiser for age, but they certainly become slower of comprehension. The president had not comprehended me when I explained the locks to him, or he had forgotten what he had once understood. But it is no matter, provided your trouble be not thrown away.[2] Mr. Eakin will take care that it shall not, and you must [*torn*]ly permit it.

I thank you sincerely for your kindness to little William Strickland.[3] One day or other we may see more of one another. It will not be my fault if we do not, for I shall try to effect it. God knows when I may again be in Washington. Whenever I am I shall certainly call upon you. Believe me very truly Yrs.

B. H. Latrobe

ALS: BHL Papers, Library of Congress (167/C4). Addressed to Lenthall in Washington.

1. John Lenthall (c. 1762–1808) was born in England, where he gained experience in mining and cotton manufacturing as well as aspects of engineering and architecture. He married Jane King, daughter of Robert King, Sr., city surveyor of Washington, D.C., about 1800. BHL hired Lenthall in April 1803 as clerk of the works at the U.S. Capitol, thereafter relying greatly on Lenthall's expertise as a builder. Lenthall was crushed to death on 19 September 1808 when the Supreme Court vault in the basement of the Capitol fell after the centering was removed. BHL published a eulogy of Lenthall, dated 20 September 1808, in the *National Intelligencer,* which is printed in BHL, *Correspondence,* 2. Hamlin, *Latrobe,* p. 278n.

2. The reference to locks here may concern the proposed naval dry dock and Potomac Canal extension, perhaps suggesting Lenthall's participation.

3. William Strickland (1788–1854), architect, engineer, and engraver, was the son of John Strickland, the carpenter who worked for BHL on the Bank of Pennsylvania and the Chesapeake and Delaware Canal (see BHL to Lenthall, 5 May 1803, below). BHL later stated that "William came to me in August 1801. On July 1, 1803, I carried him to Newcastle, and began to provide for him in almost every respect." He worked as a pupil in BHL's office until difficulties arose with his family in the summer of 1805. Looking back on this, however, Strickland himself related that he remained somewhat longer, leaving when he was 19 years old (i.e., about 1807). During that time, Strickland worked on the south wing of the U.S. Capitol, "the planning and commencement" of the works at the navy yard in Washington, and "especially . . . the very extensive and laborious surveys" for the Chesapeake and Delaware Canal and Elk River feeder. In early 1810 BHL, temporarily in Philadelphia, paid Strickland for copying a set of drawings of the navy yard steam engine. Although BHL greatly admired Strickland's talent—he later described him as "an excellent draughtsman, perhaps the best of those I have educated"—the young man's intractableness eventually forced BHL to discharge him. Strickland nonetheless

went on to become one of the principal exponents of the Greek Revival in America, designing such important Philadelphia buildings as the U.S. Custom House (1819), the Second Bank of the United States (completed 1824), and the Merchants' Exchange (1834). It was over the competition for the Second Bank of the U.S. design later in BHL's life that BHL and Strickland became estranged. BHL to Strickland, 11 Aug. 1805, and BHL to William Eustis, 10 June 1812, both in LB (42/E8, 98/G1); BHL to Paul Hamilton, 12 May 1810, RG 45, National Archives (200/D1), with Account, LB (74/G10); William Strickland, incomplete autobiographical sketch, J. K. Kane Papers, APS; Agnes A. Gilchrist, *William Strickland: Architect and Engineer, 1788–1854*, enlarged ed. (New York, 1969).

The Surveyorship of the Public Buildings

EDITORIAL NOTE

In early 1803 the existence of the United States Capitol, not one-third finished, and of the national capital itself was uncertain. In February 1803 Congress considered retroceding the District of Columbia to Virginia and Maryland, a proposal that induced fears (and some hopes) of a permanent removal of the seat of government from the struggling, inchoate "city" of Washington. Congress also considered the possibility of consolidating the public offices, a move that would have resulted in a revision of the Capitol. The building and the city got a reprieve, however, when on 3 March 1803 Congress appropriated $50,000 for "repairs or alterations" in the Capitol and for other public works, to be carried out under the direction of the president.[1] Three days later Thomas Jefferson, who had had the opportunity of evaluating Latrobe's professional abilities at close quarters in the planning of the naval dry dock the preceding fall, wrote to Latrobe asking him to accept the position of "Surveyor of the Public Buildings of the United States at Washington."[2]

As surveyor of the public buildings from 1803 to July 1811, Latrobe's primary concerns were the revision and completion of the Capitol and the President's House, both of which had been begun according to plans the architect found it necessary to alter significantly. After the British burned many of the important buildings of the city in 1814, Latrobe was employed once more, this time as "Architect or Surveyor of the Capitol of the United States," a position he held from April 1815 until his resignation in November 1817.

Although the commissions seemed to hold great promise for the architect, Latrobe encountered innumerable obstacles and frustrations, particularly at the Capitol, leading him just before his death to characterize his accomplishments there as merely "*la difficulté vaincue.*"[3] Nonetheless the Capitol gave Latrobe the

1. *Annals of Congress*, 7th Cong., 2d sess., pp. 415, 421, 486–91, 493–507, 515–17, 1601–02.
2. Jefferson to BHL, 6 Mar. 1803 (Public), below.
3. BHL to Rudolph Ackermann, 4 Aug. 1820, quoted in "Memoir of Benjamin Henry La Trobe," *The Repository of Arts*, 2d ser., 11 (1821):32 (microfiche add.).

opportunity to work on a scale that none of his other buildings offered him. More than any other single work, it was the Capitol that brought on his maturation, his emergence as a great architect. Latrobe's first tour as surveyor plunged him into an oftentimes frustrating collaboration with Jefferson. The concrete results on Capitol Hill—principally, the Hall of Representatives in the south wing, and the Supreme Court chamber and the Senate chamber in the north wing—would hold singular interest as the joint creations of these two giants. More important, nothing affected Latrobe's maturation more decisively than his exposure to Jefferson's preferences in regard to domes. In part, this exposure made direct contributions to Latrobe's store of architectural possibilities, and, in part, it confirmed or promoted opposing ideas of his own. In the course of his second term as surveyor Latrobe designed grander versions of his earlier courtroom and Senate chamber; he devised a new Hall of Representatives, based on his own thinking as modified under the influence of Jefferson's earlier decisions; and he increased the number of fine ancillary rooms beyond those he had previously created. But it was Charles Bulfinch who completed the execution of the building. Latrobe's most important achievement at the Capitol, in the end, was to have established the form of the greatest set of Neoclassical interiors in the nation.

In 1803 there supposedly existed a governing design for the building by Dr. William Thornton that George Washington himself had approved in 1793. Over the course of ten years a very different conception of the building had taken shape, with whatever degree of Washington's approval, and it amounted to a compound of ideas that had come at various times from Thornton, Étienne Sulpice Hallet, Jefferson, and perhaps other men. The pervasive notion in 1803 was that in execution the Capitol ought to adhere to the design that Washington had approved, and this was understood to be the composite plan, not the obsolete Thornton project that the president had first chosen in 1793. But as of 1803 there existed no set of drawings that pulled the ideas together by genuinely defining the whole and its component parts. For that reason, the word *design* fits only loosely.

In 1803, the basic features of the proposed building included the north wing, already executed, principally containing a Senate chamber laid out on an approximately semi-elliptical theatrical plan and articulated by a colonnade over an arcade; a south wing for a hall of Representatives on an elliptical plan, again with a colonnade over an arcade, the hall to be covered with a dome imitating that of the Halle au Blé; and a "center building." On the east, or secondary, front, the center building was to merge with the north and south wings via two elements set slightly back, the "north recess" (built) and the "south recess" (unbuilt), devised for vestibules, staircases, and rooms to serve the two wings. On the west, the center building was to project to form the principal front. The center building was to consist primarily of a domed central rotunda (once more with a colonnade upon an arcade) which Thornton had devised as a kind of monument to George Washington, and under which or in which Thornton hoped, from an early date, to put Washington's tomb; on the east front, a relatively shallow octastyle portico, inspired, in combination with the rotunda dome, by the Pantheon; on the west, a circular "grand conference room," intended for the assembly of the two houses in the presence of the president, and meant to be treated externally as a kind of peripteral circular temple; and, over the conference room, probably a lofty, circular, temple-like superstructure, with a dome that would have towered over that of the central rotunda.

The north wing had gone into service for the congressional session of 1800–01. The Senate occupied its permanent chamber on the east side, while temporary accommodations for the House of Representatives were provided on the west side. In 1801, the Supreme Court, lacking a building of its own, also moved in, supposedly as a temporary measure. Also in 1801, on the foundations of the south wing, James Hoban built the elliptical arcade of the Hall of Representatives and roofed it to serve as a temporary chamber for the House; at the same time, he constructed a temporary covered passage, with waterclosets, between the wings. Hot in warm weather, the new temporary House chamber speedily won the nickname of the "bake oven." Unfortunately, the builders of the north wing had not, on the whole, built well. The walls, of Aquia sandstone from Virginia and brick, did prove solid, but the wing had been laid out incorrectly, and the wooden internal construction soon began to rot, a problem exacerbated by a leaky roof, to the additional detriment of the plasterwork. The south wing fared still worse, for even its foundations and the "bake oven" suffered from defective construction. An unsightly, decaying assemblage of pieces—such was the U.S. Capitol when Latrobe arrived in Washington in March 1803 to undertake the work.

In truth the surveyorship was no plum; it came with an annual salary of only $1,700. It provided an imposing title, but it did not offer Latrobe the hope of great artistic glory. Latrobe did not embrace the surveyorship eagerly, as his letters show. He realized that accepting the position would be wholly imprudent if he could not work mainly by proxy and if the government did not supplement his salary with other commissions. Under these conditions, Latrobe accepted. The documents of 1803 do not address the important matter of the degree of artistic independence Latrobe was to possess in the surveyorship. He later stated that his understanding was that he "should deviate as little as possible from the plan approved by General Washington."[4] Jefferson later recollected that it was his policy "to admit no innovations on the established plans, but on the strongest grounds."[5] The case may well be that Jefferson, from the outset, did indeed allow for some alteration from the received proposal, but that Latrobe had different ideas as to what constituted strong grounds.

Although as surveyor of the public buildings Latrobe spent most of his energies on the Capitol, he was also responsible for the President's House at the other end of Pennsylvania Avenue. Like the Capitol, in 1803 the house stood in need of repair and completion. Designed by James Hoban in 1792 in the Palla-

---

4. BHL, *A Private Letter to the Individual Members of Congress, on the Subject of the Public Buildings of the United States at Washington* (Washington, D.C., 1806), dated 28 Nov. 1806, in BHL, *Correspondence*, 2.

5. Jefferson to BHL, 14 Apr. 1811, in BHL, *Correspondence*, 3.

dian tradition, the President's House derived from the plates in James Gibbs's *Book of Architecture* (1728), from Leinster House in Dublin (1745–47), and ultimately from Colin Campbell's Wanstead House in Essex (begun c. 1715). The most pressing problem with the President's House was the leaking slate roof. Latrobe remedied this defect by reroofing the building with sheet iron from the rolling mill attached to the Philadelphia Waterworks, also the source for sheet iron for the Capitol and Monticello. Later work involved the construction of low, one-story Palladian wings connecting the President's House with the adjacent Treasury and War Office buildings. Although Latrobe disapproved of this scheme of Jefferson's ("the style of the Collonade [Jefferson] proposes is exactly consistent with Hoban's Pile,—a litter of pigs worthy of the great Sow it surrounds, and of the Irish *boar,* the father of her"), he executed it with minor modifications.[6]

The roof and the wings were not the only defects in the President's House. Latrobe viewed the entire building with distaste, objecting to both its style and scale; it was, he wrote, "a mutilated copy of a badly designed building."[7] Not until 1807 was the architect able to begin effecting some important changes in the design, furnishings, and surroundings of the building. The grounds were graded and planted in 1807–08 to insure privacy within the park. During the Madison administration, Latrobe designed furniture and other interior decorations for the President's House. The architect also advocated the construction of north and south porticoes to make the entrances to the presidential mansion grander and more impressive. Although not according to his design, the porticoes were completed in the 1820s after Latrobe's death and grew to be two of the most prominent, thoroughly recognizable national symbols.

6. BHL to John Lenthall, 3 May 1805, BHL Papers, Library of Congress (178/F13).
7. BHL to Philip Mazzei, 29 May 1806, in BHL, *Correspondence,* 2.

FROM THOMAS JEFFERSON (PUBLIC)

Washington Mar. 6. 1803.[1]

Sir

Congress have appropriated a sum of money (50,000. D) to be applied to the public buildings under my direction.[2] This falls of course under the immediate business of the Superintendant, mr. Monroe, whose office is substituted for that of the board of Commissioners.[3] The former post of Surveyor of the public buildings, which mr. Hoben held till the dissolution of the board at 1700. Doll. a year will be revived.[4] If you chuse to accept of it, you will be appointed to it, and would be expected to come on by the 1st. of April. Indeed if you could make a

flying trip here to set contractors to work immediately in raising freestone, it would be extremely important, because it is now late to have to
engage labourers, and the quantity of freestone which can be raised,
delivered and cut, in the season is the only thing which will limit the
extent of our operations this year. I set out tomorrow for Monticello and
shall be absent 3. weeks, but I shall be glad to recieve there your answer
to this. Accept my friendly salutations and respects.

[Th: Jefferson]

P.S. On the raising of the freestone be pleased to consult Colo. D. C.
Brent, who can give you better information and advice on the subject
than any other person whatever, having been much concerned in the
business himself.[5]

ALS: Mrs. Gamble Latrobe Collection, MdHS (167/C8). The signature has been cut out of
the document.

1. On this day Jefferson scheduled a meeting with William Thornton, original design-
er of the Capitol, to discuss and view his plans of the building. Jefferson to Thornton, 6
Mar. [1803], Thornton Papers, Library of Congress, quoted in Noble E. Cunningham, Jr.,
The Process of Government under Jefferson (Princeton, N.J., 1978), p. 40.

2. *Annals of Congress*, 7th Cong., 2d sess., p. 1601.

3. Thomas Munroe (1771–1852) was the son of William Munroe, a prominent Annapolis, Md., merchant. Settling in Washington, D.C., about 1791, he became the clerk of
the District's Board of Commissioners. When the board was abolished in 1802, he was
appointed superintendent of the city and served in that position until 1815. In 1799 he
became postmaster of Washington, holding the office until President Andrew Jackson
removed him in 1829. In 1832 he was an unsuccessful candidate for mayor on the anti-
Jackson ticket. An active participant in the business and commercial affairs of the city,
Munroe was a founder of the Columbia Manufacturing Company (1808), one of the
incorporators of the Washington Bridge Company (1808), and an officer in the Bank of
Columbia of Georgetown (1796), the Patriotic Bank, and the Bank of the Metropolis. CHS,
Records 6 (1903):157–59; Wilhelmus Bogart Bryan, *A History of the National Capital from Its
Foundation through the Period of the Adoption of the Organic Act*, 2 vols. (New York, 1914–16),
1 : 345–46, 2 : 165.

4. James Hoban (c. 1762–1831), born in Ireland, immigrated to the U.S. after the
Revolution and worked in Philadelphia and South Carolina. In 1792 his competition
design for the President's House was chosen and he was employed to build the structure
for 300 guineas annual salary. While working on the President's House, Hoban served as
surveyor of the public buildings, and also undertook the design and construction of the
Great, or Blodget's Hotel in Washington. In 1802 he was elected to the Washington City
Council, on which he served intermittently until 1826. In the fall of 1808, he penned a
scathing attack on BHL's work on the public buildings (for which see BHL to Jefferson, 23
Sept. 1808, n. 4, in BHL, *Correspondence*, 2). He was in charge of rebuilding the President's
House after it was burned by the British in 1814.

5. Col. Daniel Carroll Brent (1760–1815), son of William and Eleanor (Carroll) Brent, was an Aquia quarrier in partnership with Col. John Cooke and a member of the Virginia House of Delegates from Stafford County. *Alexandria Gazette,* 24 Jan. 1815; Chester Horton Brent, *The Descendants of Collo. Giles Brent, Capt. George Brent and Robert Brent* (Rutland, Vt., 1946), p. 142.

FROM THOMAS JEFFERSON (PRIVATE)

Washington Mar. 6. 1803.

Dear Sir

The letter in which this is inclosed being a public one, and to be produced whenever necessary as a voucher, I have thought it would be useful to add a word in one of a private and friendly nature. From the sum of 50,000 D. we shall take between 5, and 10,000. for covering the North wing of the Capitol and the President's house. The residue of 40. to 45,000. D. will be employed in building the South wing as far as it will go. I think it will raise the external walls to the uppermost window-sills, being those of the entresols; and I have no doubt Congress at their next session will give another 50,000. D. which will compleat that wing inside and out in the year 1804. Before that period the repairs of their frigates will become so threatening that I have no doubt they will come into the proposition of the drydock to rescue themselves from heavier calls. I mention these things to shew you the probability of a pretty steady employment of a person of your character here, tho' the present job has the appearance of being for the present season only, say of 8. or 9. months; and that your being in possession of the post will put all other competitors out of the question. Should you think proper to undertake it, if you come here on a flying trip as suggested in my other letter, you can advise with mr. Monroe, who will set into motion whatever you may desire; and if you can be here finally the first week in April, you will then find me here, and every thing may be put under full sail for the season. Accept my best wishes and respects.

Th: Jefferson

P.S. I think a great quantity of sheet iron will be wanting.

ALS: Mrs. Gamble Latrobe Collection, MdHS (168/C9). Enclosed in Jefferson to BHL, 6 Mar. 1803 (Public), above.

TO THOMAS JEFFERSON

Philadelphia March 13th. 1803

Dear Sir,

I received your favor of the 6th with the most grateful sentiments.[1] It did not reach me till the 11th. I cannot better express the sense I have of your kindness, than by setting off for Washington as soon as I can leave my business with convenience, and safety. This will be in 2 or 3 days at furthest. I have already made my principal arrangements. The failure of my partners Messrs. Bollmann, has thrown the weight of our Iron concern upon my shoulders, and renders it impossible for me at this moment to say that I shall be able to accept of your generous offer.[2] But I will devote myself to the compleat organisation of the business of the Season with the same zeal and activity, as if I could go through with it: and as I shall have the honor to see you at Washington, I will give you my decission then. My sincere wish is to be employed near you, and under your direction. In the mean time, I beg you to believe me with the truest respect Yours faithfully

B. Henry Latrobe

ALS: Jefferson Papers (167/D6). Endorsed as received 21 March.

1. Jefferson to BHL, 6 Mar. 1803 (two letters of this date), above.
2. Justus Erick Bollmann (1769–1821), a native of Germany who apparently met BHL in England before arriving in the United States in January 1796, and his brother Lewis (Ludwig) Bollmann (d. post-1824) were partners in a Philadelphia mercantile firm that thrived during the Anglo-French war of 1793–1802. In 1801 the Bollmanns entered into a partnership with BHL and Nicholas J. Roosevelt to set up the steam-driven rolling and slitting mill on the Schuylkill River powered by the lower waterworks engine. The Bollmann firm failed in early 1803, following the signing of the Peace of Amiens in 1802, and their share in the mill was sold at auction. Erick Bollmann's personal life and occupation, especially after his involvement in the Burr conspiracy, are illustrated in about eighty letters BHL wrote to him from 1803 to 1816, all of which are in *PBHL, Microfiche Ed.* See BHL to Bollmann, 16 Mar., 14 Aug. 1804, both below; and BHL, *Correspondence*, 2, 3. Fritz Redlich, "The Philadelphia Waterworks in Relation to the Industrial Revolution in the United States," *PMHB* 69 (1945):245–46, 249.

TO JAMES EAKIN

Philadelphia March 13th. 1803

My dear friend,

By your packet delivered to me by Colonel Mentges,[1] I was first apprized of your illness. You know how sincerely I must have regretted it, and how rejoiced I am to hear of your gradual but certain recovery. A few days before I received your letter I had forwarded to you my acct. with the Secretary of the Navy.[2] As you had transmitted to me many of the necessary Vouchers, I fear you may have found difficulty in procuring a settlement. If when this reaches you, you have not made a remittance, I must beg that you will keep the money till you see me; for I shall be in Washington in the course of this week. Mary joins me in best wishes for your recovery. Believe me most truly Yrs.

B. H. Latrobe

Postscript. Since I wrote the letter above, I have drawn out my acct. and have signed so much of it as I can vouch for. On the other side I have written the heads of charge to be filled up by you. There will be no occasion I presume to pay King and Boyd before you get the money. King may want pressing but he must give an account, so must Boyd. If the Secretary hesitate as to the amount, pray tell him to send me on 400 or 500 Dollars on acct. immediately, for Bollmann (my partners) failure has made me devilish short of cash, for the present, although eventually I lose nothing. Tell him also that I got 500 Dollars for a weeks survey of forts at Norfolk and all my expences:[3] and that Foxall got 500 Dollars for looking at Harry Lee's mine in order to advise whether U. States should erect a foundery there.[4] Stick to him, my friend, and his liberality will get the better of his fear of the Genevan Oeconomist.[5] Another thing—Damme if I take a penny less than Will Weston got.[6]

I have another word with you. You are in this affair a commission Merchant, and entitled to 5 per Cent. I should have to pay it to any body who did the business for me, and shall my cousin fare worse than a stranger? So none of your frowns. I know you are a noble independent fellow. Don't let me be worse than yourself. This is not blarney. We all know you, as a *son*, and a *brother;* and if we did not I would beat my wife in a fit of jealousy for loving you as she does. So, my dear fellow, do me the favor to use no ceremony, but get the money for me, and do yourself justice. If you don't, I do not think I shall ask another favor of you as long as I live. Postage of course.

ALS: Gratz Collection, Historical Society of Pennsylvania (167/D1). Addressed to Eakin at the War Department, Washington.

1. Col. Francis Mentges (d. 1805), a native of France, taught dancing in Philadelphia before the Revolution. He served as an officer in the Continental army, rising to the rank of lieutenant colonel. In 1786 he was appointed inspector general of the militia of the state of Pennsylvania and was for several years adjutant general of the state. In 1800 Mentges had solicited BHL's advice on some work to be done at Fort Mifflin in the Delaware River just south of Philadelphia. BHL, *Journals*, 3 : 17–21.

2. The account with Navy Secretary Robert Smith was for BHL's commission to design a covered dry dock for the Washington Navy Yard.

3. See BHL to Jefferson, 22 Sept. 1798, above.

4. Henry Foxall (1758–1823), English-born iron founder, immigrated to Philadelphia in 1797. With his partner, Robert Morris, Jr., he owned the Eagle Iron Works on the Schuylkill River. When the federal government moved to Washington in 1800, he moved to Georgetown, where he established the Foxall (or Columbia) Foundry. Foxall's new business consisted entirely of government contracts. A devoted Methodist lay minister, Foxall gave the ground and funds for the construction of the Foundry Methodist Church in Washington in 1814. He sold his foundry in 1815, served as mayor of Georgetown (1821–23), and returned to England, where he died. Madison Davis, "The Old Cannon Foundry above Georgetown, D.C., and Its First Owner, Henry Foxall," CHS, *Records* 11 (1908):16–70; Louis F. Gorr, "The Foxall-Columbia Foundry: An Early Defense Contractor in Georgetown," CHS, *Records* 48 (1971–72):34–59.

Henry ("Light-Horse Harry") Lee owned an iron mine in Berkeley County, Va. (now W. Va.). It appears that the foundry was never built. Thomas Boyd, *Light-Horse Harry Lee* (New York, 1931), p. 193; *ASP. Military*, 1 : 159.

5. Albert Gallatin (1761–1849), a native of Geneva, Switzerland, served as secretary of the Treasury from 1801 to 1814. Friction within Jefferson's cabinet between Gallatin and Navy Secretary Smith arose from Gallatin's keeping a close watch over the expenditures of the Navy Department. See Noble E. Cunningham, Jr., *The Process of Government under Jefferson* (Princeton, N.J., 1978), pp. 61–62, 115–16, 217.

6. See BHL to Wood, 14 Feb. 1798, above.

TO ROBERT GOODLOE HARPER

Washington, March 28th. 1803

Dear Sir,

I am this moment favored with yours of the 26th. instant to which I will, in order to save the post, reply without expressing in any manner, the thanks I owe you for the flattering opinion you express of me.

It is impossible from recollection to state to you the exact expence of 265 the Waterworks in Philadelphia, nor do the published accounts of the work give a correct result. But of some parts of the work, few of which will be applicable to your situation, I can give you some idea. And to begin at the pipes of distribution.

1.) Pipes of distribution. Before any pipes were taken up for repair, I made a very careful and correct statement of what they had cost to dig the trench, lay down the logs, fill up, pave, put up hydrants and stop cocks, and found the expence to be 50 Cents some Mills per foot running. Since then all repairs 2/3ds of which were owing to contracts made with improper and inadequate agents, by H. Drinker and Th. Cope[1] have been added to the acct. of distribution, which makes the amount on the books appear greater than it ought to be.

2.) In Philadelphia local circumstances occasioned the necessity of employing 2 Steam engines. These Engines cost 30.000 Dollars, put up. The Engine houses cost 70.000 Dollars nearly, because that in Center-square is a magnificent Marble building. 15.000 Dollars would have otherwise been sufficient. At that sum the estimate was made.

3. Upper Tunnel. This Work is nearly a mile long, and is led over an Aqueduct of 3 Arches of 30 feet each. It is a reservoir of Water at all times of freshes which yield clear water though the river be turbid. It cost 22.350 Dollars including the trench and filling in. Estimate 22.500 Dollars. It is, as you know a brick tunnel laid in Cement 6 feet in diameter.

4. All the works on the Schuylkill, the lower tunnel, the Canal, and the Bason are hewn out of the solid Rock, excepting part of the latter. The Bason wall is near 200 feet long, 15 thick, built in from 7 to 15 feet of Water and founded on the solid rock. The Bason cost 23.000 Dollars, the Canal and Tunnel, *I believe,* 7.000. The whole expence, independently of maintenance for 2 Years about 200.000, also exclusive of repairs of pipes.

Now of all these Works, no part can be of any service to you, to form an idea of your probable expence excepting the Pipes. To be safe, you ought to estimate their expence at 66 2/3 cents per foot including every incidental expence of distribution. This is an expence which will be gradually incurred, for you will find it difficult to procure and lay more than 30.000 feet per Annum.

In Baltimore, where the Water will probably be taken from the foot of Jones falls, above the reach of the tide, one Engine is sufficient, say 20.000 Dollars: Engine house 8.000 or 9.000 according to the supply you contemplate. But in all events, if you do not exceed 3 Million Gallons in 24 hours 30.000 Dollars will be sufficient to effect the raising the Water in the first instance. I think you should first build a small Engine, say 12 or 15.000$s, and add another as revenue increases. The annual maintenance 3.000$.

You require no Tunnel to carry the Water along one Mile to the Center of the City, for you will be obliged by your situation, to force your Water into the pipes, regulating your force according to your distribution.

The experience acquired in Philadelphia has suggested many things which could be done better than they are done there; and if the present corporation should be inclined to listen to me, it is my intention to suggest a system of *saving* to them which may still be made. But in the outset I would beg you, and those who have influence to endeavor to prevent any attempt at a gratuitous public supply by means of hydrants. In Philadelphia this public *nuisance* is the only price at which all the other benefits of the Works could be purchased.

In the compass of one Sheet, and of one Post I cannot give all my reasons, but they are insuperable. Waste, riot, burst pipes, frozen pavements, loss of revenue, and destruction of the hydrants themselves will result from them, and in Philadelphia they will be gradually taken up, and changed for a few fountains always playing.[2]

It will be lost labor, upon the whole, to endeavor to judge of your probable expense by ours. Your levels, your supply of water, your relative situation of the water to the city are different, and nothing but a *particular* survey and estimate will do. I will certainly see you on my return: till when, believe me with true respect and affection Yrs. truly

B. Henry Latrobe.

P.S. By tomorrow's post I will send you more particulars. In mentioning the names of H. Drinker and Th. Cope, I mean not to impeach their motives or integrity but only to say that I opposed the contracts at the time they were proposed.

ALS: Mrs. Gamble Latrobe Collection, MdHS (167/D10). Addressed to Harper in Baltimore. Endorsed as received 1 April and answered soon after.

1. Thomas Pym Cope (1768–1854), a Quaker merchant and politician of Philadelphia, served on the city Watering Committee at the time BHL directed construction of the waterworks. He developed a strong dislike for BHL and was angered when the en-

gineer was unable to construct the waterworks within the time and expense limits set. Cope found morally reprehensible BHL's accepting a partnership in the Schuylkill rolling mill with Nicholas Roosevelt, the engine contractor, while at the same time giving the committee advice on the adequacy of Roosevelt's engines. Cope concluded that BHL "is a cunning, witful, dissimulating fellow, possessing more ingenuity than honesty." Eliza Cope Harrison, ed., *Philadelphia Merchant: The Diary of Thomas P. Cope, 1800–1851* (South Bend, Ind., 1978), p. 57.

2. The public hydrants were a constant problem during the early years of the waterworks. The first hydrants were failures and had to be replaced by new ones almost immediately. Still, in 1803 the Watering Committee reported that the new hydrants were easily damaged by "mischievous persons," often froze in winter, and usually stood in pools of wasted water which became ice in winter. Three years later a traveler observed: "I have seen boys, who run all day uncontrolled about the streets, playing with [the hydrants] for hours together opposite to the window of my lodgings; passengers would sometimes attempt to *persuade* them to discontinue their abuse of the water, but not till some other plan of mischief was agreed upon, would they desist for a moment." *Report of the Committee for the Introduction of Wholesome Water into the City of Philadelphia* (Philadelphia, 1801), p. 7; *Report of the Watering Committee to the Select and Common Councils, November 1, 1803* (Philadelphia, 1803), p. 4; Charles William Janson, *The Stranger in America* (London, 1807), p. 187; Eugene S. Ferguson, ed., *Early Engineering Reminiscences (1815–1840) of George Escol Sellers* (Washington, D.C., 1965), p. 6; BHL, *Engineering Drawings*, pp. 196–98.

TO THOMAS JEFFERSON

[Washington, 4 April 1803]

Dear Sir,

I herewith send you my report and the ground plan of the new wing. I fear I shall tire your patience, but I know not what I could have omitted.

I am with true respect Yrs. faithfully

B. H. Latrobe

ALS: Jefferson Papers (167/E6). Enclosed BHL, Report on the U.S. Capitol, 4 Apr. 1803, below.

ENCLOSURE: REPORT ON THE U.S. CAPITOL

Washington City 4th. April 1803.

Sir

Agreeably to your instructions I arrived at Washington on the 21st. of March, and have since that time devoted my attention to the objects proposed by your letter of the 6th of March.

After having very carefully and minutely examined the present state of the Capitol as far as it has been completed, and the foundations of the south Wing, which it is proposed to carry forward this season, I now submit to you the following report, in which, that my motives in the alterations I shall propose may be fully understood, I shall be under the necessity of entering into the consideration of the general plan at some length. I beg leave to add that the remarks to which I pray your attention, have been fully communicated and explained to [. .],[1] the original author of the plan; a communication which I felt to be due to him, not only as a matter of politeness and ceremony, but as a just tribute of respect to his talents.

In considering the general plan of the Capitol the first remark that occurs is; that by the mode in which the exterior appearance has been connected with the internal arrangement, a radical and incurable fault has been grafted upon the work, and made an essential part of it. The building has the appearance of a principal floor elevated upon a basement story. ⟨*A magnificent flight of steps leads up to the Portico on the West front, and that towards the East, though placed upon an arcade has the effect of belonging to that floor.*⟩[2] But in the interior all this expectation is disappointed. The Porticoes lead only to the Galleries and committee rooms, and to get *into* the Halls of Legislation, it is necessary to descend a flight of stairs. ⟨*On stating this remark to the author, he informed me that his first idea was that of a grand single story raised upon a basement sufficiently elevated to contain conveniently all the offices attached to the legislative bodies. On the floor of the principal story it was intended that the legislative bodies should hold their sittings. The access to this floor was to be by two grand flights of steps in the center of the East and West fronts. Reasons afterwards occurred by which he was induced to lower the altitude and diminish the diameters of his Columns: and in order that the general heighth of the building might not be thereby diminished, the Basement story was raised to one third of the whole heighth. As the diminished altitude of the principal story was no longer fitted to the high proportions of the Halls of the legislature, they were, without altering the features of the original ground plot, let down to the level of the basement story.*

On the East front the Portico, an entrance worthy of the grandest internal arrangements, being placed upon an arcade, is reduced to a mere balcony: if furnished with a flight of steps, such as it seems to demand, it will lead up to a narrow Gallery, from which the approach to the legislative Halls is by descending the internal stairs of the house. The same fault exists on the West front. The steps lead up a story too high.⟩

In the internal arrangement of the building another inconvenience   269 results from this error. The grand Vestibule, the Senate chamber, and the Hall of the representatives present but one design. For though the vestibule is circular, the senate chamber, a semiellipsis, and the Hall of representatives a full ellipsis, and though a variety may be produced by varying the detail of decoration, the same principle remains—viz, a high collonade upon a low arcade—exhibiting a poverty of design, which is as little compatible with the talents of Doctor Thornton as it would have been necessary, had the principal Halls been upon a level with the floor of the Porticos.

To correct the error of landing one story too high is impossible in the present advanced state of the work. I shall therefore dismiss the subject.[3]

The Senate chamber independently of its slight construction and the badness of workmanship is otherwise a handsome room, and should justice be done to the vestibule in the execution, Europe will not be able to exhibit a more magnificent public Saloon. It will be worthy of the intention of the building.

It is proposed that the Hall of conference shall lie on the floor of the Porticos, which obviates every objection to that beautiful part of the plan; though a basement story will be lost.

I now come to the proposed Hall of representatives which in the original plan occupies with the stair case and a few committee rooms above the Galleries, 40 feet from the ground, the whole of the south wing.

To this arrangement I think it my duty to state to you my objections, and

1.) as they respect use and convenience.

For the commodious dispatch of business by the House of representatives it appears to me that the following appartments should be closely attached to the legislative Hall.

1.) Three or four committee rooms.

2.) A chamber for the Speaker in which he may transact such business with the members or others as does not require his sitting in the chair of the House.

3.) An office for the Clerk of the House.

4.) Offices of the engrossing clerks, 2 rooms.

5.) An apartment for the door keeper where he may assort and keep printed papers for delivery to the members, distribute letters and preserve the articles belonging to his office.

6.) Another for subordinate officers of the House.

7.) Closets of convenience.

8.) Fire proof repositories of records.

9.) A lobby sufficient for the convenient retirement of a large number of members from the House, but not adapted to the purposes of a Gallery. The lobbies of the House of representatives and Senate, as hitherto used have been grievously complained against as serious nuisances, and in the Senate the Vice President[4] has given notice that he should not permit the introduction of Strangers into the lobby as heretofore during the next session.

10.) A commodious gallery, not only overlooking the House, but completely commanded by the view of the officers of the House, and accessible in such a manner that the members passing from one part of the building to another, shall never be interrupted by the persons entering or coming from the gallery.

My objections to the plan proposed originally arise from the want of all these accommodations excepting only of such apartments as may be placed in the South East recess and in the projection between the legislative Hall and the conference room which must of necessity be badly lighted, or in the attic story above the gallery, a situation remote and accessible only by a flight of 80 steps. Two only of these latter rooms are private, the two others being thoroughfares.

It has always been understood that the upper story of the north wing would supply the apartments above enumerated. But as the rooms on the Basement story contiguous to the Senate chamber will probably be appropriated to the use of that branch of the legislature, the upper stories alone will remain for the House of representatives, and a distance of at least 200 feet must be traversed to reach them. It will also be necessary that the members and officers of the House should pass through the people attending in the grand vestibule. This must be at all times unpleasant, and often highly inconvenient.

I have already mentioned the inconvenience of a lobby calculated to serve the purposes of a gallery. The lobby which is proposed to surround the legislative Hall has all the inconveniences of a lobby within the walls of the House, without the advantage of being controuled by the view of officers of the House. Its size invites a croud, of which the intervening piers prevent the view, and it is impossible to pass from the House without mingling with the persons in the lobby.

The gallery is inconvenient not only from its massy columns in front, but chiefly from the distance of the front seats from the edge of the area of the House, which unavoidably covers twenty feet of the floor from the sight of the persons in the first row of seats and still more from those behind.

2.) As they respect safe practicability.

The south wing of the Capitol consists of only two enclosures—an external wall 65 feet high, and an internal enclosure consisting below of an elliptical arcade, and above of a range of 32 massy columns with their entablature. Between these two enclosures there is no possible bond or connection excepting the floor of the gallery, and that of the proposed committee rooms, which are to be lighted by the attic windows. Although it is not eligible in any case where it can be avoided, to carry up a wall so thin, so pierced with windows to so great a heighth without support by bond with internal walls or external projections, it would be in the present instance a still more daring attempt, when a domed roof of 90 feet span by 120 is to be carried, and all its lateral thrust resisted at the heighth of 60 feet from the ground. My ideas on the safety of such a work are best explained by declaring that I want the courage necessary to embolden me to attempt it.

3.) As they respect the taste of its architecture.

It is impossible to deprive a series of 32 columns 25 feet in heighth of an effect singularly striking, and at first sight, pleasantly impressive; nor would the first effect produced be diminished by the frequency of looking at them, were the figure inclosed by the colonade an agreeable one in every point of view. But an ellipsis seen in perspective from any point not lying in one of its axes, has a distorted appearance, the parts on each side being of different figures. Nothing is so well known as that the eye judges of the forms and relative sizes of objects by the habit unconsciously acquired of reducing, their natural appearance in perspective, to orthographical projection. The eye is habituated to judge of circles and of rectilineal figures, but ellipses occur seldom; no habit exists of judging of their lines perpetually varying in the principle of their progression, and they have always a distorted effect. Experience proves the truth of this assertion, and therefore both architects and scene painters have substituted in their room parallelograms bounded by semicircles.

This is a general objection to elliptical rooms. But another objection to the elliptical form of a colonade surmounted by a spheroidal dome occurs which is of more importance. All the lines of the entablature, and
272 of every other moulding of ever so small projection are lines belonging

to parallel, or to use an incorrect phrase, concentric ellipses. If the lines be accurately drawn, they become distorted in perspective by their having each a separate and different law of curvature, for the last of an infinite series of parallel ellipses is a straight line, equal to the distance of the foci. The bad effect of the attempt even at plain elliptical domes is well illustrated by the sky light of the stairs in the north wing of the Capitol.

If the cieling of the Hall be pannelled (the most beautiful mode of decoration) it will have the distorted effect of every other elliptical pannelled dome, of which in the first revival of arts a few have been attempted, for in each tier there will be only 4 pannels of equal forms and size.

The gallery and lobby have forms the most unpleasant. The eye always judges of the form of a room by its cieling, for that is the only space in which the view can freely range. When it therefore becomes necessary to sacrifice the form of an apartment to more important arrangements, a cieling—ingeniously disposed—often hides the difficulty that has been encountered. But such an attempt would be vain, where the windows and their piers, considered relatively to the columns which form the opposite bound of the space, are disposed without the most distant reference to lines drawn either to the center, or to the foci, of the ellipsis. And that this is the case in the proposed plan, a slight inspection must evince.

Having spent several days in fruitless attempts to lay down a system of simple decoration for this apartment satisfactory to my habits of taste I have found myself wholly without the talents necessary to the task; and should be very unwilling to labor further in a field in which it is difficult to escape censure, and impossible to reap reputation.

4.) As they respect expense.

A very great expense ought to produce a permanent work: and yet if the south wing be finished in the manner proposed the whole of the internal work, excepting the arcade, the colonade and its entablature must be of timber, and of course liable to be destroyed by fire in a few hours: and the expense will be excessive.

The columns may be either of Timber, cased with plank glued up; of timber frames, lathed and plaistered or stuccoed; of bricks stuccoed; of freestone plain or fluted; or of Pennsylvanian marble. Of all these materials the latter would probably be the most eligible, and the two first the least so. The columns of the senate room which are of Plaister upon 273 frames are already tumbling to pieces. Brick columns stuccoed are extremely liable to injury, especially when exposed in a public gallery to the hands of a promiscuous croud. Freestone columns therefore would perhaps, considering their smaller expense, with their permanence, be preferred to marble, and I will proceed upon an idea of a freestone series of columns of the Corinthian or Attic order.[5] Such a column would be 2 feet 6 inches in diameter and 25 high, the whole order being 30 feet, and could not be executed with their capitals, and placed, under 1200 dollars each column, including every expense. The Entablature 5 feet high, architrave frieze and enriched Cornice, would be a work requiring the

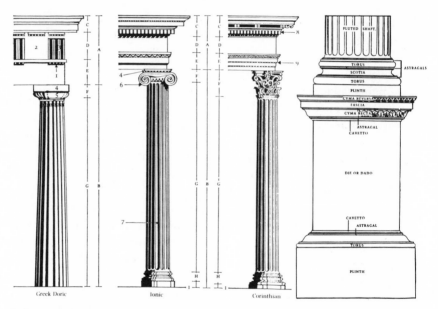

Orders A. Entablature; B. Column; C. Cornice; D. Frieze; E. Architrave; F. Capital; G. Shaft; H. Base; I. Plinth.

1. Guttae; 2. Metope; 3. Triglyph; 4. Abacus; 5. Echinus; 6. Volute; 7. Fluting; 8. Dentils; 9. Fascia.

Fig. 8. Left: The Doric, Ionic, and Corinthian orders. From *A Dictionary of Architecture,* by Nikolaus Pevsner, John Fleming, and Hugh Honour. Published by The Overlook Press, Lewis Hollow Road, Woodstock, N.Y. 12498. Copyright © 1966 Hugh Honour, John Fleming, and Nikolaus Pevsner. Right: A Corinthian base and pedestal. From John Summerson, *The Classical Language of Architecture.* Courtesy of Methuen & Co., publishers.

most expert workmen, and the most watchful superintendence in the execution. The number of massy stones required would amount to at least 200, and the number of moulds to which they must be wrought would be double that number, for every projection would require a separate mould. The *practical* difficulties attending the execution are incalculable. In a circle every stone fits every where, and the last stone which is set, is the only one the size of which is *not* arbitrary. But in an ellipsis each stone has its determined place from which if it be moved the smallest perceptible distance the line of curvature is destroyed, and the work spoiled. To calculate the value of time, care, disappointment, and destruction of materials occasioned by this circumstance is impossible, but at a moderate rate the Entablature supposing the architrave to carry the cieling of the gallery would cost 24.000 dollars.

32 columns at 1200 each are	$38.400
Entablature	24.000
	62.400.

As large as this amount appears, I believe that it would be found scarcely adequate to the completion of the work in a perfect and masterly manner.

     5.) I might also start objections to the fluttering and scanty light of that part of the room in which the legislative body must sit,[6] to the impossibility of warming the lobby and gallery, and to the probable difficulty of speaking and hearing.

Under all these impressions of the imperfections of the plan of the South wing of the Capitol, and after having bestowed much time and study in a vain attempt to preserve its principal features, and to combine with them such accommodations for the use of the legislative body as seems absolutely indispensible, I have thought it my duty to lay before you an arrangement entirely different from that proposed by the original plan.

This arrangement is explained in the plans and sections hereto annexed.[7] The form of the Hall is that of the ancient theatre (exedra), a form which the experience of ancient and modern times has established as the best for the purpose of speaking, seeing and hearing.[8] The area of the Hall rather exceeds that of the elliptical design, and will hold with ease a body of 360 members, leaving sufficient room on the floor of the House. The principal entrance to this Hall will be from the grand ves- 275 tibule, through a square lobby and colonade. On the south front will also be an entrance into the lobby behind the Speaker's chair. This lobby, intended for the retirement of members in order to confer with each other or to receive their friends, will be 80 feet in length, and can never be used as a gallery unless it should be thought proper to break the Wall into an arcade. This I presume will not be done, for if it be thought expedient that Ladies or particular friends of the members should be introduced on the floor of the House, there is ample room for them behind the last row of the seats, where a passage of 5 feet will be left open.

On the East and West fronts are the entrances to the public gallery by means of a stair case in each angle. This gallery, while it commands a full view of the House facing the members, is also under the compleat inspection of the officers of the House, whose place is at the north end of the Hall. On each side are also galleries, which may be either appropriated to public use, or reserved for the admission of particular persons.

In the north east angle of the wing is a commodious room appropriated to the clerk of the House, in which this chief clerk may sit, and in the third story above, the inferior and engrossing clerks may be accommodated. The stair case in the recess furnishes the communication with these apartments. At the north west angle is a room appropriated to the use of the speaker.

In the second story of the east, and in the second and third stories of the West front are commodious committee rooms, to each of which is attached an office for the papers and documents belonging to the Committee. It would have been desirable to have attached to this wing, a greater number of Committee rooms, but the size of the building forbids it, and should a greater number of committee rooms be wanted, they must be found in the North Wing.

By the necessary result of the general arrangement of the plan, there is an absolute want of light in all that part of the building which lies between the Wings and the center of the building. I have therefore appropriated it to a grand stair case, to closets, and to the offices of the door keeper and his assistants. The latter rooms will be lighted from the lower tier of arches of the House, the stair cases from the sky, and the closets by side lights from the staircase and from a small court which becomes necessary for light as well as domestic use, for it must contain a pump or cistern, and a sink to take off water, and it is a great error in the general design of a building insulated in every side, and which has no cellar conveniences, that no open court of convenient dimensions exists within it.

On the first floor, independently of the committee rooms, there will be: a vestibule to the grand gallery, extending from the Stair case to the court, and lighted from the latter; and a spacious repository of records over the offices of the door keeper, to which the access is from the vestibule, and the light from the stairs and open court.

The Hall of Representatives is lighted from the south front, and from a spacious lanthorn light in the center of the half dome.

The whole plan of the Wing as proposed is so arranged as to be capable of being vaulted in every part, and has been so adapted to the external elevation, that every apartment is perfectly symetrical.

I will beg leave to submit one observation on the expense which is *supposed* to attend vaulted buildings, as applicable to the present:

The external walls are not altered:

The basement story of the internal enclosure is the same:

The internal enclosure above, contains 1.120 perch of stone work, which if executed with great precision and unusual care, and allowing for arches and nich heads, will cost not more than 5 dollars per perch—say—5.600 dollars:

The colonade and entablature would cost at least 62.400 dollars—the saving therefore will be at least 56.800 dollars in this respect:

The centering of the great dome will not be nearly equal in expense to the framing of a free roof of 120 feet by 96, but allowing it to be equal, no additional expense will arise in that article:

The vault and arches of the great Hall will contain less than 100.000 Bricks. As these bricks must be laid with unusual care, and at a great hight, and must probably be brought from Philadelphia so as to cost on the spot about 9 dollars per thousand, I will estimate the expense of labor and all materials at 15 dollars per thousand instead of 13 dollars, the expense of the dome of the Bank of Pennsylvania. At this estimate, the whole vault would cost 1.500 dollars, which deducted from 56.800 still leaves a saving of 55.300 dollars. The expense of finishing in Stucco is in favor of the vault, as the whole expense of Blocking and Firring, and of all Laths and Nails, is saved.

As to the arches of the Basement story, they are so small in their dimensions, that they will exceed the expense of common well framed 277 floors immaterially. But allowing 5.300 dollars for this excess of expense, it is still clear that a saving of 50.000 dollars will be effected by the change of plan, should the Colonade and Entablature be executed in stone; and if in the cheapest manner in timber, of at least 20.000 dollars.

With these observations, I beg to submit to you the plans which accompany this letter.

I have now to state to you the measures which I have thought it necessary to pursue, in order to commence and prepare the work of the season.

Having understood that the foundation walls of the South wing, which are carried up to the level at which the Work in freestone is to begin, had not been faithfully executed, I caused them to be opened in several places, and on different levels, and find that they are on no account fit to bear the weight which is to be laid above them. The stones appear to have been loosely thrown between two thin external casings without mortar, and even without being made to bear upon each other. It is necessary therefore that the whole of this work should be taken down to the first offset; below which I am well informed that the work has been faithfully performed.

I have also caused the foundation wall of the building in which the House of representatives sat during their last session, and which seems to have been intended for the permanent Basement of the elliptical Colonade, to be opened in several places beneath the windows. I have, in every instance discovered it to be of bad workmanship, but in most of the places which I have examined, it consists also of small stones loosely thrown into a thin casing. I judge this wall to be wholly unfit to carry the weight of the colonade, and of the roof, and as the brick work, above, has been forced from 2 to 6 inches out of perpendicular by the roof, I do not hesitate in declaring it to be my opinion that the whole building ought to be pulled down to the offset, even if the elliptical colonade be executed. And this must be done, not only on account of the wretched workmanship of the foundation walls, but because, with the best workmanship, no colonade carrying a heavy superstructure can be safely constructed unless its pressure be spread over the whole foundation by means of counter arches. The fissures in the walls of the south wing are entirely owing to the omission of such precaution.

In order that no delay might injure the progress of the work during your absence, I have, with the concurrence of the Superintendant of the City, proceeded to such measures as were of the first necessity.

The whole of the foundation Walls which must be pulled down consist of small stones. They are unfit for any purpose but to work up in the Wall with larger stone, and I have therefore contracted with Mr. Elliot,[9] a respectable citizen, to furnish, at the price of $1.75 per Perch, 750 perch of large flat stone, none of which are to contain less than 3 feet on the surface, and to be from 5 to 9 inches thick. Mr. Elliot has already begun to deliver the stone. The wharfs at which materials were formerly delivered to the Commissioners being entirely out of repair, and the water in front rendered insufficient by the rubbish thrown into it, I have had the necessary repairs made to these wharves, and they are now fit to receive the rough stone, sand and other light materials. I have also repaired the bridge over the canal, and mended the road from the upper wharf to the Pennsylvania avenue.[10] The stone recovered in front of the wharves has amply repaid the expense of the work.

In respect to the work to be executed in cut stone, I find that it has hitherto been the custom to provide the stone to the Stonecutter, and to agree with him to cut and set it either by the day or by measurement. This method of doing the business is decidedly against the interest of the public. All the risks are thrown upon the public, of loss by labor in the quarry, by false measurement, by unsound stone, by the danger of navigation, and by faulty workmanship. Each of these operations requires separate and trusty agents; the attention of the architect to the work is distracted by so many distant scenes of superintendance. If an expensive stone be so faulty in its workmanship as to be rejected, though the workman lose his labor, the public lose the material. This was found to be the case, when on a trial, some tons of stones were proved to have been buried in the rubbish. Besides, in the oeconomy of the material, waste cannot be avoided when the ease of the workman is often interested in cutting up a large block, when another, with somewhat more labor would have answered the purpose.

For these and many other reasons, I beg leave to recommend a contract with Mr. Blagden for the stone,[11] cut ready to be set in the Wall, and I have prepared and delivered the terms of such a contract as I conceive to be for the interests of the work, to the Superintendant. The stone work of the South wing, erected by Mr. Blagden, and his well known character, seem to authorize the expectation that so important a contract will be well executed by him.

About 230 Tierces of New England lime have been purchased, which appears to be of a good quality.

In the supply of Scaffolding poles, ropes, sand plank and boards, no difficulty will occur. There are several sets of good Blocks in the possession of the Superintendent, but two good hoisting Engines must be made.

I have now to report to you the state of the

North Wing of the Capitol.

It is much to be feared that unless some openings be made to admit air into the Cellars, the Timbers of the floor will, in the course of a few years be consumed by what is termed the dry-rot. This is the most dangerous of decays, because when it has once established itself in the Cellar story, it never fails to climb to the top of the House unperceived untill the surface of the woodwork is broken, or some material failure in the floors betrays it. For the dry-rot will consume a fixed and painted piece of wood work, untill a shell, one tenth of an inch thick remains, without injuring its appearance in the least. This species of rot almost always begins in unventilated cellars. It is also on another account necessary that the Light and Air should be admitted to this part of the building. There is not any other means of warming the Senate chamber but by flues either to convey fire, or pipes to convey steam along the floor. The latter are the best, and now universally used in England in large apartments, as the fire flues have long been, in France and Holland.

On the state of repair of the Senate chamber and the necessity of warming it by some other means than those in use, I will report separately should you think it necessary.

The leakage of the roof, which has so much injured the Wall and Cielings of many parts of the house arises from the bad system of carrying off the water; from the bad quality of the lead used; from the joints of the sheets being soldered by which they appear to have been in many places torn; from the broken glass of the Sky lights; and from the leakiness of the Cistern.

1.) From the bad system of carrying off the Water.

All the water is at present collected from every gutter and discharged into one deep cistern. After collecting in the gutters along the parapet, it is brought under the roofs, in many gutters, into the internal Area of the roof, so that the chance of leakage is greatly multiplied. It appears to me that the very great length of gutter, and the attempt to keep the roof as low as possible, has prevented a sufficient current being given to the Gutters. The aversion to Water pipes on the outside of

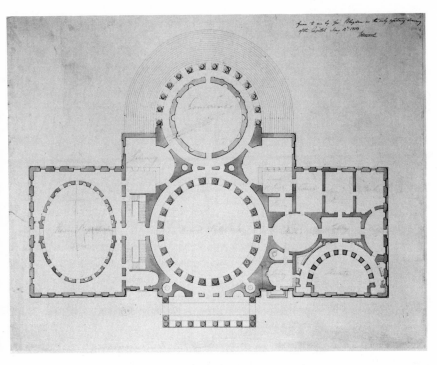

Fig. 9. [William Thornton], Revised plan of the ground floor of the U.S. Capitol, with inscription by BHL: "Given to me by Geo. Blagden as the only existing drawing of the Capitol. May 4th, 1803." Courtesy of the Library of Congress.

buildings has been another cause of this erroneous mode of draining the roof. As, however the cistern appears to have no possible use, and there are corners of the buildings in which Water pipes may be advantageously brought down, I would suggest, as the only means of obtaining a water tight roof, that the water from **A** to **B** be discharged through an external Water pipe at **B,** into a court yard which must be made in front of the brick part of the building now carried up, and which, though it was built to be pulled down again, ought to remain standing, because, in the original design no light can be received from the West to this whole pile of handsome rooms and only a scanty light from the north from a window in the corner. Besides, a court yard is absolutely necessary, *somewhere* for Privies, and other domestic purposes of Cleanliness, and I have in my plan provided for one for the South Wing. All the space discharging the Water by this pipe is coloured *blue*.

From **A** to **C** I propose to discharge the Water through an external   281

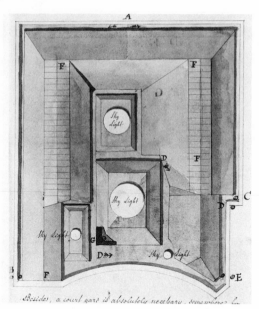

pipe in the corner of the recess where it will be entirely hidden. The space supplying this water is coloured *yellow*.

From **D** to **E** I propose to discharge the Water through an external pipe in the other corner of the recess. This space is coloured *red*.

From **F** to **G** I propose to discharge the water into the present Waste pipe of the Cistern, which leads to a drain from the Cellar story. This space is coloured *green*. All the shingling is remarkably good. It will be a great pity to disturb it, and yet I fear that it must not only be disturbed but destroyed, for I believe that all the gutters must be taken up, because, though of lead, they are coated with tar and sand so as to prevent the possibility of seeing where they are faulty altho' nothing is more evident than that they are so. When laid again, it must be with a much greater descent, and the roof will well admit of it.

All the Gutters, at present passing under the roof, will become useless. Their lead will go some way towards paying the expense of the new arrangements.

2.) Of the bad quality of the lead I have heard only from those who were present when it was laid. It must be examined when taken up.

3.) Wherever the sheets have been soldered they must, if laid down again, be cut and groved together, with a good drip.

4.) Sky lights, unless made of thick coach glass, with metal frames, always leak. Even then they are great evils, for in summer they heat the house, and in winter they become darkened and often broken by the

snow. But Lanthorn lights can always be made tight, their light is pleasant, in summer they can be opened and they cool the house, and in
Winter they retain the advantage of a common sash. I propose therefore, as the only effectual method of curing the leaks arising from the
Sky lights, to substitute in their room, Lanthorn lights, that is, lights with
upright Sashes and close tops. The sells of the sashes of the Lanthorn
must be raised sufficiently to admit of a sloping roof to them instead of
the flat, now existing. This will permanently cure leakage. I will remark
at the same time that the Sky lights, as now built, are a disgrace to the
architect and the workmen in their appearance, and ought to be altered
if on no other account.

5.) It is difficult to guess for what purpose the Cistern was intended, as it is not provided with any means of discharge. Were it on the
ground floor, or even in the Cellar story, and furnished with a good
forcing pump, it could have been made exceedingly useful in case of
fire. It is useless now even for the purposes of washing. The leak in the
Library has its rise from this cistern. It must be taken down and perhaps
placed below, and furnished with a forcing pump. The lead is valuable.
The Waste pipe will act as a rain water pipe.

Submitting the above to your consideration I am, with respect Your
faithful humble Servant

B. Henry Latrobe

DS: Jefferson Papers (167/E7). Enclosed in BHL to Jefferson, [4 Apr. 1803], above.
Endorsed by Jefferson as received 4 April.

1. The name "Dr. Wm. Thornton" appears to have been originally written here,
erased, and replaced with a series of dashes.
2. This sentence and the passage within angle brackets below were lightly crossed
out, probably by BHL.
3. Jefferson later claimed responsibility for the idea of lowering the floor of the Hall
of Representatives from the *piano nobile* into the basement of the Capitol. He stated to BHL
that he had asked and received Thornton's approval of the alteration. Jefferson to BHL,
14 Apr. 1811, in BHL, *Correspondence*, 3.
4. As vice-president of the United States (1801–05), Aaron Burr (1756–1836)
served also as president of the Senate.
5. For the Attic order, see BHL to Jefferson, 29 Mar. 1804, n. 4, below.
6. BHL's ideas of lighting reflected the impact of the Picturesque movement on his
work. The Picturesque movement rested on the conception that one can employ paintings,
principally landscape paintings, as a means of judging and even forming other kinds of
works of art. In his architecture BHL pursued the principle of interior "scenery," that is,
the idea that an architect might compose rooms as a series of spaces varying in size, shape,
color, and lighting so as to offer the moving spectator sensations parallel with those of the

traveler passing through a varied landscape. In his "Essay on Landscape" (1798), he advised the artist to "throw the principal lights into one mass" and to avoid "therefore a fluttering effect," fairly standard advice for the devotees of Picturesque drawing. He later told Jefferson that "every piece of Architecture, as well as of Sculpture, and every painting even, requires, to be advantageously seen, a *Unity of light.*" BHL, *Journals,* 2 : 477; BHL to Jefferson, 29 Oct. 1806, in BHL, *Correspondence,* 2; BHL, *Architectural Drawings.*

7. These drawings have not survived.

8. For BHL's extended comments on this matter, see BHL, Remarks on the Best Form of a Room for Hearing and Speaking, [c. 1803], below.

9. Richard Elliot (d. post-1821) was a Washington, D.C., stone quarrier.

10. L'Enfant's plan for Washington called for a canal through the city to link the Potomac and Eastern Branch. The canal was to commence south of the President's House and run east through the bed of Tiber Creek to the Capitol, where it turned south and then branched in two. One branch of the canal was to enter the Eastern Branch at Second Street, west of the proposed navy yard. The other branch was to follow the course of St. James Creek, which emptied into the Eastern Branch at Greenleaf's Point. From 1793 to 1795, the Commissioners of the District expended nearly $5,000 on the "Canal from Tiber creek to James's creek." They also constructed bridges over St. James and Tiber creeks, and four wharves on Rock Creek, Tiber Creek (at its mouth and at the foot of Capitol Hill), and the Eastern Branch. For BHL's later work on the Washington Canal, see BHL to Law and Brent, 13 Dec. 1803, below. *ASP. Miscellaneous,* 1 : 143–44, 221, 245.

11. George Blagden (d. 1826) came to the United States from England some time before 1794, when he was appointed superintendent of stonework and quarries at the Capitol. Active in the business and civic affairs of Washington, D.C., Blagden was a member of the First Chamber of the city council (1802, 1804), president of the Common Council (1812), alderman (1821–25), a trustee of the Washington public schools (1805), one of the organizers of the Columbia Manufacturing Company (1808), a director of the Washington Bridge Company (1808) and Washington Canal Company (1823–26), and a vestryman of Christ Church (Episcopal) in 1809. He was killed on 4 June 1826 in an accident at the Capitol. BHL to Elias B. Caldwell, 17 Jan. 1810 (misdated 1809), in BHL, *Correspondence,* 2; Minutes of the Board of Directors of the Washington Canal Co. 1810–31, RG 351, National Archives; Glenn Brown, *History of the United States Capitol,* 2 vols. (Washington, D.C., 1900–03), 1 : 97; William V. Cox, comp., *Celebration of the One Hundredth Anniversary of the Establishment of the Seat of Government in the District of Columbia* (Washington, D.C., 1901), pp. 298, 300–02; CHS, *Records* 33 (1932):268, 274, 285–86.

TO JOHN LENTHALL

Washington April 7th. 1803

Dear Sir,

In appointing you Clerk of the Works to the Capitol with the full approbation of the President of the United States, and of the Superin-

tendant of City of Washington I have taken upon myself the fullest responsibility for your conduct, and in order that you may not be shackled in your exertions for the public interest by the fear of the intrigues of those who may be employed during my absence in the execution of the Work, I have to inform you, that it is clearly understood by the President of the United States and the Superintendant of the city that you are to be the sole judge of the merit of the Workmen, and are perfectly authorized to discharge any man, without appeal, whom you shall judge to be unfit to be employed. You are also the sole judge in my absence of the fidelity with which contracts are fulfilled, and you are to communicate such observations as occur to you to the Superintendant of the city, who will point out to you the mode in which you are to act, in all cases of specific contract.

The specific contracts entered into are:

1.) with Mr. Geo. Blagden, for the freestone work.
2.) with Mr. Richd. Elliot for the delivery of large building stone.
3.) with Mr. Robinson for Scaffold poles.
4.) with Mr. Timothy Caldwell for pulling down the present Wall.[1]

The contracts which must be made are 1.) for the delivery of sand, 2.) of Frederic C[ount]y Lime, 3. for hauling stone. 4.) for Lumber. On all these subjects you will consult the Superintendant of the city, who has very kindly assured me that he will assist you with his advice and the very accurate knowledge he has acquired of the building resources of the city and neighborhood.

Mr. Belt has the superintendance of the Laborers. His people are employed in a variety of public work. It will be necessary that he should deliver to you a separate account of the time during which they are engaged in the work at or for the Capitol, for they must be paid thro' your certificate.

All the Stone work must be executed by the day for the reasons I have mentioned to you. You will please to consult Mr. Blagden in any case in which you may hesitate, who has very obligingly promised me his assistance to you.

Mr. Patrick Farrell, and Mr. [Robert] Mitcham will jointly, or on separate parts of the work, as you may think best, act as foremen of the Masons, at 2 Dollars per day each. Their conduct will be under your inspection and controul. It is expected that their time shall be wholly employed in the work, and its superintendence. You will please consult the Superintendant as to the employment of Mr. Wilson, who uses his name. He condemns Mr. Farrell as a workman, and is not likely therefore to act *with him* for the public interest. Mr. Farrells character is however sufficiently established.[2]

You will yourself conduct the whole of the Carpenter's work. There is a variety of work which must be done by the day, of this you will keep a *day* account; of such work as can be measured, I shall make out the account when present.

Mr. Martin will be employed by Mr. Blagden in the sharpening of his tools, and as it will be unnecessary to employ the *whole* time of a smith for *our* use, he will also do our smith's work in the Yard, in which Mr. Blagden will furnish the hearth and chimney, and we the Shed.

The heavy work of the hoisting Machines had better be done by Mr. King or Mr. Davis.[3]

As to the Wages of Journeymen, and the prices of Materials you will attend strictly to the public interest; but you well know that there is no oeconomy in hiring bad workmen, or purchasing bad materials at a low rate, and you will herein use proper discretion. In respect to workmen especially you will endeavor to have the *best,* and no bad one at any wages.

You will be guided entirely by the directions of the Superintendant of the city in all matters of account. As no money will be paid without your certificate, for which the superintendant of the city will give you a form, you will hereby obtain compleat controul over the conduct of every man employed. Mr. Blagden having undertaken a heavy contract will require money on account as his stone comes in. The other payments will be made as the contracts stipulate.

You will please to communicate frequently on all matters that occur with me by letter.[4] I am, with the fullest confidence in your talents and integrity. Yours truly

B. H. Latrobe,
surveyor of the public buildings at Washington

ALS: BHL Papers, Library of Congress (168/B7).

1. Timothy Caldwell was a prosperous Washington, D.C., brickmaker. He is possibly the same Timothy Caldwell of Lancaster County, Pa. (d. post-1839) who owned a spacious mansion at 2017 I Street, N.W. *National Intelligencer,* 31 Dec. 1802; CHS *Records* 21 (1918):116, 119.

2. In addition to his employment at the Capitol, Patrick Farrell (d. 1816) worked for BHL at the Washington Navy Yard from May 1806 until at least 1813, when BHL praised

him as "a very skillful bricklayer, and a scrupulously honest Man." In June 1808 BHL
designed a masonry bridge over Rock Creek that Farrell was to build for the city of
Georgetown. BHL to Farrell, 17 May 1806, BHL to Shadrach Davis, 17 May 1806, BHL to
John Mason, 24 June 1808, and BHL to Samuel Lane, 27 July 1816, all in LB (49/A10,
49/A11, 65/C5, 132/C10); BHL to William Jones, 2 Feb. 1813, in BHL, *Correspondence*, 3;
National Intelligencer, 17 June 1808.

    3. Probably Benjamin King, blacksmith, and Shadrach Davis, carpenter, both of
whom later worked for BHL at the Washington Navy Yard.

    4. Jefferson later described Lenthall's daily responsibilities as clerk of the works:
"Lenthall superintended directly the manual labors of the workmen, saw that they were in
their places every working hour, that they executed their work with skill and fidelity, kept
their accounts, laid off the work, measured it, laid off the centers and other moulds [&c.?]."
Jefferson to James Madison, 30 Mar. 1809, Jefferson Papers.

FROM THOMAS JEFFERSON

Washington Apr. 23. 1803.

Dear Sir

    Your letter for mr. Lenthall was received last night and will be
delivered this morning.[1] Thinking the demolition did not go on with
spirit enough I sent for him 2. days ago. He assures me the foundation
will be down this week, and the rebuilding begin on Monday. From that
day to the end of September, by which time the stone work to the top of
the [basement?] should be compleat, we have 23. weeks. I should like to
know the number of perch of stone work to be laid to the top of the
basement, to divide that on the 23. weeks, and to have a weekly report
from your agent of the number of perch laid each week, that, in your
absence, I may be quite secure that the due progress is kept up. I presume you are providing sheet iron for both buildings, the [covering] of
which had better be done as early as possible, in order if any leak should
appear, that it may be secured before winter. Will you be so good as to
order [*illegible*][2] panes of window glass 28 I. by 18⅝ I. for the President's
house. Glass of that size you know must have a due thickness. Donath in
Philadelphia[3] imports Bohemian glass from Hamburg, such as is used in
all the first-rate buildings in Europe (England excepted). He furnished
all for my house at about 21. or 22. cents the square foot. But this glass
being twice as large as mine, should be of superior thickness, and consequently superior price by the square foot. Could not a file of necessaries
be placed under each wing of the Capitol, with a deep [sewer] under-

neath of [*illegible*], and the cistern be made, by a syphon, to discharge itself through that in a [torrent] whenever it should be filled by a rain? This would be an advantageous disposition of the external waterpipes, while the internal might be reserved for fire or [*illegible*]. The defectiveness of the pipes of this house is rotting it fast at the waterclosets. Strong pipes will be wanting, and the water must be taken out from the cistern, not at the bottom, but at the sides by a syphon going to the bottom, but capable of being turned within the body of the water, so as to place it's mouth at any depth we please. My building arrangements at home require the sheets of iron bespoke of you to leave Philadelphia early in May. Not knowing if Capt. Lewis is arrived in Phila., I inclose a letter for him, and ask the favor of you to have it delivered to him on his arrival. Mr. Patt[erson], Doctors Wistar, Barton and Rush, will know when he arrives.[4] Accept my friendly salutations.

Th: Jefferson

Letterpress Copy: Jefferson Papers (168/D6).

1. BHL to John Lenthall, 19 Apr. 1803. BHL Papers, Library of Congress (168/C10).
2. Four words are illegible.
3. Joseph Donath & Co., Philadelphia merchants.
4. Jefferson to Meriwether Lewis, 23 Apr. 1803, Jefferson Papers. Prior to the commencement of the Lewis and Clark Expedition, Lewis, who according to Jefferson "wanted nothing but a greater familiarity with the technical language of the natural sciences, and readiness in the astronomical observations necessary for the geography of his route," traveled north to acquire these. He studied with surveyor and mathematician Andrew Ellicott (1754–1820) in Lancaster, Pa., and in Philadelphia with mathematician Robert Patterson, natural historians Caspar Wistar (1761–1818) and Benjamin Smith Barton, and physician Benjamin Rush (1745–1813). Albert E. Bergh, ed., *The Writings of Thomas Jefferson,* 18 vols. (Washington, D.C., 1907), 18 : 146.

TO JOHN LENTHALL

Philadelphia May 5th. 1803

Dear Sir,

Having been up for three nights, and for three days and nights having had to struggle with the apprehension of losing my wife and child, I am rather unfit to write on business. But the safe delivery of Mrs.

288 L. at last, and the birth of a chopping boy, of whom I mean to make a

carpenter and to call John, both of which you may take as compliments to yourself, enable me to answer Yours of the 1st. May, shorthandedly.[1]

Pray write to Strickland, offering him the best terms you can to take charge of the Carpenters work with you. But mind your *own* interests. You may give him the highest wages ever paid at Washington. So much for *assistance*.[2]

As to the X Walls in the South front center, that are, in Thornton's plan exactly under the piers of my plan. Their being differently placed in the Work is a new proof of the *stupid genius* of its Author. Pull up, or knock down, as you best can, and execute *my* plan. Wm. Strickland, I know, drew the angle piers confusedly in the plan sent to you, and I had no time to alter them.[3] But they must be thus: I have no time to consult the dimensions. You understand them. Both Corners to be alike. The object is to get a solid vaulted floor above. I am sorry you are so fatigued, and plagued about Materials. I hope now to be with you in about 3 weeks or a month. We may be imposed upon in 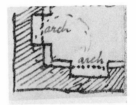 Materials this season but will not be the next. Tell Mr. Elliot that I should be glad to employ none but him; but that if he did not keep us in stone I should send on 20 Welch quarriers who are anxious to go to Washington, and upon whom I can depend as they have quarried for me here for these 3 Years. Pray present the enclosed to Mr. Munroe and remit me the amount, in a Bank post bill made payable to *my order*, which they will give you at the bank. Tomorrow more. I am now laboring at the principal story which will be different from the drawing I left you. Yours affectionately.

B. Henry Latrobe.

Pray call on Mr. Jefferson and tell him how you go on now and then, and that you hear constantly from me on all subjects of *doupt* as you spell it.

ALS: BHL Papers, Library of Congress (168/F9). Addressed to Lenthall in Washington.

1. John Hazlehurst Boneval Latrobe (1803–91) was born on 4 May. He became a notable Baltimore lawyer and philanthropist and was a founder of the Maryland State Colonization Society and the Maryland Historical Society.

2. John Strickland (1757–1820), carpenter on the Bank of Pennsylvania, was later employed by BHL as master carpenter on the C & D Canal. He had apprenticed from 1772–78 under Robert Allison (fl. 1768–1811), who was best known for his work on the

Court Room at the State House (Independence Hall). John Strickland later became an official of the Practical House Carpenters' Society, a rival of the Carpenters' Company of the City and County of Philadelphia. Agnes A. Gilchrist, *William Strickland: Architect and Engineer, 1788–1854* (Philadelphia, 1950), p. 1; Louise Hall, "Loxley's Provocative Note," *Journal of the Society of Architectural Historians* 15 : 4 (Dec. 1956), p. 27; Luther P. Eisenhart, ed., *Historic Philadelphia* (Philadelphia, 1953), p. 22n.

3. BHL refers to his "Plan of the Cellar story of the South Wing of the Capitol at Washington" dated April 1803 (Prints and Photographs Division, Library of Congress; 270/B4), reproduced in BHL, *Architectural Drawings*.

TO JOHN LENTHALL

Philadelphia May 6th. 1803

My dear Lenthall

"Thou art careful and troubled about many things."[1] What *I* am most troubled about is; that you may not injure your health by your exertions. Take care of yourself for your wife's sake, and for mine. Try to tempt Strickland to join you. Now Mrs. L. is in the straw, I shall only wait here till she can bear the motion of a carriage and then start. She promises to do bravely.

As to the Base block, let not Mr. Blagden alter his order, but set it in 3 courses of 12 inches as he has prepared it. If it be too high we can bury 6 inches and perhaps we may find them useful to get some additional slope towards the New Jersey avenue.

As to the difference between the E. and W. sides in the North wing, it is not *nearly* of the same importance, as that our *internal* arrangements should be right. I would therefore *rather* sacrifice the coincidence of the West fronts of the wings, than derange the internal plan, which depends on this, that the East and west *windows* be exactly opposite to each other, in the centers of the groins of the Gallery lobbies. To effect this, the Pilasters must be also opposite, and of course the Intercolumnations of the East and West fronts be equal. You state however to me that in the North wing the intercolumnations of the West front are 4 inches wider than those of the East, and that the center Intercolumnation is equal. Thus, as the diameter of the Pilasters are equal, it follows, that the most Southern pilaster of the West front is 1 f. 4 i. more to the South, than the corresponding pilaster on the East front. Is it not so? Now, if I recollect right, only *one* pilaster is carried up at the South termination of the West front,

and the return seems to have been intended to start from the place of the south or last pilaster. This is, to be sure, villainous but as we cannot botch on another pilaster I suppose we must proceed as intended by our predecessors.

Under these circumstances, it is my advice and opinion, that the pilasters on the West front of the South wing be arranged exactly like those of the East front, as to the size of the intercolumniations, notwithstanding that from thence will result, a length of West front 1 f. 4 i. shorter then on the North wing. We may risk this the more safely, as the Center part of the front projects; and we shall thereby gain the advantage of working symmetrically as to our internal arrangements, whether the new or the old plan be eventually followed.

As to the projection of 22 inches in the base block of the return on the north front, it appears to me that it was intended to contain, (1.,) the projection of the Rustic piers, 1 f. 3 i., (2.,) the projection of the base Mouldings of these piers which is 5 i., and (3d.) the projection of the Base block beyond this moulding 1½ in., *in all* 21½. For the returning angle must necessarily be a hollow vile corner, as that of the recess on the East front: thus * : alias, a pissing corner.

I believe this is the best solution that can be given of your question as to the 22 inch projection. I wish you would compare it to the East recess, and see whether I am right.

As to the redundant 16 inches, it must be lost either in throwing the return a little out of square, or by making the South dead wall, which Thornton stole from Hatfield,[2] 16 inches wider than that to the North. This difference no one will perceive.

I am inclined to carry up the Wall within the court, **A**, that is from **B** to **C** in plain Ashler, but at all events not in brick, as at the North end. Pray communicate this whole discussion to Geo: Blagden, and take his opinion on it. You know you stop at the door **C.**

As I am writing on a confused subject, and I fear in a confused manner, I will recapitulate.

1.) The West front of the South wing is to be exactly in all its dimensions a copy of the East front of the same wing. The *detail* to follow the west front of the North wing.

2.) The return, on projection to the Westward to follow the same projection of the North wing suffering the base block to project 21 or 22 inch before the dead [wall] of the Work. The difference which will exist, of 16 inches in the distance of the South return from the Center line of the building, beyond that of the North return from the same line, not to be regarded at present.

3.) The Wall North of the return to be carried up in plain Ashler.

However, as you say you have got *all* the piers flushed on this side, and the piers must regulate the pilasters, *if* your piers be set out agreeably to the West front of the North wing, and not to the East front, they must go as they are, but depend upon it they will plague us on the principal story. Perhaps the piers are wide enough to admit of a shove of the upper pier on each to the Southward, especially as they are arched together and a little overhanging is of no consequence. This is for *your decission.*

As to the wood house cannot we move it to the Northward and Eastward of the Gangway, there? ▣ And the necessary there ☒, digging a temporary bog hole.[3] Something of the sort must be done unavoidably. Or cannot you move the wood house and contract the Sh— house.

If you want a little money for yourself to make you easy on *any* score, I will send you an order for a few hundred dollars, to be *accounted* for to *me*. Don't on any account suffer any *private* plague divert your mind from your *public plagues*. I do not know that any thing of the kind exists but I would cure it if I could.

As to your tail and your Nobby's[4] tail, I would advise you, since you dread the loss of only *one*, not of both of them, to tie them fast together. This will give a good chance, and you may always find one by the other, as a good housekeeper finds her keys by the sticks tied to them.

God bless you my good friend. Believe me very affecty. Yrs.

B. H. Latrobe.

Remember me most kindly to Geo: Blagden.

ALS: BHL Papers, Library of Congress (168/G1). Addressed to Lenthall in Washington.

1. "And Jesus answered and said unto her, Martha, Martha, thou art careful and troubled about many things."Luke 10 : 41.
2. George Hadfield (see Wood to BHL, 22 June 1797, n. 1, above).
3. Vulgar expression for privy hole.
4. Lenthall's horse.

REPORT ON A PORTRAIT OF GENERAL WASHINGTON[1]

Philadelphia May 6th. 1803

To the American Philosophical Society, the undersigned Committee, to whom was referred the consideration of the merits and Value of a Portrait of General Washington, painted by Gilbert Stuart Esqr. report:

That the Portrait is equal if not superior to other copies of the bust of Mr. Stuarts whole length portrait of General Washington, made by himself, which your committee have seen. The picture possesses the strong likeness and the spirit of the original, and it having been painted about 6 Years ago the present state of the coloring proves that more than usual attention has been paid to the goodness and durability of the colors which have been used.

The commendation of your committee can add nothing to the acknowledged merit of all Mr. Stuart's performances, nor is it necessary to remark on the peculiarities in the drawing in this individual portrait, for they are those which the original possesses.

The price of the portrait as it includes the frame, is below that of other portraits of the same kind, by the amount of the value of the frame which may be about 16 Dollars.

Upon the whole, as it is now impossible to obtain an *original* portrait of this illustrious Member of the American Philosophical Society,[2] your Committee are of opinion, that it is not probable that a wish of the Society to possess his likeness will ever be better fulfilled than by the acquisition of that now offered.

B. Henry Latrobe
William Stephen Jacobs[3]

ADS: American Philosophical Society Archives (168/G11). Both signatures are in autograph.

1. On learning of the death of George Washington, the American Philosophical Society held a special meeting on 27 December 1799 and resolved that a portrait of Washington be procured. The portrait that was presented to the society by Gilbert Stuart (1755–1828) is a copy of the familiar "Athenaeum Head," a highly idealized representation of Washington in his old age when the loss of his teeth had changed not only the shape of his face but his expression as well. The original portrait, which is now in the Boston Museum of Fine Arts, was painted in the early fall of 1796. The society received the copy on 15 April 1803 and referred it to BHL, William Jacobs, and William Hamilton "'to report on the merits, previous to any order for its purchase.'" The report, signed by BHL and Jacobs, was read and approved on 20 May 1803. The portrait now hangs in the Assembly Room of the APS in Philadelphia. Minutes, APS Archives; John Hill Morgan and Mantle Fielding, *The Life Portraits of Washington and Their Replicas* (Philadelphia, 1931), pp. 274–75.

2. Washington was elected a member of the American Philosophical Society on 19 January 1780.

3. William Stephen Jacobs (1772–1843), physician and chemist, was born in Brabant, Austrian Netherlands, and came to Philadelphia in 1794–95. He received his Doctor of Medicine degree from the University of Pennsylvania in 1801 and was elected a member of the American Philosophical Society on 16 July 1802. He served as librarian of the Chemical Society of Philadelphia before moving in 1803 to St. Croix where he practiced medicine. Minutes, APS Archives; Biographical File, APS.

TO JOHN LENTHALL

Phil[a]delphia May 14th. 1803.

My dear Lenthall

The check on the Bank of the U. States for 141$ 66 cts. I have safely received, in your letter of the 11th. May.

As I do not keep Copies of my letters, I cannot exactly tell in *what* manner my wish to keep the West front of the South Wing, *equal and similar* in all respects to the east front of the same wing, rather than to the West front of the North wing can have *frightened* you. My reason is this, that the two lobbies on each side, E. and W., may be in every respect alike, and that we may not, in carrying up the building, be plagued by different dimensions on the opposite fronts. However, I herewith discharge you from all obligation to make them *equal* and *similar:* and for this reason, that as the difference in the fronts, amounts between the S.W. angle and the center of the West door only to 10 inches, it may be *wasted* away among the groins and groin piers without ill effect.[1] I am now laboring the principal story; and must beg you to send to me, from the *actual* measurement, the exact distances from Center [to][2] Center of the openings on all three sides. This will give me all I want to a correct drawing.

As to the old stones, more properly called rubbish, you may safely use it within the reversed arches, picking the best. What to do with Elliot I know not. I wish we could get him a partner, who understood the use of the Whip as well as of the Wedge and Sledge. If you could inform him that you had written to me, and that I thought of sending on a posse of Welchmen, unless I had more favorable accounts of him, perhaps that might produce exertion.

In the course of this week I shall send you, the hoisting machines of the Pensylvania Bank,[3] a quantity of Glass for the Presidents house, and a coil or two of Scaffolding rope to begin with. If you want any thing which you cannot so well get at Alexandria, write to me. As soon as I know what all this will cost, I shall draw on Mr. Monroe for the amount, and send him the bill of Lading. Pray tell him so with my best respects, and let me know how Mrs. Monroe does, and whether She has a boy or a girl?[4] If I had time I would write to him.

I cannot send any of the sheetiron for the roofs until I know what is the distance of the rafters from center to center. Pray send me a patch of a dozen of them with the length of the whole Rafter for a beginning. I believe I wrote to you before to the same effect.[5]

Keep the President apprized of every thing that is doing, and of the *reasons* for every thing, and believe me with great anxiety for your health, and true regard Yours

B. H. Latrobe.

I ought to write to Mr. Hatfield but have no time. If you see him remember me to him.

ALS: BHL Papers, Library of Congress (169/A3). Addressed to Lenthall in Washington.

1. The overall 16″ discrepancy between the east and west facades of the north wing was distributed evenly among the four non-axial bays of its western front, while the central bay remained equal to that on the east. Between "the S.W. angle and the center of the West door" (the latter must have been in the central bay if the surplus appeared in this interval) were two bays each four inches larger than those on the east. Thus this difference should have been eight rather than ten inches. BHL to Lenthall, 5 May 1803, above.

2. BHL mistakenly wrote "of" here.

3. BHL claimed that the Bank of Pennsylvania hoisting machines were "as good as new" and would "save much money and time and be better than [sending] a drawing" to Lenthall. BHL to Lenthall, 19 Apr. 1803, BHL Papers, Library of Congress (168/C10).

4. Fanny (Whetcroft) Munroe (d. 1858), the daughter of William Whetcroft, married 295

Thomas Munroe in 1796. They had two sons and two daughters. CHS, *Records* 6 (1903):158.

     5. BHL to Lenthall, 9 May 1803, Mrs. Gamble Latrobe Collection, MdHS (169/A1).

TO ROBERT GOODLOE HARPER

Philadelphia May 15th., 1803.

My dear Sir

    You have great reason to complain of me. But if I could with any sort of conscience take up your time in detailing the causes that have delayed my communication to you on the watering of your city, I think you would excuse me. The settlement of my connexion with Bollmann's, the accumulation of business during my absence, the necessary arrangements previously to my leaving Philadelphia for the summer for Delaware or Washington, the confinement of a week by my own illness, and its cause the dangerous though safe delivery of Mrs. Latrobe of a boy, all this has so loaded every moment of my time with engagement, that though I have written and almost copied for you a *dissertation* on *your* subject, I have not had time [to] get it ready for the Post.

    Your last communication furnishes me with accurate materials, further to enlarge and correct my remarks. I hope during this week to transmit them to you, and to be with you myself during the first days of June, when I hope to stay a day or two with you.

    I hope Mrs. Harper's health is improved, and that she is by this time breathing the country air, with your fine little boy.[1] Receive the best of assurances of affectionate respect of Yours truly

B. Henry Latrobe

Mrs. Latrobe [sends][2] her best respects to you and Mrs. H. She is doing admirably.

ALS: Morristown National Historical Park (microfiche add.). Endorsed as received 20 May and answered 23 May.

    1. Catharine (Carroll) Harper (1778–1861), daughter of Charles Carroll of Carrollton, married Robert Goodloe Harper in May 1801. Their son was Charles Carroll Harper (c. 1802–1837). Ellen Hart Smith, *Charles Carroll of Carrollton* (New York, 1942), p. 206; Dielman-Hayward File, MdHS.

    2. BHL mistakenly wrote "best" here.

TO HUGH HENRY BRACKENRIDGE

Philadelphia, May 18th. 1803.

Dear Sir[1]

You will herewith receive the designs for Dickinson College which I promised you.[2] In forming them, I have endeavored to take all the circumstances which you stated to me into consideration, and to do the best for you which they would permit. I will beg leave to state to you the principles which have governed me in the distribution, and arrangement of the apartments.

The two aspects, the most unpleasant in our climate are the North East and the North West. The extreme cold of the North West winds in winter, and their dryness, which causes a rapid evaporation so thoroughly chills the walls of every house, exposed to them, that when the wind, as is almost always the case, changes afterwards to the West and S. W., and becomes warmer and moister, the water is precipitated upon the Walls, from the air, by their coldness, as upon the outside of a Glass of cold Water in warm weather, and they soon stream with humidity. The North East winds bring along rain and sleet, and their violence drives the moisture into every wall of which the material will permit it. The unpleasantness of the winds is aggravated by the suddenness with which the Northwest commonly succeeds the North East. I have stated these things, which are indeed known to every body, in order to explain a *law*, which is thereby imposed upon the Architecture of our Country: It is, to reserve the Southern aspects of every building in the erection of which the choice is free, for the inhabited apartments, and to occupy the Northern aspects by communications, as Stairs, Lobbies, Halls, Vestibules &c.

This Law governs the designs herewith presented to you.

On the North are the Vestibule and lobbies, or passages. They protect the Southern rooms from the effect of the Northern winds. On this Aspect I have also placed the dining room, a room only occasionally occupied and for a short time, and the Schoolrooms above it, which by means of Stoves, and the concourse of Students are easily kept warm. There are indeed two Chambers in the N.E. wing on each story. If these Chambers be inhabited by Preceptors, the one as a study, the other as a Bedchamber, the disadvantages of the Aspect must be overcome by such means, of Curtains and Carpets, as a Student does not so easily acquire. The South Front affords on each story 6 rooms for Students. The angle 297

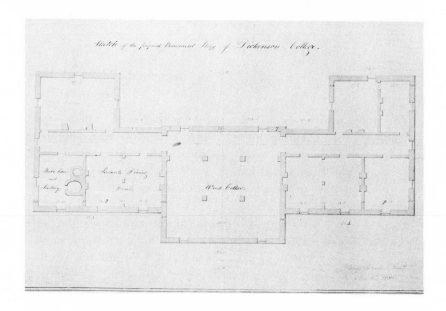

Fig. 10. Top: BHL, Plan of the basement of Dickinson College, Carlisle, Pa., 18 May 1803. Courtesy of the Dickinson College Library. Bottom: Engraving of Dickinson College, detail, from a drawing by A. Brackenridge. From *The Port Folio*, 5, 3 (Mar. 1811).

rooms will accommodate 3, and each of the other, 2 Students; in all 14 on each floor.

The Hall is intended to occupy two stories. Above the Hall a room of equal size may be appropriated to a Library, or may furnish *4* or *6* Students rooms, 2 or 3 to the South and as many to the North.

The usual mode of planning colleges, by arranging the rooms on each side of a long passage, has many disadvantages, the chief of which are the noise, the necessary darkness of the Passage, and the bad aspect of one half of the rooms. These inconveniences do not, I believe exist in the plan I present to you, and should at a future period, the celebrity of your institution encrease the number of your students, as it no doubt will, it will be better to erect new accommodations, than to obtain room by connecting the wings, in order to save expence; as has often been done.

In respect to material, I would, certainly, recommend that you should build your external walls of the lime stone of your Valley,[3] rather than of brick. The internal Walls, may with more advantage be built of brick. It will be objected that Limestone is so pervious to Water, that no Plaistering will stand upon it. I do not know that it is more so than *common* brick, but if it were, I must observe, than no material whatsoever, unless the wall be 2f. 6i. thick will prevent the damp appearance of the Walls towards the North aspects, unless they be *battened* and *plaistered* upon Lath. By battens are meant strips of 1½ inches thick and about 2 inches wide, which are fastened by Wall hooks, upright to the Walls, at the distance of 15 inches from each other, and upon which laths are nailed as upon framed work. No such precaution is necessary upon the internal walls. The Air thus enclosed between the Plaistering upon Laths, and the solid Wall being a nonconductor, prevents either the Heat or the cold of the external wall from materially affecting the temperature of the room, and the Plaistering itself will always be dry. This method has also the advantage that the plaistering on the external Walls is easily made fair and straight, whereas the roughness and irregularity of a stone Wall, is not easily got over by plaistering.

I have said thus much in order to give the Trustees an opportunity—should they adopt the plan proposed—of procur[ing] their principal materials at once. But should they contemplate to carry it into execution either with or without alteration, I shall expect that you will have the goodness to apprise me of their resolution in the course of this month, that I may furnish *such working plans* as will be immediately necessary.

I beg leave also to suggest to you and to the Trustees, that it will be impossible to conduct your building with success, oeconomy, and satisfaction, unless some intelligent, experienced, and honest Man, as superintendant of the Work, have controul over every part of it. This situation is often given to some respectable, but superannuated Workman, from motives of benevolence. Such a superintendant is indeed adequate to the counting of bricks, the measurement of Stone and Lime, and keeping an account, and often to the decission on the quality of the materials and the goodness of the Workmanship. But those things though necessary, are not all that are wanted. The great and useful business of a Superintendant, or as he is commonly called, a Clerk of the Works, consists in so directing and combining the Labors of a variety of Workmen, that they shall *all* produce the building, without Loss of time or waste of material, or dispute among themselves, or disadvantage in the performance of their contracts, by want of material, or the Necessity of waiting for each other. Such an office requires vigor of mind and body, as well as mechanical knowledge and manual skill, and whether you may meet with a person capable of filling it, the liberality or oeconomy of compensation will in part determine. I do not think you will get a *fit* man under from 12 to 15 Dollars per Week. We pay here 18$ Dollars at the public works.

I beg to repeat what I before mentioned to you, that as I conceive it to be the interest and duty of every good citizen to promote, *quoad virile,*[4] the education, and *civilization* of the society in which he and his children are to live, I will with pleasure contribute to the reestablishment of Dickinson college, every possible gratuitous personal assistance: and should you accept of this sort of contribution, nothing will be charged against you, but such *actual* expenses as may arise in the course of my giving it to you.[5] I am with true respect Yours truly

B. Henry Latrobe
Surveyor of the U. States buildings at Washington.

I must request that you will excuse the evident marks of haste in this letter; which would have been more explanatory, had not the time to which you have limited me, been so short.

ALS: Dickinson College Library (169/B1).

1. Hugh Henry Brackenridge (1748–1816), noted jurist and author, was a native of Scotland whose family came to York County, Pa., in 1753. Brackenridge studied at the College of New Jersey (Princeton), where his classmates included Philip Freneau and James Madison, graduating in 1771 (A.M. 1774). He then taught school, studied divinity, and served as a chaplain during the American Revolution. After studying law in Annapolis

with Samuel Chase, Brackenridge in 1781 moved to Pittsburgh, where he practiced law and in 1786 established the *Pittsburgh Gazette*, the city's first newspaper. From 1799 Brackenridge, an active Republican, served as judge of the Pennsylvania supreme court. He was the author of *Modern Chivalry* (1792–1815), a satirical novel considered to be the first literary work of the West.

2. On 3 February 1803 the newly built twelve-room brick classroom building of Dickinson College in Carlisle, Pa., burnt almost to the ground. At once the college trustees, including Brackenridge, embarked on a local and national fund-raising program to replace the structure. The favorable response, including donations from such men as Thomas Jefferson and John Marshall, prompted the trustees to decide on a larger building to provide lodgings for the students as well as classrooms. Brackenridge sought out BHL to design the new structure; with this letter the architect sent his drawings, including two surviving drawings (Dickinson College Library; 293/A4 ff), reproduced in fig. 10 and in BHL, *Architectural Drawings*. In the letter he also describes what he hoped to accomplish by his design.

The result was the building now known as Old West, of local grey limestone trimmed with red sandstone. The design rationalizes a type common to eighteenth-century American college building, with a long block breaking forward at center into a pedimented pavilion and sometimes extended at its ends with short perpendicular wings. BHL had encountered this type of building at the College of William and Mary (1695–1702) and at the College of New Jersey, where in 1802 he had reconstructed Robert Smith's and Dr. William Shippen's Nassau Hall (1753–56), his special point of reference in designing Dickinson College. BHL's Dickinson College building shows the fitness and quiet modernity with which he could invest a commonplace of traditional American building.

3. The Great Valley of Pennsylvania (or the Cumberland Valley as it is called in the Carlisle area).

4. Trans.: As far as is manly.

5. BHL's usual practice was to donate his professional services to religious and educational institutions. See, e.g., BHL to John Carroll and Trustees of Baltimore Cathedral, 27 Apr. 1805, and BHL to Samuel Fox, 25 May 1805, both in BHL, *Correspondence*, 2.

BHL later added a cupola to his design for Dickinson College which appears in his sketch of the building made on his trip to Pittsburgh in October 1813. See BHL, *Latrobe's View of America*.

REPORT ON STEAM ENGINES

First Report of Benjamin Henry Latrobe, to the American Philosophical Society, held at Philadelphia; in answer to the enquiry of the Society of Rotterdam, "Whether any, and what improvements have been made in the construction of Steam-Engines in America?"[1]

Philadelphia, 20th May, 1803.

Gentlemen,

The Report due from me to the Society, in consequence of the enquiry made by the Society of Rotterdam, as to the improvements made in America, in the construction of steam-engines, would have been laid before you at a much earlier period, had it not been my wish to submit several American alterations in the construction of steam-engines, which promised to be very valuable improvements, to the test of experience: and this delay has not been without its use; for it has been discovered that some of our innovations, the theory of which appeared to be very perfect, have proved extremely deficient in practical utility.

In this first report I will therefore confine myself to such improvements as have had a fair trial, in engines actually at work.

Steam-engines, on the old construction, were introduced in America above 40 years ago. Two, I believe, were put up in New-England before the revolutionary war;[2] and one, (which I have seen) at the copper-mine on the river Passaick, in New-Jersey, known by the name of the Schuyler-mine. All the principal parts of these engines were imported from England. With the Schuyler-mine engine, Mr. Hornblower, the uncle of the younger Hornblower, who is well known as a skillful and scientific engine-builder, and whose calculations on the power of steam are extremely useful, came to America. He put up the engine, which at different times has been at work during the last thirty years, and which, notwithstanding its imperfect construction, and the faulty boring of its cylinder, effectually drained the mine.[3]

During the general lassitude of mechanical exertion which succeeded the American revolution, the utility of steam-engines appears to have been forgotten; but the subject afterwards started into very general notice, in a form in which it could not possibly be attended with much success. A sort of Mania began to prevail, which indeed has not yet entirely subsided, for impelling boats by steam-engines, ⟨*and which was perhaps excited by the difficulty arising from the rapidity of many of our principal rivers.*⟩[4] Dr. Franklin proposed to force forward the boat by the immediate action of steam upon the water. (See his Works).[5] Many attempts to simplify the working of the engine, and more to employ a means of dispensing with the beam, in converting the Libratory into a rotatory motion, were made. ⟨*Not one of them, whether patented or not, appears to me to have sufficient merit or novelty to entitle it [to] recommendation or even description: and merely to enumerate them would uselessly consume your time.*⟩[6] For a short time a passage-boat, rowed by a steam-engine, was established between Bordentown and Philadelphia: but it was soon laid aside.[7] The best and most powerful steam-engine which has been employed for this purpose, excepting perhaps one constructed by Dr. Kinsey, with the performance of which I am not sufficiently acquainted, belonged to a few gentlemen of New-York. It was made to act, by way of experiment, upon oars, upon paddles, and upon flutter wheels. Nothing in the success of any of these experiments appeared to be a sufficient compensation for the expense, and the extreme inconvenience of the steam-engine in the vessel.[8]

There are indeed general objections to the use of the steam-engine for impelling boats, from which no particular mode of application can be free. These are: 1st, The weight of the engine and of the fewel. 2d, The large space it occupies. 3d, The tendency of its action to rack the vessel and render it leaky. 4th, The expense of maintenance. 5th, The irregularity of its motion, and the motion of the water in the boiler and cistern, and of the fuel-vessel in rough water. 6th, The difficulty arising from the liability of the paddles or oars to break, if light; and from the weight, if made strong. Nor have I ever heard of an instance, verified by other testimony than that of the inventor, of a speedy and agreeable voyage having been performed in a steam-boat of any construction. I am well aware, that there are still many very respectable and ingenious men, who consider the application of the steam-engine to the purpose of navigation, as highly important, and as very practicable, especially on the rapid waters of the Mississippi; and who would feel themselves almost offended at the expression of an opposite opinion. And perhaps some of the objections against it may be obviated.[9] That founded on the expense and weight of the fuel may not, for some years, exist on the Mississippi, where there is a redundance of wood on the banks: but the cutting and loading will be almost as great an evil.

I have said thus much on the engines which have been constructed among us for the purpose of navigating boats, because many modes of working and constructing them have been adopted which are not used in Europe. Not one of them, however, appears to have sufficient merit to render it worthy of description and imitation; nor will I, unless by your further desire, occupy your attention with them.

The only engines of any considerable powers which, as far as I know, are now at work in America, are the following. 1st, At New-York, belonging to the Manhattan Water-Company, for the supply of the city with water. 2d, One at New-York, belonging to Mr. Roosevelt, employed to saw timber. 3d, Two at Philadelphia, belonging to the corporation of the city, for the supply of the city with water; one of which also drives a rolling and slitting mill. 4th, One at Boston, of which I have been only 303 generally informed, employed in some manufacture. In my second report, I will notice the improvements made by the very ingenious Dr. Kinsey, ⟨*to whose merit as a general mechanic, too ample a testimony cannot be given,*⟩[10] who has erected, at New-York, an engine upon a new principle which is intended to be used in the supply of that city with water; should it on experiment, be found to answer the intended purpose.[11] He has made other improvements in the construction of steam-engines, of which I shall also give you some account. Nor ought I to omit the mention of a small engine, erected by Mr. Oliver Evans, as an experiment, with which he grinds Plaister of Paris;[12] nor of the steam-wheel of Mr. Briggs.[13]

1st. The Manhattan company's engine at New-York, is upon the principle of Bolton and Watt's double engines, without any variation. It has two boilers; one a wooden one, upon the construction of those first put up in Philadelphia, the other of sheet iron, on Bolton and Watt's construction. The Fly-wheel is driven by a sun and planet motion, and the shaft works three small pumps with common cranks.[14]

2d. Mr. Roosevelt's engine has all the improvements which have been made by the joint ingenuity of Messrs. Smallman and Staudinger,[15] with the assistance of the capital and intelligence of Mr. Roosevelt; and which have also been adopted to the engines, belonging to the water-works at Philadelphia.

3d. The engines at Philadelphia, independently of these improvements, act also upon a pump, the principal of which, though not new, has never before, I believe, been used upon a large scale; and which is worthy of being particularly described.

I shall now proceed to describe these *innovations,* for experience does not permit me as yet to call them all *improvements,* although I have no doubt, but that they will furnish hints of use to bring the steam-engine to greater perfection.

1st. THE WOODEN BOILER.

Wooden boilers have been applied in America to the purpose of distilling for many years. Mr. Anderson, whose improvements in that art are well known, appears to have first introduced them in America.[16] But it was found that the mash had a very injurious effect upon the solidity of the wood: for while the outside retained the appearance of soundness, and the inside that of a burnt, but hard surface, the body of the plank was entirely decayed. It was however still to be tried, whether simple water and steam, would have the same effect; and upon the hint of Chancellor Livingston, our present Ambassador in France, Messrs. Roosevelt, Smallman and Staudinger contrived the wooden boiler, which has been used for all the engines in New York and Philadelphia; and not without its great, though only temporary, advantages. The construction of the wooden boiler, will be best understood, by reference to the plan and section of the new boiler of the engine in Center-square, Philadelphia, which is by far the best of those which have been made.[17] It is in fact only a wooden chest containing the water, in which a furnace is contrived, of which the flues wind several times through the water, before they discharge themselves into the chimney. In the plan and section, Plate II, Fig. 1, 2, 3, 4, A is the furnace, B B B, are upright cylinders, called heaters, among which the fire passes, heating the water within them, and which, at the same time, support the roof of the fire-bed, or lower passage of the flame to the flues. C, is the take-up, or passage from the fire-bed to the flues. D the upper flue through which the fire passes from the take-up to the register E, when it enters into the chimney.

This boiler differs from the others, in the addition of the upright cylinders of the fire-bed, and in the elliptical form of its flues. The merits of this boiler are—that as the wood, in which the water is contained, is a very slow conductor of heat, a great saving of fuel is thereby effected; especially, as an opportunity is afforded, by means of the cylindrical heaters and of the length of the flue, to expose a very large surface of iron containing water to the action of the fire.[18] An idea of this saving may be formed by the quantity of coal consumed by the engine in the Center-square, which is a double steam-engine, the diameter of whose cylinder is 32 inches. The power of this engine is calculated to answer the future, as well as to supply the present wants of the city; it is therefore kept irregularly at work, filling, alternately, the elevated reservoir, ⟨*containing 7,500 Gallons of Water from which the pipes are supplied in 6 minutes, and resting about 25 Minutes during which time the reservoir is emptied*⟩[19] and stopping during the time which is occupied by the discharge of the water into the city. It may, however, be fairly rated to go at the rate of 12 strokes, of 6 feet, per minute, for 16 hours in 24, during which time it consumes from 25 to 33 bushels of Virginia coals of the best sort. ⟨*A comparison with other Engines of equal power will give an estimate of the saving effected.*⟩[20] Of the amount of the saving, I cannot venture to make an estimate; on account of the great variety of coal with which we are 305

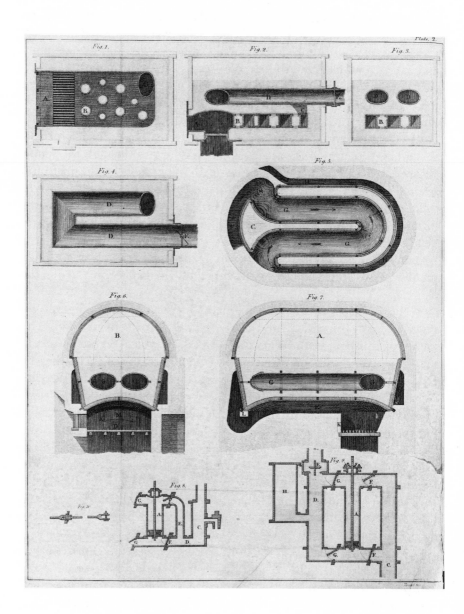

Fig. 1.

Fig. 2.

Fig. 3.

Fig. 4.

Fig. 5.

Fig. 6.

Fig. 7.

Fig. 8.

Fig. 9.

Fig. 10.

supplied, much of which is of a very indifferent quality. That there is a great saving is certain; and while the wooden boilers continue steam tight, (for that part which contains the water gives no trouble) they are certainly equal, if not superior, to every other. The wood, however, which is above the water, and is acted upon by the steam, seems to loose its solidity in the course of time; and steam-leaks arise in the joints, and wherever a bolt passes through. The joint-leaks may for a considerable time, be easily stopped, by screwing up the bolts that hold the planks together; but it is not so easy to cure the bolt-leaks; for the bolt, when screwed up, bends the top or the sides inwards, and forces new leaks, either along the corners, or at some other bolt-hole. I do not, however, believe, that every thing has as yet been done, which could be done, to obviate these defects. A conical wooden boiler hooped would not be subject to some of them: such a one has been applied by Mr. Oliver Evans to his small steam-engine ⟨*which does not otherwise contain any improvement*⟩.[21] During two years, which have elapsed since the boilers of the public engines have been erected, much has been done to improve them. Whether the last boiler will prove as perfect in its wood-work, as it is in its furnaces and flues, is still to be ascertained by experience. At present nothing can work better.

I will only mention one other circumstance, the knowledge of which may prevent similar mischief.—In the first boiler erected in Philadelphia, oak timber was used to support the sides, bottom, and top of the boilers, the plank of which was white pine, 4 inches thick. In less than a year it was discovered, that the substance of the pine plank, to the depth of an inch, was entirely destroyed by the acid of the oak. Means were then used to prevent its further action, by the intervention of putty and pasteboard; and in most cases by substituting pine timbers in the room of those of oak.

CAST-IRON BOILER

Within the last few months, a cast-iron boiler has been put up, at the lower engine, which hitherto exceeds the expectation, I had formed of the facility with which steam is raised and supported by it. The engine is a double steam-engine, of 40 inches cylinder, and 6 feet stroke.[22] The boiler has straight sides, and semicircular ends; it is 17 feet long, and 8 feet wide at the bottom; and nineteen feet long, and 10 feet wide at the height of 5 feet 7 inches. At this height, it is covered by a vault; which, in

307

its transverse section, is semicircular; and in its longitudinal section exhibits half of its plan. The bottom is concave every way; rising one foot in the center. The fire-place is 6 feet long, and at an average 4 feet wide; and is under one extreme end of the bottom. The fire-bed is arched, parallel with the bottom, leaving a space of one foot high, for the passage of the flame. At the end opposite to the fire-place, the flame descends along the bottom of the boiler, and, passing under an arch of fire-bricks, which protects the flanch of the bottom, strikes the side of the boiler at its extreme end. Here it enters a flat elliptical flue, which, passing into the boiler, follows its form, returning again and coming out near the place at which it entered. The entering part of the flue is separated from the returning flue, by a partition of fire-bricks. The flue, on coming out of the boiler, turns short round, and is carried round the whole boiler until it enters the chimney; as will be more clearly shewn by referring to Plate II. Fig. 5, 6, 7; the same letters on each figure referring to the same things. Fig. 5. *C*, a horizontal section of the boiler, through the center of the flues. Fig. 6. *B*, a transverse section of boiler at the fire-grate. Fig. 7. *A*, a longitudinal section. Fig. 6, 7. *D*, the fire-bed. *K*, a bridge-wall nine inches thick, over which the fire passes to the passage *E*, under the bottom of the boiler, being parallel both ways with the same. Fig. 7. *L* an arch of fire-bricks to support and protect the flanch from being melted by the heat. Fig. 6, 7. The fire passes from *D*, through the passage *E*, under the arch *L*, Fig. 7, to the take-up *E*, Fig. 5, 7, where it enters the upper flue *G*, Fig. 5, 6, 7, which passes through the boiler. *H*, the flue round the outside of the boiler, wherein the fire is carried until it enters the chimney at *I*, Fig. 5. The whole boiler is tied together internally by numerous braces, Fig. 10, which are forked and bolted together upon the flanches, and are indispensable to prevent the boiler from bursting. The flanches and joints of the castings are represented Fig. 6, 7.

The boiler is composed of 70 plates of iron, cast with flanches, and bolted together, so that the flanch and bolts are within the water of the boiler wherever the flame touches it; otherwise they would be burned off in a few days. The pieces are so contrived as to be of only of 12 different patterns. This boiler consumed 50 bushels of coal, and ½ a cord of wood, while rolling iron 12 hours, at 20 strokes per minute, and pumping water 6 hours, at 12 strokes per minute.[23]

I will only further observe, that this boiler requires a very active fireman; and it is my opinion, that if it were 3 feet longer, a more moderate fire would raise the same steam and consume less fuel. The permanance of this boiler renders it very superior to the wooden one; and the difference of the consumption of fuel in each, in proportion to the size of the engine, is not great.

The further improvement of the engine itself consists in a new application of an improved construction of the air-pump. I will first remark, that by the air-pump of Bolton and Watt, the condenser is only once emptied, of its water of condensation and of the air produced, in every stroke. The superiority of our air-pump consists in its evacuating the condenser twice at every stroke, thereby creating a much better vacuum, and of course adding considerably to the power of our engine in proportion to the diameter of its cylinder without encreasing friction. The drawing, Plate II, Fig. 8, will best explain the construction of this pump.

A, is the pump-barrel. B, the piston which is solid. C, the condenser. D, a pipe of connection between the condenser and the lower chamber of the air-pump. E, a pipe of connection with the upper chamber of the air-pump. F, valves opening towards the air-pump. G, discharging-valves into two hot-wells. The head of hot-water suffered to remain on these valves must be moderate, or they will refuse to open; for it must be remarked, that great part of the contents of the air-pump is an elastic gaz, which suffers compression and is not expelled, if the weight on the valve be too great. The action of this air-pump is evident from the drawing. The expulsion of the contents of each chamber creates a vacuum in the other, which draws in the contents of the condenser; and thus they act equally and alternately, agreeing in their operation with the alternate condensation of the steam in the opposite chambers of the cylinder. Experience proves this to be a real improvement.[24]

The principle which has been applied to the construction of the air-pump, is that upon which the main pump of our water-works is constructed. A section of this pump is annexed which perfectly explains it.

⟨*In all great public Undertakings personal passions do more or less mischiefs. The Philadelphia Water works have felt their influence, and to them it is owing that the pumps of the Engines remain in an incomplete state and that instead of being able to report to you the success with which the only convenience to which the pumps are liable have been removed, I must report the means which probabl[y] would be successful, and the application of which has been prohibited, to the ruin of the Contractor for the Steam engine.*⟩[25]

This pump has so many advantages that, had the corporation of 1800 permitted its disadvantages, (of which I shall presently speak,) to 309 be remedied by the means then proposed, I have no doubt, but that I might now recommend its general adoption, wherever a double steam-engine is used for pumping. The drawing in Plate II, Fig. 9, will explain its construction; *A* the working barrel. *B* the piston. *C* the feed-pipe. *D* the rising main pipe. *F* the valves which supply the working barrel. *G* discharging valves in the ascending pipe. *H* the air-vessel—The valve *E*, in the rising pipe, and the air-vessel *H*, are not added to our pumps. The want of one or other of them, has these disadvantages: as long as the engine makes only 11 or 12 strokes per minute, no inconvenience whatever is perceived in the working of the pumps. But in the engine in the center-square, which raises the water in an 18 inch pipe 51 feet, and which has less redundant power than that on Schuylkill, the attempt to work faster than 12 strokes per minute is vain; and, as it appears to me, from two causes: 1st, whenever the piston is at its utmost ascent or descent, and makes a momentary stop, the whole column of water follows the shutting valve, acquiring momentum as it falls. The range of our valves is 16 inches, the column therefore descends at an average 8 inches. It weighs near 3 tons, and to open the opposite valve against the momentum of such a column, gives the engine a shock that seems to endanger every part of it. In endeavouring to work with its full power at a speed of 20 strokes a minute, this shock is so severe, as to occasion a very perceptible stop in the return of the stroke, during which the water of condensation mounts into the cylinder. Two methods were proposed to remedy this inconvenience, which amounts to a perfect uselessness of more than ⅓ of our power. 1st, to place a large plug-valve *E*, Fig. 9, in the rising pipe close to the pump, having as much water-way through its seat at a very small rise, as the whole pipe. This valve would shut instantaneously at the end of the stroke, catching the falling column of water, and nothing would oppose its immediate return. 2d, to place an air-vessel so as to act on the whole column. By this means the fall of the water would be entirely prevented.

I regret that though this apparatus was provided, and could easily have been put up, in the course of a few days, circumstances prohibited the trial of them, and that I can only submit them as projects.[26] Could this pump be used with the same speed as the single pump, one half of the power of every double pumping engine, which works a single pump, would be saved; for the beam would need no counterpoise, and all the expense and friction of a second pump, where two are employed to balance each other, would be avoided.

I hope shortly to deliver you a second report on this subject,[27] and am with true respect yours.

B. Henry Latrobe.

Since the above was read in the Society I have constructed another and much larger iron boiler on this plan, the former having fully answered my expectation. In the new boiler I have passed the fire through a second flue above the other, which is immersed in the steam only, from which I promise myself great advantage.[28]

B.H.L.

Printed Copy: American Philosophical Society, *Transactions* 6 (1809):89–98, with plate (169/F4). A manuscript draft, labeled "Rough report," is in the APS Archives (169/C5). Read by BHL before the Society on 20 May and referred to Robert Patterson, Robert Hare, and Don Carlos d'Yrujo, who recommended publication on 15 July 1803. BHL apparently retained another manuscript draft (not found) that differed from that in the APS Archives, for he quoted from it in 1814. In 1813 Oliver Evans had claimed that BHL attempted in the report "to shew the impossibility of making steam boats useful, on account of the weight of the engine; and I was one of the persons alluded to, as being seized with the *steam mania*, conceiving that waggons and boats could be propelled by steam engines. The liberality of the members of the society caused them to reject that part of his report which he designed as demonstrative of the absurdity of my principles; saying they had no right to set up their opinion as a stumbling block in the road of any exertions to make a discovery. They said, I might produce something useful, and ordered it to be stricken out." Evans, "On the Origin of Steam Boats and Steam Waggons," *Niles's Weekly Register* (Baltimore), 3 (1812–13), addendum, pp. 2–6, quote on pp. 3–4, reprinted in *Emporium of the Arts and Sciences*, new ser. 2, no. 2 (Feb. 1814):205–17, quote on p. 210. BHL replied, "That any part of my report was rejected by the society, is utterly false. No vote whatever was taken on the subject, but the unanimous one that it should be printed, as it now lies in manuscript before me. But it is true that the following circumstance took place at the meeting of the society. To the words above quoted [the passages in paragraphs 7 and 13 mentioning Evans] I had originally added the following:—'In this engine Mr. Evans has availed himself of the experiments and discoveries of Messrs. Watt and [Jonathan] Hornblower on the ratio in which the power of the steam is encreased, a ratio of power much greater than that of the temperature of the steam indicated by the thermometer. The inconvenience and danger connected with the use of high steam as experienced in England, will probably defeat the utility of Mr. Evans's engine.'
"Professor Patterson, who was in the chair, to whom I showed my manuscript report, and who thought highly of the merits of Mr. Evans's project, requested me, however, not to throw a damp upon his experiment by such a notice of it, and I immediately drew my pen through the passage he disapproved, as a matter of civility to Mr. Patterson, for whom I feel much esteem and friendship. That Mr. Patterson, made some communication on the subject to Mr. Evans, who was not a member of the society, and could only know what passed from hearsay, appears evident: but I acquit the Professor of any share in the malignant use which Mr. Evans has made of his information." BHL to the Editor of the

Pittsburgh Gazette, 8 Apr. 1814, in *Gazette*, 15 Apr. 1814 (microfiche add.). See also BHL to Ingersoll, 17 Jan. 1814, in BHL, *Correspondence*, 3.

Significant differences between the extant manuscript draft and the printed version, which do in fact temper BHL's criticism of Evans and BHL's claims of his own successes, are shown in angle brackets and explained in footnotes.

1. In June 1802 the American Philosophical Society received the first volume of the new series of *Bataafsh Genootschap der Proefondervindelijke Wijsbegeerte te Rotterdam* (Amsterdam, 1800), accompanied by a letter from the Batavian Society dated 12 March 1802 inquiring about steam engines in America (APS Archives). On 16 July 1802 the Society directed that BHL, Robert Patterson, and Robert Leslie draft an answer to the inquiry (Minutes, APS Archives).

2. No evidence for pre-Revolutionary engines in New England has been found. Pursell, *Steam Engines in America*, p. 5.

3. The Schuyler Copper Mine in northeast New Jersey was first opened in 1719 by Arent Schuyler. In 1748 John Schuyler, having succeeded his father as owner and concerned that the quantity of water in the mine would soon prevent working it, ordered a Newcomen pumping engine from the Hornblower family of Cornwall. Josiah Hornblower came to America in 1753 with the engine and spare parts and had it operating in 1755. Schuyler persuaded Hornblower to remain in America and become head of the enterprise. After serious fires in 1760 and 1768, the engine was not rebuilt until 1793–94, when a new company, with Nicholas Roosevelt as the principal figure, began operating the mine. BHL, *American Copper Mines* (n.p., [1800]) (163/B8); Pursell, *Steam Engines in America*, pp. 5–6.

4. This passage was struck in the manuscript draft.

5. BHL apparently refers to comments in Franklin's "Maritime Observations" of 1785. Franklin suggested an improvement to an idea of Daniel Bernoulli for propelling boats, whereby water was drawn through a tube in the bow and expelled through the stern. Though inclined to use a manual pump in this scheme, Franklin added that "a fire-engine [i.e., a steam engine] might possibly in some cases be applied in this operation with advantage." BHL may also have been referring to Franklin's suggestion that *air* could be pumped by hand through a cylinder onboard a boat directly into the water—a form of jet propulsion. APS, *Transactions* 2 (1786):308–09; Brooke Hindle, *Emulation and Invention* (New York, 1981), pp. 26–28.

6. This sentence was struck in the manuscript draft and replaced by the following sentence.

7. This first American steamboat was the brainchild of John Fitch (1743–98), a silversmith, buttonmaker, clock repairman, and surveyor. Fitch's first conception of a steamboat came in 1785, and in 1786 he formed a company to support his experiments at Philadelphia. Since neither Fitch nor his technical adviser, Henry Voight, had experience with steam engines they were unafraid to try novel solutions to the problem of boat propulsion; but they also knew too little to produce an efficient engine. By 1790 they had built a workable steamboat with a condensing steam engine and reciprocating oars. That summer the boat carried passengers between Burlington, N.J., and Philadelphia, but technical and financial difficulties led to the sale of the boat, and a second boat was never successfully operated. Pursell, *Steam Engines in America*, pp. 18–22; Frank D. Prager, ed., *The Autobiography of John Fitch* (Philadelphia, 1976).

8. From 1798 to 1800 Robert Livingston (1746–1813), John Stevens (1749–1838), and Nicholas Roosevelt were associated in steamboat experiments on the Hudson and Passaic rivers. Their boat, the *Polacca*, moved in the water but was inefficient and uneconomical. BHL saw the boat at Laurel Hill, Roosevelt's New Jersey estate, probably

during his visit there in May 1800. Pursell, *Steam Engines in America,* pp. 30–31; BHL to Baldwin, 10 Oct. 1814, in BHL, *Correspondence,* 3.

9. A considerable catalogue might be made of BHL's American contemporaries who advocated steam navigation. At a minimum one should include Nicholas Roosevelt, John Stevens, Robert Livingston, Oliver Evans, Robert Fulton, William Thornton, and Daniel French.

10. This passage was struck in the manuscript draft.

11. Appollos Kinsley, who owned a small machine shop on Greenwich Street in New York, was supported by John Stevens in his attempt to build a rotary steam engine. On 16 August 1801 Kinsley reported to Stevens that he had successfully started his engine. It operated at 47 revolutions a minute and he calculated that it could raise 1440 gallons of water 70 feet every 24 hours. Archibald Douglas Turnbull, *John Stevens: An American Record* (New York, 1928), p. 151.

12. Oliver Evans (1755–1819) was the inventor of the automatic flour mill and the American developer of high-pressure steam engines. In 1802 he was a member of a committee of the Philadelphia city councils that investigated the state of the waterworks, and Evans was personally critical of the waterworks and its engineer. For his objections to this report, see bibliographic note.

About 1801 Evans conceived a small high-pressure engine with a six-inch steam cylinder, and by February 1803 he had employed it to drive his screw mill for grinding plaster of Paris in his store in Philadelphia five blocks east of the Centre Square Engine House. Evans claimed that he "could break and grind 300 bushels of plaister of Paris, or 12 tons, in 24 hours." Evans obtained a patent for his high-pressure engine the following year and established the Mars Works engine factory in Philadelphia in 1806 to produce them. His engines gained widespread use in the next decade, despite some boiler explosions, and served as the prototype for factory and steamboat engines that swept away the use of low-pressure engines in the 1820s. Evans, "On the Origin of Steam Boats and Steam Waggons," p. 211; Greville Bathe and Dorothy Bathe, *Oliver Evans: A Chronicle of Early American Engineering* (Philadelphia, 1935), pp. 68–69, 79–80; Eugene S. Ferguson, *Oliver Evans: Inventive Genius of the American Industrial Revolution* (Greenville, Del., 1980), pp. 35–39, 45–51, 63–64.

13. In 1802 Samuel Briggs patented a rotary steam engine. Pursell, *Steam Engines in America,* p. 24.

14. The Manhattan Company began to supply water to the city of New York in November 1799 using a pump powered by a horse gin. On 20 May 1801 John Stevens offered to sell a steam engine to the company. It is not clear whether this was the engine for the steamboat *Polacca* or one he intended to build. About a year and a half later an observer reported that the Manhattan Company had installed a steam engine built by Robert McQueen, a British immigrant. John Stevens to Manhattan Company, 20 May 1801, Stevens Family Papers, New Jersey Historical Society, Newark; James Tustin to Matthew Boulton, 23 Aug. 1802, extract, Matthew Boulton Papers, Birmingham Reference Library, Birmingham, England; Nelson M. Blake, *Water for the Cities* (Syracuse, N.Y., 1956), p. 59; Pursell, *Steam Engines in America,* pp. 50–51.

15. Charles Staudinger (d. 1816) was a German immigrant with considerable drawing skill who began working for Nicholas Roosevelt as a draftsman about 1797. He was trained in steam engineering under James Smallman and was a major figure in the Roosevelt-Livingston-Stevens steamboat experiments and the manufacture of the Philadelphia Waterworks engines. Eventually he became deeply involved with Robert Fulton's enterprises. For BHL's later, highly critical, characterization of Staudinger, see BHL to Lydia (Latrobe) Roosevelt, 31 Dec. 1810, LB (81/A12). BHL to Fulton, 11 Jan. 1813, LB (106/D5); Testi- 313

mony of Richard Newsham and James Smallman, c. 1815, James L. Woods Collection, Franklin Institute Library, Philadelphia; Robert Livingston to John Stevens, 10 Jan. 1800, Stevens Family Papers, New Jersey Historical Society; Thomas Pym Cope diaries, 7 July 1800, Haverford College Library, Haverford, Pa.; Pursell, *Steam Engines in America*, pp. 29, 51.

16. A contemporary distiller's manual does not mention Anderson's wooden boilers (in fact it does not mention wooden boilers at all), but it does discuss Anderson's invention of a method of preheating the liquor prior to its admission to the still, so as to decrease the time of distillation. Michael Krafft, *The American Distiller, or the Theory and Practice of Distilling* (Philadelphia, 1804), p. 37.

17. The first wooden boiler of the Centre Square engine burned out in July 1801, and a new one (which had been in preparation) was installed immediately. The plans for the first boiler are shown in Staudinger's drawings and the plans of the second boiler are reproduced as part of this paper. The dimensions of the latter boiler are uncertain, although long after it was dismantled they were reported as "9 feet high, 9 feet wide, and 15 feet long." BHL, *Engineering Drawings*, pp. 181–84, 188; Thomas Pym Cope diaries, 6 July 1801; William H. McFadden, "A Brief History and Review of the Water Supply of Philadelphia," *Annual Report of the Chief Engineer of the Water Department of the City of Philadelphia, for the Year 1875* (Philadelphia, 1876), p. 16.

18. Eleven years after BHL's report the chief engineer of the Philadelphia Waterworks, Frederick Graff, stated that he was "fully persuaded, that it far exceeds any boiler now in use at the water works, or any other which has come under my notice, both in saving fuel and the ease with which the steam can be kept up." Graff, "Steam Engine Boiler," *Emporium of Arts and Sciences*, new series, 3, 2 (Aug. 1814):275.

19. This passage was struck in the manuscript draft and replaced by the following phrase.

20. This passage was struck in the manuscript draft and replaced by the following phrase.

21. This phrase, though not struck in the manuscript, does not appear in the printed version.
Evans described the boiler as "a small boiler of cedar wood, 12 inches diameter and 20 inches in height, strongly hooped with iron: inside of this cylinder was put a cast iron furnace 7 inches diameter at the lower and 3 inches diameter at the upper end, with a flange 12 inches diameter at each end, which served as heads for the wooden cylinder: I fixed a safety valve and cock in the upper. The space between the furnace and wooden cylinder contained the water which surrounded the fire. A small fire in this furnace soon raised the power of the steam to such a degree as to lift the safety valve loaded with 152 lbs to the inch." Bathe and Bathe, *Oliver Evans*, pp. 66–67, 69, 79; Eugene S. Ferguson, ed., *Early Engineering Reminiscences (1815–1840) of George Escol Sellers* (Washington, D.C., 1965), pp. 37–38, 40.

22. The Schuylkill, or lower, engine of the Philadelphia Waterworks was in the engine house adjacent to the Schuylkill River. BHL, *Engineering Drawings*, pp. 35, 157–61, 164.

23. Roosevelt's rolling mill was located in the Schuylkill Engine House under the terms of his lease from the Philadelphia city councils. From the beginning of the mill's operation in the fall of 1802 the engine worked the mill and the pump alternately, although Erick Bollmann, the mill's first manager, recognized that simultaneous operation would be much more efficient. There is no evidence that it was ever achieved, even after the replacement of the original steam cylinder by a better one and the installation of a new set of gears for the mill. Erick Bollmann Memorandum and Letter Book, 31 Oct. 1802, George Bollman Collection, Historical Society of Pennsylvania, Philadelphia; *Report of the*

Watering Committee to the Select & Common Councils, November 1, 1803 (Philadelphia, 1803).

24. How widespread the use of the double air pump became is unknown, although BHL and Smallman used it again for the Washington Navy Yard engine. BHL, *Engineering Drawings*, pp. 223, 226–27.

25. This paragraph was struck from the manuscript draft.

26. BHL ordered the manufacture of catch valves for each of the waterworks' pumps after their trials demonstrated the jarring and energy-wasting effect of the descending column of water. Thomas Cope, a member of the Watering Committee, vehemently objected to paying for them on the grounds that they were Roosevelt's responsibility and should be included under his contract. It appears that they were never installed. Air vessels were finally attached to the rising pipes in 1810. Cope diaries, 23 Mar. 1801; BHL to Zachariah Poulson, 24 Oct. 1801, in *American Daily Advertiser* (Philadelphia), 27 Oct. 1801 (164/A1); "The History of the Steam Engine in America," *Journal of the Franklin Institute*, 3rd ser., 72 (1876):265.

27. The minutes of the American Philosophical Society do not mention a second report.

28. A second cast iron boiler was installed at the Schuylkill Engine House in the fall of 1803. After several months' operation the manager of the rolling mill, Samuel Mifflin, wrote BHL a description of the boilers which BHL described as "highly gratifying." *Report of the Watering Committee* (1803); BHL to Mifflin, 25 Mar. 1804, LB (30/F1).

The Chesapeake and Delaware Canal

EDITORIAL NOTE (PART 2)

Latrobe's 1802 fears that the Chesapeake and Delaware canal project would fail for lack of adequate funding did not at first materialize. Despite the lack of legislative aid from either Congress or the state legislatures, more C & D shares were subscribed, and by May 1803 the stockholders had bought more than the requisite half of the total 2500 shares. The C & D Canal Company was officially organized at a meeting of stockholders in Wilmington, Delaware, on 2 May 1803. Elections for company officers were held and Joseph Tatnall, a leading Delaware industrialist, was chosen president. On 3 May, the board of directors held its first meeting and began preparations for the canal survey.[1]

A Committee of Survey was appointed on 7 June 1803 consisting of President Tatnall and directors Kensey Johns of Delaware, William Tilghman and Joshua Gilpin of Pennsylvania, and George Gale and John Adlum of Maryland. The committee, along with the engineers or surveyors, was to "examine and survey" the possible routes for the canal; to determine the elevation and amount of water in the Elk and Christina rivers and White Clay Creek, which would be used as feeders for the canal; to ascertain the terms on which the waters of the streams and the land for the canal could be obtained; and to employ at least two surveyors to assist the engineers "in making the intended Rout of the Canal."

1. "First Minute Book of Stockholders meetings," 2 May, 3 May 1803, C & D Canal Company Papers.

Latrobe and Cornelius Howard of Baltimore were the engineers appointed to work under the survey committee's direction.[2]

Latrobe and Howard met with the survey committee at Elkton, Maryland, on 5 July 1803, at which time the committee agreed to pay the engineers eight dollars a day, the maximum allowed by the board of directors. Within six weeks Latrobe reported to Joshua Gilpin on his and Howard's progress (see BHL to Gilpin, 14 August 1803, below). In September, the survey committee authorized Latrobe to employ John Thomson of Pennsylvania as an assistant on the surveys. He also hired surveyor Daniel Blaney of Delaware. In addition, the engineer had help in his office. "Plotting, mapping, and calculations" had to be performed with the information gathered in the field.[3] His office assistants, or "clerks," were not the experienced men his surveyors were, but rather "pupils" whom he was training in the architecture-engineering profession: Robert Mills, William Strickland, and Lewis DeMun.

The tasks of surveying the numerous proposed routes for the C & D Canal occupied much of the fall of 1803. In January 1804, the board of directors appointed Latrobe engineer of the canal. He directed the construction of a five-and-a-half-mile feeder canal which was to supply the main canal with water from Elk River. In 1805, when the feeder was nearly finished, however, the company ran out of money as delinquent subscriptions mounted, and work on the canal ceased. The canal project remained dormant for nearly two decades. It was revived shortly after Latrobe's death, at which time new surveys were made by William Strickland, Latrobe's former pupil, and other engineers; the canal route was relocated, and the waterway was finished in 1829.[4]

2. C & D Survey Committee Minutes, 6 June, 7 June 1803.

3. Ibid., 5 July, 19 Sept. 1803; BHL to Gilpin, 19–20 Oct. 1803, below; BHL, *Engineering Drawings*, p. 12.

4. The best study of the canal's history is Ralph D. Gray, *The National Waterway: A History of the Chesapeake and Delaware Canal, 1769–1965* (Urbana, Ill., 1967).

TO JOHN LENTHALL

Newcastle, July 10th. 1803.

My dear Sir,

You will oblige me much by dispatching William Strickland with all my instruments and papers so as to be at Frenchtown on Saturday or Sunday next; for on Monday the 18th. of July I must have them there,[1] let the expense or exertion be what it may.

I have not a moment to say more. Let him stay at Frenchtown till I meet him on Monday, or if he arrives on Saturday, let him come up to Richardson's at Elkton,[2] where he will lodge more comfortably.

Yours affectionately

B. Henry Latrobe

ALS: BHL Papers, Library of Congress (169/G13). Addressed to Lenthall in Washington.

1. For the C & D Canal surveys.
2. This may have been Daniel Richardson (d. 1805) of Elkton. *Federal Gazette* (Baltimore), 26 Dec. 1805.

TO [JOSHUA GILPIN][1]

1803, August 14.

When I wrote to you on the 4th August, I had ascertained the levels of much of the practicable ground near Frenchtown. I had discovered that there are only two practicable tracts from thence to New Castle, one to the northward, the other round the south end of the hill which abuts upon Perch creek. The northern course is so evidently the best, that it will no doubt meet with unanimous preference. Since then I have proceeded to the summit of the ridge and beyond it towards Cooch's mill.[2]

Before, I however mention to you the result of my operations, I must premise that all my levels have been proved beyond the possibility of doubt, by repeated levelling upon different courses; and having with great labor and perseverance, established several points of levels, I have invariably run every day's work up to one or other of these, and have never rested until I have produced perfect coincidence, at least within 6 inches. What I shall therefore now give to you as the result of my operations, may I think, be well depended upon.

1. The tide in Elk river varies with the winds more than with the Moon, and differs from 3 ft. 6 to 2 ft. between high and low water; I have assumed the mean tide at 2 ft. 6.

2. The high land near Frenchtown, rises in no instance above 82 feet above common high water.

3. The lowest pass from Frenchtown on to the summit, is over a very narrow ridge, the only practicable spot upon which, is 72 ft. 2 in. above high water, from thence there is a long straight stretch of level to

be had about 70 feet above high water, near which the canal may be twisted about so as to go over 72 feet.

4. From the end of this level to the summit level at Oliver Howell's in a straight line occurs no material obstruction excepting a narrow ridge from Gray's hill, rising to 78 feet 6 inches near Mr. Rudolph's farm house, and two vallies to Perch creek, sinking to 64 feet above high water.

5. The summit level at Howell's is without doubt 76.9 above the highest tides in Frenchtown, and 78.6 above the majority of high waters, such as I observed during a fortnight's occasional residence there.

6. Under all these considerations, I have thought that the best summit level that can be had, and in the course of which the fewest disadvantages are to be encountered, is that of 76 feet of elevation above high water. In 9/10ths. of the length of this range, there will be 4 feet 6 inches of bank to be made on each side, and if the canal be 42 feet wide on the surface of the water, the excavation will as nearly as possible, make a handsome embankment and road on each side. I have therefore made a compleat set of sections of all my courses, and a map on a large scale from Frenchtown to the summit level at Howell's. On this map I have noted in more than one hundred places, all of which are important as to the decision on the location of the canal, the exact elevation of the spot above high water, and I have laid down the line which in my judgement is the best, placing the locks in the points most evidently convenient— showing the necessary alterations of roads, &c.[3]

I propose the distribution of the locks to be as follows:

	feet.	inches.
Summit elevation above high water,	76	00
Difference of high and low water,	2	8
	78	8

	feet.	inches.
One tide lock to the basin in the marsh so as to raise the water over the present surface of the marsh, digging down only 2 feet 6 inches, which is necessary to get earth for embankments.	9	00
At the head of the basin,		
3 locks, 9 ft. lift	27	00

At the north end of Mr. Henderson's[4] line about		
half a mile distant from the basin, 3 locks	26	8
Near the Elkton road, 2 locks, 8 feet lift	<u>16</u>	<u>00</u>
	78	8

Of the southern course which is otherwise not a bad one, I will say nothing, as it is half a mile longer; one or other of the two must however prevail, for it is impossible to arrive at Howell's, excepting over the narrow ridge I have mentioned, if Frenchtown be the west head of the navigation.

Having arrived at Howell's, and spent a day with Mr. Howard[5] in re-examining the elevation of the summit level, which we agreed to set down as above stated, having differed only 6 inches in all our operations. I requested him to level the course of the Elk. He concluded this operation yesterday, and found the head of the upper forge to be 84 feet above the tide.

Printed Copy: Extract in Joshua Gilpin, *A Memoir on the Rise, Progress, and Present State of the Chesapeake and Delaware Canal, Accompanied with Original Documents and Maps* (Washington, D.C., 1821), Appendix, pp. 17–19 (170/A1).

1. Joshua Gilpin (1765–1841), the most knowledgeable member of the C & D board of directors (1803–24), was a Philadelphia merchant and Brandywine paper manufacturer. He made two trips (1794–1801, 1811–15) to Europe, where he observed the latest technological advances in papermaking and canal engineering. In 1804 he was elected to the American Philosophical Society. Gilpin was largely responsible for keeping the C & D canal idea alive after the company's collapse in 1806. Joseph E. Walker, ed., *Pleasure and Business in Western Pennsylvania: The Journal of Joshua Gilpin, 1809* (Harrisburg, Pa., 1975), pp. iii–iv; Biographical File, APS; Gray, "Early History of C & D," p. 242.

2. William Cooch's sawmill east of Iron Hill on the Christina River.

3. BHL's "Section of the Northern Course of the Canal from the Tide in the Elk River at Frenchtown to the forked [oak] in Mr. Rudulph's Swamp," 3–10 August 1803, is in the Geography and Map Division, Library of Congress (288/A1). On the same sheet is a large scale map from Frenchtown to the forked oak showing both the northern and southern courses for the canal. BHL's "Plot of the Ground from the forked Oak to the Summit Maple at Oliver Howell, & of the Road to the Head of the Tide in Elk River," Aug. 1803, is in the Records of the Department of State, Bureau of Archives and History, PHMC (288/A5). In the same repository are BHL's "Map of the Ground between the Summit at the Maple opposite to Oliver Howell, and at the Old School House, & Aikentown: shewing two practicable lines for the Canal," Aug. 1803 (288/B1), and four other large scale maps carrying the canal routes east of Aikentown (288/B5, 289/A1, 289/A5, 289/B1).

4. Frisby Henderson (1767–1845) was the sole proprietor of Frenchtown, which consisted of a tavern, a store, and Henderson's house. In October 1803, Henderson agreed to sell a large amount of his Frenchtown property to the C & D Company at $10 an acre if the company chose Frenchtown as the western entrance to the waterway. BHL, *Journals*,

319

3 : plate 6; Henderson, bond with C & D Canal Company, 22 Oct. 1803, 18 Apr. 1804, J. K. Kane Papers, APS.

5. Cornelius Howard (1754–1844) of Baltimore was the son of Cornelius and Ruth (Eager) Howard and the brother of Maryland Governor John Eager Howard. Dielman-Hayward File, MdHS.

FROM CHARLES WILLSON PEALE

Museum [Philadelphia] Sepr. 18. 1803.

Dear Sir

I have received your favor of the 16th. Instant and sent the Polygraph packed up in a Case directed for you at New Castle. You will find some additional improvements made to it.[1]

Fig. 11. A Peale polygraph machine, no. 57, 1806, owned by Thomas Jefferson. In the possession of the University of Virginia; photograph courtesy of the Thomas Jefferson Memorial Foundation.

Mr. Hyde had not of the Velum paper a full Ream, therefore I have sent only half a Ream, suposing you would prefer it to common Paper.[2] To know whether Gilpins paper is better than Amies, I have exchanged the uppermost half quire.[3]

I hope the alarm of fever will not continue long, the weather is now in our favor. Many Houses are already shut up, yet I believe very few persons have the fever, but as some instances prove it to be contagious, that alone is sufficient to make the timid flee to the Country.[4] I expect but little company to the Museum for 6 or 8 weeks, my only consolation for this loss, is, that consequently I shall have fewer interruptions in my labours.[5]

I am with due respect your friend

C. W. Peale

Cost of haf a ream of paper   2,00

Packing Case   <u>46</u>

Dol. 2,46/100

Polygraph Copy: Peale Letterbooks (microfiche add.). Addressed to BHL in New Castle.

1. In the summer of 1802, Englishman John Isaac Hawkins (1772–1855) invented the polygraph in Bordentown, N.J. "The polygraph was a portable writing desk, surmounted by a 'gallows' from which two or more pens were suspended. The pens were so hung as to move freely and in unison," enabling one to make legible, simultaneous copies of letters. Before he returned to England in June 1803 Hawkins made over the American rights to the machine to Peale (1741–1827), the famous portrait painter and naturalist, subject to a 10 percent royalty. BHL, who was the first purchaser of a polygraph from Peale, acknowledged receipt of his machine in a letter to Peale of 24 September 1803 (LB; 26/B1). BHL later suggested many improvements in the polygraph to Peale, and he helped Peale acquire customers for the machine, including Jefferson and George Read II of Delaware. But because of its expense and the delicacy of its mechanism, the invention never caught on. Peale to Raphaelle Peale, 9 Sept. 1803, Peale Letterbooks; Charles Coleman Sellers, *Charles Willson Peale*, 2 vols. (Philadelphia, 1947), 2:159–61; Silvio A. Bedini, *Thomas Jefferson and His Copying Machines* (Charlottesville, Va., 1984).

2. George Hyde, Philadelphia bookbinder and stationer.

3. The Gilpin paper mill was established in 1787 by Joshua Gilpin and his brother Thomas (1776–1853). Located on the Brandywine River near Wilmington, Del., the mill supplied about one thousand reams of paper yearly to Philadelphia. Harold B. Hancock and Norman B. Wilkinson, "The Gilpins and Their Endless Papermaking Machine," *PMHB* 81 (1957):391–405.

The Amies paper mill on Mill Creek, Montgomery County, Pa., was constructed some time before 1769 by the pioneer paper manufacturer Conrad Scheetz. Thomas Amies (d. 1839), a Philadelphia cordwainer and shoemaker, purchased it in 1798. Because of its watermark—a dove and branch—the Amies mill became known as "Dove Mill." Charles R. Barker, "Old Mills of Mill Creek, Lower Merion," *PMHB* 50 (1926):9–11.

4. Yellow fever reached epidemic proportions in Philadelphia in September 1803. By the time it subsided in October nearly two hundred had died. René La Roche, *Yellow Fever, Considered in Its Historical, Pathological, Etiological, and Therapeutical Relations,* 2 vols. (Philadelphia, 1855), 1 : 94–96.

5. Peale's Museum, established in Philadelphia in the 1780s, was the world's first popular museum of natural science and art. Among Peale's innovations were a successful method of taxidermy and the presentation of mounted and preserved animals before painted backgrounds of their natural surroundings. At first housed in Peale's home at Third and Lombard streets, and then in Philosophical Hall, the Museum in 1803 was in the State House (Independence Hall). Late in 1801 or early in 1802 BHL designed for Peale a museum building (never executed) to extend from Fifth Street to Sixth Street on the southern (Walnut Street) side of State House Yard. Charles Coleman Sellers, *Mr. Peale's Museum: Charles Willson Peale and the First Popular Museum of Natural Science and Art* (New York, 1980).

TO SAMUEL MIFFLIN

Newcastle Septr. 24th. 1803

My dear Sir[1]

I am utterly at a loss to account for the total Silence of yourself and of all my Philadelphia friends. An answer to two very pressing letters on the subject of Sheetiron for the federal City would have saved me many very uneasy hours had it even been of the most unfavorable nature; for it would have induced me to endeavor to cover the public buildings in some other manner, either as a temporary defence against the weather or as a permanent roof. I have on my return today to Newcastle received a letter from the President U.S. in which, waving expostulations, which he finds ineffectual he throws himself on my *honor,* and *regard* for him personally. Pray my dear friend, let me know what prospect you have of procuring slabs, whether I may expect *any* sheet iron this fall, and generally how things are going on.[2] Perhaps I had better buy up the English Iron which is in the Market, than disappoint the public. If I do not hear from you on Monday I shall send up an express. Forgive the urgency of this letter and believe very affectionately Yours faithfully

B. Henry Latrobe

Mrs. Latrobe is ready to strike you from the list of her friends for having been at Newcastle without calling on her.

Polygraph Copy: LB (26/A12).

1. Samuel Mifflin (1776–1829) was a Philadelphia merchant and principal partner in the rolling and slitting mill attached to the Schuylkill Engine House of the Philadelphia Waterworks. He succeeded Erick Bollmann as the mill's manager during the summer of 1803. The son of Col. Turbutt Francis and Sarah Mifflin, he subsequently assumed the name of his maternal grandfather, Samuel Mifflin (1724–81), in order to inherit his plantation, Walnut Hill. W. A. Newman Dorland, "The Second Troop Philadelphia City Cavalry," *PMHB* 54 (1930):80; Fritz Redlich, "The Philadelphia Waterworks in Relation to the Industrial Revolution in the United States," *PMHB* 69 (1945):255.

2. The rolling mill needed hammered wrought iron slabs from tilt-hammer forges in order to make sheet iron. Mifflin apparently responded to BHL's query about the supply of slabs by confirming that there was a shortage, which BHL then told Thomas Jefferson on 2 October 1803 (see below).

TO JOSHUA GILPIN

Newcastle, Septr. 24th. 1803.

My dear Sir,

I will appeal to Mrs. Gilpin herself[1] whether or no I have good cause of quarrel with you. I have written to you from Baltimore, and from Newcastle, independently of the arrangement I made with you when in Philadelphia, entreating you to send me the Maps and Fieldbooks of my survey, and have not even, as the women say, *a scrape of a pen,* in return. But a *scrape* of another sort you have furnished to me. I spent the whole of yesterday in resurveying a line, surveyed before, in order to ascertain two levels, which I could have known on mere inspection of my field-book had I possessed it; and lost my dinner into the bargain, not to mention a cold I have caught, sufficient to qualify me for a Bass singer in a Presbyterian meeting. Had Mr. Gale presided at the last Committee of survey, I know not what further scrape I should have been in.[2]

But of what use is all this. I fear that after all I cannot quarrel with you, and I am sure you will not quarrel with me. And independently of our peaceable dispositions, the possibility of your being ill, or worried by the circumstances of the city during the existence of the fever, or absent at your Paper Mill, keeps me quiet, though anxious. Lest any one of these possibilities should occur, I shall, if I do not hear from you by Monday's post, I shall send one of my pupils express to Philadelphia on Tuesday, and should you not have had a convenient opportunity of dispatching the parcel sooner, pray let it be ready for him at Your house Tuesday evening.

I shall ready to go to Back Creek about Thursday next. Today I spent in sounding off Redhook thence to Newcastle. Monday I go along the line to Peaches fishery or Mendenhall's. Tuesday and Wednesday I shall employ on a Northern course to Newcastle.

With best respects to Mrs. Gilpin believe me very truly Your faithfull hble. Servt.

B. Henry Latrobe

P.S. I believe the paper I am writing is of your manufactory. I had it of Geo. Hyde. It is very excellent.

Polygraph Copy: LB (26/A13).

1. Mary (Dilworth) Gilpin, the daughter of a Lancashire banker, met Gilpin on his first tour of Europe. They married in 1800 and came to the United States after the birth of their son Henry in England the following year. The match provided Gilpin with "a handsome fortune" and eventually a large family, eight children in all, several of whom became prominent in their own right. Gilpin genealogical charts, Historical Society of Pennsylvania, Philadelphia; Harold B. Hancock and Norman B. Wilkinson, "The Gilpins and Their Endless Papermaking Machine," *PMHB* 81 (1957):392; Joseph E. Walker, ed., *Pleasure and Business in Western Pennsylvania: The Journal of Joshua Gilpin, 1809* (Harrisburg, Pa., 1975), p. iv.

2. George Gale (1756–1815), Cecil County planter, was a C & D director. A Revolutionary War veteran, Gale had been a member of the Maryland ratification convention of 1788 (in which he voted for the Constitution) and served in the first U.S. Congress (1789–91). In 1791 President Washington appointed him supervisor of distilled liquors for the district of Maryland. As chairman of the C & D board's Committee of Survey, Gale proved a continual antagonist of BHL.

TO JOHN LENTHALL

Newcastle, Septr. 26th. 1803.

My dear Sir

Nothing could be more fortunate than that you should have been provoked *"to pull all the hair off of your head,"* by my letter,[1] at the very moment in which it was filled with the lime dusted into it by the herculean operations you describe: for Lime has a wonderfull effect in making hair come easily from the hide. And as a bald pate contributes to a man's reputation for wisdom you could not perhaps have done a better thing.

To be serious however, I am sorry that my opinion of the fitness of the Lobby flues to receive the Stove pipes that have evidently been inserted into them led me to alter my original plan of getting away the smoke of the furnaces: You have done well in adhering to it as far as respects the South flue. Indeed such is my opinion of your sound *common sense,* a principle upon [which] I wish all my works to be conducted, that I am always pleased when you, *on* the spot, and with all the facilities and difficulties of a case before your eyes, of which I perhaps know nothing undertake to judge and act for yourself. I know not indeed how it is possible to give right directions at a distance in respect to a work in which every rational law of taste and construction has been violated; and in which new blunders, and of the most improbable kind, are sure to be discovered whenever a fresh part of the work is probed. I will now endeavor to answer your letter in the order into which you have put your enquiries.

1.) It appears to me, that whatever difficulty may attend the North Lobby flue, it can't be greater than that of carrying the new flue through the forest in the roof, or worse than the risk of adding to the leaks which already are so numerous. The greater objection to this route is that the flue is only nine inches as you inform me. It will be absolutely necessary to make the iron pipe only of nine inches diameter instead of 10 or a foot, as I could have wished otherwise it will draw very sluggishly and produce but little heat. It is after much consideration, my full intention to take off the whole roof of the North wing, and to put on one of the Presidents zigzag roofs of sheetiron, which certainly are a species of roof uniting all the good qualities of the pantile, without its bad ones. To do this it is essential that our Gutters should not be obstructed by new Chimnies, or new turns round old ones. Unless therefore you meet with

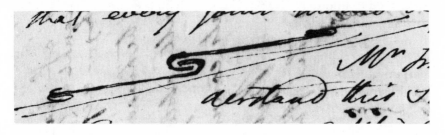

Fig. 12. Sketch of a section of proposed sheet iron roof, from BHL to Samuel Mifflin, 10 October 1803, LB.

insuperable difficulties in using the North lobby flue, you had perhaps better persist in clearing it. It is difficult on these occasions to refrain from feeling some bitterer than common indignation at the fools who contrived and executed the Work. In the course of a week or 10 days it will be time enough for me to have the angles of the knees of the flues. I will in the mean while get the straight part put together.

2.) The present situation of Philadelphia,[2] renders it difficult for me to get things done there as formerly, and I shall get the grates cast at Baltimore from which place you will also receive 5 Boxes of Glass for the Presidents house, which I have sent round by Newcastle and French-town, no opportunity to Alexandria being now likely to occur. A new foundery is established in that city, and I have already taken measures to get our work done there.

3.*)[3] There should be a simple washboard in both Mr. Stuart's rooms.[4] You may look into your tool Chest for the design. It is I think 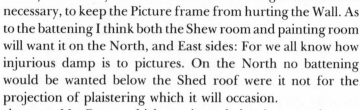 necessary, to keep the Picture frame from hurting the Wall. As to the battening I think both the Shew room and painting room will want it on the North, and East sides: For we all know how injurious damp is to pictures. On the North no battening would be wanted below the Shed roof were it not for the projection of plaistering which it will occasion.

3. My letter to Mr. Brent, which was intended to increase the motion of his workings, has had a contrary effect like a dose intended as a cathartic, which operates only emetically. I shall certainly not confine my threat to the dead letter, but take serious steps to get the public quarry into activity.[5] It is absolutely necessary that I should be here on the 8th of Octr.,[6] but on the 10th or 11th I will set off for Washington, and remain untill after the opening of the Session during which time I will make myself perfectly Master of the Quarry subject. 4.) I am much chagrined to find that Blagden is not likely to keep on his hands. What are they to do in the present state of 3 of our principal cities?[7] 5.) The hot Air holes need not be larger than 4 inches diameter. A cast Iron plate with a Register closes them. These I will have cast and filled up. Let me know their number. 6.) I am at Newcastle and perfectly well, as is my whole family. I Sincerely hope you, your wife daughter and grey Gelding be the same. Yrs. affy.

B. H. Latrobe

ALS: BHL Papers, Library of Congress (170/B10). Addressed to Lenthall in Washington.

 1. BHL to Lenthall, 15 Sept. 1803, BHL Papers, Library of Congress (170/B1).

2. The yellow fever epidemic.

3. This number, which does not appear on the polygraph copy of this letter (LB; 26/B2), was evidently added later, the asterisk intended to distinguish it from paragraph 3, below.

4. When Gilbert Stuart moved from Philadelphia to Washington in late 1803 he rented a studio that BHL had built for the artist's use on property leased by BHL (lot 15 in square 491, fronting C Street, just above Pennsylvania Avenue between 4 1/2 Street and Sixth Street, N.W., which BHL purchased in 1812). On 12 March 1805, several months before Stuart moved to Boston, BHL wrote to John Vaughan, a mutual friend, of Stuart's distressing circumstances: "He is miserably off, though his life and his residence . . . are of his own choice. . . . He has shut himself up in a little building never intended for an habitation but only for a painting room; where he boards himself, *after a fashion*, with the assistance of his Manservant, when he can get him to the place, and where he sleeps." BHL to Vaughan, 12 Mar. 1805, in BHL, *Correspondence*, 2; BHL to Lenthall, 13 Dec. 1803, BHL Papers, Library of Congress (170/G1); BHL to William Duncanson, 13 Sept. 1804, and BHL to John P. Van Ness, 13 Sept. 1804, 14 Sept. 1811, all in LB (35/C4, 35/C3, 90/C12); Caleb Boyle, advertisement in *National Intelligencer*, 8 Apr. 1808; Deed of Van Ness to BHL, 16 Jan. 1812, Liber AD, no. 29, p. 44, Register of Deeds, Washington, D.C.

5. In 1791, the federal government purchased for $6,000 an island in Aquia Creek in Virginia "on account of the freestone quarries therein." The government operated the quarries between 1792 and 1795, after which it relied on private quarries, a policy BHL continued. *ASP. Miscellaneous*, 1 : 245–46, 2 : 295.

6. For a meeting of the C & D board's Committee of Survey. See BHL to Gilpin, 10 Oct. 1803, n. 1, below.

7. In addition to Philadelphia, New York and Alexandria, Va., experienced yellow fever epidemics in the summer of 1803. René La Roche, *Yellow Fever, Considered in Its Historical, Pathological, Etiological, and Therapeutical Relations*, 2 vols. (Philadelphia, 1855), 1 : 94.

TO SAMUEL MIFFLIN

Newcastle, Octr. 2d. 1803.

Be assured, my dear Sir, that I never received your letter of the 21st. Septr. of which you have sent me a copy. This is the more unfortunate, as I have now lost above 10 days, in the business of casting the Stoves the drawings for which I will send to you this week.[1] However, the information you have now given me is too pleasant to permit me to say another word by way of regret on the subject, and I have only to thank you for your kind and immediate attention to my last.[2] I have but little time at present but I will endeavor to answer all the points in the 3 letters now before me.

1.) As one half of the steam apparatus is cast, it would be oeconomy to finish it, and I will pay for it, in the state in which it may be left, after using all the patterns [which] have been made or begun, otherwise they will shrink, and crack, and require repairs before they are used. The   327 apparatus will be wanted for the House of representatives when ever it shall be finished. Whenever I send the drawings of the stove I will give the information which may be required with them.

2.) I will by the next Post write to the Secretary of the Navy respecting Mr. Harrison's Iron, and shall no doubt obtain permission to *pick* it, on this plain principle that the United States cannot lose more by it than in its present perfectly useless state.[3]

3.) As to Mr. Jefferson's Iron,[4] in your's of the 21st. Septr. you seem to consider the prospect of obtaining it as perfectly desperate; but in your last you say that you have rolled some 1 f. 6 i. Iron for him *"about sufficient to compleat his order."* Let me now beg of you to get this iron immediately bent and jointed into the proper lengths, so as to go to Richmond by the very first opportunity. Should you find it impossible to procure a Vessel, it had better be sent by the Newcastle and Frenchtown line to Baltimore, or even to Norfolk to a safe and active correspondent who will forward it by some of the coal Vessels that are constantly plying between those places and Richmond. The quantity difficient is exactly equal to that sent. Mr. Shoemaker knows to what address in Richmond to consign it.[5] I shall write tonight to the President, telling him that his Iron is *now all rolled,* and will be sent on by the very first opportunity.[6] If you send the Iron to Baltimore, Hazlehurst Brothers & Co.[7] will be very attentive to have it sent on to Richmond.

4.) The Sheet Iron 14 or 15 inches wide must be painted, packed and sent on with a suffic[i]ent quantity of thin hoops, and screws; and also with several Cwt. of Oakum, a substance I mean in future to use under the hoops in stead of Putty.[8] Smallman understands all about this kind of Roof, and if attentive will soon get a large quantity ready to be dispatched. This Iron is to be sent to Washington, if possible by an Alexandria or Georgetown Vessel, but if the intercourse by that means is broken up, then by way of Baltimore, addressed to Thos. Munroe Esqr. Superintendant of the City of Washington.

Your letter has furnished me with materials for handsome apologies to my friends, to whom I must still write tonight. Accept my best thanks for your attention to my requests, and believe me very affecty. Yours

B. Henry Latrobe

Mrs. Latrobe begs to be kindly remembered to Mrs. Mifflin.[9] We know that you had not a moment to spare when last here, and readily excuse your not calling. Coals at Richmond 20 Cents per Bushel, I hear.

Polygraph Copy: LB (26/B10).

1. This refers to the cast iron stoves for the Senate Chamber of the Capitol, the drawings of which BHL did not send until 27 October 1803. See BHL to Mifflin, 27 Oct. 1803, with enclosure, below.

2. BHL to Mifflin, 28 Sept. 1803, LB (26/B6).

3. Navy Secretary Robert Smith later told BHL that the iron in the charge of Philadelphia navy agent George Harrison would be used at the Washington Navy Yard. Smith to BHL, 1 Dec. 1803, RG 45, National Archives (170/F14).

4. The sheet iron Jefferson ordered for his home, Monticello, from the rolling mill attached to the Philadelphia Waterworks.

5. Probably Thomas Shoemaker, Philadelphia iron merchant.

6. See following document.

7. BHL's brothers-in-law, Andrew and Isaac Hazlehurst, Jr., Baltimore merchants.

8. Sheet iron was commonly rolled in 14 inch widths during this period. Presumably the hoops, screws, and oakum ordered by BHL were used to join the sheets, but their purpose is not clear. Americans used two methods of joining sheets, standing seam and flat seam, which BHL later discussed with Jefferson. BHL to Mifflin, 2 Nov., 9 Nov. 1804, both in LB (35/G2, 36/A1); BHL to Jefferson, 9 Nov. 1804, below; Diana S. Waite, "Roofing for Early America," in Charles E. Peterson, ed., *Building Early America* (Radnor, Pa., 1976), p. 141.

9. Elizabeth (Davis) Mifflin, who married Samuel Mifflin on 21 March 1800. *PMHB* 54 (1930):80.

TO THOMAS JEFFERSON

Newcastle, Octr. 2d. 1803

Dear Sir,

I have delayed to answer your favor of the 14th. September for a few days, untill I had compleatly ascertained whether by any exertion it would be possible to procure sheet Iron sufficient to cover the public buildings and to make up the deficiency for Monticello this Autumn, and I have now the satisfaction to inform you, that all your Iron is rolled and will be sent off by the first opportunity, and that two or three Tons intended for the President's house at Washington are also ready and will be dispatched by the earliest Vessel. The fever at present raging both at Philadelphia and Alexandria renders it however doubtful when an opportunity directly to Georgetown may occur. It is my intention, that should it appear probable that considerable delay will be occasioned by waiting for a vessel, the Iron shall be sent to Baltimore, and from thence by Land, as the Iron will be sufficient to load two or three Waggons, and the expence of Transportation will not, I find on enquiry, be increased more than 8 or 10 Dollars per Ton, or about 5 per Cent on the value of the Iron.

By a letter written to you from Washington I endeavored to inform you of the exact state of the work at the Capitol, and of the difficulty of procuring stone, which has from the commencement most materially retarded the work. As I shall have the honor of seeing you at Washington in the course of next Week, I will not take up your time at present further than to say that the stoves and flues for heating the Senate Chamber will be forwarded from Philadelphia in the course of this month, and that the fever having driven away our best Coppersmith, I have ordered the pipes for the Water closet at the President's house, at Baltimore, where, by this time, they must be ready to be sent on.

The universal drought of this summer has silenced many of the best Pensylvanian forges, at least during many hours out of twenty four.[1] I must beg that you will admit this apology for the delay in forwarding the Sheet iron, to procure which, at last, has required no small degree of exertion.

I write this letter with Mr. Peale's polygraph, a machine the most useful that has, I believe, as yet been invented for the purpose of copying letters. I am not yet entirely Master of its motion so as to write exactly the same hand, which a single pen produces; but in an hour's practice I learned to write with the same ease and rapidity as with the common pen. I doubt not but that you have heard of the machine, and perhaps you possess one of them. What I have written on the other side is a specimen of the truth with which the copy is made.[2]

The young Gentleman whom you did me the favor to recommend to me has now been in my office upwards of two months.[3] He possesses that valuable substitute for Genius, laborious precision, in a very high degree; and is therefore very useful to me, though his professional education has been hitherto much misdirected. His personal character and habits are very singular. He is an enthusiastic methodist, devoting many hours of the evening and morning to prayer and singing of psalms, and though a temper violently choleric appears through the viel of religious mildness, he has himself so perfectly under command, as never to have exhibited any visible anger, though the provocations to it by the motley crew of my people have been sometimes beyond the common bounds of human patience. I think he will become a very useful citizen, though never a very amiable Man.[4]

Believe me with the truest respect and attachment Your faithful hble. Servt.

B. Henry Latrobe

ALS: Jefferson Papers (170/C1). Endorsed as received 6 October.

1. The summer of 1803, which followed an unusually cool spring (ice as late as 7 May), witnessed little rain, temperatures in the 80s and 90s, and "oppressive calms, or . . . humid and sultry winds of the south." Charles Caldwell, *An Essay on the Pestilential or Yellow Fever as it Prevailed in Philadelphia in the Year 1805* (Philadelphia, n.d.), p. 17, quoted in René La Roche, *Yellow Fever Considered in its Historical, Pathological, Etiological, and Therapeutical Relations*, 2 vols. (Philadelphia, 1855), 1 : 94–95.

2. BHL wrote the following paragraph and the close without the use of the polygraph machine; they are therefore not present on the retained copy of this letter in the Letterbooks.

3. Robert Mills (1781–1855), the famous nineteenth-century architect, was a native of South Carolina. He studied architecture with James Hoban and with Thomas Jefferson at Monticello before becoming BHL's pupil by July 1803.

4. Mills worked in BHL's office until December 1805, when he returned to South Carolina to superintend the construction of two churches of his own design. At that time BHL reassessed Mills's temperament and abilities: "He is a young Man of real worth and not despicable talents, and has improved in his profession exceedingly. . . . His religious turn seems to have made him a *builder of churches,* and the designs he has made, prove that he is capable of excelling most of those who have employed themselves in this particular branch of design in this country. I hope his success will be equal to his merit, and to his modesty which is a very amiable trait in his character." When prospects for commissions in South Carolina dried up, Mills returned to Philadelphia and to BHL's employ in 1806, where he continued until he established his independent practice in 1808. BHL to Robert Hazlehurst, 2 Dec. 1805, LB (46/C4).

FROM CHARLES WILLSON PEALE

Museum [Philadelphia] Octr. 3d. 1803.

Dear Sir

On saturday I left a publication on the Polygraphs at Mr. Paulsons, which you may see in this days paper.[1] Passing then by the Post office I found your agreable letter of the 21st. ult. The omission of carrying Letters to the Citizens, with those who do not send, or go themselves daily will subject them to a suspicion of neglects.

I am glad to see your approbation of the Polygraph after a tryal of it. It is a good beginning.

Your recommendation to finish one for George Read Esqr. I have attended to.[2] My workmen are making the necessary appendages to one of 3 pens which I have made tryal off, and found good. When I send it I shall also send you a small additional convenienty to be attached to yours.[3]

If you see Mr. Read (if it is not disagreable to you) acquaint him with   331 the Law I have made respecting payments.[4] No good man I am sure will find fault with me on that score, and I do not wish bad men to have one of my Machines.

I have received Letters from my Sons, they have left London, exhibited the Skeleton at Reading with tolerable success, from thence they intend to go to Bristol—and as nothing but War talked off in England, it is probable they will soon return to happy America, as Rembrandt calls his Country. Very likely we shall see them this fall.[5]

I am Dear Sir with much respect your friend

C. W. Peale

Polygraph Copy: Peale Letterbooks (microfiche add.). Addressed to BHL in Wilmington.

1. Zachariah Poulson (1761–1844) was a Philadelphia publisher and philanthropist. The son of a Danish father and a German mother whose families had come to America before the Revolution, Poulson learned the printing trade at a time when the Philadelphia press was engaged in the controversy with Britain over the rights of the colonies. In 1785 he became librarian of the Library Company of Philadelphia, a position he held for twenty-one years. In 1800 he purchased *Claypoole's American Daily Advertiser,* changed its name to *Poulson's American Daily Advertiser,* and continued as its editor and publisher until 1839.

Peale's advertisement offered polygraphs with two pens for $50 and those with three pens for $60, payable in advance before delivery. Peale claimed that his machine, an improved version of the one patented by John Isaac Hawkins, was "capable of being understood, and used, by any person on the first sight of it." *Poulson's American Daily Advertiser* (Philadelphia), 3 Oct. 1803.

2. George Read II (1765–1836) was the son of George Read, a signer of the Declaration of Independence. A native of New Castle and a noted jurist, the younger Read served as U.S. district attorney for Delaware from 1790 to about 1820. He served in the Delaware General Assembly from 1811 to 1813, and after 1790 owned a cotton plantation in Mississippi. Read was appointed one of the commissioners to survey New Castle in 1797. When BHL lived in New Castle (1803–04), he rented office space in Read's old house. BHL to Gilpin, 15 Nov. 1803, below; Linda Grant De Pauw, ed., *Senate Executive Journal and Related Documents* (Baltimore, 1974), p. 490; Delaware Federal Writers' Project, *New Castle on the Delaware,* 3d ed. (New Castle, Del., 1950), pp. 42, 96.

3. The "convenienty" was a lamp for using the polygraph by night. Peale to BHL, 12 Oct. 1803, Peale Letterbooks (microfiche add.).

4. In the advertisement cited in n. 1, Peale declared: "As I cannot spare the necessary time for keeping accounts, . . . in every instance I do exact payment from the Purchaser before delivery."

5. In the late summer of 1801 Peale successfully recovered two skeletons of the mammoth, or mastodon, near Newburgh, N.Y. (BHL had attended the special meeting of 24 July 1801 when the American Philosophical Society voted to assist Peale in the exhumation.) The widespread interest in the discovery among naturalists led Peale to send one skeleton to Europe in the charge of his son Rembrandt (1778–1860), who was assisted by his younger brother Rubens (1784–1865), then in training as a naturalist. The Peale brothers arrived in England in the summer of 1802 and returned to America in November 1803. While in London Rembrandt published his *Account of the Skeleton of the Mammoth*

(London, 1802) and *An Historical Disquisition on the Mammoth* (London, 1803). The skeletons are now in the American Museum of Natural History, New York City, and the Hessisches Landesmuseum, Darmstadt, West Germany. Charles Coleman Sellers, *Mr. Peale's Museum: Charles Willson Peale and the First Popular Museum of Natural Science and Art* (New York, 1980), chap. 5; *William Rush, American Sculptor* (Philadelphia, 1982), pp. 105–06.

TO JOSHUA GILPIN

Newcastle, Octr. 10th 1803.

My dear Sir

There is a passage in your last letter which I misunderstood, and which has prevented my writing to you for some time, as I daily expected to see you here. But as you did not arrive at the meeting of the Committee on Saturday last (8th)[1] I again looked at your letter, and cannot find the passage I supposed to contain the ground of my expectations. Therefore I must believe that "hope told a flattering tale," in order to disappoint *me,* and *you* too of the information I should otherwise have given you from time to time. I will endeavor to make up the deficiency, at present, though concisely.

In my last I believe I informed you that Mr. Howard had altogether declined any further Duty, and that his resignation was accepted by the last Committee, at which Mr. Gale did not attend.[2] Since then I have been engaged in the following operations:

1.) That part of the line of Canal reaching from the Summit Maple to Aikintown, and from Aikintown towards the Bear, though ascertained to be practicable required much detailed examination and as it includes all the *difficult* ground we have to go over, I determined to explore it thoroughly. This I have in a great measure accomplished though not as perfectly as I still intend it shall be done: and I find that it will probably be possible to carry the Canal over as good Ground as can be wished so as to have several, at least three reaches of two Miles each without a turn.

2. I have labored the ground from the Bear towards Newcastle exceedingly: It is on many accounts difficult, and I fear that the best and shortest line that can be effected will exceed the distance in a strait line at least one mile. There must also be of necessity one considerable Aqueduct in this part of the Work, in order to cross Read's Valley about one

333

mile from Newcastle. Otherwise nothing will be more perfect than this line of Canal if executed. As to the Embouchure of the work at the Delaware, nature has done every[thing] that Art could wish. There is a natural Basin South of the town capable of holding thirty or forty of the largest Vessels which will navigate the Canal from which two locks will discharge them into 15 feet of Water at low Water.

3.) I have surveyed a line, and a tolerably good one, to Christiana creek; but as the Creek itself is none of my making, I cannot answer for any thing below the mouth of the Canal. Having plotted Mr. Thompson's survey of the creek from its Mouth to Christiana bridge, in my office, and Mr. Thompson, (who, by the bye is, a very clever fellow, though as unpromising in his looks as the Creek about which he has been employed) having attended me during several days.[3] As Land surveyor, I have acquired a very considerable stock of information on the subject of the Christiana Navigation—more indeed than I dare venture at present to speak too loudly.

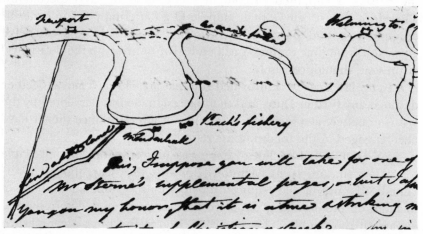

This, I suppose you will take for one of Mr. Sterne's supplemental pages, but I assure you, on my honor, that it is a true and striking miniature portrait of Christiana Creek.[4] The instruction of the Committee of survey was to find a line to Peaches fishery.[5] Mr. Howard levelled a course thither 8 miles and 6 furlongs in length from the Bear. It was however over Ground entirely impracticable. He also levelled a line to Me[n]denhall, the length of which exceeded six miles. But as neither of these lines were over practicable ground, but consisted of 3 or 4 straight courses, one of which was 2 miles in one stretch over every possible variety of surface I deviated from both, and after exploring the country between the Bear road and the Creek in a variety of directions I struck upon a line falling into the Creek above Mendenhall, the length of which from the Bear will not extend quite to six miles. It is also in my opinion the only eligible line that the country admits; and should the place at which it touches the Creek be objected to, it may be carried at a moderate expense along the marshes as far as is necessary to reach a better place. But at all [e]vents, if the Canal is to enter the Creek to the Westward of that abominable, or rather *diabolical* reach called *No man's friend* (for the Devil is by prescription, the only enemy of mankind in his own right) the point at which I propose to enter is at least as good as either Mendenhall's or Peach's.

The President of the Company[6] accompanied me during two days of this survey, much to my annoyance, for he had already discovered the best track for the Canal, and both in politeness and respect to his age and office and in duty I carried the level wherever he pointed out. But as the appearance of the ground had entirely deceived him, and the greatest part of his line lay in natural hollows, entering at the lower end and proceeding to their highest parts, it was necessary to deviate entirely and seek different Ground.

This line to Christiana Creek is not however without its difficulties which nothing but a heavy expence can overcome. For instance: the Newport road must be turned under an aqueduct erected upon the land of Vincent Gilpin,[7] or perhaps over a hollow on Geo. Read's farm. These are the only two situations that offer a passage to the road under the Canal, and neither of them can be made as good as they ought to be without great expence.

As I write to you without the smallest reserve and rather as to a private friend than a Director and Member of the Committee of Survey, I will make a few further remarks with which, as Engineer I have properly nothing to do. Mr. Tatnall has shewn less discretion, *lately*, than formerly in exhibiting his determination to effect if possible the junction of the Canal with Christiana creek. The objections to this junction appear the more glaring, the more the real state of the creek navigation is inquired into, and Mr. Tatnall is well apprised of them. In the first place he admits that the work must be a half tide navigation if carried into Christa. Creek, he admits the probability of the water decreasing annually in depth, the delay often arising from unfavorable winds in its crooked channel, the difficulty of navigation at all times: but he insists   335 that all these considerations are counterbalanced by the safety afforded by the creek to Vessels *against the ice in winter* (when by the bye the Canal and creek are both shut up) *and against privateers coming into the Delaware in time of War.* How far these are his real motives I leave you to judge from the following. If you observe the situation of Newport in the sketch I have drawn, it will appear evident, that if the canal were carried to Newport its length would not be much encreased, and that if then the neck as dotted were cut through; (a cut of about 1/4 of a mile through Marsh) the Navigation would be so straitened, as to remove the greatest objection to the Navigation of the Creek. But so great was his alarm on the mere mention of such a scheme in private conversation, and so intemperate his opposition to the idea of proposing the survey to the committee, that I thought it would be by far most consistent with discretion, to be silent on the subject. Could the probability of advantage to New port at the expense of Wilmington excite this opposition to a scheme certainly the most rational of any that has been proposed for Christiana creek?

I proposed to be concise, and yet I have filled two Sheets. I am anxious to know when I can see you. Not this fortnight I fear, and yet I should like to have a day with you before the next Committee which meets on the monday before the meeting of the Directors, at 11 o'clock at O Flinn's, Wilmington.[8]

By the carelessness of one of my Clerks, in a windy day I have lost one of my instruments. There is a Telescopic Level at Bigg's, instrument Maker front street, with a Circumferentor affixed to it for which he asks 60 Dollars.[9] It is the only instrument fit for the purpose which is to be had in Philadelphia, perhaps in the U. States, and the Company ought to buy it. That which I am now obliged to use cost me 150 Guineas, being a good Transit Instrument, an excellent Theodolite, and having a first rate Telescope. It was made for me by Ramsden, and I ought not to hazard it in doing the rough business of the Company.[10] Let me beg of you to purchase for me the Instrument at Biggs. If you think that the Company will not buy it, I will return you the money by post as soon as I get it, and the sooner, the more shall I be obliged.

I will write again soon. In the mean time believe me very faithfully and affecty. Yours

B. Henry Latrobe

P.S. I forgot to tell you that I have laid down a line, the easiest imaginable from Port Penn halfway to Back Creek, and shall compleat it next Week. But whence the supply of Water?

Polygraph Copy: LB (26/C7).

1. At the C & D board's Committee of Survey meeting in New Castle on 8 October 1803, BHL made a verbal report and presented drafts of several of the canal routes he surveyed. C & D Survey Committee Minutes.

2. BHL failed to mention Howard's resignation in his previous letter to Gilpin (24 Sept. 1803, above). Howard requested to be discharged of his duties and the survey committee agreed at its meeting of 19 September 1803 at Christiana Bridge. C & D Survey Committee Minutes.

3. The survey committee appointed John Thomson on 26 July 1803 to survey the Christina River ("Christiana Creek") from Wilmington to Christiana Bridge and to make a draft of it at seven dollars a day. On 19 September the committee authorized BHL to hire Thomson as an assistant "if he thinks it necessary." Thomson was the father of J. Edgar Thomson (1809–74), the engineer and president of the Pennsylvania Railroad. C & D Survey Committee Minutes; BHL, *Engineering Drawings,* p. 12.

4. This is probably a reference to an illustration in the ninth and last volume of Laurence Sterne's *Tristram Shandy* (1760–67). The illustration, a diagonal squiggle somewhat resembling BHL's sketch here, represents the flourish Corporal Trim made with his walking stick.

5. The instruction was given BHL and Howard at the 19 August 1803 meeting of the committee at Christiana Bridge. C & D Survey Committee Minutes.

6. Joseph Tatnall (1740–1813), Wilmington miller and merchant and first president of the C & D Canal Company, was also president of the Bank of Delaware. He and his son-in-law Thomas Lea were partners in a mill they operated on Brandywine Creek. BHL, *Journals,* 3 : 36n.

7. Vincent Gilpin (1732–1810), Revolutionary War veteran and miller, lived near Wilmington. Alfred R. Justice, comp., "Gilpin Family in England and in America," Collections of the Genealogical Society of Pennsylvania, Historical Society of Pennsylvania, Philadelphia.

8. The survey committee met in Wilmington on Tuesday and Wednesday, 25–26 October 1803. C & D Survey Committee Minutes.

9. Thomas Biggs (d. post-1821) was a mathematical instrument maker in Philadelphia. He served an apprenticeship with Benjamin Condy (d. 1798) in Philadelphia and then served for five years during the American Revolution. After the war he moved to New York and worked there for eight years, but he returned to his native Philadelphia upon Condy's retirement in 1792 to take over his business. *PMHB* 51 (1927):301–02; Silvio A. Bedini, *Early American Scientific Instruments and Their Makers* (Washington, D.C., 1964), p. 59.

10. Jesse Ramsden (1735–1800) was the premier scientific instrument maker in Britain during BHL's years there.

TO JAMES TRAQUAIR

Newcastle, Octr. 10th. 1803

My dear Sir

There is a subject upon which I have for a long time been extremely anxious, the monument now in your Yard, intended for the grave of my little daughter.[1] My friend Adam promised to see it put up at Mount holly, but the neglect of Mr. Trump to make the necessary packing cases, and when I was last in Philadelphia, and the cases were made, the absence of Adam with his mother at Lewistown prevented any thing being done.[2] As I do not know whether your Son may yet be returned, I beg leave to trouble you on this subject, and to beg that you will be so good as to attend to it, so that the monument may be put up before the setting in of the frost, for it is now more than two Years since the occasion of it occurred, and I am very unwilling on account of my own feelings, as well as those of the family that another winter should pass over without its being erected.

You will therefore confer a particular favor upon me, by getting the monument put into the cases made by Mr. Trump. If you will call on Mr. Saml. Hazlehurst, Arch near Sixth street, he will let you know when the Mount Holly boat leaves town, and provide for it being carried to the spot on its arrival there.

As to its erection, I wish a square hole to be dug not much larger than the base block of the tomb, and about 1 f. 6 i. deep. This hole must be filled with Rubble stone of which Mr. Hazlehurst has a great quantity and of which I shall take care that a supply be brought to the church Yard. The stone must be filled in dry with Sand and Water, and being levelled of to the natural Surface, the monument must be set with as close joints as possible. I believe that no clamps will be wanted, but a few dowels would be highly necessary to prevent the shifting of the blocks by the frost or violence.

By attending to this request you will oblige me beyond what I can express. I sincerely hope that the occasion of your son's absence from town has been compleatly removed, and that Mrs. Traquair is perfectly restord to that health which she so richly deserves by her indefatigable attention as a wife, a mother and a friend to the health and comfort of others.

338 I hope the quarries are in a good situation, for I shall, I hope in the

Fig. 13. Juliana Latrobe's tombstone, Mt. Holly, N.J., designed by BHL, 1801. Photograph by Stephen F. Lintner.

course of the winter, transmit to you a large order for the hollow Quoins of our locks. The principal blocks will consist of pieces about 1 f. 8 i. square and nine or ten feet long.

    How have you come off with our friends Reed and Forde, whom, may God of his infinite mercy, convert into honest men before they die.   339

Should this happen, it will render the idea that miracles have ceased, entirely erroneous. truly Yrs.

B. Henry Latrobe

Polygraph Copy: LB (26/D3). Addressed to Traquair in Philadelphia.

1. BHL's daughter Juliana was born on 29 June and died on 11 August 1801, apparently "by the carelessness of a drunken nurse." She was buried at St. Andrew's Episcopal Church, Mt. Holly, N.J. Christian Ignatius Latrobe to John Frederick Latrobe, 14 Nov. 1802, John Henry de La Trobe Collection, Hamburg, copy in PBHL.

2. BHL employed Adam Traquair (d. 1851?), son of James Traquair, as a draftsman during the architect's residence in Philadelphia. In 1835 Traquair was appointed president of the Philadelphia City Commissioners and served in that position until 1851. Robert B. Beath, ed., *Historical Catalogue of the St. Andrew's Society of Philadelphia* (Philadelphia, 1913), p. 160.

John Trump was a Philadelphia carpenter.

TO ISAAC HAZLEHURST

Newcastle Octr. 11th. 1803.

My dear Father

Since my return from Washington, three weeks ago, I have several times attempted, and actually began to write to you. But the extreme pressure of the business in which I am engaged, and the bodily fatigue with which it is attended, have always prevented my design. For it was my wish to lay before you a general view of my affairs, which though at present of very prosperous appearance, are extremely embarrassing as far as regards my arrangements for next Winter, beyond which I am hardly able to look forward.

I most entirely assent to the opinion which you expressed to Mary, while in Philadelphia, that my respectability as a member of society and as a professional Man would be best consulted by my having a fixed and known residence; and that in some principal city of the United States. Philadelphia has also in this respect the preference, as it contains the best specimens of what talents I may possess. Besides this, it would be by far the most agreeable residence to me, being the only city in which I have many personal friends, in which I can procure whatever my taste for literature or art may require, and above all in which you and all the family reside. I have not among my inducements to live in Philadelphia enumerated my interest in the Schuylkill Works,[1] and principally for two reasons; because their management, and the emoluments arising from it are in the hands of Mr. Mifflin, where they indeed ought to be, as the concern is principally a *mercantile* concern; and again, because for a Year or two, they cannot be expected to yield a profit sufficient to maintain my family even in a *decent* stile.

Indeed my desire to take a house and open an office in Philadelphia is so sincere, that sufficient business in that city or its neighborhood to enable me to pay houserent, and the hire of one Clerk would fix me. But as it is I have absolutely nothing to do there. The erection of the Pennsylvania Insurance office is a matter by which I cannot gain Two hundred Dollars, and it is attended with many most vexatious circumstances.[2] Of other public works, even on a moderate scale, there is no prospect; and since Cramond house I have not even had a transitory application to design a private building.[3]

It is the misfortune of my profession, especially here, where it is new, that I cannot act on many occasions by proxy. At Washington I have fortunately an agent, who is more than equal to the task and the trust assigned to him, Mr. Lenthall: and on this account, I have been able to execute this work in a stile equal to the most sangine expectations of the president, by only an occasional personal attendance. But it is evident that as long as the survey for the Chesapeake and Delaware Canal is incompleat I cannot employ any one in my place; and should the execution of the Work be afterwards put into my hands, I fear that for several Months I cannot for one day be absent from a work which will be at least 15 Miles in extent, and every part of which requires the utmost attention in its commencement and first progress.

After what I have already said it would perhaps appear unnecessary to say more, as my engagement with the Chesapeake and Delaware seems to preclude any residence but near the Work. But even this engagement is by no means certain. I am at present only a day laborer. If sickness, or any other accidental cause interrupt my activity for a single day, my pay ceases for that time. Even at the present moment I have no certain prospect of pay beyond the 25th of this month when the Board of Directors meet to receive my report. The ideas of oeconomy which prevail have already obliged me to swallow many very disagreeable remarks on the expenditure of the public money, and I think it *possible*, though not very probable, that when the line shall have been staked out 341 by me, some cheap Overseer, and a dozen cheap Workmen will be employed to carry on the work upon it. Should this happen I am absolutely deprived of every resource of business excepting my engagement at Washington.

It is indeed certain that nothing could in every point of view be less prudent than my continuance in this latter appointment, were either, I obliged to give much personal attention to its duties, or were the emoluments growing out of my connexion with the government confined to the Salary of 1.700 Dollars per Annum. But as my visits to Washington have been few, and of short duration, and as it is the evident wish of the Administration to throw as much profitable business in my way as possible, I have endeavored to keep my hold of this certain though moderate income, untill I shall see clearly that I can do better without it. During my last visit to Washington, the business put into my hands by the Secretary of the Navy, amounted to near Two hundred Dollars, and I left much of it unfinished.[4]

Under all these considerations, and those still more powerfully interesting which arise from my family connexion, from the disposition of my wife and my determination, as far as common sense and prudence will justify it, to make her happy and easy in her own way, as a very small return for her thousand virtues and her unlimited affection for me and my children.

Under all these considerations, I am as much at a loss what to resolve, and to what to look forward, as if I had not the understanding or decision of a Child. The house I occupy here I have on a term of only a few Months, and I ought now to secure a further term if I mean to have a home here. But untill the Directors have finally determined my situation in the execution of the Work I dare not attempt it. At Washington I could hire a genteel house for 3 or 400 Dollars per Annum but am equally at a loss on that score. At Philadelphia whither my inclination and my interests perhaps so strongly draw me, I see not even the prospect of gaining one hundred Dollars by my utmost industry. In this situation I am at present, and no one was ever more open to receive and to follow advise than I am.

I am not without the hope, as soon as the city shall be considered as safe, of paying a short visit to Philadelphia. In the mean time I must once more go to Washington, and mean to set off tomorrow, to return in a Week.

I do not recollect ever to have enjoyed a more vigorous and uninterrupted state of health than during my residence here. Indeed we have all been well, excepting our little John, who has had the slight complaints attendant on teething. Mary has, no doubt informed you that on the 4th of Octr. he cut his first and daily expects his second tooth.

With most affectionate respects to our Mother and to Robert I am Your affectionate son

B. H. Latrobe

I have written a letter to Samuel which he will no doubt communicate to you.[5]

Polygraph Copy: LB (26/D6).

1. The rolling and slitting mill attached to the Schuylkill Engine House of the Philadelphia Waterworks.

2. By June 1803 the Insurance Company of the State of Pennsylvania had arranged the purchase of a lot on which to build their office at the northwest corner of Second and Dock streets. BHL designed their new quarters in November, intending to charge $150 for his services, which included the resolution of certain difficulties involving the neighboring properties. Ultimately he received $100 or $110, representing only about 1 percent of the total cost of the work.

By June 1804 the building was complete and was described as fireproof, although its cellars were plaintively reported as insufficiently waterproof. Inside, certain walls were painted by George Bridport. The Insurance Company sold the building in 1844, and it later became Dock Hall Clothing Store. A photograph of about 1859 shows a building of five stories with white (presumably marble) lintels and sills, and although relatively tall, it was fairly standard in appearance. The building was apparently shortened by two stories in the late 1920s or the early 1930s, if not entirely rebuilt, and the site cleared about 1959. BHL to John Clement Stocker, 6 Nov., 11 Nov. 1803, and BHL to Joseph Norris, 6 June 1809, all in LB (27/B7, 27/C1, 69/C14); Philadelphia Deed Records, book EF 16 : 216, RLL 17 : 212, Philadelphia City Hall; Insurance Company of the State of Pennsylvania to President and Managers of the Board of Health, Philadelphia, 28 June 1804, in Insurance Company of the State of Pennsylvania, Letterbook 1804–07, p. 54, Historical Society of Pennsylvania, Philadelphia; Photograph, north side Dock Street looking east to Second Street, by F. DeBourg Richards, Boies Penrose Collection, Historical Society of Pennsylvania; Elvino V. Smith, *Atlas of the 5th to 10th Wards of the City of Philadelphia* (Philadelphia, 1927), plate 2; Photograph, aerial view of Dock Street area, Print and Picture Collection, Free Library of Philadelphia.

3. William Cramond (c. 1754–1843), Philadelphia merchant, married Sarah Nixon, daughter of John Nixon. Philadelphia city public health records, Philadelphia City Archives; *PMHB*, 54 (1930):49.

For Cramond BHL designed a large Gothic country house, Sedgeley, slightly northwest of Philadelphia on 28 acres of land along the eastern bank of the Schuylkill. As built, the house consisted of a hipped main block two and one-half stories high, with shorter, square pavillions extending out at the four corners. Loggias of eight columns joined these pavillions along the east and west sides, while entrance porches projected from full-height convex bays on the north and south. Gabled dormers lit the attic story. This differed 343 somewhat from the original conception seen in BHL's watercolor perspective (Fairmount Park Commission, Philadelphia; 304/B5), reproduced in BHL, *Architectural Drawings,* which appears to have been more severe and architectonic.

The Gothic detail that characterized Sedgeley made it the first American house in that style, it is generally agreed, but the disposition of its volumes is quite similar to the rest of BHL's known domestic oeuvre, all classic. It has been suggested that the choice of the Gothic vocabulary was motivated by the variety and virginity of the site, where nature rather than human intellect devised the setting. Such thinking had many precedents in England in the country houses of "men of sensibility" at the time, but its initial appearance here reveals the ambition with which BHL approached the commission, and some of the disappointment he felt at "the deformity and expense of some parts of the building, because after giving the first general design I had no further concern with it." Cramond lost Sedgeley when he went bankrupt in 1806.

Sedgeley was demolished in 1857, but the tenant house to its east still survives, much altered, in Fairmount Park at the southeast corner of Girard Avenue and Sedgeley Drive. BHL to William Waln, 1 Apr. 1805 (LB; 39/A6); Thompson Westcott, *Historic Mansions and Buildings of Philadelphia* (Philadelphia, 1877), pp. 449–53; George B. Tatum, *Penn's Great Town* (Philadelphia, 1961), pp. 75, 177; Richard Webster, *Philadelphia Preserved* (Philadelphia, 1976), p. 238.

4. This work was the construction of two navy stores measuring forty feet by eighty feet. BHL intended to cover them with sheet iron from the Schuylkill works; later, however, Navy Secretary Robert Smith informed BHL that one of the stores had been covered with cement and the other was to be raised one story and covered with shingles. BHL to Samuel Mifflin, 10 Oct. 1803, LB (26/C5); Smith to BHL, 1 Dec. 1803, RG 45, National Archives (170/F14).

5. See following document.

TO SAMUEL HAZLEHURST

Newcastle Octr. 11th. 1803.

My dear Brother,

I am sure you will readily forgive my silence since my residence in this part of the world, when you consider, that my business in the field, from which I always return in the evening excessively fatigued, and commonly without having tasted any food for 8 or 9 hours, occupies every day of my life, excepting those on which I am unavoidably obliged to remain at home to reduce my notes to paper. Nor should I even now have been able to take up the pen were I not anxious beyond expression on a subject which has made me very uneasy for some months past, though in itself it may perhaps appear trifling: I mean the placing the little monument made by Mr. Traquair upon the grave of my little daughter. As the materials and the principal part of the workmanship of this monument have been presented to me by Mr. Traquair I have been for the first twelve month obliged to consult his leisure in finishing it. During the last Summer, I have been so much absent, that after paying for packing cases, and arranging the business with Adam Traquair, early in the Spring I left it entirely in his hands. The Man however whom I had engaged, did not make the boxes, Adam went with his mother to the Seashore, and, in fact, his father keeps him in such awe, and employs every moment of his time so rigorously in his business that he has never ventured to make an exertion for me at the expense of leaving his father's Yard for a few days.

As it is however necessary that the thing should be done before the frost sets in, I have now written a very pressing letter to old Mr. Traquair,[1] and I must now beg the favor of you, to call in your walks up to Mr. Markoe[2] and urge the business, to let him know when the Mount holly boat leaves town, and to get Adam Traquair to go up with the Monument and see it safely put in its place. Our father has been so good as to say that he might sleep a night or two at Clover hill while engaged in this business. A load or two of rough stone will also be wanted from the Mount, and the use of a teem to bring up the stone from the boat. I am sure I need not, on such an occasion say much by way of apology for the trouble I give. I will beg you to communicate this letter to our father, to whom I have written, but had not room to mention this subject.

We are all here in perfect health, excepting John who has the fretfulness and slight fevers attending teething, but is otherwise as hearty a boy as ever lived. The civility of the inhabitants seems to *thaw* a little towards us, and the Read's are become kind and useful neighbors.

I am so happy to hear that little Juliana rivals her little cousin in health and good looks.[3] I hope she will live to give you and her mother the comfort we now find in Lydia, who daily grows in size fat, good conduct, and good sense. Give my love to my Sister and believe me most affectionately Yours

B. Henry Latrobe.

Polygraph Copy: LB (26/D13). Addressed to Hazlehurst in Philadelphia.

1. BHL to Traquair, 10 Oct. 1803, above.
2. Abraham Markoe (1727–1806), Samuel Hazlehurst's father-in-law, was born on the West Indian island of St. Croix and inherited the rich sugar plantations owned by his grandfather, Pierre Marcou. About 1770 Markoe moved to Philadelphia, where in 1773 he married Elizabeth Baynton (d. 1795). BHL, *Journals*, 3:81n, 82n.
3. Juliana Hazlehurst (1802–76), daughter of Samuel and Elizabeth Baynton (Markoe) Hazlehurst.

TO JOSHUA GILPIN

Newcastle, Octr. 19th. 1803.

My dear Sir,

A letter which I received from the President of the U.S. obliged me to pay a very sudden though a short visit to Washington, and as I contrived my arrival at Elkton so that I should *work* my way home, I did not receive Your favor of the 12th. till this day. I regret exceedingly that I have by this means been prevented from seeing You last Sunday at Wilmington, a pleasure for which, at the present time I would have sacrificed almost any engagement. And at this moment I cannot by any means repair the loss for the time that remains before the meeting of the Directors, is barely sufficient for me to prepare my materials for their inspection.[1] I must therefore endeavor to make up by giving you all the information I have collected since my last, and my ideas as they arise, in my usual confidential way, *premising,* that I am so thoroughly fatigued, that I cannot promise much arrangement and method in what I shall write.

The extent of power given to me by the last Committee over the operations of Mr. Thompson has had a very good effect,[2] and had I been as much trusted from the beginning the business would by this time have been finished, and in a much better stile than it ever will be now. For by properly arranging this business of the survey, I have not only been relieved from the delay and fatigue of the Land survey which ought to surround, and localize the line of level, but I have been able to go over much more ground, and more accurately than formerly. And I have not entirely depended on Mr. Thompson's assistance, for finding that there was ample room for two Land surveyors, I have engaged *with Judge John's express advice and consent* a Mr. Blaney to survey *around* and *along,* my track from Port Penn to Back Creek, and shall, at your next meeting cover the room with the multitude of my maps.[3]

Of Mr. Thompson, I will here remark, that he is a most, deserving man, with infinitely more skill, and knowledge of principle than I have yet found in any American surveyor. Had I know him at first, and had the motto of "*divide et impera*" not been too much pursued, it would have been infinitely for my ease and for the interest of the Company. But Mr. Howard was not the man, on this occasion either for me, or for the public. On most occasion, I have been able so to manage my associates so

346

as [to] produce something of advantage to the progress of the public business out of the combination of their individual skills and humours. But Mr. Howard with all his accuracy, was so reserved and solemn, and when speaking to me, for a long time under such apparent embarrassment, that I could not find out the *"handle by which to hold him."* Besides this he was without any method in his mode of keeping his field book, so that it became almost useless without being newmodelled. Being also utterly ignorant of the business of a civil Engineer, and without proper Instruments, the mode in which he carried on his survey, rendered it useless even as land survey, and as he was equal in appointment with myself, and moreover of a most ticklish temper I felt it both against my duty and feelings to attempt to instruct him. Latterly he indeed became attached to my family, and though as formal as an old Schoolmaster I by degrees conveyed my opinions on business to him in such a manner as to induce him to adopt them in some degree, and the last of his levellings is systematic and useful.

Mr. Thompson is altogether another Man. He is a good Mathematician, of course can turn his habits of business into any new course without difficulty, and under all the ruggedness of his look he has a heart, and temper that render it easy to deal with him.

Mr. Blaney is a good clever surveyor, his employment has been chiefly for the courts, of course he has the habits of great accuracy. He is recommended by Judge Johns having long done his business. I have now done with him, after 10 days employment.

So much for the Men. Now for the business. All the plotting, mapping, and calculation is done in my office and by my Clerks, assisted whenever he can spare time from the field by Mr. Thompson. It is in great forwardness, as well as a small map showing every thing we have done at one view.

My levellings from Port penn, extend about 5 Miles, and further I believe they will never go, and for the reasons I will assign to you presently.

Thursday. Oct. 20th. 1803

I was so oppressed by fatigue and toothache when I wrote the last sheet, that I fear you will scarcely be able to read it, and the haste with which I must write the present one, will render it not much more legible.

To return to Port penn: having proceeded as far as possible on that line previously to meeting the Committee of survey on the 8th., I requested Mr. Blaney to lay down the map of the country across as far as Wertz landing, intending to go on as soon as possible from the point at which I had stopped. With this business he proceeded, and it is now compleated and mapped. In the mean time I took Mr. Thompson with me, and made progress in laying down the best levels I could find towards Christiana on the day after the meeting (if I recollect right). Having satisfied myself on this course, I requested him to go to Backcreek, and from Werts landing on Back Cr. to survey the land and water to locust point, where Mr. Howard's survey ends, intending to be with him about the time he should have nearly finished, in order to use his assistance in my operations. In the mean time I further examined the very difficult ground in the neighborhood of Newcastle, with which I am not yet satisfied. In the midst of this examination, I was called to Washington from whence I am just returned. During my absence Mr. Thompson returned to Newcastle, and the whole of his survey is now nearly mapped. It appears however that Back Creek affords no eligible Debouche for the Canal. For though there is plenty of excellent Water within the Mouth of

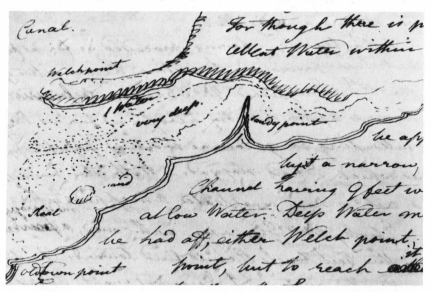

the Creek, it cannot be approached, but by a narrow, and crooked Channel having 9 feet water only at low Water. Deep Water may indeed be had off, either Welch point, or Town point, but to reach it, would lengthen the Canal so as to make it 17 or 18 miles long, which in point of expense would perhaps be objected to, although with a view to a perfect work it would be the best mode of execution. It will now be for the board to consider whether any further time and expence shall be given to the level across, as the head of the Canal appears at *present* not very practicable.

This is nearly all that has been done since my last, and when I look at it, I am surprised at its quantity. But we all have our minds engaged in the business, and feel nothing of the spirit of day laborers, although that is the footing upon which we are placed.

In respect to the contracts, you may depend upon being exactly in the situation of the Bridge Company, unless a Committee of *One,* with ample power to *conclude,* be appointed to that business.[4] No Men will treat conclusively but with *one.* I never was at a loss for proper and reasonable contracts both for labor and Materials when I was trusted to make them with reference only to *one* member of the board. I will do every thing with *You.* But do you think, that while I am surveying, and *surveying only,* and that by the day, I ought to step into the province of an Engineer and enable some cheap Workman, *put in by intrigue,* to raise himself to the direction of the work upon my labors. For independently of the enmity born me by many, altho' I never injured or willingly offended any human being in my life, although my integrity, and knowledge of business has never been disputed, and although every public Work I ever undertook has compleatly succeeded, I hear many little buzzings even here as to the conduct of the Work during its execution, and as much as I desire to be the executive officer, I can only act on terms, which may perhaps not be conceded. Some final arrangement will however be probably made by the next meeting of the board, so as to set everything agoing vigorously. I have already gained all necessary information as to the Potowmac stone.

I am much obliged to you for the trouble you have taken in respect to the Instrument. I have also received a very singular letter from Bigg's Clerk telling me with 50 Apologies that *Money only will make the Mare to go.*[5] The price is 60 Dollars, and if convenient to you to advance so much for me, I will repay you when I meet you at Wilmington, having then a large settlement to make with the board, and being unwilling to part with so much of my funds here not knowing how they may hold out in settling all my accounts with Surveyors and their Assistants.

I am sorry to hear of Mrs. Gilpins indisposition. The coolness of the weather will I hope restore her compleatly. We have escaped all serious illness though living in a new house, and a very damp one.

With very sincere respect and affection Believe me truly Yrs.

B. Henry Latrobe

Polygraph Copy: LB (26/E2).

1. In his numerous meetings with the survey committee prior to this date BHL made oral reports on his progress in the surveys. On 21 October he prepared his first written report in which he provided a "General View of Land between the Bays" and "of the general principles on which the three lines directed to be explored can be effected." BHL, C & D Report, 21 Oct. 1803 (170/C10). On 26 October the survey committee drafted its own report for the C & D board of directors in which they referred to BHL's report and maps. C & D Survey Committee Minutes.

2. See BHL to Gilpin, 10 Oct. 1803, n. 3, above.

3. Kensey Johns (1759–1848), a Federalist, was chief justice of Delaware from 1799 to 1832. He studied law under Samuel Chase and George Read, began a very successful practice, and accumulated a large estate. He served on the C & D board of directors from 1803 to 1806 and became president of the company after Tatnall's death in 1813. Gray, "Early History of C & D," p. 242.

Daniel Blaney had done survey work in Delaware in the 1790s and was hired in 1797 by the New Castle commissioners to make a survey of the town. A resident of Port Penn as late as December 1803, Blaney moved to New Castle in 1804. He charged the C & D Canal Company $78 for "13 days Service Surveying on the Rout from Port Penn to Back Creek—including one days Surveying on Christiana Creek." BHL employed Blaney on other C & D surveys and on the 1804–05 survey of New Castle (see BHL to Bird, 16 June 1804, below). Blaney served as recorder of deeds for New Castle County (1804–11) and was elected to a one-year term as clerk of the Market of New Castle in 1812. Daniel Blaney Daybook, 20 Oct. 1803, Historical Society of Delaware, Wilmington; BHL to Blaney, 4 Nov. 1803, LB (27/A7); Lucille P. Toro, "The Latrobe Survey of New Castle, 1804–1805," (M.A. thesis, University of Delaware, 1971), pp. 17–18, 32.

The only known extant map BHL presented to the survey committee along with his report of 24 October 1803 is "General Map of the Country over which the Chesapeake & Delaware Canal is proposed to be carried. Surveyed and Levelled by B. H. Latrobe Engineer, in Augt. Sepr. & Octr. 1803," Oct. 1803, Robert King delineator, RG 49, National Archives (microfiche add.).

4. Probably a reference to the "Company for erecting a Permanent Bridge over the River Schuylkill, at or near the City of Philadelphia" chartered in 1798. Several individuals, including BHL, submitted designs for the bridge and those of William Weston and Timothy Palmer were used in the construction of the stone foundations and piers and wooden superstructure. BHL may be alluding to the fact that "there being no general engineer [for the bridge], the President and Directors were under the necessity of paying more attention, than is usually required in such cases." The president and the building committee "undertook the charge of the execution of this arduous work, requiring much attention as well in the outline as in its most minute details." [Richard Peters], *A Statistical Account of the Schuylkill Permanent Bridge Communicated to the Philadelphia Society of Agriculture, 1806* (Philadelphia, 1807), pp. 19–21, 24–26.

5. The origin of the proverb is a manuscript addition to *The Second Part of Musicks*

Melodie (1609), in the British Library: "Wilt thou lend my thy mare to ride but a mile? / No, she's lame, going over a stile; / But if thou wilt her to me spare, / Thou shalt have money for thy mare. / Ho ho, say you so! / Money shall make my mare to go."

TO CHRISTIAN IGNATIUS LATROBE

Newcastle State of Delaware Octr. 25th. 1803

My dear Brother,

I again make use of the kind assistance you have before given me, by requesting you will have the goodness to chuse for my friend, Mr. George Read of this place a square pianoforte, as nearly like that which you sent to me as possible. Our climate, especially that of this place, changes from the extremes of dry to those of damp, and ranges from 0 to 91° of temperature. Notwithstanding which my instrument has stood in excellent tune ever since I have had it. I believe the leather cover lined with baize is of great service to it. If you could send me out at the same time, a copy of Pergolesi's *stabat Mater* and any good new songs the taste of which you approve you will oblige me exceedingly.[1] The annexed bill of credit for 50 pounds sterling will I believe more than cover every expense you may be at. And the sincere thanks of myself and Mr. Read must reward the kind trouble you take. Believe me your very affcte. Brother

B. Henry Latrobe

N.B. I write by the Novr. packet at length. Your sister and our children are in good health, and beg their kind remembrance. John, the youngest now 6 months old is a fine healthy fellow.

Polygraph Copy: LB (26/G11). Addressed to Christian Ignatius in London, "care of Mr. Lewis Wollin, 45 Fetter Lane."

1. Giovanni Battista Pergolesi (1710–36) was an Italian musician and composer. While in the service of the Duke of Maddaloni at Pozzuoli, he is commonly supposed to have written his arrangement of the *Stabat Mater*, a work commissioned by the Confraternity of S. Luigi di Palazzo at Naples to be sung there on Good Friday. The *Stabat Mater* is a medieval poem which came into popular use as a devotion during the thirteenth century. Originally without a musical setting, it was placed in the Roman Missal as a Sequence in 1727. H. C. Colles, ed., *Grove's Dictionary of Music and Musicians*, 3d ed., 5 vols. (New York, 1952), 4:103–07, 5:112–13.

TO GEORGE GALE

Newcastle Octr. 26th. 1803.

Sir

It was my intention to have waited upon the Committee of survey this morning, but a violent toothache confines me at home, and renders me almost incapable of business. It was my wish to have stated to the Committee that in the course of my survey, a sudden gust of Wind threw down one of my instruments, and rendered it useless; so that I must send it to London for repair. The only instrument I now possess fit for the business of the remaining survey is a Theodolite, made for me at a very heavy expence by Ramsden. Any accident which might happen to this instrument could not possibly be compensated to me, as there is perhaps not another of equal value and utility in the United States and very few of them any where. I have therefore bought a very good level, united with a Compass at Philadelphia, and now submit to the Committee, whether under the circumstances of my engagement with the Company, I may not with propriety request, that the instrument should be furnished to me at the expence of the Company. The price is 60 Dollars. In all cases in which I have been concerned, it has been the practice to furnish the more expensive Instruments, and in the present instance as I have already suffered a loss which to me is a serious one, though I wish not to claim any thing from the Committee on the score of precedent, I beg to submit to You the propriety of permitting me to charge the price of the level to Your account. I beg leave further to observe that whenever the work, shall be actually carried into execution, such an instrument as I have bought must necessarily be procured by the company, for the purpose of setting out the work to the Contractors by the Clerks of districts.[1] I am with true respect Yours faithfully

B. Henry Latrobe

I beg you to excuse, on acct. of the pain in which I write the blunders of this letter.

Polygraph Copy: LB (26/E11).

1. On 22 November 1803 the company paid Thomas Biggs $60 for the "levelling instrument." Account Book, C & D Canal Company Papers.

TO CHARLES WILLSON PEALE

Newcastle, Octr. 26th. 1803.

My dear Sir,

I did not receive yours of the 12th. of Octr. till my return from Washington a few days ago, and since then I have been so taken up in preparing to meet our Board of Directors, as to be entitled to your indulgence in not sooner answering it.[1] If any recommendation of mine can be of the smallest service to you you may depend upon receiving it as warmly as sincerely, but were I to attempt to write for the public this morning, it would be *invitâ Minerva*,[2] for though hunger is said to sharpen the wit, I am sure toothach deadens it. But in a day or two You shall receive a letter from which an extract may perhaps answer your purpose.[3]

As to Mr. Read's polygraph, you shall receive the amount per post as soon as you inform me that it is ready for delivery—before that time, I cannot well, on *your acct.* ask him for it.[4]

I have now to state to you the faults and bad habits which my own has acquired since I have used it, and mean to propose sending it back to you for another paying you whatever may be reasonable between us.
1. then: As I write with the lefthand pen, which is unavoidably necessary by candlelight, I find that if both pens be made of exactly equal length by the gage the right hand pen touches before the left reaches the paper by more than 1/16th. of an inch: so that I am obliged by repeated trials to make my pen write equally, not venturing to meddle with the regulator, to which indeed I have no key, and believing that the error lies somewhere about the frame. To the regulation of the pens rather by trial, than by the gage I do not object, as it is a practise I should always follow, rather than spoil my pens by pushing them up against the brass standard.
2. When my pens are thus regulated, I find a very troublesome defect in the Machine which I cannot better show you than by the Copy on the other side. (I then opened the paper on which I wrote so that the left side was copied on the right.) You will observe that the pen writes imperfectly at the beginning of every line, and that the defect is irregular, and rather encreases towards the bottom of every page. The defect I remedy by laying a triangular slip of paper under the left edge of the copy which raises it up in that part, and thus I manage as well as I wish, very little trouble being required in the remedy of the evil. I cannot so readily conceive the cause of this defect. Perhaps it arises from a sinking

353

in the wood in the middle of the desk, and that a block may be required under it.

4.[5] If the Pens are to be measured by a gage, I think it would be better to push them up to a mark on the surface of a piece of brass, than against a solid standard: for I find that it spoiled my nibs as long as I used it.

5. Another very essential improvement might be made thus: place the hinges of the brass frame entirely on the right half of the frame thus:

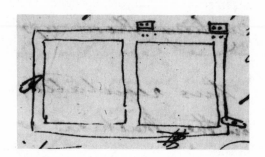

If this were done, any sized paper could be used for the original for by pushing up the sheet or pulling it down the parts to be written upon, could always be brought opposite to the copy, which must necessarily for my use be of postpaper in order to form a book which is to be bound. My reports to public bodies and in general all my public papers I wish to write upon foolscap.

With these improvements and corrections I think nothing would be more perfect than the machine. And with all its defects, nothing would now induce me to part with that which I have could I not procure another.

As my instrument has been taken excellent care of, I think you may alter it, and sell it as new furnishing me with another, for I cannot spare this even for a day to undergo the necessary alterations. I will with pleasure pay any additional charge, and send it up to you as soon as I receive the other.

I hope you will soon have Mr. Read's ready for him. I have not yet had an opportunity of getting you more orders *fixed*, but I have some for you in embryo.

I have seen your grisly bear in the papers. Has Dr. Barton given him an inspection, and what is his opinion? As to his coming from the sources of the Missouri, *"Perhaps he may."*[6]

With every wish for your compleat success in your pursuits, a success to which the success of knowledge and art in our country is in a great degree linked, I am very sincerely Yrs.

B. Henry Latrobe

Polygraph Copy: LB (26/F3). Addressed to Peale at his museum in Philadelphia.

1. Peale had requested BHL to write a testimonial on the polygraph to be used in future advertisements for the invention. Peale to BHL, 12 Oct. 1803, Peale Letterbooks (microfiche add.).
2. Trans.: Minerva unwilling, i.e., against the will of the goddess of intellectual activity.
3. BHL's testimonial of the machine was very important to Peale, who told the inventor of the polygraph that the engineer's "recommendation will be of more consequence than from twenty other persons." Over a year later, while still awaiting BHL's letter, Peale noted that a testimonial "from an architect of his celebracy will I hope have great weight with those who have doubts on the subject." BHL's letters, dated 14 May [March] and 4 June 1805, finally appeared in four Philadelphia newspapers in June 1805. (See BHL to Peale, 14 Mar. 1805, bibliographic note, in BHL, *Correspondence*, 2.) Although BHL later believed that the favorable statements did not significantly increase sales, BHL later learned from Peale's son that of the sixty polygraphs eventually sold, forty were sold by his recommendation. Peale to John Isaac Hawkins, 6 Nov. 1803, 8 Sept.–25 Dec. 1805, Peale to John dePeyster, 3 Mar. 1805, all in Peale Letterbooks; BHL to Thomas Jefferson, [28] July 1817, Jefferson Papers (233/C6).
4. Peale had informed BHL that Read's polygraph "shall be sent by the first Packet after he has complyed with my terms. I would rather not sell one of them than keep an Account." Peale to BHL, 12 Oct. 1803, Peale Letterbooks (microfiche add.).
5. BHL's numbering of the faults of the polygraph skips from two to four.
6. Peale purchased the bear for his museum on 12 October 1803 and mentioned it in his letter to BHL of that date (cited in n. 4, above). Peale's description appeared in *Poulson's American Daily Advertiser* (Philadelphia), beginning on 13 October: "This animal was born in the spring of the year 1802, not far from the sources of the river Missouri about 4500 miles from Philadelphia, in a country inhabited by an Indian nation called the Cattanahowes. He is the first of his species that ever was seen, and seems to be a separate class of White Bear, which differs from those known to and described by the naturalists, as well in point of colour as in point of inclinations. His hair is a kind of straw colour or light sorrel, neither hard nor stiff, but somewhat like wool. His inclinations are so ferocious, that he follows the tracks of men, and attacks them with undaunted fury. . . . During the short time of 2 weeks only will the Grisly Bear be seen at any hour of the day, at the Museum."

TO THOMAS SAVERY

Newcastle, Octr. 26th. 1803.

Sir[1]

Since my removal hither, the latter end of July I have been twice in Philadelphia, where I have repeatedly called at your house in vain with a view to settle my rent. On seriously considering the character of a Man who could act towards me, while confined to my bed by illness, in the manner you have done, I have concluded that it is impossible for you to have a friend in the world whom you can trust. And yet when I consider, that you were for a short time so ashamed of yourself, as to endeavor to prevail upon my servant to conceal what you had done, and that where there is *shame* there *may be virtue,* I think it possible that you may be able to appoint some one to whom I may remit, during your absence, the amount of rent to May 23d, and perhaps as much of the last quarter as will leave a balance equal to the expense of laying the water into my house which you have agreed to allow. Should you therefore be in situation as to friends to prevail on some one to receive the money for you, and will mention his name, I will in a few days afterwards cause the money to be paid to him for as I cannot prevail on any of my friends to have anything to do with You, and feel a very sufficient reluctance in that subject myself, it will be necessary for you to act by an agent.

With the sentiments towards which your own feelings will suggest as you *desert,* I am &c. &c.

B. Henry Latrobe

Mem.: When I gave notice to quit my house in Arch street belonging to Mr. Savary, in Decr. 1802, I did not owe him any thing: two Quarters became due between that date and the 23d of May. Savary was out of town for a considerable time before I moved, in the latter end of July 1803; and my attempts to see him previous to removal were vain. While confined at Mr. Hazlehurst's by a wound in my leg part of my goods being then removed, he came to town, and though I had been his tenant 3 Years and paid him regularly, besides expending 3 or 400 Dollars in improving his house, he seized immediately my horses and carriage then in the stable by a Warrant. He then called upon me for his rent, of which, ill as I was, I paid him one quarter immediately.[2] I learned what he done only some days afterwards from the coachman, whom he had attempted to bribe to silence. On receiving the rent he discharged the Warrant.

Polygraph Copy: LB (26/F8). Addressed to Savery in Philadelphia. BHL undoubtedly wrote the memorandum after disengaging the polygraph machine.

1. Thomas Savery, a Philadelphia carpenter, was on the board of directors of the Schuylkill Permanent Bridge Company.
2. In November BHL paid Savery an additional $110 toward the balance. BHL to Adam Traquair, 11 Nov. 1803, LB (27/C4).

TO SAMUEL MIFFLIN

Newcastle Octr. 27th. 1803

Dear Sir,

I have just put on board of the packet which will sail tomorrow 'morning the long promised drawings of the Stove for the Senate Chamber. The trouble of getting it cast will I hope be compleatly taken off your hands by Smallman. Newsham will make the plain part of the Pattern, and old Martin Jugiez renowned as the ugliest Man in Philadelphia will do the carving, exactly in the stile of the Stove of the Bank of Pensylvania the decoration of which I have exactly adopted to prevent tedious explanation.[1] On the other half of this letter I have written the explanation of the Drawings in order that you may tear it off and give it to Smallmann. John Brown having fitted up the Stove of the Bank of Pennsylvania will be very useful in fitting up this which I hope will be in Washington in a month.[2] I expect you of course to charge me with such expenses as will make it worth your while to do these little jobs at the Works, and I shall forward you the amount by a bill on Washington at very short sight. Believe me with true respect and affection Yrs.

B. Henry Latrobe

Polygraph Copy: LB (26/F10). Addressed to Mifflin in Philadelphia. Enclosed BHL, Description of the Plans for the Senate Chamber Stoves, below.

1. Richard Newsham was a patternmaker and machinist at Roosevelt's Soho works in the later 1790s and moved to Philadelphia to assist in installing and maintaining the waterworks engines. BHL later referred to him as "our pattern maker at the rolling mill." Testimony of Richard Newsham and James Smallman, n.d., James Wood Collection, Franklin Institute, Philadelphia; BHL to Howell & Jones, 17 Nov. 1804, LB (36/A11).
Martin Jugiez was a Philadelphia carver and gilder. *PMHB* 34 (1910):225.

357

2. John Brown was one of the workmen who helped install and maintain the steam engines of the waterworks and who remained to work at the rolling mill. N. J. Roosevelt account with James Smallman, 4 Apr. 1806, Watering Committee Papers, Archives of the City and County of Philadelphia; BHL to Smallman, 6 Feb. 1804, LB (29/D7).

ENCLOSURE: DESCRIPTION OF THE PLANS FOR THE SENATE CHAMBER STOVES

Description of the plans of a Stove for the Senate Chamber of the United States, at Washington.[1] *Two stoves wanted.* No. I exhibits the Stove on a small scale as finished. It consists of the following parts. 1.) A circular cover or top, made like a dish with a margin and a moulded lip. It is contrived to cast in a common 2 part flask all the drafts being shown on the drawing. I should be glad if this cover could be turned smooth in our lathe, should it come rough from the foundery. 2. A circular step, rebated to go under the moulded lip of the cover to which is attached an Octangular surface at right angles with projections to cover the heads of the Pilasters and a moulded lip all round. It will require much care and judgement to make a good casting of this piece, but I think it may be effected, if proper care be taken to get out the core part of the flask in

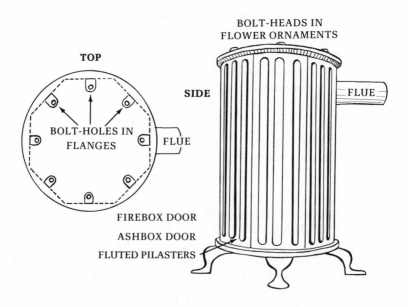

Fig. 14. Conjectural sketch of Senate stove.

time. 3.) Eight pilasters fluted as shown in the drawing of the ground plan. The bolts which hold the stove together must be so forged and cut, that the upper and lower forms the center of the rose as at the Bk. of Pensylvania, and the middle one part of the two middle beads of the Pannel: so that when the stove is together the bolts will not be perceived. The rest of the drawings explain themselves. The tops will lie on in mortar or Cement and remain steady by their own weight, as that at the Bank of Pensylvania.

5.[2] The 8 plates are perfectly plain, and require only to be well cleaned. The whole work should be well cleared of sand. I think the plates would bear sprinkling with water when hot without injury. This is the best way of getting them very smooth and clear of sand. But no risks should be run. It is of great public importance to forward this business as much as possible.

B. Henry Latrobe.

Polygraph Copy: LB (26/F11). Enclosed in BHL to Mifflin, 27 Oct. 1803, above.

1. BHL's drawings of his stoves for the Senate have not survived, but from his description it is clear that his stoves were to be cast-iron, free-standing "box" stoves, made to stand away from the wall and be vented by a circular flue connected to a chimney. Such stoves had been used in the United States from the mid–1700s. (They were *not* the same as Franklin stoves, which were partially enclosed by the fireplace and open in the front.) Box stoves were made up of at least six cast-iron plates (one for the top, one for the bottom, and four for the sides). BHL's design required eleven plates (two for the top, one for the bottom, and eight for the sides), which was not unusual. BHL's Greek Revival design was, of course, in keeping with his artistic preference and may have been original. However, Greek Revival styled stoves were seen by Benjamin Franklin in 1773 in London at the Bank of England and Lincoln's Inn, and the same style was common in the United States in the first half of the nineteenth century. Smoke from each of these English stoves descended into flues below the floors, connecting to chimneys at some distance from them.

The Senate stoves were patterned on the Bank of Pennsylvania stove, shown in BHL's north-south section of the banking hall there. This stove appears to have been directly above a furnace in the basement and similarly, despite the lack of some central floor perforation in the section, must have been fed and had its smoke exhausted from below. See Section of the banking hall of the Bank of Pennsylvania (Franklin Institute, Philadelphia; microfiche add.) and "Plan of the Cellar Story" (Historical Society of Pennsylvania; 302/A2), both reproduced in BHL, *Architectural Drawings*. Josephine H. Peirce, *Fire on the Hearth: The Evolution and Romance of the Heating-Stove* (Springfield, Mass., 1951), pp. 92, 93, 171; Joseph E. Walker, *Hopewell Village: The Dynamics of a Nineteenth-Century Iron-Making Community* (Philadelphia, 1966), pp. 156–64.

In a letter earlier in October 1803, BHL had informed Lenthall of a plan for furnaces in the cellar below the old Senate Chamber. These were to be connected with the chimneys in the lobby at the center of the north wing. The octagonal box stoves above were situated near the east wall of the old Senate Chamber. BHL's reference to perforations in the iron flues suggests that the furnaces themselves may have been near the lobby chimneys, and 359 that their flues carried warm air, but no smoke, over to the stoves. BHL to John Lenthall, 15 Sept. 1803, BHL Papers, Library of Congress (170/B1); BHL to Lenthall, 26 Sept. 1803, BHL to Mifflin, 2 Oct. 1803, BHL to Jefferson, 2 Oct. 1803, all above; BHL to Fox, 27 Oct. 1803, BHL to Burr, 13 Dec. 1803, both below.

2. BHL's numbering skips from three to five.

TO SAMUEL M. FOX

Newcastle Octr. 27th. 1803

Dear Sir,[1]

If I had had a single leisure day since I left Philadelphia you would have had a letter from me much earlier than at present. But though I have always contrived to have my hands and my head pretty full since you have known me, I have so little profitted by my former experience as to have undertaken to do more than either my mind or my body is equal to; and were it not for a thick fog which renders it impossible for me to be in the field, I should at this moment be perhaps on the road to Back creek. I have seized this opportunity therefore to remind you that I am alive, and often remember you with sentiments of respect and affection which few in this world have ever given me occasion to feel in the same degree. And tho' I shall cram a little business into this letter believe me that the business, such as it is, would not have induced me to write alone.

If you have an opportunity of seeing Mr. J. Gilpin often you must be tolerably well acquainted with the progress of the business of levelling and surveying for our Canal. In fact all that ever will be known on this subject, worth knowing is already in possession of the board. But much is still to be done for the public; that is, to justify the choice which the Directors may ultimately make to the public by thoroughly proving the impracticability of every other line but that which they shall fix upon. And this I have still to perform much to my annoyance, for, for any other purpose it will be useless. For nature has laid out the ground upon which art has to work in such a manner that nothing but very powerful efforts to counteract her will succeed. And between ourselves, and with my accustomed confidence in you which I will not permit any body to call indiscretion, the Canal must travel from Frenchtown to Newcastle if it is intended to have the *best possible* Canal. Frenchtown indeed is a

360

Debouche not quite as good as could be wished, but there is no better within the reach of the funds of the present Generation, and if even deeper water were resorted to in the lower part of Elk river, the difficulties on shore would be multiplied. Between Frenchtown and Newcastle no difficulties on Land are to be found.

How this will please our friend Levi, you can better tell than I. It is unfortunate that the father of the child should interfere in the manner in which it is to be brought into the world. If he would let it take its own course all would be well.[2] And it *will* be well I hope in spite of all the obstetrician tricks and follies that are playing. Luckily for me the decision does not lie with me, and I am determined to report nothing but facts, suppressing every shadow of opinion. Posterity and the Stockholders, or rather the stockholders and posterity will have to thank Joshua Gilpin, G. Fox, Fisher, Tilghman, Adlum, and Bayard for keeping the localists at bay.[3] Tatnall has no reserve or discretion in declaring his predetermination for Christiana. Judge Johns has a very extensive farm covering 2½ miles of the best possible route by land to the Delaware, and a situation on the very shore formed, it should seem for the entrance of the Canal by Nature. But unluckily the water of the Delaware is shoal and rendered dangerous by rocks at low water; otherwise there is no manner of doubt but that this would be the *only* place that could be thought of for it would also be the shortest cut by more than two miles. This line—which by the bye is my discovery—has its advocates out of the board, and at the board we may presume there will be some little predilection in Kinsey Johns for his own property. However, I think he will vote right. Chew is a good man, whom in fact I do not know.[4] Gale is the mischief maker, of which there is one in every public board. He is a haughty, overbearing, illmannered Encyclopedist. Heaven forbid that I should disgrace the french Encyclopedist by [having] called Mr. Gale an Encyclopedist of their class. Believe me he is no Encyclopedia writer, but only an Encyclopedia reader and retailer. If his manner to *me* were reserved for my digestion alone—for he treats me as often as he dare, as a Clerk—I should have fought him long ago: but as he is equally rude to his brother directors my shoulders are considerably lightened of the burthen. He is not worth wasting paper about, after all. Joshua Gilpin is by far the most active man at the board. Mr. Adlum is, as every where full of good sense, and good manners. How he fell in love with his colleague a man so totally different in mind, body, and habits I cannot comprehend.

If I knew exactly what *you* know of the detail of our proceedings, I could fill up the sheet with what you do *not* know. But as I mean to write to you again soon, I shall perhaps receive a line or two from you in the mean time.

Now for the business.

I have designed two small stoves for the Senate Chamber of the United States which are to be cast and fitted up in Philadelphia. Mr. Mifflin will show you the design if you will ask him. There is a geometrical elevation of the stove on one of the sheets which, owing to a little false drawing and false shading—for it is William Strickland's work—gives a clumsy representation of the thing. It has occurred to me that it would suit the library company.[5] I could on consideration put it up in the reading room so as not to make the fire in the cellar which is *let*, but under the Vestibule. This would remove the objection to this sort of stove which was formerly started; and as the patterns will be at my disposal, I will present the company with their use and with all the necessary advice and assistance in putting up the stove or *stoves*. Another time I will send you a sketch of what may be done, towards warming the rooms, which I am sure will please you, and perhaps be thought worthy of being put into practice. I shall be in Philadelphia in about a month, and will then give the assistance which may be required.[6]

We have continued here in perfect health. I hope you can say the same of yourself and Mrs. Fox with all your little folks.[7] Apropos, as the only news of importance in Newcastle let me inform you that my little John has this day cut his second tooth. May he never eat the bread of dependence upon it.

With mine and Mrs. Latrobe's sincerest respects to Mrs. Fox believe me very faithfully and affectionately Yrs.

B. Henry Latrobe

Pray is Joseph to be an Engineer or a Gentleman?[8]

Polygraph Copy: LB (26/F13).

1. Samuel Mickle Fox (1763–1808), president of the Bank of Pennsylvania from 1796 until his death, was largely responsible for securing for BHL in 1798 the commission to design and build the bank. *PMHB* 32 (1908):196–97. For BHL's eulogy of Fox and his description of Fox as the Pericles of Philadelphia, see BHL, *Anniversary Oration Pronounced before the Society of Artists of the United States* (Philadelphia, 1811), 8 May 1811, in BHL, *Correspondence,* 3.

2. Levi Hollingsworth had participated in the original American Philosophical Society surveys for a C & D canal route in 1769.

3. George Fox (1759–1828), brother of Samuel M. Fox and a member of the American Philosophical Society (elected 1784), served on the C & D board of directors from 1803 to 1806. James C. Fisher, Philadelphia merchant, was a C & D director from 1803 to 1806 and president of the revived C & D Canal Company from 1823 to 1829. William Tilghman (1756–1827) of Philadelphia, Maryland legislator (1788–93), Pennsylvania Supreme Court chief justice (1806–27) and president of the American Philosophical Society (1824–27), served as a C & D director in 1803–04. John Adlum (1759–1836) of Maryland, surveyor, mapmaker, and pioneer in viticulture, was a C & D director from 1803 to 1805. James A. Bayard (1767–1815) of Delaware, Federalist congressman (1797–1803) and U.S. senator (1805–13), served as a C & D director in 1803–04. Gray, "Early History of C & D," p. 242; *PMHB* 32 (1908):196.

4. Samuel Chew (1737–1809), judge of the Supreme Court of Delaware in 1773, later moved to Chestertown, Md., and became attorney general of Maryland. He served as a C & D director from 1803 to 1804. Gray, "Early History of C & D," pp. 241–42; *Maryland Historical Magazine* 19 (1924):229, 30 (1935):166.

5. The Library Company of Philadelphia, founded by Benjamin Franklin and his friends in 1731 and chartered in 1742, was called by Franklin the "mother of all the North American subscription libraries." In 1803 the Library Company's building stood on Fifth Street opposite Philosophical Hall (the current site of the American Philosophical Society Library). The building was heated by wood-burning stoves which, with their pipes, were stored in the garret when not in use. Charles E. Peterson, "Library Hall: Home of the Library Company of Philadelphia, 1790–1880," in *Historic Philadelphia, from the Founding until the Early Nineteenth Century* (Philadelphia, 1953), pp. 129–47.

6. Samuel Fox, who with Joshua Gilpin served as a director of the Library Company, was a member of the committee of repairs and improvements. No mention of BHL's stoves, however, appears in the minutes of the directors' meetings in 1803–04. The front cellar had been let to Messrs. Harmes & Holtzbecker, the back cellar to Jacob Shoemaker. Minutes of the Proceedings of the Directors, 7 Apr., 5 May, 7 July 1803, Library Company of Philadelphia.

7. Sarah (Pleasants) Fox married Samuel M. Fox in 1788; they had twelve children, nine of whom were born by fall 1803. *PMHB* 32 (1908):197–98.

8. Samuel's son, Joseph Mickle Fox, became an attorney, a landowner in western Pennsylvania, and a state senator. Ibid., p. 198.

TO JOSHUA GILPIN

Newcastle Octr. 28th. 1803.

Dear Sir,

By a lucky mistake of my Clerk, whom I sent to Wilmington for the maps, I am again in possession of the general Map which, it was intended, you should take with you to Philadelphia. This has enabled me to make it more perfect and to add those Memorandums which you will see on the margin, and which in the concise form in which they appear save the memory, and also prevent the trouble of constant repetition of the important facts which must decide the question.[1]

The affray of Tuesday last has completely unsettled me.[2] All my family arrangements are at a stand, and I am now preparing myself to quit the service of the company, as soon as the survey is finished. I will take care that it shall be without fault or blemish, so that in what every way I may be disposed of, I will carry with me out of your service the reputation of integrity, and industry which I brought into it. For with a known and declared enemy at the board, who is without even the manners of a Gentleman, it is impossible for me to think of fighting my way through an undertaking, to succeed in which a mind is required unharrassed by illtreatment, and undisturbed by angry sensations. Besides it is a situation in which I have never as yet been placed; and for which my temper is not [suited]. Some unguarded moment will occur in which my language and my conduct in presence of the board will be beyond what is due to the respect I owe the members as a body and as individuals. My resentment at the manner in which I am treated by the Chairman will call forth expressions beyond the bounds of prudence or respect. I am so well acquainted with my own mind, as to foresee that I shall not always be able to speak as prudently as I did on Tuesday last, and when I have once committed myself by expressions which make the *board* inimical to me, I am lost as a professional man. And as public boards, from a natural *esprit des corps,* and, from principle, always hang together I plainly see, that even with justice on my side, I have no chance.

I am not however so much of a coward, as to quit the *field,* when I quit the active service. I shall always be a Stockholder;[3] nor shall I ever forget how much I owe to the kindness of yourself, and to the politeness of my fellow citizens of Philadelphia who are in the direction. Nor do I intend that any triumph shall attend the public mention of the name of the man who has defeated me. If repentance be a good thing he shall have enough of it.

I know nothing of what has been done by you. Untill I receive my instructions, I am forwarding the drawings which I can consider as finally settled. This will employ the whole of this week, and the *next,* if I do not hear sooner from the Secretary or Chairman. On Tuesday I shall have the pleasure to correspond with Mr. Gale should I not hear from him before that day.

No instrument has as yet arrived. I shall wait a day or two longer, and then forward to you a draft on Philadelphia for the amount, if it does not arrive. I know Biggs of old—he is determined to be on the safe side. After laying out above 100 Dollars at his shop, he refused my Clerk a case of instruments value 2 Dollars till he brought the money.

By the packet which leaves this tomorrow morning I shall send to you the General Map, for which you will have to send to the Warehouse tomorrow evening. I suppose it is again opened at Market street wharf.

Believe me with the truest respect Yrs. affectionately

B. Henry Latrobe

Polygraph Copy: LB (26/G4). Addressed to Gilpin in Philadelphia.

1. "General Map of the Country over which the Chesapeake & Delaware Canal is proposed to be carried. Surveyed and Levelled by B. H. Latrobe Engineer, in Augt. Septr. & Octr. 1803," Oct. 1803, Robert King, Jr., delineator, RG 49, National Archives (microfiche add.). This map was probably presented at the survey committee meeting on 24 October 1803, but this passage indicates that it was primarily intended for display to current and prospective stockholders in Philadelphia. The "question" regards which of the several potential routes should be chosen. BHL probably commissioned King to execute the map during his mid-October trip to Washington.

2. In a notation in his letterbook (26/F2) BHL referred to the survey committee meeting of Tuesday, 25 October 1803 at which occurred "a dispute which the treatment of the Chairman of the Committee [George Gale] had long provoked, but which broke out in the Committee from the following cause. I submitted *considerations* to the Board loosely written down, intending them for discussion during my absence, should the board think proper. The first was in substance as follows: *Shall the level be carried from the point where it now stops, . . . on the line from Portpenn to Backcreek* since Mr. Thompsons *survey of that creek has proved the Navigation of the Creek to be impossible during a Westerly wind, outwards?* I then stated the time it would take to compleat the survey—After reading the Question in my presence; The chairman asked imperiously: And pray, Sir, who is to direct the survey, You, Sir, or the board?" In a letter to his father-in-law recounting the meeting BHL reported that he had "replied that no Gentleman in the room had a right to speak to me in such a tone and the feelings of no man, pretending to good breeding ought to permit him to use it." BHL to Isaac Hazlehurst, 30 Oct. 1803, LB (26/G12).

3. BHL usually attended the C & D stockholders meetings and on 2 June 1806 he was appointed secretary of that year's annual meeting. First Minute Book of Stockholders Meetings, 2 June 1806, C & D Canal Company Papers.

TO ADAM TRAQUAIR

Newcastle Octr. 29th. 1803

Dear Adam

You have exceedingly obliged me by your attention to the little Monument of my daughter. In a letter to your father, I gave particular directions as to the manner of making the foundation, which I suppose you found no difficulty in getting accomplished. Accept my thanks for your trouble. The politeness you met with at Cloverhill was not more

due to the occasion that carried you there than to your own good conduct, and to your modesty, a quality in you which though by no means
necessary to the making a large fortune, is of infinite use in procuring
and preserving friends among those who know how to discover and to
value merit.

In my present engagements your assistance would be very valuable
to me. And as both I and Mrs. L. feel for you the affection due to a child,
your society in our family would be as valuable, during my necessary
absences, as your professional assistance. But at present, it cannot be
worth your while to come hither, nor could your father I suppose easily
spare You. When the work is well under way, perhaps I may find a
situation for you in every respect eligible, and I am constantly looking
forward to some arrangement suitable to you.

I will in a few days forward to your father a particular account of the
number and size of the blocks wanted but I cannot possible think of it
today.[1] I shall be in Philadelphia in about a fortnight. Believe me most
affectionately Yours

B. Henry Latrobe.

[*On the retained (polygraph) copy of this letter BHL noted:*] In a postscript, a
request to bring my son Henry from Mr. Drake's school in order to his
coming hither on a visit.[2]

Polygraph Copy: LB (26/G7). Addressed to Traquair in Philadelphia.

1. See BHL to James Traquair, 6 Nov. 1803, below.
2. Richard Drake was schoolmaster at Grove Academy on the Lancaster Turnpike
near Philadelphia. BHL's son Henry was enrolled in Drake's school until June 1804, when
BHL sent him to study under the Rev. William Du Bourg at St. Mary's Academy in
Baltimore. BHL to Drake, 4 Feb. 1804, BHL to Vaughan, 18 Mar. 1804, and BHL to Du
Bourg, 11 Apr. 1804, all below.

TO RICHARD DRAKE

Newcastle Octr. 30th. 1803

Dear Sir,

As the weather is now becoming cold Mrs. Latrobe wishes that her
366 Son Henry may come hither for a week, both that we may have the

pleasure to see him, and in order to get his cloaths into compleat order for the winter. For this reason we request that Mrs. Drake will be so good as to let him bring with him every article of wearing apparel and linnen which he possesses, that it may be mended or replaced as occasion requires. You will also oblige me by transmitting my account for his school expenses for the first quarter which is now, some time ago, past. In order that I may remit to you the amount.

Mrs. Latrobe requests that should any part of his linnen require washing at the moment of his departure it may be sent as it is, well knowing that boys are apt to soil their linnen sufficiently, and not being nice about his appearance on the present occasion.

Believe me with true respect

B. Henry Latrobe

Polygraph Copy: LB (26/G8). Addressed to Drake at the "school, Lancaster turnpike, near the six mile stone."

TO JOSHUA GILPIN

Newcastle Novr. 4th. 1803

Dear Sir

I am sorry you have had so much trouble with Mr. Bigg's Clerk. I have at last got the Instrument, which will answer my purpose admirably, though it is truly made for the American market as to filing, gilding, and engraving. It could not have been sold, I believe, in London.

It was my determination never to have plagued you again with the name of Mr. Gale. But I think it right to give you a piece of information which I have received from Mr. Hyat of Aikintown, who is a rich and respectable Man, and holds all the land West of the Buck road through which the Canal will pass for half a Mile.[1] He tells me that Mr. G. being present at the Elkton races, became exceedingly warm in general conversation on the subject of the Land bonds,[2] and made two declarations which are in everybodies mouth—one, that sooner than carry the Canal through anybody's land *to oblige him, he* would go 300 Yds. round, and then, that *he* would not vary the line one perch to save any man's property. I found the temper of the Land holders so much altered since my last 367 visit, that I could not get a single bond which had been promised, signed, and these silly declarations were pleaded in excuse for the refusal. I have taken some pains to remove this bad impression, and hope to succeed still in getting bonds for all the Land but Solomon Underwoods, which, unfortunately extend two Miles.[3]

While waiting for Mr. Roche's intelligence,[4] I have staked out the whole french town line, and found a much better way over Belton run, so as to make it a matter of a very few thousand extraordinary, perhaps 3.000$. On Monday I go to Back Creek, but for want of my presence when the resolution was formed respecting Locust point and *Walsh* point as Roche calls it, it cannot as it stands be complied with as it involves an impossibility. I shall however act up to its meaning. Believe me very affecty. Yours

B. Henry Latrobe

N.B. The Instrument arrive[d] on Wednesday Novr. 2d. 1803

Polygraph Copy: LB (27/A13). Addressed to Gilpin in Philadelphia.

1. Probably John Hyatt (d. 1805), one of the trustees of the Glasgow Grammar School. BHL to Isaac Hazlehurst, 14 Jan. 1805, LB (37/C3); J. Thomas Scharf, *A History of Delaware, 1609–1888,* 2 vols. (Philadelphia, 1888), 2 : 953.

2. The land bonds were conditional bonds obtained from landowners along the proposed canal routes. The bonds set a price for the land which the company would pay within a certain period should the land be needed for the canal. C & D Survey Committee Minutes, 6 June, 5 July 1803.

3. Solomon Underwood served in the Delaware militia during the Revolutionary War. In 1803 he was one of the trustees of the Glasgow Grammar School. *Delaware Archives,* 5 vols. (Wilmington, Del., 1911–19), 2 : 805; Scharf, *History of Delaware,* 2 : 954.

Later BHL and Kensey Johns bought Underwood's 115-acre Pencader Hundred farm, situated where the feeder was to join the canal. This speculative venture came to naught when the canal project collapsed in 1806. BHL to Nicholas Van Dyke, 5 Jan. 1816, LB (128/F11).

4. BHL was awaiting instructions from the survey committee written by Edward Roche (d. 1821), stockholder and secretary of the C & D Canal Company, concerning the engineer's surveys including that of the land between Long and Perch creeks "only between *Welch point* and *locust point.*" (See Map 4.) BHL reported that Roche, who had a "microscopic memory," "appears by his letter to be a character fitted to cut a good figure *as a Secretary,* in a play." BHL to Gilpin, 29 Oct., 1 Nov. 1803, both in LB (26/G10, 27/A5); First Minute Book of Stockholders Meetings, 1 May 1803, C & D Canal Company Papers.

TO JAMES TRAQUAIR

Newcastle Novr. 6th. 1803

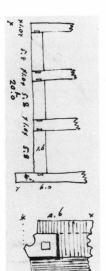

My dear friend,

If you cannot understand the sketch in the Margin my friend Adam will explain it to you. But as every Scotch stone cutter is born with the intuitive knowledge of the manner of cutting the hollow Quoin of a lock, little need be said to you on the subject.

I must however beg you to remember that at present I have only undertaken to make the necessary surveys for the Company,[1] and it is as little prudent in me to give them any of the information which they might expect from me if I were their Engineer, as it would be to lead you into the risk of providing the necessary blocks without giving you fully to understand that I have no power to contract with you. I must however say so much that there is little doubt of your doing this business, and I have prepared Mr. Gilpin the Sam. Fox of our board as to intelligence, and gentlemanly conduct, to converse with you on the subject. I beg you will be so good as to let Mrs. L. have a set of Chimney ornaments, which Adam will chuse for her. She is so little fond of frippery that unless I undertake to provide her some she will pass for a woman only by her dress. I have therefore resolved to spend 14 to 15 Dollars on her mantle piece, as she saves me twice as much a Year in beads, feathers and Gewgaws.

Yours affectionately

B. Henry Latrobe

Please to call on Mr. Gilpin Chesnut street about 8th. when he comes to town.

Polygraph Copy: LB (27/B5). Addressed to Traquair in Philadelphia.

1. C & D Canal Company.

TO HENRY SHEAFF

Newcastle, Novr. 7th. 1803

Dear Sir[1]

You will much oblige me by filling the two demijohns herewith sent, the one with Port wine the other with Madeira, and send them down by the Newcastle packet as soon as convenient, *sealing them well:* for we know *by experience* how apt the liquor of Demijohns is to run out at the Cork on board of a Vessel.

Yrs. very respectfully

B. Henry Latrobe

Polygraph Copy: LB (27/B8). Addressed to Sheaff in Philadelphia.

1. Henry Sheaff (d. post-1818) was a Philadelphia wine merchant.

TO CHARLES C. WATSON

Newcastle Novr. 7th. 1803

Dear Sir[1]

I should be much obliged to you, if you would send me down two fashionable under Jackets of flannel, and one fashionable Kerseymere Waistcoat. The choice of the pattern and make I leave to you, provided they be not too flashy.

Yrs. truly,

B. Henry Latrobe

Polygraph Copy: LB (27/B8). Addressed to Watson in Philadelphia.

1. Charles C. Watson (d. post-1830) was a Philadelphia draper, mercer, and tailor.

TO JOHN LENTHALL

Newcastle, Novr. 11th. 1803

My dear Sir

I received Yours of the 31st. Octr. just at the moment when I was setting off for as inhospitable, and wild a country as the peninsula can boast, for no other purpose than to explore it in order to satisfy the public that *no canal* can be carried over it. For so much are our courageous Stockholders swayed by public opinion, and local interests, that it is not sufficient that I have laid down a line of navigation where it is evidently most cheaply, most advantageously, and by the shortest course to be effected, but I must also go over every range of ground proposed by every projector who has impudence or interest enough to make himself heard. Neither my time therefore, nor my humor permitted me to answer it immediately, but I take the first opportunity after my return to write to you; not to answer any of your enquiries, for your letter contains none but to ask questions.

1.) Pray has any of the Stove pipe arrived? I have ordered a few Sheets of the Same Iron to be sent on to make the knees, which you will of course do more accurately than we could.

2.) Is any of the plain roof Iron and hoops arrived, for the President's house. I have had notice some time ago of both these articles being ready to be forwarded from Philadelphia.

3.) Was the failure of the cieling of the Senate Chamber owing to an old injury by former leaks, or to the leakage of the present Session. If the latter, I much fear *we* shall, that is, *I* shall get into disgrace for not getting on the new roof in time. But could I have found water for the forges, I should soon have found iron for the roof.

4. Have you covered up your Walls? or rather roofed them with the Scaffolding boards?

5. How goes on Stuarts job?

As to what People say, I don't care a straw, provided I have nothing to say against myself. Now it has regularly happened to me in the course of every work in which I have been engaged, that the talkers have chosen those subjects for censure and defamation, in which I was invulnerable, and have appeared entirely ignorant of those little errors, miscarriages, and deficiencies with which all large works more or less abound. It happens, that at Washington, the only possible fault that could be found is the neglect of the roofing, although even that was unavoidable. And on this subject nothing I dare to say, will be said, though the shaking of the old Walls, may perhaps furnish gabble enough.

The Directors of our Navigation, have appointed the 21st. of this month,[1] after which day, I hope to get to Washington, not on a scampering visit, but to sit down leisurely, and think of the business of the next season. Among other thinking, I must think seriously of the Quarries.

As to Elliot if you would treat him to the bottom of this page, it would give him something to digest. If you are of opinion that the dose will do him good, pray let it be administered.

I hope that both of us may become rich in the course of a few years, so as to afford to be idle: I, that I may arrive at a state of life different from that of a strolling Player, You, that you may cease to scratch the hair from your head, and wear the skin from your soles. Of all the Maggots, that are gnawing at this dutch cheese of a Planet of ours, You and I are among the most lively. But what we are put into the cheese for, except to gnaw at it, God only knows. Heaven bless thee thy wife, child and pony, is the prayer of Yours affecty.

B. H. Latrobe

ALS: BHL Papers, Library of Congress (170/E1). Addressed to Lenthall in Washington. Enclosed BHL to Richard Elliot, 30 Oct. 1803, below.

1. The C & D directors met on 21–24 November 1803 (see BHL to Gilpin, 15 Nov. 1803, n. 10, below).

ENCLOSURE: TO RICHARD ELLIOT

Newcastle Octr. 30th. 1803

Mr. Elliot

Sir, I should owe you a very humble apology for walking away without measuring your stone, had your candor been sufficient to have informed me that the flat drew more water than it ought. I have requested Mr. Lenthall to explain to you. As it is, your conduct owes an humble apology to your integrity.

B. H. Latrobe.

ALS: BHL Papers, Library of Congress (170/E4). Appended to BHL to Lenthall, 11 Nov. 1803, above.

TO CHARLES WILLSON PEALE

Newcastle, Novr. 12th. 1803.

Dear Sir,

I am so much from home, and when at home, so much engaged, that my correspondence with you cannot be so regular as I wish. On my arrival the day before yesterday from Back Creek, I found that Mr. G. Read's Polygraph had arrived, and a letter was yesterday delivered to me by the Steward of the Packet inclosing the key. I have the pleasure to inform you, that the Instrument has given the utmost satisfaction. I shall particularly attend to its performance, as Mr. Read is my friend and neighbor, and shall from time to time mention to you whatever strikes me as worth your knowing.

Before I saw your use of a square brass tube for the *Penframe* bar, I had resolved to advise you to several little alterations in the construction of the detail of the machine. The more of the brass work you can *cast*, the cheaper, and the more accurate will it be. I would therefore recommend you to make your *Pen bar* a *round* brass tube of above 1/2 an inch to 3/4 in. diameter. If the machine is to be for 2 pens, turn the bar in a lathe, smooth and handsome, (and it should be turned in all cases) and then taper it a little at each end. The crank that holds the pen, independently of the pen tube, and the two arms, should then be cast in one piece with a socket about 3/4 i. long, thus:

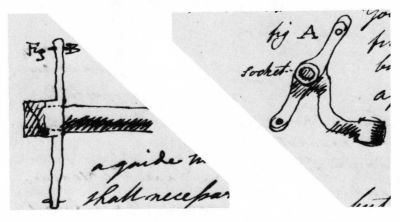

You see I cannot command my hand sufficiently to draw with your Polygraph but you will understand that fig: A is a side View of the piece, and fig. B a front View showing it as fixed to the bar. The hole in the   373

socket must not be cast but drilled afterwards in a frame with a guide hole to the drill shank, so that the socket shall necessarily be square with the arms. The hole for the pentube must also be drilled. The expence of two very good Brass Patterns, one right, one left, will not be more than of two pieces as you now make them, and the superior accuracy, and expedition with which you will file up the castings and fit them, besides the superior neatness of the Workmanship will be cheaply purchased by the trouble of making them. Mr. King of front street if you mention my name to him as an introduction will execute them for you very neatly and reasonably.[1] These pieces may be fixed to the Penbar, either by pins through the socket and bar, or by a screw at the end of the bar, or, which is the easiest way, by driving a Mandril into the tube and thus spreading it at the mouth in the nature of a rivet. If even the machine were rendered heavier by this means, you have only to strengthen the cord of suspension. Another part of the machine which you may easily cast, is your pulley blocks and the standards in which the first pivots work. In the case of three pens, a separate cast piece will be necessary for the middle pen.

The open frame of a 3 pen Machine, and indeed of one of two pens, is very liable to put the machine out of order by the casting of any of its three uppersides. Would it not be well to brace them thus:

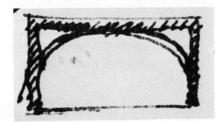

by two brass segments let in flush and well screwed on. But I think you had perhaps let the evil occur before you go to the expence of curing it.

I see no use whatever in the standing gage where there is an ivory one. The things are in the way of the sleeve, and the holes in the frame to receive them weaken it, and render it liable to warp.

Your place for the Candle is a bad one. The shadow of the Machinery is thrown upon the writing. The best place for the Candle is on the left hand on a table. The Polygraph, in a study should have its own stand, and a slider to pull out on the left hand to hold a candle or two, or a patent lamp.

I am glad Rembrandt is returning. England is indeed in an unhappy state. I have seen a very sensible Man from thence, who has given me a very melancholy picture of the state of things there. There are a thousand reasons, independently of those suggested by humanity that induce me to dread a change of government in that country.[2] The government, and the manufactures are so interwoven that one cannot fall without pulling the other after it. And it is a thousand times better for us that our workshops should be on the other side of the Atlantic while we are farmers and merchants, than that any of our citizens should be employed in making pin points, while others are employed in making pin's heads.[3] The division of labor, which successful manufactures require is a division of knowledge and of independence; every man has but a very little. Believe me with great respect Yrs. truly

B. H. Latrobe

Polygraph Copy: LB (27/C8). Addressed to Peale in Philadelphia.

1. Daniel King, Jr. (d. post-1816) was a Philadelphia brass founder.

2. In 1803 the head of government in Britain was Henry Addington (1757–1844), who had succeeded the younger William Pitt (1759–1806) as first lord of the treasury and chancellor of the exchequer on 14 March 1801. During Addington's ministry the Treaty of Amiens was signed (March 1802), which brought a temporary end to the decade-long war between Britain and France. The war resumed in May 1803, however, and Pitt and his followers became increasingly critical of the defense measures adopted by the government. On 30 April 1804, Addington declared his intention to resign, and Pitt was asked to form a new government.

3. BHL is alluding to Adam Smith's *Wealth of Nations,* in which the pinmaking industry is used to illustrate the increased productivity made possible by the division and specialization of labor. BHL gives a Jeffersonian twist to the illustration that Smith certainly did not intend, however. Smith, *An Inquiry into the Nature and Causes of the Wealth of Nations,* ed. Edwin Cannan (New York, 1937 [orig. publ. 1776]), pp. 3–5. Thomas Jefferson, *Notes on the State of Virginia,* ed. William Peden (Chapel Hill, N.C., 1955 [orig. publ. 1787]), pp. 164–65.

TO JOSHUA GILPIN

Newcastle Novr. 15th. 1803

Dear Sir,

By this time I presume you are again in Philadelphia. I will however venture to write a letter *at* you, in order to find out whether I may again write *to you*. My letters, if not worth anything more, are at least a Chronicle of the Canal facts as far as I am engaged in them, and an expression of my respect for you.

I did not receive the instructions of the Committee till a week after they ought to have been in my hands.[1] I employed this time in correcting the faulty parts of the upper line, with which I am now tolerably satisfied. Immediately however, after the receipt of my instructions, I took the first tolerable weather to proceed with my lower line. On consideration, I resolved to begin at the Old Courthouse point, and to run forward till I should arrive again at Sam Sutton's where I had left off formerly. Accordingly, I went to Frenchtown on Tuesday the 7th. of November, and arrived there early in the morning, with an intention of going down in the Baltimore packet as far as the mouth of Back Creek. One of my principal objects was to view the river Elk previously to the proposed survey of its Channel and Western shore. It was about half flood when we embarked; the wind strong at S. West, so that both Wind and tide were full against us in the narrowest part of the Channel. The Packet drew 8 feet some inches water aft, being a little out of Trim. Notwithstanding all this, we beat down to the turn of the Channel near Locust point. The wind by this time blew a Hurricane, and the Sloop carreened 2 streaks on the deck under Water at every Trip. Our Captain, too eager to make the most of the Channel, and perhaps a little flurried by the violence of the Wind, run her ashore a little above Locust point, and the Storm increasing to an alarming degree we got the Sails down, and lay snug in a bed of mud till 2 or 3 o'clock, when we carried out an anchor, and easily got afloat again. The wind being moderate at that time we easily [were] soon out of the upper reach, and the Channel then favoring our course we got down to Pierce's point. Here the breeze died away entirely, and it was eight o'clock and quite dark before we got opposite to Courthouse point. We were set ashore about a Mile below the point, and marched up in a body to Mr. Alxr. Craig's, a farmer, and shallop owner. In his miserable log and framed hut, (for these are terms applicable [to] every farm house hereabouts) we found the females [of] his family, pictures of Ague and fever, who gave us excellent beds and a good *warm* fire in a room through which the Wind found its way by a thousand creeks[2] of Glass and Walls. After prayers and breakfast, (our good host being a strict Methodist), we went in a small batteau to the point, the wind blowing violently, and the cold benumbing our fingers. In spite of the bitter weather I went to work immediately on my arrival, and proceeded that day as far as Mr. Jesse Forde's, who lives among the heads of Herring Creek in Bohemia Manor, about a Mile west of the Church. His house of Brick was tumbling down with age, and was if possible more a Temple of the winds than Mr. Craig's. His Coffee however, his hung beef, and his beds were excellent, and rendered still more so by a most friendly welcome. Mr. Forde is a man of superior manners, and belongs to a large family of Fordes in this part of the world who are all said to be very clever fellows. They are a good breed. Though this country is chiefly inhabited by Methodists Mr. Forde made an exception, and we were not detained by prayers or Psalm singing, but made good our way to very near the Buck road.[3] I am so little used to dine on these expeditions that I had almost forgotten to tell you, that breakfast and supper at the distance of 11 hours from each other was all the refreshment we got on either of these days. On the evening of the second day we proposed lodging at the Buck.[4] But we found the Landlord in great distress, and he could not give us even food. His wife was on the point of death, two days before, he had buried one of his Children, who had been carried off by the hooping cough, and another was given over, in the same disorder. As I had my carriage with me, I therefore run home to Newcastle the rest of the party had to beg lodging and food among the neighbors. Hospitality is always found (except at Newcastle) exactly in the proportion in which it is wanted. We therefore always see it the virtue of savages, and of those whom a scanty population, and the difficulty of purchasing accomodations places on the verge of savage life. But when population increases, and the markets of convenience come nearer to each other, hospitality declines and at last disappears.[5] There is therefore only one Man to be mentioned, *infamiae causâ*,[6] who ever refused us the necessary refreshment, and accomodation. His name is Abraham *Short*, he lives one mile W. and by W. of the Bear tavern, in a large brick house: *Hic niger est, hunc tu, Gilpine, caveto!*[7]

Our journey was finished on Saturday night last. Since then weather, and necessity has confined us to the Office, for our papers are growing very voluminous, and no room in my house which I can spare being 377 large enough, I have hired an office in the neighbourhood, in Mr. Read's old house.

Independently of the completion of the levelling across from Back Creek to Port penn, the opportunity which my expedition gave me of *observing* the Channel of the Elk river, and the probability of a good harbor between Frenchtown and Townpoint was valuable, and was not neglected. My opinion at present is this. The present landing at French town is badly situated, but the situation in which I have placed the tidelock in my Map is the best on the whole river for the Debouche of the Canal, and for this reason: that it is nearly opposite to that part of the Channel, which gradually varies from a South, and west to a West direction then turning again to South, and easterly course so that in any wind, a boat can get out having 10 feet water, at low water. And should the tide be stronger than the wind, a bridge from the lock to Locust point, will clear the boats by means of a horse from all difficulty. Below locust point the Channel does not approach the Eastern shore any where near enough to be reached by any works of moderate, or even reasonable expence, untill you come to the Capes of Back Creek.

As to either Welchpoint or Townpoint, though the Ship Channel off either of them is certainly an excellent harbor for a Fleet of large Vessels, neither of them afford protection in Elk river for smaller craft against any wind whatever, with these exceptions. During a North East storm, Boats may lie in the narrow Channel of Backcreek in 7 feet to 9 at low Water under Welch point, but a Storm from the Westward of North or the Eastward of North East renders this situation quite insecure. In a violent wind from South West to South East, there is Shelter on the North side of Town point, in 7 to 9 feet water, and in a North East storm, the same sort of security is to be had on the South side of the point. But altogether the whole situation is not by any means eligible as a harbor excepting for Merchant Vessels, and that in the Stream. These observations will occur to any one who views the place in a Storm, as I did, and they are confirmed by Mr. Craig who lives on the spot, who has navigated these waters for ten Years, and who is interested in bringing the Canal near his Property.

These are difficulties of the Waters, the difficulties of the land are also considerable. If the Canal *debouch* at the Point, which is in fact the only place at all eligible it must then proceed South Eastward along the narrow neck for about 2½ miles. Thence it will be necessary either to go southward to avoid the numerous head branches of Herring creek, keeping the ridge which approaches within 3/4 of a mile of Bohemia, or to bank over the two main Vallies of Herring creek, in order to keep a straighter direction. I pursued the latter course, making for the flat ground which separates the waters of Back Creek and Bohemia East of the Waters of Herring Creek. Over this ground the level was carried in a tolerably straight direction, as far as Back Creek which was crossed, and the level carried along the north bank. The South side of this Valley however offers perhaps better ground though it increases, I believe the distance. The ridge separating the Delaware and Chesapeake waters cannot be passed at the low place discovered by Mr. Howard.

Having been relieved by Mr. G[ale] from any concern about supplying the Canal with Water when he told me, "*mind your business, which is to lay out the Canal, and I will undertake that it shall be filled with Water.*" It is perhaps of little consequence that I should remark, that the line of Canal through the whole of Bohemia Manor, between the drafts of the creeks will require a summit level of 80 feet at least, of 4 to 5 feet higher than the upper Canal. This agrees exactly with the hypothesis assumed in my report, of a regular ascent to the North West throughout the highest grounds of the peninsula.[8]

The instruction of the last Committee respecting a connecting line between the upper line, and a debouche at Welchpoint, having been so worded as to prescribe an impracticable duty, I have endeavored to prepare to execute the *intention* of the Committee, as I understand it, and have employed Mr. Blaney to survey the ground between Long Creek and Perch creek, the only range over which such a line could perhaps be carried. We are now reducing this survey to paper and as far as we have gone, it looks rather unpromising. All the ridges are, I fear too high, and if the ridge be quitted, the drafts of the Creek become the sources of great trouble, and expence, and the work is much lengthened.[9]

I shall appear before the next board with a large Mass of additional information, and shall propose a number of arrangements which I hope will meet with more attention than the last.[10] It is indeed not my business to urge the matter, but I cannot help feeling a personal interest in the success of the work which is superior to any motives of personal prudence which might sway me. I fear that the lethargy of the board is already sowing the seeds of embarrassment, if not of miscarriage.

You must have had very unpleasant weather on your expedition 379 with Mrs. Gilpin, if you indeed have undertaken it. I hope that with or without it health is reestablished in your family.

Believe me with the truest respect Yours affecty.

B. Henry Latrobe

Polygraph Copy: LB (27/D1). Addressed to Gilpin in Philadelphia.

1. The written instructions by Roche. See BHL to Gilpin, 4 Nov. 1803, above.

2. Obsolete word for crack or fissure.

3. Methodism had become the predominant religion in northeastern Maryland by the last quarter of the eighteenth century. It was especially strong in that part of Cecil County north of the Elk River. However between 1787 and 1808 "there is reason to believe that Methodism increased quite as rapidly on . . . [Bohemia] Manor and in Sassafras Neck" as it did in northern Cecil County. So strong was Methodist influence in North Elk Parish, that no Episcopal minister filled the vacancy there between 1801 and 1835. Johnston, *History of Cecil County*, pp. 453, 458.

4. The Buck was a tavern operated by Peter Hendrickson. Today it is one of the variant names of Summit Bridge, a settlement in New Castle County near the Chesapeake and Delaware Canal, nearly six miles north of Middletown. L. W. Heck et al., *Delaware Place Names* (Washington, D.C., 1966), p. 107; Henry C. Conrad, *History of the State of Delaware*, 3 vols. (Wilmington, Del., 1908), 2 : 467.

5. For an earlier and lengthier discussion of American hospitality by BHL, see BHL, *Journals*, 2 : 329–32.

6. Trans.: For infamy's sake.

7. Trans.: He is black, avoid thou this man, Gilpin.

8. BHL, C & D Report, 21 Oct. 1803 (170/C10).

9. BHL requested Blaney's services on 4 November 1803. Blaney charged the C & D Canal Company $60 for "6 days Surveying up Long Creek and the Country between Long and Perch Creek" and "4 days service Plotting in Mr. Latrobe's office." BHL to Blaney, 4 Nov. 1803, LB (27/A7); Daniel Blaney Daybook, 18 Nov. 1803, Historical Society of Delaware, Wilmington.

10. The survey committee of the C & D board of directors met on 21–23 November, while the full board met on 22–24 November. BHL attended each day, submitted several drafts and plans, and made a report on his survey work. On 22 November the survey committee ordered the secretary to provide a book into which BHL's reports could be entered. The following day BHL was ordered to make surveys of Elk River, White Clay Creek, and Christina River for the feeder that would supply the main canal with water. BHL, C & D Report, 21 Nov. 1803 (170/E6); C & D Survey Committee Minutes, 21–23 Nov. 1803.

TO JOHN LENTHALL

Philadelphia Novr. 27th. 1803.

My dear Lenthal,

Did you never hear the proverb, Once a Captain, always a Captain? This is all the answer I give to you on the subject of your *Monody* about your fighting in the Ranks.

You have in the next place, not said a word to me about Stewart's painting room. Pray let me know how that matter stands. You must want money by this time, and it is fit I should send you some. You may expect it as soon as I again hear from you.

As to the public quarries I can say nothing about them till I come to you, and God knows when that will be. Some time however in December. I have great reason to be dissatisfied with my Canal directors. But I have put my hand to the plough and dare not look back. Their next meeting will make me a Delaware man or a Washingtonian.[1]

The wooden column idea is one with which I never will have anything to do. On that you may rely. I will give up my office sooner than build a temple of disgrace to myself and Mr. Jefferson. But he has certainly too much good sense to persevere in his conceptions, after hearing all that is to be said against them.[2]

You are also perfectly silent upon the subject of the tumble from the cieling of the senate Chamber. Pray give me a hint about the real cause of that disaster.

The boxes which have arrived contain the stove pipe. I have not sent any spare Iron, but there is some spare pipe, of which you must make the knees yourselves. You know how the Stove pipe makers manage. They dip the pipe into Water under the required angle and then mark and cut it. The stoves will soon follow. They are just ready.

A quantity of Iron is prepared for the roof of the President's house and sent on. I hope to be there very soon after its arrival. Also a quantity for the new roof of the Sen: Chamber.

Pray ask Mr. Brent in my name, whether he will or will not continue during the next season to deliver stone at the old price. If he says *yes,* or if he says *no,* tell him that I will agree to no contract but *at* the old price. I would add, that at that price I would take *all* that he can raise, if the appropriation *were already made.* But as it is not I can only promise on condition that it *be* made.[3]

I forget whether I ever informed you that I mean to put a compleat 381 new roof over the Senate Chamber, leaving only the floor. Of this I shall on my arrival give you a drawing, and if possible put it in hand.

I have been brought hither by business, added to a most distressing family occurence. My brother in law[4] has been for sometime past been in a very bad state of health, and for these two or three days past I have not been able to leave his bedside as his hourly dissolution has been expected. Better hopes of his recovery since yesterday permit me to answer your letter of the 11th. Novr. which I have now had about 4 days by me.

The best cement for the pipes is blood and iron filings and lime mixed up into a paste. But if the pipe fit well together common mortar will do. The Air holes need not be cut untill the Stoves arrive and then I shall be with you.

As to your office, You must have a better next Season. God bless you my dear fellow. It is for the sake of such Men as You, of whom I have in the course of my life met with 3 or 4 that I sometimes wish that I were great and powerful. As it is, I abound in little else but good intentions and kind wishes. Yours very truly

B. H. Latrobe

ALS: BHL Papers, Library of Congress (170/F1). Addressed to Lenthall in Washington.

1. For the results of the 24–25 January 1804 meeting of the C & D board of directors, see BHL to Isaac Hazlehurst, 4 Feb. 1804, below.

2. BHL encountered several difficulties in attempting to establish a tradition of monumental masonry architecture in America: a dearth of stonecutters; the fact that work on the Capitol was begun in Aquia sandstone, which varied in quality and durability; and the lack of a developed quarry industry. In addition, Jefferson did not share BHL's dedication to the principle of permanent, incombustible construction, and BHL therefore also had to contend with Jefferson's willingness to employ perishable materials, such as wood.

3. For Brent's attempt to force up stone prices, see BHL, Procuring Stone for the U.S. Capitol, [17 Feb. 1804], n. 1, below.

4. Robert Hazlehurst (1774–1804) who had assisted BHL on the Susquehanna survey expedition in the fall of 1801.

TO THOMAS JEFFERSON

Philadelphia, Novr. 30th. 1803

Dear Sir,

The difficulties I have met with in my surveys and levellings for the Canal which is to unite the Bays of Chesapeake and Delaware, have *forced* me to pay much less attention, otherwise than by correspondence to the duties with which you have intrusted me, than I could have wished. I am now here solely for the purpose of urging the progress of those works which must be performed *here*, and find that much Iron has been sent on to Washington for the roofs, and that the stoves are ready to go by the next Vessel. I will not take up your time now with the details; I am exerting myself to be at Washington in a fortnight at most, and hope eventually, not to disgrace the confidence you have placed in me.

All the Iron specified in the enclosed bill having been forwarded to Monticello, Mr. Mifflin, the principal partner of the Rolling Company, has requested me to solicit, that, whenever convenient You would please to pay the amount of the enclosed bill, to Mr. Jo. Lenthall to whom an order is endorsed upon it; and who will forward the amount, as it is impossible to dispose here of a bill on Richmond. Mr. Mifflin hopes this arrangement may not be inconvenient to you.

Fully sensible of the great obligations I owe to you, and regretting exceedingly that the duties of my engagement to the Ches. & Del. Canal Company has prevented that constant personal attention to my business at Washington which I so must desire to bestow upon it, I hope to receive the assurances of your indulgence, when, in the course of a very short time, I shall wait upon you.

I am with true respect Your faithfull hble. Servt.

B. Henry Latrobe

ALS: Jefferson Papers (170/F7). Endorsed as received 4 December.

TO ANDREW HAZLEHURST

Newcastle Decr. 1st. 1803.

My dear Brother,

On the 26th. of Octr. I wrote to you a long letter, the subject of which was *that* upon which we had a conversation the last time I saw you. Our Brother Isaac whom I have seen in Philadelphia informs me, that you have never received this letter. I have therefore enquired at the Post office, and the Postmaster not only remembers my bringing it to the office but is ready to swear that he put it into the mail. Now as this is not the first time that letters to and from me have miscarried since my residence in Newcastle, and as the letter itself is of a nature highly improper to be seen by third persons, for it contains the fullest effusions of our mutual confidence, I must beg of you to enquire at your post office about it, and procure a written certificate from the Postmaster respecting it. I suspect the fault to be at Wilmington and am determined to go to the bottom of the matter. If the Postmaster will do nothing pray send me your own certificate that you did not receive such a letter. By means of this Certificate and that of the Postmaster of this place, I shall, I hope, institute an enquiry which will prevent similar miscarriage.

I returned this morning from Philadelphia, where I have left your Sister, after spending a most melancholy week in second street. Isaac, I presume has communicated to you every thing respecting the situation of our poor Brother Robert. The convulsions which attacked him on Friday last, and continued for 8 or 10 hours, and which appeared likely to terminate so fatally *may* perhaps be the consequence of excessive bleeding. It is difficult to say whether they are so or not, for they were precisely a repetition, but with less violence, of those which so much alarmed the family a month before, and what is more remarkable, the term was exactly that of a *lunar* month. I therefore rather incline to the opinion that they belong to the disease, which is nothing more or less than a violent tendency of the blood to accumulate in the vessels of the brain; for when no pulse could be felt in the extremities, the carotid arteries (in the neck) beat strongly and notwithstanding the excessive loss of blood which he had suffered before the paroxysm (Thursday) the flushing of the face, a certain symptom of delirium, returned again on Sunday.

The system of cure adopted by the Physicians is that pursued and I believe *generally* with success in all similar cases. They have endeavored by Mercury, bleeding at the veins of the arms and feet, and especially by cupping and by a regimen most severely abstemious, to reduce his system to the lowest possible state of debility. The mercury has however had little or no effect, and it appears by the color and consistence of his blood, that the bleeding has also been attended with less success than could have been expected. He has indeed an iron constitution, the struggle is lamentably severe. The convulsions of Friday last exhausted him however so entirely that for 36 hours he appeared alive only by a faint breathing, and the weak tho' rapid beating of his pulse. He then gradually began to move and recover, and the first notice he took was of the cry of *fire* in the streets. We hoped from his manner, that he would possess his reason on his recovery; for his first expressions were perfectly adapted to the occasion that called for them. But he has since disappointed us, though he is very calm in all he says and does. The young Ladies of his acquaintance and principally Miss Bordley seem to fill his thoughts.[1]

It is not necessary, nor is it indeed possible to describe to you the distress that pervades the whole family, and hastens the old age of our father and Mother. The death of our friend would indeed be less grievous than his continuance in his present state, or indeed perhaps to his recovering an uncertain sanity.

You have no doubt heard of the birth of little Abraham Markoe. He is an uncommonly fine infant, but little Juliana is an arrant Vixen, ruined in temper and neglected in her dress by a silly and impertinent Irish jade.[2] Upon the whole indeed I do not think the Hazlehurst blood improved by the Creole mixture.[3] Sam himself with a heart as noble, and generous as ever beat in a human breast, has changed his *outside character.* You will never hide your virtues by *gilding* your conduct or I am much mistaken in you. God bless you my dear fellow. Write to me soon, and believe me most affecty. yrs.

B. H. Latrobe

Polygraph Copy: LB (27/F4). Addressed to Hazlehurst in Baltimore.

1. Elizabeth Bordley (1777–1863) was the only daughter of John Beale Bordley (1727–1804) and Sarah (Fishbourne) Mifflin. She married James Gibson in 1817. Elizabeth Bordley Gibson, *Biographical Sketches of the Bordley Family, of Maryland,* ed. Elizabeth Mifflin (Philadelphia, 1865), pp. 3–6, 111.

2. Abraham Markoe Hazlehurst (1803–45) and Juliana Hazlehurst (1802–76), children of Samuel and Elizabeth Baynton (Markoe) Hazlehurst. Hazlehurst genealogical charts, MdHS.

3. A reference to Abraham Markoe, who was a native of St. Croix. See BHL to Samuel Hazlehurst, 11 Oct. 1803, n. 2, above.

TO CORP & CASEY

Newcastle, Decr. 1st. 1803

Gentlemen,[1]

I have received your letter of the 28th of Novr. and should reply explicit to your question, had I the necessary information—respecting the instruments by which I may be held as security for Mr. Roosevelt.[2]

But it is necessary to inform you that on this subject I have received nothing from my friend Roosevelt but *general assurances;* and although I have repeatedly asked for copies of the papers, I have been satisfied to depend upon the integrity of his character of which I never have had reason to doubt. If you will therefore have the goodness to transmit to me, at my own expence, copies of the original bond, of the papers executed under any power of attorney of my own, or of any other papers in which I may on this occasion be interested I will immediately on receipt thereof remit your expences, and soon afterwards a clear and explicit answer to your enquiry. I am with much respect Yrs. etc.

B. H. Latrobe.

Polygraph Copy: LB (27/F8). Addressed to Corp & Casey in New York.

1. Samuel Corp and James Casey were New York merchants who (with Nicholas J. Roosevelt, John Stevens, Arent Schuyler, and Robert R. Livingston) were incorporators of the Soho Company in 1801. Corp was a native of England who came to New York shortly after the American Revolution. Helen M. Morgan, ed., *A Season in New York, 1801: Letters of Harriet and Maria Trumbull* (Pittsburgh, 1969), p. 71; Harry B. Weiss and Grace M. Weiss, *The Old Copper Mines of New Jersey* (Trenton, N.J., 1963), p. 21.

2. These financial arrangements arose out of Nicholas Roosevelt & Co.'s 1799 contract with the Navy Department, by which the firm agreed to supply copper bolts, sheathing, and other articles for the recently authorized seventy-four gun ships. Over a period of eighteen months Roosevelt was advanced about $50,000 on this contract, including $30,000 on a note endorsed for him by Corp and Casey. Roosevelt's security for this loan was his share and BHL's share in the Schuylkill rolling mill at Philadelphia, where he intended to roll the copper. BHL gave Roosevelt a power of attorney to mortgage his share in the mill because he recognized that the copper contract was vital to the success of the rolling mill as it was originally planned. (Once in production late in 1802 the mill rolled only iron.) Roosevelt invested much of the Navy Department's advances in the rolling mill, but in the spring of 1801 the new Jefferson administration cancelled the contracts for the seventy-fours. Roosevelt's creditors saw he was overextended and began inquiries about his assets and the security of his notes. Eventually Corp and Casey were satisfied without requiring BHL to give up his rolling mill share, but Roosevelt's account with the Navy Department was not settled until 1813. BHL to Robert Smith, 17 Oct. 1808, and Smith to BHL, 1 Nov. 1808, both in RG 45, National Archives (microfiche add., 197/A9); BHL to Smith, 21 Nov. 1808, in BHL, *Correspondence,* 2; BHL to Paul Hamilton, 18 July 1811, and BHL to Robert Fulton, 1 Feb. 1813, both in LB (87/E4, 107/A12); *Naval Documents Related to the Quasi-War between the United States and France. Naval Operations,* 7 vols. (Washington, D.C., 1935–38), 4 : 118–19; *ASP. Naval Affairs,* 1 : 79; Fritz Redlich, "The Philadelphia Water Works in Relation to the Industrial Revolution in the United States," *PMHB* 69 (1945):256.

TO THOMAS LAW AND WILLIAM BRENT

Philadelphia, Decr. 13th. 1803

Gentlemen[1]

As my residence is principally at Newcastle in the State of Delaware, I did not receive your polite letter of the 5th. of this month till my arrival here, yesterday evening. I cannot offer any apology to you for the delay which has taken place in not sending to Washington the designs and estimates of the projected Canal long before the present date, but the extreme pressure of my engagements in the State of Delaware, relative to the Canal of communication between the bays of Chesapeake and Delaware.[2] I have however made all the necessary designs, and shall devote the time that remains between my return to Newcastle, on Friday next, and my departure to Washington in the middle of next week entirely to the completion of your business. You may therefore depend on seeing me on, or before the 20th. of Decr. fully prepared with every information that my talents or experience enable me to give.[3]

I beg you to accept my thanks for the polite indulgence with which you have excused my delay hitherto, and to assure you of the respect with which I am Gentlemen Yr. faithful hble. servt.

B. Henry Latrobe

Polygraph Copy: LB (27/F12).

1. Thomas Law (1756–1834), Washington speculator, spent his early years in India, where he became prosperous. He came to America in August 1794 and visited Washington, D.C., in 1795, when, impressed by the prospects of the city's future growth, he invested heavily in city lots. Law married Eliza Custis, Martha Washington's granddaughter, and their Washington home still stands. Law's unsuccessful real estate investments and the failure of his sugar refinery in the city did not deter him from continually promoting the new capital. He was an important supporter of the Washington Canal, serving on its board of directors (1812–24, 1826–27, 1830), and became a friend and associate of BHL's. Minutes of the Board of Directors of the Washington Canal Co., 1810–31, RG 351, National Archives; Allen C. Clark, *Greenleaf and Law in the Federal City* (Washington, D.C., 1901), pp. 223, 263–64; Constance McLaughlin Green, *Washington: Village and Capital, 1800–1878* (Princeton, N.J., 1962), pp. 19, 28; Harold Donaldson Eberlein and Cortlandt Van Dyke Hubbard, *Historic Houses of George-Town and Washington City* (Richmond, Va., 1958), pp. 406–09.

Col. William Brent (1775–1848), brother of Washington Mayor Robert Brent (c. 1763–1819) and State Department clerk Daniel Carroll Brent (c. 1770–1841), was a clerk to the commissioners of the District of Columbia (resigned 1801) and clerk of the District Court in Washington from 1805 to 1848. An active politician, Brent held many city posts including city councilman (1802–04) and alderman (1831–40). Like Law, Brent was an ardent promoter of Washington City. He was a stockholder of the Bank of Washington

387

(1809) and served as a director of the Washington branch of the Bank of the U.S. (1806, 1808, 1810) and of the Washington Canal Company (1815–31). He was a member of the first board of trustees of the Washington public schools and promoted cultural activities in the capital. Minutes of the Washington Canal Co.; Chester Horton Brent, *The Descendants of Coll. Giles Brent, Capt. George Brent and Robert Brent, Gent.* (Rutland, Vt., 1946), pp. 137–38; CHS, *Records* 1 (1895):122, 5 (1902):30, 70, 8 (1905):29, 31, 38, 16 (1913):138, 24 (1922):68, 25 (1923):116, 30 (1928):20, 33–34 (1932):270, 294, 35–36 (1935):116, 39 (1938):36n; William V. Cox, comp., *Celebration of the One Hundredth Anniversary of the Establishment of the Seat of Government in the District of Columbia* (Washington, D.C., 1901), pp. 298, 303–06.

2. The Washington Canal Company was chartered by Congress in 1802 to construct a canal from the Eastern Branch (Anacostia River) near the navy yard to Tiber Creek, where it entered the Potomac near the President's House. That same year President Jefferson requested BHL to examine the possibility of supplying water for the proposed navy yard dry docks by means of a canal from the Little Falls canal on the Potomac River. BHL's elaborate and beautifully detailed plans apparently influenced the Washington Canal promoters, who approached him in early 1803 to design their waterway. By July 1803 BHL and his assistants, Robert Mills and William Strickland, were at work on the plans. But the engineer soon returned to Delaware to begin the surveys for the C & D Canal, and work on the Washington Canal ceased until early in 1804. [Thomas Law], *Observations on the Intended Canal in Washington City* (Washington, D.C., 1804), Appendix, pp. 12–16; BHL, Report on Proposed Naval Drydock, 4 Dec. 1802, above; Robert Mills diary, 2 July, 3 July, 5 July, and 10 July 1803, Special Collections Division, Tulane University Library, New Orleans. BHL's Potomac Canal Extension plans are in the Map Division, Library of Congress (267/A1).

3. BHL finally left for Washington on 30 December. He spent most of January and February in the capital city on business relating to the Capitol and the Washington Canal. In February he completed a report and several plans of the waterway. With this data in hand canal promoters began their subscription drive. But neither BHL's report and neatly delineated plans nor the forceful arguments of Thomas Law in his promotional pamphlet *Observations on the Intended Canal in Washington City* were able to encourage the requisite number of investors to subscribe. The canal project lay dormant for five years before it was revived again, this time to be successfully completed under BHL's direction. BHL to Isaac Hazlehurst, Jr., 28 Dec. 1803, LB (29/A10); BHL, *Engineering Drawings*, pp. 19–23. BHL's 1804 Washington Canal plans are in the Map Division, Library of Congress (280/A1). His original February 1804 report has not been discovered, but portions of it were published in the *National Intelligencer*, 26 May 1809 (microfiche add.). Another extract from the report, including some of the material in the *National Intelligencer* extract, was published in the version of Law's *Observations* (microfiche add.) reprinted in CHS, *Records* 8 (1905):159–68.

TO NICHOLAS J. ROOSEVELT

Philadelphia Decr. 13th. 1803

My dear Sir

On my arrival here yesterday evening, I received your favor of the 8th. Decr., which might otherwise have remained unanswered for a long time, as my residence at present is at Newcastle. I am sorry that our correspondence has been so long interrupted. I need not assure you that my attachment to you, whatever may be the difference of our opinions on matters of business remains unaltered, through all the disappointments, sufferings and apprehensions for the future that have attended our connexion, and to which I see no end.

As to the proposal you suggest I will certainly make it though without the most distant prospect of success. As to the influence which my ideas may have had upon the purchasers of Bollmanns interest, you form a wrong estimate if you suppose that it has extended beyond merely arrangements of machinery, and of manufacturing schemes. I had no means of influence. Bollman's arrangements with Mr. Casey, in which my opinion was taken necessarily became the terms with the new partners, and the negociations between all parties were so involved with each other, that no new Ground could be taken.[1] All I could therefore do was to advise professionally, and to get the money I had borrowed of my friends to support the works between the failure of the old and the organization of the new works repaid. On this occasion I have made most injurious pecuniary sacrifices, with the detail of which it is useless to plague you.[2]

As to the answer I shall receive from our Partners it will be this: We are willing to rate the two shares at 15.000 Dollars, to pay all the debts and to relieve the two shares by gradual reimbursement, but we will do no more; much less will we engage to pay 5.000$ per Annum, while the Works barely maintain themselves but have no profit, (which is the case at present), and to continue to do so for 10 Years, during which time a fire may destroy them, so as make the shares, for which no more than 30.000 Dollars have ever yet been asked, cost us 50.000. I will however as I have already said, make the proposal, and if I cannot obtain its adoption, endeavor to know the terms on which they would agree to buy them, without stipulating anything.

I have not yet informed you, that I received about 10 days ago a letter from Messrs. Corps and Casey on this subject. I have declined in the letter I have written to them giving any answer untill I should have copies of all the papers under which I may be liable to them, and have requested them to furnish me with such copies at my own expense.[3] And here the bills retained by them will come into question and all the evils which I formerly predicted, and of which you made so light will come into view. What they may amount to, and how they will influence the future life of a Man like myself, whose infant family is likely become 389 numerous, you, who are so alive to your own situation, will no doubt be well able to anticipate.

The most distressing circumstance in anything that can be said or written to you on this subject is, that you appear to consider it, (as it certainly has been between *you* and *me,* as *friends,*) as a matter not of business, of figures, and of calculation but of *sentiment,* when treating with others, who never felt, or pretended to feel friendship for you. The disinterested, and *lumping* settlements of mutual confidence and generosity, have always been expected by you from Men, whom you must have known well enough, to have looked for nothing from them but mercantile exactness, and whom you could not possibly believe to have any reasonable motive to depart from the usual mode of settling money concerns. Among these I reckon Bollmann. Believe me with very sincere affection Yours truly

B. Henry Latrobe

ALS: LB (27/F14). On 26 December 1803 (see below), BHL explained to Roosevelt that he had inadvertently sent most of the polygraph copy. The dateline, salutation, and the first seven lines of the text of the polygraph copy (as well as a notation that Roosevelt was addressed in New York), were retained in the Letterbook.

1. Upon the bankruptcy of the mercantile house of Erick and Lewis Bollmann in the spring of 1803 their share in the Schuylkill rolling mill was put up for sale. Apparently James Casey had first investigated purchasing it, since he and Samuel Corp already held Roosevelt's and BHL's shares as security. However, the actual purchasers were William Cramond and Samuel Mifflin, Philadelphia businessmen. BHL to Richard Peters, Jr., 14 Feb. 1807, LB (55/A12).

2. BHL later stated that he paid out on the Schuylkill rolling mill's account a total of $2,764.83. BHL to Erick Bollmann, 11 May 1816, LB (130/C11).

3. BHL to Corp & Casey, 1 Dec. 1803, above.

TO AARON BURR

Philadelphia, Decr. 13th. 1803

Sir,

Soon after my appointment to the direction of the public buildings at Washington, I did myself the honor to address a letter to you at Charleston on the subject of rendering the Chamber of the Senate of U.S. more commodious, and especially on the means of warming it more effectually. I much fear that this letter, which I transmitted by a private hand did not reach, it being probable that you had left Charleston before it could arrive.[1] In the mean time the early meeting of the Legislature rendered it necessary that the best means which I could devise should be pursued towards accomplishing the latter object, and with the approbation of the President of the United States, the works which, I must regret, are not yet compleated were commenced. The faulty construction of the Capitol rendered it absolutely necessary, to open windows for the admission of light and air into the Cellar story under the Senate Chamber. It was then discovered that some of the timber of the floor was in a state of decay, that the Cellar was filled with stones and rubbish in many places to its whole depth, and that, owing perhaps to alterations in the first designs, walls of enormous Mass but of little use occupied some of the most useful space. The removal of these obstructions required considerable time and labor, and the erection of the furnaces intended to warm the room above, the clearing of flues, and the building of one entire Stack could not be speedily accomplished. The pipes, and the Stoves themselves could only be made in Philadelphia or New York, and the yellow fever which prevailed in both those cities, was another cause of delay. In spite therefore of my utmost exertion the object is only just now on the eve of being obtained, the stoves being cast and ready to be sent forward by the first Vessel.

I have troubled you with the recital of this detail in hopes that it may plead my apology with You and with the Members of the Senate, and I have no doubt but that when the stoves shall be fixed and other arrangements made, the Senate chamber will be equally and pleasantly warmed in each part of it.[2] Independently of the erection of the Stoves, it is necessary compleatly to ciel the Cellar story, and I have given directions to my agent Mr. Lenthall to prepare everything for this purpose, and he will wait upon you with this letter to receive such directions as you may think proper to give.

The fund from which the expenses of this work have hitherto been defrayed is the sum of 50.000$, placed at the disposal of the President of the United States for the purpose of compleating and repairing the public buildings &c. &c. at Washington, by an act of the last Legislature. In order that this fund may go the greatest possible extent toward the completion of the buildings themselves, I beg leave to submit to you, whether the expenses attending the Stoves and in the erection of furnaces and flues in the Cellar, as well as the Stoves themselves, which   391 more evidently may be considered *as furniture* might not be charged to the contingent fund of the Senate. I am sure that you will acquit me of any intentional indiscretion in making this suggestion. Previously to the statement of my accounts of the manner in which the funds intrusted to me have been expended, I considered in a great degree my duty to state to you my ideas on this subject for your consideration, and hope, on my arrival in Washington in the course of 10 days, to be guided by your direction and advice. An account of what these expenses have amounted to, will if you require it, be made out by Mr. Lenthall.

I am with the truest respect Your much obliged hble. Servt.

B. Henry Latrobe

Polygraph Copy: LB (27/G12). Enclosed in BHL to John Lenthall, 13 Dec. 1803, BHL Papers, Library of Congress (170/G1). A similar letter to Thomas Jefferson (14 Dec. 1803, Jefferson Papers; 170/G6) was also enclosed in the Lenthall letter.

1. In spring 1803 Burr apparently visited his daughter and confidante Theodosia (1783–1813), wife of South Carolina planter-politician Joseph Alston (c. 1779–1816), at their Charleston townhouse. Matthew L. Davis, *Memoirs of Aaron Burr with Miscellaneous Selections from His Correspondence*, 2 vols. (New York, 1852), 2 : 218–22.

2. On 6 February 1804, BHL reported to James Smallman: "We have got up the Stove. It is very well put together excepting that it is 3/4 of an inch wider at the top than at the bottom. My eye saw the defect at once. I hope it will escape the notice of the Senators" (LB; 29/D7).

TO WILLIAM LOUGHTON SMITH

[Philadelphia] Decr. 17th. 1803.

Dear Sir,[1]

I have written the enclosed in the hurry of my departure.[2] To write hastily on a subject upon which to say only *a little* is almost worse than saying nothing, is always bad policy. I hope you will have the goodness however to receive the enclosed as a sincere if not a useful Mark of my esteem, and believe me with true respect Yrs. truly

B. H. Latrobe

ALS: Papers of William Loughton Smith, South Carolina Historical Society (171/A1). Addressed to Smith in Philadelphia.

1. William Loughton Smith (1758–1812), South Carolina Federalist, served in the South Carolina House of Representatives (1784–88, 1808) and the U.S. House of Representatives (1789–97). He also served as minister plenipotentiary to Portugal (1797–1801). Smith was a strong promoter of internal improvements, especially in South Carolina, and he invested large portions of his wealth in both the Catawba and Wateree (Canal) Company and the Santee Canal Company. He requested BHL's recommendation in 1804 for an engineer for the Catawba Company (see BHL to Smith, 21 Mar. 1804, below). Smith acted as an intermediary between BHL and the Santee Canal Company directors in 1809–10, when BHL served as a consultant for the company. Smith later became president of the company. BHL to Smith, 7 Dec. 1809, 10 June 1810, both in LB (71/G10, 75/D12); BHL to Smith, 13 Feb. 1810, in BHL, *Correspondence*, 2; George C. Rogers, Jr., *Evolution of a Federalist: William Loughton Smith of Charleston (1758–1812)* (Columbia, S.C., 1962), pp. 133, 306, 361–62, 362n, 396.

2. See enclosure, below. This was a letter of introduction written to Wheeler, a director and later president of the Dismal Swamp Canal Company, for Smith. Smith had purchased twelve shares of Dismal Swamp Canal Company stock in 1792 and wished to inspect the company's works on his trip from Philadelphia to Charleston, S.C. Smith never did view the canal on this trip, but he did keep abreast of the canal's progress through correspondence. See BHL to Smith, 21 Mar. 1804, below. Rogers, *Evolution of a Federalist*, pp. 235, 361.

ENCLOSURE: TO LUKE WHEELER

Philadelphia Decr. 16th. 1803.

Dear Sir[1]

Mr. William Smith, our late Minister at the Court of Portugal, is not unknown to you in his public Characters, I beg your leave to introduce him *personally* to Your attentions, with full confidence that the pleasure of his acquaintance will make you a return for that politeness and information which no one at Norfolk will be more willing and able to shew him, than yourself. And I will frankly acknowledge, that independently of the pleasure I feel in being at all instrumental in promoting the acquaintance of two such Men with each other I have on this occasion the particular object to procure for Mr. Smith the most disinterested, and correct account of the actual state of the Dismal swamp Canal, which can be given.[2]

In order to lead to a correct explanation of those points upon which I have given to Mr. Smith the best professional opinion which I could form at the distance of time which has elapsed since my last visit to Norfolk, I will take the liberty to state what I have said on this subject.

1.) There appears to me to be an error in the line chosen as the route of the Canal. The *debouche* in Deep creek may have been well chosen, but the Pasquotank empties itself into the Sound so near the

Ocean, that a very dangerous and long Voyage, through the Sound in *stout Vessels* must be accomplished before the entrance of the Canal can be reached. The Cargo must then be shifted into the flatbottomed Canal boats in which they may reach Norfolk, *in calm weather*. All this will render the Navigation *coastwise* as eligible at least as that of the Canal in Summer, for all Vessels coming from the Roanoke, or from the Head of Albermarle Sound; and even in boisterous Weather it will be preferred in many cases to the shifting of the Cargo which is necessary in order to proceed by the safer and shorter course, by the Canal.[3]

2.) The folly or fraud of the Contractor in erecting a Mill on the edge of the Bank of Deep Run to which the Canal served as the Race, appeared to me likely to throw up a Bar in Deeprun below the Tide lock which would prove a fatal obstruction to the passage of the Boats at all times of tide, excepting highwater and if I recollect right this circumstance has actually occurred.[4]

3.) When I saw the Canal, I think in 1798, it was perfectly dry, and the Nature of the Soil appeared to me to be such, that unless made watertight by puddling it must necessarily be dry during the latter part of every Summer, unless supplied from the lake, if indeed the lake be high enough to be capable of being led into the Canal.[5]

These seem to me the principal reasons why the Canal, as at present laid out cannot be a source of much public advantage or private emolument. To much of the detail of the work I have also professional objections, but they are of inferior consequence.

My object in stating nothing but objections is not to injure the interests or reputation of a Work which if it were judiciously planned and faithfully conducted is of infinite consequence, and would be of incalculable advantage to the Union, to your town, and to the Stockholders. But to those who are interested in the Work, and upon whom its completion depends it is of importance that they should know the *weak* parts of the scheme. Those that are *strong,* are sufficiently prominent and exhibit themselves.

I take this occasion to assure you that I recollect with grateful pleasure the polite attentions I have so often received from you and the instructive and agreeable hours I have spent in your Society.[6] Believe me very truly Yr. faithful hble. Servt.

B. Henry Latrobe

ALS: Papers of William Loughton Smith, South Carolina Historical Society (171/A3). Enclosed in BHL to William Loughton Smith, 17 Dec. 1803, above.

1. For Wheeler, See Design of the Pennock House, Norfolk, [8 Sept. 1799], n. 1, above.

2. The Dismal Swamp Canal Company was chartered by both Virginia (1787) and North Carolina (1790) for the purpose of connecting Norfolk with Albemarle Sound by a canal through the Dismal Swamp that would link Deep Run estuary, near Norfolk, and the Pasquotank River, which empties into Albemarle Sound. Canal construction was sporadic and the waterway was opened for boating in 1805 even though it was not completed. BHL, *Engineering Drawings*, p. 137.

3. BHL sketched his remedy for this problem in a drawing he made several days later. His proposal called for a longer canal with a southern entrance closer to the mouth of the Roanoke River, thus eliminating difficult voyages for small rivercraft or canal boats over the open waters of Albemarle Sound. BHL, "Sketch of Canals *executed* or *proposed* near Norfolk," 19 Dec. 1803, APS, reproduced in BHL, *Engineering Drawings*, p. 138.

4. To correct this error BHL proposed a northern entrance to the canal that bypassed the Deep Run estuary altogether and emptied directly into the Elizabeth River near Norfolk. Ibid.

5. BHL actually saw the canal in late March 1796 and again in June 1797 while on an expedition for the Dismal Swamp Land Company. Since no accurate survey had been taken of the canal by this time, BHL and the canal company did not know that Lake Drummond was higher than the canal and could have been used for a water supply. BHL, *Journals*, 1 : 80, 238; BHL, *Engineering Drawings*, p. 137.

6. This is a reference to the hospitality Wheeler extended to BHL on his arrival in Norfolk from England in March 1796. BHL repaid this hospitality by tuning Wheeler's pianoforte. BHL, *Journals*, 1 : 79.

TO KENSEY JOHNS

Saturday, Decr. 24th. 1803

Dear Sir,

I have now completely finished my operations upon the Elk and White clay, having traced the line of the feeder from the Elk; and in addition to my former survey on the White clay, having levelled from the paper Mill up to Rankins dam.[1] The result will, I believe, be the abandonment of White clay. For it will be necessary to bring the Water from Rankins Dam or very little below it, and above Newark, such difficulties present on both sides of the Valley that the expense of overcoming them would be enormous. I have also explored the situation for the Aqueduct to pass Christiana, and find that this work would be extremely expensive, on account of the breadth of the Valley, and the flat of the land on the West side at the only convenient part to which the feeder can be brought from the Eastward.

The course of the Elk feeder on the contrary will be over good   395 ground and deep cutting be required in only three places of no great length, and nowhere of greater depth than 16 feet. The unfortunate rain of yesterday prevented my proceeding to Hog Creek, and I must now defer what I still have to do till my return from Washington. I shall be unable to call upon you today but hope to see you tomorrow in the Course of the day. I am with much respect Yrs. truly

B. H. Latrobe

Polygraph Copy: LB (28/A9).

1. The paper mill, run by Baltimore booksellers and stationers Thomas and Samuel Meteer, was on White Clay Creek at Newark, below Symington's millpond. Rankin's mill was "built on the west side of Whiteclay creek in a very narrow part of the valley." BHL, C & D Report, 26 Jan. 1804 (171/B9); Marie Windell, "News Notes and Book Reports," *Delaware History* 6 (1954):173.

TO HENRY VOIGHT

Newcastle, Decr. 24th. 1803

Dear Sir,[1]

By the Packet which leaves this place this morning I have sent addressed to you, Captain Mudge's account of the Trigonometrical Survey made in England, in which the description and Drawing of a Transit Instrument is contained.[2] You will find it in many instances different in principle from yours, but I think it will be useful to you. The book is on many other accounts valuable. You are welcome to keep it as long as you may find it useful, when I shall be happy to receive it again. I expect to be in Philadelphia the latter end of January when I will endeavor to see you. On sending to the Warehouse at Market street Wharf, the packet will be delivered to you. I am with true respect Yours truly

B. Henry Latrobe

Polygraph Copy: LB (28/A11). Addressed to Voight as chief coiner of the mint, Philadelphia.

1. Henry Voight (1738–1814) was born in Germany, trained in clock making, and for a time employed at the Royal Mint in Saxony. He emigrated to the United States before 1770 and became David Rittenhouse's assistant at his Norriton observatory near Philadelphia. He participated in John Fitch's attempt to build a workable steamboat (Fitch regarded him as a "Mechanical genius") and in 1793 he became the chief coiner at the

United States Mint in Philadelphia. Instrument making and repair were occasional activities for Voight. For BHL's estimate of Voight, see BHL to Bollmann, 21 June 1809, in BHL, *Correspondence*, 2. Silvio A. Bedini, *Early American Scientific Instruments and their Makers* (Washington, D.C., 1964), p. 62; Bedini, *Thinkers and Tinkers: Early American Men of Science* (New York, 1975), pp. 140, 326–27; Frank D. Prager, ed., *The Autobiography of John Fitch* (Philadelphia, 1976), pp. 115–16.

2. William Mudge et al., *An Account of the Operations Carried on for Accomplishing a Trigonometrical Survey of England and Wales, from . . . 1784 to . . . 1809*, 3 vols. (London, 1799–1811). The second volume, covering the years 1797 to 1799, was published in 1801.

TO SAMUEL HARRISON SMITH

Newcastle, Decr. 24th. 1803

My dear Sir[1]

I thank you sincerely for your very friendly letter of the 20th. Decr. I am wholly at a loss to account for the extreme irregularity of the Post by which so many of my letters written about the end of October have miscarried; and I think ourselves extremely fortunate, in being still in time to avail ourselves of the means pointed out by Mrs. Smith[2] to furnish our lodging. Be assured that we shall not easily forget how much we are obliged to her. As to your friendly invitation to alight at your house on our arrival I fear that the *number* of our family will render it impossible for us to think of accepting it, for we have besides ourselves, a *baby*, our daughter and nurse with us.[3] The latter is a *White* woman, accustomed to sleep with our daughter, and if they could anyhow be accomodated for a night at Mr. Woodward's, the difficulty would be less.[4] We are far from intending to be ceremonious on this occasion. Next to the pleasure of ministring kindness, is certainly that of accepting it from those we esteem. We will therefore on second thought actually alight at your door, and trust to your, and Mrs. Smith's management for our [first] accomodation.

I have desired Mr. Lenthall to lay us in wood, and in a day we shall be easily fixed. If the weather which is at present terrible, permit us we shall set off Monday. But I look forward to so much delay from bad roads, that I shall think ourselves well off if we reach Washington before the end of the Year.

Believe me with true respect Yours very affecty.

B. H. Latrobe

Polygraph Copy: LB (28/A12). Addressed to Smith in Washington.

1. Samuel Harrison Smith (1772–1845), a leading Republican newspaper editor, was educated at the University of the State of Pennsylvania (A.B., 1787). In 1796 he established the *New World* (Philadelphia) and the following year began publication of the *Universal Gazette* (Philadelphia). At Jefferson's request he moved to Washington in 1800 to establish the *National Intelligencer and Washington Advertiser,* the Jefferson administration's unofficial organ. Smith remained editor of the *Intelligencer* (to which BHL occasionally contributed) until 1810. Involved in many civic and business affairs, Smith was elected a member of the First Chamber of the Washington City Council (1802–04, 1806), serving as its president in 1804. William V. Cox, comp., *Celebration of the One Hundredth Anniversary of the Establishment of the Seat of Government in the District of Columbia* (Washington, D.C., 1901), p. 298.

2. Margaret (Bayard) Smith (1778–1844) was a leader of Washington society and the author of several novels and periodical pieces. Many of her letters were published as *The First Forty Years of Washington Society,* ed. Gaillard Hunt (New York, 1906). Although initially on very friendly terms, the Latrobes and the Smiths later became estranged over BHL's unsuccessful attempt to use his influence with his kinsman Pennsylvania Gov. Simon Snyder to have Mrs. Smith's brother Andrew Bayard continued in office as an auctioneer of Philadelphia in 1808. Mrs. Smith was also a close friend of Mrs. William Thornton, and relations no doubt had already become strained as the dispute between BHL and Thornton developed. BHL to Snyder, 20 Nov. 1808, LB (67/B10); BHL to Samuel H. Smith, 22 Sept. 1809, in BHL, *Correspondence,* 2; Hamlin, *Latrobe,* pp. 311–13.

3. Catherine (Kitty) McCausland (d. 1815) worked for the Latrobes as a nurse, maid, and housekeeper from 1802 until she died from burns received when her clothes caught on fire in the Latrobe kitchen. BHL to John McCausland, 26 Dec. 1815, and BHL to Henry S. B. Latrobe, 16 Jan. 1816, both in LB (128/E11, 129/B5); Hamlin, *Latrobe,* p. 417n.

4. William Woodward's hotel was on Pennsylvania Avenue west of Sixth Street, N.W. CHS, *Records* 7 (1904):95–96.

TO NICHOLAS J. ROOSEVELT

Newcastle, Decr. 26. 1803

My dear Sir,

I have lately procured one of Mr. Peale Polygraphs, a Machine which makes by means of a second Pen, fixed to a double set of parallel joints a very perfect copy of whatever is written by the first which is attached to the same set of joints. By this machine which cost 50 Dollars, I am able to obtain copies of all my letters without the privacy or expense of a Clerk. The blunder by which you have received a mutilated letter is owing to my having accidentally sent you the copy instead of the original of my last letter, and half a page of which was made under the end of the foregoing letter which I had written.[1] By this accident the assurances of my sincere affection and of my regret at the interruption of our correspondence have not reached you, and as nothing I could have said to that effect would have been beyond my feelings, I trust that you will believe them, without a transcript of that part of my letter.

On the subject of proposals to our new partners, I should have given you their answer, if I had thought it would have been an agreeable one to you, or have lead to any thing practicable. It is this: we do not want the *encumbered shares,* we will not buy them on any terms, but Mr. Roosevelt shall have our shares on the terms he asks for *his.*

As to the business of the Mortgage to Corp and Casey it is a very sore subject with me. Had all the notes been returned my renunciation of my shares, when I gave you a power of Attorney to dispose of it *for your own use,* would have compleatly exonerated *me* from any danger from that quarter. Of what has been done under that power I am wholly ignorant and you well know, that you have never *given* me any *clear* account of it, though I have often requested it. The sort of *half* confidence with which you have sometimes expected me to be satisfied has been *justified* by you, as necessary and when I had once embarked with you, I had given up the power to stop. Messrs. Corp and Casey have not thought proper to comply with my request to have copies of the papers, nor have they even answered my letters. I can therefore say nothing, on the subject of *How* all this is to wind up.

You have laid particular stress on the words *us* and *our* difficulties. *My* difficulties are confined to the notes in the hands of Casey, and of *McClure* on Smith's account.[2] But should your difficulties extend beyond mine, and my abilities ever extend by my difficulties, you know where there is a *hand* and a *heart* ready to give you every assistance in my power.

Mrs. Latrobe unites with me in the sincere affection for you and Mrs. Mark.[3] Six Months ago she received from her a letter that cost her many tears, and which she has never answered. I have lived at this place and in the neighborhood since July, being engaged in the preparatory measures necessary to be taken before the Chesapeake and Delaware Canal can be carried in execution. Hitherto the expenses of my rambling life have eaten up the profits of my employ. You would very much oblige me by consigning to Mr. Hazlehurst my book of the city hall, sending it by water, and giving him notice by Post: and also if you satisfy my curiosity as to the manner in which that building is going on.[4] Believe me very affecty. Yrs.

B. H. Latrobe   399

Polygraph Copy: LB (28/A14). Addressed to Roosevelt in New York.

1. BHL to Roosevelt, 13 Dec. 1803, above.
2. In 1800 the young Philadelphia chemist Thomas Peters Smith went to Europe, having borrowed $1,000 from William Maclure for his traveling expenses. BHL endorsed Smith's note as well as helped outfit Smith for the trip. When Smith died in 1802 on the return voyage, BHL became liable for the debt. BHL to Roosevelt, 21 Mar. 1807, LB (55/G10); BHL, A Drawing and Description of the Bay Alewife and the Fish Louse, 18 Dec. 1799, n. 1, above.
3. Rosetta Mark, wife of New York merchant Jacob Mark, who was a business partner of Roosevelt's. Hamlin, *Latrobe*, p. 169n.
4. New York City Hall, for which see BHL to [Colhoun], 17 Apr. 1802, n. 4, above.

REMARKS ON THE BEST FORM OF A ROOM FOR HEARING AND SPEAKING

[c. 1803]

My dear friend,[1]

I take with pleasure the opportunity you have offered me, of shewing to you the respect which four years connexion with you in the public service,[2] has produced for your person and character, by giving to you my ideas upon the subject you propose to me with a view to the meeting house intended to be erected by your society.

You wish to know in what form a room to contain about 1.600 persons should be built with a view to the ease of the speaker and of the hearer, and in which the situation of the speaker is not fixed.

This question has not occupied the attention of architects as much as its importance deserves. Even Vitruvius dismisses the subject in two paragraphs at the end of his chapter on Theatres, recommending only that a *place* shall be chosen in which the voice is neither rendered confused by a distinct echo, nor by its continuance beyond the utterance of the speaker: for this is in my opinion the full meaning of the somewhat obscure passages. What he means by the (*loci consonantes*)[3] in which the voice being supported *from below* is heard with greatest advantage, I am at a loss to determine, nor do I find it satisfactorily explained either by his English or his German Translators. (See Vitrivii Lib. V Cap. VIII).[4]

Among the modern writers on Architecture I do not know any one who has treated this subject, in a manner to have impressed its merit upon my memory; or who has thereby acquired any public celebrity. I should be glad if I could refer you to some such authority, rather than risk mistake in proceeding entirely upon my own reasonings and experience, especially upon so short a notice, and with so little time for preparation and study as I possess.

⟨The Species of rooms under consideration are of three kinds.⟩[5]

1st.) Such as have a place appropriated to a single speaker, as Churches, Chapels, and lecture rooms.

2d.) Such as have a considerable part of the room appropriated to the speakers, as Theatres, Courts of Justice, and Music rooms.

3.) Such as are appropriated to Debate and discussion as the halls of Legislative assemblies, of Litterary societies and the meeting houses of the Society of friends, in which the place of the voice is unfixed and uncertain.

⟨On the two former I shall not, at present say any thing, as the third only is the object of your enquiry.⟩

The principal circumstances upon which the affect of sound depends are, 1st.) the size of the room, 2.) its form, and 3.) the materials of which the Walls, cieling and floor consist. Under the latter head must be considered the greater or less croud by which it is occupied.

1st. Size, Under the same circumstances of form, and materials it is evident that the difficulty of hearing and speaking must increase with the size of a room. But as the object to which the room is appropriated decides in all cases the question of *size*, nothing is left to Art in that respect.

2. The form then becomes the next consideration.

Philosophers have taken it for granted, that sound is propagated by circular undulations similar to those which are seen on the surface of water into which a stone is dropped. Many circumstances attending the propagation of sound agree exactly with this hypothesis. For if a stone be dropped into stagnant water the circles will be concentric and equally distinguishable at equal distances from the center as a sound produced in a still atmosphere; if into a running stream, they will be stretched down by the stream and become excentric, being distinguishable in the same direction and strength with the sound of a bell in a windy day. But sound is also subject to the laws that govern the progress of light, being liable to reflection, perhaps also to refraction. Science, I believe has made very little progress on this subject, compared with its extent, for sound has also I think, a very intimate connexion with Mathematical forms, I had almost said with Chrystalisation, as may be observed by   401 sounding a tone in unison or concord with that of a Glass plate upon which Sand has been very equally sifted.[6]

The property of sound however on which the merits of the present question will rest, is its reflectibility, or in common language, its proper-⟨ty of echoing. Of this there are two kinds, the Echo of direct reflection and the Echo of undulation.⟩

I.) Direct Echo.

So little has this subject been examined, as far as I know, that I believe it is generally thought that a room in which there is a perceptible Echo, cannot be well constructed for the hearer or speaker. If this were true, it would follow, that the voice of the speaker could be best heard where there is as ⟨little echo as possible, as for instance, in a space crouded near the⟩ Speaker, with hearers, the various and soft surface of whose bodies reflect no vibrations, and surrounded with scattered trees in which the sound is dispersed and lost. Experience however proves, that to attempt to speak or to hear in such a situation is a most laborious undertaking. We may therefore safely conclude that *Echo* may be useful both to the speaker and hearer; although, in an ill constructed room ⟨it may be made to⟩ counteract the distinctness of sound.

⟨Echo may be hurtful in two ways. When single or only double by following the voice at a very perceptible distance of time, or by being often repeated and that at perceptible distances of time. But it follows that the greater the number of coincident echoes, the greater is the distinctness of the voice.

The distance of time at which voice⟩ will be repeated by the Echo depends upon the distance of the Hearer from the Speaker, and upon the sum of the distances of the echoing surface from the hearer and the Speaker: consequently, the indistinctness of the sound which arises from the first cause, will depend upon the size of the room; for in a large room some of the Walls, and the Cieling, which are the Echoing surfaces, must be at a great distance from the speaker and hearer.

The rapidity however at which sound travels is so great that I do not think from my own experience much indistinctness can arise in the largest rooms which have any where been built, from the time which elapses between the original Sound and its Echo. For if there be but two Echoes, which is the smallest number possible, they cannot much confuse each other. I conceive rather that the multitude of echoes which are produced by some forms of rooms is a much more effectual cause of indistinctness. In considering this part of the subject I have been led to a very minute and laborious mathematical investigation of the number of echoes produced by different formed rooms, with differently shaped cielings and under different relative positions of the hearer and speaker. I will not take up your and my time by transcribing these details. There result agrees exactly with my experience, and I shall therefore give it with confidence, observing that I do not take the floor at all into consideration.

1.) The smallest number of Echoes which can possibly be produced is in a Cylindrical or round room with smooth Walls, open at the top, that is without a Cieling, whether the speaker be on an exact level with the hearer or not. In this case there will be only two echoes, let the hearer and speaker be where they will. The Voice that strikes the Wall at two opposite points, will be reflected or echoed to the hearer. From every other point, it will pass the hearer.

2. In a circular room with a flat cieling there will be only 3 original Echoes: two from the Walls and one from the cieling but there will be also a ring, circular or eliptical according to the situation of the hearer and speaker, from which the echo from the cieling will be reechoed, and the Voice will reach the hearer in innumerable coincident Echoes. Of course as the distance of time between the original echoes will be almost imperceptible, and the second echoes will arrive at the same instant (or very nearly) the impression of the voice will be strong and distinct, and such a room is well constructed.

3. A square and oblong room with a flat cieling will have 5 echoes. These echoes will according to the relative situations of the speaker and hearer, and their consequent greater or less coincidence produce a better or worse effect. But it never can be a powerful one even if they were all coincident for their number is limited.

4.) A square or oblong room, with an arched ciling will produce four echoes from the Walls and a line of nearly coincident echoes from the cieling. This line will always be an eliptical curve and there will be parts of the audience whom these last echoes will never reach and to whom this cieling will give no better advantage than a flat one. Therefore although such a room is certainly better than the former, its construction is still defective.

5. Polygonal rooms, as hexagons, octagons and dodecagons &c.,   403

with flat cielings will have first and second echoes equal in number, to that of their sides and one echo from the cieling; many of these Echoes will be so nearly coincident that such a room is always of a good construction with a view to speaker and hearer, and the more numerous the sides the better the construction, as approaching more nearly to that of the Cylinder.

6. Elliptical rooms commonly but falsely called Oval if the Elipsis be drawn in the usual manner and composed of 4 segments, or even if correctly drawn with a trammel, partake of the advantages of Cylindrical rooms in proportion to the greater or less difference of their diameters, those in which this difference is the least possessing them in the greatest degree.

7. Compound rooms, such as consist of parallelograms with Bows, or circular ends, are better than mere squares or oblongs, in proportion to the number of sides they present to the Voice to produce echoes that are exactly or nearly coincident.

8., But, if it could be used when built the best possible room for speaking and hearing taking only the direct echo into view would be a hollow Globe. For let the situations of the speaker and hearer be where they will, a ring of first echo perfectly coincident will be produced, and rings of reechoes, *ad infinitum* many of them nearly coincident would follow. So that the first impression of the sound would be distinct and immensely powerful, and perhaps overcome the hum and buz of the more distantly following reechoes.

9. But as such a room is impracticable, that which most nearly approaches it, must be next to it in perfection. Such a room is a Cylinder covered with a half globe or semi-spherical dome. Such a room has all the advantages of the second, with the addition of innumerable rings of first and secondary echoes produced by the dome. In proportion as a room approaches this form, it approaches perfection.

II. Echo of undulation.

I cannot speak on this species of Echo so distinctly as on the former. Of its existence there [is] no doubt. I mean by the echo of undulation, the support and even increase of the original undulatory vibration by which the sound was produced; by its being repelled by the Walls and Cieling of a room. As these undulations are supposed to be circular they must of course be broken and interrupted by straight Walls. But circular Walls and cielings meeting them in the same or nearly the same lines, return them as they came. This is the cause of the long continuation of sound in such rooms, in which the undulations can often be distinctly and separately heard, and is also the reason why such rooms are noisy and ill adapted to the distinct hearing of *more* than one sound at a time. They are therefore as bad music rooms, as they are excellent for the exhibition of orations, or the singing of single tunes. They are peculiarly pleasant to the speaker, who finds him self supported at ease and, as it were, floating upon the sound of his own voice.

In what I have said above I have supposed the Walls of my rooms to be plain surfaces uninterrupted by Windows, Galleries, Columns, Pilasters or Cornices. In proportion as these things are necessarily, or from false taste, crouded into the room, in that proportion its perfections are destroyed. What is injurious to the object, or inconsistent with the use of a building can never be ornamental. Simplicity is one of the first of Architectural ornaments, and the highest atchievement of study and of taste; and to the attainment of the object you have in view it is as conducive, as it is consistent with the manners of your society.

I will now mention from memory the properties of a few of the buildings which I have seen, and which may elucidate the principles I have laid down.

1.) The Pantheon, or Church of Sta. Maria di Rotonda at Rome, is a circular room about 140 feet diameter, 70 feet high in the Cylindrical part and 70 in the dome, which [is] a half Globe. During the bustle of a procession there is a noisy buzz in the Church; but when the officiating priest raises his single voice nothing could be more clear and melodious. From this I should conclude it to be an excellent speaking room.

2.) All the churches in Italy, France and Germany, which I recollect having domes over the transept, alarm a stranger by the sound of his own voice, if he whisper only in a common low tone. In very numerous private and public saloons covered with domes I remember the same effect.

3. One of the most beautiful rooms, and perhaps the best lecture room in the world for speaking, hearing, and seeing, is the Anatomical Theatre in the Rue Faideau at Paris.[7] Its plan is a half circle, and it is covered by a half dome. This form, though I would perhaps not recommend to you must have great advantages. The Board of Architects, with   405

Kersaint at their head, in their report to the National Convention of France, upon the public Buildings, (and which I possess but cannot just now find) proposed to convert the unfinished Church of St. Madelaine into a Building for the meeting of the National Legislature: and I find that they have designed for their hall of debate a semicircular room covered with a segment half dome. In this report the first Architects of France have expressed an opinion that such a room is the best adapted for the purposes of deliberation.[8]

4. The Hal au bled or Corn Market at Paris was (for it has lately been burned)[9] a circular building covered with a semispherical dome. I recollect only two circumstances which are to our present purpose. I spoke with great ease to my companion notwithstanding the buzz of business, and I understood distinctly the words of a ridiculous though violent quarrel across the hall.

5. There are many circular rooms covered with domes in the Bank of England[10] and other public buildings in London, all of which have this in common. They ring with the sound of feet and voices, so as to produce a confused buzz, and the sound of your own voice appears louder to yourself than in the open air.

6. Surry Chappel, a polygon belonging to Mr. Hill's congregation in Southwark, London, though interrupted by Galleries and pillars, and the Octagon Chapel at Bath, are remarkably good speaking rooms, if I may judge by the immense effect of the voices of two zealous preachers whom I heard in each of them.[11]

7. I could mention many other buildings in Europe but the Bank of Pensylvania is at hand for an experiment. I find that the buzz of business which drowns conversation has created a prejudice against such a room. But at Mr. Woolcot's[12] dinner when the Chairman spoke, or a song was sung, the clearness, and the precision of the voice was striking beyond expectation. The rattle of dollars, and the feet of Customers is indeed confusedly heard at present, but the real fact may be easily ascertained after the hours of business of the day is over.

From what I have said you may infer that I would recommend a circular, domed, meeting house to your society, as the best adapted to the ease of hearer and speaker, and also as containing the most space within the least quantity of walling. The proportions of such a room are also of consequence. But to ascertain what are the best, it would be necessary to go into the design, which would exceed your enquiry and my immediate leisure.

With the sincere hope that these remarks may not be altogether useless to you,[13] I am Yours very respectfully

B. Henry Latrobe.

PS. Since I wrote this I have been informed that Professor Chladni of Berlin has written an excellent treastise on this subject.[14] I have taken great pains to procure the only copy of his work which is in America but without success.[15]

ALS: American Philosophical Society Archives (157/E10). BHL's letter to Thomas Parker of 8 February 1804 (below) indicates that Parker was the recipient. Although the letter is signed, numerous corrections, deletions, and interlineations, as well as the lack of a dateline and an address folio, suggest that it may be a draft. The cover sheet of the document was endorsed by BHL "Remarks on the best form of a room for hearing and Speaking" and was endorsed "1797," erroneously, in a different hand. The document postdates the news of the burning of the Halle au Blé in October 1802 (see n. 9) and was apparently written well before BHL's letter to Parker of 8 February 1804.

1. Thomas Parker (c. 1761–1833), a Philadelphia clock- and watchmaker, served at various times on both the Select and Common Councils, was active in the Abolition Society, and was president of the Mechanics' Bank from 1814 to 1819. "The Elfreth Necrology," *Publications of the Genealogical Society of Pennsylvania* 2 (1900):200.

Parker, a prominent Quaker, had requested BHL's opinion on the best form of a room for hearing and speaking for the Arch Street Meeting House, Philadelphia. In his response BHL discussed a topic—the practical application of theoretical acoustics to architectural design—which at this time was virtually unexplored. The unanswered queries in Aristotle's *Problemata*, the brief comments of Vitruvius in the first century A.D. (which BHL refers to below), and the seventeenth-century geometric ray diagrams of Athanasius Kircher (which display linear paths of reflected sound), had but touched on the subject, and BHL lamented the lack of an authoritative work. It was in this context that BHL made his first attempt to explain the principles of correct architectural design for good acoustics. The ideas BHL outlined below were reiterated in 1804 by his pupil Robert Mills, then in BHL's office, when Mills was designing the Congregational Church in Charleston, S.C. (see BHL to Mills, 12 July 1806, n. 2, in BHL, *Correspondence*, 2). The subject was later discussed after the mid-1820s by such writers as David B. Reid in England and Joseph Henry in America, and quantitative experiments on absorption, reflection, and reverberation of sound in rooms were first conducted towards the end of the nineteenth century. Mills, "Communication recd. from Mr. Robert Mills on the subject of the Ceiling of St. Michael's Church & on the Doctrine of Sounds," 15 Oct. 1804, in *Journal of the Society of Architectural Historians* 12 (1953):27–31; E. G. Richardson, "Notes on the Development of Architectural Acoustics, Particularly in England," *Journal of the Royal Institute of British Architects*, 3d ser., 12 (Oct. 1945):352–54; Frederick Vinton Hunt, *Origins in Acoustics: The Science of Sound from Antiquity to the Age of Newton*, with a foreword by Robert Edmund Apfel (New Haven, Conn., and London, 1978), pp. 32–37, 123, figs. following p. 140.

2. Parker was apparently a member of the Watering Committee during the entire period BHL was engineer to the Philadelphia Waterworks.

3. Trans.: consonant places.

4. BHL refers to the only surviving work, *De architectura,* of Vitruvius, the influential Roman writer on classical architecture.

5. Angle brackets enclose passages that were copied out by someone other than BHL to replace the less legible original passages.

6. Ernst F. F. Chladni (1756–1827) first described this phenomenon in *Entdeckungen über die Theorie des Klanges* (Leipzig, 1787).

7. This was Jacques Gondoin's anatomical theater at the École de Chirurgie (1769 ff.), an influential neo-antique theater.

8. Armand Guy Simon de Coetnempren (1742–93), comte de Kersaint, French mariner and statesman, published *Discours sur les monuments publics, prononcé au Conseil du département de Paris, le 15 Décembre 1791* (Paris, 1792). Also published with the *Discours* were five "*mémoires,*" signed by Molinos and Legrand, one of which was "*projet et description du Palais national,*" which recommended converting Pierre Contant d'Ivry's incomplete church of the Madeleine in Paris into a palace for the French national assembly.

9. The Halle au Blé burned on 16 October 1802.

10. Domed rooms at the Bank of England were designed by Sir Robert Taylor and his successor there, Sir John Soane. BHL probably found Soane's Bank Stock Office (1792–93) particularly noteworthy. John Summerson, *Architecture in Britain, 1530 to 1830,* 4th rev. ed. (Harmondsworth, England, 1963), pp. 218, 286–87.

11. William Thomas's Surrey Chapel (1782–83), on Blackfriar's Road, was executed for Rowland Hill (1744–1833), a popular and unorthodox preacher. Thomas Lightoler designed the Octagon Chapel at Bath (1767). Damie Stillman, "Church Architecture in Neo-Classical England," *Journal of the Society of Architectural Historians* 38 (May 1979): 103–19.

12. Probably Oliver Wolcott (1760–1833), who served as secretary of the Treasury from 1795 to 1800.

13. The Arch Street Meeting House was erected between 1803 and 1811 according to a design by Owen Biddle, Jr. The structure consisted of two rectangular wings with flat ceilings connected by a center building. Lee H. Nelson and Penelope Hartshorne Batcheler, *An Architectural Study of Arch Street Meeting House, Fourth and Arch Streets, Philadelphia, Pennsylvania* (Philadelphia, 1968).

14. *Die Akustik* (Leipzig, 1802).

15. For the evolution of BHL's theories of acoustics and the application of his ideas to his architectural projects, particularly the Hall of Representatives in the U.S. Capitol, see BHL to John Lenthall, 21 Nov. 1807, BHL to Samuel Harrison Smith, 22 Nov. 1807, BHL to Christian Ignatius Latrobe, 1 Dec. 1807, BHL to William Bibb, 14 Dec. 1807, BHL, Report on the Public Buildings, 23 Mar. 1808, all in BHL, *Correspondence,* 2; BHL to William Stedman, 5 Jan. 1808, LB (62/A10); and BHL, Article on Acoustics and Architecture for the *Edinburgh Encyclopaedia,* [Dec. 1811], in BHL, *Correspondence,* 3.

TO ISAAC HAZLEHURST

Washington, Jany. 9th. 1804.

My dear Father

Since I left Philadelphia I have more than once sat down to write to you, but have always been prevented by the obtrusion of business. Since my arrival in this city the whole of my time has been taken up in arranging the accumulated accounts that relate to the public buildings and I have now nearly [fought?] my way through them. The work that has been done during the last Summer gives very general Satisfaction. Congress have not yet appropriated anything for the next season but there is no doubt but that they will, though Oeconomy, and impeachments have hitherto employed the greatest part of their thoughts.[1] At this season this city cannot fail to be pleasant as to society, of which there is so much, and such variety, that a *choice* may be made. Mary has written to her mother, and has, I believe, given you an account of our own arrangements. We have met with some little difficulties, principally arising from the detention of our trunk for 5 or 6 days after our arrival, during which time we were in great distress for a change of dress, and also from our inexperience in the very important article of marketing. To live here systematically during the winter, it would be necessary to bring hither many articles from Philadelphia, hams, beef, candles, sugar, in fact everything that comes under the denomination of *stores*. In our lodgings which are very convenient in every respect we can however make tolerable shift, laughing now and then at our embarrassments, and determining never to be out of humor.

The only real source of uneasiness, which we feel indeed very severely at present, is our ignorance of the situation of poor Robert. His having escaped the spasms when last expected, is a circumstance so much in his favor, that we cherish the hope of his being on the recovery. Andrew promised to transmit the accounts from Phila. to us, but we have not yet had a line from him. We hope soon to hear from our Mother. I go tomorrow to the Quarries. On my return I shall have much to communicate, for which I have not time at present. Believe me most truly Your afft. Son

B. H. Latrobe

Love to our Mother and you.

Polygraph Copy: LB (29/B1). Addressed to Hazlehurst in Philadelphia.

1. As part of the Republican effort to curb the power of the Federalist-dominated judiciary, Congress contemplated and initiated impeachment proceedings against several Federalist judges during Jefferson's first administration. The House impeached the alcoholic and insane John Pickering (1738–1805), judge of the federal district court of New Hampshire, in March 1803, and the Senate tried him during the first two weeks of March 1804. He was found guilty and removed on 12 March 1804, the day the House passed a resolution for the impeachment of Samuel Chase (1741–1811), associate justice of the U.S.

Supreme Court. Chase's trial took place from 4 February to 1 March 1805, when he was acquitted. (For BHL's involvement with designing fittings for the Senate Chamber for the Chase trial, see BHL to Burr, 17 Dec. 1804, below.) Early in 1804, proceedings against Richard Peters (1744–1828), judge of the federal district court of Pennsylvania, were also considered, but charges were never brought. See Richard E. Ellis, *The Jeffersonian Crisis: Courts and Politics in the Young Republic* (New York, 1971), chaps. 5–7.

TO ROBERT SMITH

Washington, January 9th. 1804

Sir,

In consequence of the conversation with which you honoured me yesterday, I beg leave to lay before you the following proposals, relative to my proposed engagement in the service of the Navy department. In making them I have taken into view the situation which I already hold as Surveyor of the public Buildings of the United States, by which I am enabled to offer you my professional Services on the terms herein specified:

And in order that no doubt may exist as to the nature and extent of the Services which I shall hold myself bound to perform under such proposed engagement, I will beg leave to specify them:

1.) I will, whenever required, give to You my professional opinion in writing on any work which is proposed to be, or has been already executed, furnish all the plans and descriptions of future undertakings which shall be required by you, and if put into execution, be responsible for their perfect construction either under my own personal direction or that of an agent, for whose fidelity and skill I hold myself answerable; I will ascertain by measurement or account all bills and charges against the Navy Department arising out of works under my direction; and in general perform all those duties *in detail*, which are necessary to the perfection of public works, and which cannot be enumerated in words; to the best of my abilities.

As my permanent residence is not in the City of Washington, I hold myself however bound to attend personally at the Navy Yard whenever called upon, on receiving 6 days notice by Post. It is impossible, as, I hope it is unnecessary to define the exact degree of *personal* attendance which may be sufficient for the full performance of my duties. It is my intention never to be guilty [of] neglect.

These duties, and such others, as, though not mentioned, reasonably arise out of the nature of my engagement, which is intended to preclude the necessity of any professional advice, direction or superintendance, which I might perform or give, unless specially required by You I will engage to perform for the annual salary of one thousand five hundred Dollars.

The expense of a responsible and resident Agent or Clerk of the works, of other Clerks which with Your consent may be employed, of office expences, of travelling or any other expenses, in the service of the Navy department (excepting my own expenses whenever attending my duty in Washington, or travelling thither) are not included in the above sum.[1]

I am with true respect, Your faithful hble. Servt.

B. Henry Latrobe

Polygraph Copy: LB (29/B11).

1. Soon after the date of this letter BHL assumed the oversight of the layout and architecture of the Washington Navy Yard as part of his duties as surveyor of the public buildings. After BHL moved to Washington in 1807, he became engineer to the Navy Department at a salary of $1,000 per year, although his duties remained the same. His salary was raised to $1,500 per year in 1811, and he resigned in 1813. BHL to William Jones, 2 Feb. 1813, and BHL to John Rodgers, 23 Mar. 1815, both in BHL, *Correspondence*, 3.

TO JOSEPH TATNALL

Newcastle, Jany. 23d. 1804.

Dear Sir,

The excessive fatigue which I underwent while exploring the Elk and Whiteclay feeders, joined to the severity of the Weather during that time, has so far injured my health, that I have ever since been subject at times to the most violent rheumatic pains in my back and thighs, and since my return from Washington, I have been so ill, as to be unable at this moment to walk without assistance. I fear therefore that it may not be in my power to attend the Board of Survey or the Directors, although I shall make every possible exertion to do so. My accounts I have transmitted to the Secretary, and in order to explain the manner in which my time has been employed, I send to you the extract on the other side, which is taken from my Diary.[1] You will, if you think it necessary, have   411 the goodness to use it for explanation, although I do not conceive, that, *without it,* any doubt of the correctness of my Statement will be entertained. The fact is that the business which has been performed, considering the terrible weather, and the roughness of the country, could not have been gone through without the most persevering exertion.

I am with true respect Yours faithfully

B. Henry Latrobe.

P.S. You will please to observe that in a Map which encloses a Country 18 Miles in Latitude and 20 in Longitude, much time is taken up in *making the Work close,* as the phrase is. As my work would be useless, unless correct, I have always run over the doubtful lines in the field.

Polygraph Copy: LB (29/C2). Addressed to Tatnall in Wilmington.

1. The C & D board of directors met in Wilmington on 24–25 January 1804. The survey committee of the board met on 26 January and passed BHL's accounts for $570 for services and expenses. For the diary extract, see below. C & D Survey Committee Minutes; BHL to Isaac Hazlehurst, 4 Feb. 1804, below.

ENCLOSURE: DIARY EXTRACT

Extract of the Diary of B. H. Latrobe, Engineer.

1803.	Days
Novr. 22d. 23d. 24th attending board of Dir. Ches. and Del. Canal Wilmington	3
25th.–28th, in Philadelphia, and on the road.	
28th. 29th. 30th. Decr. 1. In the office, and verifying an important point of level between Christiana Cr. and the Bear, in which an error was discovered.	4
Decr. 2d. 3d. 5th. 6th. 7th. 8th. 9th. 10th. in the field on Whiteclay and Elk rivers.	8
4th. 11th. made the necessary sketches, sections, and calculations for proceeding	2
12th. 13th. 14th. 15th. 16th. in Philadelphia. 13th. 14th. proceeded with the necessary calculations and sections for the Elk feeder.	2
18th. 19th. employed in the office at Newcastle.	2
20th. 21st. 22nd. 23d. 24th., In the field, laid down the Elk feeder.	5

26th. 27th. explored alone the situations of the two
   reservoirs to correct doubts   2
28th. 29th. in the office and in running a level of
   verification from the Christiana road to the Mill pond
   on Mill creek, being the completion of the corrections
   necessary on the Christiana line   2
30th. Went to Washington.
1804
Jany. 4th. 5. 7th. 9. 11th. 13th. 14th. 16th. engaged in the
   office solely upon the Maps, calculations, and the
   general Map.   8
21. 22d. 23d., at Newcastle engaged in completing the
   Map of the whole survey, and the accts. and report.[1]   <u>3</u>

                                                    Days.   41

Polygraph Copy: LB (29/C4). Enclosed in BHL to Tatnall, 23 Jan. 1804, above.

   1. BHL, C & D Report, 26 Jan. 1804 (171/B9).

TO RICHARD DRAKE

Washington Feby. 4th. 1804.

Dear Sir,
   I did not receive yours of the 23d. Decr. 1803 untill my return to
Newcastle whither it has been sent, and which place I had left on the
30th. of last Decr. Not finding a convenient mode of remittance from
that place, I have delayed answering you till my return hither, and now
take this earliest of opportunity of enclosing a Draft of the Cashier U.S.
Bank at this place on the Bank of U.S. in Philadelphia payable to your
order for 102$.85, by mistake instead of 105$.85. I beg you will have the
goodness to charge me with the 3$ deficient in your next account, and
excuse the delay of this remittance, which should have been immediate,
had your letter reached me before I left home in December.
   Your account of the conduct, and the progress in his studies which
you give of my Son, is very gratifying. On his late visit to us at Newcastle
I had indeed great reason to know how much both he and his parents
owe to your attention to his manners, as well as to the improvement of
his mind.   413

The talents which Henry appears to possess have led me to believe that a school in which the higher ranges of literature and science are taught might qualify him, at an earlier period than usual for the study of one of the liberal professions, and I have for some time endeavored to inform myself of the comparative merits of the different seminaries which are scattered over our country. There are none to which I have not objections. Mr. Dubourg's seminary at Baltimore unites advantages however, which incline me to give it the preference,[1] and though I much wish that he could remain for a Year at least longer under your tuition, yet as he cannot be admitted after passing his 11th. Year, which expires on the 19th. July next, I shall be under the necessity of removing him a little before that day. You will I am sure properly appreciate my motives, and the gratitude for your attention to my Child with which I am Your faithful hble. Servt.

B. H. Latrobe

Polygraph Copy: LB (29/C8). Addressed to Drake at the Grove Academy near Philadelphia.

1. For William Du Bourg and St. Mary's Seminary, see BHL to Du Bourg, 25 Mar. 1804, below.

TO ISAAC HAZLEHURST

Washington, Feby. 4th. 1804.

My dear Father,

You will perhaps have thought me inattentive to you, that I did not write to you from Wilmington. But you would easily excuse me, if I could describe to you the state of body and of mind in which I was during the week which I spent in Delaware. The extreme fatigue which I have undergone during the last 3 or 4 Months has certainly produced an unfavorable effect upon my constitution, and I require the repose in which I now indulge myself to recruit my health. On my arrival at Newcastle after a very fatiguing journey, I was so unwell, and so afflicted with rheumatic pains from head to foot that I could scarcely walk across the room for four days, during which I was however obliged to attend 414 closely to business. The Directors had made a board on Tuesday, but I could not get to Wilmington till Wednesday noon. My accounts had in the mean time been the subject of discussion, as usual. They were however passed. This has always been the most unpleasant part of the business which I have to transact: for as Mr. Gale has always refused to admit me to explain, the minds of the Committee are always irritated by the discussion of suspicions before I can get an opportunity to remove them. For instance, I find that it was asserted that I had been guilty of *fraud* in charging the 24th. of Decr. as spent *in the field,* while a receipt for money received on that day at Wilmington proved that I had been *there.* The fact was, that I was in the field all the morning, and in the evening rode 6 miles to Wilmington for money to pay my Men, which I received about 5 o'clock. I mention this as one of many facts which may be stated by Gale or Adlum, for they both left Wilmington before I was called to explain my account. You may easily imagine into what a situation of mind such circumstances throw an irritable man, sick, and distant from his family. Independently of settling accounts, the board discussed the subject of the route of the Canal. But as the board was not full it was postponed. However they resolved to begin to work at the feeders.[1] Another subject more interesting to me was the question, Who shall be the Engineer? I was required to give in my proposals; and while I was drawing them up two of the Philadelphia Directors had the goodness to communicate to me, *privately,* the course of the debates and the highest sum proposed to be given. To this I therefore conformed, and asking 3.500 per Annum. I was elected. Gale and Adlum immediately resigned their seats in the committee of survey and left Wilmington.

Till that moment the Board had in fact done nothing. I had never been present at any of their debates on the subject of the Work. I was now called in. I found the most violent contrariety of opinions prevailing, for no other reason, but because Mr. Gilpin perhaps was the only one who practically understood the subject. In a few minutes however it was easy to make them comprehend, that without entering on the Main question of the line of the Canal, the Canal of supply, or the feeder might be determined on, and begun. This was therefore done, and I will now venture to predict that the work will go on vigorously and successfully.

In being appointed Engineer *after* the receipt of my proposals, they have virtually been adopted. A Committee is appointed to make a Contract with me. In the mean time, I am getting my business here into such a train that I may leave it for several Months. I shall return to Delaware 415 about the 1st. of March, and pay a visit to Philadelphia, as soon after as I can, when I hope to find your hopes of our Brother Robert sanctioned by considerable progress in his recovery. We daily think and speak of him, and his situation throws a cloud over all our sensations, and renders the gaiety of this place far less attractive than it would otherwise be. God grant that he may soon be restored to us.

I have now seriously to think of my summer residence. The most central situation, and indeed the only healthy one on the line of the Canal is the top of Iron hill. I am now in treaty for 50 or 60 acres of land on the very summit, on which there is a squared log house lately built, and a very good spring. These are indeed the only requisites towards habitability which are present on the hill, but at first we must make great shifts, and gratify ourselves, for the want of conveniences by looking at the grandest prospect in America, and enjoying the ease with which I can get home every night from the most distant part of my work. I have indeed no other choice in respect to health but between Newcastle or Ironhill. This map will explain the situation.

If I lived at Newcastle The distance would be as under compared to those from Iron hill. NB. The feeder will begin at Elk forge.

Newcastle		Ironhill	
To Frenchtown	17	Do..........................	7
To Elk forge..................	18	Do..........................	4
To Christiana Creek where the Canal will enter	4	Do..........................	8
To the South end of the feeder.	13	Do..........................	1
		To Newcastle...............	10

It is evident therefore that by living on Ironhill the greatest distance
which I should have to travel from home would be to Newcastle 10 miles,

should the Canal go thither (which I believe it will not). While if I lived at Newcastle the greatest part of my work, and all that is to be done this Year would not be nearer than from 18 to 13 Miles from home. From Ironhill none of my business will be more distant than from 7 to 1 mile for two Years.

There are several other advantages attending this situation. The Main post road passes the door. Near us that is within 4 Miles is Elkton, Newark and Christiana bridge, and Aikintown within 2 Miles. Mr. Couch a most intelligent, valuable and friendly Man within 1/2 Mile.[2] Several other respectable neighbors, Mr. Hyatt, Mr. Alexander, Mr. Gilpin within 2 Miles.

It is indeed necessary to dwell on all these advantages for I am aware of many unpleasant circumstances which we must get over as well as we can. One resource we shall always have, our mutual love and esteem, which will be the same every where, and under all possible circumstances.

Our distance from Philadelphia will be 42 Miles, where we may easily reach in one day at any season.

We are here kept in agitation by a dispute among the Ladies about precedence. Mrs. Merry claims the precedence of all other Ladies including the wives of the Secretaries, in which she is supported by the Marquis and Marchioness D'Yrujo. As the consequences of this dispute, contemptible as it is, may become serious, I will in a few days give you the particulars at large, so that you may form some judgement on a subject on which reports are so various.[3]

I cannot close my letter which has grown to an unreasonable length without thanking you, and our mother most affectionately for your kindness to Henry who I hope will make himself worthy of it. Our best love to Samuel and Betsey and to Isaac. Believe me most truly and respectfully Your affecte. Son

B. Henry Latrobe.

Polygraph Copy: LB (29/C10).

1. The board agreed with BHL's conclusions in his 26 January 1804 report that a five and one-half mile feeder from the Elk River would be the best means of supplying water to the highest level of the main canal. BHL told Joshua Gilpin that the Elk feeder would begin at Elk Forge, where "the Water must be taken from the upper forge Dam on the West side and carried across the Creek [Elk River] at the forge over an Aqueduct of one Arch and of moderate expense. The Reservoir has an admirable situation near Oliver Howells. . . . Such a Canal as this feeder from Elk forge will bring infinite custom to the main Canal, as lime stone is within a few miles of it, and the head will be only 38 miles from

Lancaster." In his report BHL claimed that "the Elk yields water sufficient to pass 3 boats in one hour or 72 in one day" through the main canal. BHL, C & D Report, 26 Jan. 1804 (171/B9); BHL to Gilpin, 26 Dec. 1803, LB (28/B7).

2. William Cooch (b. 1762), New Castle County Republican and owner of a saw mill on the Christina River, replaced James A. Bayard on the C & D board of directors in 1804. An active board member ("He seems to enter into the business . . . with spirit"), Cooch served on the Committee of Works and on occasion supervised the construction of the feeder. For BHL's description of Cooch's volatile personality, see BHL to Isaac Hazlehurst, 15 Sept. 1805, in BHL, *Correspondence*, 2. BHL to Cooch, 14 Mar. 1804, and BHL to Levi Hollingsworth, 10 June 1804, both in LB (30/B10, 32/G7); John A. Munroe, *Federalist Delaware, 1775–1815* (New Brunswick, N.J., 1954), p. 246n; Mary Hollingsworth Jamar, comp., *Hollingsworth Family and Collateral Lines of Cooch-Gilpin-Jamar-Mackall-Morris-Stewart* (Philadelphia, 1944), p. 24.

3. At a dinner at the President's House in December 1803, Jefferson offered his arm to Dolley Madison, the wife of the secretary of state, and escorted her to the table while ignoring Mrs. Anthony Merry, the wife of the British minister. A few days later the Merrys experienced the same lack of distinction at a dinner given by the Madisons. Claiming that custom gave the wives of ministers precedence over the wives of cabinet members, Merry interpreted these actions as a deliberate slight against his government. The Merrys subsequently refused to attend any official dinners unless they received advance assurance that they would have the precedence they deserved. The Federalist newspapers in Washington took the side of the Merrys and reiterated their claim that they were the victims of a deliberate anti-British policy. Merry referred the matter to his superiors in England, who proved unwilling to let such a trivial matter affect the relations between the two countries. It was this incident which prompted the Jefferson administration to draw up explicit rules of etiquette for the guidance of the executive officers. With their emphasis on unceremoniousness and social equality, these rules gave formal expression to the Jeffersonian principle of "pell mell." Dumas Malone, *Jefferson the President: First Term, 1801–1805* (Boston, 1970), pp. 376–92.

TO GEORGE DAVIS

Washington Feby. 6th. 1804.

My dear Sir,[1]

February is again come round, and with it the Quarter's rent of the Theatre. Do you think I shall *this* time come in for a share of it? If your friendly endeavors could prevail I know I should not be disappointed. You can however, if you please, jog the memories and consciences of the Members in my behalf. I have written a polite letter to Mr. Biddle on the subject. A small purchase which I have made renders it a matter of great importance to me that I should not be entirely disappointed, and I should even be willing to give up part of my just claim, rather than hang on much longer. The sum I want is 400 Dollars. If you can keep so much locked up for me till my arrival in Philadelphia a few weeks hence, I would make a strong push for it myself. Pray give me the best lift you can in the meantime.[2]

We are here as busy in paying visits, and receiving them, in playing loo, and in quarrelling about etiquette as you please. By *we* I do not mean myself or even my family, but the great world in general. *We* have this advantage, that without a Theatre, *we* are acting a dozen farces at once, some of them tragi-comedies, others pure burlesque. As to the article of a Theatre, I must however tell you that an attempt to build one was made last Summer, and although it is not quite finished, yet, as my wife observes, it *has been open some time*, for the roof was never put on. Bernard was to have brought hither a company, but he failed in getting *a house*.[3]

We are here in lodgings. The rooms are good and convenient enough, they have only one fault which if we dealt in Tongues and Hams would be a great virtue, for we could smoke them either in the parlor or bedchamber. We have closed our fireplaces with a broad pine board, but without much effect: and I do not find that our *board* puts us into better humor with our lodging. Otherwise the talents which are collected in this city, and the idleness of everybody, which precludes all symptoms of the bank fever, a disorder which creates so many dull faces in your commercial towns, added to an excellent road in all weathers makes the place agreeable enough. For my part I am everywhere a drudge, and considering hard labor, great responsibility, and scanty pay, as things of course, I endeavor, with the best humor I can muster, to scramble along among the rest, and could I look with cheerfulness to the state of our good father's family, I should find more amusement here than in any town in America.

As to News, the newspapers are such cormorants as carry off every thing worth and not worth telling so fast that you must be content with this very old but very true story, that I am, with true esteem and respect Your faithful friend and Servt.

B. Henry Latrobe

Polygraph Copy: LB (29/D11).

1. Treasurer of the Chestnut Theatre, Philadelphia.

2. In 1791, Thomas Wignell and Alexander Reinagle formed a partnership to establish a new theater in Philadelphia. The New, or Chestnut, Theatre was completed in 1793 on the north side of Chestnut above Sixth Street, and it opened in February 1794. For the

next seven years the theater operated with great financial difficulties and "in a state of architectural incompletion." In February 1801, BHL was chosen as architect to plan the extensive alterations to the theater, which were carried out principally in that year. The most important of the alterations was the addition of two brick side wings, connected to stone-faced entrance pavilions that were joined by a Corinthian colonnade. Because of continued financial difficulties, however, the proprietors had not paid BHL his fee of $800. Besides this offer to reduce his claim by half, BHL later sought to gain his remuneration by threatening "to sell the claim at the Coffeehouse by auction" and by putting "the business into the hands of an Attorney." BHL may eventually have been paid for his work, for in July 1806 he offered his thoughts on the completion of the front of the theater. BHL to Davis, 10 Mar. 1804, BHL to Charles Biddle, 6 Feb., 2 May 1804, BHL to J. R. Smith, 5 Feb. 1805, BHL to Richard North, 1 Apr. 1805, and BHL to Agents of the Trustees of the New Theatre, 9 July 1806, all in LB (30/B6, 29/D9, 31/G9, 37/F7, 39/A2, 49/G4); BHL to Davis, 2 May 1804, below; Abe Wollock, "Benjamin Henry Latrobe's Activities in the American Theatre (1797–1808)" (Ph.D. diss. University of Illinois, 1962), chap. 4; *William Rush, American Sculptor* (Philadelphia, 1982), pp. 31–35.

Charles Biddle (1745–1821), merchant and state official, was president of the proprietors of the Chestnut Theatre and a director of the Bank of Pennsylvania. Wilfred Jordan, ed., *Colonial and Revolutionary Families of Pennsylvania*, new series, vol. 4 (New York, 1932), pp. 73–74.

3. BHL was on the Theatre Committee in Washington and participated in the parade and ceremonies on 23 June 1803 when the cornerstone of the Washington Theatre was laid. John Bernard (1756–1828), English-born actor and theatrical manager who had played comedy roles on the Philadelphia stage since 1797, moved to Boston rather than Washington in 1803. In 1806 he became joint manager of the Federal Street Theatre there. The lack of a permanent acting troupe in Washington, however, did not completely deprive the city's residents of dramatic entertainment. Each year when the Philadelphia Company of actors went on tour they performed for two months in the capital city. *National Intelligencer*, 24 June 1803; Constance McLaughlin Green, *Washington: Village and Capital, 1800–1878* (Princeton, N.J., 1962), p. 45.

TO THOMAS PARKER

Washington, Feby. 8th. 1804

My dear friend

You will probably recollect that when the Society of friends were about to erect a Meeting house for the Women in 4th street, you wished for my opinion on the best form of a room for hearing and speaking, and that I gave you this opinion in writing very much at large.[1] I have since once or twice troubled you with a request that you would be so good as to furnish me either with the original, or with a Copy of the Manuscript. It was the result of much reflection, and never having been of any use to your Society, I think I have a right, as to them, to claim that it should be returned, but in respect to You, I only ask Your good offices as a favor. Being now about to design the future hall of the House of Representatives of the United States, this Paper would be of infinite service to me. I have indeed no possible leisure to enter into the subject as I did when applied to by You. Let me now intreat you to devote as much time to the recovery of this manuscript as may be necessary. When I last spoke to you, it was in the hands of S. Coates[2] or of some other friend in the Committee. I am sure, that if your health and leisure permit you will cheerfully take this trouble for me, and if you knew how important a service you can thereby render me, you would use your endeavor for me on this occasion. Should you succeed in procuring the manuscript, I beg you to send it to me per post without regard to the postage on so large a packet.

I hope you and Mrs. Parker with your family are well. I am here for 3 Weeks or a Month longer. Believe me very sincerely and affectionately Your faithful friend

B. Henry Latrobe

Polygraph Copy: LB (29/D14). Addressed to Parker in Philadelphia.

1. See BHL, Remarks on the Best Form of a Room for Hearing and Speaking, [c. 1803], above.
2. Samuel Coates (1748–1830), Philadelphia merchant and president of the Pennsylvania Hospital. *PMHB* 32 (1908):421.

TO JAMES COCHRAN

Washington, Feby. 8th. 1804.

My good friend:[1]

I should have written to you from Wilmington when I was last there, had I not been so unwell that I could not undertake it. The Directors of the Chesapeake and Delaware Canal Company have now resolved to go to work in the course of this spring, if not on the main Canal, however on the feeder which will supply it with Water either from the Whiteclay or Elk rivers. I have recommended you to Mr. Gilpin of the Committee as a Man in whom the Company may confide, both as to knowledge of business, and as to faithful execution of any thing You may undertake. 421

He will probably send for You. I beg you will endeavor by the reasonable terms You propose to become engaged with the Company. I shall feel infinitely easier in my own situation, if I have again the assistance of those whose labors have so es[sen]tially contributed to the success of my own.

As the Undertaking is in a great measure new, I wish you would consider whether you could not provide your own utensils of every kind. I have had a Wheelbarrow made by Jo. Grimes with a cast iron wheel.[2] The pattern is at your service. As you can give undeniable security, I dare to say an advance to help you in the purchase of plank, and of boards for shelds,[3] scantling for ladders &c. &c. could be procured of the board. We must begin quietly at first. The principal part of the ground is stiff clay, but there is also rock and deep digging to be encountered. I shall be in Wilmington the latter end of this Month. I wish you could then meet me. I mention generally the nature of the work that you may turn your thoughts that way. You must however, before you make any proposal see the ground. God bless you. Call upon Mr. Gilpin, in Chesnut street when you come to Philadelphia. Mr. Davis can tell you where he lives.[4] Believe me sincerely Yours

B. Henry Latrobe

Pray see your friend Mr. Smith of Chesnut hill and take him with you.

Polygraph Copy: LB (29/E2). Addressed to Cochran in care of John Davis, Philadelphia Waterworks. Enclosed in BHL to Gilpin, 20 Feb. 1804, below.

1. James Cochran, respectable and wealthy public works contractor, was employed by BHL on the Schuylkill Basin construction for the Philadelphia Waterworks. In 1810 BHL hired him as the principal contractor for digging the Washington Canal and recommended him for the construction of the National Road, a large portion of which Cochran was responsible for. In 1816 BHL recommended Cochran to the Virginia Board of Public Works: "He is an unassuming, and rather humble man in his pretensions. With much energy and most admirable temper in the management of his men, he is one of the most modest in his deportment to his employers. His integrity and sobriety are proverbial where he is known. In fact after so many Years acquaintance with him, and after having paid to him some hundred thousand dollars on behalf of the public, I have not once found him deficient in a single good quality. He is an Irishman, and can collect, for the service of a public work, more of his country men than any other, and govern them with more effect. I consider him as by far the first Man, I have ever known in his line of business. He is also, what is called, *a good Scholar.*" BHL to James Madison, 8 Apr. 1816, in BHL, *Correspondence,* 3.

2. John Grimes (d. 1808), who had worked on the Philadelphia Waterworks, was later

employed as a contractor on the C & D Canal feeder. On 25 March 1804 BHL wrote Grimes, "As to the Wheelbarrow, it is not *exactly* on my model, but it is very well. The load is not near enough to the Wheel. It can be easily altered" (LB; 30/F3). BHL later described Grimes as "one of the best Carpenters I ever knew." BHL to Charles Goldsborough, 18 Mar. 1807, BHL to Mrs. Grimes, 5 Mar. 1808, both in LB (55/G8, 64/A1); BHL, *Engineering Drawings*, p. 14.

    3. Obsolete form of shield, in the sense of temporary shelter.

    4. John Davis, for whom see BHL to Relf, 9 June 1804, n. 4, below.

TO THOMAS VICKERS

Washington Feby. 10th. 1804.

Dear Vickers,[1]

When I was in Wilmington about 10 days ago I begin to write to you, but I was then so ill, and so hurried that I could not compleat my intention. I am still far from well, and the hurry and fatigue of my journey seems to have rendered repose for some few weeks necessary, otherwise I should have been again at home if I could get away from hence, next Week.

The Committee have resolved to commence with the feeders, a very wise and proper resolution. It is necessary that the stream which is to be used should not at present be mentioned, at least untill all the necessary purchases are made. I will however describe to you what must first be done, in order that you may prepare yourself and your hands to be ready to begin.

The first work to be executed, will be an Aqueduct over a rapid Creek. The arch will be 40 feet span. The foundations on the solid natural rock. A slight earthen dam will serve for a Coffer dam, (unless I am much deceived) on each side, formed of the Earth thrown out in digging. All the hills around are full of stone. I have examined it as well as I could, and I think we shall find near at hand, some that will hammer into Arch and Quoin stone. The exterior appearance of the Work will be most perfectly plain. The width of the work about 36 or 40 feet, the Water Way of the Canal over the Aqueduct being 16 feet.

You will want several good hands as Quarriers and Hammermen. 423

You had perhaps better speak to some of your best workmen at the Bridge and the Quarry at the upper ferry;[2] For the first month or six Weeks you will undoubtedly be chiefly employed in the Quarry.

I know nothing of the facility of making bricks in the neighbourhood of the Work. But it might be well to speak to Ridgeway upon the probability of getting a Contract for burning 2 or 300 thousand bricks on the spot for the numerous Culverts which occur in the first three Miles. On this however nothing can be done untill the sort of Stone to be had in the neighborhood is examined. Perhaps we may find flat stone fit for flooring and arch stones.

I write these lines to you chiefly with a view to enable you to look out for proper Men to begin with, and also to request you will call on Mr. Gilpin and have a full conversation with him on the subject. See also James Cochran on whom I have the fullest reliance, and whom I wish to engage as an Example to all our other Contractors.

I hope your family are well believe me very truly Your sincere Friend

B. H. L.

Polygraph Copy: LB (29/E5). Enclosed in BHL to Gilpin, 20 Feb. 1804, below.

1. Thomas Vickers (d. 1820), Philadelphia mason, became experienced in hydraulic or watertight cements while working under William Weston in the 1790s. BHL secured his employment on the Philadelphia Waterworks where in 1799 he constructed the brick tunnel connecting the Schuylkill and Centre Square engine houses. Vickers also supervised construction of both piers of the Schuylkill Permanent Bridge at Philadelphia. BHL appreciated Vickers's abilities to make and use hydraulic cement, an art known to the Romans but only beginning to be learned again in the Western world. BHL, *Engineering Drawings*, pp. 14, 32, 65.

2. Construction on the Schuylkill Permanent Bridge was started in 1801. By 1804 the masonry work had been largely completed, and the bridge was ready for use by the beginning of 1805. [Richard Peters], *A Statistical Account of the Schuylkill Permanent Bridge, Communicated to the Philadelphia Society of Agriculture, 1806* (Philadelphia, 1807), p. 78.

PROCURING STONE FOR THE U.S. CAPITOL

State of the Prospect of procuring Stone
for the Capitol for the Year 1804.

[17 February 1804]

1. From Messrs. Brent & Cook.[1] These Gentlemen are the only contractors who may with certainty be relied upon. The require an advance of 2000$. on a contract made with them Feby. 17th. 1804 for 1000 Tons delivered in Washington, at 8$ per Ton for all stone of one Ton and under, 8.25 above one Ton to 1½ Ton and 8.75$, for all stone of greater weight. The *average* of their supply will probably cost 8$. 10cts. which is 44 Cents per Ton more than last Year. But should the public Quarry yield good Stone, the bills may be so regulated as to take no stone of them exceeding 1 Ton weight.

2.) The public Quarry, is opened and promises well.[2] We may depend on 600 Tons good stone at 7$.25 Cents average. The *next* season, I flatter myself to be entirely supplied from thence.

3.) We have bought for Cash a quantity of stone ready quarried at Acquia, about 150 Ton, which when brought hither will cost only 5$. per Ton.

4. Robertson has contracted to deliver from a very good Quarry now open 400 Ton of extra-fine stone for the Cornice and Capitals at 9$. per Ton. I consider this as an advantageous Contract as that species of stone does not appear in any other Quarry. Of this stone I expect with certainty not more than 250 Ton as Robertson is not entirely to be depended upon.[3]

5. Stewart at Acquia, labors under disadvantages in working his Quarry, which render the fulfillment of his contract for 250 Tons precarious. His stone however is very good, and he will make a great exertion this Season. 8$ per Ton[4]

6. Conway of Acquia has good stone, but having no great force, may not perhaps compleat his Contract for 300 Tons. 8$ per Ton[5]

7. Richardson of Fredericsburg has an excellent Quarry, and were he not engaged in building the New Jail, might furnish a very large Quantity of stone. But I fear he will disappoint us, and as he wants a large advance, I hesitate about contracting for 500 Tons at 7$ 66 cts.—the Quantity and terms which he offers.[6]

Cook & Brent enter into their Contract, *at the risk* of its being avoided if no appropriation be made by Congress to the prosecution of the public Works.

Recapitulation.

			Tons
Cook & Brent,			1.000
Public Quarry			600

	Ton			
Robertson, contract 400,		say		250
Stewart, do. 250.		say		100
Conway do. 300		say		200
Richardson offers 500				000
Purchase by Cash at Acquia				150
Total to be depended upon				2.300

This quantity will compleat the South wing, according to the best judgement I can form, on a subject the most complicated and difficult to be calculated, that can be conceived.

As I have said above, I expect the public Quarry to compleat the work in future Seasons.

B. Henry Latrobe
Survr. Public Bldgs. U.S.

ADS: Jefferson Papers (177/D8). Date derived from following letter, paragraph seven.

1. Col. Daniel Carroll Brent (see Jefferson to BHL, 6 Mar. 1803 (Public), n. 5, above) and Col. John Cooke (c. 1755–1819) of Stafford County, Va., who was married to Mary Thomson Mason, daughter of George Mason. Cooke & Brent's quarry was in Aquia, Va. Earlier, Cooke & Brent attempted to force a general raise in private charges to $10 per ton of stone from the Aquia quarries. BHL outmaneuvered them, however, by reopening the government-owned quarry on the island in Aquia Creek. BHL to Jefferson, 15 Jan. 1804, Jefferson Papers (171/B1); BHL, *Journals*, 3 : 83.

2. BHL abandoned the idea of using the government-owned quarry in 1804. He later told John Lenthall that "it would have very much distracted our attention. . . . I think we will take it up again next Winter." BHL to Lenthall, 6 May 1804, BHL Papers, Library of Congress (174/C9).

3. BHL wrote Aquia quarrier William Robertson (17 Feb. 1804, LB; 29/E11) inform-

ing him that he would receive an advance for his stone as soon as he provided "sufficient security." A visit to Robertson's quarry in August 1806 provided BHL with some of the data he employed in his paper, "An Account of the Freestone Quarries on the Potomac and Rappahannoc Rivers," APS, *Transactions* 6 (1809):283–93, printed in BHL, *Correspondence*, 2. For BHL's description of his "adventures" at Robertson's house, see BHL, *Journals*, 3:78–80.

4. Col. William Steuart (Stewart) (1780–1839) was, according to BHL, "the most wealthy and respectable Stonecutter at Baltimore." His father, Robert Stewart, was the "proprietor of an acre, containing the best Stone on the Island" in Aquia Creek. Steuart supplied stone for the Capitol in 1804 and 1805, though some of it, "which on drying falls to pieces" was rejected. BHL later called on Steuart for stone for the Baltimore Exchange and Washington Canal (both 1816) and for a burial monument he designed for Gov. William C. C. Claiborne's wife, daughter, and brother-in-law (1811). Steuart was active in Baltimore politics where he served in the Maryland House of Delegates and was mayor of the city (1831–32). BHL to Thomas Jefferson, 15 Jan. 1804, Jefferson Papers (171/B1); BHL to Steuart, 25 Aug., 3 Sept. 1805, 17 Jan. 1811, 1 July 1816, all in LB (43/B3, 43/F10, 82/F9, 132/A6); BHL, *Journals*, 3:243; Dielman-Hayward File, MdHS; Wilbur F. Coyle, *The Mayors of Baltimore* (Baltimore, 1919), pp. 37–38.

5. BHL wrote Thomas B. Conway (17 Feb. 1804, LB; 29/E10) that Blagden was to contract with him for the delivery of 300 tons of stone "to be delivered at such Wharf as shall be pointed out in the Potowmac or Eastern branch before the 1st Decr. 1804 at Eight Dollars per Ton, which is the Sum I have agreed to pay Messrs. Brent & Cook, and which I must therefore agree to pay to you."

6. George Richardson claimed to "have enough [stone] to build the City of London," but after George Blagden inspected and reported on Richardson's quarry, BHL concluded that the quarrier was "something of a *braggart*. For how could he assert that he had Stone sufficient to build a city, if it is clear only 4 feet in depth. I hope he may be better depended upon in what he *does* than in what he says." On 17 February, BHL wrote Richardson declining his proposal to provide stone for the Capitol. BHL to Richardson, 31 Jan., 17 Feb. 1804, and BHL to Blagden, 16 Feb. 1804, all in LB (29/C6, 29/E13, 29/E8).

TO THOMAS JEFFERSON

Washington Feby. 18th. 1804[1]

Dear Sir,

Since I last had the honor to wait upon you nothing has occurred upon which I feel myself authorized to take up your time, and though I have often been in your house, I have not found it necessary to trespass upon your leisure for directions.[2]

In the mean time, every thing has been prepared to begin the roof as soon as the Weather promises to be fair. The lead for the Gutters has been cast and the iron Work prepared. My time has been employed in

427

the accounts in the designs necessary for the ensuing season, and principally in the negotiations for stone.

I now take the liberty to send you a sheet of sketches which explain the effect of different dispositions of the plan of the House of Representatives, lighted a la Halle de Bled.

The best proportioned room would be the circle of 80 feet No. III. But its excessive rise above the Balustres renders it perhaps inadmissible, independently of the narrowness of the intercolumnation if 32 Columns be the number adopted.

No. II in which the Intercolumniation is in the mode of Eustyle gives columns too slight in appearance for the weight of the dome, and lowers the room too much. The Elliptical room No. IV has all the faults formerly enumerated with very slender Columns.

In No. I I have taken great pains to ascertain the line in Perspective of a Dome upon an Eliptical plan, segment 120 Degrees,[3] Columns (as in Doctor Thornton's plan 3 feet Diameter), as it would appear along the Pensylvania avenue. It must be observed that the Capitol hill is only 78 feet above the tide, though its abruptness gives it the air of much greater altitude, and that therefore any roof projecting much above the parapet is seen easily at the distance of 1/2 a mile which distance reduces the angle of Elevation to a very few degrees.

I take the liberty to lay these sketches, and a paper on the State of the Stone contracts before you this evening and will wait upon you early tomorrow morning.[4]

I have been very seriously ill for the last fortnight of an species of intermitting headach, which has contributed to delay my business. I am with true respect Your very hble. Servt.

B. Henry Latrobe

ALS: Jefferson Papers (171/C3). For dating problem, see n. 1.

1. Jefferson endorsed this letter: "Latrobe B. Henry. Washn. Feb. 18. 04. recd. Feb. 17." BHL may have postdated the letter.

2. BHL had seen the president on 15 January to discuss with him the attempt by the Aquia quarriers to force up the price of stone. BHL's frequent visits to the President's House were probably to supervise the repairs there. BHL to Jefferson, 15 Jan. 1804, Jefferson Papers (171/B1).

3. Presumably BHL here refers to a shallow dome whose profile describes a segment of a circle, the angular extent of whose arc (or, possibly, whose angle of springing) he specifies here in order to determine its rise. A 120° curve (along the longer axis of the ellipse?) by either method would spring obliquely, and would give less height to the dome than would the vertical springing of a dome of a semicircular profile.

4. The sketches are now lost; the paper, [17 Feb. 1804], is printed above.

REPORT ON THE PUBLIC BUILDINGS

To the President of the United States.

Washington, Feby. 20th. 1804

Sir,

On the 4th. of April 1803, I had the honor to lay before you, a general report, on the State of the public Buildings in this City.[1] I now beg leave to submit to you an account of the progress that has been made in the works directed by you in consequence of that report: and in order more clearly to explain the subject, I beg to recapitulate concisely what I formerly stated.

I. *On the North Wing of the Capitol.*

On a careful survey of the North wing of the Capitol it was found, that the want of Air and light in the Cellarstory, had began to produce decay in the Timbers, that the roof was leaky, and the cielings and walls of several of the Apartments were thereby injured, that it would be impossible to render the Senate Chamber, the extreme coldness of which was matter of serious complaint, more warm and comfortable without the construction of stoves or furnaces below the floor for which purpose it would be necessary to carry up additional flues, and to remove a very large quantity of rubbish from the Cellars; and that the Skylights were extremely out of repair.

During the course of the last Season therefore openings have been made into all the Cellars, the decayed timbers have been replaced where immediately necessary, the floors that required it have received additional support, the Senate Chamber has been rendered more comfortable by the introduction of warm air, by the erection of a stove, by the exclusion of cold air from the Cellar by plaistering, and should the plan adopted after the experience of the present Session be approved, another Stove is ready to be put up. All the Cellars have been cleared and the rubbish removed. In respect to the roof, the best repairs which could be made without unroofing the whole wing, have been made, and the leaks rendered of less importance: but the early meeting of Congress,[2] and the magnitude, and the doubtful completion as to time, of a thorough repair by taking off the whole upper part of the roof, induced me to postpone this operation. Every preparation however is made, and the lead which covers so great a part of the roof will contribute greatly to defray the expense of this thorough repair.

429

The skylights have also been *only* repaired, but it is necessary to substitute in their room Lanthorn lights, with upright Sashes and close tops. This Work has also been deferred, and for the same reasons.

General repairs of those parts of the building which were hastily and slightly executed previously to the removal of the seat of Government were also necessary, and they have been made.

II. On the South Wing of the Capitol.

On the 4th. of April 1803, it was necessary to report to you, that on opening, in order to examine the Walls of the Cellar story of the South wing of the Capitol the workmanship was found to have been so unfaithfully performed, as to render it absolutely necessary to take them down to the foundation, and that even the greatest part of the Materials were too bad to be used again. Previously therefore to the commencement of the work upon this Wing all the old external Walls were removed. The new Work was executed with the best Materials and in the most durable manner, that could be devised. Great disadvantages were encountered at the commencement of the Season. The long intermission of public Work, had scattered the Workmen, and the supply of materials was difficult and tardy. The work however which has been done, is considerable. The Walls have been raised to nearly half the heighth of the Ground story. The preparations for further progress, should the Legislature direct the same, are also great, and materials are now collected on the Spot nearly sufficient, and already prepared to finish the external Walls of the lower story. The rapidity and greater oeconomy with which the work will in future proceed are also an advantage gained. A system for the supply of materials is now organized, a great number of excellent Workmen are collected, and the expense of Machinery, scaffolding, and utensils defrayed.

The Hall in which the House of Representatives are now assembled was erected as part of the permanent building. I am however under the necessity of representing to you, that the whole of the Masonry from the very foundation is of such bad workmanship and materials, that it would have been dangerous to have assembled within the building, had not the Walls been strongly supported by shores from without. For easy examination the Wall has been opened in several places, and an actual inspection will immediately explain the state in which it is.

Besides the Work done to secure the present Building, it has been lighted in the best manner which the construction of the roof will admit, in order to remedy the diminution of light by carrying up the external Walls.[3] The increase of the number of the Members of the House this Session, rendered it necessary to take up the Platform, and to enlarge the space for seats.[4] This has also been done, and forms part of the Expenditure of the Season.

In my former report, I took the liberty to suggest the propriety of considering whether any and what improvement of the original plan of the Work, might be necessary for the better accomodation of the House of Representatives in the South Wing of the Capitol, so as to bring the Offices attached to the house nearer to the Legislative Hall. The attention You have already been pleased to give to this subject encourages me to suggest the necessity of an ultimate decision previously to the Commencement of the Work of the ensuing Season.

III. The President's house.

Agreeably to Your desire that the Monies appropriated by the Legislature should be devoted as much as possible to the erection of the Capitol and to the accomodation of the Legislature, the expenditure on the President's house has been kept as low as possible.

In my former report to You on this building[5] I stated, that the Roof and gutters were so leaky as to render it necessary to take off all the Slating; to take up all the Gutters and to give them much more current; and to cover the building with Sheet iron, as uniting safety against fire with oeconomy; to strengthen and tie together the roof which having spread, has forced out the Walls; to put up the Staircase, which was already prepared; to sink a Well for the purpose of procuring good Water, of which the house was in absolute Want; to glaze those Apartments which required it, and to complete some accomodations wanted in the Chamber story.

All these Works, except the complete repair of the roof have been done. The work on the roof, is however in progress, and the funds remaining in hand are estimated to be sufficient to complete this object.

The Superintendant of the City has favored me with the necessary information to give the following Statement of Expenditures, up to this day.

The expenditure of monies out of the fund of 50.000$, on the roads, and on objects not placed by You under my direction,......................		4.832.63
On the North wing of the Capitol,		
a. In repairs	1.513$.22 ½	
b. On the Senate Chamber........	1.168 .34 ½	
		2.681.57
On the South Wing		
a. Repairs &c. of the Hall of Representatives	555.13 ½	
b. Materials, Labor, and superintendance of the Work of the South Wing	31.190.23 ½	
	31.745.37	31.745.37
On the President's House.		
Repairs, and Works enumerated above		2.251.67
Balance, estimated to be sufficient to discharge unsettled and outstanding accts., to complete existing contracts of last Season, to pay advances on new Contracts, and prepare to lay in a Stock of new materials............		8.488.76
		50.000

The above statement, collected in many instances from running, and unsettled accounts, is necessarily liable to corrections in detail, which cannot however in any case, materially affect the results stated.

The Season is now at hand in which preparations for the Work of the present Year should be made. I therefore respectfully submit the premisses to Your consideration, and am Your faithful humble Servt.

B. Henry Latrobe
Surveyor of the public Buildings
of the United States at Washington

P.S. I beg leave to add, that to compleat the Work *in freestone* of the South wing, which is the most expensive part of the building, the sum of 30.000$ will be sufficient, according to the best Estimate which can be made.

ADS: Records of the U.S. House of Representatives, RG 233, National Archives (171/C11). Jefferson submitted this report to Congress on 22 February 1804. A polygraph copy submitted to the Senate is in the Records of the U.S. Senate, RG 46, National Archives (171/D11). The report was published in *Message from the President of the United States, Transmitting a Report of the Surveyor of the Public Buildings at the City of Washington* ([Washington, D.C.], 1804), pp. 5–10 (171/F2). The report also appeared in the *National Intelligencer* on 7 March 1804.

1. Printed above.
2. On 16 July 1803 Jefferson issued a proclamation calling for Congress to convene on 17 October, rather than 7 November, primarily for the purpose of ratifying the Louisiana cession treaty with France and arranging for the administration of the newly acquired territory. *Annals of Congress*, 7th Cong., 2d sess., pp. 270, 700, 8th Cong., 1st sess., pp. 11–15, 17–18, 369, 382.
3. The temporary House chamber completed by Hoban in late 1801, the "bake oven," appears originally to have been lit from the sides through its elliptical arcade. BHL here describes his introduction of a temporary scheme of top-lighting in the existing wooden roof for the 1803–04 session of Congress. Glenn Brown, *History of the United States Capitol*, 2 vols. (Washington, D.C., 1900–02), 1 : 28. See also BHL to Jefferson, 21 May 1807, n. 5, in BHL, *Correspondence*, 2.
4. As a result of reapportionment based on the 1800 census and of the admission of the new state of Ohio, there were 142 members in the House of Representatives of the Eighth Congress which met in December 1803. This was an increase of 36 members over the Seventh Congress which met in 1801–03.
5. No previous report on the President's House has been found.

TO JOSHUA GILPIN

Washington Feby. 20th. 1804.

My dear Sir

I did not receive your very obliging letter of the 3d of Feby. (with the postmark of the 8th.) till the 11th. Had I been well enough to have even read it through and considered its contents as they deserve, I should then have answered it. But the fatigue I have undergone during the last 4 Months, the illness which I had at Newcastle and the injury which I suffered from two long journies in bad health, and in bad weather have for the last 15 days reduced me to the necessity of keeping my room, and for more than half the day, my bed. A rheumatic headach, a species of intermittent, to which I had been annually subject for many years past, again seized me on my return hither, and with such violence, that I have sometimes almost lost my senses. I am within these two days somewhat better, but not by any means well. I am indeed wholly unable to think of travelling for a few days to come, and am obliged to beg you to put off Your meeting for a week longer, that the bark, and repose may have a little more chance in restoring me.[1] I shall write to the same effect to Mr. Tatnall and to Mr. Johns.[2]

In respect to the very friendly advice your letter contains it is too reasonable not to be followed by me to the utmost extent. I will say little on this subject but when you shall have known me as a man of business a little longer, you will have ample reason to believe that neither pride nor self interest are the reins by which I am guided, and that a hint from an upright, and candid friend is more efficient than a decree of the most powerful board.

That I have not forgotten the business of the Canal (which indeed I now consider to be the principal business of my life) will be evident from the two letters which I enclose, and which I wrote 10 or 12 days ago, with an intention of then sending them to you.[3] But all attention to business was soon interrupted by the excessive pain I suffered for the first half of every day, and the languor which depressed me for the other. They may however perhaps be still useful. I am exceedingly anxious about Cochran whom I consider to be one of the pillars of our concern. Tomorrow when I hope to be still better in health and spirits I will answer the whole of your letter very fully.

We have here no news. Jerome and Madam Buonaparte have amused us considerably for the last fortnight. She is certainly pretty, and her youth and singular fortune may excuse her if she be not very wise. Of her it may be said, *Bella te vedo, saggia te credo*.[4] She has much scandalized the lovers of Drapery and disgusted the admirers even of the naked figure.[5] I have ventured in the evenings, when I have generally been a little better, once or twice into the gay societies of this place, and have witnessed some of the absurdities which the new etiquette has introduced. I am not of opinion that the first treatment, as to precedence, of Mrs. Merry was correct or politic. Nothing was indeed intended, but then nothing was considered as it ought to have been. She has now withdrawn from all evening Society excepting of one or two families, but the Marchioness D'Yruijo who does go into society has now taken up the claim to *universal* precedence, and some times meets with a little mortification and disappointment. Trifling as this business is, it is exceedingly to be regretted, for it will *color* our intercourse with the British court at a moment when every thing ought to be the most perfect good humor. My *paper* and my *head* remind me to close. You shall soon again hear from me. I propose setting out from hence on the 1st. March not to return for many Months. My best respects attend Mrs. Gilpin. Believe me most sincerely Yrs.

B. H. Latrobe.

Polygraph Copy: LB (29/F2). Addressed to Gilpin in Philadelphia.

   1. For BHL's detailed description of his annual bouts with the headache, see BHL to Dr. Henry Huntt, 10 Jan. 1816, in BHL, *Journals,* 3 : 134–39.
   2. BHL to Joseph Tatnall, 20 Feb. 1804, and BHL to Kensey Johns, 20 Feb. 1804, both in LB (29/F6, 29/F12).
   3. BHL to Cochran, 8 Feb. 1804, and BHL to Vickers, 10 Feb. 1804, both above.
   4. Trans.: "I see thee beautiful; I believe thee wise."
   5. In 1803 Jerome Bonaparte (1784–1860), Napoleon's youngest brother, visited the United States, where he met and married Elizabeth Patterson (1785–1879) of Baltimore. They arrived on the Washington social scene when the Merry "affair" was still the talk of the town. Jefferson gave a dinner at which he escorted the new bride to the table, further infuriating the Merrys when they heard about it. The beautiful Mme. Bonaparte wore "the highest, and scantiest, of Parisian fashions." Men who dared to steal a glance at her "said 'they could put all the clothes she had on in their vest pocket.'" "Lovers of Drapery" were those who admired Mrs. Merry's style of dress: "a mélange of satin and crepe and spangles with shawl fantastically draped from head to heels." Merrill D. Peterson, *Thomas Jefferson and the New Nation: A Biography* (New York, 1970), pp. 732–33.
   Napoleon disapproved of his brother's match and, because Jerome was still a minor, he annulled the marriage in 1806 and provided Elizabeth Patterson with a large annual pension.

TO CHARLES WILLSON PEALE

Washington Feby. 22nd. 1804

My dear Friend

   I was in hopes that before now I should have had the pleasure to give you at least a dozen orders for Polygraphs so many of my friends have *talkd* about buying. At last however I can send you *one* but you will be obliged to break thro' your law of not forwarding one without the Cash. It is for the President of the United States. It must be made as perfect as your best, but different in one respect. Instead of one drawer to draw out on the left hand, it must have two drawers each of half the length, one to draw out to the right the other to the left. It must have a binding frame and half a ream of paper as usual. Please to send it by the first Vessel

435

bound to Alexandria to the care of *Mr. Lewis Deblois Merchant Alexandria for the President of the United States,* enclosing a bill of lading by Post to Mr. Deblois.[1] As soon as it arrives the President will send you the Money. You had better write to him and enclose him a Bill. I am ashamed to say that I had not the Courage to ask for it beforehand.

I have in the mean time lent to the President my own Polygraph, much to mine and my Wifes inconvenience, whom I have now restord to her former post of Copying Clerk. You will I am sure so far oblige me as to send me another of the most approved Construction to New Castle to be there by the 6th of March at latest. As soon as the President U.S. receives that which you will make for him my old one will be sent to you from Alexandria. You will recollect that it is of the first Construction with three bars. Tomorrow I hope to find you another order. Believe me most sincerely Yrs.

B. Henry Latrobe

P.S. I consider myself responsible to you for the amount of a Polygraph until you receive mine from the President and for all extra expenses.

Letterbook Copy: LB (29/F14). In MEL's hand. Addressed to Peale in Philadelphia.

1. Lewis Deblois, a Boston and later a Washington, D.C., and Alexandria, Va., merchant, was appointed a justice of the peace for the District of Columbia by John Adams in March 1801, one of the so-called "midnight appointments." Deblois served as a director of the Washington branch of the Bank of the United States from 1806 to 1811, and he was an agent and consul representing Portugal in Washington and Alexandria from 1808 to 1819. BHL dealt with Deblois for both household goods and materials for his federal commissions, and the families of the men were good friends as well. CHS, *Records* 5 (1902):260, 8 (1905): 29, 31, 38.

TO THOMAS JEFFERSON

[The following paragraph is a memorandum BHL wrote in his letterbook at the head of his rough draft of this letter (29/G6).]

The following letter was occasioned by an interview with Dr. Thornton, in consequence of a prior conversation with the President o[n] the subject of the plan. The President, from the beginning of these discussions, has hung back from any alteration. Delicacy to Dr. Thornton proved to be his motive for this conduct. He had promised to see Thornton on the objectionable parts of the design. I hoped to prepare the way for an amicable adjustment of the business by a prior meeting. My ill success appears as follows:

Washington Feby. 27th. 1804.

Dear Sir

I judged very ill in going to Thornton. In a few peremptory words, he, in fact, told me, that no difficulties existed in his plan, but such as were made by those who were too ignorant to remove them and though these were not exactly his words, his expressions, his tone, his manner, and his absolute refusal to devote a few minutes to discuss the subject spoke his meaning even more strongly and offensively than I have expressed it. I left him with an assurance that I should not be the person to attempt to remove them, and had I had immediate possession of pen, ink, and paper, I should have directly solicited your permission to resign my office.

I owe however too much to you to risk by so hasty a step, the miscarriage of any measure you may wish to promote, and I shall devote as before my utmost endeavors to excite the disposition in the Committee, to which I am summoned tomorrow morning, in favor of the appropriation.

In respect to the plan itself, it is impossible to convey by words or drawings to the mind of any man, that impression of the difficulties in execution which 20 Years experience creates in the mind of a professional man. I fear I have said already too much for the respect I owe to your opinions, though much too little for my own conviction. The utmost praise which I can ever deserve in this work is that of *la difficulté vaincue,* and after receiving your ultimate directions all my exertion shall be directed to earn this degree of reputation.

My wish to avoid vexation, trouble, and enmities is weak, compared to my desire to be placed among those whom you regard with approbation and friendship. If you therefore, *under all circumstances,* conceive that my services can still be useful, I place myself entirely at your disposal. I am with sincere respect Your faithful hble. Servt.

B. Henry Latrobe   437

PS. In order to pass my accounts it will be necessary to produce a regular appointment from you to my office. May I beg you to give the necessary directions for this purpose.[1] I ought to leave Washington on Wednesday morning.[2]

[The following paragraph is a memorandum BHL wrote in his letterbook at the end of his rough draft of this letter.]

After writing this letter and before I drew up my report to the Committee on the President's Messages respecting the public Buildings (see Reports Feby. 28th. 1804)[3] but having had an interview with Mr. Blagden and Mr. Hatfield as to the facts which I have therein stated, I met the Committee.[4] As soon as it broke up the President's letter of the 28th Feby. 1804 was delivered me.[5] I answered it immediately, explaining in many instances the utter absurdity of the plan especially in respect to the Conference room, which though drawn in the plan of the Ground-story belongs to the story above,[6] and to the want of light in the two rooms of this shape  on each side of the Conference room.[7] I also stated what had passed verbally before the Committee, and that I was required to give it them in writing. Of this letter I have no Copy. In the evening I had an interview with the President, when after much conversation he appeared convinced of the absurdity of many parts of the plan and the impracticability of others, and desired me to transmit to him drawings of a practicable and eligible design retaining as much as possible the features of that adopted by General Washington.

ALS: Jefferson Papers (171/G9). Endorsed as received 27 February.

1. Jefferson made the following notation on this letter: "his appmt. to commence Mar. 15. 1803." The president apparently wrote a new letter of appointment for BHL and backdated it to 15 March 1803. Jefferson to BHL, 15 Mar. 1803(4), Jefferson Papers (172/F14).
2. BHL left for Wilmington, Del., on Thursday, 1 March 1804.
3. Printed below.
4. The committee consisted of Philip R. Thompson (1766–1837) of Virginia, John Smilie (1741–1812) of Pennsylvania, Benjamin Huger (1768–1823) of South Carolina, John Campbell (1765–1828) of Maryland, and Richard Cutts (1771–1845) of Massachusetts. *Annals of Congress*, 8th Cong., 1st sess., p. 1044.
5. See following document.
6. BHL's letter to Jefferson of 28 February 1804 (below) deals more generally with the matter of floor levels.

The plan which BHL inscribed in May 1803 as "Given to me by George Blagden as the only existing drawing of the Capitol" (Prints and Photographs Division, Library of Congress; fig. 9) is of the ground floor, as indicated by the eastern door to the recess of the north wing, as well as by the eastern porch interrupted by the porte cochere below. Both Senate and House chambers are shown on this level, as is the stair-fronted western conference room. A western elevation, thought to belong to the same Thornton design, however, shows this peristylar conference room elevated to the principal story; this probably explains BHL's observation about a confusion of levels here. Glenn Brown, *History of the United States Capitol*, 2 vols. (Washington, D.C., 1900–02), 1: pl. 31.

All three principals involved here agreed that Thornton, initially, had placed the legislative chambers on the principal story. At some point before the completion of the north wing in 1800, Thornton had acceded to Jefferson's desire to lower the legislative chambers to the ground floor, but the exterior and the plan were not, to BHL's thinking, completely adapted to the new arrangement. Shortly before BHL's appointment, however, Jefferson was considering reversing his decision, and in response Thornton prepared a proposal to again elevate the chamber story (Prints and Photographs Division, Library of Congress; 270/B1). BHL, Report on the U.S. Capitol, 4 Apr. 1803, above; Thornton, *To the Members of the House of Representatives of the United States* [Washington, D.C., 1805]; and Jefferson to BHL, 14 Apr. 1811, in BHL, *Correspondence*, 3.

7. In place of the southernmost of these two rooms flanking the conference room (Hadfield's libraries; see BHL to Jefferson, 28 Feb. 1804, below), BHL had already proposed a courtyard adjoining a circular ground stairway in his plans of the previous year. BHL to Lenthall, 6 May 1803, above.

FROM THOMAS JEFFERSON

Washington Feb. 28. 04.

Dear Sir

I am sorry the explanations attempted between Dr. Thornton and yourself on the manner of finishing the chamber of the house of representatives have not succeeded. At the original establishment of this place advertisements were published many months offering premiums for the best plans for a Capitol and President's house. Many were sent in. A council was held by Genl. Washington with the board of Commissioners and after very mature examination two were preferred and the premiums given to their authors Doctr. Thornton and Hobans, and the plans were decided on.[1] Hobans', has been executed. On Dr. Thornton's plan of the Capitol the North wing has been executed, and the South raised one story. In order to get along with any public undertaking it is necessary that some stability of plan be observed. Nothing impedes progress so much as perpetual changes of design. I yield to this principle in the present case more willingly because the plan begun for the Representative room will in my opinion be more handsome and commodious than any thing which can now be proposed on the same area. And tho the Spheroidical dome presents difficulties to the Executor, yet they are not beyond his art, and it is to overcome difficulties that we employ men of genius. While however I express my opinion that we had better go through with this wing of the Capitol on the plan which has been settled, I would not be understood to suppose there does not exist sufficient authority to controul the original plan in any of it's parts, and to accomodate it to changes of circumstances. I only mean that it is not adviseable to change that of this wing in it's present stage. Tho' I have spoken of a Spheroidical roof, that will not be correctly the figure. Every rib will be a portion of a circle of which the radius will be determined by the span and rise of each rib. Would it not be best to make the internal columns of well burnt bricks moulded in portions of circles adapted to the diminution of the columns. Ld. Burlington in his notes on Palladio tells us that he found most of the buildings erected under Palladio's direction and described in his architecture to have their columns made of brick in this way and covered over with stucco.[2] I know an instance of a range of 6. or 8. columns in Virginia, 20. 9. high well proportioned and properly diminished, executed by a common bricklayer. The bases and Capitals would of course be of hewn stone. I suggest this for your consideration, and tender you my friendly salutations.

Th: Jefferson

Polygraph Copy: Jefferson Papers (172/E7).

1. For more on the Capitol competition, see Wells Bennett, "Stephen Hallet and His Designs for the National Capitol, 1791–94," *Journal of the American Institute of Architects,* 4 (1916):290–95, 324–30, 376–83, 411–18; Fiske Kimball and Wells Bennett, "The Competition for the Federal Buildings, 1792–1793," ibid., 7 (1919):8–12, 98–102; Kimball and Bennett, "William Thornton and the Design of the United States Capitol," *Art Studies,* 1 (1923):76–92; Jeanne F. Butler, "Competition 1792: Designing a Nation's Capitol," *Capitol Studies,* 4 (1976):11–96.

2. Richard Boyle (1695–1753), third earl of Burlington and fourth earl of Cork, *Fabbriche antiche designate da A. Palladio date in luce da Riccardo, Conte di Burlington* (London, 1730). In fact this method had been used for the colonnade at Jefferson's Virginia State Capitol in Richmond. Fiske Kimball, *Thomas Jefferson, Architect* (New York, 1968 [orig. publ. 1916]), p. 43.

TO THOMAS JEFFERSON

Capitol, Washington, Feby. 28th. 1804

Dear Sir,

The circumstances that attend the conflict between my wish to promote your views respecting the Capitol, and my conviction of the necessity for forming a plan different from that which is *now* said by Dr. Thornton to be the plan approved by General Washington are among the most unpleasant which I have ever had to struggle with. It cannot in my opinion be stated that *any* plan, that is any *practicable* plan exists, or ever existed. I do not allude to the spheroidal dome. I will undertake to execute it under all my impressions against it, and I have so much confidence in myself, that I hope to produce a thing not entirely displeasing. If the house be raised to the level of the top of the basement story, I will withdraw all further opposition to the colonade, and its eliptical form, but it will *then* be absolutely necessary to cut off the angles, and thereby to strengthen the external Walls.[1] Of my ideas on this subject I will in a few weeks send you compleat drawings, which I hope will perfectly satisfy your wishes, because the eliptical form, and the Colonade, the principal features of the Work will remain. But perhaps I may still be favored with an interview with you.

In a contest, similar to that in which I am engaged, first with Mr. Hallet,[2] then with Mr. Hatfield, Doctor Thornton was victorious. Both these men, men of knowledge, talents, integrity and amiable manners were ruined. Hatfield had the best expectations in England, when he was called to this country. The Brother of Maria Cosway, and the protege of the Queen, and of Lady Chesterfield (who on her death left him a legacy of £1500) could not have failed in making a figure in his profession, had he remained at home.[3] I knew him slightly there. He is now starving in Washington, and Hallet was ruined some Years ago. After seeing Dr. Thornton yesterday I procured Mr. Hatfield's letter to the Commissioners in which he states his opinion of the plan. His ideas, and almost his words are those I have often repeated.[4] He remained Superintendant of the work for three Years. During this period the original plan disappeared. Hatfield proposed a New Elevation rejecting the basement. The circular domed Vestibule is Hatfields, the two Libraries of this shape are his. His style is visible in many other parts of the Work. All this has been retained while the basement, wholly incompatible with this plan, and loading it with absurdities and impracticabilities remains. All this can be proved by the most authentic documents. If I felt the slightest respect for the talents of the original designer *as an architect*, I should be fearless as to myself, but placed as I am on the very spot from which Hallet and Hatfield fell, attacked by the same weapons, and with the same activity, nothing but a very resolute defence can save me.

The Committee have just risen. Their enquiries have been most minute. I produced the plan given me by Doctor Thornton. I mean the ground plan. Its absurdities are still more glaring than its insufficiency as a guide, by which to execute the work. I was asked whether that was the original plan? I said, no, and had I said otherwise I should have failed in my duty to myself and to truth. I was asked for the original plan? It is not to be found. Whose plan was that which I exhibited? I detailed the authors of the different parts. Is it a good plan? No! What are its faults? I confined myself to the total want of offices and accomodation of every kind. How can they be remedied? By raising the floor one story higher. More questions were asked, and answered agreeably to truth, without fear or self interest, for it is my interest in this city, peaceably to act and speak to every body but yourself, directly contrary to my judgement.

As the result of the meeting it was understood, that an appropriation of 50.000 Dollars should be recommended. I stated the necessity of removing the Earth about the public offices and the President's house. I was desired to put in writing all that I had verbally stated, in one report, as to the Capitol, and in a separate report, as to the removal of the Earth. It was also asked whether I would recommend a plan, whether the President knew the inconveniences of the present one, and had conceived the means of remedying them? I answered that I had stated them fully to You, that the idea of raising the floor of the house appeared reasonable to you, that I had however no authority to commit your opinion on the subject, that I was persuaded that such alterations would be made by You as would produce the best accomodation possible to the house.

In the report which I shall make tomorrow,[5] I shall be under the necessity of speaking the truth as to the history of the plan and the causes of the defects of the building. I am prepared for open war, and shall suffer less by it than I have already done by that conduct that keeps greater talents than I possess out of sight. I shall recommend *nothing*, but *generally* say that all the inconveniences and deficiencies stated, *may be easily remedied* without altering the external appearance of the building.

I am also desired to state the probable expence of completing the work. On this point I shall only say that in the third Year the South wing will undoubtedly be finished probably in the *second,* and that two more appropriations of 50.000 Dollars will *probably* compleat it.

The haste which, I fear is visible in the expressions as well as writing of this letter, I beg you to pardon and to believe me with the truest respect Your much obliged hble. Servt.

B. Henry Latrobe.

ALS: Jefferson Papers (172/A1). Endorsed as received 28 February.

1. Early in the previous year BHL had proposed a semicircular antique theater, without a colonnade, for the House of Representatives. This plan having been rejected, cutting off the angles around an elliptical chamber would be required to solidify the corners of the south wing in order to buttress the projected dome, whose thrusts would tend in all directions rather than primarily toward the recess and rotunda. See BHL to Jefferson, [4 Apr. 1803], enclosure, above.

2. Étienne Sulpice Hallet (1755–1825), a French architect who came to America in the late 1780s, submitted designs in the Capitol competition of 1792. He won the second prize and was commissioned to revise those of the winner, Thornton, and to supervise the construction of the building. Conflict with his supervisors, the District of Columbia commissioners, soon resulted in his dismissal in 1794.

3. Maria (Hadfield) Cosway (1759–1838) was an artist, musician, and composer. She was the wife of the noted British painter, Richard Cosway, and a close friend of Thomas Jefferson. Helen Duprey Bullock, *My Head and My Heart: A Little History of Thomas Jefferson and Maria Cosway* (New York, 1945), pp. viii–x, 15, 194.

The Queen was Charlotte Sophia (1744–1818), younger sister of Adolphus Frederick IV, duke of Mecklenburg-Strelitz, who married King George III on 8 September 1761.

Lady Chesterfield was Anne Thistlethwaite (d. ante-1800), the first wife of Philip Stanhope, fifth earl of Chesterfield (1755–1815).

4. George Hadfield's critique is in Hadfield to the Commissioners of the District of Columbia, 27 Oct., 28 Oct. 1795, both in RG 42, National Archives.

5. See following document.

TO PHILIP R. THOMPSON

Washington Feby. 28th. 1804

To the Chairman of the Committee of the House of Representatives in Congress, to whom was referred the Message of the President of the 443

United States of the 22d of February 1804, transmitting a report of the
Surveyor of the Public buildings of the 20th. of February, 1804.

The Report of the Surveyor of the public Buildings

Sir,

In compliance with my duty, and your desire, that I should give you
such information respecting the original plan of the Capitol as approved
by General Washington, of the accomodations provided therein for the
house of Representatives, together with my opinion as to such alterations as might further conduce to render the house as commodious as
possible, I beg to submit to you the following report.

By the act of Congress of the 16th. July 1790 establishing the permanent seat of Government, it is enacted, among others, "that the President shall appoint three Commissioners" who shall "*according to such
plans as the President shall approve*" &c. "prior to the 1st day of December
1800 provide suitable buildings for the accomodation of Congress" &c.[1]

General Washington, at that time president of the United States did
approve the plan of Doctor Thornton, and by that approbation this plan
became, as it were, a part of the Law, and ceased to be liable to alteration,
untill the act of Congress of 1802–1803, which appropriated 50.000$
towards the completion of the Capitol, and other public purposes, and
authorized "*alterations*" in the plan.[2]

Of the plan approved by General Washington no drawing can at
present be found among the papers belonging to the office.[3] From the
evidence of the foundations which were taken up during the last Season,
from some which still remain, and especially from the testimony of all
those who were first employed in the execution of the Work, it appears
that, it differed from that which is now to be had, in many essential
points. The evidence of the books of the Office proves that it was not
considered as practicable. As its author was not a professional Man, it
was put into the hands of Mr. Hallet, whose knowledge, and talents as a
practical architect are proved by his designs, still in the office, that its
deficiencies might be corrected.[4] Mr. Hallet however, was not continued
in the public service. Mr. Hatfield afterwards succeeded to the superintendance of the Capitol. Of his judicious attempts to correct the radical
errors of the original design, as far as it could be understood from the
imperfect sketches, which were put into his hands, instances are every
where to be found in the North wing of the Capitol; and it is to be
regretted that his endeavors, upon the whole, failed, and that the public

have lost the benefit of his talents. After the departure of Mr. Hatfield, the public became indebted to Mr. Geo: Blagden, of whose integrity and abilities, as the principal Stone Mason, his work bears honorable testimony, for the excellent execution of the Freestone work of the North wing.

Under the hands of Mr. Hallet, and of Mr. Hatfield, the original design, as far as its erection was attempted, received improvement, and considerable alteration. The various stiles of each architect show themselves in the work, and prove the truth of the preceding statement.[5] The parts belonging to each might be pointed out in detail, if it were interesting or necessary.

When the President of the United States did me the honor to employ me in the direction of the Work, my first endeavor was to procure the drawings necessary to understand and execute the original design; for which purpose I applied to the Author, and received only a ground plan.[6] No information as to the execution of any part of the work, being given by this plan beyond what was already built, I searched the papers in the office, and applied to the persons formerly employed in the Work. I was every where disappointed, *and found that no drawings from which the design could be understood or executed existed,* and that the plan of which I was possessed, independently of several parts being wholly impracticable, did not agree with the foundations which were laid.[7] I was also informed, and the most indisputable evidence was brought before me, to prove, that no sections, or detailed drawings of the building had ever existed excepting those which were from time to time made by Messrs. Hallet and Hatfield, for their own use in the direction of the work.

From what I have said, it is evident, that I am unable to give you any information as to the plan approved by General Washington. But supposing the plan, now in my possession to be similar to that which he did approve, as far as regards the South wing, I will submit to you my opinion respecting the accomodations provided therein for the House of Representatives of the United States.

The whole area of the South wing, being about 108 by 84 feet in the clear, is in the plan given to me as the original design, appropriated to the hall of representatives and to a spacious lobby around it. The room in which the House now sits is the area intended for the accomodation of the house in Session, the Windows are to be open Arches, as in the Senate Chamber, leading into the Lobby, and the space between the Wall of the present house and the external Wall, is designed for the Lobby of the House. Upon the Wall, on which the present roof rests,   445

Columns have been designed to support the roof, while the whole space between the Columns and external Wall, was appropriated to an immense Gallery surrounding the house, in form and size exactly equal to the Lobby below. A better idea of the intended Hall cannot be conceived, than by imagining the present Senate Chamber to be doubled and formed into a compleat Ellipsis, presenting a range of arches below and of Columns above, the lobby and Gallery, being situated as in the Senate Chamber.

To this arrangement I think it my duty to state to you the following objections:

I. As they respect use and convenience.

For the commodious dispatch of business it appears to me that the following apartments should be closely attached to the legislative Hall.

1. A number of committee rooms.

2. A chamber for the speaker in which he may transact business with the Members or others, when not sitting in the Chair of the house.

3. An office for the Clerk of the House.

4. Offices for the engrossing Clerks.

5. An Apartment for the door keeper in which he may assort and keep printed papers for delivery to the Members, distribute letters, and preserve the articles belonging to his office.

6. Another for subordinate Officers of the House.

7. Closets of convenience.

8. Fireproof repositories of records.

9. A Lobby sufficient for the convenient retirement of a large number of Members from the house, but not adapted to the purposes of a Gallery. The lobbies of the House of Representatives and Senate, as hitherto used have been grievously complained against as nuisances, and the President of the Senate has not permitted the introduction of Strangers into the House as heretofore.

10. A commodious Gallery, not only overlooking the house but completely commanded by the view of the Officers of the House.

My objections to the present plan arise from the want of all these Accomodations in situations contiguous to the house, and the want of some of them altogether. The North wing is too remote to supply this want consistently with the convenient dispatch of business.

I have mentioned the inconvenience of a lobby calculated to serve the purposes of a Gallery. The lobby which is proposed to surround the

Legislative hall has all the inconveniencies of a Lobby within the Walls, without the advantage of being controuled by a view of the house. Its size invites a croud of which the intervening piers prevent the View.

II. I might add objections as to the safe practicability of such a plan, as to its appearance and as to the difficulty of warming the house, but I will not trespass upon your time, by the enumeration of professional objections.

The alterations which may be made in the plan, so as to obviate all these objections and to supply all conveniences, have already been laid before the President of the United States and have received his serious consideration. They are consistent with the preservation of the exterior appearance of the house, and at an expense not greater than that of the plan proposed.

The great feature of this alteration is to raise up the floor of the legislative hall to the level of the present library,[8] and to use the whole lower story, as the situation for Committee rooms and Offices. The speaker and the Clerk of the House would have offices level with the floor of the house. In contemplation of such improvement the Walls of the house have been carried up last Summer, and should the Legislature direct the further prosecution of the work, there can not be a doubt but that the expenditures will be so directed by the President of the United States, as to produce a work, permanent, convenient, and not inconsistent with the dignity of its purpose.

I beg leave to state to You, Sir, on this occasion that during the progress of the Work the House of Representatives may be conveniently accomodated in the Library and the alterations necessary may be made at a small expense. The library may be removed into the Committee room adjoining to the South.

If the system now established for the supplying of materials be not interrupted, and the numerous Workmen now collected be kept together, I have no doubt but that the South wing will be compleatly finished for the permanent accomodation of the House in the Year 1805. But as it may be unadviseable to occupy the building while still damp, the fall of 1806 may be considered as the period at which the house will assemble in their new Hall.

I am with true respect Your faithful hble. Servt.

B. Henry Latrobe.
Surveyor of the Public buildings of the Un. States at Washington. 447

PS. In my report to the President of the United St. I have mentioned that 30.000$ would be sufficient to finish the Work in *Freestone only* of the South Wing. This sum will not be expended on the Freestone work during the present Year. It is my opinion, from the best estimate which I can make in the present state of the business that two annual Appropriations of 50.000 each will compleatly finish the South Wing before the end of 1805.[9]

B. H. Latrobe

ALS: Records of the U.S. House of Representatives, RG 233, National Archives (172/B1). Printed in *Report of the Committee to Whom was Referred on the 22d. ultimo, the Message from the President of the United States, Communicating a Report of the Surveyor of the Public Buildings at the City of Washington* ([Washington, D.C.], 1804), pp. 7–14 (172/D6).

1. "An act for establishing the temporary and permanent seat of the Government of the United States" was approved on 16 July 1790. BHL quoted from sections two and three of the act: "That the President . . . be authorized to appoint . . . three commissioners, who, or any two of whom, shall . . . according to such plans as the President shall approve, . . . prior to the first Monday in December, in the year one thousand eight hundred, provide suitable buildings for the accommodation of Congress, and of the President, and for the public offices of the Government of the United States." *Annals of Congress*, 1st Cong., 2d sess., p. 2234.

2. See Jefferson to BHL, 6 Mar. 1803 (Public), n. 2, above.

3. Washington had expressed his approval of a Thornton design he had seen in January 1793, and official sanction was given these plans in March. This set of drawings cannot be definitively identified with any of the existing drawings attributed to Thornton, though, and BHL, in his letter of the same date to Jefferson (above), described them as having "disappeared." They were presumably withdrawn by Thornton, replaced by drawings of his revised design, made in 1795 et seq. The design Washington approved is thought to have resembled Thornton's revised design much more than it had Thornton's initial two designs, which dated from 1792. Fiske Kimball and Wells Bennett, "William Thornton and the Design of the United States Capitol," *Art Studies* 1 (1923):89–90.

4. Hallet's post-competition drawings are in the Maryland Historical Society and the Prints and Photographs Division, Library of Congress. See Wells Bennett, "Stephen Hallet and His Designs for the National Capitol, 1791–94," *Journal of the American Institute of Architects* 4 (1916):411–16.

5. President Washington himself had been of this opinion in 1795, when he wrote, "the present plan is no bodies but a compound of every bodies." Washington to the Commissioners of the District of Columbia, 9 Nov. 1795, in John C. Fitzpatrick, ed., *The Writings of George Washington from the Original Manuscript Sources, 1745–1799*, 39 vols. (Washington, D.C., 1931–44), 34:359.

6. Thornton's ground plan with the inscription in BHL's hand, "Given to me by Geo. Blagden as the only existing drawing of the Capitol May 4th. 1803. B. H. Latrobe," is in Prints and Photographs Division, Library of Congress (fig. 9).

7. The cornerstone had been laid in September 1793 with construction of the foundation then already underway for some months while the design continued to evolve. The

plans by Thornton and Hallet known to BHL had failed to keep pace with this evolution. Kimball and Bennett, "Thornton," p. 88; Glenn Brown, *History of the United States Capitol*, 2 vols. (Washington, D.C., 1900–02), 1:14.

8. Since January 1802 the Library of Congress had been located in the galleried chamber on the west side of the north wing, initially used by the House of Representatives. This was on the principal floor, raised above smaller, ground story rooms that were at the same level as the original Senate Chamber. William Dawson Johnston, *History of the Library of Congress, Volume I 1800–1864* (Washington, D.C., 1904), pp. 33–34. For its later locations, see BHL to Michael Leib, 4 Feb. 1811, n. 2, in BHL, *Correspondence*, 3.

9. After receiving and studying BHL's report, Thompson's committee reported on 6 March recommending a $50,000 appropriation for the public buildings, and on 16 March the House passed the $50,000 appropriation bill. *Annals of Congress*, 8th Cong., 1st sess., pp. 1093, 1195. For opposition to the bill in the Senate, see BHL to Lenthall, 28 Mar. 1804, and BHL to Jefferson, 29 Mar. 1804, both below.

TO THOMAS JEFFERSON

Washington Feby. 29th 1804.

Sir

The situation of Mr. Lenthall as Clerk of the Works at the Capitol and Presidents house, combines, the duties formerly performed by seperate persons. For instance, Mr. Williams was employed to collect materials at 800 Dollars per Annum, Mr. Blagden measured and superintended the Stone work at 3$.66 Cents per day; the Carpenters 2$.33 cts., the Sculptor or Carver at 3$, each kept their day account. Mr. Lenthall now performs all these duties. Mr. Blagden works by contract, and Mr. Lenthall directs and measures his Work. He cannot therefore on the principle of precedent, be placed on the footing of any person forme[r]ly employed.

The advantage of employing *one* person to controul the supply and working up of materials is so evident that the regular system established in Europe, is to employ a Clerk of the Works under the Architect or Surveyor, exactly for the performance of the duties, undertaken by Mr. Lenthall. I have successfully followed the same system in America, thereby saving to the Public, the high wages of many Agents, and avoiding their Counteraction of each other. The uncommon merit of Mr. Lenthall appears to me to entitle him at least to the wages formerly enjoyed by Mr. Blagden, while attending only to the stonework. I beg however to   449 submit the case to your decision. His accounts have not been settled, owing to the doubt respecting the salary he merits.[1]

I am very respectfully

B. Henry Latrobe
Surveyor of the Public buildings.

LS: Jefferson Papers (172/E13). Endorsed as received 2 March. Letter is in Lenthall's hand; a draft, in BHL's hand, is in LB (29/G12).

1. Over a year later Jefferson responded to BHL's request and approved of paying Lenthall first $3.66, then $4.00 a day, retroactively. Jefferson to BHL, 10 Mar., 3 Apr. 1805, both in Jefferson Papers (178/A1, 178/C4).

TO JOHN LENTHALL

Newcastle, March 8th. 1804

Dear Lenthall

After a horrible journey, I got hither, on Monday last. Pray how is Mrs. Lenthall, for that *concern* is uppermost with me, as I suppose it must be with every husband and father who has humanity and friendship, about him. In the next place have you found or caught Nobby. In the third will you ask Mr. Munroe to give you a copy of the Debit side of my account, that I may be certain of the correctness of my own entries. On receiving it I shall immediately forward to him my account with all its Vouchers which I have now got.

What hopes of an appropriation? I am laboring at the plan, retaining the Elliptical Colonnade. My conscience urges me exceedingly to throw the trumpery, along with my appointment into the fire. When once erected, the absurdity can never be recalled and a public explanation can only amount, to this that *one* president was blockhead enough to *adopt* a plan, which *another* was fool enough to *retain*, when he might have altered it.[1] The only discovery which I have made, in *elaborating* the thing, for you must know I have already got it into compleat order, is, that the Doctor[2] was born under a musical planet, for all his rooms fall naturally into the shape of fiddles, tamborines, and Mandolines, one or two into that of a Harp.[3]

Now for the business on which I took up the pen at first. Please to send me, by return of Post, the distance of the Elliptical wall externally from the face of the base block at each of its diameters, with the thickness of the Wall, and also the space between the two Wings, at the Base

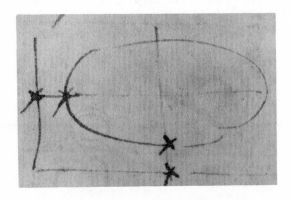

block, so as to find the extent of the Center building. Believe me very affecty. Yrs.

B. Henry Latrobe.

Mrs. L. desires to be remembered to You and Mrs. Lenthall.

ALS: BHL Papers, Library of Congress (172/F4). Addressed to Lenthall in Washington. Endorsed as received 11 March and answered 12 March.

1. Washington and Jefferson.
2. Thornton.
3. BHL's tastes showed a distinct predilection for more elemental geometric shapes, a standard characteristic of the more rationalistic phase of Neoclassicism, as compared with the Thornton/Hallet taste evident in the existing plans of the Capitol. Elliptical shapes, with their seeming distortion from the primitive purity of circles, were especially suspect to this later eye, but with Jefferson BHL had added a practical objection to his stylistic one—namely the more demanding construction of the continually varying detail following the ellipse. See BHL to Jefferson, [4 Apr. 1803], enclosure, above.

TO HENRY VOIGHT

Newcastle, March 10th. 1804

Dear Sir,

Will you have the goodness to let the bearer have my Theodolite. I should be exceedingly obliged to you if it has been convenient to you to put it in order, already, or to finish it before my Clerk leaves town. At the same time I send you another invalid, the last of my regiment but one, and that a very bad recruit, so that if I do not get the Theodolite I shall be utterly at a loss how to go on with the Campaign.

I hope you found the book useful to you.[1] You may keep it as long as you please, and return it at any time by the Newcastle packet.

Believe me very truly

B. Henry Latrobe

Polygraph Copy: LB (30/B2). Addressed to Voight in Philadelphia.

1. See BHL to Voight, 24 Dec. 1803, n. 2, above.

TO JOHN LENTHALL

Newcastle, March 10th. 1804

My dear Friend

I have by some accident lost or mislaid the memorandum given to me by Weirick respecting the things wanted for the roof.[1] As it is, I know, of importance that he should get them by the first opportunity, will you be so good as to desire him to enclose a Copy of the list to Mr. Mifflin (directing to Mr. *Samuel* Mifflin, Market street) to whom I have already written on the subject, and who will attend to their being immediately forwarded.[2] I wish also, that he would count the bays of the Rafters, (leaving out, one half of the Gussets), and multiplying the numbers of bays, by the length of the Rafters, he will thus obtain the *length* of Iron wanted making a proper allowance for laps. This will be a better direction as to the quantity of Iron wanted than the number of squares. He should at the same time send an account of the quantity, or rather *length*, in hand at Washington. The Iron for the Gutters will also soon require to be ordered. The operation of laying the new Gutters will require nice consideration. I shall, one of these days devote a letter expressly to the subject.

I have been laboring hard at the plans for the Season, and have at least so far pleased myself as to be ready to lay the drawings when finished before the President. Instead of the Ellipsis I am going to propose two semi-circles abutting against a Parallelogram in the Center. Of this I can make a very good thing of the sort: As Old Mr. Izzard, who hated the New Englanders said of Mr. Coit from Connecticut. Coit had made a speech in Congress in favor of a motion of Izzard's. Don't you think that's a good sort of Man, asked Mr. Harper. N-N-Neneno! said Izzard who stuttered violently, He-he-he's a googood man of a G-G-God-damn'd bad sort. This I say of my plans, no more.[3]

I might as well be in the territory of the West Louisiana as to my knowledge of what is going forward in respect to the appropriation. If that falls through I shall have to bear all the blame of it. Do give me a mess of news in your next as to the Canal,[4] Dr. Thornton, Mrs. Lenthall, Nobby, and the appropriation.

It would be extremely convenient if Mr. Munroe could contrive that my letters to you should go post free. Pray talk to him on the subject. I think I could direct them to him in such a Way as to distinguish all those that are for you, and as they are all on public business, the public should pay. I am very willing to pay for your letters myself, but not so for my own, not being quite so sure of their value.[5] Believe me very affecty. Yours

B. Henry Latrobe

ALS: BHL Papers, Library of Congress (172/F9). Addressed to Lenthall in Washington. Endorsed as received 15 March and answered 17 March.

1. Nicholas Weirick, Philadelphia carpenter, was hired to do the sheet iron roofing of the public buildings in Washington. Shortly before BHL sent him to the capital, Weirick, "a Dutchman . . . had the misfortune to fall bolt upright from the top of our new boiler; by which accident he has been so shaken, as to Swell to an enormous size, and turn almost black." Weirick recovered quickly, however, and in early 1804 went on to Washington where he could "work all Winter when the Weather is moderate." BHL to Lenthall, 13 Dec. 1803, BHL Papers, Library of Congress (170/G1); BHL to Samuel Mifflin, 8 Jan., 6 Feb. 1804, and BHL to James Smallman, 6 Feb. 1804, all in LB (29/A11, 29/D3, 29/D7).
2. BHL to Mifflin, 10 Mar. 1804, LB (30/B4).
3. BHL may have heard this anecdote from his friend Robert Goodloe Harper. The incident probably took place between 9 February and 3 March 1795, the only time when Representative Harper of South Carolina, Representative Joshua Coit (1758–98), Connecticut Federalist, and Senator Ralph Izard (1742–1804), South Carolina Federalist, were serving together in Congress.
4. BHL's Washington Canal plans and report, which he had completed in February 1804 while in the capital city, were finally made available for inspection by prospective investors in mid-June 1804. Efforts to capitalize the canal scheme that year, however, failed. See BHL to Law and Brent, 13 Dec. 1803, n. 3, above. *National Intelligencer*, 15 June 1804.
5. Munroe was the local postmaster in Washington as well as superintendent of the city.

TO ERICK BOLLMANN

Newcastle March 16th. 1804

Dear Sir

I have not for many months past received a letter from you, which does not contain some reproach or complaint. I ought not however to quarrell with your last, which I have just received (d. March 2 but without postmark) for your reproaches have dwindled from moral lectures, to reproofs on account of my monopleuretic[1] letters. This surely is unjust for your last 4 letters do not amount to more than one side and a half. In my last however I told you *why* I had not come to Philadelphia, when I intended: I am now very uncertain as to the time of my going thither, but think it will be within 10 days. It depends on the meeting of the Canal committee, and that hangs upon the health of Mr. Gilpin.[2] I will write to you as soon as I can determine. I have been here a week from Washington. Mr. Law is returned a good sort of wild Man, on bad terms with his wife—a separation talked of &c. &c.[3] How are your Children? I shall conclude on this side *once* more. My next shall be longer. Yours very truly

B. H. Latrobe.

Polygraph Copy: LB (30/C9).

   1. One-sided.

   2. The Committee of Survey finally met in Philadelphia on 7 April 1804. They requested BHL to complete all the surveys for the feeders and various canal routes that remained unfinished and "to furnish a compleat Report of his whole operations in the service of the Company." BHL reported that the survey of the feeder was "so far compleated" that work on it could begin immediately. Joshua Gilpin and BHL were then "authorized to enter into contracts with one or more gangs or bodies of diggers to Commence digging immediately" upon the feeder. C & D Survey Committee Minutes.

   3. In the spring and summer of 1803, Thomas Law had gone to England, where he unsuccessfully attempted to raise capital for the Washington Canal Company. He and his wife, Eliza Parke Custis (Martha Washington's granddaughter), were divorced in 1810. *Federal Gazette* (Baltimore), 28 Apr. 1803; *National Intelligencer*, 5 Sept. 1803; Hamlin, *Latrobe*, pp. 309–10.

TO JOHN VAUGHAN

Newcastle, March 18th. 1804.

My dear Sir,

I recd. Yours of the 14th. on the 16th., and regret exceedingly that Mr. Wm. Smiths letter did not reach me sooner.[1] I returned from Washington, hither, on the 5th. of March. Mr. Smith's letter is dated the 9th. of February, and from the time which is already elapsed, and must still elapse before my answer can reach him, I fear all my exertions to be of service to the Company may come too late. However I will tell you what I have done.

I have immediately written to Mr. Adam Traquair to hunt up my *eleve*, Mr. Fr. Graff; and to order him hither immediately.[2] I shall also write to Graff himself, though I fear he may not be in town at this moment.[3] I shall then know from himself whether he be willing to undertake the work, and on the terms proposed. If he is, the Company will obtain the assistance of *the best Superintendant, I ever knew,* of a man upon whose integrity and knowledge I had calculated largely in the superintendance of the Chesapeake and Delaware Canal, and whom I would not spare did I not conceive his own interests likely to be promoted by having a separate command.

As you are at head quarters, I must now beg you to write immediately to Mr. Smith, and beg him to decide, by return of post, whether *Mr. Graff,* if his services can be obtained, shall immediately proceed for Charleston, *and bring with him two or three practical and Laboring blowers of rock,* men who will be infinitely useful, and cannot probably be got on the shores of the Catawba. I shall keep Graff here untill I hear again from Mr. Smith, unless I find him willing to run all risks.

You may easily conceive how much I am flattered by the good opinion which Mr. Curwen entertains of my Son Henry. I have heard much of the kindness of the family to the boy, from himself, and took the liberty some time ago to thank Mr. Curwen by letter, as I ought to thank you also for the introduction to all the favors he has received.[4]

My idea of removing Henry from Mr. Drakes school does not arise from the slightest objection to the school itself. On the contrary I feel myself highly obliged by the attention which Mr. Drake has paid to the improvement in learning, the manners, and the morals of my Son, and of which no stronger evidence can exist, than the knowledge he has actually acquired, and the behavior he observes whenever he returns

455

home. But as it will be necessary for him to apply diligently, and at an early age to some profession by which he may procure a livelihood, and he is already well founded in those rudiments of literature which are taught at Mr. Drakes, it is my wish to send him to Mr. Dubourg's Academy at Baltimore where he will enter upon Mathematics, Natural history and philosophy, improve in classical knowledge, and learn French, Spanish, and German.[5]

It may appear ridiculous to push forward a boy of 11 Years old at this rate, but the course of my own education, was at least as rapid; and yet, with talents very inferior to those of my son, a disposition much less *sober* and persevering, and opportunities for folly and dissipation which he knows nothing of, my understanding of Geometry and Trigonometry was as perfect at 12 Years old as it is at this moment. This is the only and the true reason of Henry's removal, which by the bye will not be immediate. I have written to Mr. Drake to this effect and though he has not answered my letter, he cannot but be satisfied of my respect and esteem.[6] Yours very affecty.

B. H. Latrobe.

P.S. Tell Mr. Smith that Aveilhe has invented the perpetual motion. That will satisfy him as to the value of any of his discoveries.[7]

I shall write myself as soon as I have Graffs answer.

Polygraph Copy: LB (30/C11). Addressed to Vaughan in Philadelphia.

1. William Loughton Smith had written on behalf of the Catawba and Wateree Company of South Carolina to ask BHL to suggest an engineer to direct the navigational improvement of the river. For BHL's reply, see BHL to Smith, 21 Mar. 1804, below.
    2. BHL to Traquair, 18 Mar. 1804, LB (30/C10).
    Frederick Graff (1775–1847), engineer, was the son of Jacob Graff, a bricklayer. Frederick was apprenticed as a carpenter before he became BHL's draftsman and assistant on the Philadelphia Waterworks and the Bank of Pennsylvania. Henry Simpson, *The Lives of Eminent Philadelphians Now Deceased* (Philadelphia, 1859), pp. 431–36.
    3. BHL to Graff, 18 Mar. 1804, LB (30/C14).
    4. BHL to Mr. Kirwan, 16 Nov. 1803, LB (27/E4).
    5. See BHL to Du Bourg, 25 Mar. 1804, below.
    6. BHL to Drake, 4 Feb. 1804, above.
    7. Smith wanted to learn the value for the Catawba Company of a "machine for boring holes in rocks under water" that John Baptiste Aveilhé had patented on 24 August 1803. Thomas Green Fessenden, *The Register of Arts, or a Compendious View of Some of the Most Useful Modern Discoveries and Inventions* (Philadelphia, 1808), p. 394.
    BHL was not alone in believing that Aveilhé purported to have invented a perpetual motion machine. A contemporary list of patents noted that on 14 October 1802 Aveilhé patented a "machine for raising water [a perpetual motion!!!]." Ibid., p. 392.

TO JOHN VAUGHAN

Newcastle, March 21st. 1804

My dear Sir,

Graff, and yours of this morning are both before me. He accepts of the engagement, if still in time, but as there must elapse at least 21 or 23 days before we can have an answer, he will, if the Catawba Company be already provided, lose the chance of an engagement with the Chesapeake & Delaware Canal Company, as I must immediately look out for another in his room, and as Mr. Jo. Strickland, the father of my William, is the Man in my view the disappointment to him will be serious.[1] What shall we do. Graff must I believe run the risk of staying. He will deliver you this, and you can have some conversation with him, and if necessary, you will write to Mr. Smith again on the subject. He will bring a letter to Mr. Smith, which I beg you to forward.[2]

As to Aveilhé, I know nothing of his borer. Though there is no difficulty in boring and blasting rocks under Water, *and without a Coffre Dam in most Cases,* yet it certainly is right, as you observe, *to see* before judgement is pronounced upon the discovery even of a *perpetual motion man.* Now I really know nothing of the borer of Aveilhé, but enclose a letter to him on the subject which you may read, seal and send, if you approve it.[3] When I have his answer, I will give you my *serious* opinion.

What can I do for you about this Cement business. I cannot get Higgins anywhere, not in the Library at Washington where I enquired.[4] On the *General subject* I can give you my own ideas, and experience, if that is worth you having.

Henry was at Mr. Hazlehursts on Sunday. I thank you for your enquiries after him.

Believe me very truly Yours

B. Henry Latrobe

Polygraph Copy: LB (30/D10). Addressed to Vaughan in Philadelphia.

1. On 21 March 1804 BHL wrote John Strickland offering him the postion of C & D clerk of the works (LB; 30/D9). But Strickland's position was to be temporary, for as early as 7 April 1804 the C & D survey committee discussed the possibility of employing Robert Brooke as clerk of the works. In May the committee agreed to Brooke's terms and a contract was signed. After Brooke's arrival at the project, Strickland's role was limited to that of master carpenter. C & D Survey Committee Minutes, 7 Apr., 23 Apr., 10 May 1804; BHL, *Engineering Drawings,* p. 14.

2. See following document.

3. BHL to Aveilhé, 21 Mar. 1804, LB (30/D12).
4. Bryan Higgins, *Experiments and Observations Made with the View of Improving the Art of Composing and Applying Calcareous Cements and of Preparing Quick-Lime* (London, 1780).

TO WILLIAM LOUGHTON SMITH

Newcastle, March 21st. 1804

Dear Sir

Your favor of the 9th. of Feby. I did not receive till the 16th. of the present Month. As it came to me by the hands of Mr. Vaughan, I instantly wrote to him all I could at that moment say on the subject of an Engineer for the Catawba Company.[1] By a letter just now received from him I find that he sent to you a Copy of what I wrote. I need only therefore add, that Mr. Graff, the Gentleman whom I had in view is now with me, and accepts of the terms offered in your letter, and should my letter come to your hands, time enough, he will, on your further determination to employ him, immediately set out for Charleston, and bring with him two or three of my most steady hands, whose experience in the business of blasting rocks I well know, from the services they have rendered me, in that sort of Work.

Of Mr. Graff's ability to execute the Work you will require of him, (independently of my own confidence in him) it may be well to give you an idea, by recounting his professional history.

Mr. Graff came into my office while I was engaged in supplyg. the City of Philadelphia with water. He saw, and partly superintended the excavation of the Schuylkill bason and tunnel. The tunnel is a work of 400 feet in length driven through the solid granite, forming a passage into the Engine Well 8 feet high and 4 f. 6 i. wide, for the admission of the Water from the river. The Canal leading to the Tunnel is 40 feet wide 12 to 16 feet deep, and about 200 feet long also blasted out of the solid Rock. Of all the tools, utensils, and Machinery used in this Work, and of the best method of working he thus acquired a perfect knowledge. Finding his talents and integrity deserving of full confidence, I appointed him Superintendant of the Pennsylvanian bank at the most difficult period of that Work, and when my absence was often of considerable duration, and I freely acknowledge that the perfect execution of that building is considerably indebted to his indefatigable attention. He

458

then went to Norfolk to superintend the erection of the United States bank, which he begun and finished *alone,* and to the perfect satisfaction of all concerned.[2] Since then I have looked to him for the resident superintendance of the Chesapeake and Delaware Canal. I consider it as very unfortunate for this work that an independent situation, as *Principal* which your Work offers him, is likely to deprive me of his Services. But his merit, and his integrity ought to be where it can be of most service, and on that account, I will part with him.

You will find him modest, and diffident of his own abilities. He was brought up to the *actual execution* of business, when, in his 18th. Year, he met with an accident which lamed him. I then first heard of him, and placed him in my office without expecting much from him. I have however now the pleasure of considering him as the first of my *élevés,* and as my friend. Should he feel himself ever at a loss, all that my experience can supply, is fully at his service.[3]

I have never seen Aveilhé's boring machine. To bore and blast under water is not a very difficult operation, or very expensive. But it no doubt may admit of improvement, and I have written to him for an account of his invention, upon which I will give you, then, my opinion. I have however but little expectation of anything valuable from a man who pretends to have discovered the perpetual motion, and whose machine erected for this purpose, is the most convincing proof that could be adduced of his total ignorance of the first principles of mechanism. In sending the Model of his Machine to the Philosophical society, he very wisely requested, *that* no experiment of its operation should be made.[4]

Mr. Wheeler will, I doubt not, with pleasure transmit to You a faithful account of the state of the Dismall swamp Canal. I beg to assure you, that it will be highly acceptable to me to be honored with your commands whenever you conceive that I can render you the smallest service. I am Dear Sir with true esteem Yours faithfully

B. Henry Latrobe

Polygraph Copy: LB (30/D14). Addressed to Smith in Charleston, S.C.

1. BHL to Vaughan, 18 Mar. 1804, above.

2. A set of Graff's drawings of the Norfolk branch of the Bank of the United States is in the Winterthur Museum, Wilmington, Del.

3. BHL sent Graff his "final appointment" on 25 April 1804, and Graff arrived in Charleston in May. It was not long, however, before the appointment provided embarrassment to BHL and disappointment to Graff. About a year after his arrival Graff quit his position with the Catawba Company and moved back to Philadelphia. Catawba Company

President John F. Grimke blamed Graff's departure on the young engineer's "being hypochondriacally inclined." When Graff returned north he became manager of the Waterworks; eventually he was placed in charge of building its replacement, the Fairmount Waterworks. BHL to Graff, 25 Apr. 1804, LB (31/D13); *Mirror of the Times, & General Advertiser* (Wilmington, Del.), 13 June 1804; Hamlin, *Latrobe*, p. 175; *ASP. Miscellaneous*, 1:791.

4. The minutes of the American Philosophical Society do not record the receipt of any perpetual motion machine. For BHL's later meeting with Aveilhé, see BHL to Vaughan, 1 May 1804, below.

TO ROBERT PATTERSON

Newcastle, March 25th 1804

Dear Sir,

I will take the liberty to trouble you with a few enquiries on the subject of Oliver Evans's Steam Engine because I know that, with your liberal Spirit to promote the growth of Science wherever it may be planted, you have considerably contributed to methodize the attempts of Mr. Evans to improve the Steam engine: and although the conduct of Mr. Evans towards me has been injurious to me to the most serious extent, and has placed an insuperable bar between us; I certainly should promote, to the utmost, any *real* improvement of which he may be the inventor, and as far as my recommendation and example goes, be the means of forwarding his individual interests.

When I left Philadelphia, Mr. Evans pretended to no more than to have brought Hornblower's ideas and calculations on the subject of Steam into practical use:[1] he had namely erected a wooden boiler of such dimensions, and strength, as to resist a force of Steam much greater than that raised by Bolton and Watt, and that to render the weight of the atmosphere of less comparative importance than in *their* Engines.

If Mr. Evans means, by what he calls in his advertisement his *New principle,* the practice of working without condensation, I believe I should scarcely admit the principle to be New, because in the course of Bolton and Watt's experiments, they have tried all that appeared likely to be advantageous in the results of Hornblowers experiments; and the dispute and Lawsuit which took place between Hornblower and them brought the matter fully before the public.[2]

460   If however in the course of Mr. Evans's experiments, a different

principle has been discovered, either in the application of the steam to the Machinery, or the construction of the boiler, I will not only candidly examine the same but if I find Mr. Evans's pretensions to be well founded, I will *adopt his principle,* and pay him for it; and thus heap firy coals upon the head of my adversary. Since Mr. Evans's advertisement has appeared, I am overrun with letters of enquiry on this subject, to which I have answered generally, *Ignoramus.*[3] You will very much oblige me by taking the trouble to give me some concise account of this business, when your leisure will admit. *I* might indeed, for the customary fee, obtain a Copy of the Patent, but I prefer your account of the matter to the *author's* description.

I hope to be in Philadelphia soon but my motions are so uncertain, that I dare not with confidence calculate on it. Please to give my respects to Mrs. Patterson, and the rest of your very amiable family[4] and believe me very affectionately Yours

B. Henry Latrobe

Polygraph Copy: LB (30/E9). Addressed to Patterson in Philadelphia.

1. Jonathan Carter Hornblower (1753–1815) was an English engineer who in 1781 patented a two-cylinder steam engine which derived its power from the expansive force of steam.

2. Evans's notice appeared in the Philadelphia *Aurora* on 5 March 1804. Hornblower's engine, in which steam was condensed successively in two cylinders, was much like Boulton and Watt's patented separate condenser engine. Boulton and Watt continually threatened legal action for infringement of their patent, but the issue never came to trial. In 1792 Hornblower applied to Parliament for an extension of his patent but was challenged successfully by Boulton and Watt. L. T. C. Rolt, *James Watt* (London, 1962), pp. 122–24; Eric Robinson and A. E. Musson, eds., *James Watt and the Steam Revolution* (London, 1969), pp. 155–61, 163–72.

3. I.e., we do not know.

4. Patterson married Amy Hunter Ewing of Greenwich, N.J., in 1774. They had eight children.

TO WILLIAM DU BOURG

Newcastle, Delaware March 25th. 1804.

Reverend Sir[1]

Sometime ago I requested a friend of mine in Baltimore to inquire of you whether my Son, who is now eleven Years old, could be received 461 at your Seminary.[2] Not having received any answer to my application, I take the liberty to apply to yourself, and to entreat the favor of you to inform me whether after your next Vacation you can receive him, and in the meantime consider him as a Candidate for the first Vacancy. I have Your proposals before me, with all the terms of which I shall be ready to comply. Perhaps it may be some recommendation to You of my son, if I mention, that independently of an excellent disposition, good habits, and good talents which he possesses, he is descended, from French Ancestors of respectability, my older Brother being at present the representative of the House of Boneval, and I believe the eldest of that family.[3] I do not mention this as being of the smallest importance [in] point of merit, but merely as pointing out a claim to your attention, which m[ay] perhaps have some little weight with the Principal of a French Institution.

I am with the truest respect Your obedt. hble. Servt.

B. Henry Latrobe B.
Surveyor of the Public Works
of the United States

Polygraph Copy: LB (30/E13). Addressed to Du Bourg in Baltimore.

1. The Rev. Louis William Valentine Du Bourg (1766–1833), a native of Santo Domingo, had studied and taught with the Sulpicians in Paris. He arrived in Baltimore in 1794 and joined the Sulpician order the following year. Du Bourg served as president of Georgetown College from 1796 to 1798 and was head of St. Mary's Academy (later College) in Baltimore from 1799 to 1812, when he was appointed administrator apostolic of New Orleans. In 1815 he became bishop of Louisiana and the Floridas. Du Bourg returned to France in 1826, became bishop of Montauban, and was archbishop of Besançon when he died.

2. St. Mary's Seminary was founded in Baltimore in 1791 by French Sulpicians. In 1799 Du Bourg established St. Mary's Academy (later College) in association with the seminary, and in 1803 the college was opened to all American students regardless of creed. All three of BHL's sons attended the college: Henry sporadically from June 1804 to 1808, when he received an A.B.; John H. B. in 1818 before he left to attend West Point; and Benjamin, Jr., from September 1821 to July 1823, when he graduated with an A.B. *Memorial Volume of the Centenary of St. Mary's Seminary of St. Sulpice, Baltimore, Md.* (Baltimore, 1891), pp. 82, 97, 104; "Catalogue des Ecoliers de l'Academie" (in "Day Book, 1799–1805"), and "Students of St. Mary's College, from June the 4th 1818," Sulpician Archives, Baltimore.

3. BHL here perpetuates an erroneous family belief that the Latrobes descended from Count Henri Bonneval, a French nobleman. It was thought that Bonneval had a son named Jean Henri Bonneval de la Trobe, who fled first to Holland and then to Ireland following the revocation of the Edict of Nantes (1685). Christian Ignatius Latrobe later recalled that BHL, who "had more family-vanity, than I, . . . took some pains to find the

origin of our race, in the Registering Offices in France." BHL's correspondent in France informed him that the Bonneval family "resided on their own Estates in Languedoc, a branch of which . . . was called La Trobe, '*which emigrated* into *foreign parts*' and there the genealogical acct. of that branch stops." BHL and other members of his family apparently believed that the Jean Latrobe (b. 1670) who left France after the revocation was the representative of that foreign branch of the Bonneval family. In fact, the Latrobe family originated in the province of Guienne and was not related to the Bonnevals. BHL's belief in the tradition was so strong that he frequently appended the name (with one *n*), or the initial B., to his signature, and several of his children carried the name (Henry Sellon Boneval, John Hazlehurst Boneval, and Juliana Elizabeth Boneval). Christian Ignatius Latrobe to John Frederick Latrobe, 1 Feb. 1820, John Henry de La Trobe Collection, Hamburg, copy in PBHL. See also Genealogy in BHL, *Journals,* 1 :lxv–lxvii.

TO JOHN LENTHALL

Newcastle, March 28th. 1804

My dear Lenthall

I absolutely am incapable of saying anything in answer to your letter of the 25th.[1] Not that I care a straw about the public, and very little about the public buildings, but I care a great deal about *you,* and as you say, the conduct of the Blockheads in the Senate, will certainly ruin all the individuals who were not original proprietors of the Soil of the City. As to our business I give it up for lost at once. We must now contrive to make what money remains cover the Presidents house, and when that is finished, knock off altogether. As to yourself, while I have business worth your doing, or services worth your acceptance I will stick by you. A few days will show what course we must in future pursue. I am sorry I was not in Washington, when this mischief was about.

If Mr. Anderson, means to accomodate congress in the president's House, what does he mean to do with the President. There is absolutely not a house in Washington into which he could go, excepting Mr. Tayloe's.[2] But I suppose the Amendment was only intended to defeat the whole bill.

If however the H. of Repr. should agree to the Amendment, then the President being left to shift for himself we must set our wits to work to Stuff the H. of Repres. into the Room formerly inhabited by the Mammoth Cheese: and I think the preparation for that Maggot breeding Assembly, has been very properly made, by fixing the Cheese for two Years where the Speaker may sit for one.[3]

But the subject is really not worth the Paper.

In the meantime I have compleatly reduced the whole South Wing into System, and have made *all* the Drawings. Tomorrow I shall send off a set of these Drawings to the President which are necessary to explain my ideas. I shall accompany them with a letter in which I shall use the utmost freedom consistent with respect in treating the general subject.[4]

Pray let me know instantly the *ultimate* decision. Believe me very sincerely Yours

B. Henry Latrobe

Our best wishes attend your good Wife who with her children continues I hope in good health &c.

PS. I have written to Mr. Otis about the stoves.[5]

ALS: BHL Papers, Library of Congress (173/A1). Addressed to Lenthall in Washington. Endorsed as received 1 April and answered 2 April.

1. Apparently Lenthall had described the Senate debates over the appropriation bill for the public buildings. On 16 March, the House passed the appropriation bill and it was read for the first time in the Senate. The following day Sen. Robert Wright (1752–1826) of Maryland introduced a bill for the temporary removal of the capital to Baltimore. Wright intended his proposal to act as "a spur to the inhabitants of Washington to effect a more complete accommodation of Congress." A lengthy debate on the removal bill took place on 19 March before the measure was defeated. Among the removal bill's supporters was Sen. Joseph Anderson (1757–1837) of Tennessee who then proposed an amendment to the appropriation bill which required the money to be used for "finishing the President's House in such manner as will accommodate both Houses of Congress; and for the purpose of renting, purchasing, or building a suitable house for the accommodation of the President." The Senate passed the amended bill on 24 March 1804, but the House refused to concur. The Senate refused to rescind its amendment and a stalemate ensued during which Lenthall wrote his letter of 25 March to BHL (not found). *Annals of Congress*, 8th Cong., 1st sess., pp. 278–79, 282–88, 299–301, 1235–36.

2. John Tayloe (1771–1828), a staunch Federalist and one of the wealthiest men in America, was a successful "patron of the turf." He established the racetrack in Washington and was president of the Jockey Club there. BHL prepared a design for a Washington home for Tayloe, but the house was built in 1799–1800 according to a plan attributed to William Thornton. The house, the so-called "Octagon" at 1799 New York Ave., N.W., was near the President's House and served as a temporary residence for the Madisons after the British burned the President's House in 1814. BHL, *Journals*, 2:555; Diane Maddex, *Historic Buildings of Washington, D.C.* (Pittsburgh, 1973), pp. 35–39.

3. The "mammoth cheese," which was over 4 feet in diameter, 15 inches thick, and weighed 1235 pounds, was made by Elder John Leland's Baptist congregation in Cheshire, Mass., in the summer of 1801. The "Cheshire cheese," as it was sometimes called, was presented to Jefferson at the President's House on New Year's Day, 1802. The term mammoth was being popularized around this time by Charles Willson Peale, who was mounting his huge specimen in his Philadelphia museum. Republican newspapers played

up the event under the heading, "The Greatest Cheese in America, For the Greatest Man in America." The cheese was still on display the following New Year's Day, though sixty decaying pounds had been removed. It was apparently removed from the President's House by early 1804, though its ultimate fate is unknown. For a more detailed discussion of the cheese and the less publicized "mammoth veal," see Dumas Malone, *Jefferson the President: The First Term, 1801–1805* (Boston, 1970), pp. 106–08.

4. BHL to Jefferson, 29 Mar. 1804, below.

5. Samuel A. Otis (1740–1814) of Massachusetts, father of Federalist party leader Harrison Gray Otis, was secretary of the U.S. Senate, a position he held from 1789 until his death. BHL wrote Otis concerning the Senate Chamber stoves, the grates of which had been designed for burning coal. Wood, however, had been burned in the stoves during the 1804 session. BHL urged that coal be ordered for the next session, but if wood was to be used, Otis should notify BHL so that he could "have the grates so altered as to burn it with Oeconomy." BHL to Otis, 28 Mar. 1804, RG 46, National Archives (173/A6).

TO ROBERT PATTERSON

Newcastle March 28th. 1804

My dear Sir

I am extremely obliged by your kind and prompt attention to my enquiry concerning Mr. Evans's Steam engine. I am indeed disappointed in not hearing any account from you of an improvement in the principle or construction of the Engine. For I sincerely wish that he or some one else may succeed in producing more power from *less fuel,* so as not to encounter thereby greater inconveniences than the advantage gained. There is however in all that Mr. Evans has done *nothing new.* It would be necessary, in order to give his patent effect, to pass a law regulating the load which those who do not use his patent shall carry on the safety Valve, and restricting them from taking of the bonnets off the condensing Nozzles in working, and also describing the sort of boiler that they shall use. But after all, the Encyclopedia alone, though the account of what has been done in England is imperfect, is sufficient to render the patent nugatory.[1] I hope soon to be in Philadelphia when I shall have the pleasure to show you how we have contrived to save *half of our fuel* at the lower Engine house. We have among other contrivances carried a fire flue through the Steam over the Water in the large boiler.[2]

While in Washington I had frequent interviews with the President who desired me to present to you his respects whenever I should see you. He has an unruly set in Congress to deal with. Believe me very affecty. Yours

B. Henry Latrobe

Polygraph Copy: LB (30/F10). Addressed to Patterson in Philadelphia.

1. The most recent edition of the *Encyclopedia Britannica* available to BHL had an article on steam engines which thoroughly discussed the development and operation of Watt's and Hornblower's engines. *Encyclopedia Britannica*, 3rd ed., 18 vols. (Edinburgh, 1797).

2. In the fall of 1803 Roosevelt installed two new cast iron boilers in the Schuylkill Engine House of the Philadelphia Waterworks. *Report of the Watering Committee to the Select & Common Councils, November 1, 1803* (Philadelphia, 1803); BHL to Samuel Mifflin, 8 Jan. 1804, LB (29/A11).

TO THOMAS JEFFERSON

Newcastle, March 29th, 1804

Dear Sir,

I herewith transmit to you, a separate Roll containing drawings: being the plans and sections of the South Wing of the Capitol according to the ideas which I explained to You when I had the favor of seeing you last.[1] I fear however that these and any other preparations for proceeding with the public Works may be useless, for by a letter from Mr. Lenthall I learn, that the appropriation bill has passed the Senate with an amendment, enjoining the removal of Congress to the President's house. This amendment must either be fatal to the bill when returned to the house of Representatives, or divert the expenditure of the appropriation from the Capitol, to I know not what sort of an arrangement for Congress and for the President—if it should pass into a Law.

However, as it is impossible to think or speak with *legal* respect of the Yeas in such a measure or to suppose that such a law should pass both houses, I will take the liberty to explain the drawings as concisely as I can.

No. I. Fig. 1. is an exact copy of the plan proposed by Dr. Thornton for the arrangement of the Ground floor into Offices and Committee rooms, from the plan given to me by You, which is too large for the Roll, or I should have sent it back.[2]

It is liable to these remarks. 1.) The author had forgotten that the space enclosed by the Elliptical Wall becomes a dark Cellar; the Hall of Legislation being raised into the story above. Therefore 2.) The doors leading into it are useless if not absurd. 3.) None of the rooms can be furnished with fireplaces excepting in the outer wall, and it is now too late to open them there, on account of the solidity of the Work and the size and hardness of the Stones of which it is composed. 4.) No Staircase to the Gallery can be carried up behind the speaker's Chair, between the outer Wall and the Eliptical enclosure, for want of room, and there is besides not heigth enough to admit a revolution and a half so as to land right in the Gallery. I wave other very numerous objections.

Fig: 2. shows that the arrangement of Columns either of 32 or 24 in number, has no possible reference to the piers and windows either considering them according to the lines of true eliptical radiation, which are laid down, or according to perpendiculars from the line of the Wall.

Fig. 3. Shows the distortion which the bases and Capitals of the Columns would undergo in perspective if made truly square, and in regularity of form if made perpendicular upon the lines of eliptical Radiation.

To avoid all the inconveniences arising from the Eliptical form, with the additional expense resulting from them; to obtain the means of carrying up flues for fireplaces wherever required; to add many conveniences to the *domestic* comforts of the legislative Hall; to give decision of character to the place appropriated to the Chair, and yet to preserve *the principle,* and the great feature of the original design,[3] I have ventured to convert the elipsis, into two semicircles abutting upon a parallelogram, in the manner more distinctly seen in No. III than in the plan of the Ground floor, No. II. I beg however to add, that should you deem this change inadmissible, the Elipsis may be restored without altering the Office floor, as represented in No. II.[4]

The great difficulty in arranging the Office floor arises from the immense space inclosed by the Wall supporting the Colonnade above, the exclusion of direct light from this part of the building, and from the narrowness of the irregular area which surrounds it. The manner in which I have endeavored to conquer this difficulty is best explained by the Plan itself. The Clerks office is a very roomy apartment, and will be perfectly well lighted even in its second range, for the windows are opposite to large and high arcades. The Colonnade above rests either on the piers themselves, or on the short and stout arches between them; 467

where they are capable of carrying any conceivable burthen. Behind the second range are Vaults for Records. The only places where there is room for the Gallery stairs is in the angles. Two spiral staircases of 10 feet diameter occupy two of the angles. Through the Center of the building from East to West, a wide Coridor borrows a strong light from the two Common antichambers to the Committee rooms. There are three Committee rooms on each side, well lighted and warmed.

To all these Offices a wide Coridor leads from the North, borrowing a very sufficient light from the Clerks office. On each side of this Coridor are Cellars for fuel, communicating by staircases with the lower Cellars. It was impossible to light this part of the building from the North, and indeed the use to which I propose to convert it, will render the Office floor very convenient, as to its *domestic* arrangement.

The privies are spacious and borrow a very excellent light from the stairs. I propose to construct them on your plan with an air drain. The light is so high that those who ascend the stairs cannot look into the privies.

The total want of light in those parts of the Building, which lie behind the Recesses, and between the Corps de Logis and the wings, has produced all the bad arrangement, and the waste of room which is found in the plan of the North wing. In the South it seems to have been proposed to fill up this space with four Spacious Staircases all leading only to the Gallery, and with a room, which though measuring 50 feet each way, seems to be of no possible utility and which can be lighted, by only one Window in a Corner.[5]

I have taken the liberty to alter the whole of this part of the plan, by placing a handsome Vestibule, the scenery of which will be very striking, on the East front. This Vestibule will be amply lighted by the Skylight of the staircase with which it communicates. The staircase leads up to the Hall of Representatives. On the other side the Stairs communicate with, and light the Vestibule and Corridor of the Offices.

The residence of the Doorkeeper, or of some officer of the house within the building has always appeared to me to be a matter of very great importance: and the practise of Europe points out its advantages. I have therefore appropriated the dark part of the house to this purpose, and by introducing two Courts on each side of the house for the admission of light and air, I think the healthiness of the building is promoted; 468 For I must observe, that no opening what soever is intended to be made in any part of the building on the West side between the two Wings: The space occupied on the East by the two Recesses, being filled up on the West by two blank Walls without Pilasters or break of any kind. The reason assigned for this interruption of the General design is *because* it is necessary that the Columns of the Rotunda should be three feet longer than the Pilasters, in order to get rid of the blocks (Des)[6] on which the Pilasters are raised. This contrivance which throws the Columns out of all proportion to the Entablature, is one of the innumerable bad consequences of a design radically defective in the harmony of its exterior decoration, with its internal distribution.

The Groundstory being 20 feet high, admits of two excellent stories for the Doorkeepers dwelling. The Windows of this house being placed in the Courts, are not seen externally, and require no proportions agreeing with the external openings.

No. III. Is the plan of the hall of Legislation, and of the surrounding apartments. The Gallery is raised 7 feet above the floor of the house. The lobby is on a level with the house. The doorkeeper and Sargt. at Arms have their separate rooms. The Speaker has a handsome Chamber, and the Members a retiring or drawing room. The access from what is called the Grand Vestibule is through a circular Apartment which distributes light to the door of the House.

The arrangement upon which it may be necessary particularly to remark, is the Closet and Gallery behind the Speakers Chair. Independently of the convenience of this apartment and of the Gallery, for the admission of Ladies, and persons of distinction, the arrangement is useful and even necessary, 1.) To strengthen the long south Wall of the house, 2.) to carry up the flues of the fireplaces on each side of the speakers Chair, 3. To give a *Center* to the room marked by distinct features: On the opposite side, the same arrangement carries up two other flues from fireplaces on each side of the door of entrance. Without some such contrivance, it is impossible to place a single fireplace within the Area of the house the Columns not being of a diameter sufficient to carry up a 14 inch flue without being discolored by the Heat and Steam of the fire.

No. IV. Is a Section from East to West exhibiting the length of the room, with the effect of the Alteration from the Eliptical form. The Columns are of the Attic order, a very beautiful specimen of which is to be found in the Clepsydra at Athens, commonly called the Temple of 469

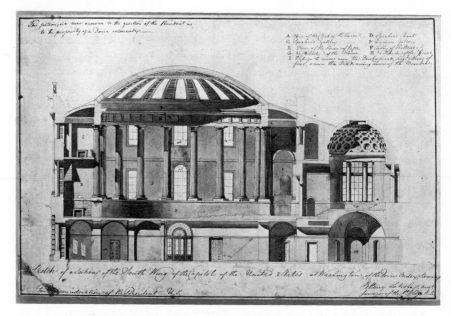

Fig. 15. BHL, Section of the south wing of the U.S. Capitol, [c. 29 March 1804]. Courtesy of the Library of Congress.

the Winds, (see Stuart's *Athens*).[7] The bells of the Capitals may easily be cast in one piece in Iron with the upper row of plain leaves. The lower may be cast separately and fixed with Copper rivets.

No. V. Exhibits a Section of the Room from North to South, of the Doric order.[8] The specimen of the Doric Order which you showed to me was in a work which I do not possess, but it is so similar to Vignola's representation of the Doric of the Theatre of Marcellus, that I shall use his proportions in speaking of it.[9]

1.) Heighth of the Columns. The Pilasters externally are 30 feet high. The architrave of the attic windows is 3 f. 10 i. below the soffit of the external architrave. Therefore the internal Columns, to allow an architrave of the same width to the upper windows, cannot be lower than 26 f. 2 i.

2. *Diameter.* If the Columns be Eight Diameters high, the Diameter must be 3 f. 3 i. But they may be stretched so as to be only 3 feet in diameter. The Module then will be 18 inches and the minutes 1½ inch each.

470   3. *Entablature.* The Entablature is always 2 Diameters or 4 Modules,

and as the Columns have an extraordinary proportion in length, it cannot be compressed. It must be 6 feet high.

The Architrave	1 Mod.	1 f. 6 inches
The Frieze	1 1/2	2. 3
The Cornice	1 1/2	2. 3
	4.0	6. 0
Width of the Triglyph	1 Mod.	1. 6
Of the Metope to be square	1 1/2	2. 3

Therefore the Intercolumnation with *one* Triglyph would be = 2 Triglyphs (3 ft.) 2 Metopes (4 f. 6 i.)—in all 7.6 from Center to Center: and deducting one Diameter leaves 4 f. 6 i. for the Intercolumniation.

Again. The Intercolumniation with 2 Triglyphs = 3 Triglyph. (4 f. 6 i.), 3 Metopes, (6 f. 9 i.)—in all 11 f. 3 inches—deduct one Diameter, leaves 8 feet 3 inches for the Intercolumniation.

Now the distances of the Centers of the Columns either on the Eliptical plan, or the plan now proposed, will fall out to be very nearly 10 feet. To enlarge or diminish the diameter of the Area one foot will always make only 4 inches difference of distance between the Centers of the Columns. No great advantage can therefore be gained for the better arrangement of the Triglyphs and Metopes by such an expedient. And it so happens that the distance of 10 feet from Center to Center is very unfavorable in this respect: For with one Triglyph the Metopes are too long by much, being 2 f. 3 i. by 3 f. 6 i., and with two, much too high being 2 f. 3 i. by 1 f. 10 i. I fear these are fatal objections to the Doric order in this place, as the irregularity is too great to be hidden by any moderate enlargement or diminution of the highth of the frieze.

The roof as designed is, I think as flat as it can be made so as to give sufficient slope to the Sashes. I should make them narrower in a design for execution.

Could all the Windows of the Walls be stopped up, the effect of this building would be indeed beautiful, but as it is, I fear the building is to much *a la lantherne.* The flutter of light which is so exceedingly injurious to the effect of paintings, is equally, if not more so, to the effect of architecture.[10]

Upon the whole, I have to solicit your favorable opinion of the industry which has produced them, if you cannot give it to the merit of these drawings. It is a greater labor to correct errors in Art, than to avoid 471 them by beginning a new design. If the same liberties are allowed *pictoribus atque poetis*[11] they ought to be governed by the same laws in the construction of their works. A poet who after writing down his *sentiment,* were first to work at the metre, and then settle the Grammar of his lines, would not be more unskillful, than the Architect, who having conceived the *purpose* of his building, were to make two separate labors of the arrangement, and construction of his work; and yet the whole design of the Capitol may be compared to the work of a poet, in which you never find sense, metre, and grammar in the same line, though each of them may be found separately. In the mind of an Artist who deserves the name, the operation of the brain which produces a design, is a simultaneous consideration of the *purpose, the connection and the construction* of his work.

I have to beg your indulgence on acct. of the extreme length of this letter. I sincerely hope that Congress may not have rendered the whole discussion of the Subject entirely useless.

Dr. Thornton, after all that has passed, has sent me one of his pamphlets on the subject of Negro emancipation.[12]

With the sincerest and most grateful respect I am Your faithful hble. Servt.

B. Henry Latrobe

ALS: Jefferson Papers (173/A11). Addressed to Jefferson in Washington. Endorsed as received 6 April.

1. Only one of the drawings, No. V, "Sketch of a Section of the South Wing of the Capitol of the United States at Washington, of the Doric Order, Roman style," survives (Prints and Photographs Division, Library of Congress; 272/B5). This drawing (fig. 15) is reproduced and discussed in BHL, *Architectural Drawings.*

2. Thornton's plan for an office story below the principal one, if it was not the surviving Thornton drawing BHL received from Jefferson the next year (Prints and Photographs Division, Library of Congress; 270/B1), must at least have resembled it.

3. I.e., the colonnade.

4. Although only one of the drawings BHL submitted to Jefferson has survived (see n. 1, above), similar drawings prepared for John Lenthall are extant. BHL's plan of the ground floor of the south wing (Prints and Photographs Division, Library of Congress; 270/B5 [see fig. 16]), records the main features of Jefferson's No. II. Similarly, BHL's surviving plan of the principal story of the south wing (ibid.; 270/B6) must have approximated Jefferson's No. III, while his east-west section (ibid.; 272/B4) would be close to Jefferson's No. IV. All three surviving drawings are reproduced and discussed in BHL, *Architectural Drawings.*

5. The more southerly of "Hadfield's . . . two Libraries." See BHL to Jefferson, 28 Feb. 1804, above.

6. Obsolete form of dies.

7. The Tower of the Winds was an octagonal clock tower built in the first century B.C. by Andronicus of Cyrrhus. Clepsydra was the name of a Greek instrument that used water to measure time. The columns of the "Attic" order are in James Stuart and Nicholas Revett, *The Antiquities of Athens*, 3 vols. (London, 1762, 1787, 1794), 1: chap. 3, plates 3, 4, 7. "The capitals belong to a late variant form [of Corinthian], decorated only with a single row of acanthus leaves beneath a row of tall, narrow leaves, and the abacus is square." (See fig. 17, left.) A. W. Lawrence, *Greek Architecture*, 2d ed. (Harmondsworth, England, 1967), p. 237.

8. See fig. 14 and n. 1, above.

9. Giacomo Barozzi da Vignola (1507–73), Italian Renaissance architect, published an authoritative treatise, based on Vitruvius's work, on the five orders of classical architecture, *Regola delli cinque ordini d'architettura* (1562). This work includes a plate which details the Doric order of the Theatre of Marcellus in Rome (first century B.C.).

10. BHL preferred to consolidate areas of light and to contrast them more forcefully against darker parts. See BHL, *Journals*, 2:477, and BHL, *Architectural Drawings*, Introduction: The Picturesque.

11. Trans.: To artists and poets. The source is Horace, *Ars Poetica*, 9–10: *Pictoribus atque poetis | quidlibet audendi semper fuit aequa potestas*, i.e., To artists and poets there has always been equal power to dare anything.

12. Thornton's Quaker antecedents and his humanitarianism led him as early as 1788 to support emancipation through colonization. His pamphlet, *Political Economy: Founded in Justice and Humanity* (Washington, D.C., 1804), advocated the abolition of slavery. In later years he was active in the American Colonization Society. See Gaillard Hunt, "William Thornton and Negro Colonization," American Antiquarian Society, *Proceedings*, new ser. 30 (1920):32–61.

FROM THOMAS JEFFERSON

Washington Mar. 31. 04

Dear Sir

Congress having appropriated another sum of 50.000 D. for the public buildings it becomes necessary to settle the plan of operations for the summer.[1] The following are my ideas on the subject.

Capitol. The walls to be completely finished this summer. For insuring this every effort must be exerted from this day forward, the supplies of stone pushed with all the energy possible, and the cutting and laying to keep pace with the supplies.

The roof to be prepared in the course of the summer, so that it shall be ready to put on the walls on the 4th. of March of the next year.

The columns, entablature, and inside house-carpentry in general to be compleated this summer ready to put up. As I shall be returned by the beginning of May, I suppose that will be in time to decide finally on the order of the columns and entablature.

473

The roof of the North wing to be thoroughly repaired. Is it necessary to aim at something like a symmetry with the roof of the South wing? Or is that practicable at all?[2] Perhaps this may lie a month till my return.

President's house. During my absence they may finish the roof and rectify the gutters so as to put an end to the ruinous leaks. Larger glass may be provided for compleating the glazing of the house. Flooring boards be procured for laying the floors of the great room and the rooms above it. By the time they are in place I shall be returned and can direct the construction of a kiln for seasoning them.

There are some other small matters which may await my return.

No new appropriation being made for the highways, we must turn every expence we can (past as well as future) relating to the buildings on the new fund, and reserve what remains of the old one for the roads to which they are applicable.

I have packed your Polygraph in a box and delivered it to mr. Barnes to be sent by a trusty captain to Philadelphia to the care of mr. Peale. I received Brunell's which indeed was a beautiful thing, but I found at once it was ineffectual and returned it with yours. I am now writing with one I received from mr. Peale, which has some advantages over yours, but is very stiff, and wants the adjusting screw for the pen. Brunell's had that improvement.[3] With my thanks for the use of your machine accept my salutations and assurances of esteem and respect.

Th: Jefferson

Polygraph Copy: Jefferson Papers (173/C1).

1. On 27 March, the last day of the session, the Senate finally voted to rescind its amendment requiring the President's House to be made into a legislative hall and agreed to the House appropriation bill for the public buildings. *Annals of Congress,* 8th Cong., 1st sess., pp. 305–06.

2. In order to minimize the fundamental inequality of the roofs of the wings, Jefferson apparently recommends here either that the House's dome not rise visibly above the parapet (to the nearby viewer), or that the two wings be capped with similar domes. The latter alternative may be visible in an east-west section on a sheet of problematic date, but probably made by BHL within a few years of this letter. Sections through the north wing (Prints and Photographs Division, Library of Congress; 272/B6), reproduced in BHL, *Architectural Drawings.*

BHL's proposed lantern over the House dome, soon to be a major bone of contention with Jefferson, would also prove difficult to match symmetrically, due to the eccentricity, in the plan of the north wing, of what would be the top-lit Senate lobby. The displacement of the northern lantern would hardly be noticeable when viewing both domes together from either front, however.

3. John Barnes (1730–1826), a wealthy Georgetown merchant and philanthropist, was Jefferson's intimate friend and confidential agent. CHS, *Records* 7 (1904):39–42.

Sir Marc Isambard Brunel (1769–1849) was a naval officer, architect, and civil engineer. Born in Normandy, he left France in 1793 and settled briefly in New York. He moved to England in January 1799, and in May of that year he secured a patent for a writing and drawing machine.

Rembrandt Peale procured one of Brunel's machines in London for his father, Charles Willson Peale, who lent the machine to Jefferson in March 1804. *PMHB* 28 (1904):141–43.

FROM THOMAS JEFFERSON

Monticello Apr. 9. 04.

Dear Sir

I received three days ago, your favor of Mar. 29.[1] and have taken the first leisure moment to consider it's contents and the drawings they refer to, and I approve generally of the [*illegible*] distribution of both the floors, with some exceptions [*illegible*][2] below. But we must for the present defer whatever is external [to] the North wall of the South wing that is to say, the Vestibule, the speaker's chamber, the withdrawing room for the members and the corridor and staircase between them; 1st. because all our efforts will be not more than sufficient to finish the South wing in 2 summers and 2dly. for a more absolute reason, that the object of this appropriation is to finish the wing. There having been no idea in the legislature of doing any part of the middle building for the present a temporary staircase may be put up in the place of the Vestibule and upper corridor. I perceive that the Doric order for the Representatives chamber must be given up on account of the difficulty of accommodating it's metop and triglyph to the intercolumnations resulting from the periphery of the room: and as the Senate chamber is Ionic, we must make this Corinthian, and do the best we can for the capitals and modillions. I suppose [*illegible*] will be the best. The following are the exceptions or rather the doubts as to some of the details of the plans.

I have approved the Speaker's chamber and Drawing room for the members. Would it not be better to assign for the [for]mer the Sergeant's room, and for the [latter the Doorkeeper]'s? On the lower floor would it not be better to convert the lobbies of the [galleries to representa]tives rooms, opening from the anti chambers, and let the entry to the staircase 475 be directly thro' the corner window adjacent to it?[3] [*illegible*] I think less than the semicircle would be enough. I return you the Drawing and pray you to push the works with all the force which can be employed in the order proposed in my last letter to you.[4] Accept my friendly salutations and assurances of respect.

Th: Jefferson

Letterpress Copy: Jefferson Papers (173/D1).

    1. Printed above.
    2. About three words are illegible.
    3. BHL apparently chose not to make this alteration in his plan, retaining the rooms as lobbies for the staircases. BHL to John Lenthall, 26 Apr. 1804, BHL Papers, Library of Congress (174/A4), and BHL, "Plan and Section of the Stairs of the Gallery of the Hall of Representatives," 28 Feb. 1805 (Prints and Photographs Division, Library of Congress; 271/A4), reproduced in BHL, *Architectural Drawings*.
    Following this, half a line, or about five or six words, is illegible.
    4. See preceding document.

TO JOHN CARROLL

Newcastle Del. April 10th. 1804

Revd. Sir,[1]

My friend, Mr. Fitzsimmons of Philadelphia has given me an opportunity of shewing my high respect for Your character, and for the Church which is so much indebted to your Pastoral Care, by putting into my hands (by favor of the Count deMun) the plan, or sketch of the Cathedral Church proposed to be erected at Baltimore.[2] Having promised Mr. Fitzsimmons to give to You *my undisguised* opinion on this plan, and being entirely ignorant of its Author, and moreover proposing to myself no possible advantage from any professional assistance which you may please to accept from me, but the honor of having been useful to you, I do not doubt your ready confidence in the honesty, if you should hesitate as to the correctness of my opinions. I will therefore concisely lay them before you.

    1.) If the tower or dome be intended to be constructed of stone or brick, the building is altogether impracticable, for there is neither Room for Arches over the Columns, nor strength in the Columns themselves to support it.

476

2. If of Timber, it must decay within 50 Years: and if it be not burned before it is finished, it will require constant and expensive repair and painting, and never have the least dignity in its appearance.

3. As far as I discover from the extreme imperfection of the plan, there are 54 Columns of the Corinthian Order, and of 30 feet high, in the building. If these Columns be constructed of Acquia Stone (the cheapest sort of Material) they will cost at least 1.000 Dollars each Column, when set, in all 54.000.$ for the Columns alone.

Further, I cannot judge of the expence; for the drawings give no information as to the Material or mode of finishing.

I could easily point out many fatal objections to the design as far as it can be understood, but these are perhaps sufficient, and I should be sorry to hurt the feelings of the Author, should you propose to him to correct all that I think objectionable. I beg also to do justice to the taste which appears in many parts of the design.

Permit me now to propose that you will have the goodness to furnish me with the size, and the *form* of the building you would prefer, and the number of conveniences you wish to be attached to it; as vestry, Committee rooms, treasury, &c. &c. Also the Amount of your present, or probable funds, and a plot of the *place* in which it is to be built, and the avenues leading to it. I will then take the liberty of offering to You a plan, which though it will probably possess less elegance, shall however not be deficient in practicability.

I have the honor to be with the truest respect Your very obedt. hble. Servt.

B. Henry Latrobe

ALS: Archives of the Archdiocese of Baltimore (173/D8). Addressed to Carroll in Baltimore. Endorsed as answered.

1. John Carroll (1735–1815), first Roman Catholic bishop of the United States and archbishop of Baltimore, was a member of the influential Carroll family of Maryland. He studied for the Jesuit priesthood in Europe, returned to America, and served with Benjamin Franklin on an unsuccessful mission to Quebec (1776) to attract the Canadians to the American cause. After the Revolution Pope Pius VI named him prefect-apostolic (1784–85) of the American Church and in 1790 he went to England to be consecrated bishop. Carroll founded Georgetown College (1789) and urged the Sulpician fathers to found St. Mary's College in Baltimore (1803). He began collecting for a cathedral in Baltimore in 1795 and in 1804 he welcomed BHL's offer to design the structure. By the time of his death Carroll had established the Catholic Church as a viable American religious organization, free from excessive foreign influence.

2. Thomas Fitzsimmons (1741–1811), prominent Philadelphia politician and businessman, had emigrated from Ireland in his youth. A Federalist, philanthropist, and

president of the Philadelphia Chamber of Commerce, Fitzsimmons was a leading member of the city's Catholic community.

Count Auguste DeMun and his brothers Lewis and Amadée were royalist French army officers who fled France during the Revolution for Santo Domingo. With Toussaint L'Ouverture's uprising in the 1790s they fled once more, this time to the United States where they became good friends of BHL. For Lewis DeMun, BHL's pupil and assistant, see BHL to Cooch, 5 Aug. 1804, n. 1, below. BHL to Auguste DeMun, 16 Mar. 1804, LB (30/C5).

William Thornton may have made the cathedral design to which BHL refers. Mrs. Thornton's diary for 1800 records that Carroll approached Thornton after the board of trustees of the cathedral congregation had received several designs that they did not like, and that Carroll seemed pleased with the project that Thornton produced. CHS *Records* 10 (1907):121. For a detailed analysis of BHL's later design and construction of the Baltimore Cathedral, considered to be his architectural masterpiece, see The Baltimore Cathedral: Editorial Note, in BHL, *Correspondence*, 2; and BHL, *Architectural Drawings*.

TO WILLIAM DU BOURG

Newcastle Del. April 11th. 1804

Reverend Sir

Having been in Philadelphia for some days past, I have not received your very polite letter till yesterday. I congratulate myself on the prospect you open to me of placing my Son Henry under your care, and regret that by some means, I was kept so long ignorant of the vacancy which was open to him. Letters directed to this place have frequently been lost previously to the late new arrangements of the post office as respects our town.

The School at which my Son is at present in the neighborhood of Philadelphia[1] closes its course of *annual* instruction about the beginning of June. It was my wish to have sent him immediately to Baltimore, but as there is to be an exhibition on this occasion his Master is very anxious to retain Henry till then, and seems unwilling to lose the credit which his partiality to Henry leads him to expect from his progress under his instruction. As soon therefore, as his Year is expired, that is about the 15th or 16th June, I will with much pleasure attend him to Baltimore, and have at the same time the honor of making myself known to you.

Although the Ancestors of my Son were certainly of the Roman Catholic persuasion, his mother was a Protestant of the Church of England. She died before he was two Years old, and he was educated by her Relations till his 9th. Year;[2] and as his present excellent Mother is also a

478

Protestant, he has continued to attend the service of the English episcopal Church. He therefore is wholly ignorant of those peculiarities of Doctrine which distinguish these Churches from each other, and, in fact, at his age, if a sincere respect for Religion, without any *detailed* knowledge of its dogmas be rooted in the mind, it is as much as can perhaps [be] expected from the modes of instruction in religion which at present prevail, and which are not the best calculated to counteract the fashionable examples of infidelity which every where surround even our children. For my own part, the disposition of my self and of Mrs. Latrobe, towards the Catholic religion is best evinced by the *chance* we give to our child to adopt it, by sending him to your School: and I confess freely, that I would rather see him do honor to the benevolence of our Creator, by the cheerfulness of a Catholic, than disgrace the benignity, the mercy, and the justice of God, by the Religious Gloom of some Protestant Sects. On this subject however, I shall have the honor to explain myself when I see you.

I beg to thank you for the agreeable and flattering opinion you are pleased to [. .] of my own character. To be thought well of by such Men as yourself is a happiness to which no virtuous Man can be indifferent.

Accept the Assurances of my most per[fect] esteem.

B. Henry Latrobe B.

Polygraph Copy: LB (31/C2). Addressed to Du Bourg in Baltimore.

1. Richard Drake's school.
2. After the death of his first wife, Lydia (Sellon) Latrobe (c. 1761–1793) on 25 November 1793, several of BHL's relations felt it was too scandalous for him to be living with his children and their young and *"very pretty"* nursery maid. BHL therefore decided that as a temporary solution his daughter Lydia should live with one of her paternal aunts and his son Henry should reside with his maternal aunt Elizabeth (Sellon) White. BHL to Erick Bollmann, 30 Aug. 1805, in BHL, *Correspondence,* 2; Christian Ignatius Latrobe to John Frederick Latrobe, 10 Apr. 1794, John Henry de La Trobe Collection, Hamburg, copy in PBHL.

FROM WILLIAM THORNTON

City of Washington 23rd. April 1804.

Sir

It is with extreme regret that I think myself under the necessity of addressing you, but as I am unwilling to offend any Gentleman without provocation, so am I equally disinclined to receive unnoticed any Insult. Never was my Surprise so much excited as on reading this Day, for the first time, your Letter to the Committee of Congress dated the 28th. of Feby. last.[1] My uniform behaviour to you in the City of Washington I did imagine would have precluded you from offering any thing like insult or even incivility; but I am sorry to be obliged to declare that your Letter to the Committee is, as it respects me, not only ungentlemanly but false.[2]

I am Sir with due respect,

W: Thornton

Copy: William Thornton Papers, Library of Congress (microfiche add.). In Thornton's hand, addressed to BHL in Philadelphia, and endorsed "No. 1."

1. Thornton probably read the published version of BHL's report to Thompson of 28 February 1804 (printed above).

2. The insult must have been felt in BHL's references to "radical errors," "imperfect sketches," "wholly impracticable parts," and "deficiencies" in the evolved designs nominally referred to as Thornton's, though altered by Hallet and Hadfield. BHL's specific objections to the plan, at least some of whose features Thornton, too, had opposed, must also have stung the doctor. BHL to Thompson, 28 Feb. 1804, above.

Thornton would respond in greater detail in a pamphlet published early the next year. Thornton, *To the Members of the House of Representatives* ([Washington, D.C., 1805]). See also Thornton to BHL, 27 June 1804, and BHL to Thornton, 13 July 1804, both below.

TO GEORGE HADFIELD

Newcastle, April 28th. 1804

Dear Sir,

By mistake I carried the enclosed copy of a letter to Newcastle with me. You have conferred an obligation upon me by its communication, which is now the more importance as I am now at open war with Dr. Thornton. He has written to me a letter in which he asserts my report to the Committee on the public buildings to be *false,* in terms which according to the fashion ought to produce a *rencontre* with a brace of pistols.[1] But though he is a capital fellow *at a long shot,* I shall not be near enough to him for a few weeks to come within his compass. In the mean time, if you could go over your drawings, and as nearly as possible ascertain, what is *his,* and what stolen property in the plan now *said* to be the

480

original plan I should be infinitely obliged to you. The contest which must now inevitably ensue, is highly disagreeable, but I shall enter into it without reluctance if it in any respect can lead to the removal of that load of calumny with which you have been treated. My opinion of You can be of little consequence, while you possess such talents, taste and knowledge, as are more easily admired by me, than rivalled: All that is necessary to be done is to expose the truth. Believe me in haste very respectfully Yours

B. H. Latrobe

Polygraph Copy: LB (31/E13). Addressed to Hadfield in Washington.

    1. See preceding document.

TO WILLIAM THORNTON

Newcastle April 28th. 1804.

Sir,

    Open hostility is safer, than insidious friendship. I cannot therefore regret the declaration of War contained in your letter of the 23d. April.[1] For a considerable time I have been convinced that an open rupture with you would be more honorable to me than even that show of good understanding which has prevailed between us; and which was kept up last winter by the respect of my wife for the Ladies of your family:[2] a respect which led me to accept an invitation to a Ball at your house. For the civility of this invitation, and for three or four former invitations to your table, in which the hospitality of your disposition ranked me with every other stranger of respectability who visits the City of Washington, I feel myself indebted and particularly for the transmission of your essay on Negro emancipation; a mark of respect, as unintelligible on any principle of consistency, as it would have been flattering had it been possible for it to be Sincere.

    The terms used by you in your letter, would preclude further remark, did you possess the sort of memory recommended by the proverb to persons of your character.[3]

    It seems however necessary to remind you of your conduct to me the day after you consented to the alterations proposed in the South 481

Wing of the Capitol in April 1803,[4] and of the insults you then offered me; of the coolness which since subsisted between us: of the frequent attempts which I, notwithstand[ing] made to come to an amicable discussion of the subject; and especially of the insulting audience with which you honored me in the public passage at the door of the Patent office;[5] when I called upon you for no other purpose but to know to what alteration in the plan you would consent, and what answer I could give to the Committee, to their enquiry after the *original plan approved by General Washington.*

When I accepted the office which has connected my Character with the successful and honest management of the public Buildings at Washington, I was informed that I had nothing to do with you or your plan. Thinking however that much was due to your feelings, and to your reputation, and perceiving much superior talent, and, as I thought much goodness of heart under the confusion of your conversation, and rubbish of your language, I determined to consult, and advise with you on every thing I did. In this determination I persevered notwithstanding my ill success with you. Those who despise you most in Washington can bear witness to my perseverance in this resolution. My last call upon you is the strongest proof how far I was willing to go. The insulting treatment I received closed all further prospect of amicable arrangement, which I might have expected from your politeness or your understanding.

I now stand on the Ground from which you drove Hallet, and Hatfield to ruin. You may prove victorious against me also; but the contest will not be without spectators. The public shall attend and judge. I shall not court public discussion. It is in my *power* however, more than in my inclination to show you in a more ridiculous light, even, than were I, as is the fashion after such a correspondence, to call you to the field. But you have other accounts of that sort to settle before it can come to my turn. There is a certain advantage which I shall gain by your declared enmity. Your standing in society is such that in proportion to your abuse of me I shall be respected and to your denial of my assertions they will be believed. And you must also be a gainer by the present state of things. Hitherto your detraction has been limited to the circle of those, whom you thought unconnected with me, you can now indulge it without restraint, and wherever you please. I am Sir with due respect &c.

Letterbook Copy: LB (31/F10). In a clerk's hand.

1. Printed above.

2. Thornton's wife, Anna Maria (Brodeau) Thornton (c. 1775–1865), and her mother, Ann Brodeau. CHS, *Records* 18 (1915):151, 171, 181; Elinor Steanus and David N. Yerkes, *William Thornton: A Renaissance Man in the Federal City* (Washington, D.C., 1976), pp. 16, 39.

3. BHL is probably alluding to the aphorism, "A liar should have a good memory," which appears in Quintilian (42–118), *Institutiones Oratoriae,* bk. IV, 2, 91. Other versions of the aphorism can be found in the works of Montaigne, Corneille, and Algernon Sidney.

4. Presumably BHL refers to his astylar semicircular theater plan for the House, proposed in his report of that month. See BHL to Jefferson, 4 Apr. 1803, enclosure, above.

5. Thornton was appointed superintendent of the patent office in the State Department in 1802 and retained that position until his death in 1828.

TO THOMAS JEFFERSON

Newcastle, April 29th. 1804

Dear Sir

I had not the honor of receiving your favors of the 30th. March, and the 9th. April,[1] till 5 days ago, having been in the lower parts of the peninsula during the beginning and middle of the Month. My attendance on the Board of Directors of the Ches: and Delaware Canal at Wilmington has since then prevented that immediate attention to them which it was my duty to pay.[2]

Previously to your approval of the general ideas of the plan, proposed in the designs transmitted to you, I had furnished Mr. Lenthall with a rough sketch, which would prevent any thing being done, inconsistent with what you might approve. I had also so arranged the construction of the new design, that it became feasible to make great progress in the external Walls, without pulling down the present building immediately. Every thing has accordingly been done under the idea, of permitting this erection to stand for the present.[3] My ideas respecting the best and most rapid means of compleating the South Wing are not in favor of postponing the removal of this part of the work. I shall lay them before you fully, and with that candor which I owe to your past goodness towards me, and to my gratitude, and duty.

In the first place, however, I will answer Your letter of the 9th. April, which relates to the new design and its proposed modifications. 483

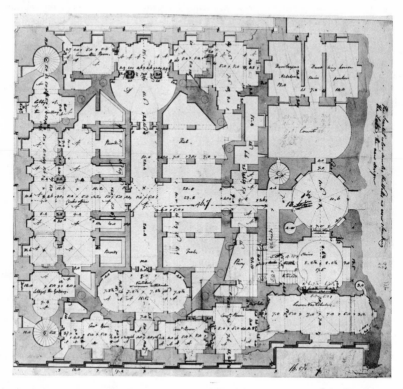

Fig. 16. BHL, Plan of the ground floor of the south wing of the U.S. Capitol, March 1804. Courtesy of the Library of Congress.

1.) The suppression, for the present, of the part of the design behind the recess; may be made without any detriment, provided the ends of the

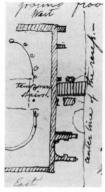

Walls which proceed Northward from the long Walls which bound the [South][4] Wing on the North side be carried up in the two lower stories (i.e. the Cellar story and ground floor). If this is not done, it will be necessary to encrease the thickness of this long wall, which is also 70 feet high, considerably, to enable it to resist the lateral pressure of the Arches, and especially of the Roof. This encreased thickness for so great a higth and length would consume more material and labor than the erection of the ends of the Cross Walls of the recessed part of the building.

The temporary stairs will lead up opposite to the centre of the North side, where the present covered passage is. Should you consent to this arrangement which will be both oeconomical, and much the safest and strongest mode of carrying up the Work, the Wall must go up only 3 feet thick, as designed. The opposite *South* Wall, is 4 feet thick besides the internal and external piers which make it 7 feet between the windows.

2.) The Doric order being given up, and the Corinthian adopted, I must consider in what manner the Capital can best be made: There would be no difficulty whatever in casting the Attic capital of the Clepsydra, because all the upper plain leaves would be cast with the bell, and the lower, raffled, leaves could be easily rivetted on, being cast either in Brass, or Iron. The capital would, thus, require only 2 patterns and moulds. But the Volutes of the Corinthian Capital would require many moulds, and very nice Manipulation, and besides there are the 1.) thin

Fig. 17. Left: Attic capital, Tower of the Winds (Clepsydra). Right: Corinthian capital, Choragic Monument of Lysicrates (Lanthorn of Demosthenes). From James Stuart and Nicholas Revett, *The Antiquities of Athens*, 3 vols. (London, 1762, 1787, 1794), 1 : chap. 3, pl. 7; chap. 4, pl. 6.

485

leaves under the angle volutes, 2 setts, turned opposite ways. 2. the husk from which the Volutes and leaves spring. 3.) The long leaves of the second range, and 4.) the short leaves of the lower range. 5.) The short leaves under the center Volutes, and 6. The rose over the Center Volutes on the Abacus in all 12 different parts requiring separate modelling and separate Moulds. I conceive therefore that capitals carved, might be as cheap, as if cast. This I submit to your consideration. The Athenian capital I allude to, is of the best Age of Athenian architecture, as is to be found in the 1st. or 2d Volume of Stuart's *Athens*.[5] The exterior decoration of the house furnishes a very good specimen of Corinthian Architecture. Should you however prefer the same order for the Hall of Representatives I will immediately proceed to make the necessary drawings, and take the steps to have the Capitals executed during the present season.[6]

3.) The Gallery, certainly may be contracted to a much less size. The floor of the lobby, as of the Gallery is *the top* of the Arches of the Ground floor. The Seats of the Gallery are raised in Timber upon this level, and may be extended or contracted at pleasure. A very capacious Gallery seems in every respect inelligible. That which I had exhibited in the drawings was extended as far as I supposed it would ever be carried.

4.) The Doorkeepers, and Sargeant at Arms rooms may be appropriated easily and conveniently to the purposes you propose. These Officers may be accomodated with railed boxes at each end of the Gallery, for the purpose of distributing papers and letters to the Members, and of keeping the store of stationary.

The Gallery Lobby might have been converted into a Committee Room in the manner proposed without much difficulty: but I much fear it is now too late, as the construction of the Corner of the Building is already otherwise adapted, and it is so Massive, and the Stones of which it is composed so large, that considerable expence and derangement of the general operations would ensue were it attempted. The Jaumbs of the Window are now contracted, in order to throw the light into the stairs, and they must both be pulled down to enlarge the opening into a doorway. Independently however of this difficulty, permit me to submit to You, whether the entrance to the Gallery, would not be too mean, if carried diagonally, in the manner required, if the alteration be made, the last step being also within a few feet of the external threshold. The Lobby in bad weather seems necessary as a kind of resting place, and as the Gallery may possibly, as in England, be under the regulation of a

486

particular officer, at the Door, some such apartment as the Lobby appears convenient.

The mode of proceedure proposed in your letter of the 29th. March has been hitherto followed.[7] But I cannot help thinking that the ultimate completion of the building will be very materially retarded, by suffering the present building to stand during the present season. Nothing also is more certain, than that the work will be executed in a manner not entirely safe, unless the whole can be made as much as possible, to go up together, and get its general settlement gradually and uniformly.

And in order to meet the very serious objections made to removing the House back to the Library, permit me to state to You, that when I appeared before the Committee on the proposed appropriation, I distinctly explained to them the necessity which there appeared to be, of this removal, and found no opposition to it. I proposed that the books should be placed in the adjoining Committee room, in the brick part of the House which still would answer the purpose of a Committee room. Their is ample room round the walls of this apartment for the cases, and for any addition to them that is likely to be made within the next two Years.

The Library itself is sufficiently large to contain all the Members of the House, without crouding them, even with the addition of the new Members. Claxton,[8] who is an excellent officer though not a very good contriver was convinced of this fact, last Summer when it was discussed whether or no the removal should take place. It was the opinion of the Committee, (Mr. Thompson, Coutts, Smilie, Huger, and another member from Baltimore whose name I cannot recollect[9]), that no uneasiness would arise in the House on this account, nor any ill effect, but rather the contrary, as to a future appropriation.

Should you be satisfied on this head, permit me to state to you further the good effect which would result to the work from clearing away the whole of condemned part of the building.

1.) The Materials would come into immediate use as far as they are good, and a very large expense would be saved in making the necessary centering, the greatest part of which would come out of the small timbers of the floor and roof, which cannot again be employed in the new roof and floors.

2.) The whole work could be set out accurately, and carried up regularly.

3.) Twice as many hands could be employed in forwarding the work, as can possibly be employed on the external Walls alone. And the 487 external Walls would notwithstanding be carried during the whole season to as great a higth as if built separately.

4. The workmen employed over so large a space can be so distributed as to cooperate to the greatest advantage, while in the very nature of the work to be done on the outer Walls, the Labor which can be employed on the backing, depends upon the cutting and setting of the freestone; and that again up [on] the supply and the *order* of the supply from the Quarries. And it is impossible to avoid irregularity, and of course want of system in the progress of this part of the Work for it can not be known, *what* number of Masons and Laborers will during any given time balance the Stonecutters and setters employed. Now if the internal Work could progress at the same time, there would always be a recruit of Masons to be got from within the building when the external walls required it, and whenever the Stonecutters were behindhand, the Masons would find employment below. Under such arrangement, there would be no limits to the number of Workmen which we could employ but the difficulty of procuring them, and the fear of exceeding the appropriation by the expenses.

5.) Another most important consideration is, that if the house sit in their present Hall the next Session: more than two Months during which the Work might go on, will most certainly be lost. If the winter even set in early, we may continue to lay stone till the middle of December, and very probably, the Men need not be discharged till Christmas. But if the present building stand, the work must stop in October. If our Men have a chance of making a *long* Season, we shall have the command and choice of them, if not, they will quit us in August and September, to go to Works, from which they will not be discharged till the frost puts an end to all manner of business. The effect of this last circumstance was felt towards the close of the last season: and although congress break up on the 3d March 1805, time will be lost even then in making the preparations to begin with the first fair weather.

6. But the most powerful argument in favor of beginning the *whole* Work this season is this: That if there be any possibility of putting the Legislature into their new Hall at the end of the Year 1805 it can only be, by getting all the work up to the floor of the house finished this season: so as to begin early in 1805 to set the columns which surround the Hall. Every preparation which can possibly be made this season in procuring and preparing the Carpenter's work, cannot so forward the business as

to place it within the reach of practicability to pull down the present erection and carry up the new one in one Season. I do not believe that it could be done in Europe, much less here. But if the Cellar and Ground story can be got so forward this summer, as to begin the next with the upper floor, some hope may be entertained of completing the Work in 1805: although I should not even then be very sanguine.

If therefore, let the mode of proceeding be what it may, One Session must almost inevitably be held in the Library. I most respectfully submit to you, whether it would not be better, to ensure the solidity of the Work, by carrying it up throughout regularly, than to take the chance of the *possibility* of compleating it in two Seasons, a chance which is a very uncertain one, at the risk of injuring and cracking the Walls by its unequal settlement.

Whatever the result of your consideration of this subject may be, the utmost exertions will be made to push the work to the utmost.

I have lately received a letter from Dr. Thornton on the subject of the answers, which I gave to the Committee of the House of Representatives.[10] In these answer I repressed as much as possible the truth as respected the original plan, and thought I had spoken of it with delicacy. His letter to me is, among those who admire the fashion, an unequivocal challenge to the field. I am however perfectly easy as to matter in controversy, and apprehensive of nothing but lest the publicity of a regular dispute, which he appears willing to court should be unpleasant to you.

With sentiments of the most grateful respect, I am Your much obliged hble. Servt.

B. Henry Latrobe.

P.S. The Work on the Canal to unite the Chesapeake and Delaware bays will be begun this week.

I am now engaged assiduously in preparing the plans in detail for the Capitol, which I shall forward gradually, as they are drawn or wanted.

Mr. Peale has made some important alterations in his Polygraph, by which among other advantages it is very much reduced in size. I desired him to write to You on the subject and to send one improved to the utmost to You at Washington. I am now so accustomed to the steel pen that I prefer it. The leaden Inkholders however are bad things. The 489 lacker rub of the lead being disolved by the ink discharges the color, for which reason I cannot use my Polygraph till I replace them with Glass. The 6th. Volume of the *Ph. Transactions* APS will be out next week.[11]

ALS: Jefferson Papers (174/B1). Addressed to Jefferson in Washington. Endorsed as received 4 May.

    1. Jefferson to BHL, 31 (not 30) Mar., 9 Apr. 1804, both above.

    2. BHL had spent part of the month completing surveys requested by the C & D survey committee at their 7 April meeting. At meetings with the C & D board of directors on 24 April and with the survey committee on 25 April, BHL submitted a lengthy report with detailed estimates of the costs of the various proposed canal routes. In his report BHL recommended that the western terminus of the canal be at Welch Point, and he detailed its advantages over Frenchtown. His preferred route was to extend northeast to the Bear Tavern and then directly to New Castle on the Delaware River. BHL, C & D Report, 24 Apr. 1804 (173/F11); C & D Survey Committee Minutes, 25 Apr. 1804.

    3. On 16 April BHL sent Lenthall drawings for the cellar story (not found) and the ground story (fig. 16), as well as a rough section, possibly the surviving east-west section (see BHL to Jefferson, 29 Mar. 1804, n. 4, above). BHL had yet to receive Jefferson's decision on whether the elliptical shape of the House chamber would be retained, and whether he could proceed with the demolition of the lower portions of the "bake-oven," although he did get word of Jefferson's approval of the raising of the House chamber to the principal floor. He therefore devised a plan that would accommodate either shape, as well as phased construction. BHL to Lenthall, 15 Apr., 26 Apr. 1804, both in BHL Papers, Library of Congress (173/E8, 174/A4).

    4. BHL erroneously wrote "North" here.

    5. BHL contrasts the easily fabricated Attic capital from the Clepsydra, or Tower of the Winds (fig. 17, left) with a richer Corinthian type. Ultimately employed were capitals modelled on those of the Choragic Monument of Lysicrates (fig. 17, right), or "Lanthorn of Demosthenes," but his enumeration of parts suggests that BHL was looking at a more conventional Corinthian capital. A description of the Lysicrates capitals would be less likely to cite "husks," short leaves under the center volutes, or "roses" over them. Both the Clepsydra and Lysicrates capitals are detailed in the first volume of James Stuart and Nicholas Revett, *The Antiquities of Athens*, 3 vols. (London, 1762, 1787, 1794), 1:chap. 3, pl. 7, chap. 4, pl. 6. A more conventional Corinthian capital, that at the Library of Hadrian at Athens, also appears in the first volume of *Antiquities*, chap. 5, pl. 8. See BHL to Lenthall, 29 Oct. 1804, and BHL to Jefferson, 17 Nov. 1804, both below.

    BHL's allusion to "the Athenian capital," probably to that at the Tower of the Winds, misplaces that building in the era of the acknowledged Greek masterworks on the Acropolis, but, like the library, it dates to the much later, Roman period.

    6. Jefferson made the following notation at this point in the letter: "The Capital of the Clepsydra may do, but not the entablature. It has no modillions. The frize of the lanthern of Demosthenes."

    7. Jefferson to BHL, 31 (not 29) Mar. 1804, above.

    8. Thomas Claxton, doorkeeper of the House of Representatives.

    9. John Campbell. See BHL to Jefferson, 27 Feb. 1804, n. 4, above.

    10. Thornton to BHL, 23 Apr. 1804, above.

    11. The first part of volume six of the American Philosophical Society *Transactions*, which contains BHL's Paper on Two Species of Wasp, 21 January 1803, and his Report on Steam Engines, 20 May 1803 (both above), was printed in May 1804. The complete volume, however, did not appear until 1809. Minutes, 18 May 1804, APS Archives.

TO JOHN VAUGHAN

Newcastle, May 1st. 1804.

My dear Sir

By mere accident I was so fortunate as to receive your favor of the 27th. by Mr. Aveilhe, whom I met in the streets of Wilmington the day before yesterday, just as I was leaving the town. I went with him into a Tavern and had twenty minutes conversation with him. He is a very different Man from what I expected: for in the first place he is not the inventor of the perpetual Motion—and in the next he has real merit as a man of mechanical and mathematical knowledge. He showed me a drawing of a pump which is a very good thing, though not so simply managed as our Engine pump in Philadelphia. I will endeavor to serve him though I fear it cannot be in the boring line—for he asks too large a Sum (6000$) for the use of his Patent in So. Carolina, a Sum which no Company will be willing to give.

I thank you for the transmission of Mr. Smiths letters. I have engaged Mr. Graff and he will go out in a few days to Charleston. He will be a real acquisition to the Company. I am sincerely sorry to part with him.

I have no books belonging to the Philosophical Society unless it be the Volume of the Rotterdam Transactions on which my Steam Engine paper was grounded, and which I think was returned when the paper was read. Please to let me know whether you have it. Tousard's paper is in my possession. I believe I have it here. I will hunt it up, and try to report upon it. At all events you shall have it again soon.[1] The Concretion found in the Duodenum of the horse is among my things in Philadelphia, and cannot be got at unless I were present. Seybert ought to finish his Analysis: my Drawing is finished somewhere. I fear no very early conclusion of our operations can be expected respecting the said concretion, but I will endeavor to think of it.[2]

I have not heard from Kingsley. He is a Man of Genius. I must write again, for I am anxious that his merit should be known, and his ideas be improved by others, consistently with his interests.[3]

Depend upon it that I do not forget you. But be not weary of reminding me of my duty. Every moment of my time is indeed at present engaged. I shall have more leisure I hope in a month hence.

I have never heard of a similar improvement in the boiler to ours in Centersquare having been used by Meux in his brewery. I should suppose it a good thing, the more, on this account.[4]

I fear our friend Drake does not make out very well with his school, but continues so as to be pushed for money. Perhaps he is not very punctually paid by some of the parents. I recommended a scholar to him just before I left Philadelphia, I fear an unruly subject.

Tomorrow I hope to put the first spade into the ground by way of setting out the feeder of our Canal for the inspection of our Committee. *Quod felix faustum secundumque sit.*[5]

Believe me very affectionately Yours

B. H. Latrobe

Polygraph Copy: LB (31/G3). Addressed to Vaughan in Philadelphia.

1. Anne Louis de Tousard (1749–1817) was a French military engineer who served under Lafayette in the American Revolution. He later planned and superintended construction of fortifications at West Point, N.Y., and Fort Mifflin, near Philadelphia. In 1801 he remodeled the garrison at West Point into a military school. Norman B. Wilkinson, "The Forgotten 'Founder' of West Point," *Military Affairs* 24 (1960–61):177–88.

Tousard's paper, entitled *"Mémoire Sur les Epreuves des Canons de fonte de fer,"* dated 4 January 1802, was originally presented to the American Philosophical Society on 15 January 1802, when Erick Bollmann was requested to translate it. The paper was referred to BHL on 18 February 1803. He was doubtless a member of the committee appointed on 20 July 1804 to translate and abridge the paper, for he wrote to Vaughan on 9 January 1808 that he was sending to Vaughan the paper with Bollmann's translation (LB; 62/C5). The original paper and translation are in the APS Archives.

2. Adam Seybert (1773–1825), pioneer American chemist and mineralogist, received the M.D. from the University of Pennsylvania in 1793 and then continued his studies at London, Edinburgh, Göttingen, and Paris. Seybert was a member of the Chemical Society of Philadelphia and of the American Philosophical Society from 1797, serving as one of the secretaries of the APS from 1799 until 1808 and as a councillor in 1810 and 1811. Seybert ran a drug and apothecary shop in Philadelphia, perhaps the first laboratory in America to manufacture mercurials. He later served in the U.S. Congress (1809–15 and 1817–19).

On 21 January 1803, the American Philosophical Society referred to Seybert and BHL a letter from Hugh G. Shaw to John B. Smith with an accompanying calculous concretion found in the duodenum of a horse. The stone, which was 9 inches long and weighed 18 pounds, 4 ounces, was lost or thrown away by BHL's servants. BHL sent a report and drawing of the stone (not found) to Robert Patterson in 1808. Minutes, APS Archives; BHL to Patterson, 9 Jan. 1808, LB (62/C6).

3. Probably Appollos Kinsley, for whom see BHL, Report on Steam Engines, 20 May 1803, n. 11, above.

4. Richard Meux was senior partner of the Meux Reid (or Griffin) Brewery in Liquorpond St., London. The steam engine at the brewery "was one of the few erected in a major brewery in London before 1800 which had not been supplied by Boulton and Watt from Birmingham." Arthur Woolf, the engineer in charge of the machinery at the brewery, "utilised the waste steam for heating water; . . . installed cast-iron boilers, and converted a small engine from Fenton, Murray and Wood into a compound-motion. It is possible that he erected at Meux's the first of Richard Trevithick's high-pressure engines to be installed beyond Cornwall. . . ." Peter Mathias, *The Brewing Industry in England, 1700–1830* (Cambridge, England, 1959), pp. 61, 95–96.

5. Trans.: And may it be happy, favorable and propitious.

TO GEORGE DAVIS

Newcastle, May 2d. 1804

My dear Sir,

Nothing but the most pressing business could have so long prevented my acknowledging your most friendly remembrance of me in the Message on the subject of my Claim upon the Theatre,[1] by Mr. S. Hazlehurst. I received it however only a few hours before I set out for this place, to meet a number of Men wishing to commence the digging of our Canal, and though I endeavored to follow it by calling at Mr. Biddle's house, I was disappointed. He was from home, and I could not possibly remain in town. I have again written to him.[2] My former letter[3] he did not answer, and should the present application remain unnoticed, it is [my] determination to sell the Claim at the Coffeehouse by auction. I have good advice on this subject and both my patience, my temper, and my humiliation are at an end. Your kindness on this occasion I shall never forget. Believe me most truly Yours

B. Henry Latrobe

Polygraph Copy: LB (31/G10). Addressed to Davis in Philadelphia.

1. The Chestnut Theatre. See BHL to Davis, 6 Feb. 1804, above.
2. BHL to Charles Biddle, 2 May 1804, LB (31/G9).
3. BHL to Charles Biddle, 6 Feb. 1804, LB (29/D9).

TO JOSHUA GILPIN

Newcastle, May 3d 1804

Dear Sir,

I have been very little at home since I last saw you, otherwise I should have written to You before. I copied my report for you before I left Wilmington.[1] Judge Johns carried the copy home with him in order to take one from it, and he has since informed me, that he sent it to You by Mail a day or two afterwards.

The Spades and shovels, and the steel, as also six Wheelbarrows have arrived at Christiana bridge, and I have forwarded them to the Work. I expect hourly Wheeling plank bought by Strickland in Philadelphia. I have met with a lot of excellent Scantling which had lain long on hand here, and a parcel of 2 i. white pine plank for Wheeling, at

493

Christiana Bridge, much below the present Philadelphia Market price, both of which I have engaged, after consulting Mr. Tatnall.

Yesterday I went to the Forge,[2] to set out the first stretch of the Work. Watson the first Contrac[tor] attended with 5 or 6 hands and cut the center line.[3]

I did not however permit him to begin work, but advised him to go to Philadelphia, and get a dozen sodding spades in order that we may have every advantage of the excellent sods which the meadow affords. In the mean time I have put all his hands into the quarry.[4] My real reason for postponing the commencement of the Work was the wish that the Committee might be present at the first serious operation. I am going to write to Mr. Tatnall from whom you will no doubt hear if he can himself attend. Next Wednesday we could begin. I hope you can then be here.

The want of accomodations for the Men is the most serious Evil we have to contend with. Strickland is here and at work but Carpenters are scarce, and I have written to Mr. Vickers to send two or three rough hands from Philadelphia.

I regret exceedingly that the operations of the Company cannot go on with the vigor, which we could employ, with ample funds. I am morally sure that I could finish the feeder in November, could I act up to the means within my reach, as to Men and arrangement.

There are several original papers among those in my possession of which you have no copies, and which are part of the history of the Canal. I will send them to You. I am now engaged in the Office in making Sections as required, and it is also become necessary to make a compleat map of all our operations, the surveys being now I think finished.

I shall apprize you regularly of all my operations from time to time, and consult you on every new step that seems necessary. I hope a Committee may meet at Elkforge on Wednesday next.[5] Believe me very affectionately Yrs.

B. H. Latrobe

Polygraph Copy: LB (31/G13). Addressed to Gilpin in Philadelphia.

1. BHL, C & D Report, 24 Apr. 1804 (173/F11).
2. The Elk feeder began at Elk Forge, now the village of Elk Mills, Md., on the Elk River. The Elk Forge Company, which had been organized in 1761, was a successful business concern that owned large areas of woodland that provided the charcoal for its two forges. The C & D Canal Company had to purchase from the forge company the right to the Elk River water at the forge. Johnston, *History of Cecil County*, pp. 347–48, 385.

3. William Watson had worked for BHL on the Philadelphia Waterworks. BHL reported to the survey committee that on 2 May he had also set out the line of the second section of the feeder to be done by contractor Joseph Pollock, another Philadelphia Waterworks veteran. BHL sent C & D President Tatnall the contracts for Watson and Pollock, "good honest Men, whom I have known for five or six Years but I was unwilling to give them too much, as I am not so sure of their Management as of their honesty." C & D Survey Committee Minutes, 10 May 1804; BHL to Joseph Tatnall, 15 Apr. 1804, LB (31/C6); BHL, *Engineering Drawings*, p. 14n.

4. The quarry, which was to provide the stone for the canal's masonry work, was about a quarter of a mile south of the beginning of the feeder where the proposed aqueduct was to cross Elk River near Elk Forge. BHL, *Engineering Drawings*, p. 15.

5. The survey committee met next on Thursday, 10 May 1804, in New Castle. There BHL was directed to prepare a report on the workmen's housing problem, to erect a carpenter's and blacksmith's shop and toolhouse at the work site, "to compleat the contracts for digging and finishing the Feeder," to buy the necessary gunpowder, and to complete "the purchase of the Lands on the line of the feeder and reservoir." C & D Survey Committee Minutes.

TO CHRISTIAN IGNATIUS LATROBE

Newcastle Delaware, May 7th. 1804

My dear Brother,

It was and still is my intention to have written to you a long letter, in order to bring up old scores. I have received three letters from you within the last 4 or 5 Months which the haste in which I write prevents my referring to. The last is dated March [6th.?] I do not recollect whether any of them came by Mr. Gill. I have received also a bound book, containing the *Dies irae,* Dawn of Glory, and your Airs, for which I most sincerely thank you, as for every letter you write to me.[1] I have found it utterly impossible to write to you since my last of the 12th. of October.[2] Since then I have seldom been at home. In July last I undertook the greatest work at present projected in America, the Union of the Delaware and Chesapeak bays by a Canal of 8 feet Water, and a few days ago the first turf was cut. Previously to this engagement, as I have already written to you, I had been barely kept alive by my magnificent appointment of surveyor to the public buildings of the United States, an office attended with enormous expense and a small salary, and which has hitherto furnished me with most laborious employment in detecting the villanies and correcting the blunders of my predecessors. My present engagement promises me something like the means of an income beyond the support 495 of my family. I have not yet been able to obtain payment of the Sums due to me by the Corporation of Phila. and the proprietors of the Theatre, so that the brilliant appearance of my success covers only vexation, and poverty. In the mean time, I am so pressed with business, and so happy in my family at home that I have no time to think much of my vexations. The *Pigou,* Collet is just coming from Philadelphia and I hasten to write these few lines as a Cover to your Sisters letter which I mean to put on board as the Ship passes by.

The conduct of the Sellons to me and my children, in not even rendering an account of the money accumulating in their hands in unpardonable and almost dishonest, and the neglect of John Sellon in not returning your visits is ungentlemanly. I mean to put them into Mr. Silvester's hands, if I do not soon hear from them. William, I know is not better than a bankrupt. If justice were done, he should pay, principal and interest, to my children of at least £20.000. But they will never get a penny.[3]

In the course of this Year, you shall hear from me in the way you wish. I will write by every packet, for my employment, will in future give me the leisure I have hitherto wanted. In June your Sister goes to her Mother's to be confined. We are going on in this respect much as you do. Love to my Sister. Yr. affectionate Brother

B. H. Latrobe

Polygraph Copy: LB (32/A8). Addressed to Christian Ignatius in London. Sent via the ship *Pigou,* Captain Collet. Enclosed "letter from Mrs. L. giving an account of family affairs and personalities."

1. Among Christian Ignatius Latrobe's published musical compositions were Lord Roscommon's translation of the *Dies Irae* (1799), *The Dawn of Glory* (1803), and *Six Airs on Serious Subjects, words by Cowper and Hannah More.* In a letter to John Frederick Latrobe, to whom he also sent copies of his compositions, Christian Ignatius describes his *Dies Irae* as "a sort of cantata or little oratorio—which has been performed here [London] with the applause of all who love melancholy music" (14 Nov. 1802, John Henry de La Trobe Collection, Hamburg, copy in PBHL).

2. BHL to Christian Ignatius Latrobe, 25 (not 12) Oct. 1803, above.

3. When BHL married Lydia Sellon in February 1790, her father settled £1,000 on her, "secured on his Estate in Portman chapel." In addition, at his death in the summer of 1790 he bequeathed to Lydia a share of the residue of his estate, the share estimated to be worth £2,500. After Lydia's death and BHL's departure for America, the estate was held by Lydia's brothers John Baker Sellon (1762–1835) and William Marmaduke Sellon in trust for BHL's children Henry and Lydia. BHL was eventually able to collect a portion of the estate. BHL, *Journals,* 1:201–13; BHL to Christian Ignatius Latrobe, 4 Nov. 1804,

below; BHL to Christian Ignatius Latrobe, 3 Nov. 1805, 1 Dec. 1807, 10 Jan. 1808, and BHL to John Baker Sellon, 4 Feb. 1806, all in BHL, *Correspondence*, 2; BHL to Martha Sellon, 20 Dec. 1806, and BHL to Henry S. B. Latrobe, 27 Nov. 1807, both in LB (53/A7, 60/E10).

John Silvester (1745–1822) was BHL's London attorney. BHL, *Journals*, 1 : 251.

TO THOMAS MUNROE

Newcastle May 13th. 1804.

Dear Sir,

Having been from home for a few days, I received Yours of the 9th only just now on my return. On the other side I send you a copy of my letter to Mr. Robertson, from which it will appear that on the 17th. of Feby. I was ready, and by the terms of the letter obliged myself to contract with him for fine stone on terms formerly proposed, (namely 9 Dollars per Ton) and at 8 Dollars for common stone, not intending to order of him any blocks, which under the terms of Cook and Brent's contract would have raised the price above 8$ by their *extraordinary weight*.[1] I remained in Washington till the 1st. of March, and during the intermediate time Robinson,[2] if I recollect right, was in Washington, but showed no intention of entering into Contract: Nor has he, it seems, taking any steps to enter into a specific contract, untill the offer of Mr. Stuart of Baltimore to supply us *with the fine stone*, put the public out of his power. Before that time it appeared more than probable, that we should be entirely dependent upon him for the Capitals of the Pilasters, and for the carved Work generally.

While things were in this state, I received frequent letters from Mr. Lenthall complaining that Robertson and the small Contractors hung back and did not compleat the bargain made with them by entering into specific Contracts for determined quantities of stone; and it was my intention to have written to them on the subject when I heard of Mr. Stuart's disposition to supply us. Nothing seemed to me to come in better time, and as I considered the letter of the 17th of Feby. to be a call to enter into *immediate* contract on the terms specified, and by no means as an instrument *then*, and *forever afterwards*, binding on the public, while Robertson was left to do as he pleased; I immediately wrote to Mr. 497

Stuart, requesting him to apply to Blagden, and Mr. Lenthall, and should he agree to the terms granted to Messrs. Cook and Brent, to enter immediately into Contract.[3] I had previously arranged with Mr. Lenthall that the Contract should [be] for 600 Tons, including the necessary quantity for carving. I also send You a copy of my letter to Mr. Stuart, enclosed.

These are the facts, and leaving it to You to act upon them as you may think best, I will take the liberty to state my opinion to be: that the contract with Mr. Stuart should be compleated and no contract made with Robertson and for the following reasons:

1. Because, though Messrs. Cook and Brent *may* at present believe him capable of complying with his engagements, and worthy of public confidence, they did not think so when I was negotiating for the supply for the whole Season. At that time, as I am ready to aver, he was stated to be a man well disposed and sanguine, but not to be relied upon either as to his *means,* or his *character and talent* as a Man of business.

2. Because he has already proved himself to be a man disposed to make the most of the public necessities, by hanging back untill a powerfull rivalship rendered it prudent for him to come forward.

3. Because, the proposal for a contract offered by me on the 17th. of February being tacitly though absolutely declined by a silence of three Months nearly, we have now an opportunity of making a Contract with a Man who has the means, the disposition, and has already taken the measures, necessary to execute his engagements, and whose Character is besides too well established as a punctual and solid Man of business to leave a doubt of his exertions, and success in the performance of what he undertakes.

4. Because I think that these little Quarriers want a rap on the Knuckles.

I may however add, that as the President of the United States has approved the Plan proposed for the completion of the South Wing a large quantity of good Stone will be wanted for the internal Columns, bases, and Mouldings and that we shall not have too much stone, even if a Contract with Stuart for 600 and with Robertson for 400 Ton be entered into, beyond our Contract with Cook and Brent. But if only *one* Contract is to prevail, I think that it will prove to be sound Oeconomy to give Stuart the price agreed for with Cook and Brent, in preference to giving Robertson that offered to him.

498   I have written in haste in order to save the post. You will excuse the

traces of hurry, and accept the most sincere assurances of my respect and affection. Yours truly

B. H. Latrobe

P.S. In answering Mr. Lenthall, I have referred him to this letter to You, as I cannot possibly enter into detail with him, before the post goes out.[4]

NB. Enclosed are sent the Copies to Stuart and Robertson.

Polygraph Copy: LB (32/B10). Addressed to Munroe in Washington.

1. BHL to William Robertson, 17 Feb. 1804, LB (29/E11).
2. I.e., Robertson.
3. BHL to William Steuart, 7 May 1804, LB (32/B4).
4. BHL to John Lenthall, 13 May 1804, BHL Papers, Library of Congress (174/D4).

TO JOSHUA GILPIN

Newcastle May 14th 1804

Dear Sir

The Maps go by this mornings Packet. Permit me to request Your great indulgence as to the Sketch book. It is not fit to be seen by any body but yourself.

The sooner we get the Gunpowder by Levi Hollingsworth's shallop the better, and the sooner I get *my Gothic hints,* and Gilpins picturesque scenery the more I shall thank you. Perhaps you will trust me with two or three of the Volumes.[1]

With much esteem and truth Believe me Yours affecty.

B. H. Latrobe.

Polygraph Copy: LB (32/C11). Addressed to Gilpin in Philadelphia.

1. The "*Gothic hints*" may have been BHL's early ideas or sketches for a Gothic design for the Roman Catholic cathedral of Baltimore. See BHL to Gilpin, 19 May 1804, below. "Gilpin's picturesque scenery" refers to the writings on the Picturesque by the Rev. William Gilpin (1724–1804), English clergyman and a distant relation of Joshua Gilpin. Gilpin genealogical charts, Historical Society of Pennsylvania, Philadelphia.

TO ISAAC HAZLEHURST

Newcastle, May 14th. 1804

My dear Father,

The two last letters which Mary has received from our Mother give us hope that not only the life of our poor Robert is out of danger, but that he is also better in other respects, and that a favorable crisis may have taken place in his disorder. It appears at least certain that for the last four Months he has gradually recovered the command of his mind, and I think it is clearly ascertained that the state of his bodily health so entirely governs the cast of his ideas, that a course of medecine or of diet may probably be adopted under which his compleat restoration may be looked for, with more confidence, than hitherto. It happened unfortunately that at the moment of our receiving the intelligence of the late return of his spasms the visit of Mr. Gilpin and of the other Gentlemen of the Canal Committee took me from home. It was impossible to put off my engagements as more than 50 Workmen were waiting for me at Elkforge. I was obliged to leave my wife in the greatest distress, and by no means in good health. The letters of her mother however and her new hopes have restored her tranquillity, and she is this day as well as ever. I sincerely hope this favorable state of things will continue and improve, tho' we hardly now dare hope for the pleasure of seeing you here next week as we expected.

The Committee who now manage the Canal affairs with Mr. Gilpin at their head, proceed in a manner infinitely more advantageous to the Stockholders and pleasant to me than their predecessors Mr. Gale & Co. It is singular that the Work was commenced on the 2d. of May, the day on which 5 Years ago I begun the Waterworks. We have now above 50 Men employed at Elkforge and on the first Mile from thence, all of them hands who have formerly been under my direction. I have now no doubt of finishing the feeder, 5 Miles long, this season, and perhaps also the Grand Reservoir near Aikentown.

The question which now agitates everybody in this State, on one side, or the other, is whether the Canal shall terminate at Newcastle or in Christiana Creek. If the nature of the Ground, the better Navigation, or the expense were alone consulted, there is no doubt but Newcastle would be determined upon as the best situation for the mouth of the Canal. And yet, as the subscription is almost entirely made up by the Christiana interest both here and in Philadelphia, I much doubt whether the whole scheme would not fall through unless the work be made to terminate in Christiana Creek: and as it would even then be highly useful to the public, though more expensive and circuitous than if taken at once into the Delaware, I think the Christiana interest must prevail.

We are not entirely without hopes of seeing you here next week, and sincerely pray that the health of our brother may not prove the cause of our disappointment.

Mary joins me in most affectionate respects to You and our Mother Believe me very truly Your affecte. Son

B. H. Latrobe.

Polygraph Copy: LB (32/C12). Addressed to Hazlehurst in Philadelphia.

TO JOHN CARROLL

Newcastle May 16th. 1804

Reverend Sir,

I had the honor to receive yours of the 6th. May on my return home, and with the information you have given me, shall find great pleasure in giving you such assistance, as, whatever professional talent I may possess, will enable me to yield. At the same time I beg leave to assure you, that far from thinking You under the smallest obligation to me in this respect, nothing can be more sincere and lively than the sense I have of the honor I receive in Your confidence and good opinion, nor a more flattering reward for my labor, than your acceptance of my mite of service. Though I have never had the happiness of a personal introduction, Your character has been too long known and revered by me, not to render the present opportunity of intercourse most valuable to my feelings.[1] I am with the truest respect and high esteem Your faithful hble. Servt.

B. H. Latrobe.

ALS: Archives of the Archdiocese of Baltimore (174/D7). Addressed to Carroll in Baltimore and sent via Lewis DeMun.

1. Nearly a year would elapse, however, before BHL finally sent his first designs for the cathedral to Carroll. BHL to Carroll, 16 Apr. 1805, in BHL, *Correspondence*, 2.

TO JOSHUA GILPIN

Newcastle, May 19th. 1804

My dear Sir

Among the multitude of your engagements, I cannot quarrell with you if you have forgotten my Gothic Cathedral, and my Gilpinian landscapes; and indeed my time having been spent chiefly at Elk forge, I have not been able to think of either of these things. But the Gunpowder which has not yet arrived is a more serious subject, and I must intreat you to send us a barrell as soon as possible.[1] I must also beg you to send me the Contracts. The Work is half finished as far as the point of the first Rocky hill, and I am now distressed for the presence of Thos. Vickers or of his partner. I enclose a letter to him open, which will render you the information I should otherwise give you.[2]

The only Man of our three Contractors who thoroughly understands his business is Mr. Cochran. The two others are very industrious, but give me great trouble in watching and instructing them. I am determined in future to recommend no one to a Contract who has not had actual experience either in Europe, or under Mr. Weston. By the first of June I should have a considerable stretch of the work filled with Water could I possibly get the first Culvert constructed by that time.

We are well supplied now with everything but Wheelbarrows. I have contracted for part of the number ordered by the Committee with Mr. Howard a good Wheelwright at Elkforge.[3] The Country people begin to court the people employed at the Works as much as at first they shunned them. Not a single instance of misconduct has occurred.

I hope you received my sketch book and the Maps by the packet. Pray do me the favor to write to me soon enclosing the contracts. Much of the Work already ought to be measured.

With best respects to Mrs. Gilpin believe me very truly Yours

B. H. Latrobe

P.S. I this moment hear the melancholy News of the death of my brother in law Mr. Robt. Hazlehurst. I may perhaps visit Philadelphia before the 1st. June.

Polygraph Copy: LB (32/D8). Addressed to Gilpin in Philadelphia.

1. The gunpowder eventually arrived by summer. Although the first quantity of powder was from another source, during the summer and fall of 1804 the C & D Canal Company purchased 900 pounds of powder from the new Eleutherian Mills of E. I. du Pont de Nemours & Co., near Wilmington, Del. At the time of its final purchase on 17 October 1804, the C & D Canal Company had accounted for 12 percent of the sales of du Pont powder. BHL, *Engineering Drawings*, p. 15n.

2. BHL to Vickers, 20 May 1804, LB (32/D10).

3. William and Thomas Howard made (at $5 apiece) and repaired over fifty wheelbarrows for the canal project in the summer of 1804. C & D Committee of Works Journal, 10 July, 22 Sept., 27 Sept. 1804.

REPORT ON THE CHESAPEAKE AND DELAWARE CANAL

2d. of June, 1804.

Gentlemen,

Agreeably to your resolution of the 24th. of April I have the honor to lay before you maps and profiles of the line of Canal from Frenchtown and Welch point to the meeting of these two canals—from this point to the vicinity of the Bear—thence to Christiana Creek near Mendenhall's and also to New Castle, with estimates of these several sections.

A former resolution of the Committee of Survey required of me a general report on the whole business committed to me for the purpose of its being laid before you at your present meeting—with this resolution I now beg leave to comply.[1]

At the first meeting of the board of Directors for the transaction of business in June 1803 Mr. Howard and myself were appointed to explore all the ground over which it was judged to be most likely to find a good line of canal between the waters of the Chesapeake and the Delaware. The arrangements previous to our undertaking this business delayed the commencement of our operations till the middle of July when the gentlemen of the committee of survey rode over the several proposed lines and pointed out the leading objects of examination.

The instructions of the Committee were confined in the first instance to the examination of the ground between several principal points on each bay and of the feeder. They were from time to time extended to all the following lines,

Chesapeake	Delaware
1. Back creek at or near Wertz' landing	Port Penn.
2. Back creek at the nearest convenient point below Wertz	Port Penn.
3. Old Court House point the south cape of Back Creek	Port Penn.
4. Welch Point	New Castle.
5. Welch Point.	Christiana Bridge
6. and 7. Any convenient point at which there might be deep water between Locust and Welch point }	New Castle and Christiana Creek
8. Frenchtown	vicinity of New Castle particularly Red Hook
9. Frenchtown	New Castle
10. Frenchtown	Christiana Creek

When these instructions were given several other routes had been under consideration by the board and were the subject of conversation with the engineers, altho they are not mentioned in any formal communication. As it is the object of this report to bring into view the whole of the proceedings with the reasons on which they have been founded; and public attention having been frequently directed to these lines it appears necessary not entirely to omit mention of them. They are principally the following:

Chesapeake	Delaware
1. Head of Chester.	Duck Creek.
2. Sassafras.	Appoquinimink.
3. Sassafras.	Drawyer's Creek.
4. Bohemia.	Appoquinimink.
5. Bohemia.	Drawyer's.
6. Sassafrass or Bohemia.	Silver Run.

The first of these lines was deemed to open into the bays too far from Philadelphia and from the mouth of Susquehanna to be eligible. Against all the rest there was, independently of every other one general objection the bars at the mouths of Appoquinimink, Drawyer's and Bohemia.

The excessive expence and uncertain result of what has been called the thorough cut, precluded the adoption of that plan.[2]

In the operations intrusted to the engineers the following leading principles were understood to be for their general government.

1. The canal to be carried into water at each end of 8 ft. deep at least, at low water.

2. The canal itself to be 8 feet deep below the surface of the water.

3. The canal to be fed either by Elk river, Christiana creek, White-clay creek or by all those Streams.

The business of exploring the ground was begun at the tide at Frenchtown. The surveys formerly made at the expence of the American Philosophical Society for the same purpose had already pointed out the practicability of several lines of Canal, but on principles which the experience of European engineers during the time since elapsed, has exploded or corrected the first leading fact which it was necessary to ascertain was the level of the ridge which divides the waters of the bays of Chesapeake and Delaware, and much time was spent by Mr. Howard and myself in levelling up from the tide and back again and in performing every operation necessary to correctness. We finally agreed to fix the height of a point on the lowest pass of the ridge on the upper line near Oliver Howell's at 70 ft. 9.5 in: above the high water of Chesapeake at common tides and from thence to determine all other levels of the summit southward.

In the course of the operations to ascertain this level, it was proved that any line of canal commencing at Frenchtown must necessarily pass near a remarkable maple in front of the house of Oliver Howell because the vallies of Perch creek on one side and the high ridges from Gray's hill on the other, allow no other course.

It then became requisite to know how high it would be necessary to proceed up the Elk, Christiana or Whiteclay to secure a supply of water for a summit level of about 76 feet, whether the supply could be brought to the canal on that level, or whether it would be better to lower the summit by deep cutting. Accordingly Mr. Howard levelled up to the upper forge on Elk and found the elevation of the water of the dam to be 84 ft. and that of the lower to be 70 feet above the tide of Chesapeake. It appeared therefore necessary to obtain the water of the upper forge. 505

In examining the ground towards Christiana creek I found it difficult and uneven and ascertained that Fisher's mill dam would not be sufficiently elevated for a supply—above Fisher's the creek branches out and its water cannot be easily collected. Whiteclay creek being also afterwards explored I found that nothing short of Rankin's dam above Newark had sufficient elevation, that very uncommon difficulties presented themselves in the construction of this feeder, and that independently of local difficulties—the feeder would be more than double the length of one from Elk.

It being known that the Canal could be certainly supplied with water from the upper forge dam on Elk river, if carried on a summit level of 76 ft. Mr. Howard proceeded to determine the elevation of the range of the highest land between the two bays so as to intersect by this line of levels all the routes between the two bays which it was proposed to explore.

He found that in proceeding from Howell's along the ridge in a S.E. direction, the ridge increased in elevation till he approached the heads of the waters of Back creek running into Elk river and of St. George's discharging themselves into Delaware.

From this point southward he found a depression of the ridge extending for above a mile; the lowest point being only 62 ft. above the tide in Chesapeake. The ridge from this point southward became again elevated. All these facts were afterwards verified by levels taken in my subsequent operations.

Mr. Howard afterwards ascertained the respective levels of the ridges which separate the waters of Christiana creek and Delaware and sounded the Elk at Frenchtown, making a survey of the shore and of Perch creek.

The general elevation of the highest land being accurately determined the surveys and levellings were now directed to the actual determination of the lines of canal. And in order to ascertain the best situations on the waters of the two bays, at which to enter the tide water, Mr. John Thompson of Springfield Pa. was employed to make surveys and take all the soundings of Christiana creek and Back creek from their mouths to the end of tide navigation and to survey the east shore of Elk river from Locust point to Welch point. This task he executed with great skill and fidelity. In the necessary land surveys his assistance and also that of Mr. Daniel Blaney of Port Penn were very useful.

It would be very uninteresting and unnecessary to describe the great variety of levels which were unavoidably taken in order to discover the lines of canal which have from time to time been laid before you as practicable or eligible. Their whole length taken together exceeds 300 miles. For altho the top of the country is plain and preserves nearly the same level it is intersected by so many watercourses and broad ravines, and so much abounds in intricate swamps, that great difficulties occurred in finding the most eligible levels. The very great choice of ground even, increased the necessary extent of examination. It was also proper to go over every line more than once, in order to verify former levellings and insure the necessary accuracy.

I will now recapitulate the leading object of all the operations performed by me under the direction of the Committee of survey, beginning with the most southern lines and proceeding northward.

The first line of levels carried over the ground between Port Penn and Back creek had for its object a canal from Port Penn to Wertz' landing or its vicinity on Back creek. It was soon found that no good line of canal could be found in this direction on account of the numerous and deep ravines of St. George's as well as of Back creek which intersect it; for this reason and in order to shorten the difficult navigation of the creek it was given up and a lower point on Back creek at the mouth of Hog creek was chosen as the point to which to carry the work. This line was connected with another leading into the deep water of Elk river at Old Court House point. Both these lines were found very practicable but the elevation of the ground of part of Bohemia manor is so much greater than of the depressed part of the ridge over which the feeder must be brought, that a steam engine seemed the best and least expensive method of supplying the summit level of the Canal. This great elevation of the ground was unexpected and more than usual pains and time have been expended to examine every part of the neck between Back creek and Bohemia river: the fact is however fully verified.

By the range of levels which had been taken along the next ridge, it had been discovered that there were only two modes by which a canal north of Back creek could pass it without an enormous deep cutting. The one to cut thro it near Oliver Howell's at or near the place above mentioned; the other to follow from Oliver Howell's the ridge in its S.E. course, for above 2 miles as far as F. Elsebury's spring which is the most distant head of St. George's—to cut thro it at that point—to keep on the 507 southern side of another ridge which divides the waters of Christiana creek from those of Red Lion and St. George's and to pursue its direction to the N.E. nearly as far as the Bear tavern where the lines to Christiana creek, to New Castle or to Red Hook separate. The latter of these routes was first explored and many collateral lines were run towards the Delaware between the ravines of St. George's and Red Lion as well as towards Christiana. The result of these operations was that it would be better to cut thro the great ridge near Oliver Howell's than to follow this circuitous track which tho it offered no obstructions to the work by deep cuttings or embankments, would be more expensive by its length than the direct course across the head waters of the South Branch of Christiana between Oliver Howell's and the Bear.

It then became my principal duty to explore this part of the ground before entering on either end of the work. In the course of this examination it was found that the general depression of the ground among the ravines of Christiana creek would permit the summit level to be fixed at 74 feet above the tide in Chesapeake; and all my subsequent operations were calculated to this elevation of the summit.

The only places between Oliver Howell's and the Bear which present any difficulty are a valley and brook west of Aitkentown—Belltown brook in its broad valley—and a brook and valley on the land of Kinsey Johns Esq: All these waters have spread branches to the southward below the junction of which the line of canal must necessarily be carried. Aqueducts in all these places and at Belltown brook a considerable embankment are required—under these aqueducts however the public roads may be passed and thus the expense of bridges will be saved.

Having carried the levellings as far as the Bear tavern, the shortest distance by which the Delaware could be reached appeared to lead to Hamburgh a distance of only 2 miles in a straight line. But in levelling the ground for a canal I found that the straight line which would nearly follow the road was intercepted by 2 broad depressions leading towards Red Lion. To avoid these it was necessary to keep to the N.E. by which means a line to Red Hook became much shorter and passed over much better ground and the land close to the river affords every advantage which could be desired at the termination of the work, and must certainly have been chosen in preference to any point of discharge, had the water in the Delaware been of sufficient depth within a moderate distance from the Shore; but a broad flat beginning a little below New Castle, extends a great distance into the river, and passes in front of Red

508

Hook, Hamburg and all the landings from thence almost as far as Reeden point.

To discover good lines of Canal to New Castle and Christiana creek required a very long and attentive examination of the ground. In going to New Castle the branches of Mill creek spreading chiefly to the N.W. opposed great difficulties on that side of the creek, the best line was found on the S.E. side where the ground over which the Canal must be carried is remarkably level and straight as far as Mill Creek marsh. This marsh must be crossed by an embankment which will be more or less expensive according to the course of the canal after crossing. It will be 24 feet high and 400 yds. long if a circuitous route be taken thro lands and hollows of small value, and only 14 feet high if carried thro very valuable private improvements.

The ground towards Christiana creek is of a very different nature—a high ridge lies between Mill creek and Christiana creek under which the numerous branches of Mill creek have their rise, and on the south of which is situated the Bear tavern. This ridge cannot be advantageously passed but at one place on land of Nicholas Vandyke Esq: The depressions caused by the waters of Mill creek prevent a straight course of the canal but the levels are not otherwise unfavorable. The crossing place at Mr. Vandyke's is also very short, and the deep cutting of no great importance.[3] The greatest difficulties occur on the other side of the ridge in the valley of Christiana creek, they arise from deep ravines on the lands of Enos, Read and Gray deceased, and of many lines which may be followed to reach the creek none are entirely free from them.[4] It will however appear by the map and sections that by minding the line of canal into the vallies or by a few short embankments they may be easily overcome and a very excellent canal be made into the deep water of the creek near Mendenhall's.

I have only to remark further on the lines to New Castle and Christiana that in both instances the mouth of the canal will be admirably placed upon the tide navigation, and that the works in each instance will be nearly the same expense.

In the first operations of the engineers the ground about Frenchtown was well explored—of two practicable lines to reach the summit that tending to the north from the mouth of the canal was found far the most eligible and least expensive. But both of them have their difficulties and that which is proposed for adoption has three aqueducts of moderate size within the first mile.

One of the last lines of levelling which has been performed is that from Welch point to join the upper line at the ridge, the length of this line exceeds that from Frenchtown by more than 3 miles. But in other respects it has none of the difficulties of the former in its whole course of near 8 miles. It passes over level ground easily dug and requires not even a culvert in the whole distance; nor will it materially exceed the line from Frenchtown in expence.

The board after very minute investigation on the subject of the feeders and after laborious examination of the different grounds by the engineer having purchased the waters of Elk for the supply of the canal I shall omit a particular description of what has been done on Whiteclay and Christiana creeks.

The Elk rises in the hilly country and in order to bring it to the summit by the best route, 3 ridges must be cut thro—one at Bell hill, another on Mr. Cachot's land and the last on land of Richd. Updegrove being a connecting ridge of Gray's hill with Sandy Hill.[5] Compared with similar works which have been executed in Europe, or even with the cut thro the Sand-hills near Philadelphia,[6] these cuttings are trifling—the deepest of them Bell hill does not exceed 12 feet.

The actual work on the Feeder commenced at Elk Forge on the 2d. of May. The weather has been so unfavorable since then as to retard the digging work very considerably. Great progress however is already made in the first 1/2 mile. In the commencement of every great work, there are many inconveniences to overcome. The want of tools and accomodations was at first seriously felt. At present we are better supplied with utensils and more are daily procured; temporary and portable houses have also been erected so as to remove that difficulty of accomodation in a very great degree.

The operations carried on under your directions in the field commenced in July 1803 and were pursued without intermission during the months of August, September, October, November, and December—they were again taken up in March and April 1804. The country minutely explored is of about 18 miles average breadth, between the waters of the two bays, and 12 miles average width.

The time thus expended has furnished minute information upon all that is practicable in the way of inland navigation throughout the upper part of this peninsula—so that independently of the means of deciding on the line of the present work the utility of the survey will reach to every future attempt to extend its benefits by lateral canals, and save a very heavy expence in future surveys of the ground.

I have the honor &c. &c.

B. H. Latrobe.

Copy: C & D Canal Company Papers (174/E11).

1. The resolution was made at the 7 April 1804 committee meeting. See BHL to Bollmann, 16 Mar. 1804, n. 2, above.

2. BHL discarded the idea of a "thorough cut" or lock-free, sea-level canal in his first written report to the survey committee in October 1803. Such a canal would require the removal of 1,760,000 yards of earth for the one-mile pass through the ridge. Concluded BHL: "one mile would more than exhaust the whole Capital of the Company." BHL, C & D Report, 21 Oct. 1803 (170/C10).

3. Nicholas Van Dyke (1770–1826) of New Castle, brother-in-law of Kensey Johns, was attorney general of Delaware from 1801 to 1806. A Federalist, Van Dyke represented Delaware in the U.S. House of Representatives (1807–11) and the U.S. Senate (1817–26).

Besides digging and banking on Van Dyke's land, BHL called for "Removing the Barn, repairing and underpinning the same" at a cost of $200. BHL, C & D Report, 24 Apr. 1804 (173/F11).

4. George Gray's property was marshland. Culverts and locks had to be constructed at a cost of $5,000 on the lands of Jo. Enos and George Read. Ibid.

5. For BHL's troubles in attempting to acquire Jacob Gachot's and Richard Updegrove's lands, see BHL to Gilpin, 9 Sept. 1804, below. Updegrove was one of the first Methodists in the Elkton area, and services were held at his house near the state line about 1799. Johnston, *History of Cecil County*, p. 459.

6. This was probably part of the Delaware and Schuylkill Canal on which deputy engineer Robert Brooke reported in 1795: "At the lower end of the canal, in the vicinity of the city, through the distance of two miles and three-quarters, there have been two hundred and fifty thousand cubic yards of earth and gravel, and partly rocks, removed out of the bed of the canal, and ten culverts built and completed." *ASP. Miscellaneous*, 1 : 859n.

TO SAMUEL RELF, EDITOR OF THE
PHILADELPHIA GAZETTE

New-Castle, June 9, 1804.

Sir,[1]

The attempt, which is become so common, to carry on public works by the help of newspaper *puffs*, reflects disgrace, as well upon the taste, as upon the credulity of the public; and does little honor to the judgement of those who employ so contemptible a mean of success. I am led to   511 this remark by seeing in your Gazette of the 7th June, a letter dated Charleston, May 23, in which is announced the arrival of Mr. Graff in the following words:[2]

"With great pleasure we announce the arrival of Mr. Graff, in the service of the Catawba Company who has been strongly recommended to them by Mr. Latrobe, as a proper person to open the navigation of the Catawba and Wateree. Mr. Graff has had ample experience in similar works, *having carried a circular perforation of six feet diameter for nine hundred feet, through a solid rock, to favor the transmission of the water of Schuylkill to the grand reservoir* in Philadelphia for supplying the city with water for domestic purposes."

In this passage nothing is true, but the employment of whatever weight there might be in my recommendation in favor of Mr. Graff, that he has ample experience in similar works, and that he has arrived in Charleston. But should Mr. Graff, ever read the exaggerated description of the works at Philadelphia, and of the part he had in their execution he will, I am sure, feel the severest mortification, and almost repent his acceptance of the situation that has exposed him to it. In those who know Mr. Graff, and are acquainted with the detail of the Philadelphia water works this letter will naturally induce the persuasion, that in the warmth of friendly feelings, and of high professional respect for my pupil, mixed with some personal vanity, I had ventured to extend the limits of my commendations, and of the difficulty of executing the water works far beyond the bounds of truth.

In referring however to the copy of my letter in his favor now before me,[3] I find, that in order to explain the nature of Mr. Graff's professional experience, I have *described* the works cut in the rock at Philadelphia; and have stated, that they are *about* 600 feet in length; that they were carried on while Mr. Graff was in my office, and that the performance of his duty in the office made him well acquainted with the principles and methods of executing works in solid rock. This being the branch of knowledge which in clearing the rocky bed of the Catawba will be most useful to the Company, I endeavored to prove that Mr. Graff possessed, by showing *how* he had acquired it; namely, by daily attendance at the works on the Schuylkill during the whole progress. But the tunnel itself was executed by Mr. John Lewis, and the Canal in the rock, chiefly by Mr. James Cochran. Mr. John Davis, then clerk, now manager of the water-works, a man, whose skill and integrity in his present employ, does so much credit to himself, and to the city such essential services, had the immediate superintendance of the work.[4]

As to the extent of the work itself, the most exaggerated and unauthorized assertions are made by the writer of the Charleston letter. The *perforation* is not "circular," it is not "six feet in diameter," it is not "nine hundred feet long," it does not "transmit the water to the grand reservoir," the *grand reservoir* has no existence.

In my letter of recommendation, the collective length of *all the works* in the rocks, is stated at 600 feet about, including the tunnel, the canal, and the engine well. I wrote from memory, and may therefore be mistaken; instead of nine hundred feet, the tunnel is not I think 400 feet long. Its size is about what I stated, 8 feet high, 4 feet 6 inches wide.

Judging of the feelings of Mr. Graff from my own, and from my knowledge of his unaffected modesty, and scrupulous respect for truth, I have thought it necessary to rescue *his* name, as well as mine, from their connection with a palpable mistatement: and I beg the editors of such papers as have copied the letter from Charleston to insert this also.

Those who deal in the article of *puffs*, whether in the shape of letters or of reports, rob themselves of all credit for understanding and veracity. The cheat is easily discovered by all who know, and strongly suspected by all who do not know, the work or the person puffed. Besides they inflict the most cruel mortification upon those engaged in the design or direction of public works. Every professional Man whose self-respect is founded on a true estimate of his own skill and science, knows much better than his bitterest enemy, to what extent the measure of public applause is filled beyond his real merit. If a public work ultimately succeeds, boundless praise is given to *one* man only.

This is sufficiently mortifying to the man, whose mind has virtue and modesty to admit, that unassisted by the suggestions, and the various talents of those employed under him, he would have been incapable of designing and directing so perfect a work. The consciousness and acknowledgement of what such a man owes to others, and the friendship and esteem growing out of this kind of obligation, is one of his most exquisite pleasures. The *puffers,* laying about them with clumsy violence, and striking the public, themselves, and those they attempt to protect, injure the cause they pretend to serve, bring themselves into contempt, and destroy the feelings of those they intend to praise. The water-works of Philadelphia, which were begun and brought to maturity without any 513 such assistance, and which, on the contrary were during their whole progress attacked and abused by the same kind of writers differently employed, are the best proof of how little avail is the aid of puffing, or the opposition of calumny. Such statements as have lately appeared on the subject of the inland intercourse of Pennsylvania, and the official reports [of] the several boards to whom the public works have been entrusted, where they do honour to the writers, promote the success of the works of which they treat, by enlightening the people into their true interests.[5]

As to Mr. Graff, the Catawba Company are truly fortunate in possessing an engineer of his rare merit. He is a Pennsylvanian by birth, and there can be no doubt but that his native state will be at some future period, benefitted and honoured by his professional and personal character.

B. Henry Latrobe

Printed Copy: *Relfs Philadelphia Gazette. And Daily Advertiser,* 13 June 1804 (microfiche add.).

1. Samuel Relf (1776–1823), Federalist journalist and author.

2. The same letter from *The Times* (Charleston, S.C.) with minor variations (e.g., Graff appears as De Graff) was also published in *Mirror of the Times, & General Advertiser* (Wilmington, Del.), 13 June 1804.

3. BHL to Smith, 21 Mar. 1804, above.

4. John Davis (1770–1864) was born at Avebury in Wiltshire, England. He had a grammar school education and by his own account was later "practically engaged in engineering, and architectural pursuits and employed by those Eminent and distinguished Gentlemen, Messrs. James and Sam. Wyatt of London." In 1793 he immigrated to the United States with his wife and child and the next year settled in Philadelphia. Recognizing Davis's skills, BHL appointed him clerk of the works at the commencement of the Philadelphia Waterworks construction (summer of 1799), and he became superintendent of the waterworks in 1803. Davis was consulted by the projectors of the Baltimore Waterworks during the fall of 1804, and the next spring he became engineer and president of that enterprise, a position he held until 1816. He had numerous engineering and millwrighting commissions in the Baltimore area, and from 1816 to 1839 constructed and superintended the Cumberland Road Turnpike from near Hagerstown, Md., to Cumberland, Md. Davis, "Autobiography of John Davis, 1770–1864," *Maryland Historical Magazine* 30 (1935):11–39; Nelson M. Blake, *Water for the Cities* (Syracuse, N.Y., 1956), p. 74; *Report to the Common Councils, on the Progress and State of the Water Works, on the 24th of November* (Philadelphia, 1799), p. 15; Richard Xavier Evans, ed., "The Daily Journal of Robert Mills: Baltimore, 1816," *Maryland Historical Magazine* 30 (1935):365–66.

5. BHL may have had in mind the *First General Report of the President and Directors of the Chesapeake and Delaware Canal Company*, published in June 1804, which was reprinted in *Relfs Philadelphia Gazette* on 19 June 1804.

TO ISAAC HAZLEHURST

Newcastle, June 10th. 1804

My dear Father

You will, I am sure, excuse my silence for the last 10 days, when you consider how extremely the late election and the consequent measures of the new Bd. of Directors have occupied almost every moment of my time.[1] I have been indeed very little at home since my return from Philadelphia. The progess of the Feeder is such as to require much of my time at the work itself.

You have no doubt heard of the ultimate decision of the directors in favor of a Canal from Welchpoint to Christiana Creek. Welchpoint is about 5 Miles below Frenchtown, and forms the North Cape of Back creek. This is in every respect the best starting point on Elkriver and there can be no doubt of the correctness of the decision of the board in its favor: As to Christiana creek I confess that policy *certainly* rendered that decision necessary more than the true merits of the case. Had the Christiana interest been offended, I believe the whole work would have failed. And the work will be very excellent if carried to Christiana, although there can be no doubt, that Newcastle has in respect to situation and oeconomy claims to a decided preference.[2]

The decision on this has had a very remarkable effect in quieting every body's mind in this neighborhood, and I feel the advantage of being no longer tormented by a thousand teazing and often very impertinent conversations on the subject. I have also got rid of the labor of survey, and am now in a regular routine of business and a regular Salary, commencing with the first of March. Another effect has been produced, as it were by magic. Mr. Adlum and Mr. Gale, finding their efforts against me entirely in vain, have met me, at their last meeting with the utmost civility. One of the new directors is Mr. Couch who lives at the foot of Ironhill, a man of large property, and excellent talents, with whom I have been on a very intimate footing ever since my residence in Delaware. All these circumstances render my situation infinitely more pleasant than formerly.

At home we have continued well. Henry is still with us. John is cutting teeth. Lydia is daily making me look older by her size. My dear Mary is well. In three weeks she must I believe be with You, when I hope also to spend some time in Philadelphia.

515

Mr. Ch. Kanote who delivers this is the person who has had a dispute with Porrit. Porrit himself has never made his appearance. Randle gives him an excellent character for honesty, but says he understands nothing of Canal business having been bred to the Blanket business in England, and only undertaking *Labor* here. Randle accounts for his dispute from the extreme obstinacy of Porrits character. He is now almost too late, most of the work of the Season being already given out. I have agreed with Randle for a Mile, *about*, jointly with one Coxsy another sturdy Englishman, whose health seems able to brave any thing.[3]

We think and speak of you and our Mother every day, with that interest and affection which we so much owe to You, especially at present. Mary joins in the most dutiful respect to you with Your affecte. Son

B. Henry Latrobe

Polygraph Copy: LB (32/G4). Addressed to Hazlehurst in Philadelphia.

1. Most of the original C & D directors were reelected: Kensey Johns of Delaware, John Adlum and George Gale of Maryland, and James C. Fisher, George Fox, and Joshua Gilpin of Pennsylvania. The new board members were William Cooch of Delaware, William Hemsley of Maryland (see BHL to Jo. Helmsley, 29 Oct. 1804, n. 1, below), and George Roberts of Pennsylvania.

2. BHL informed George Read that the three Maryland directors (Adlum, Gale, and Chew) and Kensey Johns favored the New Castle terminus while the Pennsylvania directors (Gilpin, Tilghman, Fox, and Fisher) and Tatnall and Bayard voted for the Christina debouche. The engineer remarked that "the Majority even acknowledge that the point was knotty." BHL to Read, undated, folder four, Read Papers, Historical Society of Delaware, Wilmington (171/A13).

The board's decision was published in its annual report, *First General Report of the President and Directors of the Chesapeake and Delaware Canal Company, June 4, 1804* (n.p., 1804).

3. BHL told Gilpin that contractors Charles Randle and John Coxey (Cocksy) were "thoroughbred English Gangsmen . . . also Men of integrity." Randle had worked on the Grand Junction Canal in England, built by William Jessop. BHL later recommended him to Secretary of the Treasury Albert Gallatin to assist the commissioners in laying out the National Road. Randle was also employed on the Washington Canal, another project directed by BHL. BHL to Joshua Gilpin, 28 Mar., 2 Sept. 1804, and BHL to Frederick May, 10 Feb. 1814, all in LB (30/F12, 35/A8, 114/G10); BHL to James Madison, 8 Apr. 1816, in BHL, *Correspondence*, 3.

In a memorandum to Randle (29 Mar. 1804, LB; 30/G3), BHL outlined some of the contractors' responsibilities to his laborers: "The Country affords little convenience for lodging Men. The best plan will be to fix upon some elevated spot, and to build sheds: to lay in a stock of beef pork and potatoes, and perhaps of liquor for the Men, and to establish a careful person to manage the provisions and take care of the Utensils on the spot. The Men had also better lodge in the Sheds. The Ground along the feeder is very healthy."

TO JOHN BIRD

Newcastle June 16th. 1804

Sir,[1]

I am highly flattered by your Letter of this morning on the subject of regulating the levels of the Streets, and furnishing to the corporation a correct Plan of the town of Newcastle. I will with pleasure undertake this service, and hope to be able to compleat the object proposed to me by the tenth of August next.[2]

The compensation I should willingly leave to the corporation to fix, after the business is done. It shall not however exceed One hundred Dollars, independently of the wages of two Assistants in levelling.[3]

I beg leave to suggest, that a well bound book containing about 3 Quires of the largest Elephant paper will be necessary to record the Survey in detail, a sheet of which I send herewith. This book should be immediately provided.[4]

I am with true respect Yr.

B. H. Latrobe

Polygraph Copy: LB (33/A5). Addressed to Bird in New Castle.

1. John Bird (d. 1810), who leaned towards the Republicans in politics, was elected to the New Castle town commission in 1798 and 1804 and to the state senate in 1801. He was a partner in the New Castle mercantile firm of Riddle and Bird which did much of its business with the U.S. Navy. Bird died suddenly after the firm failed in 1810 after losing government orders for naval supplies. John A. Munroe, *Federalist Delaware, 1775–1815* (New Brunswick, N.J., 1954), pp. 213, 252; Delaware Federal Writers' Project, *New Castle on the Delaware* (New Castle, Del., 1950 [orig. publ. 1936]), pp. 85, 89; Lucille P. Toro, "The Latrobe Survey of New Castle, 1804–1805" (M.A. thesis, University of Delaware, 1971), pp. 20, 25.

2. In 1804 the Delaware General Assembly passed legislation providing for an extensive survey of the town of New Castle to be undertaken by the town commission. The commission met on 13 June 1804 and appointed two of its members, John Bird and Henry Colesberry, a committee to ask BHL if he would perform the survey and what his terms would be. Toro, "The Latrobe Survey of New Castle," pp. 21–22, 25.

3. BHL actually employed three assistants: Robert Mills, William Strickland, and Daniel Blaney. Blaney worked eight days in September 1804 assisting BHL "in Surveying and measuring the Horizontal distance of the different Streets" in New Castle. Daniel Blaney Daybook, Sept. 1804, Historical Society of Delaware, Wilmington; Toro, "The Latrobe Survey of New Castle," pp. 28–32.

4. On 18 June 1804 the commissioners accepted BHL's terms and agreed to furnish the laborers and stones for the survey as well as a parchment book for the map and drawings. With the assistance of Mills and Strickland, BHL produced a plan of the town (14 pages, each 16″ × 20″) that included every house that stood in 1805, with sections of each street showing both the existing gradient and that proposed by BHL. The architect

also wrote an essay in which he explained his plan and discussed the future growth of the town. The plan and essay are in the Division of Historical and Cultural Affairs, Hall of Records, Dover, Del. (261/A1). The most thorough treatment of the New Castle survey is Toro, "The Latrobe Survey of New Castle."

FROM WILLIAM THORNTON

City of Washington 27th. June 1804

Sir

I did not hear till today of your Arrival in this City, or I should before now have noticed your Letter.[1]

How much sooner you may exult in an open declaration of enmity it is nevertheless distressing to me that any person should conceive he had reason to call me his Enemy. You mention some Instances of incivility on my part. I remember none ever intended, nor any act that could be so construed except in the Lobby of the State Office, when I must own that your perseverence in Alterations of the South Wing of the Capitol (which I thought unnecessary after those I had made) did for a moment put me out of patience, and the pressure of public Business upon me at that time prevented perhaps the Attention I ought to have paid to your wishes; but the want of attention is all you can charge with. I made use of no Insults. I am more affected by your charge of insincerity than by all the malevolent aspersions contained in your Letter. I had at the time I sent you my pamphlet no Enmity to you, for I had not then seen your Report to the Committee of Congress. I was sincere in the Expression of my good wishes toward you and your respectable Lady. The pointed Injury you had intended me must have been the Cause of your suspecting my sincerity, and your Feelings towards me must have been bitter indeed to dictate your subsequent Invectives.

You accuse me of having driven Mr. Hallet and Mr. Hadfield to ruin. Mr. Hallet was dismissed from public Service on the 28th. of June 1794. My Commission was dated Septr. 12th. 1794.[2] Mr. Hadfield resigned his Employment on the 24th. of June 1796, which the Board accepted on the 27th. At his own request he was restored to the Superintendance of the Capitol on the 29th. Septr. 1796, and though his behaviour to me was what few would have overlooked, yet on his apology, which he made voluntarily, I was the first to reinstate him. He was

518

afterwards dismissed by the Board for reasons not necessary to mention.[3] I consider him a man of taste and am not his Enemy. You charge me with detraction, but I deny it, and should be sorry to compare my Character with yours in that respect. You say I have some Field Business to settle. I know of none. I received several months ago a challenge, which I accepted, and I waited in the Country the Appointment of the time and place by the Seconds. My Antagonist was in the mean time bound to the peace: but before Heaven I declare that no Information ever came from me *direct or indirect* relative to the Affair, and my Family I believe have never yet heard of it. I am thus, and shall always be prepared to repel any attack from any Quarter.

I am Sir with due respect,

W: Thornton

Copy: William Thornton Papers, Library of Congress (microfiche add.). In Thornton's hand and endorsed "No. 3."

1. BHL to Thornton, 28 Apr. 1804, above.
2. Thornton served as a commissioner for the District of Columbia from 1794 to May 1802.
3. Hadfield was dismissed on 28 May 1798 after the commissioners refused to recognize his claim that he had a professional right to supervise the construction of the Treasury and Executive Offices that he had designed.

TO KENSEY JOHNS

Philadelphia, July 8th. 1804

Dear Sir,

Since I last had the pleasure to see You, I have been so variously placed and engaged, that it seems to me almost impossible that no more than a fortnight should had elapsed. My departure from Newcastle was indeed rather precipitate. The situation of Mrs. Latrobe required her immediate removal, and the pressure of the business required to be disposed of previously to my departure, not only forbad me to join in the happy scene which then occupied your family, but rendered it impossible for me even to comply with the ceremonial of a short bridal Visit. Permit me now, though late, to express my sincerest participation in the satisfaction which you and Mrs. Johns must feel in an event, which opens to you and to Your amiable daughter the prospect of so much happiness. 519

Immediately after my arrival in Philadelphia, I prepared to visit the works, and came to Elkton by the mail the next day. I there made all the necessary arrangements with Mr. Brooke,[1] and the other persons engaged in the service of the Company, and proceeded to Baltimore, where I have placed my son at the French college. This school was first recommended to me by my friend Mr. R. G. Harper, and my own personal enquiries confirm the good opinion which his excellent judgement had occasioned. As you once spoke to me on the subject of schools, with a view to the education of your eldest Son,[2] I cannot but point out to you, that in making a comparison and choice, the french college at Baltimore is well worthy of consideration even with our best Eastern and Northern academies. The terms for board, and instruction in French, belles lettres, languages, natural science, and mathematics, are 200$. per Annum. Accomplishments are separately paid for, as drawing, music, dancing &c. The advantage of learning to speak French fluently is a great one. There are now 80 scholars, about 1/3 Americans.

I did not get back to Elkton till last Saturday week, June 30th. Finding every thing to go on well, I came on hither. Mrs. L has been very unwell, but as she remained in suspence I spent two days last week at the works, and returned hither only yesterday. I found *the want of money* excessive. Of 2.300 odd Dollars reported to be due on the 4th. of June only 1.700$, (700) in hand 1000 by draft, have been paid to me. I have advanced since about 150$. By an estimate, I also reported that 6.000 Dollars would probably be wanted before the 17th. of July. You may therefore easily imagine what a chasm is to be filled. Were money in plenty I should have by this time had a complete navigation, from Elkforge to the Lancaster road *to lay at the feet of the Committee.* You will no doubt have seen my report to Mr. Cooch and my draft for 2.000 Dollars. Let me beg you to give me your signature, and your exertions in the financial department. I hope to be with you in the course of a few days or a week, that is, as soon as my family affairs will permit. Mrs. L. begs to be particularly recommended to Mrs. Johns,[3] with whom joins in sentiments of the most perfect respect. Yrs. Truly

B. Henry Latrobe.

ALS: Mrs. Gamble Latrobe Collection, MdHS (175/A2). Addressed to Judge Johns in New Castle.

1. Robert Brooke (1770–1821), clerk of the works on the C & D Canal, was a Philadelphia surveyor who had been William Weston's "Assistant Engineer" on the Delaware

and Schuylkill Canal in the 1790s. In 1805, BHL described this "little dapper Man": "If this Man were cut open, I believe you would find a pendulum swinging in his chest, instead of a heart. He swings along at such an even pace that no one can derange him. He obeys orders with scrupulous punctuality right or wrong, takes care to have every thing in writing, pays no body without a signed order of myself or the Committee, though the debt be ever so just or evident, is as immovable as a post, *and is never in a scrape.*" BHL to Thomas Tingey, 6 Apr. 1805, LB (39/A10); BHL, *Engineering Drawings*, p. 14; *Encyclopedia of Pennsylvania Biography*, 32 vols. (New York, 1914–67), 6 : 1857–58.

   2. Johns's eldest son, Kensey Johns (1791–1857), graduated from the College of New Jersey (Princeton) in 1810 and attended the law school at Litchfield, Conn. He went on to practice law, serve in Congress (1827–31), and in 1832 replace his father as chancellor of Delaware. Johns's younger son, John Johns (1796–1876) also graduated from the College of New Jersey (1815) and later became the fourth bishop of the Protestant Episcopal Church in Virginia and president of the College of William and Mary.

   3. Ann Van Dyke, daughter of Delaware President (Governor) Nicholas Van Dyke (1738–89), married Kensey Johns in 1784.

TO JOHN LENTHALL

Philadelphia, July 13th. 1804.

My dear Lenthall

   I have had your letter two or three days by me; and though, I have had a severe share of distressing circumstances in the course of my life to school me, I am at present so situated that I can scarcely command my own mind long enough to answer you properly, or to think distinctly on any subject whatever. My wife, who is otherwise well, has expected her delivery *daily* for the last 10 days. 4 days ago, her mother died after a few hours illness of an inflamation in her bowels. She is ignorant of it. The event is to me distressing beyond measure, to her father it will be almost fatal. I have the task of maintaining my usual conduct. She is cheerful, laughs, and even sings sometimes. I shall certainly go mad. Pray tell this to the president.

   The Columns *including the Plinth* which will be continued all round, and form a kind of *blocking* above the Moulding of the Pedestal-inclosure of the house will be 26.7½ inches high, ten diameters. 26.7½ = to $\frac{26.625}{10}$ = 2.6625, or 2 ft. 7¾ about. This, I think we must assume as our diameter; and in the lower block enough additional allowance must be made for the projection of the Cincture. What it must be, you will find in Chambers.[1] The Columns must be diminished in a straight line without 521 swell ⅙th. $\frac{2.6625}{6}$ is .44&c. = 5¼, therefore diameter at the neck is 2 ft. 2½. As I never diminish pilaster I follow the general practice of the Greeks and make them ¹⁄₁₂ narrower than the lower diameter of the Columns, or 2⅝ i. in the present instance, so that the Pilasters, ought to be, instead of 2 f. 6 i. as I have it, in the drawing, 2 f. 5⅛ i., and it were well, if you could alter the impost piers accordingly, although, *in them* it is not a matter of any importance. The Order will run thus

Highth *exclusive* of plinth,	26f.2
Lower diameter	2.7 ¾
Upper do.	2.2 ½
Quantity of diminution 1/6th	5 ¼
Width of Pilaster	2.5 ⅛

I fear my head is not composed en[oug]h to be correct.

I will in a short time send you the order compleat.

As to the Tunnels, it is impossible to leave a hole in a 9 inch Culvert, unless it be enclosed in a Circle or Elipsis.[2] The strength of a Culvert is in the pressure inwards being every where resisted by its circular form. A straight [*illegible*] destroys this.

In your answer say nothing of the situation of my family, lest Mrs. L. should see it. Your rule of diminishing the heighths of the blocks is very excellent, and must be adopted. I had not thought on the subject, and doubt whether I should found one as good.

Yours affecty.

B. H. Latrobe

ALS: BHL Papers, Library of Congress (175/A7). Addressed in Lenthall in Washington. Endorsed as received 16 July and answered 21 July.

1. Sir William Chambers, *A Treatise on the Decorative Part of Civil Architecture* (London, 1791).

2. BHL wished to follow Jefferson's suggestion that he construct for the south wing privies an "air drain" that could serve also as a wheelbarrow passage during construction of the wing. BHL to Lenthall, 26 Apr. 1804 (misdated 1803), BHL Papers, Library of Congress (174/A4).

TO WILLIAM THORNTON

Philadelphia, July 21st. 1804

Sir,

Your letter of the 29th. June was put into my hands on the evening of the 30th., at the same moment that brought me a few lines from my family.[1] The situation of my wife was such as to oblige me to leave Washington by the Mail of the next morning, and the business necessary to be previously arranged, made it impossible for me to answer your letter on the same evening.

On my arrival in Philadelphia, another still more unfortunate event occurred, which has hitherto interrupted all my correspondence. At the time when Mrs. L. expected hourly to be confined to her Chamber, her Mother was suddenly carried off by an inflamation of the bowels. This misfortune has not yet been fully communicated to her. She has been brought to bed, and is still in a situation very far from health.[2]

I have thought it right to give you this explanation, because I am well aware that your letter ought to have received an immediate answer; and also in return for the explanation you have given me of an affair, in which general report appears to have done you great injustice. On this part of the subject which your first letter, by its expressions, has introduced it is not my intention to say more at present.

If you wish for further light on your character as an underhand destroyer of reputation, I refer you generally to your conscience, and particularly to your recollection of a visit to Mr. Stuart's painting room, with my pupil Mr. Mills. If this be not enough, I have a volume of additional facts ready for you.

Having thus noticed the principal points in your letter, I can not help expressing my opinion that any further correspondence between us will not only be unnecessary, but tend to encrease the irritation of the minds of each of us. The primary cause of our difference can never be removed. In 1798 you told me, that you had only studied architecture for one fortnight in the Library of Philadelphia, previously to your designing the Capitol.[3] That you should be so very imperfect therefore in the theory, and wholly deficient in the practise of the Art, cannot astonish me who have from my childhood studied and for 15 Years practised the profession, and yet daily feel how very far my acquirements in the science, and execution of this complicated art, are below those of many Men whom I have known. Nor am I surprised that you

523

know as *much* as you actually do, when I consider the quickness of your talents and the grasp of your memory. As it is impossible that you should ever be on a level with me, excepting in your own opinion, and equally so that I should revert to the ignorance of the art with which I began to study 25 Years ago, in order to descend to your scale of knowledge, you must forever consider me as a presumptuous tyrant in the profession, while my opinion of your designs of your principles, and of your conduct, in respect to the buildings and the artists of Washington remains exactly what is [*illegible*].[4] I avoid unpleasant explanation. The cause of our quarrel being therefore permanent discretion points out that conduct to each which it will be most for our interests to observe. If you think you can gain any thing by publicity, I am not pledged *always* to observe the delicacy which dictated my report.[5] I am with due respect Your hble. Servant

B. Henry Latrobe

Polygraph Copy: LB (34/A9). Addressed to Thornton in Washington.

1. Thornton to BHL, 27 (not 29) June 1804, above.
2. On 17 July MEL gave birth to Juliana Elizabeth Boneval Latrobe (1804–90).
3. In an earlier draft of a letter to Thornton (not sent, LB; 34/B2), BHL remarked that William Maclure had introduced him to Thornton in 1798. Although Thornton is known to have designed the building for the Library Company of Philadelphia in 1789, he had no formal training as an architect. On 12 October 1802 he wrote, "I saw a publication for a plan of a public library in Philadelphia offering a premium for the best. When I trevelled [*sic*] I never thought of architecture. But I got some books and worked a few days, then gave a plan in the ancient Ionic order, which carried the day. The president and secretary of state published [in 1792] a premium of a gold medal of $500 and a lot for a house in the city of Washington for the best plan and elevation of a capitol of the United States. I lamented not having studied architecture, and resolved to attempt the grand undertaking and study it at the same time. I studied some months and worked almost night and day, but I found I was opposed by regular architects from France and various other countries." CHS, *Records* 18 (1915):150, 175–76.
4. BHL had shown that he was not entirely without appreciation of Thornton's talents six years earlier, when he remarked in his journal that the Capitol design, "though . . . faulty in external detail, is one of the first designs of modern times." Nevertheless he was decidedly opposed to the authority of Thornton's Capitol designs, considering the doctor's admitted innocence of practical matters, and ultimately to the taste Thornton demonstrated there. BHL, *Journals*, 2 : 378.
5. For the outbreak of a newspaper war between the partisans of Thornton and BHL, see BHL to Jefferson, 9 Nov. 1804, below.

TO GEORGE READ

Philadelphia July 22d 1804.

My dear Sir

A series of most distressing circumstances have kept me from returning long before now to Newcastle. Previously to her confinement, Mrs. L was so unwell, that I returned from Washington immediately to Philadelphia. I paid afterwards a flying visit to the works, but could not devote a day to a visit to our residence at Newcastle. A few days after my return, Mrs. Hazlehurst, my wife's mother, died very unexpectedly at Cloverhill of an inflammation of the bowels after 18 hours illness. At that time Mrs. L. was in hourly expectation of her labor. The loss we had suffered could not therefore be communicated to her, nor is she yet apprised of it, tho' she believes her mother to be dangerously sick. On Tuesday last she was safely delivered of a fine little Girl, and would be uncommonly well if her breasts were not in a very dangerous state. Thus has my mind been most severely harrassed by domestic distress, while my absence from my public engagements is scarcely less afflicting to me. Tomorrow morning however it is my intention to go to Elkton,[1] and before I return hither I mean to have the pleasure to see you.

I have had little time or inclination to go into public since my arrival in Philadelphia. With the highest respect for his eminent talents, and the truest esteem for his benevolent and social heart, I have not been able to work myself up into the fashionable pitch of grief for the death of Mr. Hamilton. Other folks besides myself are also refractory, and the Clergy among others seem to have resolved on an insurrection against the public melancholy.[2] I hope you have taken the matter properly to heart in Delaware. For my own part, since Bonaparte has turned out such a rascal, I am more than ever convinced, that the fear of great talents, which caused the Ostracism of Aristides is less reprehensible and injurious to republics, and better founded on a true estimate of human nature, than that republican frenzie which often raises [a] meritorious individual to an altitude above the power of the people to pull down again.[3] On this account I disapprove both of posthumous, and of contemporary adulation.

With best respects to Mrs. Read,[4] believe me truly Yrs.

B. H. Latrobe

Polygraph Copy: LB (34/A13). Addressed to Read in New Castle.

1. BHL intended to meet Kensey Johns at the works later in the week "to compleat the purchases [of land for the canal] in Maryland" which he had hoped "to be able to arrange" by then. BHL to Johns, 22 July 1804, LB (34/B1).

2. Hamilton died in New York City on 12 July from a wound he received in the duel with Aaron Burr that had taken place the day before. Many Philadelphians mourned Hamilton's passing, and the citizens asked the city's clergymen to remonstrate against duelling in sermons on Sunday, 22 July. On the eighteenth ministers of the Episcopal, Presbyterian, Catholic, Baptist, Reformed, and Jewish faiths met, resolved that they opposed duelling, and declared that individual clergymen might speak upon the subject, but they resolved that offering prayers and thanksgivings "or otherwise noticing a late mournful event . . . would, as we conceive, be, for various reasons, at this time highly inexpedient." *Aurora,* 18 July, 20 July 1804.

3. Aristides the Just (died c. 468 B.C.), Athenian statesman and general, was ostracized in 483. Recalled in a general amnesty three years later, Aristides fought successfully with his countrymen against the Persians.
Napoleon Bonaparte declared himself emperor in May 1804.

4. Mary (Thompson) Read, daughter of Gen. William and Catharine Ross Thompson, married George Read II on 30 October 1786.

TO ROBERT GOODLOE HARPER

Philadelphia July 22d 1804

My dear Sir

Your letter of the 25th. of June I received only yesterday. The state of the roads between Washington and Baltimore was such, that the Mail arrived about 1/4 before 2 o'clock, and I had scarce time to get myself shaved before we again proceeded.[1] By this means your letter remained at the Compting House of Messrs. Hazlehurst till a few days ago, a most melancholy event having brought my brothers hither at a moment's warning. Mrs. Hazlehurst my mother in law was taken ill about dinnertime on the 10th. with violent vomiting. In the evening she wrote to her husband an particular account of her case and added a lengthy postscript the next morning. She was weak but easy all the day, and thought herself quite well at night, but about 11 o'clock, attempting to cross the room she sunk into a chair and expired without a groan. This happened at Cloverhill. Mr. H. was in town, and on his arrival, the 12th. he found her a corpse. His distress cannot be described. At his age to lose the companion of all his pleasures and pains for nearly 40 Years! She was 62 and till her death enjoyed the most perfect health. The loss falls most severely on my father, but to Mrs. Latrobe it is also a most serious 526 misfortune. At present she is however ignorant of the death of her mother, although she believes her to be dangerously ill. For at the moment when the news arrived she was in hourly expectation of being confined to her Chamber. The Physicians thought it best to postpone the communication and to endeavor to prepare her for it. On the 17th. she was safely delivered of a very healthy little Girl, and is doing very well. I dread the moment when it will be necessary to tell her the truth, which cannot now be much longer conceald.

Your letter prevents all procedure for the present. The plan and estimate[2] shall be transmitted in 10 days from hence. I will write to you then more at large; my spirits are low, and the restraint I have lived in for the last fortnight has benumbed all my faculties. With best respects to Mrs. Harper, and the truest affection believe me truly Yrs.

B. Henry Latrobe.

ALS: Mrs. Gamble Latrobe Collection, MdHS (175/B1). Addressed to Harper in Annapolis. Endorsed as received 24 July, answered 1 August, and "Informed him of the Contents of my 2d letter, which he [appears?] not to have received."

1. BHL had arranged to meet Harper on Sunday, 25 June "unless something very extraordinary occurs to prevent it." BHL to Harper, 10 June 1804, Mrs. Gamble Latrobe Collection, MdHS (174/G2).
2. The plan and estimate for the Baltimore Waterworks have not been found.

TO JOHN LENTHALL

Philadelphia, Augt. 5th. 1804

My dear Sir

For the last fortnight I have been absent from this city having been engaged in bringing up the business of the Canal where I have now above 200 Men at work. I received therefore your two letters of the 21st. and 29th. of July at once on my return, and I sit down immediately to answer them, regretting exceedingly that they were not sent after me into the Country.

1.) I do not see any thing in your arrangement of the dimensions of the blocks of the internal columns but what is *perfect*, and I shall therefore regulate all my ideas and designs accordingly.

2.) The rules that determine the proportions of what is called *the*   527 *orders,* were, no doubt, arbitrary, among the ancients, as to all *matters of detail.* Palladio and his successors and contemporaries endeavored to establish fixed rules for the most minute parts of the orders. The Greeks knew of no such rules, but having established *general* proportions and laws of form and arrangement, all matters of detail were left to the talent and taste of individual architects. This is amply proved in all their best buildings. Of this license in detail, I think it right to avail myself on all occasions.[1] There are however practices in respect to some of their arrangements which Palladio and his school, have totally rejected, although among the Greeks they were so general, as scarcely to have been arbitrary. Among these were, the straight contour of the Columns: the perpendicularity of pilasters, called by the Greeks *Antes:* the total omission of Pilasters, excepting at the angles[2]: *the projection of the frieze beyond the diminished shaft of the Column, 1/12th. of the lower diameter.* I have prefaced the introduction of this latter rule, by the preceding remarks, lest you should think that the design I shall propose is an arbitrary innovation. I do not know of a single building in Greece or Asia minor in which the practice is not followed, and its effect is admirable. When looking at a Collonade in profile, if the frieze which determines the place of the entablature be perpendicular to the diminished end of the Column, it necessarily must happen that the building will appear to *batter* or lean back. But if the frieze, and of course the Architrave come forward to the mean line of the Column, the building immediately assumes a bold perpendicular appearance. This is practically exemplified on a large scale in the Pensylvania and United States banks. I have constructed the former on the Greek principles. The latter has its frieze perpendicular to the small end of the Columns. Even the most ignorant perceive and acknowledge the superior effect of the former.[3]

This will account to you for my having made the pilasters only 1/12th less in width than the diameter of the Columns. Their upper end, being 1/12th larger than the upper diameter of the shaft, their mean thickness will be the same. The frieze line will be perpendicular to the shafts of the Pilasters and of course project 1/12th diam: beyond the diminished shaft of the Column. As to the bases, it naturally follows, that those of the Columns will be larger than those of the Pilasters. This has not a bad effect, for the *quantity,* of Base will still appear to be in a favor of the Pilaster. At least it has that effect at the Bank of Pennsylvania. For though I know that the diameter of the Base of the Column is 3 inches more than the width of the base of the pilaster, I have often looked at them for a considerable time, and still the base of the Pilaster has had the effect of being quite as wide, *at the least*. And this must necessarily happen, because the light on the base of the Pilaster continues along its whole width, while that on the base of the Column occupies but a small portion of the surfase. In fixing the Subplinth or Base block on which the Colonnade is to stand, its width must be sufficient to receive the bases and plinths of the Columns. It will then of course be sufficient for those of the Pilasters.

As to the *continued* Plinth, a difficulty is certainly created at the pilaster which would not exist if I had followed the Greek method of entirely omitting the plinth. I retained it in compliment to what I know to be the taste of the President of the U.S. in a place where a deviation from the Palladian fashion would be very conspicuous. But the difficulty you have pointed out will I fear oblige me after all to reject it, or otherwise make some alteration. I am now engaged in making your further drawings and shall devote the whole week to them. This point will come then in course, as also the agreement of the impost pier with the Pilaster. Wm. Strickland is here and very busy in drawing and copying.

3.) The line from which 6f. 3 i. is to be measured for the springing of the niches in the staircases is the level of the Landing which is laid down in the Section of the Circular stairs drawn on a seperate small paper.

4.) I cannot today say any thing on the subject of the Iron roof. It rains so as to render it impossible for me to go to the works on Schuylkill. Tomorrow I will however write fully, and in the mean time give the gutters consideration.

5.) King as you say is but a bag of wind as to promises. I have reason to know it. I saw him here a fortnight ago. He gave me an order for round Iron, and we went to considerable trouble to prepare to manufacture it. Since then we have not heard a word as to quantity or dimensions. He is one of those who are *good* when necessity forces them to work, and good for nothing when necessity ceases. It will do him good to receive a lecture from me on the subject of his neglects. I will write to him stating the dissatisfaction of the President U.S.[4]

Thus for your letter of the 21st. now for that of the 29th.

1.) I had no doubt of our finding the old eliptical wall to be awkwardly adapted to the new work. There can be no better means adopted to eke it out, than those you propose, as I evidently find, on inspection of the plan, on which I have laid down the Walls, as formerly described and 529 measured by You. As to small slices you judge rightly. They are weak and worse than Corbeling.

2. I have now before me the Sections you wish me to examine. Unless your Copy differs from mine, you will find in the Section E. and W. No. II looking Northward that part which has this shape drawn to be arched exactly as you propose with only this difference that I have not proposed to carry up piers in the places *X* but have sprung the dotted arches from the solid Wall, in order to save the trouble of car-rying up piers; the arches are 10.10 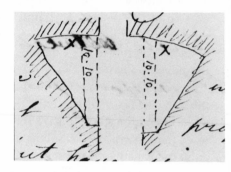 inches span. These arches spring from the lower springing line, and carry a 9.8 foot barrel arch sprung the other way from the upper springing line, as in the long passage.

In the same situation at the other end of the passage I proposed a groin, but your method will certainly be less expensive and therefore preferable.

4. It was my intention to have carried the footing across the 8 f. 8 opening to the 10 f. 6 i. pier in the angle, and to have placed the reversed arch upon this footing. But in consequence of your suggestion, I have again considered this part of the work, and conclude, that as the re-versed arches are of use principally to give an extent of foundation to the small piers in the Center in order to prevent their settlement under the weight of the arches below and the Columns above, and as the solid work in this Cellar story in the space between the second and third Columns from the Pilaster is by its bond equal in effect to a Counter arch—the Counter arch from the 10 f. 6 i. pier maybe safely omitted as you propose.

5. The manner in which you have set out the Staircase will I fear make the Gallery doors too small for if, in the rough, they are only 3 feet open, they will finish only 2 f. 9 i. I should not at all find my optics offended by seeing the door wider than the Niche opposite to it. Its finishing, and every part of its detail and use will be different; Suppose therefore we still make it 3 f. 6 i. which will give us a good roomy door of 3 f. 3 i. opening.[5]

6. In Philadelphia there is the same complaint as to want of hands as

in Washington. However I could from hence and from Delaware send you half a dozen, if another part of your letter did not apprize me that you[r] means of payment are considerably decreasing. There is something [in] false oeconomy that not only defeats itself, but is certain to produce the effect of extravagant profusion. As soon as I can again carry my family home to Newcastle, which will now be in 8 or 10 days, I shall pay you a visit. I am clearly of opinion that the external walls should be kept back as much as possible. But I know the President thinks otherwise. In this instance I am more astonished at his perseverance in wrong, than ever before. I must still try to move him.

I will write to you again in the course of a few days when you shall receive the sections and other deficient plans. Yesterday I communicated to Mrs. Latrobe the loss she has suffered. We are all much distressed, but time is a certain cure for affliction. I have written to you a long and you will think a tedious letter. But I wish you always to be Master of my reasons as well as of my wishes. Yrs. affecty.

B. H. Latrobe

ALS: John H. B. Latrobe Papers, Library of Congress (175/C6). Addressed to Lenthall in Washington. Endorsed as received 8 August and answered 17 August.

1. Andrea Palladio (1508–80), Italian Renaissance architect, wrote the vastly influential *I Quattro Libri dell'Architettura* (Venice, 1570), which was translated into English (*Four Books of Architecture*) in 1715. Adolf K. Placzek described Palladianism as "the conviction, first of all, that a universally applicable vocabulary of architectural forms is both desirable and possible; secondly, that such a vocabulary had been developed by the ancient Romans (Palladio's knowledge of Greek architecture was scant), and thirdly, that a careful study and judicious use of these forms will result in Beauty. This Beauty, according to the Palladians, is therefore not only derived from ideal forms and their harmony; it is also rooted in historical correctness; and it includes the most practical, reasonable solution of the specific problem on hand." Palladio, *The Four Books of Architecture*, ed. Adolf K. Placzek (New York, 1965 [orig. publ. 1738]), pp. v–vi.

With the discovery of varied and evolving orders in Greek architecture, Palladian notions about the static universality of the orders were thrown into serious question. BHL, in his view that classical proportions were arbitrary, seems in accord with the premises of Claude Perrault, who, in his late seventeenth-century commentaries on Vitruvius and other writings had already challenged this idealism. Perrault distinguished an intrinsic beauty, especially of materials and workmanship, from a customary beauty of forms, once arbitrary, but elevated by their long association with such intrinsic qualities. This approach challenged many of the more transcendent sanctions attached to the orders, and its relativism has been recognized as a particularly modern view. Joseph Rykwert, *The First Moderns: The Architects of the Eighteenth Century* (Cambridge, Mass., and London, 1980), chap. 2, esp. pp. 37ff.

2. Greek columns did in fact have subtly swelling curves in the vertical profiles of their shafts, but this feature, entasis, was not nearly as pronounced in the most prominent buildings of fifth-century B.C. Athens as it was according to Palladio's formula. A. W. Lawrence, *Greek Architecture,* 2d ed. (Hammondsworth, England, and Baltimore, 1967), pp. 170–71; Palladio, *Four Books of Architecture,* p. 12.

In Greek architecture an anta is distinct from a pilaster, typically being used on a wall that adjoins a porch or a colonnade. It is not usually capped by a full-fledged capital drawn from one of the conventional orders.

3. The First Bank of the United States, the first important building in America to be faced entirely in marble, was designed by Samuel Blodget and built in Philadelphia in 1795–97. For BHL's initial reaction to the Bank of the U.S. in 1798, see BHL, *Journals,* 2 : 373.

4. Benjamin King, who came from Carron, Scotland, a village well known for its extensive iron works, worked for BHL on the Capitol and at the Washington Navy Yard. For BHL's more extensive description of King, see BHL, *Journals,* 3 : 67–69. BHL wrote King a somewhat chiding letter requesting him to complete his work on the President's House, especially on the water closet. BHL to King, 5 Aug. 1804, LB (34/C4).

5. The following note, apparently in Lenthall's hand, appears at this point in the received copy: "N.B. This has been misunderstood, the Door has been allowed to be 3.6 wide."

TO WILLIAM COOCH

Philadelphia Augt. 5th. 1804

Dear Sir

The extreme fatigue which I had undergone during my stay in the neighborhood of the feeder, and the unpleasant intelligence I have had to communicate to my family on my return, so deranged me, that I could not sit down till this day to perform my promise of giving you a full account of the actual state of the Works and of the directions and super-intendance which may be usefull during my absence. I will now endeav-or to comply with your wishes in the clearest manner possible.

1.) The experience of the fresh of last Tuesday (the 31st. July) had appeared to point out the necessity of constructing the Eastern abutment of the Aqueduct immediately, as a protection to the very important and expensive embankment. The drawings of this work are in the hands of Mr. DeMun,[1] if he has not already delivered them to Mr. Vickers. In the present instance it will be necessary to request Mr. Vickers to set his Men immediately to work to dress the stones requisite for this part of the work according to the drawing. Mr. Strickland[2] will probably have to make moulds for the stones of the pier head of the butment, which differ so far

 from those of the middle piers as to run out parallel with [the] side of the Aqueduct, instead of forming a point. A Mould will also be wanted for the coping of this projecting part, see the drawing, as also for the upper course, below the springing line, upon which the Askew-back must be roughly cut. If this Abutment be carried up this season, the remainder of the Aqueduct may, if the Committee think proper, be postponed till next spring.

The bridge must by this time be perfectly finished, and ready to receive the Earth.[3] It is of great importance that the towing paths South of the Bridge should be cleared and properly trimmed as the water collected on the narrow Offset now left runs into the Canal and gullies the banks. This Earth was always in part intended to make the road over the Bridge. The quantity required will be chiefly for the lower side. It will not be large. What afterwards remains will make the Canal across the Aqueduct.

The second Culvert must about this time be so far finished as to admit of carrying the Canal across it. The Trunk which has been put through the bank at the first Culvert is too high to discharge all the water from the Canal. I much wish that the Trunk which formerly passed through the stank across the Canal at the first Culvert may be laid through the bank at the second, so that the top of the Valve may be level with the bottom of the Canal. It will be some time before we can connect this part of the work with the upper Canal, and we may frequently have occasion to fill and discharge it.

I have laid out the work for Mr. Cochran a considerable distance into the Wood of Mccaslin and [James] Springer. I have also wished him to employ a detachment of his Men in the wood at the place where a Quarry has formerly been opened, and have instructed DeMun and Strickland[4] to set out this part of the work and fix his Slopeboards for him. My object is to procure Stone for the five succeeding Culverts, the last of which will be in Gilpin's field East of the Lancaster road.[5] This part of the work cannot be well delayed. Mr. Strickland[6] fully knows my intentions. I will only repeat, that under the Quarry, and along the steep bank the Center of the Canal must be in 6 ft. digging.

Cochran's contract ends within the wood at a run over which is a Culvert, and there Clegg and Binnerman's begins. They have both worked under Mr. Weston, and therefore ought to understand their business. But I have not yet seen them at work, and DeMun should look

533

sharp after them, especially as to the depth and manner of their puddling in their low Ground next to the Run:[7] He must see that they clear away all roots and rubbish from the bottom of their puddle gutter, and especially that they dig below the Gravel which I believe abounds at that place. Their is one principle in the construction of this feeder of which we should never lose sight, its *Water-tightness*. We shall not have so much water as to afford to lose any of it, and no labor is so dreadful, and vexatious, as the breaking up of a Canal to search for, and repair leaks. They often are to be found a very considerable distance from the place at which they break out; and no expense or care can well be too great in the first instance which will ensure against them.

Watson begins his work in the Maple swamp. My uneasiness lest his work should not be water tight is extreme. The bottom of the Maple swamp is a bed of coarse gravel. The puddle Gutters must be dug through it into sound Clay, and all the old Stumps and Roots be carefully removed. Watson is a clever fellow, but endeavors to push on so rapidly as to require attention to his proceedings.

After Watson comes Pollock, whose cut is of that kind in which he cannot do wrong unless he by bad management, injures himself.

Sands who next succeeds, is so pushing a Man that in his puddling on each side of the Culvert he will require much attention.[8] I believe however that he has already finished the greatest part of the work that requires puddling before the Culvert shall be constructed. He ought, if he has not yet done it, to finish all that part of his work which lies East towards Randle and Cocksy's contract, throw a stank across the head, and fill it with Water. This will then be a reservoir for Randle in his puddling across the low Ground, without which he absolutely cannot proceed. In coming out of the Wood there is a turn which Sands has managed badly. About a Yard is required to be cut out on the North Bank: for at every turn the Canal should be a little wider. The part marked thus  must be cut off to a good sweep. By to-morrows post I will continue these remarks. I fear I may be too late to send this today unless I conclude.[9]

Believe me with the sincerest respects Yours faithfully

B. H. Latrobe

Polygraph Copy: LB (34/C8). Addressed to Cooch in Delaware.

1. Three BHL drawings (plan, elevation, and section) of the Elk River aqueduct are in the Robert Brooke Papers, New York Public Library (290/A1).

Lewis (or Louis) DeMun, a native of Santo Domingo, received a military education in France, served briefly in the royalist cause during the French Revolution, fled to Santo Domingo, and then came to the United States, where he attended St. Mary's College in Baltimore. He entered BHL's office as a pupil (c. 1802–03) and worked on a variety of the engineer's projects, including the C & D Canal, the Washington Navy Yard, the U.S. Capitol, and the Baltimore Cathedral. On the C & D he acted as draftsman, surveyor, and courier. He made a number of trips back and forth to Wilmington, where the company funds were kept, to procure money for the contractors. BHL very much admired DeMun's character; in 1805 he wrote his brother, Auguste: "In this money getting country, a friend who does not consider it the object of human existence to scrape dollars together, and who has a heart as well as a pocket, is an invaluable companion to one, whose nature, education, and habits have also taught him a different doctrine. Such a one is your brother Lewis." In April 1806 BHL recommended DeMun to Secretary of the Treasury Albert Gallatin, who needed an engineer to survey the coast of the Territory of Orleans (now Louisiana). DeMun received the appointment. By 1808 he had gone to Cuba, where his brothers were living, but by June 1809 he was back in Philadelphia and in 1812 was residing in Upper Louisiana. In 1816 he was "engaged in a great Land concern West of the Mississippi." BHL to Auguste DeMun, 16 Mar. 1804, 8 Apr. 1805, BHL to Francisco Sarmiento, 21 Aug. 1808, and BHL to William Eustis, 12 July 1812, all in LB (30/C5, 39/B9, 65/F9, 100/F7); BHL to Lewis DeMun, 29 Apr. 1806, 21 Aug. 1808, 21 June 1809, all in BHL, *Correspondence*, 2; BHL to James Madison, 8 Apr. 1816, in BHL, *Correspondence*, 3; C & D Committee of Works Journal, 15 Jan. 1805; Hamlin, *Latrobe*, pp. 214–15; *ASP. Commerce and Navigation*, 1 : 840–42.

2. John Strickland.

3. This masonry road bridge built by Vickers a few hundred feet south of the aqueduct site is standing today (see BHL, *Engineering Drawings*, p. 17). It is made of roughly hewn stone in a segmental arch of 15-foot span across the canal with stone abutments on either side. Little remains now of the original roadway of packed earth. BHL, *Engineering Drawings*, pp. 15–16.

4. William Strickland.

5. John Gilpin (1765–1808), wealthy Maryland farmer and cousin of Joshua Gilpin, was elected to the C & D board of directors in 1805 and assisted in supervising the construction of the feeder that year. BHL to Isaac Hazlehurst, 15 Sept. 1805, in BHL, *Correspondence*, 2; Gray, "Early History of C & D," p. 242; Gilpin genealogical charts, Historical Society of Pennsylvania, Philadelphia; Mary Hollingsworth Jamar, comp., *Hollingsworth Family and Collateral Lines of Cooch-Gilpin-Jamar-Mackall-Morris-Stewart* (Philadelphia, 1944), p. 33.

6. John Strickland.

7. BHL later referred to Clegg and Binnerman as "men of unexceptionable character." BHL, C & D Report, 1 Oct. 1804 (176/B1).

8. Hugh Sands, "a very clever fellow, who worked with Weston 3 Years," was "a man of considerable property, who had also executed large contracts on the turnpike roads near Philadelphia." Sands was occasionally absent from the feeder and therefore BHL "employed Jo. Callaghan and Geo. Martin, remarkably steady and quiet men, as foremen." BHL to Joshua Gilpin, 28 May 1804, LB (32/F10); BHL, C & D Report, 1 Oct. 1804.

9. On 10 August BHL wrote Cooch (LB; 34/D5) that MEL's illness prevented him from writing further on the state of the works, but that he hoped to see him on 13 or 14

August. BHL, however, did not arrive in Delaware until 18 August. BHL to John Strickland, 18 Aug. 1804, LB (34/E10).

TO HENRY S. B. LATROBE

Philadelphia Augt. 6th. 1804

My dear Son

Your letter of the Year 1804, for you date your letters by Years, not by days as other people do, gave me in some respects much pleasure. The expression of your feelings on the severe loss we all have suffered is that of a grateful heart; and no one has more cause of gratitude than yourself.

In other respects however I have several observations to make to you. First, your letter is so badly written, that I could hardly read it; it is absolutely a string of blots from beginning to end. This cannot possibly be necessary. Mr. Dubourg will surely supply you with good pens, and, when you chuse, you can write as good a hand as any boy of your age. If my hearing from you depends upon your writing full gallop and in the hurrying slovenly stile of your letter of the Year 1804 I have nothing further to say. I would rather you wrote badly than not at all, but I think your own pride will prevent your sending me such another letter, when you can do so much better.

In the next place, I am sincerely sorry that you misunderstood my last letter as to the further Subscription of five dollars, *beyond the ten,* to your Ball alley, by supposing that I meant them as a present to You.[1] My intention was to add five dollars to my first Subscription of ten Dollars, if it should be found that the first subscription was not sufficient. You will have to bear this disappointment and for a reason with which you yourself have furnished me. You must allow that your weekly allowance of a quarter of a dollar is sufficient for all your traffic in cakes and apples, upon a moderate scale. It is more than you have ever been allowed before. But you say that the Shoeblacks consume it. I am sorry that you, or any of your Schoolfellows should submit to such an imposition. If these Negro boys belong to the house, they are no doubt both clothed and fed by the institution; and any contribution they may levy on the scholars goes to enable them to buy cakes &c. and to *gamble* at pitch and toss. If they do you any little services, a fivepenny bit once in two or three weeks would be a very proper gratuity to them and from 60, or 80 boys would indeed be a large revenue. But it is shameful to you and to the School if you permit them to make any large deduction from your weekly allowance. You ought rather to clean your own shoes, as I did daily, when I was at College, as well as my Schoolfellows, many of whom were of noble families. When I see you I must further enquire into this matter, and if necessary speak to Mr. Dubourg, on the subject. You must therefore, my dear Henry, make your arrangements of finance before your vacation, without calculating on any extraordinary revenue for the present, and when you come home in about a week or ten days we will talk the subject over with your mother.

Your dear Mother thanks you for your letters. She is not at present able to answer them, and you must continue to write to her, till her health and spirits will permit her to write in return. I expect to be in Newcastle within a week from hence. I am not afraid to trust you to come thither by the packet alone. You will apply to your uncle Andrew to dispatch you to whom I shall write on the subject.

If your uniform is made bring it with you that your Mother may see you in all your paraphernalia of cravat and the other apparatus.[2]

Your affectionate father

B. Henry Latrobe B.

Polygraph Copy: LB (34/C14). Addressed to Henry in Baltimore.

1. Alley ball, long popular at St. Mary's, was an American version of the French game, "boule." Resembling English lawn bowling or Italian boccie, it was played in an alley with a large wooden ball and several smaller wooden balls.

2. After receiving another letter from Henry on 10 August, BHL wrote his son: "Your present epistle is written so much better and does you altogether so much credit, that I am almost sorry that I treated you a little severely about your last." BHL to Henry S. B. Latrobe, 11 Aug. 1804, LB (34/D8).

TO ERICK BOLLMANN

Philadelphia, Augt. 14th. 1804.

Dear Sir,

I received your kind letter of the 11th. yesterday. It is the first which has reached me since our last meeting at Mr. Jones's in Market street. I am therefore entirely ignorant of the request contained in yours, writ- 537 ten, as you say, about a month ago. This letter must be either at Mr. Hazlehurst's counting house at Newcastle or at Washington, if it has arrived at all. You may be fully assured that had I received it, I should have punctually answered it. But so ignorant have I been, even of your residence, that I supposed you, on information I received a fortnight ago, to have been at Lancaster.

Since I last saw you several events have occurred, which have much embarassed and distressed me. On the 20th. May Mr. Robert Hazlehurst died. Tho' his life could no longer be hoped or wished for under the circumstances of his case, the remembrance of his former conduct, talents, and warm affections contributed to afflict his family exceedingly. About the middle of June I brought my family to Philadelphia, in expectation of returning to Delaware in a Month or 6 weeks at most. But I had miscalculated, and I shall only return tomorrow. On the 11th July, at the moment, when Mrs. L. hourly expected to be put to bed, her Mother died, after an illness of only 18 hours. Her disorder was a cholic followed by an inflammation, and subsequent mortification of the bowels. Mr. Hazlehurst was in town, and did not arrive at Cloverhill till after her death. As difficult as was the task, it was necessary to conceal from Mrs. L. the death of her mother as long as possible, and though she has long believed her dangerously ill she has known of her death only a few days. During these events, I have been alternately here, in Delaware, and at Washington. On the 17th. July my wife was brought to bed of a little Girl whom we have named Juliana Elisabeth, and who has been remarkably healthy since her birth, notwithstanding the most sickly season for children ever known, and the very bad effect of her family distresses on the health of her mother. Among the numerous deaths among the Children of my acquaintance, I will here mention that Mr. S. Mifflin has lost his youngest child, and that his eldest, Charles is now dangerously ill.[1]

You can easily imagine that during all this time, hurried about by my business and occupied at home with the most unpleasant family occurences, and for a long time keeping up a system of deception when it was difficult and almost impossible to deceive, or to account to my wife for the total silence and absence of her friends, my time has not been pleasantly spent. And indeed from the very nature of my profession, ill suited to the regularity and quiet of domestic comfort, I ought, rationally, to give up for life all hopes of ever arriving at a state of existence in which I can enjoy *leisure,* even of a few hours a day with regular certainty, or pursue my plan of employment for my individual gratification or amusement. This whole Year has to me been a series of disappointments. I bought a few Acres on the Summit of Ironhill a situation healthy, romantic, and in the very center of my business. 500 Dollars would have added, two or three rooms to a Log house already built. I even collected materials. But my good father-in-law violently opposed the idea of the expense, and *the total seclusion from society*, which, he predicted, would attend my scheme; and as the strongest argument against it, he gave us one of the best houses in Wilmington, which belongs to him, to live in rent free. The house is out of repair, and though he has given me 200$ towards repairing it, the expense of a new roof, &c. &c. will be nearly equal to my proposed improvements on Ironhill. But what is worse, I shall thus have my family at the distance of 19 Miles from my business, I shall see them seldom, and live half my life at a tavern. At Ironhill, uninterrupted by that nuisance called society, I should have been able to dispatch all my business in a few hours of the morning, and have devoted the rest of my time to improving study. And yet it was impossible for me to persevere in my own plan, so much more rational, oeconomical, and agreeable. Even my wife who entered with enthusiasm into my ideas, had no powers to persuade her father to consent to the arrangement. He persisted in pleading the necessity of my living in a situation and style to call for the respect from the public which is always paid to apparent or real independence as to property. And as a man of the world he perhaps reasons right. To obtain it I must now reside in the midst of the gossip of a small town, laboring with out satisfaction, and always in a hurry when from home, and when in Wilmington, watched by a director of the Company,[2] who never thinks that I can labor enough.[3]

I have now fully answered your kind enquiries after myself, and have filled a sheet with that sort of Egotism with which friendship cannot be offended. In your situation of which you have given me an account, I feel myself exceedingly interested. By a Mr. Vallcourt of Natchez who has been here, I had heard that your connection with Tarascon and OHara had not succeeded, and indeed that those Gentlemen have no confidence in *Steam Engines*.[4] And yet from all I have learned, not only from you who may be supposed to be interested, but from many others, no prospect of certain gain from the employment of moderate capital appears fairer than an Establishment of the kind you propose. I have given lately a letter of recommendation to Mr. Vallcourt to Mr. Roosevelt.[5] His head is full of Steam boats. He has got into the hands of Oliver   539

Evans. I have discouraged all his sanguine prospects and if Roosevelt talks candidly to him on the subject of steamboats he will probably think of other employment for his capital.

As to Roosevelt, a fatality does certainly appear to attend him. Not having received Your last letter, I do not understand that part of your present one which relates to the English scheme. I have not heard a word of the Sawmill for two Years. Does it still exist? Has Roosevelt any share in it? When I saw him last, he evidently appeared to have given up his hopes of personal advantage from it.

The Rolling works are still going on and profitably if the Corporation pays up their charge of maintenance. But without that they are a losing concern, *as yet.* I have not been there since my last arrival in town.

If you possessed a mind capable of enjoying the present without looking to the future I should believe you to be now happier than you have been for the last two Years. And even with your future views, I sincerely hope you are so. At all events what you actually enjoy, is *positive enjoyment.* It's very calm and repose appears to me, who have so long lived in *medio tempestatum, quasi navis, agitata, conturbata, maximis procellis,* (the words of a Mass by Hasse)[6] so enviable, as to balance every thing. In a few Months more, I shall now have freed myself in a great degree from all encumbrances of former engagements. I should be glad to hear from you soon as to the subject of your lost correspondence. Believe me in the mean time very sincerely Yours

B. Henry Latrobe.

You wish my letter to be written with a goose pen. Is there a greater goose, or a *flightier* Goose than is in some respects the amiable and indefatigable Polygraphist Peale.

Polygraph Copy: LB (34/E3). Addressed to Bollmann on Long Island, in care of Nicholas J. Roosevelt, N.Y.

1. Charles apparently died within the year for a new son born on 19 July 1805 was named Charles. *PMHB* 54 (1930):80.
2. Joseph Tatnall, C & D Canal Company president.
3. In the fall of 1804, BHL had the necessary carpentry work done on his Iron Hill house and the following summer he and his family resided there. C & D Committee of Works Journal, 10 Dec. 1804, 9 Jan. 1805; BHL to Christian Ignatius Latrobe, 3 Nov. 1805, in BHL, *Correspondence,* 2.
4. Louis Valcourt of Natchez had heard of Oliver Evans's steam engine and steamboat plans, and came east to purchase an engine while a partner built a boat. Evans sent the engine to New Orleans, but the boat (which was to be floated to New Orleans) was stranded

at Natchez by a sudden fall of the Mississippi's level. The engine was then sold to William Donaldson of New Orleans who installed it in a sawmill. Patrick N. I. Elisha [Oliver Evans], *Patent Right Oppression Exposed; or Knavery Detected* (Philadelphia, 1813), pp. 170–72.

Louis Anastasius Tarascon, who emigrated from France in 1794, and his brother John A. Tarascon, Jr., were Philadelphia merchants interested in opening up the Ohio-Mississippi river navigation to direct trade between Pittsburgh and the West Indies and Europe. Both men, in partnership with James Berthoud (d. 1819), were involved in a Pittsburgh boat-building business, John A. Tarascon Brothers, James Berthoud & Co., established about 1801–02. Tarascon, Jr., and Berthoud later promoted the development of Shippingport, Ky. Tarascon, Jr., and James Berthoud & Co., *An Address to the Citizens of Philadelphia on the Great Advantages which Arise from the Trade of the Western Country to the State of Pennsylvania at Large, and to the City of Philadelphia in Particular* (Philadelphia, 1806); Henry McMurtrie, *Sketches of Louisville and Its Environs* (Louisville, Ky., 1969 [orig. publ. 1819]), p. 158; Henry Simpson, *The Lives of Eminent Philadelphians, Now Deceased* (Philadelphia, 1859), pp. 911–12; Leland D. Baldwin, *Pittsburgh: The Story of a City* (Pittsburgh, 1937), p. 131.

OHara is probably James O'Hara (1752–1819), a prominent Pittsburgh businessman, who was engaged in, among many concerns, ocean-going trading vessels, owning one in 1796 and building one at his shipyard on the Monongahela River at least as early as 1805. For more on O'Hara, who later became a friend and associate of BHL in Pittsburgh, see BHL, *Correspondence*, 3. Florence C. McLaughlin, "Margaret Townsend Scully's Trunk," *Western Pennsylvania Historical Magazine* 53 (1970):371–72.

5. In the letter, BHL described Valcourt as "a Gentleman of merit in every point of View." BHL to Nicholas J. Roosevelt, 13 Aug. 1804, LB (34/D13).

6. Trans.: In the midst of storms, like a ship, agitated, disturbed, by greatest gusts. John Adolph Hasse (1699–1783), German composer, is noted primarily for his fifty-six operas, although he also wrote oratories, masses, and instrumental music.

TO THADDEUS O'HARA

Newcastle, Septr. 2d. 1804.

Sir,[1]

I have very lately received yours of the 28th. July by Mr. Jo. Aull, having been from home for the last two Months.[2] Your former letter, I answered verbally to Mr. Smallman, stating to him what I now take the liberty to repeat.[3]

The business of the Canal Company is carried on by very few Officers, A Clerk of the Works, who is a perfect surveyor and accountant, two other Clerks who must be good Draftsmen, and the Master Carpenter, Mason, and Smith.[4] These are the only appointment over which I have the smallest influence, and as you do not profess any of the Arts necessary to fill them, you would, no doubt feel uneasy and at a loss even

541

if you were in one of these situations. The execution of the digging &c. &c. is performed by persons qualified by long experience in these kind of works, from whom security is expected for the due performance of their Contracts. It is also necessary that they should per[form] a considerable quantity of work before they become entitled to receive any money, thus leaving a part of their earnings as security in the hands of the Company.

From what I have thus candidly stated, it must be evident to you, that with the sincerest dispositions to serve you, I want the power. The case would be otherwise if our work were performed by day Laborers. A Number of Superintendants would then be required, in whom fidelity and a knowledge of accounts would be the necessary qualifications, and nothing would have given me more pleasure than to have taken so respectable a Man as yourself into the employment. I regret that there is not now an opportunity of this kind likely to arise. I am with respect Yours

B. H. Latrobe

Polygraph Copy: LB (35/A5). Addressed to O'Hara in care of James Smallman, Philadelphia.

1. Thaddeus O'Hara was a teacher in Philadelphia from 1802 to 1805.
2. O'Hara to BHL, 28 July 1804, C & D Canal Company Papers (175/B8). John Aull was BHL's landlord in New Castle.
3. O'Hara had been introduced to BHL by Smallman. O'Hara to BHL, 28 July 1804.
4. The master smith was Peter Bath, a Philadelphia blacksmith. BHL to Bath, 1 May, 22 May 1804, both in LB (31/G8, 32/E8); C & D Survey Committee Minutes, 10 May 1804.

TO JOSHUA GILPIN

Newcastle, Septr. 9th. 1804.

Dear Sir,

I have written to you two long letters on the progress of the feeder in which I have entered into considerable detail.[1] I hope that you have received both, together with a parcel of drawings by the packet. About the latter I am anxious, because your good opinion of them gave them a value, otherwise, I hope *you*, as well as myself, may safely consider our correspondence to be upon terms not requiring the regular ceremony of

542

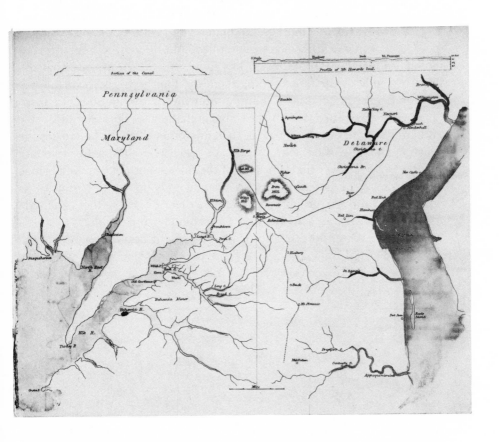

Map 4. Vicinity of the Chesapeake and Delaware Canal, showing canal and
feeder route adopted in 1804, from Joshua Gilpin, *A Memoir on the Rise, Progress,
and Present State of the Chesapeake and Delaware Canal, Accompanied with Original
Documents and Maps* (Washington, D.C., 1821).

alternate letters. I at least write with a view only to your information and my own gratification in corresponding with you.

My last letter carried me to the Lancaster road. Since it was written I have found it necessary to condemn the puddling of one of the Contractors for 50 Yards in length and to oblige him to cut it out and repuddle it. The readiness with which he complied, and the perfect repair he has made, induced me to suppress his name. In a few days, we shall fill nearly a mile of canal, extending from the Lancaster road Northward. At the Lancaster road itself, I am now laying the foundations of a turning bridge to be thrown over the Canal at that place. This kind of Bridge is better adapted to the situation than any other. The Canal crosses the road at an angle of 60 degrees, and at a place where the natural surface of the Earth is lower than the level of the towing path. An arched bridge would therefore be extremely disadvantageous both on account of its great rise, and of the obliquity of the situation. Below the Canal is a Valley, which after a heavy rain is absolutely impassable, so large a Quantity of Water descends from a large flat and swampy country to the Eastward called Cat's Swamp. At some period, not far distant, a bridge must be erected over this Valley. When this is done an arched bridge may also be thrown across the Canal.

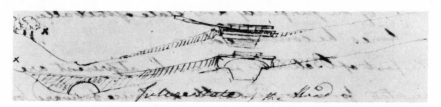

The road at X is at present so steep as to require lowering from the summit 12 or 13 feet. When this is done, there will be an ample supply of Earth for raising the road on the opposite side.

It will not I think be necessary to put up the Swing bridge untill the feeder becomes navigable and therefore, as there is plenty of timber, fit for no other purpose on the company's Land adjoining, it will be best to throw a temporary bridge of logs over the Canal a little to the South, where the ground is higher and thus save for a few years the wear and tear of the more expensive Swing bridge.

From the Lancaster road across Mr. Gilpin's Land the Canal is in very great forwardness as far as the foot of Bellhill. In this place two Culverts are necessary, one of one Arch to carry off the Wash of the hill and of a Valley coming from the North, the other of two Arches to discharge the waters of Cat's swamp, the force and quantity of which after a heavy Gust, are incredible, if the perfectly dry state of the Valley at all other times be considered.

At the foot of Bellhill our works at present are interrupted for a considerable distance forward. From the foot of the Hill to the Summit the Land belonging to Mr. Basil Cunningham. The Company purchase it for 30 Dollars per Acre, and 75 Dollars for the Timber. Over the Summit of the hill passes the road to Newark and Christiana bridge from Elkton. The Canal crosses the road obliquely where the cutting will be about 26 feet deep, so that the heighth of the bridge will be considerable. Thence the small farm of Chr. Thomas descends the hill to its foot, where other Land of Mr. Gilpin, abounding in the most beautiful springs, occupies the Valley. By an exchange of a triangle which is cut off with Christian Thomas, and a payment of 40 Dollars for his growing crop all difficulty of obtaining his land is removed. On the other side of the Valley comes Gachot. A few Years ago he bought his farm of 365 Acres for £725 (1966$), or for 5$.33 ct. per Acre. He asks of the Company £100 per Acre for about 8 Acres, half of which is in good Clover, and tolerably good Meadow, the rest in rocky and uncultivated cripple. A Jury must determine between us. Beyond Gachot Thos. Cunningham's Land extends to the Post road, and Richd. Updegroves thence to the Maryland line. Both these Gentlemen have sold their Land to the Company for 30$. per Acre. Thos. Cunningham receives besides 100$. in lieu of a bridge, as his farm is completely intersected for half a mile in length. Joseph Pollock has already been at work for about a week on the terms of his former Contract on Richard Updegroves Land South of the postroad, and William Watson will begin tomorrow on Cunningham's Land North of the road.[2]

I have now once more to explore and accurately determine the course of the feeder from the ridge to the Reservoir, a distance of about a Mile. This will be the work of the next fortnight.

The work we have done is considerable, but I do not for a moment hesitate to say, that had we only a *tolerable* command of funds, we should have already completed the Work as far as the Maryland line, excepting only across Gachot's land. Nor can there be any doubt of the perfect completion of the work of the feeder by Christmas if we can possibly command 4 or 5000 dollars now, and from 1.500 to 1.800 Dollars per week afterwards. Mr. Brooke who is gone to Philadelphia, and whose talents and character will be invaluable to the Company, will save me the unpleasant statement of our most necessitous and almost disgraceful situation. The failure of the West butment of the Schuylkill bridge which I have no doubt is greatly exaggerated, has called Vickers to Philadelphia. He will also say something to you on the subject of finance. He has not yet received any thing on account of his wages, and I have ventured to draw upon you in his favor for 250$., and also for 80 Dollars to be distributed to the families of those of our Masons who are under contract to remain till the work is finished, and who we cannot therefore permit to suffer. Besides they are first rate workmen and we should find it very difficult to replace them.

Next week I hope to remove to Wilmington. I was in hopes of seeing you at the works before now. Pray let me know when I may expect that pleasure. I shall write to you again next Sunday, unless I see you before that time.

Give our best respects to Mrs. Gilpin, and believe me very sincerely Yrs.

B. H. Latrobe

Polygraph Copy: LB (35/A13). Addressed to Gilpin in Philadelphia. On the retained copy BHL noted: "Enclosed two drafts in favor of Thos. Vickers for 80$, and 250$."

  1. BHL to Gilpin, 26 Aug., 2 Sept. 1804, both in LB (34/G7, 35/A8).
  2. More than two weeks later BHL reported to Kensey Johns that Basil and Thomas Cunningham and Richard Updegrove had not yet been paid for their land and that they were growing impatient. In addition to the purchase price of the lands, the C & D company also had to pay for the crops growing on them. When the company officials and the farmers disagreed on the value of the crop, arbiters were appointed to settle the matter. BHL felt that the arbiters' decision that Updegrove's corn and fodder were worth $50 was too high: "It is so generally supposed by adequate judges that no more than 20$ would have been given between individuals for the same crop, that I have avoided entering upon Cunningham's corn, although it would be much more convenient to have been now at work in the field." BHL to Johns, 26 Sept. 1804, LB (35/C10); Arbitration between C & D Canal Company and Richard Updegrove, 19 Sept. 1804, Salem County Historical Society, Salem, N.J.

TO WILLIAM DU BOURG

Newcastle, Septr. 11th. 1804

Reverend Sir,

The time of the vacation of your college being nearly expired, I take 546 the liberty to consult you on the course of studies on which my Son

Henry ought to enter for the ensuing Year. He arrived at Elkton with a violent Hooping cough, so that it was impossible for us to receive him into our family but at the risk of the life of his youngest sister, who is only 2 Months old. He has spent the vacation therefore in our neighborhood with two or three of our friends living at a distance from each other, and the constant change of air, and proper medecines have nearly restored him. This circumstance, however, has prevented my becoming at all acquainted with the progress he has made under your care. I have been unusually pressed by business, and have only seen him occasionally. I am therefore wholly unable to advise or propose any thing on the subject of his future studies. Nor have I by me the prospectus published by you sometime ago my papers having been already conveyed to Wilmington, [to] which I am myself going to live.

I will [here][1] beg leave to offer to you some general remarks and should you find that my ideas can be useful in giving a direction to his occupations at School, suited to his talents and future prospects, I shall be happy.

There are many reasons which induce me to propose bringing Henry up to the practice of the Law. It may be called the profession which governs this country, but independently of views of a political tendency, the situation of his maternal property will render this study peculiarly useful to him. With this view the study of Languages and of polite literature ought perhaps to be his principal object.

But although I could wish his studies to have this direction, I do not think that his natural disposition would make him a Lawyer. He would rather I believe become acquainted with *things* than with *words*. I could therefore with pleasure see a trial of his talents in Mathematics attempted. I am ignorant at what age you usually begin this Study with your pupils. It is generally one of the last in American schools. I think it might advantageously be commenced more early. I remember that, getting hold of a few plain instructions at 8 Years of age, I made myself a tolerable geometrician about that period; and at 12 I was almost Master of the *Mathesis pura,* having studied it from an irresistible propensity, and with very little help.

Those parts of Your instruction which may be called accomplishments, and for which a separate entrance is to be paid, are I think Music, Dancing, Drawing, but I forget whether the German or Spanish language are included. You will please to judge whether he ought now to study either of those languages, and act accordingly. Music and Drawing   547 are studies which may be begun at any time, and untill I can have the pleasure to see You, I am willing that he should still postpone them. But on many accounts I wish him to be taught Dancing. My principal reason is his extreme bodily inactivity, which whether it arise from bad habit, or be constitutional has within the last 12 Months grown upon him exceedingly, and threatens to ruin his health.

To this subject permit me to request your kind attention. When with us in June last, he spent great part of his time, when he could escape, on the bed, and those of our friends with whom he has lately spent his time, complain, that it is impossible to make him take any exercise. With a view to correct this evil, I subscribed for him with great pleasure to the erection of the Ball Alley, and I hope he will enter into its amusements with ardor.

If you will have the goodness to transmit to me an account of such expenses as arise out of my Son's additional instruction, you will oblige me, and when I have the pleasure to see You, which will now, I hope, be in the course of 10 days, I will discharge them.

As much as you must be troubled with the long letters dictated by parental anxiety, you will I am sure believe me, when with the utmost sincerity I beg you to believe that the fullest confidence in your talents, your principles and Your virtues, render me perfectly happy under every treatment and instruction You may give to my Son. I am with the truest esteem Yours faithfully

B. H. Latrobe

Polygraph Copy: LB (35/B12). Addressed to Du Bourg in Baltimore.

1. BHL inadvertently wrote "have" here.

FROM THOMAS JEFFERSON

Washington Oct. 5. 04.

Dear Sir

I returned here on the 30th. Ult. and confess myself much disappointed in the progress of the Capitol. Mr. Lenthall urges the general sickness among his hands as the cause, and from my entire confidence in his diligence I have no doubt as much has been done as could be by the hands he had. The error has been in not engaging others so as to keep up a sufficient number constantly at work. I am particularly mortified that scarcely any thing has been done of the interior walls. The only ground on which I consented to pull down the chamber of the H. of R. was the strong representation that the work could not be depended on unless both the external and internal walls were carried up together so as to make good bond and to settle all together. This representation by persons of the art I relied on as my apology to the members of the legislature to whom I had given reason to believe their chamber needed not to be taken down this year. On this it was taken down, yet the work has not been carried up together, and I know not what I shall have to say. Mr. Lenthall says mr. Munroe understood from a letter of mine that every thing was to stop that the external walls might be pushed. But there is some mistake in this, as my letter used these very words "I think with mr. Lenthall that the interior walls should be raised to the height of the basement story to support the external walls."[1] However the important object now is to avail ourselves to the utmost of the remainder of the season. To do this we are to consider 1. what force our funds will employ thro' the season. 2. whether that force can be procured. 3. whether the materials can be procured. I am afraid the utmost which can be done is to raise the interior as high as the cellar walls. Even this will make some shew, and, as so far a support to the exterior walls will so far exhibit a reason for the demolition of the house. But to accomplish this there is not one day to lose, nor can any step be taken toward accomplishing it till you come. I hope therefore you will come immediately, aid us in deciding what may be attempted, and put it under way. Mr. Lenthall will exert faithfully whatever means are put into his hands, but he is too diffident to undertake the first decision. Nothing but the greatest exertion can render possible the completion of the work the next year, and the cramming the Representatives into the library a second and long session.

The gutturs of this house also await you, and in the mean time are constantly pouring floods of water into it. The covering of the house is unfinished for want of some strips for the joints. Every thing relative to this house and the highways which was not considerably advanced, was stopped early in August on the alarm I received from mr. Monroe on the state of our funds, that the Capitol might be pushed to the utmost.

A word now on my own affairs. My works at home will shortly call for 100. sheets of rolled iron 16. I. wide and 11. f. 8 I. long. Can you furnish them in the course of 3. or 4. months? The amalgamating 2. sheets together at their ends in the manner of the inclosed paper, is an operation certainly well understood at the iron works. But if they cannot be obtained of the length desired in this way or in a single roll I must be content to tuck them together in the common way. Accept my salutations and assurances of esteem and respect.

Th: Jefferson

Polygraph Copy: Jefferson Papers (176/B4).

1. Jefferson to Thomas Munroe, 4 Aug. 1804, District of Columbia Papers, Library of Congress.

TO THOMAS JEFFERSON

Octr. 11th. 1804.

Sir,

I am just now arrived in the city, and will wait upon you as soon as I can make myself acquainted with the exact state of the public Works.

I left Washington on the 30th. of June last. On the 12th. of July, Mrs. Latrobe's mother died suddenly. On the 17th she was brought to bed of a daughter and continued so unwell for a month that it was improper to communicate to her the loss she had suffered. After visiting her father, I left Philadelphia to come hither the latter end of August, but during my absence from the Canal of the Chesapeake and Delaware, circumstances had arisen which detained me at Newcastle till the 16th. Septr.[1] when I again set off in the Mail taking with me my son Henry, who is a scholar at the French Academy at Baltimore. Before we reached the Susquehannah he was so ill that I was obliged to take him to the house of a friend where in a few days his life was despaired of. I have remained with him till his mother who was at her father's could come down to him and he was declared out of danger.[2]

Altho' I have by correspondence and drawings endeavored to do my duty, the peculiar and distressing occurences that have kept me from Washington, appear sufficient from the possibility of similar detentions to deprive me of your confidence in my being a fit person to be entrusted with the duties assigned to me. With these impressions upon my mind, I hope you will forgive my having detailed to you personal inconveniences that ought not perhaps to weigh against any public injury that has been sustained.

With the sincerest desire rather to lose every thing than your good opinion I am most respectfully, Your hble. Servant.

B. H. Latrobe

ALS: Jefferson Papers (176/B7). Endorsed as received 11 October.

1. In addition to his work on the canal during this period, BHL conducted portions of the New Castle survey which he had been commissioned to do earlier in the year (see BHL to Bird, 16 June 1804, above). BHL, "Notes of Survey of the town of Newcastle," 1 Sept. 1804–21 May 1805, Robert Mills Papers, Tulane University Library, New Orleans (175/E1).

2. BHL described Henry's illness as "a bilious fever of the most violent kind." BHL to John Lenthall, 30 Sept. 1804, BHL Papers, Library of Congress (176/A13).

TO JAMES TODD

Wilmington, Octr. 26th. 1804

My dear Sir,[1]

I herein enclose a drawing for your seal, which I hope will meet with Your approbation and that of the Directors of Your Bank.[2] The language of Allegory is like the Indian language of signs. It is *poor* in expression, and to those who do not understand it, appears nothing but ridiculous grimace.[3] In the drawing I send you, you see a woman holding a stick with pigeon wings tied to the end of it, and two snakes wrapped round it, a tea waiter in the other hand, a pointer by her side, and standing on the wharf in the midst of Market truck and bales of goods. But he that is initiated in the mysterious language of Allegory sees in a moment, that the female figure with the mural crown, and the caduceus of Mercury in her hand, must represent a commercial city. Her shield which covers and protects the produce of the land, and which is decorated with the arms of Pennsylvania shows her to be the emblem of Philadelphia. Her attribute, the dog, the symbol of watchfulness as well as of fidelity, attends her. All this is further explained by the houses, steeple, and Ships in the back Ground.

These ideas occurred to me, and were put upon paper, before I recollectd, that a seal ready *cut* and dry may be bought cheap, designed

551

by Mr. Blodget.[4] It represents a dog chained to a money chest fast asleep. I forget where I saw it, but it was intended and engraved for one of the banks, and might be heard of on enquiry.

As to the execution, I hope the engraver will exceed my drawing in distinctness, and especially keep the principal figure as much before the accompaniments as possible. In the buildings, I particularly beg he will follow my lines. The error of most seals and medals, ancient and modern, is faulty perspective.[5]

With true and affectionate respect Believe me Yours truly

B. H. Latrobe

Polygraph Copy: LB (35/D11). Addressed to Todd in Philadelphia.

1. James Todd, who had once served as clerk to the Philadelphia Select Council and as first bookkeeper of the Bank of North America, became cashier of the Bank of Philadelphia at the time it was organized in August 1803. He held the position (at an annual salary of $2,000) until November 1805, when he sailed to Georgia to restore his health. It was then discovered that the bank's accounts were very much out of order, and that Todd had applied the bank's money to his personal use. There is no evidence that he ever returned to Philadelphia. Nicholas B. Wainwright, *History of the Philadelphia National Bank: A Century and a Half of Philadelphia Banking, 1803–1953* (Philadelphia, 1953), pp. 18–19.

2. At the request of Todd, BHL designed a seal for the Bank of Philadelphia. His drawing has not been found. BHL to Todd, 8 Sept. 1804, LB (35/B5).

3. For BHL's later comments on allegory, see BHL, *Journals*, 3:263–66.

4. Samuel Blodget (1757–1814), merchant, economist, and amateur architect, made his fortune in the East India trade in Boston before moving to Philadelphia in 1792. He designed there the building for the First Bank of the United States (see BHL to Lenthall, 5 Aug. 1804, n. 3, above). He submitted a design for the U.S. Capitol in 1792, served as superintendent of buildings in 1793, and promoted various Washington undertakings, such as a national university to be built with proceeds from lotteries he sponsored. For BHL's later comments on Blodget's deprived financial condition, brought on by the failure of the lotteries, see BHL, *Journals*, 3:71.

5. The following spring BHL thanked Todd for sending him an impression of the seal "taken from my design." BHL regretted that the engraver, John Reich, had "totally altered the character of the figure, and instead of a grave sober female, *dressed* in decent fashion, he has given us a dancing Bachante—one of her breasts bare and scarce any chance of hiding the other should She move an inch from the spot. Her head besides is much too small for her body, and her arms for her legs. When standing upright her fingers ought to reach a *little* below the middle of the thigh." Nevertheless, BHL noted that "the execution of the Seal is superior to any thing I have yet seen in America." BHL to Todd, 17 Nov. 1804, 18 May 1805, both in LB (36/C9, 40/B11).

The current seal of the Philadelphia National Bank, the successor to the Philadelphia Bank, conforms closely to the description BHL gives here. The figure appears to have been altered, as she now has a fully-robed upper torso. Photocopy of seal in PBHL.

TO JOHN LENTHALL

Wilmington, Octr. 29th. 1804.

My dear friend

Pray send to me as soon as possible the sizes of the blocks ordered for the internal Capitals, and also of the architrave and Frieze blocks. I have drawn the Capital halfsize; it is an enormous thing, and as I have followed the Greek rather than the Roman style, in spite of Sir William Chambers, I am not quite sure that your blocks will suit my drawings.[1]

Yours very affecty.

B. H. Latrobe.

ALS: BHL Papers, Library of Congress (176/C3). Addressed to Lenthall in Washington. Endorsed as received 1 November.

1. Sir William Chambers (1723–96), dean of the architectural profession in eighteenth-century Great Britain, published his *Treatise on Civil Architecture* in 1759. Described as "the Englishman's Palladio and Vignola," the work appeared in two more editions during Chambers's life and four more in the nineteenth century. In the third edition with the expanded title, *A Treatise on the Decorative Part of Civil Architecture* (London, 1791), Chambers attacked the Greek Revival movement which had been triggered by the publication of the first volume of James Stuart and Nicholas Revett's *The Antiquities of Athens* (London, 1762). In a typical statement of his ideas, much opposed by Grecophiles like BHL, Chambers declared: "Indeed, none of the few things now existing in Greece, though so pompously described, and neatly represented, in various publications of our time; seem to deserve great notice; either for dimension, grandeur of stile, rich fancy, or elegant taste of design; nor do they seem calculated to throw new light upon the art, or to contribute towards its advancement." Chambers, *A Treatise on the Decorative Part of Civil Architecture*, ed. John Harris (New York, 1968 [orig. publ. 1791]), pp. i, 19.

TO JO. HELMSLEY

Wilmington Octr. 29th. 1804.

Dear Sir,[1]

The president of the Ch. and Del. Canal Company very obligingly communicated to me your letter of the 22d. of this month. In this letter you state that many of your friends who have subscribed to this great work begin to doubt the probability of its completion, and are therefore reluctant in advancing money to a scheme which may probably never become productive.

If it were in my power to remove such impressions by any state- 553 ments of facts which can not be known to subscribers at a distance, I should be very wanting to my duty were I not to use every means in my power to diffuse correct information, and you will therefore I am sure excuse the trouble I give you by this letter. And I am certain, with you at least, no suspicion will arise that my statements will be colored by self interest, for independently of my character which is well known, and which I hope is sufficient, the annual mode of my compensation secures me against any idea of its being my interest to precipitate the completion of the work.

There are three principal causes which separately or jointly may cause a failure of the work.

1. Want of money, arising from nonpayment of subscriptions, or a deficiency in the numbers of subscriptions.

2. Natural difficulties which cannot be overcome by the amount subscribed and paid.

3. Misconduct in those employed, in the execution and direction of the work.

1. On the first head, I must first remark, that the fear which keeps back subscriptions, least the work should fail, is the most certain mean of ensuring its failure. It is however fortunate that no such fear seems to operate where the largest subscription has been made, in Philadelphia. Mr. Gilpin has already collected the greatest part of the third payment, and calculates that before Christmas he will certainly get in the fourth, so as to have 50.000 Dollars in the Treasury between that time and the present. I may with confidence assert that the works will not before Christmas require more than 20.000 Dollars, including all outstanding demands. This will leave a fund of 30.000. The subscription to the Ch. and Del. Canal, has not been, like those to other Canals, raised by the union of large and wealthy mercantile houses in the scheme. It is made by a very numerous body of men, of moderate, but permanent fortunues, and also by some wealthy men. We are not therefore liable to ruin, by great bankruptcies in our commercial towns, such as those of Morris & Nicholson in Philadelphia or Aquila Brown in Baltimore.[2] Those who have paid up to the third installment, may be considered as pledged, by the money they have already embarked in the Scheme, to go through with it. A very great Majority of Philadelphian subscribers have gone thus far, and of all the Philadelphia Subscriptions Mr. Gilpin does not calculate that there are more than 117 (if I recollect right) that are likely to be behindhand. Of these he also thinks that the greatest part will come in wh[en] the collection is put into the hands of a Lawyer.

As it is a doubt whether the Delaware subscribers can be legally compelled to pay up the amount of their shares, and Mr. Bayard, has unfortunately set the example of refusal I will say nothing on the expectations to be entertained of much assistance from this quarter. And yet it is very certain that the rivalry of the towns of Wilmington and Newcastle may still be used by the Company in such a manner as to obtain prompt payment of at least one half of the present subscriptions, and probably, a very large encrease of them. This is a delicate subject, but thus much may be boldly said, that in a contest between two parties, the wish of each of whom, if obtained, will conduce perhaps *equally* to the public interest, *that* party ought to prevail, which makes the greatest exertions. The Wilmington subscribers have been notoriously deficient in their payments. Those on the South of Christiana do not profess an intention to pay unless compelled, *or* unless the Canal go to Newcastle. Both modes of obtaining payment are in the power of the Board.

On the Maryland payments I can say nothing to you, who can so much better judge of the probability of their being completed. That the Subscribers are compellable by law seems to be agreed. This therefore though a last resource is a certain one.

If all the subscriptions already made were paid up, I think (though I am not certain) that the funds of the company would exceed 400.000 Dollars. As there can be little doubt but that additional subscriptions will still be obtained, and it is also certain that some will be lost, I will make a deduction of 50.000 Dollars from this sum, and suppose the present efficient fund of the company to amount to no more than 350.000 Dollars. The purchase of the waters of Elk takes from this sum 66.000 Dollars, the expense of the feeder, will not be 40.000 dollars. Towards the main Canal will then remain the sum of 250.000 Dollars or thereabouts. It appears to be the sentiment of many of the Board, that the work, after bringing the feeder to the point at which it will meet the Canal, should proceed westward to the Chesapeake bay. This certainly will be the wisest mode of proceeding. The distance then from the feeder to Welchpoint will be 8½ miles. In this distance there are no Aqueducts, no Culverts, in short no expense but that of the digging, of banking, and of the locks. In each Yard in length of the Canal, there will be at a very large average 45 Yds. of digging, or 79.200 Yds. in a Mile. By the work already executed it is proved that it will not cost more than 20 Cents per Yard to dig and trim the Earth, and make the towing path. This makes the expense per Mile 15.800 Dollars, say 16.000, which for 8½ Miles is 136.000 Dollars. Of the correctness of this estimate I can venture to be confident, and the principles on which it proceeds are so plain, that you may easily judge of them.

In the distance between the feeder and Welchpoint, are 9 locks. 8 of them may be built at the expense of 5 thousand dollars per Lock, but to be full say for the 8 locks	136.000
	500.000[3]
The last Lock or tide Lock, will be much more expensive, and subject to increased expense from Accidents. It ought to cost only 20.000 Dollars, being a work of the same Nature and difficulty with the Wall and Sluice of the Basin in Philadelphia which cost that sum.[4] But to cover unforeseen accidents say	34.000
	220.000
Balance to carry the Work Eastward	30.000
	250.000

When the work shall have proceeded thus far, which without some very unforeseen accident to prevent its progress will be in the fall of the Year 1806, a perfect navigation will have been effected from within 38 Miles of the town of Lancaster, and a much less distance from the vallies of Conestogo, and Pequay, in Pennsylva., to *Baltimore*. The question then occurs, will not the subscriptions then deficient be made up in Philadelphia, to complete the work, or will the mercantile interest tamely look on, and see the course of business to Baltimore gain an establishment, which nothing but the completion of the work can prevent. It is fair to suppose that then the subscription of 500.000 Dollars will be at least efficiently filled. 13½ miles will then be unfinished,

towards which the sum remains of		30.000
Subscription deficient		150.000
		180.000
13 ½ miles of Canal at 16.000, is	216.000	
8 Locks as above	50.000	
3 Aqueducts at 10.000$	30.000	
1 Tidelocks	34.000	
Incidents and purchase of Land	20.000	
	350.000	
Deficiency		170.000
		350.000

In every article of the above estimate, I have purposely made the largest possible allowances, and have gone far beyond my own experience of expense, even in the feeder now under progress. The means which all companies that have arrived so near the completion of the object of their incorporation, as the expenditure of their Capital will bring the Ches. and Del. Canal Company, are by experience found to possess of increasing their stock by additional subscriptions, or their funds by borrowing Sums of money on the security of their corporate property, will no doubt be easily procured in the present case. The example of the Waterworks in Philadelphia and especially of the Schuylkill bridge are recent instances, of the effects of exertion after the capital had been expended.[5] And the national work in which our Company are engaged is an object of such superior importance, and promises such superior profit to either of the former, that there can, I think, be no doubt of success in making up the deficiency stated on the other side. My hopes in this respect are besides founded on the experience of my whole professional life. For of all the public works on which I have been employed, not one has remained unfinished, and yet I may also say that, not *one* has been finished without the necessity of raising a capital beyond that originally contemplated, the estimate made by me having, with all the attendant expenses, not coming professionally into my view, always exceeded the proposed capital.

In discussing this first difficulty of finance, you will perceive that I have not [*illegible*] endeavored to bring the expense of the work by any management of my statements within the compass of the capital. The estimate offered to the board this last spring was an estimate in detail, the present sketch is a gross average estimate, and yet it will be found that they come nearly to the same amount—670.000—with the addition to the former of the purchase of waterrights, of the feeder, and of incidental expenses which were not included.[6]

2. I now come to the natural difficulties of the Work. The principal of these are in the feeder are already overcome. To the length of the Canal, there are more natural difficulties in the construction of the feeder, than in any work of the same kind which has fallen under my observation. We have had rocks of the most difficult kind to remove, to force the work across sandy valleys, and along the brow of hills, steep, and ill calculated to retain the Water. To embank and cross a gravelly swamp which require great expense in making the work tight, to cut through hills 25 feet deep, to pass through other lesser ridges, and to pass three deep valleys. The greatest part of this work is done, and seven large Culverts are built to carry off the Land water. We have been at 557

work only 5 Months, and have expended 16.000 Dollars, great part of which is for Utensils and buildings, which at the commencement of such a work are always a very heavy expense. All the difficulties above stated are overcome excepting the deep cutting and the passage of one Valley. What remains to be done of the feeder is easy and level cutting, the aqueduct, which is begun, a lock, and three bridges. All these works are included in the estimate of 40.000$.

As to the Main Canal, the only *difficult* Works are the two tide Locks. The Aqueducts are expensive but there is no difficulty in their construction, nor in that of the other Locks. The digging is over the most favorable ground which it is possible to conceive.

3. As to the persons employed, I can say, without hesitation, that our Stone Mason, who will have to construct the Locks, is the most able man in his business that I have ever known. His talents, and integrity are equal to his experience, and from his infancy he has been employed in heavy works in Water. Such a Man it would have been difficult to have procured, had not Mr. Vickers been engaged. In his branch of business I may assert the same of Mr. Strickland, our carpenter, and of Mr. Brooke, the clerk of the works, too much cannot be said, as to his accuracy, attention to business, and integrity. As a practical surveyor and leveller he is invaluable.

Among the Contractors there are three Men to whom the whole execution of the Canal might safely be committed, James Cochran, Charles Randle, and John Cocksy. They perfectly understand their business, and are capable of managing any number of Men. The work they have performed already is their best praise.

Upon the whole view of the subject, it is evident, that there exists no serious difficulty but in the department of finance: and it appears also, that before this difficulty will be felt, so much of the work will be compleat as to force through the remainder. At all events, it appears to be much too early to despond while so large an efficient source of money is to be procured from Philadelphia. Those who from fear of their neighbors, keep back their payments, act certainly unwisely. They contribute thereby all in their power to produce the failure they so much dread.

In a few days I will send you a drawing of the feeder, specially pointing out the work which is done, and what is incomplete. I wish however you could view it yourself. I am sure you will approve it, as to quantity and quality.

558   I have written this letter while laboring under a violent cold and

headache which has driven me home from the works. This must excuse much in it. I beg You to believe me very sincerely Yours faithfully and respectfully

B. Henry Latrobe

Polygraph Copy: LB (35/E4). Addressed to Helmsley "near Centerville E. Shore Maryland."

1. Perhaps a relative of William Hemsley III (1766–1825), of "Cloverfield," Queen Anne County, Md. (county seat, Centreville), a C & D director. Edwin M. Barry, "The Old Wye Mills, 1690–1956," *Maryland Historical Magazine* 52 (1957):37.

2. The financial firm of Robert Morris (1734–1806) and John Nicholson (c. 1757–1800) failed in 1797.

Aquila Brown failed during Baltimore's mercantile depression of 1798–1803. Gary L. Browne, *Baltimore in the New Nation, 1789–1861* (Chapel Hill, N.C., 1980), pp. 30–31.

3. I.e., 50,000.

4. The basin in the Schuylkill River for the Philadelphia Waterworks.

5. The original estimate for the waterworks was $127,000, but by 1806 the project had cost a total of $349,016.50. The Schuylkill Permanent Bridge Company was originally capitalized at $150,000, but total expenditures reached nearly $300,000. BHL, View of the Practicability and Means of Supplying the City of Philadelphia with Wholesome Water, 29 Dec. 1798, above; [Richard Peters], *A Statistical Account of the Schuylkill Permanent Bridge, Communicated to the Philadelphia Society of Agriculture, 1806* (Philadelphia, 1807), p. 28; Hamlin, *Latrobe*, p. 171.

6. The detailed estimate for the proposed canal from Welch Point to Christina River was for a total cost of $534,725. BHL, C & D Report, 24 Apr. 1804 (173/F11).

TO NICHOLAS J. ROOSEVELT

Wilmington, Novr. 2d 1804

My dear Sir

I received your letters of the 2d and 24th. October only today, on my return from the Works on the Chese. and Del. Canal. Your first letter was delayed by my having lately been at Washington, so that it travelled a roundabout journey.

I assure you that I know as little about the negotiation with the corporation as you do.[1] I have seen Mr. Mifflin only twice within these three months. He then told me that Stephen Girard, who carries on the negotiation on the part of the corporation carefully avoided committing himself by any proposal.[2] My opinion is that nothing short of withholding the water will bring the matter to an issue. Of the details I am wholly 559 ignorant, and I conceive that a personal interview will be wholly without effect, unless the principles of settlement are previously well understood and agreed upon.

The matters to be settled between the concern and the corporation cannot possibly be brought to conclusion in a few days. Just the subcommittee of the watering committee must assent to an arrangement, then comes the watering committee itself, then the common council, and the Select council, all avaricious, unjust, ignorant, and proud. The supreme court will inevitably have to decide the matter, or an action for withholding the Water. This is my firm and decided opinion formed at least two Years ago, and confirmed by all that has since happened.

As to arrangements with our partners, I have already *committed myself,* and still retain the opinion I gave in writing and which is at all events binding upon *me.* I can do no more in the business.

In respect to Corp & Casey, the matter is so simple, that your mode of treating it always surprises me. I became your security by accepting bills to a large amount. I had no interest but that of my reputation and friendship in the completion of your contract with the corporation. The bills were protested. By an arrangement with the Navy department the security was changed as to the persons who had it and ruin was postponed. That ruin must one day or other fall upon the drawer and acceptor. The only indemnification I hold is the share in the works. We shall see what it is worth when our partners state their account. I am in their power. I cannot even *give away* my share because it is mortgaged. There was some comfort while the Bankrupt law existed. That is repealed.[3] It is a fearful abyss to look into. But a batchelor need not care about it.

It will be wholly out of my power to be in Philadelphia for a month to come. Whenever I have any prospect of getting thither I will write to you. Believe me

Polygraph Copy: LB (35/F13).

1. Roosevelt's contracts with the city of Philadelphia for the two waterworks engines were complex and were never fulfilled. The first contract, of 23 May 1799, required that the engines be able to pump 3,000,000 gallons of water to an elevation of 50 feet above ground level every twenty-four hours, and that Roosevelt operate and maintain both engines for five years in return for fixed maintenance payments by the city. A second contract, of 24 December 1799, granted Roosevelt the right to make the Schuylkill engine larger than needed for the city's water supply in order that he could use the so-called "extra power" to operate a rolling and slitting mill. Roosevelt's rent of the building and

extra power was to be deducted from the city's maintenance payments. Although Roosevelt completed the engines and built his mill (in partnership with BHL and the Bollmanns), the Watering Committee of the city councils determined that the engines would not pump the minimum amount of water and they refused to begin maintenance payments. Roosevelt, in turn, claimed that he had expended far more in manufacturing the engines than the city had advanced to him, demanded that the city councils pay him the difference, and gave up operating the Centre Square engine while retaining control of the Schuylkill engine and mill.

Since the expense of operating the Schuylkill engine for rolling and pumping exceeded the mill's income from the sale of sheet and rod iron, Roosevelt and his partners were deeply concerned about coming to an agreement with the city. Discussions dragged on, however, until they were hastened by the city's seizure of the Schuylkill Engine House in September 1805 because the engine was not ready to pump when water was needed to fight a serious fire. In January 1806 Roosevelt accepted a payment of $16,000 to renounce all claims and agreements with the city, and the rolling mill equipment was removed and sold. *Report of the Committee Appointed by the Common Council to Enquire into the State of the Water Works* (Philadelphia, 1802), pp. 21–36; *Report [of the Joint Committee to Whom was Referred the Memorial and Remonstrance of Nicholas J. Roosevelt]*, (Philadelphia, [1801 or 1802]); *Report of the Joint Committee, Appointed by the Select and Common Councils for the purpose of Superintending and Directing the Water Works* (Philadelphia, 1802), pp. 11–13; *Aurora*, 24 Sept. 1805; *Gazette of the United States* (Philadelphia), 1 Oct. 1805; Minutes of the Select Council, 31 Dec. 1805, Archives of the City and County of Philadelphia; BHL to Roosevelt, 8 Jan. 1806, LB (47/B1); BHL, *Engineering Drawings*, pp. 50–52.

2. Stephen Girard (1750–1831), a native of Bordeaux, France, was a Philadelphia merchant, financier, and philanthropist. In June 1804 he had commenced negotiations with Mifflin, Roosevelt's agent. Girard to Mifflin (draft), 25 June 1804, Girard Papers, APS.

3. "An Act to Establish an Uniform System of Bankruptcy throughout the United States" (passed on 4 April 1800, *Annals of Congress*, 6th Cong., 1st sess., pp. 1453–71) was repealed on 19 December 1803 (ibid., 8th Cong., 1st sess., p. 1249).

TO ROBERT MILLS

Wilmington Novr. 3d. 1804

Dear Sir

You must inevitably have accused me of neglect in not having during the 6 weeks since I left Newcastle in some way or other noticed you. But the circumstances that have filled up the interval have been so different from what I expected that neither my time nor my plans have been in my own power. When I left Newcastle it was with the hope and intention of returning in a week, and I did indeed return as far as Wilmington on my road thither. There I heard that my son Henry was 561 sick, and for 14 days afterwards, I attended him at the house of Mr. Wallace near Elkton. As soon as he was tolerably recovered I went to Washington and since then have been so pressed by the business of the Canal as to have found it impossible to attend to anything else. Yesterday however I should have visited Newcastle had I not been prevented by one of the most oppressive Catarrhs with which I have ever been afflicted, and which scarcely permits me to see what I am writing.

As I hope now that I am perfectly settled here I must now plan the winter campaign for the office. Winter is the best season for studying the theory as Summer is to attend to the practice of our prefession, and as I shall spend most of my time for the next four months in the office, you will perhaps not find that period to be uselessly or unpleasantly spent with me. I shall endeavor immediately to find out convenient board and lodging for you, DeMun and William in my neighborhood, which if agreeable to you you may then occupy.

I have now to request, that you will please to procure all the things in the office to be moved into my former dwelling. Mrs. Latrobe has written to Mrs. Hall who occupies it, and who will assign a room for them.[1] All the small articles which are not used by you for the few days that you may stay in Newcastle had perhaps best be packed in a box and sent hither by Pusey. It would give me great pleasure to see you on Tuesday or Wednesday at the Canal where I shall then be, and continue till Thursday evening. Perhaps it will be convenient to you to move the office on Monday.

I am so unwell that I can scarcely see to write. I will only add, that notwithstanding the apparent neglect of which I have appeared to have been guilty, no one more sincerely values and respects your many excellent qualities, or feels more friendship for you than Yours faithfully

B. Henry Latrobe

Polygraph Copy: LB (35/G5). Addressed to Mills in New Castle.

1. BHL wanted his things moved from the office he rented from George Read II to his "former dwelling" that he was renting from the Aulls.

TO CHRISTIAN IGNATIUS LATROBE

Wilmington, Novr. 4th. 1804. State of Delaware

My dearest Brother

Yesterday I received your kind letter d. Lyme Regis Aug. 25th. inclosed in one to your Sister. I hasten to answer it, but she cannot I fear write to you at present, being engaged most busily in arrangements consequent to our moving to this place, and having a long letter to write to her father on business which cannot be postponed. She thanks you in the mean time most affectionately; and will write soon. Your letter mentions mine of the 7th. of May as the last you have received. I wrote to you again on the 29th of May by the *Active,* and as you mention the death of our Brother Robert Hazlehurst which I announced only in my last I presume you have received it also.[1] Since then I have not written, absolutely for want of time when I had an opportunity, and for want of opportunity when I might have had time. The work I am engaged in, the Ches: and Del. Canal, employs me sufficiently as you may easily suppose, independently of my public appointment at Washington. But were I at Philadelphia, and in a situation to hear of all the means of forward[ing] a letter, I should find infinite pleasure in writing weekly. This you believe, I am sure, and no apology is worth postage across the Atlantic. And now regularly to your letter.

You are perfectly right in the difference you imagine that there is between doing business here and in England in my profession. Had I, in England, executed what I have done here, I should now be able to sit down quietly and enjoy *otium cum dignitate.*[2] But in England the croud of those whose talents are superior to mine is so great, that I should perhaps never have elbowed through them. Here I am the only successful Architect and Engineer. I have had to break the ice for my successors, and what was more difficult to destroy the prejudices which the villanous Quacks in whose hands the public works have hitherto been, had raised against the profession. *There,* in fact lay my greatest difficulty. I have now arrived at a point in the public opinion which is troublesome. Three Years ago, I presented a design for the new city Hall at New-York. It was I think my *best* design. It was rejected, a vile heterogeneous composition in the style of Charles IX of France, or Queen Elizabeth of England was adopted, the invention of a New York bricklayer and a St. Domingo Frenchman in partnership. I am vexed beyond expression at the circumstance, for this vile thing is now slowly rising from the ground, and will 563 occupy one of the grandest situations in the world.[3] *Now,* this very city of New York, have appointed a Committee to solicit my undertaking their business *on my own terms* and I have been obliged *twice* to refuse them, on account of my present engagements.[4] If it please God that I live a few Years longer I shall be able to welcome half a dozen more Babies to a table which I shall easily be able to cover with food. For the next six or eight Months, I must indeed work hard, having to make the Men who are to execute, as well as the designs of my works. Now and then indeed I pick up a ready made English artisan, the rest I manufacture out of American Carpenters, who, to do them justice are incomparable Jacks of all trades. Before I close this Chapter on my professional labors, let me tell you, that from all the *Blarney, Flummery, Flattery,* and other sorts of praise with which I am crammed, I turn with disgust, but to receive the affectionate testimony to my talents which your letter to my Mary contains, I would at any time labor a Year without pay. In this, I am vain, nay I feel proud, for I know you are sincere.

2. The business of my children's property is now growing serious for the amount from the Chapel property since the death of their Grandmother must be considerable. I want none of it, but let it be vested for them in American stock, provided you, or Judge Washington be a Trustee. Pray consult Mr. Sylvester. My long letter on this subject is all I can say on it. It is a sort of business which I well know you cannot transact with pleasure; and had I any friend to whom I could possibly intrust I would not plague you with it. As to Jack Sellon he was certainly an honorable Man when I knew him. What he may be after 10 Years more practice of the Law, I cannot tell. Suppose you write to him. But I will not dictate to you. My duty to my children alone could induce me to give you so disagreeable a commission.[5]

I heartily sympathise with you respecting your daughter Agnes.[6] These little creatures are in fact emanations of ones one soul, and hang by invisible, but strong ties to the parent stock. Of six I have lost two, both incapable of solving a problem in Euclid, and yet I would rather have heard of the death of Herschell,[7] than parted with either of them. I have erected a little marble monument in a single Block of 2 feet by 18 inches over the tomb of little Juliana. Her name, and a little Basso relievo, representing a Butterfly, of course a Machaon, just escaped from its Chrysalis is all that adorns it.[8] It is now three years Ago, and I could still drop a tear over it. May you, my dear Brother, keep what you have got, especially your Girls. Since I wrote to you, my dear Mary has presented to me, on the 17th. July another little Juliana Elisabeth, a fine healthy child. She did not then know, nor for 3 weeks afterwards that on the 11th. July she had lost her Mother, after 18 hours illness. Her brother Robert had been then dead 6 weeks only. The death of this most excellent woman, notwithstanding all that is to be said religiously, philosophically, and medically on the subject is a great calamity to us all: To me, most particularly of all the family, excepting only her husband. He is now 64. For the last ten Years he had ceased to visit *anybody*. All his evenings were with her. He is now alone. My dear wife is still most deeply afflicted. But she is a Woman of so superior a cast, that I often feel quite little before her. There is a greatness in all she does and "feels the sorrows, but not as they who have no hope."[9] She is now singing to her Baby over my head so as to prevent my writing. With the voice of an angel and an intonation so true, and *learned* even, the child is a fool to sleep at such a concert.

decies repetita placebit.[10]

    I have now only room left to assure You of an affection which can cease only with my life. If from the days of our old Grand Uncle Count Boneval Pacha of Belgrade we have been an eccentric breed, we have never ceased to have affectionate hearts.[11] Love to my Sister and all Your children from Yr. affcte. Br.

B. H. Latrobe

Polygraph Copy: LB (35/G8). Addressed to Christian Ignatius in London. Endorsed by BHL: "Enclose this letter to Mr. S. Hazlehurst to go by the first Vessel, if possible by the *Active.*"

    1. BHL to Christian Ignatius Latrobe, 7 May 1804, above, and 29 May 1804, LB (32/F9).

    2. Trans.: Leisure with dignity.

    3. For the New York City Hall, see BHL to [Colhoun], 17 Apr. 1802, n. 4, above.

The "New York bricklayer" was John McComb (1763–1853), architect and son of builder/architect John McComb (1732–1811). Besides the city hall, the younger McComb was best known for his work on several churches, educational buildings, lighthouses, and residences in and around New York City, including "The Grange" designed for Alexander Hamilton in 1801–02.

The "St. Domingo Frenchman" was Joseph François Mangin (d. post-1818), who served in New York in 1794 as an engineering adviser for the city's fortifications. Two years later he became a city surveyor. New York City Hall was Mangin's most important commission. He was primarily responsible for the design and the competition drawings, while McComb supervised the construction.

4. On 4 June 1804 the New York City Common Council appointed a committee "to employ some suitable person to report the plan of a Tunnel or canal most proper to drain the waters from the low lands, between the East and the North [Hudson] Rivers." On 9 June and 27 July the committeemen, at the instance of Aaron Burr, wrote BHL requesting his services. BHL declined both offers but not without suggesting a plan for the city's drainage that included "establishing a system of dry and wet docks, which, with those *natural* advantages which New York possesses beyond any other city in the United States, would preclude all possible rivalry in commercial conveniencies, by any other port." BHL to Wynant Van Zandt, Jr., Jacob Morton, and Clarkson Crolius, 17 June 1804, Wynant Van Zandt Papers, New York Public Library (174/G5); BHL to Van Zandt, Jr., 5 Aug. 1804, LB (34/C6); I. N. Phelps Stokes, *The Iconography of Manhattan Island, 1498–1909,* 6 vols. (New York, 1926), 5 : 1423–24.

5. For the estate due to BHL's children, see BHL to Christian Ignatius Latrobe, 7 May 1804, n. 3, above; for a description of John Baker Sellon and his legal accomplishments, see BHL, *Journals,* 1 : 207.

6. Anna Agnes Latrobe (1797–1827), died unmarried.

7. William Herschel (1738–1822), the foremost British astronomer in BHL's time, who discovered the planet Uranus in 1781. Christian Ignatius knew Herschel and had visited him in 1792 "at Slough, and peeped, thro' the Dr.s telescope, at the Moon, Saturn and several fixed Stars, till my head run dizzy." Christian Ignatius Latrobe to John Frederick Latrobe, 25 Sept. 1792, John Henry de La Trobe Collection, Hamburg, copy in PBHL.

8. See fig. 13, above.

9. 1 Thess. 4 : 13: "But I would not have you to be ignorant, brethren, concerning them which are asleep, that ye sorrow not, even as others which have no hope."

10. Trans.: Ten times repeated it will be pleasing.

11. For BHL's mistaken notion that the Latrobes descended from the noble Bonneval family, see BHL to Du Bourg, 25 Mar. 1804, n. 3, above. Count Claude Alexandre Bonneval (1675–1747), "a french Man by birth, who quitted that service being accused of Sodomy," fought for Prince Eugene of Savoy and the Holy Roman Empire against the French in the War of the Spanish Succession. In 1718 he was appointed to the imperial council of war; but his licentiousness and indiscretion resulted in his removal and, later, in his imprisonment followed by exile. He moved to Constantinople where he converted to Islam and was made a pasha and commander of a large army that defeated the Austrians on the Danube. His memoirs (*Memoirs du Comte de Bonneval,* 2 vols [London, 1737]; *Mémoires of the Bashaw Count Bonneval, from His Birth to His Death . . . Written by Himself and Collected from His Papers* [London, 1750]) are spurious. Marginal note by John Percival, first earl of Egmont, in Capt. J. Worth to Lady Percival, 30 Aug. 1724, Additional Manuscripts 47030, folio 91, British Library. See Heinrich Benedikt, *Der Pasha Graf Alexander von Boneval (1675–1747)* (Graz, Austria, 1959).

TO THOMAS JEFFERSON

Novr. 9th. 1804, Wilmington

Dear Sir,

I arrived at this place from our works on the Canal yesterday, having daily attended at the postroad from the 3rd. of Novr. to the 5th. in hopes that I should have been able to procure a passage to Washington. But the stages were so crouded with the Members going to Congress that I could not get a seat, and on the 5th. both lines were preengaged for three days to come. It was then too late to go to Washington previously to the next meeting of our board on the 20th.[1] On my return hither yesterday I was mortified to see the enclosed written on the 24th. of Octr. on my table where I had left it to be taken to the postoffice.[2] I have also a letter from our Roller[3] of which the following is a Copy.

"I have applied to Jones & Howell,[4] and am informed that the Iron which they sent to the President U.S. was connected in the usual way thus  from your letter I understand that it must be weld- ed in this manner and then bent down. As I am fearfull of some  mistake, send me a pattern in paper. (I did send him the pattern, which he must have dropt in opening the letter.) We are now rolling Iron for the purpose, and of course can finish it without delay."

One of the partners having been here yesterday, I made another pattern which I sent up by him, and he will omit nothing to procure proper information from Jones & Howell and to have the business done Satisfactorily. He says that all the Iron will be packed in three weeks, ready to be put on board.

I shall go to Philadelphia in the course of a day or two after the 20th. and leave Mrs. L. with her father while I go to Washington. I will then select the stoves you wish to be sent you, with great pleasure. This is the section of the Rittenhouse Stove, if I mistake not.[5]

By a paragraph in the *Aurora*, I observe that the management of the public buildings at Washington *has* been made the subject of animadversion in the *Federalist*. I have not seen the article, but from the paper in which it has appeared, it cannot but operate as praise.[6]

This letter is the polygraphic *copy* with the short *quill,* by a machine made for me about three months ago. The quill is almost worn out, but the whole letter has been written without touching the adjusting screw a proof that the machine may be made to work very correctly. Along the left end of the sheet on this side there has been a remarkable sinking (boucle) which has occasioned blanks.[7] I am with the sincerest respect Yr. faithfully

B. Henry Latrobe

Polygraph Copy: Jefferson Papers (176/D1). Addressed to Jefferson in Washington. Endorsed as received 13 November. BHL retained the ALS in his letterbook (36/A4).

1. The C & D board met in Wilmington on 20–26 November 1804 and "fully employed every moment of" BHL's time. There he submitted his progress report of 20 November on the feeder (see below). BHL to Nicholas J. Roosevelt, 23 Nov. 1804, LB (36/A13); BHL to Jefferson, 26 Nov. 1804, Jefferson Papers (176/E5).
2. BHL to Jefferson, 24 Oct. 1804, Jefferson Papers (176/C1).
3. Samuel Mifflin.
4. Philadelphia iron merchants.
5. Jefferson had asked BHL "to select for me in Philadelphia 3. of the handsomest stoves, of the kind called Open stoves, or Rittenhouse stoves, which are in fact nothing more than the Franklin stove, leaving out the double back and flues formed in that for supplying warm air. The Rittenhouse stove is the one commonly used in Philadelphia, and was the model and origin of the Rumford fireplace, which is a Rittenhouse stove in brick instead of iron." Jefferson wanted the stoves for Monticello to be ordered from Jones & Howell and sent to Richmond. Jefferson to BHL, 3 Nov. 1804, Jefferson Papers (176/C9); BHL to Jones & Howell, 11 Nov., 17 Nov. 1804, both in LB (36/C1, 36/C11).
6. In the fall of 1804 an attack on BHL attributed to Thornton appeared in the *Washington Federalist* (Georgetown, D.C.). It was countered in the Philadelphia *Aurora* on 2 November by William Duane's resounding condemnation of alleged abuses by the former

District of Columbia commissioners and his praise of BHL's work. (BHL clipped the *Aurora* piece and pasted it into his letterbook [35/E2].) Although Duane ascribed the *Federalist* attack to "a person in a subordinate situation at that city [Washington], and who was deeply concerned in the original works" there, the *Federalist* replied on 7 November, denying that Thornton had been responsible and reiterating its belief that "the United States have been unnecessarily put to the expence of about twenty thousand dollars, principally for the corrupt purpose of giving a job to Mr. Latrobe." Thornton shortly thereafter published a letter, dated 1 January 1805, *To the Members of the House of Representatives of the United States* [Washington, D.C., 1805], in which he answered the criticisms BHL put forward in his report to Philip R. Thompson of 28 February 1804, above.

7. After completing the letter, BHL filled in the blanks on the left margin.

TO CHARLES GHEQUIERE

Wilmington, Novr. 12th. 1804

Dear Sir,[1]

I am going to ask a favor of you, which your politeness to me gives me reason to believe you will excuse, and which you[r] connexions of business in France will I hope render as little inconvenient to you as possible.

When I came to America 10 Years ago I brought part of my library with me, the remainder being sent in another vessel about 1.500 valuable books, and several instruments was captured by the French and sold, so that I never could recover any part of it. By this means I have lost many professional books. This loss would have rendered me almost incapable of doing business here, had not my memory been tolerably good, and I even designed and executed the bank of Pennsylvania without any assistance from books; the part of my library which I had saved been then in the custody of a friend. Whether I am growing more lazy, or more aged, or whether the increase of my business is the cause, I find a recurrence to books daily more convenient, and there are two or three works which are become almost indispensibly necessary to me. I have made several attempts to procure them, but have failed, the promises of my friends who have gone to France having been lost at Sea, I suppose.

Knowing the extent of your negotiations in France, I therefore take the liberty to request of you *as a matter of business* to import for me, if 569 possible early next spring the following Works, which are expensive ones and not to be had but at Paris, I believe.

1.) *L'Architecture Hydraulique, par* M. Belidor.[2] This is an old work and perhaps scarce, of course, dear.

2. All the works of M. Peronet.[3] Perronet was without exception the greatest Bridgebuilder in the world. His works are voluminous, and the numerous plates render them expensive. I could wish to have *them all.*

3. *Recueil et Parallêle des edifices de tout genre, anciens et modernes, par* Durand, two Volumes, one of plates the other of description.[4]

I expect that these works will amount to about 400 Dollars. In order to be certain of procuring perfect and good impressions, it would be well perhaps, if your correspondent were to employ some Man of letters to hunt up the works among the booksellers.

I need not say with how many thanks I shall honor your order for the Amount. Begging once more that you will excuse the liberty I have taken, believe me truly Your faithful hble. Servt.

B. Henry Latrobe

The drawing of the Cathedral will be with you in about 14 days.[5]

Polygraph Copy: LB (36/C4). Addressed to Ghequiere "(Kunkel & Chequiere Merchts.)" in Baltimore.

1. Charles Ghequiere (c. 1754–1818), a native of Hamburg and a Baltimore merchant since the end of the Revolutionary War, was in partnership with H. Kunckel. He was a trustee of the Baltimore Cathedral from 1795 to 1806. *American and Commercial Advertiser* (Baltimore), 14 Aug. 1818; John Thomas Scharf, *The Chronicles of Baltimore* (Baltimore, 1874), p. 209; *Cathedral Records from the Beginning of Catholicity in Baltimore to the Present Time* (Baltimore, 1906), p. 109.

2. Bernard Forest de Belidor (c. 1697–1761), *Architecture hydraulique, ou l'art de conduire, d'élever et de ménager les eaux pour les différens besoins de la vie* . . . , 4 vols. (Paris, 1737–53). This work considered elements of both civil and military engineering which involved harbors, canals, waterworks, and other public works in or near water. As a compendium of best practice and a model of rational analysis of problems, *Architecture hydraulique* had a major influence on European engineering well into the nineteenth century.

3. Jean-Rudolphe Perronet (1708–94) was trained as an architect and joined the French government's Corps des Ponts et Chausées in 1735. The Corps was responsible for the construction and repair of state bridges, highways, canals and other public works. In 1747 Perronet became head of the Corps' training school, which eventually became the famous École des Ponts et Chausées. He became chief of the entire Corps in 1763. His three-volume work on bridges related his actual experience in construction: *Description des projets et de la construction des ponts de Neuilly, de Montes, d'Orleans et autres, du projet du canal de Bourgogne* . . . , 3 vols. (Paris, 1782–89).

4. Jean Nicolas Louis Durand (1760–1834), *Recueil et parallèle des édifices de tout genre, anciens et modernes, remarquables par leur beauté* . . . , 2 vols. (Paris, 1799–1800).

5. BHL did not send his earliest surviving set of cathedral plans to Baltimore until the following April. BHL to John Carroll, 16 Apr. 1805, in BHL, *Correspondence*, 2; BHL to Ghequiere, 16 Apr. 1805, LB (39/C7).

FROM THOMAS JEFFERSON

Washington Nov. 12. 04.

Dear Sir

It would be well to recieve from you as early as possible the report you propose to make for Congress as to the progress, state and further cost of the public buildings. I am apprehensive of a more serious opposition to another appropriation than has ever been made. Perhaps after you shall have sent me the report, and it is referred to a committee it may be expedient you should come up yourself to give them the information necessary for their own conviction, and to enable them to carry conviction to the house. Accept my salutations and respects.

Th: Jefferson

Polygraph Copy: Jefferson Papers (176/D6).

TO THOMAS JEFFERSON

Wilmington Novr. 17th. 1804.

Dear Sir

I returned home last night from the Canal and found your favor of the 14th.[1] Our directors meet on Tuesday next the 20th. instant, and will probably sit the two following days. As soon as the board breaks up, I shall set off for Washington, and arrive with the Mail. There are a few articles of information which it will be necessary for me to obtain before I can compleat my report, as to the exact expense, and its distribution to the different purposes of fitting up the library, carrying on the South wing, and rendering the President's house habitable, the quantity of work done to the present time, the nature and extent of the preparations for the next season, &c. &c. To obtain this information I should be on the spot, and if the few days of my unavoidable detention here, could be given to me, I should be prepared with my report on the day after my arrival, for I shall bring with me the report compleat as to every thing that is not detail.[2]

I have packed up and sent to Baltimore the Volume of Stuart's *Athens* containing the choragic Monument of Lysicrates, in order to consult on the best material and method for the erection of the top of the work. I have already bestowed much thought upon it, and have not satisfied myself how economy and any like an exact imitation can be united, for it is a most complicated piece of Sculpture.[3]

I am with the sincerest respect Your faithful hble. Servt.

B. Henry Latrobe.

ALS: Jefferson Papers (176/D9). Endorsed as received 18 November.

1. Jefferson to BHL, 12 (not 14) Nov. 1804, above.
2. See BHL, Report on the Public Buildings, 1 Dec. 1804, below.
3. Despite his earlier recommendation of Attic capitals, BHL acceded to a preference, probably Jefferson's, for the richer Corinthian capitals of the Choragic Monument of Lysicrates (fig. 17, above) for the House of Representatives columns. See BHL to Jefferson, 29 Apr. 1804, above.

REPORT ON THE CHESAPEAKE AND DELAWARE CANAL

20th. November, 1804.

Gentlemen

I herewith present you 2 statements agreeably to your resolution at your last meeting, the first of which exhibits the outstanding debts of the Company to all manner of persons excepting only the Contractors amounting to $ 5,456.82

The other is a gross estimate formed upon as exact ⎫
a measurement as could in the present state of the ⎬   20,174.96
work be taken of its different sections, amounting to ⎭   on which is paid

                                                              10,508.75
                                            Balance due $ 9,666.21

Independently of these sums there is a small debt due to persons employed in surveying levelling setting out and measuring. This duty has been performed by Mess. De Munn and Strickland my pupils, the former of whom has resided at the work previously to the arrival of Mr. Brooke and ever since.

On the first of these statements I have to remark that it is no otherwise incorrect than as it is rendered so by the impossibility of settling correctly the accounts of men unused to figures and receiving explanation with difficulty and delay—such as laborers workmen and Carters. The incorrectness however is not considerable and the shortness of time and principally the distance of abode and the engagements of the carters have alone prevented a correct settlement at the present day.

The second statement tho approaching to an accurate measurement of the work done cannot be considered as a settlement of the accounts of the different contractors. The extreme irregularity of the ground over which the feeder is necessarily led—and the great variety of soil—renders the measurement of this work more than usually complicated. The labor and price necessarily varies according to the open or woody nature of the surface, the depth of the digging, the distance of the wheeling, the depth and width of puddling all which is specially provided for in the existing contracts. The weather whether windy or wet, has been often unfavorable to the measurement. I beg however to assure the board, that not a day has been unemployed by Mr. Brooke, his assistants, or myself which could be usefully employed in the field to the accomplishment of the general measurement of the work and in its *general* correctness I believe confidence may be placed.

While every attention has been paid to this object, the work has also been carried on without hindrance. At your last meeting it was in a state to require close attention to its progress. Cochran required the remaining part of his contract to be staked out. Clegg and Binnerman had completed their first take and wanted a new extent of digging. Grimes had come down to the postroad to begin cutting thro the dividing ridge of the Peninsula. Randell and Cocksy having completed the puddles N.W. of Bell hill moved to the valley on its S.E. side in order to finish the puddling there while the weather would permit. Watson and Sands in passing the vallies at Thos. Cunningham's called for great attention to the levels, and Pollock had to carry up the ramps for the future bridge at the post road.

From the nature of these works part of our time was necessarily 573 employed in the field operations necessary to direct them and I hope if more has not been done towards *exactness* of measurement the board will please to believe that it was impossible.

If the work which has been done this season be considered in its particular parts, I may I think confidently assert that in expence it comprises at least 2/3ds. of the feeder. There are still two parts of the work untouched which will be expensive and tedious but which if they can be begun and carried on this winter may be completed by spring—I mean the deep cutting thro Bell hill and thro Gachot's land. The rest of the work presents a continued and nearly finished series of canal from the aqueduct to the ridge at Updegrove's.[1]

Of the aqueduct the eastern butment is in very considerable forwardness, and will be raised to the springing course if the weather permit this week. There the work will be closed for this season and serve in case of an ice fresh next spring as a bulwark to defend the embankment. A very large body of stones has been boated from the rocky hill, and now lies at hand on the embankment to carry on the work.

The Canal may be considered as complete from thence to the Rocks. The passage bridge with its ramps has long been finished.

The work from one end of the Rocks to the other is compleated excepting only the dressing. It is my intention to lay before you verbally my reasons for discontinuing this work at present, and will only now mention that they are founded on the value which this part of the work possesses as a quarry accessible by the Canal at each end and promising a sufficient supply of excellent stone for a very large part of our Locks below.

From the Rocks to the Lancaster road and indeed to Bell Hill, there remains only one part unfinished. It is in the Contract of James Cochran who will complete it in 2 weeks at farthest. There will then be a continued extent of boatable water from the Rocks to Bell hill and tho the whole will in the Spring require some trimming and dressing, the work to be done is so trifling, as not to occasion any prospect of delay in the early use of the work.

On the Lancaster road the walls of the permanent swing bridge and its abutments are intirely finished. Untill the Canal however shall be navigable it would be perhaps better to wear out the temporary bridge which has been erected, than to lay the platform and put on the Swing bridge now.

An expensive part of the work has been, the culverts and drains
necessary to carry off the water falling to the North and West of Bell hill.

The nature of the soil as well as the narrowness and depth of the digging, and the strength and size which was necessary in the culverts have been the cause of the consumption of much time labor and materials. All these works so important to the safety of the work during the winter are intirely finished and the necessary trunks thro the banks are laid, nor do I apprehend that any danger can accrue to any part of the Canal or its bank from the utmost severity of weather.

Beyond Gachot's land no water above the level of the bank can be procured.[2] This occasions expence in embanking, and therefore the level of the work beyond has been carried so as to require no puddling.

The work at present tho continuous is less finished than that to the N.W. of Bell hill; it may be considered as 3/5ths. finished.

At the post road the ramps to the future bridge have been laid off and will be carried up without expence the earth being furnished by the Canal. On the size and construction of this bridge I have to request your direction.

Beyond the ridge in the state of Delaware the next part of the Canal which can be executed is at the foot of the swamps on the boundary line of Z. Ferguson[3] and Theodore Thomas. It is necessary in the first place to provide for the drainage of the whole work thro the swamp, before any part of it can be cut. Agreeably therefore to permission obtained of Theod. Thomas, Clegg and Binnerman are engaged in cutting a trench across the Company's land to the leading draught or run a little to the Eastward of the line. When this is complete and the back drains are dug I have no doubt but the work may be carried on during the whole of winter.

The reasons, arising from the large calls upon the Company from other quarters and the unavoidable delay in procuring the lands over which the feeder passes, have necessarily led to the endeavor to keep down the number of men employed and with it the daily expence of the work. This has indeed been a matter of some difficulty. At a moderate profit on the labor of each man, it is evidently the interest of the Contractors to engage as large a number of laborers in the work as possible. To reduce this number below a certain point is to render the work unprofitable perhaps ruinous to them at a moderate price and the inconvenience recoils upon the Company. That much more could have been done had those reasons not existed is certain and whenever they shall be removed the rapidity with which the work will proceed will be much more striking than it has hitherto appeared.

At the commencement of the work about the middle of May the

575

dread of the neighborhood to receive the workmen of the Canal into their houses rendered it necessary to provide extensively for their accomodation. The uniform good conduct of these men has now so altered the case that for a considerable time past no new accomodations have been called for. Many log houses have also been erected along the lines by the labor of our people themselves to which the Company have only found boards for the roofs. As the work proceeds into Delaware more accomodations must be provided, the range thro which the canal passes being very thinly inhabited. On the other hand the charge for utensils will be most considerably diminished by the completion of the rocky part of the work, the quarry expences alone calling for tools for blowing and breaking stone.

The Company are now provided with an ample stock of wheelbarrows and wheeling plank, shovels, mattocks, picks, crowbars, and spades. In the deep cutting carts of a particular construction will be required. The person who has furnished all our best wheelbarrows and who is a thorough bred Canal carpenter John Bindley has now established himself on the line and works by the day under Mr. Strickland.[4] These articles may therefore be now provided at the most moderate expense.

In reviewing the conduct of the individuals employed on the work during this season I hope the board will find reason to think it worthy of commendation. Three of the contractors join consummate skill in their business to perfect integrity and industry;[5] the rest with less experience and requiring more instruction have performed their work perfectly well in all its parts and promise to be highly useful to the success of the undertaking.

It will rest with the board in how far the Men who have now made all their arrangements to remain for some years attached to the work, who have provided for their winter's housing and provision, and who may be perhaps not easily collected if again scattered, shall take their chance of continuing the work during the winter. It may, if the board think proper, be closed. The advantages and disadvantages which will attend either line of conduct may be compared on hearing a large mass of verbal information which I have to lay before you.

I am &c.

B. Henry Latrobe.

Copy: C & D Canal Company Papers (176/D12).

1. Richard Updegrove assisted in the feeder construction by "making, finding Materials and putting up 100 pannel of post and Rail fence along the Canal thro his Plantation" for $50. C & D Committee of Works Journal, 29 Dec. 1804.

2. Jacob Gachot continued to frustrate the canal company's efforts to acquire his land along the feeder line. He refused to lower his price (see BHL to Gilpin, 9 Sept. 1804, above) and BHL urged the C & D directors to decide quickly on whether to pay Gachot's exorbitant price or go to a jury to decide the land's value. The engineer predicted that delay would result in suspension of "the operations of the Company for nearly one Year." BHL's warning went unheeded, however, and as late as February 1805 he was asking the board to take up the question of Gachot's land. By that time, however, the directors were more concerned with the economic survival of the company than with the acquisition of Gachot's acres. BHL to Kensey Johns, 1 Nov. 1804, LB (35/F2); BHL, C & D Report, 23 Feb. 1805 (177/G7).

3. Zebulon Ferguson rented a log house to the C & D Canal Company for the accommodation of the workmen. C & D Committee of Works Journal, 12 Jan. 1805.

4. BHL had ordered wheelbarrows from Bindley as early as 9 April 1804 (LB; 31/B6), and by 10 May nine had already been delivered (C & D Survey Committee Minutes). In May John Coxey, soon to be hired as a contractor on the feeder, assisted Bindley in his wheelbarrow contract. BHL recommended to Coxey that Bindley settle near the feeder: "He shall have as much to do as will compleatly employ him for the next 3 or 4 Months." BHL to Coxey, 26 May 1804, LB (32/F5).

5. James Cochran, Charles Randle, and John Coxey. See BHL to Helmsley, 29 Oct. 1804, above.

REPORT ON THE PUBLIC BUILDINGS

To the President of the United States

The Report of the Surveyor of the public buildings
of the United States at Washington.

Washington Decr. 1st. 1804.

Sir,

In reporting to You on the manner in which the work on the public buildings of the United States has been conducted during the Year 1804, I cannot avoid expressing my regret that[1] a sensible portion of the appropriation by Congress has necessarily been expended in pulling down or repairing what was done insufficiently, previously to the Year 1803.

The application of the public money to the separate objects of the President's house, and the Capitol, including the alteration, removal, reerection or repair of the works, will be separately stated in the accounts of the superintendant of the city to be rendered to the Treasury. But as these accounts will not be closed untill the 1st. of January 1805, he has furnished me with the following statement, up to the present day, of payments in the present year out of the Appropriation for 1804, and a Balance of the Appropriation of 1803 not expended in that year *vizt.*

CAPITOL, including all alterations additions and repairs in north wing (except fitting up Representatives chamber)	$44,548.20
For Fitting up Representatives chamber	689.23
PRESIDENTS HOUSE	11,928.29
PAYMENTS ON ACCT. for sundry materials, on Acct. of the particular Application whereof has not yet been rendered	500.00
	57,665.72

1. The President's house.

It is well known that the Presidents house was inhabited before it was finished; and that it still remains in a state so far from completion, as to want many of those accomodations which are thought indispensible in the dwelling of a private citizen.[2] Of the inconveniencies attending the house, the greatest was the leakiness of the roof, which had indeed never been tight. The rain water which entered the building in every part, had injured the furniture exceedingly, and ruined many of the cielings. This important defect arose from two principal causes: the very injudicious manner in which the gutters, and the troughs conveying the water to the Cistern were constructed, and the badness of the Slating.

The Gutters are of lead. The Sheets were soldered together: the fall or current of the gutters was much too small: the openings in the roof through which the water passed into the troughs were so contracted as to be incapable of discharging the water of a moderate rain, consequently it overflowed and found its way into the building: the troughs were of boards lined with lead, soldered at the joints, and laid with very little current: and all the lead was of bad quality and badly cast. All and each of these causes occasioned leakage in the Gutters and troughs. It requires very little theory or experience to know that, wherever solder is used in leaden Gutters, leakage is inevitable. In Water Cisterns, and pipes, solder is necessary, and the joints made with it are sound and permanent, the temperature of the Water they contain not being subject

578

to great variation. But in gutters and flats, alternately exposed to the scorching sun, and to severe frost, the use of solder is every where inadmissible, but peculiarly so in our climate. It is besides very expensive, and in no well constructed building is it necessary. In the president's house, five feet of additional current was easily procured, and by that means the new gutters were laid without solder, and with proper grovings and drips.[3]

The first part of the season was so uncommonly wet, that no very early measures could be taken to make a thorough repair of the roof. The attempts at temporary repair, made with a view to save the furniture and cielings of the house, did not succeed, and tended only to prove the absolute necessity of a complete alteration of the whole system of guttering, and of providing new lead for the whole building. Such a general repair is always troublesome and difficult, and was much more expensive than it would have been to have executed the work right at first. It is now finished, and the roof is free from leaks. It will, I have no doubt, remain so.

The second Cause of leakage was the Slating. The quality of the Slates was bad, but their size, especially towards the ridge, was more injurious than their bad quality. The upper courses, for a considerable distance down the roof did not show more than from 2 to 2½ inches in width, and a large majority of these Slates were only from 1½ to 3 inches in breadth.[4] Slated roofs are always difficult to repair, but such a roof could not be repaired at all; and there were also other reasons, which rendered it necessary at all events to remove so heavy a covering as slate.

I am uninformed[5] why the particular mode of construction which renders this roof so heavy and so high was adopted. If strength was proposed, capable of bearing a covering of slate laid in mortar, it has not been attained, for the framing has every where given way, and at the Eastern end of the house, where there are no internal Walls it has failed so much as to force out both the front and the back Walls very considerably. It appeared therefore necessary, in the first place to secure the timbers as well as the Walls by strong ties of Iron; which being fixed, both are now perfectly safe. In the next place it became highly proper to take off the load of Slates and mortar, even had they not leaked; for they seemed to be the principal cause of the failure of the Timber framing. In the covering which was to supply the place of Slate, *lightness* was the principal requisite: but safety from fire, and oeconomy were also necessary considerations. Shingles and tiles were therefore out of the ques- 579 tion, as well as lead; and the choice was confined to Copper, Tin, and painted Sheetiron. Of these, Sheet Iron was by far the cheapest, and with a little attention to its painting, quite as permanent, as the two former. 100 superficial feet of Slating in Mortar weighs about 15 Cwt., of Sheet Iron, exactly 147 lbs. So that the building, the roof containing 12.600 superfl. feet, could be relieved of a weight of about 82 Tons. These reasons induced the adoption of a Sheet iron roof, which has accordingly been put on.

The repair or rather the total renewal of the roof of the Presidents house, forms the principal part of the expense of this building for the season. It has however been further requisite to make a new drain from the house, of such dimensions and construction, as to prevent it from being filled up as before, and the building from being flooded from the circumjacent grounds. The cost of this improvement, and the finishing of one of the Chamber apartments in the second story, bears a small proportion to the former Sum.

2. The Capitol.

In my former reports to You, I stated the propriety of reconsidering the plan of the South wing of the Capitol; and on the reasons given in that Report, and in a letter to the Chairman of the Committee of the house of representatives appointed to enquire into the subject, the plan, which has been the Ground work of all that has been done during the Season, was approved and adopted.[6] By the arrangements of this new design, the House of Representatives will sit on the principal story of the building the whole of the Ground Story being appropriated to the offices of the house: a situation the most contiguous which could be obtained, and far preferable for Offices to the North wing, or the Attic Story.

Various causes have conspired to prevent our carrying up, this Season as large a Mass of building as was expected. The first and principal of these have been the time, labor, and expense of pulling down to the very foundation all that had been formerly erected. Bad as the workmanship appeared before the Walls were taken down, the measure of removing them entirely was still more justified by the State in which they were found to be on their demolition. Even the materials, with exception of the bricks, were not of any important value to the new work. The stone was fit only to be used as common rubble, and most of the Timber, was in a state of decay, from the exclusion of Air.

Another cause of delay in preparation, and an important one, was the late period at which the appropriation was made. The extreme wetness of the beginning of the Season, and the floods which filled up some of the quarries, and retarded the working of others, afterwards operated much against the progress of the building, and threw great difficulties in our way. After the work had begun, we were again interrupted by the sickness which prevailed, and which at one time threatened, by depriving us, of many of our best workmen, to put a total stop to the work.

Under all these inconveniences, and others arising from the nature of the building itself, the work has been carried on. The best mode of proceeding would undoubtedly have been to have carried up the interior with the exterior walls. But the former building stood within the area of the Wing. Had the external walls been suffered to remain on the level at which the work was closed, at the end of the Year 1803, till the inner building could be removed, and the internal Walls carried up, little progress could have been made in the former, during the present Season, and the Stonecutters would have been idle. It was therefore thought best to carry up all the external walls by themselves, thereby forwarding the more slow progress of the ornamental work in freestone, and to construct them in such a manner as to prepare for good bond with the interior work, and for the support of the Vaults, the pressure of which they will be required to resist. Thus has the work been raised to the level of the Selles of the Attic windows externally, and by far the most tedious and expensive part of the work in freestone has been completed, excepting the Cornice and the Capitals of the Pilasters. Of the cornice a large portion is also wrought, and of the 30 Capitals, 16 are finished.

Of the interior parts of the building all the foundations are laid, and brought up to the floor of the Cellar story on the North side, and although they do not appear to view, the work done in them is very considerable. The whole south half of the Cellar story is Vaulted, and ready to receive the Walls of the Basement or Office story.

Preparations to a very great extent have already been made, in order to proceed vigorously with the building as soon as the will of the national legislature shall be known to that effect, and the Season will permit. All the freestone for the external walls, Entablature, and Ballustrade is provided, and the greatest part of it on the Spot. For the internal Colonnade all the Stone is ordered, most of it quarried, and much already brought to the building. Early in the season the public Quarry on the Island in Acquia Creek was opened, and much useful Stone quarried: and it would have been much to the advantage of the 581 public, had the extent of the appropriation permitted us to have prosecuted this work. But it was found that to clear out the rubbish of former workings, and to provide for the conveyance of the stone to the waterside, altho' ultimately a measure of oeconomy, would have made too large a deduction from the funds required to carry on the building itself, and contracts for stone with individuals were therefore preferred.

In the arrangements for erecting so large an edifice as the South wing of the Capitol, and for pulling down or repairing extensive works of former construction, it was not easy, perhaps it was impossible, so to proportion all the various contracts and engagements for Labor and materials to the funds appropriated to their ultimate liquidation, as to keep within their limits, and at the same time to make exertions equal to the public expectation, arising out of their extent.

In the present instance, the contracts which are made, and which are in the progress of their completion will exceed in amount what remains of the appropriation of last Year. I must however at the same time observe, that the stock of materials wrought and unwrought, which are now actually at the building, exceeds greatly this deficiency. Should the National Legislature, on view of the solid, permanent, and incombustible manner in which the work has been executed, and on consideration of the evidences of fidelity to their duty which those engaged in the Labor of the work have every where exhibited, think proper to proceed with the completion of the building, it would much tend to the early occupation of their house, by the house of representatives if an appropriation exceeding 50.000 dollars were made for the next Season. Such an appropriation, while it would give larger limits to the exertions which might be made, would by no means disturb that system of oeconomy which has hitherto been pursued; but would rather conduce to the more advantageous and provident purchase of all our materials. And it is especially to be considered, that too early and extensive provision cannot be made for those parts of the work, which must necessarily be of wood. The time is now at hand at which further delay would be injurious and expensive, and should the Sum necessary for this provision, added to the arrears which are or will become due on outstanding contracts, be defrayed out of a future appropriation of *only* 50.000 Dollars, the progress of the solid parts of the building will be materially injured, and must to a certain extent, be put off to another season beyond the next.

In my letter of the 28th. of Febry. 1804 to the Chairman of the Committee of the house of representatives to whom the subject of the public buildings was referred, I presumed that three annual appropria-

582

tions of 50.000 Dollars each would be sufficient to finish the Southwing of the Capitol. This estimate was given under statement of the extreme difficulty of estimating a work of this kind. One of these appropriations of 50.000 Dollars has been granted. But from the detail of the statements I herein submit to You it will appear, that the whole of it could not possibly be made applicable to the actual *progress* of the work on the Capitol.

Having thus endeavored correctly, and minutely to report the progress of the work on the public buildings during the past Season, I now most respectfully submit to You all the views of the past, and for the future which the facts suggest.[7]

B. Henry Latrobe,
surveyor of the public buildings of the
United States at Washington.

ADS: Records of the U.S. Senate, RG 46, National Archives (176/G6). Jefferson submitted this report to Congress on 6 December 1804. Another copy in BHL's hand is in the Records of the U.S. House of Representatives, RG 233, National Archives (176/F5). An incomplete draft in BHL's hand with some alterations by Jefferson is in BHL Papers, Library of Congress (176/E9). The report was published in *Message from the President of the United States, Communicating a Report of the Surveyor of the Public Buildings at the City of Washington, on the Subject of the Said Buildings, and the Application of the Monies Appropriated for Them* (Washington, D.C., 1804), pp. 5–13 (177/A10). The report also appeared in the *National Intelligencer* on 19 December 1804.

1. The rest of this sentence was altered at Jefferson's suggestion to replace what BHL had originally written: "So large a Sum will appear to have been exhausted in pulling down and repairing works, the original cost of which has been very great; and which, had they been designed with judgement, or executed with integrity, ought not to have required any further expenditure for many Years to come. And although the defence or crimination of the personal Characters of those who are or have been employed in the public works cannot now be of any use to retrieve the loss and the disgrace which have been incurred, I feel so much at least to be due to the trust with which I have been honored, and to the conduct which I have endeavored to pursue and enforce, as to say, that, having discovered in all those parts of the work which have been pulled down, or have called for repair or alteration, the traces either of gross ignorance, or of fraud, or of both, every exertion has been used to prevent similar censure from attaching itself to the present and future expenditures on the public buildings." BHL, Report on the Public Buildings, 1 Dec. 1804, incomplete draft, BHL Papers, Library of Congress (176/E9).

2. At this point in his original draft BHL added a footnote: "There are no Cellars in the house, no place in which linnen can be dried, not one of those conveniences which are afforded by an inclosed Yard." Ibid.

3. Before Jefferson changed it, this sentence read: "And in the President's house especially 5 feet of additional current could easily be procured, had only ingenuity been employed." Ibid.

4. BHL had originally begun this sentence with the clause, "It will scarcely be believed that," which Jefferson struck. Ibid.

5. This phrase is Jefferson's; BHL had written, "It is not easy to comprehend." Ibid.

6. BHL, Report on the U.S. Capitol, 4 Apr. 1803, and BHL to Thompson, 28 Feb. 1804, both above.

7. The House tabled this report on 6 December; eleven days later a committee consisting of Philip R. Thompson, Benjamin Huger, Richard Cutts, Roger Nelson (1759–1815) of Maryland, John Cotton Smith (1765–1845) of Connecticut, Peterson Goodwyn (1745–1818) of Virginia, and Thomas Plater (b. 1769) of Maryland was appointed to examine and report on it. *Annals of Congress,* 8th Cong., 2d sess., p. 836.

TO NICHOLAS J. ROOSEVELT

Wilmington Decr. 17th. 1804

My dear friend,

I have been absent three weeks, and you can therefore easily forgive and account for my long silence. I shall be in Philadelphia on Monday evening the 24th. Decr. and stay till the 2d January. If you can then meet me we will talk over all our matters including that on which you have written to Mrs. Latrobe. Since my return I have not had time to bestow much consideration on anything. (I got back on Friday and finding my father in law here (who has only just returned home) again) I could not answer your letter before now.

On the subject on which you have written to Mrs. L, we had better *talk* than *write*. Perhaps it will be still better *to laugh—13 Years and 6 months.*[1]

In the mean time, if there is any thing certain under heaven, it is that You hold the first place in our esteem, good opinion, and friendship. Mrs. Latrobe joins in affecte. respects with Yours

B. Henry Latrobe

Polygraph Copy: LB (36/D9).

1. Roosevelt had fallen in love with BHL's thirteen and a half year old daughter, Lydia. BHL tried to discourage the relationship at first, but it eventually culminated in marriage in 1808. For a description of the wedding day, see BHL to Isaac Hazlehurst, 16 Nov. 1808, in BHL, *Correspondence,* 2.

TO AARON BURR

Wilmington Decr. 17th. 1804

Sir,

By this Mail, I transmit to you the drawings of the proposed arrangements in the Senate chamber agreeably to the plan sanctioned by

You at Washington.[1] The drawings are for the purpose of executing the work and I regret that the Shortness of the time, and the accumulation of my business here, has not permitted me to make fair Copies for your inspection. It shall still be done if agreeable to You.

I have directed Mr. Lenthall, Clerk of the Works to wait upon you to receive your orders; and have written to him at large as to their execution.[2] You will find him a very intelligent Man, capable of understanding, and putting into practice any idea you may please to suggest to him. I have to request that you will please to give him the drawings when you can spare them, as I could not procure a Copy to be made.

The appropriation for the public buildings being entirely exhausted, may I take the liberty to request, that you will please to mention to Mr. Lenthall the funds, from which the payments on account of the work to be done, will be made. We are not only out of Money, but out of Credit, and in every thing relating to the public buildings, such is the distrust in the intentions of Congress to make further appropriations, that I do not believe that a single workman can be hired without a full explanation of the means of payment.

I shall be in Philadelphia next week, and shall send on all the Cloth, Baize, and Fringe wanted *per Mail.*[3]

With the truest respect I am Your faithful hble. Servt.

> B. Henry Latrobe
> Surv. P. Bldgs. U.S.

Polygraph Copy: LB (36/D10). Addressed: "The Vice president U.S."

1. As presiding officer of the Senate, Burr was in charge of the arrangements for the Senate trial of U.S. Supreme Court Justice Samuel Chase, who was impeached on 4 December 1804. Looking to England for precedents, particularly the recent impeachment proceedings against Warren Hastings in Parliament, Burr desired to rearrange the Senate Chamber so that trappings of grandeur conveyed to the participants and spectators the solemnity of the occasion. Apparently BHL and Burr discussed the arrangements on 13 December, the day BHL left Washington for Wilmington. A rough sketch by BHL of his proposed rearrangement of the Senate Chamber for the trial is in PBHL (314/B1). *Annals of Congress*, 8th Cong., 2d sess., pp. 747–62; Richard Ellis, *The Jeffersonian Crisis: Courts and Politics in the Young Republic* (New York, 1971), p. 96.

2. BHL to John Lenthall, 17 Dec. 1804, BHL Papers, Library of Congress (177/B13).

3. As it turned out, Burr adopted a design by Samuel Blodget rather than BHL's. BHL later told Lenthall that Burr "regretted that my design was not adopted, *on account of the difficulty of fixing my Gallery,* and that a much worse but more economical and easy plan had been of necessity preferred. Lord! how this world is given to lying!" BHL to Lenthall, 26 Jan. 1805, BHL Papers, Library of Congress (177/F1).

BHL, as surveyor of the public buildings, carried out the work of fitting up the chamber for the trial according to Blodget's design. The work cost $2,000. For a description of the chamber during the trial, see *Annals of Congress*, 8th Cong., 2d sess., p. 100. *In Senate of the United States. April 2, 1806. Mr. Bayard, from the Committee to whom was Referred, the Account Rendered by John Lenthall for B. H. Latrobe, against the Senate for Expenses in Fitting up the Senate Chamber for the Trial of the Impeachment of Judge Chase* ([Washington, D.C., 1806]).

TO PHILIP R. THOMPSON

Wilmington, Del. Decr. 30th. 1804.

Sir

In answer to your letter of the 21st of Decr. I beg leave to state to You that the sum necessary to finish that part of the South wing of the Capitol which is now in progress is *109.100* Dollars, and of that part which corresponds to the Recess in the North wing, *25.200* Dollars in all *134.300$*.

This estimate is founded upon the best calculation that can be made of a building so complicated in its construction, of which the material and workmanship of many parts are of such a nature that a small alteration of dimension or arrangement, may occasion a considerable difference of expense. It is, I believe the most accurate that under all circumstances can be made, and I do not expect that it will be exceeded.

On this occasion I beg leave respectfully to submit to you the following remarks.

Of the appropriations which have been made by Congress towards the erection of the Southwing, that of the Year 1803, could not be entirely expended in that Year; partly because a considerable time elapsed in making the arrangements to resume a work so long suspended; partly because we were obliged to discharge our workmen and close the Season in the month of October, in order that the House of Representatives might not be disturbed in their occupancy of the part of the building which then stood.

The appropriation of 1804 with the balance of that of 1803 has on the other hand not only been expended but exceeded. No hindrance to the progress of the work to the end of the Season occurred, and it was besides impossible so to arrange the very large contracts for stone and other materials, and so direct the Labor of the work, as to stop at the point at which the appropriation was exhausted. For even at the moment at which it was perceived that an expense beyond the appropriation would probably be incurred, it was absolutely necessary to the security of the work during the winter, to carry up the Walls to a certain level, to

586

compleat the vaults on the South side, and to incur much other unavoidable expense. I think it also proper to mention that independently of monies due for labor; some of our most respectable contractors, having made arrangements which it was highly against their interest to interrupt while the prospect of completing the building by further appropriations was open, have proceeded in their contracts, with a perfect knowledge that the last appropriation was exhausted, as well as with a full confidence that what has been so far carried on, would be completed.

In both these seasons however we have experienced an extreme difficulty in collecting good workmen, though from different causes. In the first (1803) the city could not at first furnish those we wanted, and after collecting a sufficient number we were obliged to discharge them again before the working season ended. This last circumstance, and especially the lateness of the appropriation operated against us in the season of 1804. Lest we should again labor under similar disadvantage, I consider it to be my duty most respectfully to represent to you the advantages that would result to the work by an early appropriation, approaching more nearly to the estimated expense of the house. The objects in view would be accomplished, if congress in their wisdom should think proper to grant the Sum of 100.000 Dollars for the use of the public buildings during the next Season. Such an appropriation will indeed be the only means of insuring to the house of representatives the occupancy of their Hall at the session of 1806, and of preventing their being confined for more than *one other* season to the inconvenient situation of the Library.

In the above estimate I have included that part of the building which is not yet begun, but which will contain the access to the House, and correspond to the recessed part already erected in the North wing, because, it were well to begin this part of the work as soon as possible, if it should appear to the President of the United States that its progress will not retard that of the House itself. I must also remark that no Sum is therein estimated for fitting up and furnishing the new House. I am with great respect Your faithful hble. Servt.

B. Henry Latrobe.
Surveyor of the public buildings at Washn.

P.S. The above sum of 109.100$ includes the amount of all outstanding debts.[1]

ALS: Records of the U.S. House of Representatives, RG 233, National Archives (177/C5). A copy made by BHL for Jefferson with some variant wording is in Jefferson Papers (177/C10). The letter was published in *Letter from the Surveyor of the Public Buildings at the City of Washington, to the Chairman of the Committee appointed the Seventeenth Ultimo, on a Message from the President of the United States, on the Subject of Said Buildings* ([Washington, D.C., 1805]), pp. 3–5 (177/D2). It also appeared in the *National Intelligencer* on 14 January 1805.

1. The House passed its appropriation bill for the Capitol on 15 January 1805; the Senate amended it and the final act was approved on 25 January. The law provided almost all of what BHL had requested: $110,000 for completing the Capitol's south wing and $20,000 for "necessary alterations and repairs" on the north wing and on "other public buildings at the City of Washington." *Annals of Congress,* 8th Cong., 2d sess., pp. 41, 985, 1662.

Index

Compiled by Lisa Mae Robinson

Page numbers in boldface indicate biographical sketches.

Mr. Traquair, Stonecutter }
Philadelphia }   Newcastle Nov. 6th

My dear friend,

If you cannot understand the sketch
in the Margin, my friend Adam will explain
it to you. But as every Scotch stone
cutter is born with the intuitive know
ledge of the manner of cutting the hollow
drain of a lock, little need be said to you
on the subject. —

I must however beg you to remember
that at present I have only undertaken
to make the necessary surveys for the Com
pany, and it is a little prudent in me to
give them any of the information which
they might expect from me if I were their
Engineer, as it would be to lead you into the idea
of providing the necessary blocks without giving
you fully to understand that I have no power to
contract with you. I must however say so much
that there is little doubt of your doing this busi
ness together, & I have prepared Mr. Gilpin the
Sam. tary of our board as to intelligence &
gentlemanly conduct, to converse with you on